The Philosopher's Gaze

The Philosopher's Gaze

Modernity in the Shadows of Enlightenment

DAVID MICHAEL LEVIN

University of California Press

BERKELEY   LOS ANGELES LONDON

University of California Press
Berkeley and Los Angeles, California

University of California Press, Ltd.
London, England

© 1999 by the Regents of the University of California

Library of Congress Cataloging-in-Publication Data

Levin, David Michael, 1939–.
   The philosopher's gaze : modernity in the shadows of enlightenment/
David Michael Levin.
      p.   cm.
   Includes bibliographical references and index.
   ISBN 0-520-21780-2 (alk. paper).
   1. Philosophy, Modern.   2. Vision.   I. Title.
B846.L48   1999
190—dc21   98-43812
                                                           CIP

Manufactured in the United States of America

08 07 06 05 04 03 02 01 00 99   10 9 8 7 6 5
4 3 2 1

Written in remembrance of centuries of victims
brought by the inhumanity of moral
and cultural blindness,
by eyes narrowed in brutal lust, rage, and hate,
into depths of pain and suffering—or to even darker
cruelties engraved in dust and ashes

Written with letters shrouded in black

Contents

Acknowledgments

I am grateful to the Agence Photographique de la Réunion des Musées Nationaux for providing a photograph (© Photo RMN) of *Un Philosophe Occupé de Sa Lecture,* a portrait by Jean-Baptiste-Siméon Chardin on exhibit in the Musée du Louvre.

I am grateful to Alfred A. Knopf for permission to use "On the Road Home" and "Crude Foyer," as well as some lines from "Credences of Summer" and "Auroras of Autumn," quoted from *Collected Poems* by Wallace Stevens. Reprinted by permission of Alfred A. Knopf Inc. I am also grateful to Faber and Faber Limited, which holds British Commonwealth rights to this text.

I

FORESHADOWINGS

Outside the Text
Thoughts on a Painting by Chardin

In *Un Philosophe Occupé de Sa Lecture* (1753), Jean-Baptiste-Siméon Chardin depicts a well-dressed, corpulent man comfortably seated at his desk and absorbed in contemplation whilst reading a book. The painter's philosopher seems to be in repose, untroubled by the thoughts that are passing through his mind. The atmosphere of the painting is soft, the lighting gentle but sufficient to illuminate the book.

Since the dawn of books, the philosopher's gaze has been absorbed in the reading of books: reading the Book of Life, the Book of Nature, reading the prescriptions of morality by the natural light of Reason, translating the presence of the Good into an archive of books for eyes to read.

But what do philosophers see when they turn away from the books they are reading and writing? And what are they seeing and reading when they return from the world to their library of books?

According to Jacques Derrida, "il n'y a rien hors du texte." But this does not mean that the philosopher's thought is restricted to the solitude of the library. On the contrary, his assertion breaches the walls of the library, making an opening that compels the philosopher to assume responsibility for the world outside. If the world outside is a text, then the philosopher is responsible for its interpretation: for what is seen, what is made visible by thought, and what kind of response the condition of the world outside elicits. But in truth this means: no inside, no outside. No escape from the other.

In this book, the one I have authored with these questions in mind, we will undertake a reading of some philosophical texts, searching for inscriptions—or rather the tracework of inscriptions—indicating the claims of moral responsibility that bind our perception, imagination, and memory. In an important sense, therefore, our examination of the philosophical gaze constitutes an effort to break out of that peculiar absorption in the book which defines the philosophy of consciousness, the philosophy of subjectivity. It is this philosophy, conceived as a certain discipline, a certain praxis of the philosophical gaze, that has participated in the making of the modern world.

Blindness, Violence, Compassion?

Where are his eyes?" Lear cries, asking this of the other who is himself. The King is naked in the state of madness. And he is blind. But thus blind, he is beginning truly to see. It will, however, be all too late (*King Lear*, Barnet, 1.4.246–50).

T. S. Eliot: "I see the eyes but not the tears / This is my affliction."[1] With these simple words of remorse, the poet confesses an inability to be touched and affected by the suffering he sees. He also, however, reveals the suffering that this limitation, or the recognition of this limitation, causes him. Thus is revealed after all, in the very depth of his affliction, an irrepressible compassion, an unmastered operation of alterity, secretly at work. What must we say about philosophers? When have philosophers seen the tears? When have they given thought to what, without words, tears are saying? Is the history of philosophy a history of blindness, a discourse disfigured by traces of this terrible, unavowable affliction? Is there something inherent in the philosophical gaze that compels this affliction to remain unavowable?

In his "Lettre sur les Aveugles à L'usage de Ceux Qui Voient" (1749), Diderot wrote this:

> Since the blind are affected by none of the external demonstrations that awaken pity and ideas of grief in ourselves, with the sole exception of vocal complaints, I suspect them of being, in general, unfeeling toward their fellow men. What difference is there to a blind person between a man urinating and a man bleeding to death without speaking? Do we ourselves not cease to feel compassion when distance or the smallness of the object produces the same effect on us as lack of sight does on the

blind? Thus do all our virtues depend on our way of apprehending things and on the degree to which external objects affect us! I feel quite sure that were it not for fear of punishment, many people would have fewer qualms at killing a man who was far enough away to appear no larger than a swallow than in butchering a steer with their own hands. And if we feel compassion for a horse in pain though we can crush an ant without a second thought, are these actions not governed by the same principle?[2]

In 1927, in San Gabriel de Jalisco, Mexico, this is what the eyes of a child had to see: "The mother covers his eyes so that he cannot see his grandfather hanging by the feet. And then the mother's hands prevent his seeing his father's body riddled by the [death squad's] bullets, or his uncle twisting in the wind over there on the telegraph posts. Now the mother too has died, or perhaps has just tired of defending her child's eyes. Sitting on the stone fence that snakes over the slopes, Juan Rulfo contemplates his harsh land with a naked eye. He sees horsemen—federal police or *Cristeros*, it makes no difference—emerging from the smoke, and behind them, in the distance, a fire. He sees bodies hanging in a row, nothing now but ragged clothing, emptied by the vultures. He sees a procession of women dressed in black" (Eduardo Galeano, *Memory of Fire*).[3]

In 1932, during the Indians' struggle in Izalco, Guatemala, for the right to vote, this is what the children were forced to see: "Soldiers beat to death the Indian chief José Feliciano Ama, leader of the revolution in Izalco. They hang Ama's corpse in the main plaza and force schoolchildren to watch the show" (ibid., p. 91).

How much longer must our children's eyes suffer this blinding violence? Where is the redeeming vision?

Minima Moralia

At the very end of *Minima Moralia*, Theodor Adorno wrote: "The only philosophy which can be responsibly practiced in face of despair is the attempt to contemplate all things as they would present themselves from the standpoint of redemption. Knowledge has no light but that shed on the world by redemption: all else is reconstruction, mere technique. Perspectives must be fashioned that displace and estrange the world, reveal it to be, with its rifts and crevices, as indigent and distorted as it will appear one day in the messianic light. To gain such perspectives without velleity or violence, entirely from felt contact with its objects—this alone is the task of thought." If, however, this task is imperative, it is also "utterly impossible," for, as Adorno acknowledges, "it presupposes a standpoint removed, even though by a hair's breadth, from the scope of existence, whereas we well know that any possible knowledge must not only be first wrested from what is, if it shall hold good, but is also marked, for this very reason, by the same distortion and indigence which it seeks to escape."[1]

I can think of nothing which better conveys the hope and the despair in which and with which this book was written. I do not know what redemption is. If its light is present, I cannot be sure that I see it; but my eyes have seen all too much hatred, cruelty, and oppression—and the unmistakable evidence of suffering that human beings have caused one another. If to see this much—or rather, to be *able* to see this much—may be taken to attest the presence of the light of redemption, then perhaps the reflections engraved in the darkness of this text will contribute in some small way to letting this light become more visible and more effective, so that it can give to our moral task the lucidity and evidence it requires.

In some small way. Like Adorno, I think we must turn our thought to small things, expecting only small sparks of light. Perhaps, then, the most that we may reasonably hope for from a work of philosophical thought such as this is that it point out, mindful of the fact that there are consequential shades of meaning, some of the shadows that double-cross, and yet also foreshadow, the future of modernity in an enlightenment always still to come.

II

INTRODUCTION

The Discursive Construction
of the Philosophical Gaze

In the *Phaedo*, Plato writes that Socrates must "be careful not to suffer the misfortune that befalls people who look at and observe the sun during an eclipse. For people may harm their eyesight unless they look at its image [εἰκών] reflected in water or in some similar medium."[1] But he also meant, allegorically, a danger even greater, in a sense, than the one that could befall one blinded by the sun: the danger, namely, that befalls one who is spellbound by shadows, reflections, and images—the illusions that hold our gaze in the material world. Thus the affirmation of a turning-away, decisive for the philosophical gaze: "I thought of that danger, and I was afraid that my soul would be blinded if I looked at things [τά πράγματα] with my eyes or tried to apprehend them with any of my senses. So I thought I must have recourse to λόγοι and examine in them the truth [ἀλήθεια] of beings."[2] In this testimony, Plato remarks the distinctively philosophical movement (a conversion, or turning, a περιαγογή) of vision—the progression from the activity of eyes obsessed with and entangled in the visible world to a contemplative, theoretical vision dedicated to knowledge of the Forms, timeless, eternal Ideas visible only to the discursive intellect of the rational psyche.

For Plato, to *see* the Forms of the Good and the True is to *know* the Forms of the Good and the True. And to know these Forms, one cannot help but be morally good and care about (care for, love) the truth. In *The Republic*, Socrates addresses his interlocutor, saying:

> For surely, Adeimantus, the man whose mind is truly fixed on eternal realities has no leisure to turn his eyes downward upon the petty affairs of men, engaging in such strife with them that he becomes full of envy and hate, but fixes his gaze upon the things of the eternal and unchanging order, and seeing that they neither wrong nor are wronged by

one another, but all exist in harmony as reason bids, he will endeavour
to imitate them, and, in so far as possible, to form himself in their likeness and assimilate himself to them. Or do you think it possible not to
imitate the things to which anyone attaches himself with admiration?
(Book VI, 500b–c)

Commenting on this passage, Charles Taylor writes that "reason reaches its
fulness in the vision of the larger order, which is also a vision of the
Good. . . . Once reason is substantively defined, once a correct vision of the
order is criterial to rationality, then our becoming rational ought not most
perspicuously to be described as something that takes place in[side] us, but
rather better as our connecting up to the larger order in which we are
placed."[3]

This conversion of vision involves a certain ascent: obedient to the axis
that connects earth and sky, the dialectical movement that begins with two
eyes caught in the confusion of the sensuous, material life of the world and
ends in the asceticism of the philosopher's monothetic, contemplative gaze,
fixed on, and also fixed by, the immutable Forms, begins well with the humility of a gaze looking up at the stars: "for I conceive that, as the eyes are
designed to look up at the stars, so are the ears to hear harmonious motions" (*Republic*, book VII, 530).

In his *Critique of Practical Reason*, Immanuel Kant invokes the stars to
evoke, to awaken, the moral sensibility:

Two things fill the mind with ever new and increasing admiration and
awe, the oftener and steadily we reflect on them: the starry heavens
above me and the moral law within me. I do not merely conjecture
them and seek them as though obscured in darkness or in the transcendent region beyond my horizon: I see them before me, and I associate
them directly with the consciousness of my own existence.[4]

What must be the effect, then, of the ever increasing hiddenness—or, say,
withdrawal—of the starry heavens and the horizon? Kant's words are
provocative, calling for a critical look at our contemporary life-world. This
is a world in which, increasingly, our city lights and industrial pollution
shut out the light of the stars, while our tall city buildings and hurried way
of living keep us alienated from the incommensurability that is the measure of the horizon. In contrast to the life Kant knew in eighteenth-century
Königsberg, our lives of today are no longer measured by the height of the
stars and the depth of the horizon. How then can the character of the
philosopher's vision be tried and measured, challenged and questioned?

For Plato, the contemplative vision of the philosopher, a "perception" of the absolute Good and the absolute Truth, can initially be understood, however, only in terms of an analogy that depends on an understanding of the perception of sensuous Forms (*Republic*, book VII, 532). Unlike the worldly knowledge we achieve with eyes still attached to the earth, the knowledge achieved by the philosopher's gaze is a knowledge free of images, shadows, reflections: it is a knowledge free of all sensuous and material limitations, and it is a knowledge free of perspectivism and its "distortions," grasped all at once and once and for all (book VI, 500–11).

For philosophers from Plato to Descartes, Hobbes, and Locke, the philosopher's vision is an expression of the "natural light" of reason (*Republic*, book VII, 532). This light is an inner light, generated by the power of reason. Emotions are said to be dark and confusing, but reason sheds its light on things and leads us to clarity and enlightenment. If, as Plato says (at *Republic*, book VI, 508), light is the "noble bond" between sight and the visible world, gracefully withdrawing from notice into the invisibility of a condition taken for granted, the *light of reason* is that which binds us to the ideality of a vision exceeding the visible in its reach and range, a vision that can never be satisfied with what has taken place within the realm of the visible.

This light of reason, once, long ago, a manifestation of the joy attending an indwelling sense of divinity and imaged as the aura or aureole that surrounds the head, but now too reduced, too secular, too subjective, too disenchanted, to be experienced and rendered in this way, now takes *nothing* for granted—unless this be the event of the gift of light itself, that light by grace of which a field of visibility is first opened up for the projective activity of vision. Today, having repudiated the light of this wondrous event as mythic nonsense and extinguished the inner light of reason in the brightness of mere metaphor, vision must now pass through a medium it can only understand in the languages of physics, optics, and biochemistry, focusing on the objects made visible by the event of a gift it ignores.

In "Philosophy and the Crisis of European Man," Edmund Husserl said: "Man becomes the disinterested spectator [*uninteressierter Zuschauer*], overseer of the world; in other words, he becomes a philosopher."[5] For Plato and Aristotle, the philosopher's gaze must be disciplined; it must be steadied in a calm and dispassionate state. As Plato says in the *Meno*, to be steady in virtue, reliably disposed, to know what virtue is, one needs a "steady" gaze.[6] But it is not only a question of steadying the gaze; its object too must be such that a steady, calm, dispassionate gaze is possible. Thus the object must be an ideal Form, timeless and unchanging. Only then can the gaze participate in the world of perception and be a guide to virtuous action.

This ascetic philosophical gaze, informed by a theoretical fixation on the Forms, has today, of course, lost its compass: the Forms have been swept away by the winds of subjectivity, cynical if not skeptical about the claims of objective reason. Without its proper object, such a gaze vanishes, probably forever, leaving the traces of its once glorious sovereignty only in the dark ink of letters that now, contrary to original intention, can only mourn and commemorate its historically fated passage.

The gaze of today makes its way through a thoroughly disenchanted landscape, attentive only to the objects at the end of its immediate interests. We take its measure not by the bounds of the horizon, nor by the boundless depths of the beyond, into which the horizon opens, but by the calculated ratios of loss and gain. The glitter of false gold, the dazzling display of civilization's latest instruments and commodities, the ornaments of material culture, hold the gaze in their power, blinding it to the suffering that demands the light and the darkness of truth, that by grace of which alone all our ways of seeing are first made possible. Lost in the subjectivity of perspectivism, we lose all perspective on our lives. We are easily distracted by our obsessions, the objects they inhabit rendered visible according to the laws of desire and an economy of illusory promises.

To the extent that the world is as it is in correspondence to the character of our vision, to the extent that the world is as it is as a function of this vision, its projection and reflection, one way to change the world would be to change the way we see things. Perhaps no one has articulated this point with more eloquence than Michel Foucault. In an interview subsequently given the title "Questions of Method," Foucault said: "My project is to contribute to changing certain things in people's ways of perceiving and doing things, to participate in this difficult displacement of forms of sensibility and thresholds of tolerance."[7] And in *The Use of Pleasure*, he wrote: "There are times in life when the question of knowing if one can think differently than one thinks, and perceive differently than one sees, is absolutely necessary if one is to go on looking and reflecting at all."[8]

In his *Ethics*, Spinoza formulated as a proposition of some importance the thought that "the more capable the body is of being affected in many ways, and affecting external bodies in many ways, the more capable of thinking is the mind."[9] All the commentaries by philosophers have ignored the implicitly radical significance of this proposition: the necessary implication of the body in the transformations that would constitute the "improvement" or enlightenment of the mind. All the commentaries have concentrated their attention on the capability and enlargement of the mind. But the strict parallelism that obtains between intellect and body means that, for every alteration of the mind, there must be a corresponding alteration of the body. And there is no reason to suppose that alterations of the body must be conceptualized only from the standpoint of the mind. Suppose, then, the possibility of a more enlightened, more ethically capable embodiment. What would this involve? What would it be like? How, for example, might we conceive a vision more capable of being affected in many ways, and affecting external bodies in many ways? How might a gaze with an historically different character be brought into being, preparing, perhaps, for the advent of a new epoch, a new beginning for humanity, and for the entire world of our beholding?

Borrowing one of Hegel's numerous "heliotropes," vision-generated, vision-saturated tropes especially frequent in his thinking about the philosophy of history, we may want now to ask ourselves how—in so far as it is within the reach and range of our present historical capabilities—we would like to, and actually might, alter the (intentional) character of our vision, to "greet together the dawn of a better time."[10]

Since the time of its beginning, Western philosophy has been a philosophy of light, vision, and enlightenment. Its principal methods have been intuition, reflection, speculation, and insight, while evidence has served as its measure of truth, and clear and distinct ideas have represented its objective. Moreover, in the discourse itself, metaphors drawn from light and vision have figured in ways that cannot always be eliminated by substitution without altering truth or meaning. This connection between philosophical thought and discourse has recently been subjected to critical questioning. To a considerable extent, the stimulus for such questioning has come, I think, from the so-called linguistic turn in philosophy, which has obliged philosophers to turn their critical reflection onto the rhetorical features of philosophical discourse, its own ways of using language, and its hitherto unexamined assumptions about the relationship between writing and thought. The turn to language must be situated, however, within a much larger narrative. If it has unquestionably been stimulated by new technologies and a revolution in the forms of communication that is releasing ever new potentials, it has also been promoted by new conditions of social life—multiculturalism, ethnic diversity, and other forms of social heterogeneity, which have made it necessary for democracies to improve the processes and procedures of social recognition and communication on which the legitimacy and effectiveness of their political institutions ultimately depend.

To be sure, the philosophical gaze is no longer turned away from the world, directed upon the timeless essences of an absolute, objective order. Nor is it obsessed with a movement of radical transcendence, be this a new theology, a new theodicy, or even the image of a future utopia. But the return of the gaze to the immanence of worldly matters, its inevitable subjective turn, acknowledging its historicity, its situatedness, its relativity, its finitude, has not been an easy transition. Deprived of the theoretical objectivity it once enjoyed, deprived of the omniscience and omnipotence it once could claim, denied the benefit of radical transcendence, how can the philosopher's gaze continue its critical function? How can it assume a position of authority? How can it justify a claim to truth? What happens to this gaze when it is reduced to perception, taking place without higher refuge in the midst of the commonplace? And in the name of what more enlightened potential for vision can the philosopher undertake the rational reconstruction of ordinary sight? How can the philosopher justify programs for the reform of visual perception, making it less susceptible to illusion and deception—or at least more guarded, more cautious in its claims?

In *The Social Contract*, Jean-Jacques Rousseau indicates how important it is that citizens learn to "see objects as they are, and sometimes as they ought to appear."[11] How, then, can the philosopher address our perception, so that we see through ideological distortions, recognize the power plays behind false appearances for what they really are, and subject the political processes of democracy to the public scrutiny that keeps them open and honest? How can the critical method of dialectical thinking be embodied in looking, seeing, and observing?

In *Minima Moralia*, Adorno remarks that "knowledge must indeed present the fatally rectilinear succession of victory and defeat, but should also address itself to those things which were not embraced by this dynamic, which fell by the wayside—what might be called the waste products and *blind spots* that have escaped the dialectic. . . . What transcends the ruling society is not only the potentiality it develops but also all that which did not fit properly into the laws of historical movement."[12] (Foucault's peculiar optics could be read as continuing precisely this project.) Overcoming blind spots recalls a thesis that Karl Marx advanced in his 1844 manuscripts: "The cultivation of the five senses is the work of all previous history."[13] Marx argued there that "sense which is subservient to crude needs has only a restricted meaning. . . . Thus, the objective realization of the human essence, both theoretically and practically, is necessary in order to *humanize* man's senses, and also to *create* the *human senses* corresponding to all the wealth of human and natural being."[14] The present book, continuing the project I began in *The Opening of Vision,* is intended as a contribution to the philosophical understanding of what is involved in the cultivation of sensibility and the humanization of the senses. What is needed is [1] the theoretical reconstruction of the enlightenment potential in our naturally bestowed capacity for vision and [2] the equally important theoretical reconstruction of the historico-cultural conditions in which these capacities, the gift of nature, were or were not permitted realization, development, and fulfillment. The second task requires that we think about the perceptivity of our vision from the standpoint of a certain *Leidensgeschichte,* a history that brings to light the traces of suffering and violence. For what is in question, what is at stake, here, is ultimately the *moral disposition and character* of our way of seeing—the humanization of the natural eye. Thus, what is needed is a philosophical critique of our *capacity* to see and of the way of seeing by which, for the most part, we actually live our lives: an undertaking in many ways like the philosophical project that Jürgen Habermas articulated in his appendix to *Knowledge and Human Interests,* except that, instead of the redemption of dialogue, it is a question of the redemption of vision as a cultural inheritance. Here is what Habermas says:

> Only when philosophy discovers in the dialectical course of history the traces of violence that deform repeated attempts at dialogue and recurrently close off the path to unconstrained communication does it further the process whose suspension it otherwise legitimates: mankind's evolution toward autonomy and responsibility. My fifth thesis is thus that *the unity of knowledge and interest proves itself in a dialectic that takes the historical traces of suppressed dialogue and reconstructs what has been suppressed.*[15]

In a sense, this is a task that calls for a critical theory of collective memory, a re-collection (*anamnesis*) of what our culture has refused to recognize and to see. With nature's gift of sight comes a certain calling—and the pressure of a normativity grounded only in the gift of nature itself. Through this calling, we are enjoined to take historical responsibility for our ability to be responsive.

In a note to one of the letters written for *On the Aesthetic Education of Man,* Friedrich Schiller asks us to consider:

> How can we be fair, kindly and humane towards others, let our maxims be as praiseworthy as they may be, if we lack the capacity to make strange natures genuinely and truly a part of ourselves, appropriate strange situations, make strange feelings our own?[16]

Keeping in mind the time of these letters—for otherwise we might worry about the operation of a certain quite subtle form of egoism, even in this benevolent thought—I want to say that I appreciate the question that Schiller poses. It is, however, ambiguous. I will argue that we have already been given a certain rudimentary corporeal schematization of this capacity and are therefore, in this sense, not without it. But the documents of a repeated barbarism that our civilization has failed to overcome make it impossible to deny, when we interrogate the archives of thought, that the philosopher's elevated gaze has done little to clarify and exhibit its potential, bringing before our vision a different way of being with others.

The present book is an attempt to call attention to our perceptive capabilities and examine the historical prospects in the light of their promise. To this end, the chapters of this book will be reflecting on the different forms of the gaze as they figure in the thinking of some important philosophers.

Although the chapters are united by their commitment to a certain critical point of view and are sequenced according to a certain argumentative logic, they may nevertheless be profitably read, I believe, quite independently of this order.

The Importance of Phenomenology

The art of storytelling is coming to an end. . . . It is as if something that seemed inalienable to us, the securest among our possessions, were taken from us: the ability to exchange experiences.

One reason for this phenomenon is obvious: experience has fallen in value. And it looks as if it is continuing to fall into bottomlessness. Every glance at a newspaper demonstrates that it has reached a new low, that our picture, not only of the external world but of the moral world as well, overnight has undergone changes that were never thought possible. . . . For never has experience been contradicted more thoroughly than strategic experience by tactical warfare, economic experience by inflation, bodily experience by mechanical warfare, and moral experience by those in power.

Walter Benjamin, "The Storyteller"[1]

[T]he dying out of experience [is] something that ultimately goes back to the atemporal technified process of the production of material goods.

Theodor Adorno, *Notes to Literature*[2]

[T]he question of experience can be approached nowadays only with the acknowledgement that it is no longer accessible to us. For just as modern man has been deprived of his biography, his experience has likewise been expropriated. Indeed, his incapacity to have and communicate experience is perhaps one of the few self-certainties to which he can lay claim.

Giorgio Agamben, *Infancy and History: Essays on the Destruction of Experience*[3]

Since I consider my work to be a contribution to hermeneutical phenomenology, I would like to say something about how I understand the use of this method.

PHENOMENOLOGY AS A HISTORICAL MOVEMENT

Phenomenology is a method with its own history. As Husserl first conceived it, the end of phenomenology was to reveal the constitution of meaning in a transcendental realm: although phenomenology must begin in the life-world, its assignment was to arrive at a pure transcendentalism. With Heidegger and Merleau-Ponty, however, phenomenology abandoned transcendental reduction, not only beginning but remaining in the life-world: in their work, phenomenology thus became existential. But this transformation is not enough: once the project of phenomenology has been situated in the world, it becomes necessary for it to go through a third moment of evolution. It must now become genuinely experiential: capable of articulating experience in all its hermeneutical intricacy, working with the dimensionality of experience to engage and bring forth from its depths newly emerging meaningfulness. It is only when phenomenology has truly understood experience and learned to become experiential, learned how to work with our experience in a way that carries it forward into new configurations of meaningfulness—only then will it have become what from the very beginning it always intended and claimed to be. In a certain sense, this third moment represents a recognition of phenomenology as Hegel conceived it: a hermeneutical work of the spirit, revealing its ever-changing reflexive configurations. But, of course, without any commitment to an immanent end and a dialectic of progress.

PHENOMENOLOGY AS A HERMENEUTICS

In the past, hermeneutics has been understood exclusively in relation to the interpretation of texts, or, say, cultural discourses. In my work, however, hermeneutics constitutes the essential phenomenological structure of perception, since the phenomenon never presents itself all at once and, correlatively, perception is always a process of delimited explication, a bringing-forth and bringing-out that is always situated in the "untimely" interplay of presence and absence, concealment and unconcealment. Phenomenology cannot be faithful to the "truth" of the phenomenon unless it is, in this sense, hermeneutical. Moreover, if we would like to be able to work with a structural distinction between shallow experience and deeply thoughtful experience, or a distinction between primordial experience prior to consciousness and experience reflectively retrieved, we will need a phenomenology that is hermeneutical in the sense defined here. But if experience is never ready-made, hermeneutics must not be reduced to the discovery of what is already present, merely taking away its hiddenness. Thus we will be thinking, here, about our looking and seeing, as organs with a capacity for engaging hermeneutically—disclosingly, revealingly—with the being of whatever we may be given to behold. The problematic at stake in the hermeneutics of texts and cultural discourses, namely the avoidance of an imperialism of the same in our relation to what is other, is no less at stake, I believe, when it is a question of our gesturing, our seeing and hearing. Here, too, the violence inherent in the logic of identity all too easily dictates the conditions of our perceptivity.

ON EXPERIENCE

Many philosophers have claimed empirical, experiential grounding for their thought. However, in spite of good intentions, their thinking has often not only failed to correspond to experience, but to a surprising extent even subverted and betrayed it, without, however, formulating any critical position in relation to its authority. I will not attempt, here, to defend this thesis by narrating once again the history of philosophy. Instead, I will begin my argument with some reflections on the method of phenomenology as it was formulated by Husserl at the beginning of the twentieth century.

What brought Husserl to the threshold of phenomenology was the problem of meaning: clarifying the meanings of our words by tracing them back to their origin in the acts of transcendental consciousness through which these meanings were first constituted, and reiterating the meaning-forming process, this time with an explicitly reflexive awareness of the way transcendental subjectivity functions in the process. "Back to the things themselves!" he proclaimed, boldly asserting that the phenomenological method, which he formulated in terms of a sequence of "reductions," is the only authentic positivism, the only true empiricism, and the only way to a realm of knowledge worthy of being called the "science" of all sciences.

Husserl's battle cry summons us to return to the experience of subjectivity and to insist on its claim to a certain validity and legitimacy. In a time when objectivity has become the dominant paradigm of knowledge, truth and reality, excluding or even denying all reference to experience, this battle cry has played a crucial historical role, a progressive historical role, challenging the hegemony of this paradigm, reaffirming the critical function of subjectivity, and renewing the promise of a rational redemption of lived experience.

But Husserl's phenomenology is ultimately more concerned with the task of securing for our knowledge an absolute grounding in the meaning-constitutive activity of transcendental consciousness than it is with the task of showing us how to reflect on our own experience just as it is lived. In fact, the latter task is not merely rendered subordinate to the task of laying an absolute foundation; it is ultimately annulled. What might have served as a method for reflectively contacting and working creatively with the

reflexively critical constitution of our experience as we actually live it became, instead, a method in the service of a metaphysical program: the rational reconstruction of knowledge by means of an intuitively immediate
demonstration that the meanings of our concepts were originally constituted, and can again (*nachträglich*) be constituted originarily, outside (or,
say, independently of) the material and causal conditions of the natural
world, by the pure activity of the transcendental ego.

We need to retrieve the progressive, critical spirit behind Husserl's affirmation of subjectivity and his formulation of the phenomenological
method. Thus, for example, we need his "principle of all principles," formulated in §24 of his *Ideas: General Introduction to Pure Phenomenology:*
that phenomenologically self-evident seeing (*Anschauung*) is the source of
authority (*Rechtsquelle*) for all knowledge, and that whatever presents itself in this way is simply to be accepted as it gives itself out to be, although
only within the limits in which it then presents itself. We also need his
methodological suspension of the "natural attitude," for this enactment of
a certain critical distance with regard to conventional wisdom and the culturally predominant interpretation of our reality must be effected *before*
this principle can be put to work. But these steps require that we unhitch
the method from his metaphysical agenda.

What becomes of phenomenology when it is released from the task of
tracing the origin of meaning back to the activity of the transcendental ego?
Does it necessarily lose its critical potential? Does it necessarily forfeit its
autonomy in relation to the opinions, beliefs, convictions, and knowledge-
claims constitutive of the natural attitude? Does it necessarily fall back into
dogmatic naturalism or realism? Does it necessarily surrender to the forces
of irrationalism?—Or does it finally, rather, win for subjectivity, for our experience as we actually live it—and that means, also, for the phenomenon
itself and as such—the recognition, the rights, and truth that are due?

Benjamin and Adorno lamented the withering of experience that is happening, today, at an alarming pace. Why should we care? Why does this matter? What can be done, if anything, to end this process of destruction? What
I think we need today—today, perhaps, more than ever—is a method that
can recognize and affirm the meaning of our experience as we actually live
it: a method that not only can recognize and affirm this, but can also show
us how to work with our own reflexively constituted critical interpretation
of this experience in a way that engages its immanent tensions and conflicts
and carries it forward into a new configuration. When released from its
metaphysical destination, phenomenology can then be seen as a powerful
agent of enlightenment, a powerful force, already at work within the social,

political, and cultural movements of modernity, on behalf of rights and liberties—and the self-fulfilling enlightenment of the individual.[4]

Now, to be sure, phenomenological reflection is not foolproof; it cannot guarantee that reflection will necessarily cut through all possible forms of self-deception and self-delusion, all possible frames of ideological distortion, all possible forms of historicism and the limitations imposed by narrow cultural perspectivism. But in fact, if the phenomenological suspension of the natural attitude cannot guarantee our release from the pride and prejudice that prevail in our life-world, neither can the reduction to transcendental consciousness. Not even Husserl's transcendental reduction could be demonstrated to guarantee absolutely the critical distance and autonomy of phenomenological reflection. However, it can be argued that the phenomenological method is more likely, in general, to encourage and support the reflexively critical realization of experiential truth than the methods of the objective sciences. And this is sufficient to give phenomenology a critical role of the utmost importance in ethics, morality, politics, and culture.

In "Subject and Object," Adorno acknowledges that the rational reconstruction of the transcendental subject seems to set up a neutral and autonomous theoretical position, a position of spectatorial distance, from which the conditions of every society and culture can be critically judged and resisted; but he is equally conscious of the fact that this is really an otherworldly position outside time, space, and history, a false or illusory position, nothing more than the philosopher's fantastical dream of omnipotence, of being able to see with God's eye and God's infallibility. All knowledge is situated, perspectivally conditioned and limited. There can be no getting around this fact. What therefore is needed, he concludes—I think rightly—is neither the assumption of a transcendental subject (a transcendental position) nor the erasure of the subject-position (a move which would in effect establish an omnipotent positivism with no place for resistance, for negativity), but rather the recognition of a concrete, embodied, innerworldly subject, and consequently the possibility of an "immanent critique," grounded only in this subject's reflexively critical experience and transcending prevailing conditions from within. "For society," as he says, "is immanent in experience, not an *allo genos*. Nothing but the social self-reflection of knowledge obtains for knowledge the objectivity that will escape it as long as it obeys the social coercions that hold sway in it, and does not become aware of them." "Social critique," he adds, "is a critique of knowledge, and vice versa."[5] Adorno understands that this will be difficult, that it will require a commitment to ongoing resistance and struggle. But, as he argues with admirable dialectical skill, the assumption of the position of a transcendental subject ultimately cannot solve the problem of critical distance and autonomous reflection, the problem of how a critical social theory, and a correspondingly critical reflective practice, can function while *inside* a given social and cultural system.

Rather than positing some hypothetical transcendental subject to preclude a priori the possibility of ideological deception, prejudice, and the social imposition of meaning, and to guarantee, again a priori, the critical suspension of the "natural attitude" and the position of an autonomous social critic, we could instead commit ourselves to working toward a theory and practice of phenomenology that would understand and promote the critical potential inherent in our perceptive capacities as embodied subjects who are thrown into the world and living through situations, responsible for responding appropriately to the claims of whatever gives itself to perception in the interplay of concealment and unconcealment. In question is our capacity for perceptive, hermeneutically revelatory interaction.

CONTINUING THE ENLIGHTENMENT PROJECT

Every one of the liberation movements that have swept across the Western world in this century is indebted to a *praxis* that can only be called, in effect, the living incorporation of hermeneutical phenomenology. What I mean is that every one of these movements essentially involves the empowerment that comes from *rejecting* the socially imposed constructions that have been interpreting or determining the meaning of one's experience, one's individual and group identity, and *learning* how to think, feel, and act from one's own reflexively critical constitution of lived experience. For centuries, most people have been *told* what it is that they are or should be experiencing; told, also, *how* they should experience the socially constructed—hence ideologically hegemonic—interpretation of what they are experiencing. Liberation from the sociocultural imposition of meaning therefore essentially involves the subject (whether individual or collective) in a phenomenological gesture, whereby experience just as it is actually lived is finally recognized and its existential meaningfulness is respected as such. The power of phenomenology consists in the fact that it insists on recognition and respect for the reality of our experience as lived: it thereby legitimates and empowers the reflexive, critical capacity of subjectivity in its struggle to twist free of the oppressive cultural interpretations that have been imposed on it. In this sense, phenomenology is already an ethics, already a politics. For me, then, the significance of phenomenology is that it offers a disciplined method for working hermeneutically and critically with lived experience in order to draw out its implicit or latent enlightenment-potential and carry this critical potential forward in ways that are felt to be life-affirming and felt to contribute to the flourishing of meaningful life.

But this project can be realized only if, following Heidegger's formulation in the "Introduction" to *Being and Time*, we give Husserl's "principle of all principles," and his battle cry, "zu den Sachen selbst!," a much more radical interpretation. Because Husserl's approach is captive to a metaphysical program, it cannot entirely avoid imposing meaning on experience, forcing it into a narrative that in many ways can be distorting. Phenomenology, therefore, must be, as Heidegger says, drawing on the word's Greek etymology, an approach to experience, an approach to the phenomenon, that *lets* it show itself from out of itself. As Heidegger formulates the phenomenological method in *Being and Time*, it becomes, finally and for the first time, truly empirical, in the radical sense of truly *respecting* the phenomenon as it gives itself. And this means respecting not only its dynamism, its essential becoming, its *physis*, the openness of its nature as the ever-emerging, but also respecting its self-concealment, its withdrawal from the realm of its appearing.

The radicality of the phenomenological method formulated in *Being and Time* consists in the fact that it *detaches* the method from Husserl's metaphysical program, so that it can be entirely given over to hermeneutic articulation, the caring and thoughtful unconcealment of the phenomenon. But Heidegger's fidelity to the hermeneutics of being also depends on a far-reaching critique of the philosophical tradition: on a critique of the domination of the assertion, the constative mode of discourse; a critique of the metaphysically enshrined structure of subject and object; and a critique of the correspondence theory of truth. For phenomenology cannot be entirely devoted to serving the hermeneutic presencing of the phenomenon unless it recognizes the aletheic dimension of truth, the prior event of opening that lays out a field of conditions for the perception and assertion of truth, and recognizes a mode of discourse that is not assertive, not constative, but poetizing, metaphoric, appropriate to the hermeneutics of that which presents itself and that which, as origin, as the event that gives and inaugurates the field for this presence, itself withdraws from truth, a self-concealing background that cannot be retrieved as origin nor reduced to the structure of the objective.

Although Heidegger could see in the history of philosophy the repetition of a certain foreclosure, a move that again and again betrayed the wonderful opening laid out, as the task that calls for thinking, with the very broaching of the question of being (Why is there being, anything at all, rather than nothing?), he did not at first realize that his own treatment of this question in *Being and Time* repeated this history of betrayal, articulating the ontological question only to impose a framework of conditions for response that immediately deny the very opening which the question set in motion. It is as if I wanted to get to know you and therefore invited you to tell me about yourself—not by letting you talk freely and by listening in a respectful, open silence, but instead by submitting you to an intense interrogation structured entirely according to my own terms, obliging you, for example, to restrict your answers to the set of questions I had already formulated in advance of our encounter and to use only the vocabulary that I wanted you to use.

After the publication of *Being and Time*, Heidegger soon came to realize that the "analytic of Dasein" which followed his formulation, in the "Introduction," of a very radical phenomenological methodology repeated the betrayal of the *Seinsfrage* that he had lamented in his history of philosophy. In other words, he recognized in his own work a repetition of the very same foreclosure that he reproached in his precursors. For instead of waiting to receive in an open way what comes from the asking of the question; instead of letting what comes with (from) the question of being simply show itself from out of itself, he had forced the phenomenon, the presencing of being, to show itself in terms of the existential structures constitutive of *Dasein*. This betrays the very hermeneutical openness to the moment of truth that his critique of the correspondence theory of truth and his introduction of the prior event of aletheia was intended to secure. Heidegger's so-called turning therefore involved an attempt to twist free of the enframing of the question of being in terms of the existential structures posited in his analytic of *Dasein* and an attempt to return to the question of being, working with it, this time, in the radically phenomenological way he had formulated in his "Introduction," henceforth maintaining the most rigorous responsibility for responding to the claim of the question of being as an opening question that calls for a response from our perceptual faculties which would be correspondingly open. The question of being demands an open hermeneutic receptivity to whatever might come, whatever might emerge, from the self-concealing openness into which the question throws us. Thus, as Vladimir Jankélévitch says, "hermeneutics must not be reduced to a linear induction, nor even to a mere chiasm, for it must engage us in the tortuous meanders of a labyrinth."[6]

III

THE PHILOSOPHERS

1   Descartes's Window

Deeply mistrustful of the dogmas of epistemology, I love to look
now out of this window, now out of that.

> Friedrich Nietzsche, *The Will to Power*[1]

As a monad, the Dasein needs no window in order first of all to
look outward toward something outside itself; not because, as
Leibniz thinks, all beings are already accessible within its capsule,
so that the monad can quite well be closed off and encapsulated
within itself, but because the monad, the Dasein, in its own being
(transcendence) is already outside, among other beings, and this
implies always with its own self. . . . Due to this original
transcendence, a window would be superfluous.

> Martin Heidegger, *The Basic Problems of Phenomenology*[2]

For to objectless inwardness, as to a "spectator", truth appears as a
strange and enigmatic drama even when he tries to assure himself
of it through introspection.

> Theodor Adorno, *Sören Kierkegaard:
> The Construction of the Aesthetic*[3]

I

> In my room, the world is beyond my understanding;
> But when I walk I see that it consists of three or four hills and a cloud.[4]

In this poem, "Of the Surface of Things," Wallace Stevens moves between
two kinds of poetic vision. Tempted at first by what the disengaged contemplation of the world seems to offer, the poet is finally compelled to renounce his sovereignty and surrender to a sensuous engagement with the
world. The poet's experience of being drawn out of his withdrawal recalls
for me the fragments of two stories about vision written by Franz Kafka
and found after his death. They are short enough to tell in their entirety.
One is a fragment entitled "Absent-minded Window-gazing":

> What are we to do with these spring days that are now fast coming on?
> Early this morning the sky was gray, but if you go to the window now
> you are surprised and lean your cheek against the latch of the case-
> ment. The sun is already setting, but down below you see it lighting up
> the face of the little girl who strolls along looking about her, and at the

same time you see her eclipsed by the shadow of the man behind overtaking her. And then the man has passed by and the little girl's face is quite bright.[5]

The other is called "The Street Window":

> Whoever leads a solitary life and yet now and then wants to attach himself somewhere; whoever, according to changes in the time of day, the weather, the state of his business, and the like, suddenly wishes to see any arm at all to which he might cling—he will not be able to manage for long without a window looking on to the street. And if he is in the mood of not desiring anything and only goes to his window sill a tired man, with eyes turning from his public to heaven and back again, not wanting to look out and having thrown his head up a little, even then the horses below will draw him down into their train of wagons and tumult, and so at last into the human harmony.[6]

II

In *History and Spirit: An Inquiry into the Philosophy of Liberation*, Joel Kovel commented that "Descartes's thought provides a window on the emerging despiritualization in Western culture, especially as it affects notions of the self. Thus, a critique of this despiritualization requires a critique of Descartes."[7] The textual passage that we will be examining in precisely this light is taken from Descartes's *Meditations on First Philosophy*:

> Si par hasard je ne regardois d'une fenêtre des hommes qui passent dans la rue, à la vue desquels je ne manque pas dire que je vois des hommes, tout de même que je vois de la cire; et cependant que vois-je de cette fenêtre, sinon des chapeaux et des manteaux, qui pourroient couvrir des machines artificielles qui ne se remueroient que par ressorts? mais je juge que ce sont des hommes; et ainsi je comprends par la seule puissance de juger qui réside en mon esprit ce que je croyois voir de mes yeux.[8]

This text is also, I think, the mark of another kind of passage: the defining emblem, or perhaps, rather, since it is in part, here, a question of a certain cultural malaise, the cultural "symptom" of a decisive historical passage from one worldview to another—to one, namely, that we would undoubtedly call, referring to a cultural worldview that is proudly proclaimed in the writings of Descartes, the modern.[9] And that means also: the outlook of the emerging class, the bourgeoisie, with its distinctive style of domestic life, enjoying the sovereign spaces of interiority.

After arguing, in the second of his *Meditations on First Philosophy* (1641), that it is only through the intellectual operations of the mind that we can know the identity of a piece of wax, since what we see with our eyes is merely a disconnected series of very different qualitative states, Descartes says:

> We [commonly, and in "ordinary language"] say that we see the same wax, if it is present, and not that we simply judge that it is the same from its having the same color and figure. From this we should conclude that I knew the wax by means of vision and not simply by the intuition of the mind; unless by chance I remember that, when looking from a window and saying I see men who pass in the street, I really do not see them, but infer that what I see are men, just as I say that I see wax. And yet, what do I see from the window but hats and coats which may cover automatic machines? Yet I judge these to be men.[10]

Words written in the peculiarly elevated tone of the philosopher, words through which we are supposed to hear the voice of Reason, a dispassionate voice, adopting a tone that registers the self-mastery of stoic virtue, a tone that is calm, affectively neutralized, steady and even, strictly impersonal. Words that speak of the philosopher's gaze, words that bespeak the distinctive character of this gaze. As we have seen, and may have noticed, this gaze, poised on the threshold of the modern age, inaugurated a new science and a new philosophical attitude.

In "The Crisis of European Man," Husserl wrote, on the eve of the Holocaust, that "man becomes the disinterested spectator, overseer of the world, he becomes a philosopher."[11] Now, this is *not* merely a reaffirmation of the "theoretical" gaze of the Platonic or Aristotelian philosopher.[12] For, unlike the gaze of the Greeks, the gaze by which Husserl defines the philosopher—a gaze that is modeled after that of Descartes—is not just directed at ideals and universal essences, but is also turned on human beings, and accordingly constitutes a philosophical *response* to the presence of others.

Such an uncanny, *unheimlich* gaze! How did it end up so far from our homes, so far from the warmth and friendliness of the hearth?

Heidegger gave much thought to how both the experience of vision and the conception of vision evolved in the history of philosophical discourse. Commenting, for example, on what happened to the Greek *theorein*, the philosopher's pure beholding, when it was appropriated by the Romans, he argues that, "In *theoria* transformed into *contemplatio*, there comes to the fore the impulse, already prepared in Greek thinking, of a looking-at that sunders and compartmentalizes." If Plato rejected the earlier, essentially mythical experience of vision and left behind its attitude of enchantment, its sense of wonderment, in order to practice *theoria*, a steady and attentive gazing upon the eternal aspect of that which presences in a mental state that is calm, dispassionate, and disciplined, in the period *after* Plato, the gaze of

ilosopher increasingly became a form of empirical observation, dis-
recursor of the gaze which founded modern science, and which Heidegger describes as a "challenging" of the real.[13]

In his *Rules for the Direction of the Mind,* published in 1628, some thir-
teen years before the *Meditations,* Descartes is already deploying such a
strongly visual rhetoric to formulate the method he wants to follow that it
would not be inappropriate to say that his rules are rules for the disciplin-
ing of inner and outer vision. Rule II reads: "Only those objects should engage our attention, to the sure and indubitable knowledge of which our
mental powers seem to be adequate."[14] Although the rhetoric of vision is
not explicit in these words, his subsequent discussion inscribes these "mental powers" of "attention" within the logic of vision. Thus, he writes of
obeying "the light of reason," a "natural light," in order to overcome "confused reflections" and achieve a "mental vision," a "vision-like knowledge,"
"a clear vision of each step in the process," a vision in which what we claim
to know will shine forth in its unquestionable "evidence."[15] What he wants
is "intuition": "not the fluctuating testimony of the senses, nor the misleading judgment that proceeds from the blundering constructions of the
imagination, but the conception which an unclouded and attentive mind
gives so readily and distinctly that we are wholly freed from doubt."[16]

The irony, of course, is that, while he, like Plato before him, disparages the
ability of "the senses" to convey the truth about our world, he nevertheless
depends on visionary experience—just as Plato did—to model the mind's access to truth. And, with words that conjure up the allegorical images of Plato's
cave, he warns that "those who become accustomed to walking in darkness
weaken their eye-sight so much that afterwards they cannot bear the light of
day."[17] This, he says, could only be a symptom of extreme "mental disorder."[18]
There is an unacknowledged assumption, throughout Descartes's work, that
social order, the rational moral order, depends on, requires, a well-ordered rational vision. The major problem with this derives from the fact that it privi-
leges an objective, impersonal, instrumental conception of the "rational," a
conception appropriate for mathematics and the natural sciences, but not for
the philosophical understanding of individual experience and social life.

Here is Rule V, in which a reference to vision figures explicitly: "Method
consists in the order and disposition of the objects towards which our mental
vision must be directed if we would find out any truth."[19] Although this rule
could be interpreted as proposing a method for the ordering of a purely *logical*
space, it is questionable whether it would even make sense to someone who is
deprived of visionary experience. In the hope of beholding the truth and
achieving "perspicacity," Descartes limits himself, in accordance with Rule IX,

to "viewing single objects distinctly," inasmuch as "he who attempts to view a multitude of objects with one and the same glance sees none of them distinctly."[20] Thus is our vision to be tutored, made obedient to the tuition of science, measured by the principles of geometry and the laws of physics: it is to be straight, linear, focused, and ray-like. (In the *Ideas: General Introduction to Pure Phenomenology*, Husserl describes "intentionality" in precisely the same terms.[21] The phenomenological faithfulness of these descriptions is, however, extremely problematic—and less excusable than in the work of Descartes.)

Such a conception will advance the science of optics and serve clinical medicine; but it will not address the ethical, social, and cultural dimensions of vision: what people see when they look at someone whose skin is of a different color; that people can shut their eyes to poverty and other evidence of social injustice; that people can avoid seeing another's pain and hurt; that people often see others through stereotypes, rather than as individuals; that people do not take the time really to look at the world around them; that people gifted with the capacity to see well can be so blind. Descartes's interpretation of the scene at his window lucidly reveals what Max Horkheimer, in his discussion of "The Problem of Truth," called the "indwelling inhumanity of philosophy."[22]

Nine years later, in 1637, Descartes saw the publication of his *Discourse on the Method of Rightly Conducting the Reason and Seeking for Truth in the Sciences*. Here, briefly and in passing, he unwittingly associates his method, not with the reality of our *two* eyes, but with the *singular* eye, an uncanny third eye, that mythical, mystical, monocular eye of traditions we can be sure he scorned. Thus we find him following a method that has him "looking with the eye of the philosopher on the diverse actions and enterprises of all mankind"[23] and undertaking arduous journeys into distant lands, "trying to be a spectator rather than an actor," as he puts it, "in all the comedies the world displays."[24] Perhaps we need to see the *comédie humaine*. But do we not also need to see the tragedy? How could a spectator with a Cartesian eye look at our world, a world darkened by so much suffering, so much tragedy—and really *see* it? Is it perhaps the calling of philosophers to show through their example the virtue in a way of seeing that is conducive to a life of rationality and a world of social order? But why is it assumed that detachment and affective neutrality will never themselves be responsible for cruelty and violence? Why is it assumed that only the dispassionate gaze of Reason can see the world *clearly*, and such as it is? Why is it assumed that feeling, that sense and sensibility, can only cloud and confuse our vision? And why is it always assumed that our vision can learn nothing from the dark? (Rule IX, *Rules for the Direction of the Mind*: it is "a mental disorder which prizes the darkness higher than the light.")

In Part II of the *Discourse*, there is a revealing discussion of urban planning, an allegorical digression in which Descartes indulges his urge to play with words and images:

> One of the first of the considerations that occurred to me was that there is very often less perfection in works composed of several portions, and carried out by the hands of various masters, than in those on which *one individual alone* has worked. Thus we see that buildings planned and carried out by *one architect alone* are usually more beautiful and better proportioned than those which many have tried to put in order and improve, making use of old walls which were built with other ends in view. In the same way also, those ancient cities which, originally mere villages, have become in the process of time great towns, are usually badly constructed in comparison with those which are regularly laid out on a plain by a surveyor who is free to follow his own ideas. Even though, considering their buildings each one apart, there is often as much or more display of skill in the one case than in the other, the former have large buildings and small buildings indiscriminately placed together, thus rendering the streets crooked and irregular, so that it might be said that it was chance rather than the will of men guided by reason that led to such an arrangement.[25]

Although he scorns a city with irregular streets and unpredictable alleyways, he nevertheless allows *himself* to stray from the straight and narrow logic of pure thought to contemplate, in an extended analogy, the layout of cities and towns. Translated into architectural principles, Descartes's vision of Reason clearly supports a hierarchical social structure and a monarchical politics. Ultimately, his analogy could even seem to suggest a law and order imposed by a totalitarian, if benevolent, rationality.

"I learned," he tells us, "to believe nothing too certain by which I had only been convinced by example and custom. Thus, little by little, I was delivered from many errors which might have obscured our natural vision and rendered us less capable of listening to Reason."[26] But what does he see, what imagine and think, when his ears listen to Reason and his "natural vision" of the truth is not "obscured"? Near the end of his *Discourse*, the peregrinations of his thought, perhaps less disciplined, less linear than he believes, take him into speculations that we shall need to keep in mind when we return to the passage with which we began. After noting that the human body is a machine, or may be seen as one, Descartes writes this:

> If there were machines which bore a resemblance to our body and imitated our actions as far as it was morally possible to do so, we should always have two very certain tests by which to recognize that, for all that, they were not real men. The first is, that they could never use

speech or other signs as we do when placing our thoughts on record for the benefit of others. For we can easily understand a machine's being constituted so that it can utter words, and even emit some response to action on it of a corporeal kind, which brings about a change in its organs; for instance, if it is touched in a particular part it may ask what we wish to say to it; if in another part, it may exclaim that it is being hurt, and so on. But it never happens that it arranges its speech in various ways, in order to reply appropriately to everything that may be said in its presence, as even the lowest type of man can do.[27]

This is not, however, a good argument, for it depends on his hearing vocal sounds which correspond to recognizable patterns of speech, and yet he has already declared that the evidence of his senses is deceptive and cannot be trusted. Somehow, he has released the sense in communication from the necessity of embodiment.

Be this as it may, Descartes offers a second "test" for determining the difference between man and machine: although machines can do many things, and some, he admits, even better than we can do, they fall short in other ways, "by which means we discover that they did not act from knowledge, but only from the disposition of their organs."[28] But how this test overcomes the systematic doubt he would apply to the evidence of the senses he does not, for some reason, see a need to consider.

In 1641, his *Meditations on First Philosophy* appeared in print: a subtle and elegant, but also inherently precarious synthesis of rationalism and empiricism held together, perhaps, only by its equally strong refusals to submit to superstition; the authority of tradition, custom, and habit; and propositions not grounded in a rigorous methodology. Descartes grounds his faith in the nature of Reason. His distinctive synthesis of rationalism and empiricism has not been, however, without its historical effects on our own way of understanding ourselves and our relations with others.

In the first "Meditation," Descartes sets in motion a very radical process of doubt: "if I am able to find in each one [each of the knowledge-claims he examines] some reason to doubt, this will suffice to justify my rejecting the whole."[29] No matter that this reasoning, generalizing from some to all, is indefensible! He will, in the end, restrict its meaning to the realm of pure thought. Besides, he will find that there are, after all, some things that he cannot doubt: a foundation for knowledge is possible, even though our senses deceive us and cannot be depended on for the truth:

> For example, there is the fact that I am here, seated by the fire, attired in a dressing gown, having this paper in my hands and other similar matters. And how could I deny that these hands and this body are

mine, were it not perhaps that I compare myself to certain persons, devoid of sense, whose cerebella are so troubled and clouded by the violent vapors of black bile, that they constantly assure us that they think they are kings when they are really quite poor, or that they are clothed in purple when they are really without covering, or who imagine that they have an earthenware head or are nothing but pumpkins or are made of glass. But they are mad, and I should not be any the less insane were I to follow examples so extravagant.[30]

We should note, to begin with, that the rhetorical structure of this reflection, this textual passage, is remarkably similar to the rhetorical structure of the reflection, quoted at the very beginning, which it is the concern of this essay to interrogate. In the first passage, the form is: "I would be inclined to think that *p*, unless by chance I remember that . . . " In the second, the form reads: "how could I deny that *p*, were it not that . . . " In each case, there is, as it were, a temptation which he resists—a strong temptation to think something which it would make sense, common sense, to believe. And in each case, the resistance is based on a curiously disconnected thought, a very controversial thought, dogmatically assumed to be true and already demonstrated, yet introduced as if, in some way, it were coming by chance from the margins. Like an afterthought which, because of its belatedness, may be excused from the requirement that it be argued for. Or like a thought that one finds too embarrassing—as might be the case, were one obliged to spell out the argument.

But there is a much deeper connection between the two passages, and it is about this that I now want to speak. In the passage just cited, the certainty that inhabits Descartes's "natural attitude" is rendered questionable when, for a brief moment, he entertains the thought of a comparison between what he believes about himself, and in particular, about his body, and what some others believe—those whose thoughts about themselves, or about their bodies, he calls, no doubt with some sense of relief, "extravagant." In other words, he defines the rationality he will obey in his "meditations" in terms of a comparison with those whom he assumes to be unquestionably mad. The Cartesian form of rationality, then, is *defined*, as Foucault pointed out in *Madness and Civilization*, in terms of its other: the reference to madness is unavoidable, because essential to the possibility of drawing the distinction. But does this not mean that, in a certain sense, there is a *touch* of madness within reason itself? Or at least, within *this* form of reason—the one that Descartes formulates in his rules and principles for the discipline of vision?

Descartes thinks he *knows* what madness is, and what, in comparison with it, should be regarded as rational. And yet, in the second "Meditation," we find him remembering what he saw, or thought he saw, looking out the window, and rejecting the impulse—or perhaps better said, the disposition—to believe that what he saw was human beings. I use the word "rejecting," because I now want to say that I am inclined to feel that what is most uncanny, most unsettling about this meditation is that Descartes does *not* seem to be "resisting" any overwhelming "temptation." Where is the *ethical* conflict, the struggle? This is a question to which we shall be returning. He makes the radical shift, the extreme adjustment, with what seems to be the greatest of ease. And yet, what could be a greater symptom of madness than to look out one's window and see (what might, for all one knows, be) machines, instead of real people? The point I want to make is that *this,* this kind of vision, is what the rationality he has embraced leads to. Not by mere chance, not by a momentary caprice, but by the inexorable logic of the rationality to which he is committed. Instead of turning away from madness, he moves, then, into its proximity.[31] As we see, when his vision is under the rule of objective Reason, dispassionate, detached, affectively neutralized, it is radically dehumanized—and rendered terribly blind to the very *presence* of the human.

"I cannot at present yield too much to distrust," he says in the first "Meditation," "since I am not considering the question of action, but only of knowledge."[32] For a first reading, these words, taking place near the beginning of his "meditations," may seem quite innocent of consequence. But what Descartes says as he thinks about looking out the window betrays their terrible truth. The separation of thought and action, theory (*theoria*) and practice, is a fundamental requirement of the form of rationality for which Descartes is arguing. And by denying vision its contact with the world, its involvement, this requirement makes us the spectators of a terrifying world. What is problematic, here, is not the move that establishes the possibility of theoretical thought—or even the move that secures the position and vision of the spectator, and that consequently liberates vision for the election of a speculative, or imaginative purpose—but only, rather, the extension of the program *outside* its appropriate domain.

Descartes's speculative disengagement of vision, a requirement of his program, did not remain hermetically sealed within the text of his *Meditations.* On the contrary, what he could only think—seeing other people, seeing human beings, as machines, or worse, as present through nothing but hats and coats—started to become, some three hundred years later, a nightmare, as both good and evil intentions translated the vision inscribed in his text into modern reality. Could the hypothesis that Descartes comfortably entertains at the window be read as an act with a double meaning? At the same time that the hypothesis projects the mechanization of the human as a possibility it could be desirable to see, it might also, perhaps, represent an unconscious projection of anxiety regarding the direction of the age that he was himself inaugurating.

In *Sources of the Self: The Making of the Modern Identity*, Charles Taylor points out that "one of the strongest motives underlying the rise of mechanism was originally its link with 'control', at first in relation to God. But then the beneficiary comes to be seen as human as well, and with the actual seventeenth-century revolution, motives come to be inextricably intertwined."[33] The window experience metaphors the moment when the philosopher has a vision of a uniformly mechanistic world totally under human control—and begins to see even the being of humans in this light. But a fortiori, it also metaphors the moment when the philosopher begins to see "Man" as self-made, self-constructed, self-invented. In the age that Descartes inaugurated, people began to see both the world and themselves as objects of their own making.

Perhaps it could be argued, precisely by pointing to his separation of thought from action, that Descartes's experience at the window is not to be taken seriously. But for us, his heirs, seeing others as machines—or, what is worse, seeing others as nothing but hats and coats—cannot be considered as merely an innocent experiment in thought. What Descartes sees is not present. Nor is it of *his* present. What he *sees* is the future.

Is this experience at the window to be exempted, today, from challenge because it is only feigned, only a methodological fiction? Is it to be spared from criticism because Descartes is not denying that, loosely speaking, he may appropriately say that he *sees* some men, but is merely making a *philosophical* point about the strict and proper use of words—the logical or, say, grammatical point that, strictly speaking, we do not actually (or, say, "directly") *see* the men, but only infer, or deduce, their presence on the basis of always incomplete, always corrigible, always *possibly* ("for all we know") deceptive sensory evidence? Is he merely contesting the way *philosophers* are wont to think and talk about such a situation?—And exactly what difference does it make, anyway, whether he (says that he) *sees* some men walking on the street or (says, instead, that he) *judges that* there are some men on the street? Is it not a perverse misreading to take him to be *denying* that there really *are* men passing on the street? Perhaps he is intending only to call into question the philosopher's metaphysical certainty, the philosopher's epistemological theory, leaving the familiar life-world, the world of action, just as it is. In any case, one might say, all's well that ends well; and in the final analysis, there can be no grounds for quarreling, since his judgment is clearly not impaired, and its deployment leads to the reassuring conclusion that what he sees are indeed men. But I do not find this way of reading him entirely compelling. What this reading misses is the historical context—and the subtext of implications that the passage of time has brought to light.

First of all, there are, in fact, countless practical as well as theoretical consequences at stake in the difference between seeing and judging—and what some of them are it is not at all difficult to figure out. The very separation of thought and action affects, alters, *both* thought and action. Beyond this objection, however, there are many others: for example, one may question the grounds for the distinction between strict and loose ways of talking; one may challenge the requirement that perception be absolutely incorrigible; one may contest the logic of the leap that generalizes the possibility of deception from some—a few—cases of deception; and one may dispute the argument about "directly" seeing and judging by inference, beginning with the phenomenology of perception and the *experience* that it betrays. After all, what evidence is there for the assumption that seeing always—and normally—involves a process of judgment, of inference?

On the margins of his consciousness, Descartes seems to have been aware of the difficulties that his program must confront and overcome. "I dread awakening from this slumber," he writes, referring to the uncritical attitude of his "former opinions" and the difficulties involved in his method of doubt, "lest the laborious wakefulness which would follow the tranquillity of this repose should have to be spent, not in daylight but in the excessive darkness of the difficulties which have just been discussed."[34] But he does not foresee, and obviously does not dread, the terrible *moral* darkness into which his absolute separation of thought and action, with its methodologically correlative disengagement of sight, inevitably casts us.

Descartes makes a decisive—and, one might say, fateful—break with the past when he not only separates epistemology from ethics and knowledge of truth from character, but gives priority to epistemology. To be sure, this break made possible the pursuit of science as we moderns know it, allowing, for example, ways of thinking and types of research in the field of clinical medicine that had heretofore been forbidden. (In *The Birth of the Clinic*, Foucault calls attention to the use of cadavers for research and teaching.) The benefits flowing from the Cartesian vision—the ways in which this vision has made our world a better and happier world—are certainly not to be underestimated or denied. Indeed, I will be the first to acknowledge that this vision, in many ways enlightened, in many ways a precursor of the Enlightenment, has more than fulfilled its *promesse de bonheur.* The undeniable benefits are not, however, what we are concerned with here.

Here the matter for thought is rather the perversity, the pathology, in this vision: traits the character of which we cannot ignore, and must now take very seriously, because, whatever may be said in defense of Descartes, the course of history since his time—a certain "dialectic of Enlightenment"—bears witness to the monsters this way of seeing can create and all the nightmares and horrors to which it can give rise. Never, before Descartes, had anyone published and disseminated the thought that what we see when we think we are seeing human beings may really be dressed-up machines. Of course, Descartes attempts to reassure us that our capacity for rational judgment can always *correct* the evidence of our eyes. But this reassurance does not diminish the radicality of his speculative hypothesis. Could such a thought ever have occurred to the ancients, or even to the medievals? It is, I want to say, the kind of thought that could only have occurred to a modern. An amazing thought! But the wonder of it is that its revolutionary historical significance—above all as an indication of radical changes in self-image, social relations, ethical experience, and cultural self-understanding—should have passed virtually unnoticed. The separation of epistemology from ethics and the prioritizing of epistemology contributed to the acceptability of a mode of perception the character of which is grasping, possessive, and dominating. The earlier mode, more responsive, more receptive, more predisposed to be moved by ethical factors, consequently withdrew to a reduced role in our cultural life.

The subtext of alienation from others and dehumanization that is registered in Descartes's disturbing experience at the window is related to another, perhaps even more serious, or anyway perhaps more fundamental, alienation—this one from his own body as lived: "even bodies," he declares, "are not properly speaking known by the senses, or by the faculty of the imagination, but only by the understanding, and . . . are not known from the fact that they are seen and touched, but only because they are understood."[35] Now, if this experience of one's own body were actually to be lived, it would unquestionably be regarded as symptomatic of psychosis. How, then, does Descartes arrive at such a position? We can easily catch hold of his intention, the point he wants to make, namely, once again, that it is the reasoning mind which alone can lay claim to knowledge. But he can argue for this point only by assuming that we essentially experience our own bodies only through a mental act of self-observation. But Ludwig Wittgenstein quite rightly ridiculed this way of thinking: "If I am *now* in doubt whether I have two hands, I need not believe my eyes either."[36] Making a similar point in regard to grief, he asks: "If you observe your own grief, which senses do you use to observe it? A particular sense, one that *feels* grief? Then do you feel it *differently* when you are observing it? And what is the grief you are observing—is it one which is there only while it is being observed?"[37] What he was getting at is the inappropriateness, the oddity, of using the observation model for describing our self-awareness. It may be tempting to think that, since it seems to make sense for us, in our peculiarly disengaged role as philosophers, to say that we surely *know* what we are experiencing (although it would be appropriate, and in fact would be intelligible to articulate a claim to such knowledge only in very special circumstances), it "must" *also* make sense to use the observation model, which works well enough in regard to our knowledge of the *objective* world, even for the description of our bodily self-knowledge or, rather, less problematically, what I would call our bodily self-awareness. Since Descartes adopts the observations of a spectator as model for a philosophical understanding of self-awareness, it should not be surprising that he would take the spectator's observation as paradigmatic of our relationship with others. This model, in which an odd visuality in self-experience is extended to constitute a perverse relationship with others, rests on the metaphysical dualism of mind and body that Descartes introduces very early in the first "Meditation." Having posited them as two separate substances, it seems to make sense to talk about the mind's observation of the body that is essentially "outside" it. Making the body external in this way, however, turns the body into a purely *objective* body: in effect, it takes what used to be called the soul, the spirit, *out* of the body, leaving it dehumanized, mechanical, thinglike, "mine" because I can control it, but visible and observable like anything else.

In the sixth "Meditation," this relationship to the body—the body, I mean, that one *is*—receives further definition: "there is certainly no affinity (that I at least can understand) between the craving of the stomach and the desire to eat, any more than between the perception of whatever causes pain and the thought of sadness which arises from this perception."[38] No "affinity"? To be sure, there is no *logically necessary*, a priori connection between the bodily sensations of hunger and the desire to eat; but the "contingency" of the connection (in the sense that one can *rationally* imagine creatures very much like ourselves, but for whom no such connection could arise) should not tempt us into thinking that this relationship is therefore no different in its contingency than the present relationship between my desk and my chair. Given the human embodiment, and of course the crucial role of language in the formation of all our experience, the connection is anything but contingent in this sense.

Descartes proceeds to examine the implications of his program: "if I consider the body of a man as being a sort of machine, so built up and composed of nerves, muscles, veins, blood, and skin, that though there were no
mind in it at all, it would not cease to have the same motions as at present,
exception being made of those movements which are due to the direction
of the will."[39] A conjecture that he takes very seriously. These reflections
lead him to the severe and startling conclusion that "although the whole
mind seems to be united to the whole body, yet if a foot or arm, or some
other part, is separated from my body, I am aware that nothing has been
taken away from my mind."[40] It must be pointed out, however, that he had
earlier, in fact, introduced what should be considered as evidence of a deep
loss for the mind, but without recognizing it as such. I am referring, here,
to the reports from people whose legs or arms had been amputated, according to which they claimed to feel pain in the severed part. Of course,
for Descartes, this constitutes only further evidence that the senses deceive
us: it does not bespeak a terrible loss to the mind.

When Descartes continues his elaboration of the observation model, he
is led to a conjecture: "I conjecture with probability that body does exist;
but this is only with probability, and although I examine all things with
care, I nevertheless do not find that from this distinct idea of corporeal nature, which I have in my imagination, I can derive any argument from
which there will necessarily be deduced the existence of body."[41] This alienation of the "I" from its body, an alienation the possibility of which
Descartes's unexamined visualism is, I suggest, largely responsible for, encourages him to think of his relations with others in a way that reproduces
this alienation in a corresponding alienation from others: "nature teaches
me that many other bodies exist around mine, of which some are to be
avoided, and others sought after. And certainly, from the fact that I am sensible of different sorts of colors, sounds, scents, taste, heat, hardness, etc., I
very easily conclude that there are, in the bodies from which all these diverse sense-perceptions proceed, certain variations which answer to
them."[42] Only a philosopher could, or would, talk this way. In "real life,"
outside the study, such a way of talking—such a way of *looking* at other
people—would be judged mad, a subtle symptom of paranoia.

III

The window is a framework of human construction. And since, in Descartes's
text, it is a framework for viewing others, it implicitly becomes a framework
for interpersonal, and therefore moral experience. But when moral experience is represented as taking place within a framework of human construc-

tion, the text is implicitly suggesting, or at least dangerously drawing near to, the possibility that morality itself is a mere construction, something entirely man-made. In this context, the explicitly articulated visibility of the window, a visibility that turned the window into a framework for ethical and moral relationships, could hardly have avoided raising morality into consciousness in a way that would ultimately contribute to the thematization and subsequent cultural problematization of our ethical and moral life.

To see others through a window frame is to see others as beings in a picture, as in some sense man-made, the products of artifice. Why is it that, in the modern discourse of philosophy, such a way of looking at other people could hold sway for so long without challenge? How, indeed, could it even be thought intelligible? Why did it not strike people as exceedingly peculiar, peculiar enough to call for a fundamental rethinking of the premises—and of the intellectual attitude that sustains them? Perhaps because this way of looking at human beings was actually, at the time, a radically *new* way of looking, and was for some time, moreover, manifestly liberating, making visible and inaugurating hitherto unseen possibilities for great advancements in science and technology. In the historical dialectic of Enlightenment, the revolutionary significance of this moment, when Descartes committed to the printed word a way of seeing, a vision, not only free of myth and superstition, but free, also, of the cultural constraints that forbade the objectivating gaze, should not be overlooked. But if there is any lesson in the dialectic, it is that such moments of enlightenment, such moments of liberation, must themselves be overcome, since whatever is positive in their innovations eventually becomes problematic.

Wittgenstein reminds us that "the human body is the best picture of the human soul."[43] My attitude towards the other, he says, is "an attitude towards a soul. I am not of the *opinion* that he has a soul."[44] Refusing the metaphysical dualisms of mind and body, thought and action—refusing, indeed, to philosophize from the position of the disengaged rational spectator, Wittgenstein says: "Just try—in a real case—to doubt someone else's fear or pain."[45] "If I see someone writhing in pain with evident cause, I do not think: all the same, his feelings are hidden from me."[46] I want to think of such remarks as, among other things, an attempt at the discursive reconstruction of the philosopher's way of looking at the world, and therefore an attempt to alter the way philosophers have constructed vision in their discourse. Wittgenstein thinks of this as an attempt to reconstruct these two interdependent visions by reminding us of the grammar, the logic, of our discourse—and how we experience things before we are "corrupted" by the disengagement and abstractness of philosophical speculation. "Our problem," he remarks, "is not a causal but a conceptual one."[47] Descartes, however, tells us a story, forgetting that he has invented it, that places a window between him and the men on the street, a window which disengages him from the visible world, makes him a spectator, and interrupts, or rather destroys, all the causal connections that would normally be in effect.

Using imaginary conversations, Wittgenstein dispels the aura that surrounds the philosopher's pronouncements and makes us see the unfamiliar, and indeed strange ways in which philosophers have formulated their thinking: " 'I believe that he is suffering.'—Do I also *believe* that he isn't an automaton? It would go against the grain to use the word in both connections. (Or is it like this: I believe that he is suffering, but am certain that he is not an automaton? Nonsense! Suppose I say to a friend: 'He isn't an automaton.'—What information is conveyed by this, and to whom would it be information? To a *human being* who meets him in ordinary circumstances? What information *could* it give him? (At the very most, that this man always behaves like a human being, and not occasionally like a machine.)"[48]

It is very much, for Wittgenstein, a question of altering the way philosophers have been wont to see—and also the way they understand what they see. This is apparent, for example, in another dialogue he constructs, probably with Descartes's "experience" at the window in mind:

> But can't I imagine that the people around me are automata, lack consciousness, even though they behave in the same way as usual?—If I imagine it now—alone in my room—I see people with fixed looks (as in a trance) going about their business—the idea is perhaps a little uncanny. But just try to keep hold of this idea in the midst of your ordinary intercourse with others, in the street, say! Say to yourself, for example: "The children over there are mere automata; all their liveliness is mere automatism". And you will either find these words becoming quite meaningless; or you will produce in yourself some kind of uncanny feeling, or something of the sort. Seeing a living human being as an automaton is analogous to seeing one figure as a limiting case or variant of another; the cross-pieces of a window as a swastika, for example.[49]

Wittgenstein's critical strategy, here, is to ignore precisely that separation of thought and action, symbolized by the window, which Descartes posited at the beginning of his *Meditations*, and on which the persuasiveness of his entire argument ultimately depends. Wittgenstein puts philosophical discourse back into the world. He asks us to try actually looking at people the way the philosopher proposes. He asks us to take the philosopher "seriously," to stop using our eyes and try to see, instead, through the philosopher's eye. But, at the same time, he assigns us to enact this game *in the world we actually live in.* This, of course, shows us just how difficult it would be to take the philosopher's proposition seriously.

And yet, Wittgenstein's reference to the swastika, symbol of German National Socialism, may remind us that, in fact, there is much at stake in the philosopher's vision—that there may be a deep connection between the vision represented by Descartes's "experience" at the window and the vision that hailed the swastika and murdered millions of Jews, gypsies, and homosexuals in a Holocaust of such monstrous evil that it is impossible to imagine it.

IV

In *Minima Moralia: Reflections from a Damaged Life,* Theodor Adorno commented that "the possibility of pogroms is decided in the moment when the gaze of a fatally wounded animal falls on a human being. The defiance with which he repels this gaze—'after all, it's only an animal'—reappears irresistibly in cruelties done to human beings, the perpetrators having to reassure themselves again and again that it is 'only an animal.'"[50] How does it happen that large numbers of people can be convinced that the human beings they see are only "animals," or are without human feelings, human consciousness, the human soul—like machines? How can such a vision take hold of a nation?

In "The Child's Relations with Others," Merleau-Ponty observes that, "if I like, I can always be strict and put in doubt the reality of the other's feelings towards me; this is because such feelings are never *absolutely* proved."[51] And he adds that "the normal, non-pathological attitude consists in having confidence above and beyond what can be proved, . . . by means of the generosity of the *praxis*, by means of an action that proves itself in being carried out."[52] Such confidence, however, is precisely what Descartes must deny himself, once he has allowed his window to separate his thought from the possibility of action. Thinking that one is seeing is not at all the same as actually seeing, but Descartes's *epokhé* entails their equivalence, or even their identity.[53] Nor can the act of perception be separated from the object towards which it is directed without turning it into an act of imagination. The very essence of perception lies in the inseparability of act and object.[54]

This is but one of the problems that Merleau-Ponty brings out in his examination of Descartes's treatment of perception, and, more particularly, one's visual perception of others. The perception of others "cannot be accounted for if one begins by supposing an ego and an other that are *absolutely* conscious of themselves, and each of which lays claim, as a result, to an absolute originality in relation to the other that confronts it."[55] Absolute consciousness and absolute originality could only be possible if each of us were to be shut up within ourselves, in a private "world" so self-contained and independent that we would have no interactions whatsoever with anything outside ourselves. The clinical correlate of this philosophical solipsism is the pathology of autism. But it may also be useful to think of this philosophical conception as a portrait of pathological narcissism—an extreme form of arrogance and conceit that is manifest in the perception of others. It is thus just as much an objection to narcissism, to its defensiveness and paranoia, and its painful dialectic of vulnerability and aggressiveness, as it is an objection to the philosophical position taken by Descartes to say, as Merleau-Ponty does, that "we must abandon the fundamental prejudice according to which the psyche is that which is accessible only to myself [oneself] and cannot be seen from outside."[56] This means that the other's "psyche" is not, for me, a private consciousness closed in on itself and accessible only to her.

Wittgenstein takes a similar position, formulating his critical remarks in terms of the visualism responsible for this way of thinking, or at the least complicitous in its tenacity: " 'I cannot know what is going on in him' is above all a picture."[57] "If God had looked into our minds, he would not have been able to see there whom we were speaking of."[58] It will be argued, then, that a "picture" is indeed involved, not only in the sense Wittgenstein means it here, but also in the more "literal" sense for which I shall be arguing in my discussion of Heidegger, viz., that a radically different ontology and epistemology take hold of cultural life with the beginning of modernity, and that in the course of this historical shift, our experience itself becomes increasingly "pictorial." What this means more precisely and in more detail we shall be considering later.

Merleau-Ponty's response to Descartes is to articulate our experience as we reflexively live it in a phenomenology that shows "the surpassing of narcissism"—and even, in fact, what I have called its "double-crossing."[59] "My eye for me," he points out, "is a certain power of making contact with things, and not a screen on which they are projected."[60] Descartes's philosophical gaze is a gaze that refuses such contact—and becomes, in fact, inhuman and dehumanizing: "the other's gaze transforms me into an object, and mine him, only if both of us withdraw into the core of our thinking nature, if we both make ourselves into an inhuman gaze, if each of us feels his actions to be not taken up and understood, but observed as if they were an insect's. This is what happens, for instance, when I fall under the eyes of a stranger. But even then, the objectification of each by the other's gaze is felt as unbearable only because it takes the place of a possible communication."[61] Descartes stands at the window, silently looking out. Even though he is prepared to recognize the speech of the other as an irrefutable evidence of the other's humanity, he makes no attempt to go outside, to meet the "men" he seems to see, to talk with them. The philosopher *prefers* the distance of vision, even when this distance means uncertainty—even when it means dehumanization.

"The social is already there when we come to know or judge it."[62] Before we philosophize, and while we philosophize, we are always already in communication with others.[63] This communication is, at first, unthematized, an interaction with the other taking place in a prepersonal, prereflective dimension of our experience. It is an interaction, a communication, by grace of our "intercorporeality": an experience that Merleau-Ponty has put into words which carry it forward into a more intricate meaningfulness: "it is precisely my body which perceives the body of another person, and discovers in that other body a miraculous prolongation of my own intentions, a familiar way of dealing with the world."[64] Indeed, Merleau-Ponty holds that, when I go into this experience, I will learn that "my body and the other person's are one whole, two sides of one and the same phenomenon, and the anonymous existence of which my body is the ever-renewed trace henceforth inhabits both bodies simultaneously."[65] "Vision ceases to be solipsistic," he argues, "only up close, when the other turns back upon me the luminous rays in which I had caught him, renders precise that corporeal adhesion of which I had a presentiment in the agile movement of his eyes, enlarges beyond measure that blind spot I divined at the center of my sovereign vision, and, invading my field through all its frontiers, attracts me into the prison I had prepared for him, and, as long as he is there, makes me incapable of solitude."[66] Merleau-Ponty grants that the "philosophy of vision is right in emphasizing the inevitable dissymmetry of the I-Other relation." But he insists that, "in founding the experience of the other upon that of my objectification before him, the philosophy of vision [erroneously] believed it could establish between him and me a relationship that would be at the same time a relation of being—since it is in my very being that I am affected by the view the other gets of me—and a relation of pure negation, since this objectification which I undergo is literally incomprehensible to me."[67]

"The Child's Relations with Others" resumes the reflection on this experience that Merleau-Ponty began in his *Phenomenology of Perception*.

In both works, he problematizes (much like Wittgenstein, Gilbert Ryle, and Norman Malcolm) the validity-claim of the "argument from analogy," in which Descartes takes refuge (e.g., in the sixth "Meditation") and into the proximity of which Husserl perhaps comes dangerously if ambiguously and undecidably close. His phenomenological critique involves, among other things, [1] a rejection of the assumption that I can separate the act of seeing from the world, [2] a rejection of the premise that I know about the behavior of my own body by observing myself, [3] a rejection of the assumption that the other is first and foremost an object for my observation, [4] a rejection of the premise that I enjoy privileged access to my own mind and privileged knowledge of its states and dispositions, [5] a rejection of the premise that the mind or psyche of the other is lodged inside her body, and is therefore inherently invisible, inherently hidden from me, [6] a rejection of the assumption that the mind is like a theater for the screening of private pictures, and [7] a rejection of the premise that my "own" mind, psyche, or consciousness exists in essential, a priori independence from a social life with others.[68]

But in his lectures on the phenomenology of childhood, Merleau-Ponty goes beyond critique to articulate the experience that proves Descartes wrong—experience that would not be possible if Descartes were right: "At a very early age, children are sensitive to facial expressions, e.g., the smile. How could that be possible if, in order to arrive at an understanding of the global meaning of the smile and to learn that the smile is a fair indication of a benevolent feeling, the child had to perform the complicated task I have just mentioned [namely, the argument from analogy and its decoding]."[69] He goes on to point out that, "in the case of the smile, for me to *interpret* [or, as Descartes would say, 'judge'] the visible smile of the other requires that there be a way of comparing the visible smile of the other with what we may call the 'motor smile'—the smile as felt, in the case of the child, by the child himself."[70] One of the problems with the Cartesian argument from analogy (i.e., [1] I observe the dispositions of "my body" in relation to the immediately intuited evidence of the states of my own mind, [2] I observe behavior in other bodies, bodies other than my own, that is similar to the dispositions I have observed in my own body, [3] I therefore infer the existence of other minds in states similar to my own, and [4] I therefore conclude that other beings like myself exist) is that there is no point-for-point correspondence between the image of my own body and the image of the other's body. Thus, "if my body is to appropriate the conducts given to me visually and make them its own, it must itself be given to me not as a mass of utterly private sensations [or as just another object in the world I observe], but instead by what has been called a 'postural' or 'corporeal' schema."[71]

Because Descartes makes explicit conceptual *knowledge* primary, he does not think to consider whether or not there might be an immediate, preconceptual, prereflectively felt acknowledgment of the *presence* of these others—he does not pay attention to the facticity of his *response* to what he sees. That response counts for naught. In a nursery where there is more than one infant, the crying of one of them can cause others to start crying. How can Descartes account for this "contagion of cries"?[72] How can Cartesianism ignore this "syncretic sociability," this still undifferentiated "group life"? How can it fail to see the evidence for an "initial community," already functioning prior to the phases of individuation? To be sure, the infant's display of what Merleau-Ponty calls a certain "initial sympathy" in response to the presence of others "rests," as he says, "on ignorance of oneself rather than on the perception of others," and is significantly different from the sympathy or empathy which is exercised, in later years, freely and deliberately, and which "does not abolish the differences between myself and the other."[73]

Adorno asserted that, in a repressive society, "The mechanism of 'pathic projection' determines that those in power perceive as human only their own reflected image, instead of reflecting back the human as precisely what is different."[74] There are ethical and political dimensions to the prepersonal experience of human kinship that Merleau-Ponty describes, but he does not attempt to explore them. Since I have written about these dimensions elsewhere, I will not elaborate on them here, except to say that the initial bonding of gazes to which the infant is responsive is the natural, spontaneous manifestation of a corporeal predisposition for mutual recognition in its earliest phase. But, since the process of individuation is always also a process of socialization, the further phases of development through which this predisposition must pass in order to become the mature form of recognition and respect appropriate to the ethical life of an adult in our society essentially depend on—indeed they require—the cooperation and collaboration of all the social and cultural matrices within which the infant grows up. Without favorable social and cultural conditions, without encouraging processes of socialization and learning, without exemplars in daily life, this spontaneous predisposition to see others as friendly, or as kindred spirits, or at least as human beings like oneself, may be irremediably corrupted and damaged.

When the predisposition for mutual recognition is damaged, one of the forms it may take—one of the ways in which it may be embodied—is perceptual rigidity, perceptual stereotyping. Here again, Merleau-Ponty's lectures on the phenomenology of childhood, summarized in "The Child's Relations with Others," are relevant, for he begins to formulate a fateful connection in this paper between research on the visual interactions of infancy and the damaged perception that the Frankfurt School research, conducted in the wake of the Holocaust, identified with the authoritarian personality and the oppression of totalitarian regimes.

What the Frankfurt School research found was that people whose personality makes them strongly disposed to authoritarian behavior and strongly supportive of authoritarian institutions correspondingly display perceptual habits that are distinctly authoritarian and totalitarian. They need perceptual closure (closed wholes, or totalities), insist on clarity and distinctness at all costs, and cannot tolerate ambiguities, uncertainties, complexities, and intricacy. Their perceptual forms tend, therefore, to be obsessively static and rigid, and they tend to see individuals not as individuals, but through the stereotypes of their prejudices. Their vision is accordingly disengaged from open interactions with others—not disengaged, however, as Descartes would have it, for the sake of the judgment of Reason, but disengaged, rather, so as not to disturb the fixed, automatic application of the stereotype. This *Gestalt* stereotyping tends to divide everything into extreme, absolutely irreconcilable opposites: good or evil, right or wrong, friend or enemy, me or you, we or they, with us or against us. Questions of inclusion and exclusion, identity and difference, are accordingly constantly at stake for the gaze of the authoritarian personality. This gaze is always looking for others who are either exactly the same or else predictably, stereotypically, absolutely different, others whose perceived sameness or difference will absolutely confirm the driving prejudice. This is a gaze, then, which, being intolerant of ambiguity, either reduces the otherness of the other to an absolute identity (totalitarian solidarity), or else demonizes the other's otherness, making it an otherness so absolutely different that no empathic projection, and no recognition of the humanity of the other, is possible.

Now, it should not be forgotten that Descartes's vision is a vision grounded in, and disciplined by, the judgment of a universal rationality. It is an enlightened vision, humane and benevolent, certainly not a vision of prejudice, intolerance, and hatred. But, as our examination of his writings on methodology have shown, there are some marked affinities with the authoritarian gaze, most notably in its unhappiness with ambiguity, its insistence on clarity and distinctness, its linearity, its need for fixation. (No "duck-rabbits" please!) And perhaps, too, there is an affinity in the absence of any empathy or sympathy: the Cartesian gaze is a gaze ruled by Reason alone; but it is not beside the point, I think, to note that this is a Reason without feeling, without any *rootedness* in that empathic "intercorporeality," that affectively embodied sociability, which Merleau-Ponty's phenomenology of childhood experience so nicely articulates.

I am not trying to make Cartesian vision responsible for all the horrors that, in the centuries which have followed it, the eyes of humanity have perpetrated, seen, witnessed. And yet, I cannot avoid the conclusion, as I read the history of modernity and try to understand the world I see around me, that, in some very important sense, a sense difficult to make visible in the light of strong cultural defenses and blind spots of resistance, there are deep undercurrents of influence that connect the peculiarities of Cartesian vision—its very virtues—with the malevolence of a modernity whose history has indeed been a dialectic of enlightenment, a struggle between the forces of wrath and the forces of benevolence.

V

Framing a rationalized world, Descartes's window shows us not only that reality is a construct of Reason, constructed according to a picture, a representation, but also that it is constructed to *be, and be seen as,* a work of artifice. The window is a representation of representation, an emblem of the modern age, when all that presences is to be subject to the conditions of representation, subject to a certain temporal and spatial distancing (delay, deferral, *différance*) sufficient for improved rational control. All that presences is re-presented by the ego to itself: by re-presenting what presences, the ego attempts to guarantee that it will have the encounter on its own terms.

In "The Age of the World Picture," one of his major essays, Heidegger makes the claim that

> this objectifying of whatever is, is accomplished in a setting-before, a re-presenting, that aims at bringing each particular being before it in such a way that man who calculates can be sure, and that means certain, of that being. . . . What it is to be is for the first time defined as the objectness of representing, and truth is first defined as the certainty of representing, in the metaphysics of Descartes.[75]

"Certainly," according to Heidegger, "the modern age has, as a consequence of the liberation of man, introduced subjectivism and individualism. But it remains just as certain that no age before this one has produced a comparable objectivism. . . . Essential here is the necessary interplay between subjectivism and objectivism. It is precisely this reciprocal conditioning of one by the other that points back to events more profound."[76] Events "more profound": presumably, the history of being and the advent of nihilism.

For Heidegger, nihilism defines our time, manifesting the negation of being in the realm of human experience. It is essentially related to the will to power—the rise to power of the modern ego (the modern ego-logical subject) and, at the same time, paradoxically, the domination of objectivity as the ego's paradigm of knowledge, truth and reality. This will to power has transformed the being of the human being into subjectivity, the being of things into objectivity, and the being of the world itself into a picture: "The fact that whatever is comes into being in and through representedness [i.e., being-for-a-subject] transforms the age in which this occurs into a new age in contrast to the preceding one. . . . The world picture does not change from an earlier one into a modern one, but rather the fact that the world becomes picture at all is what distinguishes the essence of the modern age [Neuzeit]."[77] Explaining what it means for the being of the world to be reduced to the being of a picture, Heidegger says: "Where the world becomes picture, . . . the world [is] conceived and grasped as picture. What is, in its entirety, is now taken in such a way that it first is in being and only is in being to the extent that it is set up by man, who represents and sets forth."[78]

Never before has the being of all that in any way is been "brought before man as the objective, . . . placed in the realm of man's knowing and of his having disposal, and [such] that it is in being only in this way."[79] In fact, this historical process has advanced so far that it has finally turned against us, and increasingly, in countless ways, major and minor, we human beings are now ourselves being turned into objects, a "standing reserve" (Bestand) for the will to power in the technocratic machine, the administrative imperatives of the "military-industrial complex." Through Descartes's window, we see the other as automaton, as machine—as perfectly, absolutely knowable, and perfectly, absolutely controllable. Ultimately, moreover, we learn to see ourselves as other, as this other. Descartes's vision is the embodiment of a rationality in the service of instrumental control.

The rise to power of the modern ego-logical subject, the modern individual, involved a cultural commitment to the will the power as the will to master, dominate, and control. But the ego's possibility of mastering, dominating, and controlling required, in turn, that objectification—reification—must be given priority, for objectification is the way that the world is brought before us in representation, made available for our technological mastering, and subjected to our domination. But the final ironic twist in the logic of this process of objectification is that it escapes our control, and we ourselves become its victims, simultaneously reduced to the being-available of mere objects and reduced to the being of a purely inner subjectivity that is no longer recognized as enjoying any truth, any reality.

If, as Heidegger suggests, the domination of technology in this process is also the domination of a certain way of seeing, then we cannot easily avoid the conclusion that the forces of nihilism at work in this domination must also be at work in our vision.[80] Heidegger accordingly calls our attention to a fateful historical moment, a moment in which a decisive shift took place in our culture of vision. The human being, who since time immemorial had been the one looked upon, becomes, at the threshold of modernity, the one looking at. This is why I want to take Descartes's experience at the window as an emblem of our time: in this narrative, we see Descartes standing at the window, standing in for the modern subject, the ego who, for the first time, affirms his pride of place as the one who looks. But the situation tells us more than this: it tells us that this way of looking is a way that can be objectifying and dehumanizing, a way that can look at others without being touched and moved by their condition—and also a way that can easily lose touch with reality.

Here, now, is what Heidegger has to say about this momentous historical shift, in which a change in ontology is connected to a change in the attitude of the gaze:

> That which is [for the ancient Greeks] does not [as in the world of modernity] come into being at all through the fact that man first looks upon it, in the sense of a representing that has the character of subjective perception. Rather, [for the ancient Greeks,] man is the one who is looked upon by that which is. . . . To be beheld by what is, to be included and maintained within its openness and in that way to be borne along with it, to be driven about by its oppositions and marked by its discord—that is the essence of man in the great age of the Greeks.[81]

The ancients allowed themselves to be, as it were, "exposed" to what presences. Their way of being was noble in its humility. Thus it would seem that, for the Greeks—and indeed, I would say, for all premodern peoples—the being of the human being can never be reduced to the condition of the *subiectum*, because the truth of their being was *unconcealment*, its participation in the interplay between the realm of the visible and the realm of the invisible—which means that it necessarily eluded total reification and its mastery and violence.[82]

"Greek man," says Heidegger, "*is* as the one who apprehends [*der Vernehmer*] that which is, and this is why in the age of the Greeks, the world cannot become picture."[83] In spite of this difference, Heidegger does not exalt the Greeks, putting them in some otherworldly paradise: it is crucial to the story he wants to tell that we see how the future, our present, was already in a certain sense implicit in the Greek way of looking: "Yet, on the other hand, that the beingness of whatever is, is defined by Plato as *eidos* [aspect, view] is the presupposition, destined far in advance and long ruling indirectly in concealment, for the world having to become picture."[84]

Unlike the Greek way of "apprehending," modern "representing" is a strategy for control. It means "to bring what is present at hand [*das Vorhandene*] before oneself as something standing over against, to relate it to oneself, to the one representing it, and to force it back into this relationship to oneself as the normative realm."[85] To "represent," he says, is "to set out before oneself and to set forth in relation to oneself. Through this, whatever is comes to stand as object."[86] To picture, to represent, is to re-present, to present again, in the sense that what presences, what gives itself to be beheld, is not received, not accepted, as it presences, as it gives itself, but is, rather, subjected to a certain delay, a certain postponement, a certain deferral, so that the ego-logical subject can give what is presencing *to itself*, can, in other words, make *itself* the giver of what it receives. In this way, the subject exercises maximum epistemic control. We might say that the emblem of such an attitude—the correlate in the realm of vision—is the stare. I think Heidegger himself may have had this analysis in mind when, in *Being and Time*, he called attention to "a fixed staring at something that is purely present-at-hand" in the context of a narrative concerned with the historical transformations undergone by the contemplative vision (*theorein*) of the ancient Greek philosophers.[87]

VI

Heidegger asserts that the problem with humanism, as the self-assertion of Man, is that it is deeply implicated in the process that has turned the world into a picture.[88] His argument is, I think, quite compelling. But the problem is complicated, because it is also precisely at this moment, when all being is reduced to the being of a picture, that the human being's relationship to other human beings—and in particular, the recognition of a common humanity that is affirmed in the very heart of humanism—becomes vulnerable and precarious. But if humanism is the rise to power of Man, and the assertion of a power that has been very self-destructive, it has also been a battle cry for the recognition and affirmation of the dignity of all human beings. And if it rebelled against the subordination of Man required by the theodicies of the ancient and medieval worlds, refusing the oppressive condition of always being visible to the gods while deprived of the power, and the right, to return the gaze, it has also turned this rebellion into a progressive struggle for conditions of symmetry that would favor respectful dialogue—and gazes of equality and reciprocity.

Heidegger argues convincingly that, "through Descartes, realism is first put in the position of having to prove the reality of the outer world [including the existence of others], of having to save that which is as such."[89] With the beginning of modernity, the existence of the world is indeed, in a sense, put in jeopardy. Read allegorically, Descartes's window opens out onto the modern age, just beginning in Descartes's time. But it is also a frame, an enclosure. And thus it is the first sign of *das Gestell*, the "enframing," the universal imposition of a totalizing order of intelligibility, which, according to Heidegger, defines the character of the modern world. But the danger is not one that realism—or for that matter, any epistemology—can overcome. Nor can a realism more robust than the one which Cartesian skepticism vanquished with a few strokes of the pen be expected to "save that which is as such" from the nihilism of a representational ontology. Something much more radical is called for. According to Heidegger, Descartes began the "completion and consummation" of Western metaphysics; Heidegger therefore believes that the currents of thought to which he gave the eloquence of his speech "can be overcome only through the overcoming of that which he [Descartes] himself founded, [i.e.,] only through the overcoming of modern, and that means at the same time Western, metaphysics."[90]

But what does this mean—the overcoming of modern, i.e., Western metaphysics? And how (if I may ask this question in another way) is radical change for the better—the *promesse de bonheur* of the Enlightenment philosophies—possible? Heidegger's answer is: "Here and now and in little things. . . . This includes holding always before our eyes the extreme danger."[91] I suggest that we take his reference to our eyes, here, as an indication that today, more than ever, there is a need for a different vision. But Western culture draws our vision in two opposing directions. And if one direction is towards the nihilism of ever-increasing reification and dehumanization, then Descartes's experience at the window may be read, in this light, allegorically, as a narrative of strategically feigned doubt and anxiety doubled by a parallel subtext, a subtext belonging to his unconscious and revealing his very *real* doubts and anxieties as he stood looking out the window of *his* world into an alien world he could already—and in a sense prophetically—see threatened by the technology of the machine and a deep ethical and cultural crisis. The other direction, then, must be towards a somehow progressively more enlightened vision. And if our hope lies in the overcoming of metaphysics, the overcoming of "picturing" and "enframing," then what I think this means in terms of our capacity for vision is that our sight must renounce its modern grounding in the epistemology of a disembodied, disengaged rationality and ground itself anew in an ethics it almost knew in ancient times, an ethics it has always, in a sense, already known, and yet, somehow, has never quite known—an ethics, in fact, that, even now, it does not know. Not quite yet.

To retrieve this possibility, we must return to the phenomenology of perception that Merleau-Ponty left us. It will be recalled that he brought out the felt intercorporeality, the felt connectedness with others, that is at work in the infant's experience. I want to say that, in effect, what he was calling to our attention, there, was a primitive, spontaneous *ethical* relationship with the other: an ethical predisposition borne by the body; a bodily attunement to and by the other; a rudimentary, bodily felt recognition of the other as both other than oneself and a part of oneself, a being different, yet of the same flesh; an "initial [capacity for] sympathy," functioning, but not yet developed.

And now I want to say that the nihilism of our time is related to the fact that the vision of modernity is an uprooted vision, a vision turned upside down. A truly enlightened and humane vision is not, and cannot be, grounded in the metaphysics of a disengaged rationality, for such a grounding can only tear vision away from its ethical roots, leaving it bereft of compassion, the capacity to be touched and moved by what it sees—what it is *given* to behold. For too long, the rationality of the philosophers has been an abstract, disengaged form of reason. But it is wrong to assume that the only way to surer knowledge lies in the disengagement of a "procedural" reason.[92] For too long, the vision of the philosophers has been a vision untouched and unmoved by what it sees—a vision that took pride in its disengagement, its *apatheia* and *ataraxia*. I would not deny that such a state can be a desirable and admirable achievement. But it can be so, I think, only in so far as it remains in touch with the feelings, the sensibility, that roots us, as human beings, in the human world. Otherwise, the vision achieved is not an embodiment of virtue, not enlightenment, but something inhuman, monstrous.

In "Interrogation and Dialectic," Merleau-Ponty observes that, "for a philosophy that is installed in pure vision, in the aerial view of the panorama, there can be no encounter with another: for the look dominates; it can dominate only things, and if it falls upon men it transforms them into puppets which move only by springs."[93]

The eyes are organs for seeing, the site of vision, and clarity. But they are also the organs through which we weep, the site of tears.[94] The eyes are "for" seeing, seeing clearly. But they are also "for" crying, for weeping. Is this connection nothing but a meaningless biological fact? I want to say that, even if we reject any metaphysical essentialism, we cannot, and must not, deny that this connection, though contingent, bears great existential significance in all known human cultures. What meaning can this be? This is what I think: that crying, the confession and seal of our belonging, our connectedness, is the *root* of vision.[95] And that, when our vision is uprooted, detached from our sensibility, our capacity for feeling, it becomes blind. It loses its ethical bearings, falls into an abyss, and sooner or later will have to face the consequences of its madness.

There is a vision whose madness consists precisely in its being driven by a rationality, a judgment, that is strictly instrumental, strictly techno-cratic.[96] And there is a vision whose madness consists in its being driven by prejudice, by re-presentation as the very structure of prejudice—a form of judgment, *Ur-teil,* divided against itself, split off from the body of felt experience, and the affective syntheses it normally vouchsafes; a form of judgment which expresses the pain of a psyche splintered into parts and incapable of the ethical syntheses and discriminations that, as the research Merleau-Ponty discusses has shown, are fundamental in the constitution of ethical relations with others.

When rooted, through crying, in sensibility, in the body of felt experience, in, therefore, an experience of our interconnectedness with all beings, vision can *see* the ethical humanity of others, can *see* their presence, without the corrective mediation of judgment. An always already ethical relationship with the other, a spontaneous responsiveness to the presence of the other as another human being, precedes and grounds the constitution of the epistemological relationship. And it is out of this responsiveness that ethical responsibility for the other can emerge and be cultivated—but only if it is deeply and securely rooted in this experience of interconnectedness, and stays in touch with its roots.

When Descartes peers out his window, what he sees, or would see, were his judgment not to correct him, are presences that could be, for all his senses can tell him, machines covered by hats and coats. As indices of the presence of human beings, nothing but hats and coats. Three hundred years later, the Nazi administrative machine turned German men into the machines of its program for genocide, the "final solution" to "the Jewish problem." And these obedient machines of the Holocaust turned six million Jews into nothing but piles of hats and coats. What did the death camp murderers see? How did they look at their victims? How could they look at the emaciated bodies of the living—and the piles of corpses, freshly produced—with eyes untouched and unmoved?

In one of his poems, T. S. Eliot wrote: "I see the eyes but not the tears / This is my affliction."[97]

VII

I have argued that it is Descartes's ocularcentric rationality which is responsible, at least in part, for his "experience" at the window—that is, for his broaching the possibility that, for all he can know from the evidence of his perception, what he is seeing are not men, but machines. But it could also be argued that, if the visualism of this rationality has drawn him into the force-field of this dehumanization, it is solely, for him, by virtue of his powers of rationality—his faculty of judgment—that he is able to avoid this conclusion. But how can Reason, the ocularcentric rationality he advocates, save him, here, from the dehumanization of others, when after all it is responsible for the madness in the dualisms of mind and body, Reason and feeling, self and other? What Descartes "sees," before being "corrected" by his rational judgment, is actually the truth about the world that this same work of Reason produced: a despiritualized, dehumanized world. What he "sees," before being "corrected" is the *madness* of this rationality.

There is, however, another way of reading Descartes's resolution of this scene at the window. That judgment, and not perception, is assigned to establish his relationship with others may be read as an indication of his vision of hope that the universality of Reason, and not the prejudices of the senses or the emotions, will—should—determine social relations among people: a vision of hope, then, for a future in which social relations would be determined by enlightened rational principles. That judgment prevails over the senses, that it is needed to correct them, may be read as an affirmation of the power of rationality—an affirmation of its freedom from the given. Unfortunately, this vision is also a vision of rational social control: a vision in which rationalization means the increasing mechanization, standardization, normalization, and engineering of the human populations. A perverse form of individualization and social progress.

An easily overlooked footnote in Merleau-Ponty's *Phenomenology of Perception* enables us to see a connection between Descartes's enframing, endistancing window, the *epokhé*, and the historically new formation of capitalism, an economy of competitive individualism based on narrow self-interest. In Descartes's fantasy of the *malin génie*, in the extreme paranoia of his metaphysical solipsism, one can see reflected the new self-understanding of the bourgeois individual. As Merleau-Ponty points out, "solipsism as a philosophical doctrine is not the result of a system of private property; nevertheless, into economic institutions as into conceptions of the world is projected the same existential prejudice in favor of isolation and mistrust."[98]

There is, finally, yet another way in which Descartes's resolution of the skeptical prospect is disturbing. Why, since he holds that only human beings are capable of authentic speech, does he not consider *speaking* to the men he "sees" on the street? Why does he allow his window to enforce a separation that excludes reciprocity, communication? What kind of judgment allows itself to be enframed in this way? And what kind of rationality is it which allows itself to be cut off from communication? In what way is the judgment of a *monological* rationality superior to, and able to correct, the *communicative* moment of perception? In *The Infinite Conversation*, Maurice Blanchot notes that a shift in paradigms from vision to speaking "frees thought from the optical imperative that in the Western tradition, for thousands of years, has subjugated our approach to things, and induced us to think under the guarantee of light or under the threat of its absence."[99]

VIII

I want to conclude by turning to what Foucault would call a marginalized and excluded body of knowledge. Turning to see what this excluded body of knowledge makes visible. Among the Native Americans of the Oglala tribe, there is an ancient ritual practice for adolescents, preparing them for their transition into the life of a responsible adult. The practice is called "crying for a vision."[100] And when the elders of the tribe speak of crying, it is not, for them, just a question of deeply *wanting* a visionary experience, and a vision by which to live their lives; it is also a question of understanding that only a vision deeply rooted in crying—in the body's deeply felt experience of the interconnectedness of all beings—can be trusted to guide one through life. There is a crying need, today, for a vision of clarity, a vision of reason; but this must be a vision of reason whose judgment, the capacity for rational discrimination and synthesis, is rooted in the body of felt experience, rooted in the vertical axis of our embodiment. When rooted in weeping, in the body of felt experience, vision becomes more deeply rooted, through the rectitude of this axis, in the ecology of the earth and the sky, the source which the judgment of reason depends on—for its first and its final measures of justice, good and evil, and for the stability of the principles by which it counsels us to live.

In his *Journals*, Emerson wrote: "Kindness is necessary to perception."[101]

2 Husserl's Transcendental Gaze

Controlling Unruly Metaphors

I know the world I converse with in the city and in the farms is not the world I think.

Ralph Waldo Emerson, "Experience"[1]

The phenomenological reduction that seeks the pure ego, beyond being, could not be secured by the effect of a writing, when the ink of the world stains the fingers that put this world between parentheses.

Emmanuel Levinas, "No Identity"[2]

See the sun again with an ignorant eye / And see it clearly in the idea of it.

Wallace Stevens, "Notes toward a Supreme Fiction"[3]

La lucidité est la blessure la plus rapprochée du soleil.

René Char, "Feuillets d'Hypnos"[4]

La question à se poser sans cesse: par où et comment rendre la nuit du rêve aux hommes.

René Char, "Aversions"[5]

The inspirations of mother earth dawn from the melancholic's night of brooding [*Grübelnacht*] like treasures from the earth; lightning-quick intuition is foreign to it.

Walter Benjamin, *Ursprung des Deutschen Trauerspiels*[6]

I. THE TRANSCENDENTAL VIEWPOINT

Can there truly be a transcendental viewing-point? Does this thought make sense? Is there not something paradoxical in the very thought that the transcendental can be identified with a viewing-point? For Husserl, the paradoxicality, the uncanniness of this thought—if it occurred to him at all—would only have multiplied his passionate questioning of the possibilities of rational life—and of the prospects for their actualization in our time. The challenge, for him, was how, as a philosopher, he could overcome the prevailing "blindness to the transcendental," the "Blindheit für das Transzendentale" that afflicts our contemporary culture.[7] Because, from his vantage point, Europe was moving at an ever-accelerating speed into the vortex of a crisis—and it was clear to him that to a greater extent than his contemporaries would see, the crisis "has its roots in a misguided rationalism"—a "verirrenden Rationalismus."[8]

In lectures given in Vienna early in May 1935, Husserl was so alarmed by the turn of events in Europe that he came out of his philosophical withdrawal and allowed himself to express, in words no longer so restrained, the dimensions of his vision, his sustaining hope and faith—almost, one might say, a dream—that, through the auspices of philosophical thought,

> man gradually becomes a new man. His spiritual being enters into the movement of an advancing reconstruction. This movement proceeds from the beginning in a communicative way, awakens a new style of personal existence in one's sphere of life, a correspondingly new becoming through communicative understanding [*Nachverstehen*]. Within this movement at first (and then later even beyond it) there grows a new sort of humanity, one which, living in finitude, lives toward poles of infinity. Precisely in this way, there arises a new type of communalization [*Vergemeinschaftung*] and a new form of enduring community [*fortdauernde Gemeinschaft*] whose spiritual life, communalized [*vergemeinschaftetes*] through the love of ideas, the production of ideas [*Ideenerzeugung*], and through ideal life-norms [*Lebensnormierung*], bears within itself the future horizon of infinity: that of an infinity of generations being renewed in the spirit of ideas.[9]

With words that, in spite of vigorous protestations, continue to echo Hegel, Husserl declares that, "only when spirit returns from its naive external orientation to itself, and remains with itself and purely with itself, can it be sufficient unto itself."[10]

Somehow, the populations of Europe, and ultimately those of the entire world, must learn to see with eyes under the rule of reason. Somehow, humanity must find its way to "a life of reason," for only that, Husserl believes, will make us "selig," "blessed."[11] And it is, for Husserl, the task of the philosopher to show the way. It is a question, he says, of "a universal responsibility," and first and foremost, the "self-responsibility" ("universale Selbstverantwortlichkeit") of the philosopher, whose assumption of this task is a necessary condition for the achievement of "autonomy" ("Autonomie").[12] One may well, then, ask: To what extent is our historical, culturally predominant way of seeing responsible for the crisis that it now can (begin to) see? What is the moral responsibility of our culturally reproduced way of looking and seeing? How—exactly—is the very "intelligibility" (my translation of Husserl's word "Einsichtigkeit") of our world-order, the very "intelligibility" of our web of sociocultural beliefs, customs, and practices, the moral responsibility of the philosopher? And how, or why, is this a responsibility for sight and insight?

For Husserl, the paradigm of rationality seems inextricably bound up with looking and seeing: so much so that it is difficult, if not impossible, to imagine expounding his ideal of reason without the rhetorical resources—the metaphors and allegorical associations—of the discourse of vision. "Self-responsibility" means, first of all, that "he who philosophizes proceeds from his own ego, and this purely as the performer of all his validities [*Vollzieher aller seiner Geltungen*], of which he becomes the purely theoretical spectator [*rein theoretischen Zuschauer*].[13] We must therefore "perform [*vollziehen*] the *epokhé* . . . ; it is through this abstention that the gaze of the philosopher [*der Blick des Philosophen*] in truth first becomes fully free: above all, free of the strongest and most hidden, internal bond, namely the pregivenness of the world."[14] And this requires that we attempt "to understand the path of motivation, the path of the bestowal and creation of meaning which leads from the mere reorientation, from mere *thaumazein*, to *theoria*—a historical fact that nevertheless must have something essential about it. We must clarify the transformation from original *theoria*, the fully disinterested seeing of the world, . . . to the *theoria* of genuine science, the two being mediated through the contrast of *doxa* and *epistemé*."[15] And we must clarify in the pure light of reason—and for a gaze absolutely committed to the purest evidence of reason—all our fundamental inherited meanings, all the inherited concepts (the *Sinngebilde*) on which our cultural life has been built.[16] For Husserl, this can be accomplished only in so far as the philosopher "withdraws into himself" in a rigorously methodical way, i.e., by means of [1] the phenomenological *epokhé* and [2] the transcendental reduction, and "establishes himself as 'disinterested onlooker' above the naively interested Ego."[17] In this peculiarly unconditioned condition, in a state of totally suspended engagement, "absolutely self-responsible," completely freed from all presuppositions and prejudices (*Vorurteile*), the philosopher is able to perform "absolute insights, insights behind which one cannot go back any farther" and thereby to reconstruct all our crucial concepts, giving them at last the rational clarification of sense (*Sinn*) that they require.[18]

Read in the context of our current postmetaphysical disposition, this philosophy seems vulnerable to challenges from many different directions. Here, though only briefly, we will consider some of the contestations formulated by Theodor Adorno, one of Husserl's most astute and most insightful critics, in spite of an occasional stubborn unfairness. In his early work on Husserl, *Against Epistemology: A Metacritique*, Adorno easily acknowledged Husserl's greatness and importance, whilst also pointing out some major problems and blind spots in the project.[19] Adorno liked Husserl's critiques of positivism and naturalism, realism and idealism; and he also, therefore, was in sympathy with Husserl's attempt to construct for his thinking an autonomous position, a critical viewing-point, outside, or at least not (totally) within the force-field of the prevailing order of reason. But he could not concur with Husserl's extreme version of transcendentalism, which not only suspended the prevailing order of beliefs, practices, and judgments, but in a certain sense entirely removed the thinking subject from the world, thereby making it impossible for the philosopher to think and enact such dialectical mediations between subject and object, subject and world as his moral conscience—or, say, moral self-responsibility— would require. Husserl, he says,

> rebels against idealist thinking whilst attempting to break through the walls of idealism with purely idealist instruments, namely, by an exclusive analysis of the structure of thought and consciousness.[20]

In fact, he argues, Husserl is the most uncompromising of all the idealists, insofar as the objective of transcendental phenomenology is "to get hold of the Absolute and, in the last analysis, to deduce with an absolute stringency everything from one absolute point [of sight]."[21]

On the one hand, Adorno could recognize in Husserl's "struggle against psychologism" the "freeing of critical reason from the prejudices contained in the naive and uncritical religion of 'facts', which he challenged in its psychological form."[22] Thus he declared: "It is this element of Husserl's philosophy in which I see even today its 'truth.' "[23] But, on the other hand, he could not overlook the abstract idealism, for which, it seemed, Husserl's ocularcentrism, his peculiar commitment to visualism, must bear some responsibility:

> There was no other philosopher in his time in whose thought terms like "dynamics" or "process" played so small a role as in Husserl's, except for his last period. He used to interpret thinking not as action but as looking at things, that is, quietly facing them like pictures in a gallery. . . . From his mathematical beginnings to the very end he was concerned only with the justification of *verités éternelles*, and for the passing phenomena he held all the contempt of the classical rationalist. In brief, he was the most static thinker of his period.[24]

Given Husserl's willingness, even if only in the realm of logic, to accept the authority of what he described, in his *Logische Untersuchungen*, for example, as a "mere looking" ("bloßen Hinblick"),[25] it is certainly difficult to deny the charges that Adorno makes.

The paradox on which Adorno puts his finger—a paradox that is also perhaps touched with a certain sense of irony—is that a position constructed precisely in order to make rational critique possible could end up too detached from its object for effective rational intervention:

> uncritically and in contemplative passivity it lays out an inventory of the thing world as that world is presented to it in the reigning order. . . . The phenomenologist correctly says of the *epokhé:* "We have properly lost nothing". . . . He declares himself satisfied with a formal title of possession over the accepted "world."[26]

Husserl's visualism encourages this passive, contemplative interpretation of reason and its task. And yet, whilst relying heavily on visualism, Husserl, like Descartes, attempts to suspend and, in effect, split off literal sight, so that he can, by a rhetorical transfer of sense, resume vision in a metaphorical sense—as the acts of a transcendentally purified Ego. Adorno does not miss this sleight of hand, tricking the incarnate eye:

> Phenomenologically speaking, it belongs to the sense of seeing that it be "with one's eyes," and would not just be casual reflection and theoretical explanation. Seeing simply could not be conceived without eyes nor hearing without ears. . . . The deictic method, which . . . seeks to seize the sense [*Sinn*] perceptually given, must expressly or not appeal to the sense organs in order to "show" in some way what may be sensed and what is sense-perception. The "I" which givenness necessarily requires is the subject as something sense-perceptually determined, one that can see and hear—and just that is denied to a transcendental or pure subject.[27]

In an important note on the transcendental suspension of the signifying body, Adorno pursues a point that Merleau-Ponty broached rather more gently in the "Introduction" to his *Phenomenology of Perception*. Similarly challenging the claim that the transcendental reduction or suspension can ever be complete, Adorno argues that

> the fact that fields of sensation are attributed to the body should be of immeasurable significance for the starting point of phenomenology, if the inferences were drawn from the description. . . . The admission of such a unity [of organ and perceptible *hyle*], however, yields up nothing less than the fact that sensation, in Husserl's doctrine the immedi-

ate, irreducible factual state of the transcendental ego, cannot be isolated from the sense organs at all. . . . The *constituens* would be as dependent on the *constitutum* as vice versa. At this point, Husserl's
analysis must cease, unless it wants to rupture the entire *epokhé* by a
finding gained within it.[28]

For Adorno, what is crucial is the dialectical mediation—and this means, on
the one hand, that there must be sufficient distance between subject and
world to make the subject relatively autonomous, but, on the other hand,
that there must be sufficient connectedness to enable the subject to engage
the world in critical interventions. In any case, even if a spectator were able
in some methodic and systematic way to "suspend" all his worldly "interests" and disengage from all his beliefs about the world, he still would not
be compelled—or even necessarily disposed—to exercise in relation to the
world a capacity for rational and critical reflection. In today's world, there
are already too many people willing to assume the position and perspective
of detached, disinterested spectator, looking at their world with eyes of res-
ignation, the downcast eyes of submission or eyes blinked shut in blind
consent.

In "Zum Ende," the concluding note to *Minima Moralia*, Adorno boldly
declares his philosophical faith and explains his understanding of the task
to which he felt himself called. The note is long, but its relevance to our
present reflections on Husserl's visualism and his assumption of the transcendental viewpoint perhaps justifies quoting it here in its entirety:

> The only philosophy which can be responsibly practised in face of de-
> spair is the attempt to contemplate all things as they would present
> themselves from the standpoint of redemption. Knowledge has no light
> but that shed on the world by redemption: all else is reconstruction,
> mere technique. Perspectives must be fashioned that displace and es-
> trange the world, reveal it to be, with its rifts and crevices, as indigent
> and distorted as it will appear one day in the messianic light. To gain
> such perspectives without velleity or violence, entirely from felt contact
> with its objects—this alone is the task of thought. It is the simplest of
> things, because the situation calls imperatively for such knowledge, in-
> deed because consummate negativity, once squarely faced, delineates
> the mirror-image of its opposite. But it is also the utterly impossible
> thing, because it presupposes a standpoint removed, even though by a
> hair's breadth, from the scope of existence, whereas we well know that
> any possible knowledge must not only be first wrested from what is, if
> it shall hold good, but is also marked, for this very reason, by the
> same distortion and indigence which it seeks to escape. The more
> passionately thought denies its conditionality for the sake of the

unconditional, the more unconsciously, and so calamitously, it is delivered up to the world. Even its own impossibility it must at last comprehend for the sake of the possible. But beside the demand thus placed on thought, the question of the reality or unreality of redemption itself hardly matters.[29]

Now, the first thing to notice is the extent to which Adorno's own thinking, here, is bound up with the rhetoric of light and vision. Although there is nothing in the text to suggest that Adorno was thinking of Husserl, it is, I think, striking how effectively it bears on Husserl's project.

Nearing the end of his life, Husserl, as we know, allowed himself to speak of our spiritual destiny, of the blessedness, the *Seligkeit,* promised by a life of reason. We also know that the life of reason meant, for him, a life in search of the unconditioned, a life, therefore, in which the apodeictic contemplation of essential truths would play a crucial role. Finally, we know that he believed such contemplation to be possible only from a position, a perspective, "removed . . . from the scope of existence," free of the worldly conditions the hidden intelligibility of which it is called upon to render manifest. These thoughts, expressed without his usual reserve in some of the texts assembled in the *Crisis,* certainly attest the depth of his anxiety, and perhaps betray a certain despair. But can we say that they constitute an "attempt to contemplate all things as they would present themselves from the standpoint of redemption"? In these late texts, we can certainly see that Husserl is resuming the great project of the Enlightenment, and that it therefore would not, perhaps, be misrepresenting his vision of transcendental phenomenology to suggest that it implies—or even in a certain sense practices and is—an ethics of lucidity. But is the light to which it aspires, or the illumination by which it is guided, the messianic light of redemption?

Would it be entirely foolish to read into Husserl's *epokhé* the motivating conviction that, as Adorno put it, "perspectives must be fashioned that displace and estrange the world, reveal it to be, with its rifts and crevices, as indigent and distorted as it will appear one day," if not "in the messianic light," then in the light of an ideal rationality, an ideal consciousness, that Husserl knows, deep down, to be impossible, but toward which, even "in the face of despair," he will nevertheless strive—and all the more passionately, the more it eludes his reach?

To be sure, Adorno enables us to catch sight of a certain performative contradiction in Husserl's thought, indeed a certain perilous darkness and unconsciousness obscured by the very brightness of the thinker's vision: "The more passionately thought denies its conditionality for the sake of the unconditioned, the more unconsciously, and so calamitously, it is delivered up to the world." And yet, in the end, does it not seem that Adorno himself effectuates an *epokhé,* a suspension of sense, closing his final note with a sentence, not at all of condemnation, but rather of admiration—the deepest respect for a thinker whose most impossible thought is wholeheartedly sacrificed "for the sake of the possible"? Adorno's final thought: "But beside the demand thus placed on thought, the question of the reality or unreality of redemption itself hardly matters."

II. HUSSERL'S OBSESSION WITH VISION

In his "Introduction" to the first volume of *Ideas,* first published in 1913, Husserl proclaims "a new way of looking at things," declaring that it is necessary that we philosophers "learn to see what stands before our eyes."[30] Years later, after a lifetime of thought, Husserl confidently announces, in his *Cartesian Meditations,* that a "science whose peculiar nature is unprecedented comes into our field of vision."[31] The phenomenological program inaugurated in the *Ideas* set the stage for Husserl's unwavering commitment to an ocular paradigm of knowledge, truth, and reality: "Immediate 'seeing' [*Sehen*], not merely the sensory seeing of experience [*Erfahrung*], but *seeing in general as primordial dator consciousness of any kind whatsoever,* is the ultimate source of justification for all rational statements."[32] We must, he says, "fix our eyes steadily upon the sphere of consciousness."[33]

Even a cursory reading of Husserl's writings, surveying his lifetime of work from the early *Logical Investigations* of 1901 through the late lectures and manuscripts of 1936, cannot but be struck by Husserl's ocularcentrism: his reliance on a vision-generated, vision-oriented rhetoric—and, as Derrida puts it, "the privilege given to vision."[34] And not only his reliance on the tropes of light and vision, but also, more extensively, his apparently inescapable dependence on metaphors of all sorts. But this dependency and reliance would not be the catastrophe that it is for his philosophical program, were it not for the fact that the logic of his visualism tempted him to envision an uncompromisingly *total* suspension or bracketing of existential referentiality and an absolutely uncompromised clarity and determinacy of meaning.

Thus, in the meaning-structures constituted within the transcendental domain of phenomenology, he will not tolerate any disruptive forms of language: no luxuriant tropes, no unruly metaphors, no shades of meaning, no formations of meaning that would give way to what Mallarmé called a "vibrating center of suspense,"[35] nothing that could not be brought within the grasp of the pure transcendental gaze. But vision, whether it be literal or figurative, a proper sense or a most improper sense, cannot possibly satisfy and fulfill the transcendental conditions that Husserl requires. For the discourse of light and vision becomes altogether incomprehensible if it needs to deny shades and shadows, horizons and darkness, viewpoints and perspectives. Husserl wants all the advantages of light and vision, wants their gift of lucidity, wants their promise of apodeictic metaphysical presence—but without any of the sacrifices which perspectivism—the reality of light and vision—imposes.

In *Time and the Other*, Levinas remarks that "De Waelhens reckons that the reason which prompted Husserl to shift from descriptive intuition to transcendental analysis resulted from an identification of intelligibility and construction—pure vision not [yet] being intelligibility."[36] He, however, reads Husserl differently:

> I think, to the contrary, that the Husserlian notion of vision already implies intelligibility. To see is already to render the encountered object one's own, as drawn from one's own ground. In this sense, "transcendental constitution" is but a way of seeing in full clarity. It is a completion of vision.[37]

But when is vision ever complete? Perhaps such completeness makes sense as a *regulative* ideal. But can it ever make sense as a *constitutive* ideal? To be sure, Husserl shifted, as Levinas and De Waelhens point out, from descriptive intuition to transcendental analysis. However, he never renounced the ocularcentrism that made his theoretism, his "strenge Wissenschaft," seem to be a feasible philosophical enterprise; nor was he ever prepared to accept the "natural" and "proper" implications of his most improper use of vision-generated rhetoric. To the end, he was as if entranced by what Adorno calls "the magic glance of intuition."[38]

Furthermore, even if it be admitted that, in a certain sense, Husserlian vision is already, as Levinas says, evidence and intelligibility, still we must insist on the fact that this vision of intelligibility is, and must be, discursively constructed. If natural vision necessarily fails the test of transcendental originality, metaphysical presence and clarity, then it can only be a question of a gaze peculiarly *constructed* in and by the discourse of transcendental philosophy. And yet, Husserl will explicitly acknowledge neither the discursive constructedness of his philosophical gaze—nor therefore the peculiar liabilities and vulnerabilities that attend this origin in a discourse, a rhetoric, irremediably contaminated by the loose talk and idle chatter of the so-called natural attitude. Levinas is therefore justified in arguing that

> Husserl will have taught us that the reduction of naivety immediately calls for new reductions, that the grace of intuition involves gratuitous ideas, and that, if philosophizing consists in assuring oneself of an absolute origin, the philosopher will have to efface the trace of his own footsteps and unendingly efface the traces of the effacing of the traces, in an interminable methodological movement staying where it is.[39]

The truth that Husserl will not admit is that he is engaged in the discursive construction of an intellectual vision—a rational intuition—and that the way this vision functions is never really immediate, as Husserl claims, but is always itself merely a transitory moment in the arduous discursive process whereby a philosophically certified gaze and, correspondingly, a philosophically admissible evidence are to be achieved. "Achieved": that means, said in language—said in a language that can never be reduced to the immanence of transcendental experience.

The transcendental purity of Husserl's language is threatened by his surprisingly free use of figurative discourse and a rich vocabulary drawn from, and inseparable from, mundane experience in the "natural attitude": terms such as "secure foundation," "founding stratum," "copy"; phrases such as "shine forth" and "reflecting back as from a mirror."[40] To be sure, Husserl is aware of his borrowings: "We spoke metaphorically of a 'mental glance' or 'glancing ray' of the pure Ego, of its turning toward or away."[41] And he warns against taking his figurative language too seriously, too "literally," i.e., too figuratively. Such language is not really proper, not really appropriate to the nature of the phenomena: "We should not hold too hard," he says, "by the metaphor of stratification; expression is not [really] of the nature of an overlaid varnish or covering garment."[42] Indeed, all "these figures of speech which have here thrust themselves upon us, those of mirroring and copying, must be adopted with caution, as the imaginativeness which colours their application might easily mislead us."[43] But such warnings and demonstrations of caution are far from sufficient: as long as any mundaneity at all clings to the words on which he depends, and as long as there are words the meanings of which cannot be limited to their explicitly meant determination, the transcendental authority of his phenomenological claims is hopelessly defended.

In "Force and Signification," Derrida questions and problematizes "the metaphor of darkness and light (of self-revelation and self-concealment), the founding metaphor of Western philosophy as metaphysics."[44] Among philosophers of the twentieth century, both Husserl and Heidegger may be charged with this ocularcentrism—although they differ in that, whereas Husserl relies mostly on constellations of meaning related to the gaze, Heidegger relies mostly on constellations of meaning related to concealment and unconcealment, and thus to darkness and light. Derrida's challenge continues, pressing a point that applies more, if at all, to Husserl than to the most eminent of his students: "In this heliocentric metaphysics, force, ceding its place to *eidos* (i.e., the form which is visible for the metaphorical eye), has already been separated from itself in acoustics. How can force or weakness be understood in terms of light and dark?"[45] It must, I think, be conceded that Husserl's method resists the recognition of force—is even designed precisely to evade or exclude the force-fields that would jeopardize a transcendental grasp of meaning. But it is not obvious that, or why, force and weakness cannot be understood within the discourse of light and dark. After all, Jewish and Christian theologies have given us many texts stained with the blood of wars, wars said to be between the forces of light and the forces of darkness.

Nevertheless, Derrida is surely correct when he argues, in " 'Genesis and Structure' and Phenomenology," that an ocularcentric philosophy generates a virtually irresistible temptation to reify, totalize, and homogenize, and reduce the forces of temporality and historicity to a state of eternal presentness.[46] Adorno advances a similar argument in *Against Epistemology*, observing that Husserl's methodological imperative to "stare fixedly at 'states-of-affairs' " turns becoming into being, processes into states, contingent events into permanent essences.[47] And Levinas, too, in *En Découvrant l'Existence*, points out the exclusion of historicity when clarity is awarded the title of supreme principle.[48]

But Husserl is not quite so easily indicted. Whatever the issue, his thinking almost always pulls him in opposing directions. In *Ideas*, for example, he reflects on the fact that, in the discourse of philosophers, "it is usual to compare attention with an illuminating light." But this reflection leads at once to the articulation of a phenomenological version of attention that registers a certain distance from earlier theories:

> What is attended to, in the specific sense, subsists in the more or less bright cone of light, but can also shade off into the half-shadow and into the full darkness. Little as the image suffices to inculcate with the proper distinctness all modes calling for phenomenological fixing, it is still significant as pointing to changes in that which appears as such. . . . [For] brightness and darkness modify its mode of appearing: they are to be found in the directing of the glance to the noematic object and the described.[49]

Although he reminds us, here, in a way that recalls William James, that attention, like the light to which it is assimilated, "can also shade off into the half-shadow and into the full darkness," there is no hint of anxiety or doubt concerning the clarity and distinctness of the boundary he wants to draw between experiences (*Erlebnisse*) that are immanent and experiences (*Erfahrungen*) that are transcendent. Nor is there any trace of anxiety or doubt concerning the possibility of achieving, through the phenomenological and transcendental "reductions," a mode of attention—immanent apperception—from which shadows and darkness would be absolutely excluded.

In spite of this persistent ocularcentrism, Husserl is nevertheless surprisingly critical—in fact strongly, sharply critical—of the so-called picture theory of the mind: neither its activity nor the product of its activity, namely meaning, can be understood in terms of the presence of images or pictures in an inner mental space. We must avoid being "misled," he says in the second of his *Logical Investigations*, "into taking the inner pictures which are found to accompany our names as the meanings of those names."[50] This reinforces the position he takes in the preceding "Investigation," where, much to his credit, he challenges us, in a rhetorical style very much like that of the later Wittgenstein, to find any mental images corresponding to the attribution of a state of understanding:

> Let a man read a work in the abstract field of knowledge, and understand the author's assertions perfectly, and let him try to see what more there is to such reading than the words he understands.[51]

He even presses this attack on the picture theory so far, here, that he declares, quite at odds with his later inclinations, that, "if the meaningful is not to be found in intuition, speech *without* intuition need not be speech deprived of thought."[52]

Moreover, whether or not two people have the same inner sensation or inner percept is not at all necessary for their ability to understand the meaning of a perceptual statement about the world.[53] By the same token, he argues, as will Heidegger some years later, against a foreshortening of intentionality—a foreshortening, that is, of our contact with the world—insisting that "I do not [at first and immediately] see colour-sensations, but rather see coloured things; I do not [at first and immediately] hear tone-sensations, but the singer's song, etc."[54] And yet, in spite of this unequivocal repudiation of image theories, Husserl still can somehow turn to describe tactile experiences as "perceptual images"![55]

In *Against Epistemology*, Adorno makes a comment on Husserl's position that brings out what might be considered the most consequential of his hidden contradictions, and he turns this critical moment, a moment in the discourse of profane illuminations, into a passage that returns us to a sacred covenant, the Jewish prohibition of images:

> If the early genuinely phenomenological Husserl convincingly polemicizes against the image and sign theories of cognition, then that polemic could also be turned against the sublimated idea that cognition is a picture of its object through resemblance or *adaequatio*. Only with the idea of an imageless truth would philosophy retrieve the prohibition of images [*Bilderverbot*].[56]

But of course Adorno's interest in retrieving this prohibition does not derive from a desire to revive a sense of absolutely transcendent divinity; rather, it comes from an intense concern, essentially political, that the doctrine of intentionality will simply perpetuate the oppressive logic of identity: if he is afraid that philosophers will continue to "fulfill" what they suppose to be utopian images by giving them a content, a noematic sense, which merely repeats the prevailing conditions of social reality, he is equally afraid that this doctrine, conceived in sympathy with a correspondence theory of truth, will, in effect, reify and fetishize the presentness of the present social reality.

III. RAYS AND BEAMS: A RATIONAL RECONSTRUCTION OF
      VISUAL INTENTIONALITY

What if Husserl had seen intentionality as the unquestionable evidence of our connectedness, as so many threads by which we are woven into the world—threads that no nightwork can unravel? Wallace Stevens saw the intertwining, and likened the effect of its binding to the effect of a tattoo:

> There are filaments of your eyes
> On the surface of the water
> And in the edges of the snow.[57]

In question, here, are Husserl's *Blickstrahlen*, his rendering of the intentionality of the gaze (be it ever so immanent) as rays and beams. It is in the texts of this rendering that we finally confront, and can no longer deny, the unsettling truth that, in the guise of rigorous, faithful, and accurate phenomenological description, leaving the phenomenon in all essentials perfectly intact, essentially as it was, Husserl is passionately engaged in a *rational reconstruction* of vision—bent on altering, or more precisely on elevating, not only the gaze of the "self-responsible" philosopher, but also, ultimately, eventually, even the ordinary, "natural" gaze of every man, woman, and child. To the extent, that is, that such ways of looking and seeing remain deeply entangled in the irrationality of images, shadows, perspectival adumbrations, and distorting reflections, instead of striving to attain, through "inwardness," the clarity and intelligibility of rational insight.

But if we must accuse Husserl of a certain unwitting sleight of hand—the sacrifice of phenomenological description and the substitution of a "rational" reconstruction—we cannot avoid the next consequential step: noticing, namely, that this reconstruction is much more than, is finally indeed something quite other than, an innocent reconstruction, merely giving the phenomenon a clarity of definition, an intentional meaning-fulfillment, more satisfying to the vanity of reason; noticing, rather, that the gaze which this modestly presented "phenomenology" discursively constructs not only is unfaithful to the phenomenon—to our experience with vision just as it is lived—but undergoes alterations, in the name of a more sublime principle of reason, which in reality have imposed untold suffering and rendered our sight capable of unimaginable monstrosities: witnessing cruelties untouched by tears; creating visions of utopia that send humanity into endless nights of living hell.

Levinas is therefore justified in arguing, in "Diachrony and Representation," that "in thought understood as vision, knowledge and intentionality, intelligibility signifies the reduction of the other [*autre*] to the same, synchrony as *being* in its egological gathering."[58] "Seeing or knowing, and taking in hand, are," he explains, "tied together in the very structure of intentionality. It remains the intrigue of a thought that recognizes itself in consciousness: the 'now' [*main-tenance*] of the present emphasizes immanence as the very excellence of this thought."[59]

Although, to be sure, affective detachment and everything that this promotes—for example, the violence inherent in reification, homogenization, and totalization, as well as the drive to achieve clarity and distinctness in the immediacy of self-evidence—certainly represent strong tendencies latent in vision that, with only a little encouragement easily assert themselves, even to the point of predominance, we need to recognize the fact that Husserl undertakes a most artful reconstruction of ordinary, everyday vision: an *artificial* construction that, blinded by a certain conceit of reason, selectively favors just *these* tendencies and proceeds in a methodical way to abstract them from the unenlightened "nature" of vision. We need, therefore, to question this construction; and since there could be other constructions, constructions that would bring out, or bring forth, other latent tendencies, making it possible for us to develop other potentials inherent in the nature of vision, we need to consider whether or not, in the final analysis, when all is said and done, the gaze that Husserl has constructed really serves the interests of reason. Reason, that is, as we presently find ourselves wanting to understand it.

Without quite realizing it, Heidegger puts his finger on the nightmare implicit in Husserl's reconstruction. In his *Introduction to Metaphysics*, Heidegger observes that, in our present epoch,

> all understanding, as a fundamental mode of disclosure, must move in *a definite line of sight*. The nature of this thing, the clock for example, remains closed to us unless we know something in advance about such things as time, reckoning with time, the measurement of time. The *line* of sight must be laid down in advance. We call it the "perspective", the *track* of foresight [*Vorblickbahn*]. Thus we shall see not only that being is not understood in an indeterminate way, but that the determinate understanding of being moves in a certain predetermined perspective. . . . We have become immersed (not to say lost) in this perspective, this *line* of sight which sustains and guides all our understanding of being. And what makes our immersion all the more complete as well as the more hidden is that even the Greeks did not and could not bring this perspective to light, and this for essential reasons.[60]

With Heidegger's words in mind, let us return to Husserl and read some passages from his published writings, beginning with the 1901 *Investigations*.

[1] As early as his *Logical Investigations*, for example, Husserl was thinking of intentionality in terms of rays: single-rayed and many-rayed objectifying acts.[61]

[2] *Ideas* I, §27, p. 92: Husserl speaks, here, without reservation, without cautionary words, of "rays from the illuminating focus of attention."

[3] *Ideas* I, §37, p. 109: "To the *cogito* itself belongs an immanent 'glancing towards' the object, a directedness which from another side springs forth from the 'Ego.'"

[4] *Ideas* I, §57, p. 156: Husserl asserts, but with scare-quotes which somehow fail to be sufficiently scary, that the Ego's "'glance' goes 'through' every actual *cogito* and toward the object. This visual ray changes with every *cogito*, shooting forth afresh with each new one as it comes."

[5] *Ideas* I, §77, p. 199: "Immanent reflection" is described as a *Blick*, a focused glance.

[6] *Ideas* I, §78, p. 207: Using, as always, as in all his writings, the masculine gender, betraying his assumption that "the philosopher" must be a man, Husserl says: "As his glance [*Blick*] turns toward the experience, it

[the *eidos,* the essence] thus becomes that which now offers itself to his gaze; and as he looks away, it becomes something else."

[7] *Ideas* I, §84, p. 223: In a section bearing the title "Intentionality as the Main Phenomenological Theme," Husserl maintains that "in every wakeful *cogito,* a 'glancing' ray from the pure Ego is directed upon the 'object' of the correlate of consciousness for the time being, [i.e., it is directed upon] the thing, the fact, and so forth, and enjoys the typically varied consciousness of it." (Also see §119, p. 310.)

[8] *Ideas* I, §92, p. 249: Husserl claims, here, believing himself to be providing a phenomenological description absolutely faithful to the phenomenon, just as it gives itself to us in our immediately lived experience, that "the attending ray [of intentionality] gives itself out as radiating from the pure Ego and as terminating in the objectivity, being directed towards or deviating from it. The shaft of attention is not separated from the Ego, but itself is and remains personal."

[9] *Ideas* I, §92, p. 247: Husserl speaks, here, of "the fixing of the beam of attention in its own appointed circuit."

[10] *Ideas* I, §101, p. 271: Now Husserl describes intentionality in terms of a "line of reflective vision," as "either a 'straightforward' or a 'reflecting' line of vision." (In *Le Temps et l'Autre,* Levinas calls our attention to "la droiture du rayon intentionnel" in Husserl's phenomenology and suggests the urgent need for an intentionality, a gaze, that connects by "detours.")[62]

[11] *Ideas* I, §122, p. 315: The Ego, Husserl says, "does not live within the theses [that it posits] as a passive indweller; the theses radiate from it as from a primary source of generation."

[12] *Ideas* I, §123, p. 318: Venturing into the realm of the concrete, Husserl gives us a moment from his own experience: "Perhaps we recall a proof, a theory, a conversation—it 'occurs to us'. And yet at first we are not turned toward it; it must emerge from the 'background'. Then a personal glance is turned single-raywise upon it."

Perhaps these passages will suffice to make the necessary point.[63] In question is whether or not intentionality has other shapes and configurations, which Husserl's rationalism cannot see: undulating waves, for example, and threads and tendrils. The more we take into account the prepersonal body of experience, the more such shapes and configurations catch our attention. Also in question: whether or not Husserl can exercise total control over what Adorno calls "the Medusa's glance": "the Medusa's glance of a sudden 'ray of vision.' "[64]

The gaze that Husserl attempts—discursively—to construct is a geometrical gaze, linear, rectilinear, straight, direct, frontal; its focus is hard, narrow, sharply pointed: precisely what tempts us to consent to the domination of *Vorhandensein*, that "theoretical" ontology which, though valuable in its appropriate domain, can also become oppressive and violent when fetishized and universalized. The gaze Husserl describes is an artificial gaze, the peculiarly unnatural product of his unacknowledged artifice. Presenting us with a carefully manufactured gaze in the disguise of a phenomenologically transcribed experience, Husserl assumes that he can bring the gaze under his "rational" control. But, whether this gaze, this intentionality of rays and beams, is meant literally or figuratively, it resists, mocks, and ultimately annihilates this attempt at control. The gaze is ultimately unruly; and even the most cautious use of ocularcentric metaphors will ultimately subvert the artifice and conceit in Husserl's rationalism. There is just no way to secure a fixed center of focus, no way to control all the shades and shadows, the mirror-play of reflections, the darkness beyond the horizon, the contingencies at the margins, the spontaneous transgressions of the periphery, the anarchy lurking in the background. (See *Ideas* I, §35, p. 107, on focal vs. peripheral intentionalities.) Even Husserl's rays and beams, at first sight so straight and direct, so perfectly suited to satisfy the imperative of lucidity, can suddenly bend and curve, twisting free of an imposed rationality. In fact, by dint of a certain magic in metaphor, utterly beyond rational control, they may even assume the sinister character that they would bear under the stress of a Cartesian madness.

"The eye," as Emerson knows it, "is the first circle; the horizon which it forms is the second; and throughout nature this primary figure is repeated without end."[65] He also says, in another essay, that "there is a property in the horizon which no man has but he whose eye can integrate all the parts, that is, the poet. This is the best part of these men's farms, yet to this their warranty-deeds give no title."[66] To be sure, Husserl understands that, as he already puts it in his *Logical Investigations*, "a great deal is marginally noticed."[67] But what about all that is *not* noticed—all that in fact is not *noticeable*? What about all the things and events that fall outside the controlled circle of the rational gaze? Husserl wants to eat his cake and yet keep it around so he can look at it and contemplate it! So at one moment, he will freely acknowledge the presence of shadows, the background, the horizon, the invisible; whilst at another moment he will blithely continue his discourse on the apodeictic character of transcendentally purified evidence, serenely avoiding any entanglement in the phenomenology of their "unruly" presence. What he gives with one hand, he takes back with the other.

What Adorno has to say, citing Benjamin, in criticism of the old masters of the dialectic—those philosophers who betray the dialectic they profess to practice by submitting it to the totalitarian logic of identity—also applies, *mutatis mutandis*, to Husserl, whose normative principle of evidence, his phenomenological "principle of all principles," is obedient to this logic for the sake of a rationality that he can conceive only in strongly identitarian terms. In *Minima Moralia*, Adorno remarks that,

> if Benjamin said that history had hitherto been written from the standpoint of the victor, and needed to be written from that of the vanquished, we might add that knowledge must indeed present the fatally rectilinear succession of victory and defeat, but should also address itself to those things which were not embraced by this dynamics, which fell by the wayside—what might be called the waste products and blind spots that have escaped the dialectic.[68]

What are Husserl's blind spots? What can he not see, not notice, because of his commitment to a rectilinear gaze, a gaze of rays and beams, a gaze that insists on maintaining its focus on the center, a gaze that will never look askance? Why is the proper gaze for a philosopher straight and narrow? Why must it abstract from worldly interests and suspend worldly involvements in order to achieve theoretical authority?

Arguing against Husserl's transcendental method, Adorno contends that the "primacy of intentionality destroys, through endless protests of concrete plenitude, the relation of philosophy to the real," because intentionality becomes a way to bind the object to the act of consciousness and pull it into the sphere of consciousness, instead of a way to think our practical engagement in and with the world.[69] For this reason, and in this sense, it cannot, I think, be denied that Husserlian phenomenology falls into an irresponsible idealism.[70]

One expression of this idealism may be read in Husserl's seemingly unproblematic assertion of the freedom and spontaneity of the phenomenological gaze. In *Ideas* I, §28 (p. 94), he remarks, for example, that "I can freely direct my glance or my acts to the natural world or to any ideal world." Again, in §35 (p. 106), he writes of "a free turning of the 'look'—not precisely nor merely of the physical but of the 'mental look' ": a turning, for example, in the direction of those backgrounded things of which we are implicitly aware.

In this regard, what I am calling the problematic implications of Husserl's thinking already appear in his *Logical Investigations*. Here is a passage from the "Third Investigation":

> The visual content *head* cannot be presented without a visual background from which it stands relieved. This impossibility is, however, quite different from the impossibility used to define non-independent contents. If we let the visual content *head* count as independent, we think that, despite its inescapable, accompanying background, it could be presented as existing by itself, and *could* therefore be intuitively envisaged in isolation. . . . The "logical" possibility remains unshaken, our visual field, e.g., "could" shrink down to this single content.[71]

Believing that he can effectuate a transcendental reduction without at all altering the phenomenon, Husserl assimilates perception to the imagination and subjects it to a "reduction" which brackets or suspends precisely that existential sense by which it is distinguishable from the imagination. Thus he is tempted to ascribe to the perceptual gaze a freedom in relation to its field of operation that makes its abstraction from the ground seem to be both feasible and reasonable: "The attempt to doubt everything," he says, "has its place in the realm of our perfect freedom." Turning the world into a mere "thesis" posited by consciousness, he continues: "We can attempt to doubt anything and everything."[72] After this, it seems to be only a short step to the conviction that a radical and absolutely total suspension of our existential involvement in the world is actually possible. Thus, in the "Prolegomenon" to his *Logical Investigations*, Husserl declared that

> a perception is . . . *possible*, in which the whole world, with the endless abundance of its bodies, is perceived at *one* glance. But this ideal possibility is of course no real possibility; we could not attribute it to any empirical subject, particularly since such a vision would be an endless continuum of vision: unitarily conceived, it would be a Kantian Idea.[73]

Of course, he acknowledges,

> the world is not doubtful in the sense that there are [specific, concrete, and] rational grounds which might be pitted against the tremendous force of unanimous experiences, but in the sense that a doubt is *thinkable*, and this is so because the possibility of non-being is in principle never excluded.[74]

But even this abstract theoretical thinkability makes sense only because Husserl's philosopher is from the beginning a disengaged spectator thinking in a "freedom" withdrawn from the world, looking at it as if from a transcendental space outside. Only in terms of this odd picture can it make sense even to talk of *thinking* "the detachability in principle of the whole natural world from the domain of consciousness."[75] What really *is* the Husserlian philosopher's "freedom"? What does it amount to? What are its ethical and political implications?

Vision, taken as paradigm of knowledge truth and reality in an ocular-centric philosophical discourse, does not inevitably or necessarily lead to a reduction of the background that renders it as just another figure. This reduction or assimilation is not inherent in the logic of vision; but it is a potential that tends to prevail, especially in our present age. Husserl's conviction that he can survey the entire world and put the world as a whole, the world in its totality, in doubt and, in effect, under suspicion *only* makes sense on the assumption that the world—the background of his present act of consciousness, the context of his present philosophical gaze—can be treated as nothing more than the sum, as it were, of all the objects that are *in* the world. But this assumption, which regards the ground as nothing other than another (albeit more comprehensive) figure, another object of intentionality, is deeply, terribly, tragically errant. We must turn to Heidegger, Husserl's student, to see and understand just how errant, how tragic, *this* way of continuing the Enlightenment project can be.

IV. EVIDENCE: A GAZE THAT LEAVES NO TRACES

What Husserl has constructed is not a blinding, sun-drenched vision, not a vision by candlelight stumbling through the shadows, and also not a vision moving gracefully by moonlight. It is a vision of the interior, a vision that the invention of electricity has made possible: it is a vision that prizes focus, fixity, centeredness, clarity, distinctness—"evidence." "Evidence," for Husserl, is the decisive goal of phenomenology, its philosophical touchstone, its "principle of all principles": "complete clearness is the measure of truth."[76] This conception of evidence, first formulated in the "Prolegomenon to Pure Logic," remained essentially unchanged in his later works. "The most perfect 'mark' of correctness," he wrote there, "is inward evidence; it counts as an immediate intuition of truth itself."[77] (Since seeing and written language are so intimately related, we should not overlook the marks around the word *mark*. What is Husserl afraid of here? What mark or trace is he attempting to scare off? What mark would he like to be able to efface?) This "inner evidence," he says,

> is called a seeing, a grasping of the self-given (true) state of affairs, or, as we say with tempting equivocation, of the truth. . . . *The experience of agreement* between meaning and what is itself present, meant,

between the actual *sense of an assertion* and the self-given *state of affairs,* is inward evidence: the *Idea* of this agreement is truth, whose ideality is also its objectivity.[78]

In "evidence," Husserl explains, "the state of affairs comes before us, not merely putatively, but as actually before our eyes, and in it the object itself, *as* the object it is."[79] Thus, there must be, on the part of the philosopher, a certain *Gelassenheit,* a certain letting-be, letting the phenomenon show itself from out of itself, as, later, Heidegger would say in his "Introduction" to *Being and Time:* "We wait, in pure surrender, on what is essentially *given.* We can then describe 'that which appears as such' faithfully and in the light of pure self-evidence."[80] What comes is worth the wait: "Every evidence 'sets up' or 'institutes' for me an abiding possession."[81] (But it is not just a question of waiting: it is clear from other passages, other texts, that, for Husserl, nothing will come if all we do is wait.) Thus, insofar as "I" construct and achieve the sight of phenomenological evidence, I enjoy the sight of "truths that are valid, and remain so, once and for all and for everyone."[82]

Such "meaning-fulfillment" (the concept is Husserl's, but it is meant, of course, in the most ascetic sense, denied all possible connotations of hedonism) requires strict adherence to the "principle of all principles." In the 1913 text of *Ideas,* this principle is formulated as follows:

> that very primordial dator intuition is a source of authority [*Rechtsquelle*] for knowledge, that whatever presents itself in 'intuition' in primordial form (as it were in its bodily reality), is simply to be accepted as it gives itself out to be, though only within the limits in which it then presents itself.[83]

("Though only within the limits . . . ": But how can Husserl's line of sight control those limits?) In the much later *Cartesian Meditations,* this principle is still considered fundamental, and its interpretation likewise remains essentially the same:

> [The "principle of pure evidence"] signifies restriction to the pure data of transcendental reflection, which therefore must be taken precisely as they are given in simple evidence, purely "intuitively" and as always, kept free from all interpretations that read into them more than is genuinely given.[84]

(When we notice—read—the word "read" here, how does our understanding of "evidence" change?) The task for the philosopher that this principle lays down is, he says, "to see and to describe adequately what he sees, purely as seen, as what is seen and seen in such and such a manner."[85] (How easy would it be—indeed, would it even be possible—to reformulate this task without the vocabulary, the rhetoric of vision, of vision, in fact, very narrowly, very artificially conceived? Moreover, in the light of Husserl's reliance on a rhetoric of seeing, how can Husserl avoid drawing the line dogmatically between the sphere of immanence and the sphere of transcendence, with regard to the "presence" of shadows?[86] "Shadows" may turn metaphorical when they are transferred into the sphere of immanence. But wouldn't there nevertheless be at least a metaphorical trace of the shadow interfering with the sovereignty of the immanent transcendental gaze?)

Now, Husserl wants to claim that, even when this evidence is incomplete, or as he puts it, "inadequate," such that more experience with the *Sache* is not only possible, but may even be reasonably expected, it can be judged "apodeictic," absolutely indubitable, beyond the logical conceivability that it could ever become questionable or doubtful. Thus, for Husserl, the non-being or being-otherwise of such evidence may also be described as "absolutely unimaginable."[87] As he states the point in his *Investigations*, "To know the ground of anything means to see the necessity of its being so and so."[88] But I would argue that, with his claims for apodeictic evidence, Husserl ultimately confuses and conflates experience as *Erlebnis* with experience as *Erfahrung*. If immediately lived experience, as lived, is inherently and necessarily a conscious consciousness, pure awareness and self-awareness through and through, then it will necessarily be unquestionable in and during the very moment of its being *erlebt*, lived. And if we wish, we could use the term "apodeictic" to refer to this unquestionableness, this "absolute unimaginableness of its non-being or its being-otherwise." But Husserl's usage of the term undergoes an unjustifiable "glissage," a slippery shift or shifty slippage of meaning; for he goes on to interpret this apodeictic character as if it could also apply to a privileged form or condition of *Erfahrung*, knowledge. Knowledge, however, whether it be empirical or transcendental, can never be regarded, unlike the lived, flowing moment of consciousness, as unquestionable, inconceivably other, apodeictic.

This problem comes to the fore with a question that Husserl himself repeatedly broaches concerning the situation in which two practitioners of phenomenology see the *Sache* differently and cannot agree.[89] It can hardly be sufficient for him to say, for example, that "it is obvious that where there is nothing, nothing can be seen; but it is no less obvious that, where there is no truth, there can be no seeing something to be true, i.e., no inward evidence."[90] For this statement is purely formal; it provides no usable criterion for settling disagreements in phenomenological practice. Hence it is incapable of sustaining the distinction between psychological certainty and transcendentally certified apodeictic evidence. Let us consider another of Husserl's attempts to think through the problem. This, too, is drawn from his "Prolegomenon" to the *Investigations:*

> I can compel nobody to see what I see. But I myself cannot doubt; I once more see, here where I have insight, i.e., where I am embracing truth itself, that all doubt would be mistaken. I therefore find myself at a point which I have either to recognize as the Archimedean point from which the world of doubt and unreason may be levered on its hinges, or which I may sacrifice only at the peril of sacrificing all reason and knowledge. I see that this is the case, and that in the latter case—if it were then still reasonable to speak of reason or unreason—I should have to pack in all rational striving for truth, all assertion and all demonstration.[91]

But if apodeictic evidence is immediately lived experience (*Erlebnis*), and not a claim about knowledge (*Erfahrung*), why is there a problem when two phenomenological insights disagree? Wouldn't such "conflict" be a problem only in so far as the moment of vision claimed—pretended—to be an apodeictic knowledge, a knowledge absolutely resistant to challenge, debate, revision, and repudiation? That Husserl frets so anxiously and obsessively over this question is a telling betrayal of the "glissage" I mentioned above, and correspondingly, an equally telling indication of his deep confusion—a confusion undoubtedly generated by, and obviously favorable to, his peculiar version of rationalism and idealism.

Like Derrida, Adorno broaches the problem of temporality. Again and again, Husserl bumps his head against this problem. However, whilst it must be said to his credit that he does not shy away from explicitly articulating it as a problem, it must also be said that he repeatedly deferred or postponed dealing with it. Thus, for example, in *Ideas* I, §81 (pp. 216–17), he describes it as "a completely self-contained sphere of problems" and blithely declares, "Fortunately, we can leave the enigmas of time-consciousness in our preliminary analyses without imperilling their rigour." Just this, of course, is what Adorno and Derrida will not allow. In *Against Epistemology*, Adorno, emphasizing, like Derrida, the impropriety of the "proper" and the impossibility of possessing knowledge as property, argues that

> non-present moments . . . are not "here", not intuitive and not absolutely singular, but distilled from some other. Always more belongs to the "proper sense" of an act than its proper sense, the canon of Husserl's method. Every act transcends its periphery in that its meant content, in order to be meant, always demands the co-meaning of an other.[92]

Levinas likewise problematizes the rationalistic (and implicitly, therefore, the Husserlian) conception of evidence, not only with regard to "diachrony" or "the impossibility of the dispersion of time to assemble itself in the present,"[93] i.e., in the reified, self-contained presentness of evidence that the absolute rational gaze assumes it can impose, but also with regard to the optics. As for the latter issue, Levinas's strategy is, first, to make the optical rhetoric of rationalism turn against itself and then to articulate his own, radically different way of approaching questions of ontology:

> the disclosure of truth is not a simple optical phenomenon. If in the quiddity of the beings that show themselves, their visibility and their being is not inscribed in the form of an attribute, it is their grouping, their co-presence, that is—and this is new!—the position of the one with regard to the other, the relativity in which the one makes a sign to the other, the reciprocal signifyingness of the one with respect to the other, that is equivalent to the coming to light of qualified quiddities themselves. The regrouping of all these significations or structures into a system, intelligibility, is the disclosure itself. The intelligibility or systematic structure of the totality would allow the totality to appear and would protect it against any alteration that could come to it from the look. And this indifference to the subjective look is not ensured in the same way for the terms, the structures, and the system. For a shadow veils the terms taken outside of the relationship in which they are implicated, the relations and the structures taken or surprised outside of the system that locks them in at the moment, when, still isolated or already abstract, they have to search for or rejoin their place in the conjuncture. . . . An order manifested in which the terms of the structures or the elements of the system hold together as an abstraction is still obscure and . . . offers resistance to the light, that is, is not fully objective. A structure is precisely an intelligibility, a rationality or a signification whose terms by themselves do not have signification (except through the already kerygmatic ideality of language). In the relationship, the terms receive a weightlessness, a grace, and something like transparency for the look, and get weighted down and occulted as soon as they separate from it.[94]

He continues his critique of ocularcentric, photocentric metaphysics, arguing that

> the intelligibility of being is always high noon without shadows, where the subject intervenes without even projecting the silhouette of its own density. Dissolving into this intelligibility of structures, it continually sees itself to be at the service of this intelligibility, equivalent to the very appearing of being. This is rational theoretical consciousness in its

purity, when the clarity of appearing in truth is equivalent to intelligibility, as in the good Cartesian tradition, where the clear and distinct ideas still receive light from Plato's intelligible sun. But the clarity comes from a certain arrangement which orders the entities or the moments and the *esse ipsum* of these entities into a system, assembling them.[95]

V. THE EIDETIC VARIATION: THE DISCURSIVE CONSTRUCTION OF THE *WESENSSCHAU*

Distinguishing between the intuition (seeing) of particulars and the intuition of essentialities (insight, *Wesensschau*), Husserl believes "that one can learn to see ideas in a type, represented, e.g., by the idea 'red', and that one can become clear as to the essence of such 'seeing.' "[96] Husserl considers individual particulars and the essences (necessary truths) which represent them to be in a certain sense interdependent and inseparable; he is, however, much more interested in essences than he is in particulars. In fact, he shows no interest in particulars as such—no interest such as the painter or writer might have, in noticing them, looking at them, watching and observing, examining and describing them—except in so far as they are the beginning of a process that enables him to achieve a clear insight into their respective essences and work on the construction of an ever more complete, ever more systematic essential ontology. Thus, he says, for example, that

> no essential intuition is possible without the free possibility of directing one's glance to an individual counterpart and of shaping an illustration; just as contrariwise no individual intuition is possible without the free possibility of carrying out an act of ideation and therein directing one's glance upon the corresponding essence, which exemplifies itself in something individually visible.[97]

Insight into the essence is achieved through ideation—or, more specifically, through a procedure that Husserl calls "eidetic variation":

> Starting from this table-perception as an example, we vary the perceptual object, table, with a completely free optionalness, yet in such a manner that we keep perception fixed as perception of something, no matter what. Perhaps we begin by fictively changing the shape or the colour of the object quite arbitrarily, keeping identical only its perceptual appearing. In other words: Abstaining from acceptance of its being, we change the fact of this perception into a pure possibility, one among

other quite "optional" pure possibilities—but possibilities that are possible perceptions. We, so to speak, shift the actual perception into the realm of non-actualities, the realm of the as-if, which supplies us with "pure" possibilities, pure of everything that restricts us to this fact or to any fact whatever. As regards the latter point, we keep the aforesaid possibilities, not as restricted even to the co-posited de facto ego, but just as a completely free "imaginableness" of phantasy. Accordingly from the very start we might have taken as our initial example a phantasying ourselves into a perceiving, with no relation to the rest of our de facto life. Perception, the universal type thus acquired, floats in the air, so to speak—in the atmosphere of pure phantasiableness. Thus removed from all factualness, it has become the pure "*eidos*" perception, whose "*ideal*" extension is made up of all ideally possible perceptions, as purely phantasiable processes. Analyses of perception are then "*essential*" or "*eidetic*" analyses. All that we have set forth concerning syntheses belonging to the type, *perception,* concerning horizons of potentiality, and so forth, holds good, as can easily be seen, "*essentially*" for everything formable in this free variation, accordingly to all imaginable perceptions without exception—in other words: with absolute "*essential universality*", and with "*essential necessity*" for every particular case selected, hence for every de facto perception, since *every fact can be thought of merely as exemplifying a pure possibility.*[98]

Since Husserl supposes that, in this process of variation, the use of fantasied particulars, fantasied possibilities, can so unproblematically substitute for actual particulars, he allows himself to declare, in a passage he might later have regretted, that,

> if anyone loves a paradox, he can really say, and say with strict truth, if he will allow for the ambiguity, that *the element which makes up the life of phenomenology, as of all eidetic science, is "fiction"*, that fiction is the source whence the knowledge of "eternal truths" draws its sustenance.[99]

He seems, here, to be acknowledging, at the very least, the *discursive artificiality* of his essential formations. That this does not strike him as problematic is no doubt an index of his comfort with an interpretation which fits so well his commitment to transcendental idealism. However, if we hold him very strictly to his words, words that, as he himself admits, spell out an ambiguous meaning, the fictionality of his "eternal truths" will mischievously subvert his strong version of rationalism. For fictionality undoes whatever rationalism, whatever metaphysical absolutism, his paradigm of "seeing" can impose.

Adorno charges that the *Wesensschau* "is no 'seeing' of essentialities, but rather a blind spot in the process of cognition."[100] His argument for this position is that the procedure turns mere facts, mere contingencies, into unalterable truths of reason:

> Facticity, the "impure", whatever is opaque to reason in producing the most obstinate resistance, i.e., with the foundation of the reality of objecthood, is sublimated into something prognosticated by reason, and thus ultimately a mere determination of reason.[101]

Marx invented a name for this process; he called it "fetishization." As both a reflection *on* the world and a reflection *of* it, philosophical discourse can all too easily fetishize what it thinks. However, according to Adorno's critical social-theoretical analysis, Husserl's constructivist treatment of categorial insight suggests that "advanced bourgeois self-consciousness can no longer be satisfied with that fetishizing of abstracted concepts in which the world of commodities is reflected for its observer."[102] Conceding the dialectical ambiguity in Husserl's work, Adorno accordingly notes that "essence does not just protect thinking from facts; it also opposes fact as sheer appearance whose validity is doubted and then posited in the epokhé, in order to bring the underlying lawfulness to consciousness."[103] Raised thus into consciousness, its reality-status temporarily suspended whilst its meaning can be examined and its origin (*Sinnesgenesis*) can be interrogated, both facts and essences can be unmasked, stripped of their fetish-character. In Husserl, then, Adorno sees the "bourgeois spirit" striving "mightily to break out of the prison of the immanence of consciousness, the sphere of constitutive subjectivity." But he also sees a dialectical contradiction or dilemma in this endeavor: it attempts this escape to freedom "with the help of the same categories as those implied by the idealistic analysis of the immanence of consciousness."[104] Adorno does not connect this critique, however, to a critique of Husserl's ocularcentrism. Had he made this connection, he might have discerned another context where the biblical *Bilderverbot* could have given rise to a healthy skepticism regarding what can be seen and encouraged Reason's emancipation from the fetishizing tendencies in seeing and its rhetoric—and discerned how, by turning thought away from vision and toward the recognition of fiction, of discursive artifice and construction, it could have rendered thought more capable of transforming the world through a phenomenological practice which begins with the assumption that the world can always be otherwise.

In *Otherwise Than Being*, Levinas also tackles the problem of essence and attempts its displacement, moving it into the force-field of "Saying" (*Le Dire*), making essence a temporal matter, a matter, at long last, for the discursive eye, the "eye that listens." For Levinas, the problem with the essence that figures in the history of philosophy from Plato through Husserl is that it has been taken out of time, "fixed in a present," and given dogmatic protection in the finality of "the Said" (*Le Dit*): "the entity that appears *identical* in the light of time *is* its essence in the *already said*. The phenomenon itself is a phenomenology."[105] "The time of the essence," he says, "unites the three moments of knowing." But, he asks, "Is the light of essence which makes things seen itself seen?" To this he wants to reply that "it can to be sure become a theme; essence can show itself, be spoken of and described. But then light presents itself in light, which latter is not thematic, but resounds for the 'eye that listens', with a resonance unique in its kind, a resonance of silence." Conscious that he is proposing something that seems very strange, he adds that "expressions such as the eye that listens to the resonance of the silence are not monstrosities, for they speak of the way one approaches the temporality of the true, and in temporality, being deploys its essence."[106] Levinas here returns the philosophical gaze to its metaphorical truth—that truth which Husserl, in a moment of abandon, a curiously "light" moment, was willing to acknowledge when he disclosed the artifice in the seeing of essences—and hence in the essences themselves.

VI. KEEPING OTHER PEOPLE IN MIND

When Husserl gives the passion of his thought to other people, what does he see? What is he moved to say? How does he keep them in mind?

> What are others, what is the world, for me?—Constituted phenomena, merely something produced within me. Never can I reach the point of ascribing being in the absolute sense to others, any more than to the physical things of Nature, which exist only as transcendentally produced affairs.[107]

Two matters of rhetoric, here, call for immediate comment. First, we should notice the "merely" and the "only": words that belittle, words that reduce, words that indicate the operation of what Adorno calls the "logic of identity." Second, we should notice how the "any more than" equates people with things, overlooking all the difference. Husserl speaks comfortably, confidently, about many things, things such as the pattern in a carpet ("Sixth Investigation," *Logical Investigations*, vol. II, §10, p. 700), "this paper before my eyes" ("Sixth Investigation," §5, p. 684), centaurs (*Ideas*, §79, pp. 207–8), "this apple tree in bloom" (Ibid., §88, p. 239), "a tree in the garden" (Ibid., §97, pp. 260–62), a table (*Cartesian Meditations*, §14, pp. 32–33), scissors (Ibid., §50, p. 111), a die (Ibid., §18, pp. 41–42), a house (Ibid., §14, pp. 32–33, §15, p. 34). When "meditating" on such things, he can proceed untroubled by the specter of solipsism. And he can continue his untroubled thinking so long as he is not obliged—or so long as he does not *feel* obliged—to recognize in the "presence" of other people an essential difference from things. Or indeed, a difference so deep, so fundamental, that even to speak of "an essential difference" somehow fails to do justice to the phenomenology of our experience: the "presence" of other people utterly shatters even the logic of the difference Husserl eventually is obliged to draw.

In Husserl's transcendental phenomenology, there is a certain moment in which the reality of other people is treated just like the reality of things: both are subject to the procedure of bracketing—the *epokhé* that suspends the existential sense which the experience normally and "naturally" carries. In other words: "Other men than I, and brute animals, are data of experience for me," so that, "from now on," everything, "not just corporeal Nature but the whole concrete surrounding life-world, is for me . . . only a phenomenon of being, instead of something that is."[108] Assuming a very odd sense of "what comes into view" for him, Husserl is prepared to accept the consequences of his procedure:

> If I keep purely what comes into view for me, the one who is meditating—by virtue of my free *epokhé* with respect to the being of the experienced world, the momentous fact is that I, with my life, *remain untouched* in my existential status, regardless of whether or not the world exists and regardless of what my eventual decision [sic] concerning its being or non-being might be.[109]

Thus Husserl can also say:

> The psychic life of my Ego (this "psychophysical" Ego), including my whole world-experiencing life and therefore including my actual and possible experience of what is other, is *wholly unaffected* by screening off what is other.[110]

In these last two passages, we can see, in the boldest, most explicit terms, the character of the vision that figures paradigmatically in the discourse of rationalism and idealism. In the name of a certain "enlightenment," we are brought face-to-face with a vision—a vision that includes a way of looking and seeing other people—that remains untouched, "wholly unaffected," by what it sees, or is given to see. But can a vision thus unaffected, thus untouched and unmoved, really be *seeing* other people at all? Can a vision protected from all vulnerability in relation to other people really be in touch with them—and in this sense, really *see* them? What kind of Enlightenment is this? And could it ever be a *kind* Enlightenment?

In *Otherwise Than Being*, Levinas draws our attention to the difficulty of registering sensibility in terms of the discourse of light and sight:

> Sensation, which is at the basis of sensible experience and intuition, is not reducible to the clarity or the idea derived out of it. Not because it would involve an opaque element resistant to the luminousness of the intelligible, but still defined in terms of light and sight. It is vulnerability, enjoyment and suffering, whose status is not reducible to the fact of being put before a spectator subject. The intentionality involved in disclosure, and the symbolization of a totality which the openness of being aimed at by intentionality involved, would not constitute the sole or even the dominant signification of the sensible. The dominant meaning of sensibility should indeed enable us to account for its secondary signification as a sensation, the element of cognition. We have already said that the fact that sensibility can become "sensible intuition" and enter into the adventure of cognition is not a contingency. The dominant signification of sensibility is already caught sight of in vulnerability.[111]

Caught sight of—but only, in the end, to be betrayed! For our vulnerability in relation to others, our susceptibility to being touched and moved by their visible presence, "cannot be defined," as Levinas rightly insists, "in terms of intentionality, where undergoing is always also an assuming, that is, an experience always anticipated and consented to, already an origin and *arkhé*." Levinas grants that "the intentionality of consciousness does not designate voluntary intention only." However, as he points out, "it retains the initiating and incohative pattern of voluntary intention. The given enters into a thought which recognizes it or invests it with its own project, and thus exercises mastery over it."[112] (We should recall, here, Husserl's words, "my eventual decision," in the passage about the *epokhé* just cited above.)

To be sure, Husserl recognizes in the world the signifying *traces*, essentially distinctive, of the human presence, pointing out, many years before Heidegger's *Daseinsanalytik* in *Being and Time,* that, by virtue of an act of heeding (*Achtsamkeit*)

> we find facing us in the natural setting, and therefore *as members of the natural world*, not natural things merely, but values and practical objects of every kind, cities, streets with street-lighting arrangements, dwellings, furniture, works of art, books, tools and so forth.[113]

In Husserlian phenomenology, some things do get named, but only as typicalities, essential types. There is no narrative interest in looking at them; no interest in deeply examining their histories, no interest in deploying a descriptive phenomenology to reflect critically on their social roles, the emotional and cultural values they evoke, or their place in our lives: they are bare particulars, or exemplars of a type. And yet, it must be noted that even the little which Husserl accomplishes with regard to the phenomenology of values breaks the powerful spell of the philosophical obfuscations and diremptions that accompanied the technological, industrial, and commercial innovations of the seventeenth century and continued with ever-increasing effects—reification, division of labor, commodity fetishism—into the century of Husserl's own lifetime. In this regard, Husserl stands virtually alone among philosophers of the early twentieth century: with only some brief passages, he redeems the *perception* of values, complicating the nondialectical distinction between facts and values and insisting that we must see values *in* the world and at the other end of our practices. Reflecting on the fact that we *see* values, that we *see* things *as* valuable, and that we *see that* things have value, Husserl says:

> When consciously awake, I find myself at all times, and without my even being able to change this, set in relation to a world which, through its constant changes, remains one and ever the same. It is continually "present" for me, and I myself am a member of it. Therefore this world is not there for me as a *mere world of facts and affairs*, but, with the same immediacy, as *a world of values, a world of goods, a practical world.* Without further effort on my part, I find the things before me furnished not only with the qualities that befit their positive nature, but with value-characters such as beautiful or ugly, agreeable or disagreeable, pleasant or unpleasant, and so forth. Things in their immediacy stand there as objects to be used, the "table" with its "books", the "glass to drink from", the "vase", the "piano", and so forth. . . . The same considerations apply of course just as well to the men and beasts in my surroundings as to "mere things". They are my "friends" or my "foes", my "servants" or "superiors", "strangers" or "relatives", and so forth.[114]

In *Ideas* I, then, he allows that we see human values quite "directly" and "immediately." And yet, in his later *Cartesian Meditations*, it is questionable whether he thinks that we may properly claim to see *other people* directly and immediately. Groundbreaking though this descriptive phenomenology is, however, we should not lose sight of its deficiencies. There is a certain quite uncanny detachment here in this passage, something almost audible, if not visible, to the "listening eye," something that I might be tempted into calling a theoretical alienation. Whilst the writing directs our attention to the "immediate presence" of social and cultural values, the presence of *other people*, the very people in whose lives these values obtain, seems to have only a very attenuated, virtually ghostly reality—as if

Husserl could more easily see the *traces* of their presence, the *traces* of their existence, than their presence, their existence, itself. The things that Husserl sees are things of value, things that human beings value—but the people themselves are strangely absent, missing.

There is something vaguely disquieting, even when he writes on the subject of love:

> Just as noetically a ray of love proceeding from the Ego splits up into a
> bundle of rays, each of which is directed toward a single object, so too
> there are distributed over the collective object of affection as such as
> many noematic *characters of love* as there are objects collected at
> the time.[115]

How faithful to the experience of love shall we say this description is? Does its difference from our experience as lived in the "natural attitude" deepen our understanding—or our experience? What is involved in *seeing* love this way? Is this (supposed to be) the description of a love that sees, that is not hopelessly blind? My questions, here, are perhaps a way of suggesting that we do not know quite how to read such a passage.

Whatever suspicions and reservations the passages we have looked at thus far may have encouraged are only multiplied by Husserl's attempt to settle the question of solipsism in the fifth—and the last—of his *Cartesian Meditations*. His efforts to dispel (or should we rather say "dis-spell"?) the impression of solipsism, of an uncanny transcendental monadology, only make matters worse, leaving this reader with the disquieting sense that the presence of other people is all too much like the spectral presence of ghosts. Or perhaps like the deceptive presence of a waxwork likeness—the "charming lady," for example, that Husserl amusingly admits he mistook for a "real" one as he walked through the Panopticum Waxworks![116] Despite his rationalism, despite his transcendental idealism, he could not resist the *jouissance* in being fooled by such dissimulation. As Gabriel Chappuys, secretary to Henry IV of France, once put it, expressing the essential spirit of the Baroque in words with which René Char and a Heraclitean Heidegger might easily have concurred,[117] dissimulation can be "a veil made of honest shadows and violent respects which serves not to form falsehood but to give respite to truth."[118] Be this as it may, "the other," Husserl tells us, speaking treacherously in the first-person language of phenomenology, "is a 'mirroring' of my own self—and yet not a mirroring proper, an analogue of my own self and yet again not an analogue in the usual sense."[119]

As we know, Husserl claims that an apodeictic evidence "excludes otherness."[120] Perhaps in the domain of logic, the rationality of this exclusion is unproblematic. But when, in the context of his phenomenological treatment of our experience of other people, this rationality, based as it is on apodeictic seeing, on insight, stubbornly dominates the meditation, the excluding of otherness becomes the principal barrier to a faithful articulation—whatever that is—of our experience. The Husserlian is forced to say that, strictly speaking, our experience of (being with) others is not, and cannot ever be, truly rational. Adorno accordingly makes the astute observation that "the shadow of what Husserl has excluded falls necessarily over the protected zone of purity—and the fundamental operation of his philosophy is one of exclusion; it is defensive through and through."[121]

The more our reading becomes entangled in Husserl's struggle, in the fifth of his *Cartesian Meditations*, to articulate "his" experience of other people, the more we are likely to agree with Adorno's judgment that the project is doomed from the very beginning:

> The more recklessly the subject insists upon identity, the more purely
> it strives to establish its mastery, the more threateningly looms the
> shadow of non-identity.[122]

(Notice how, here and in the preceding quote from his study on Husserl, Adorno expresses his critical thoughts in terms of shadows, a figure of speech that can only be intensely threatening to a phenomenology wedded to lucidity.)

The other person "brings to mind the way my body would *look* 'if I were over there.' "[123] He seems to be utterly out of touch with the oddity of this way of experiencing and describing the presence of the other. Struggle as he might, Husserl cannot satisfactorily articulate our experience with other people, because he cannot in the final analysis renounce a phenomenology generated by the logic of identity. There is no way to work with "analogical apperception," "analogizing apprehension," "similarity," "mirroring," "pairing," and "the associative transfer of sense" that will break through the solipsism of Husserl's philosophical point of departure, the monadic transcendental Ego. Not even his recognition of a "passive synthesis of sense" can settle the problem; instead, it only intensifies the paradox, the philosophically generated enigma. The truth is that Husserl cannot even *see* others clearly, because his vision is terribly distorted by the optics of his commitments to rationalism and idealism. In Merleau-Ponty's "Working Notes," published in *The Visible and the Invisible*, we find a line which reads:

> Blindness (*punctum caecum*) of "consciousness."[124]

In what ways is the philosopher's own purely theoretical gaze a tragic instance of this very blindness?

VII. AFTER THE DREAM

In his *Philosophy of History*, Hegel argued that, if one looks at the course of history through the optics of Reason, the events of history, seemingly without order, will begin to reveal their immanent rationality, their intelligibility in accordance with the cunning of Reason. Although Husserl wanted to distance himself from Hegel, his protests only confirm the proximity, for his faith in the power of rational vision, marked in fact, despite all differences, by his appropriation of the word "phenomenology," would not be surpassed in the slightest degree by that of his predecessor. But precisely this adequation, this correspondence between the way of looking and the object of this gaze, makes the vision of the gaze to some extent responsible for that which it sees. There is a certain theoretical way of looking at the world, a way that, in its mirrorlike reflecting, and in spite of its serene rational detachment, its assumption of theoretical neutrality and non-complicity—or should we rather say, precisely because of this methodic disengagement?—becomes finally inseparable from the web of causes which have brought forth in time the very conditions of cruelty, violence, and destitution on which it is ultimately compelled to reflect.

Perhaps Husserl was only one nightmare away from the darker, but also more messianic perspective expressed by Novalis, who wrote, for the *Athenaeum Fragments*, that, "a transcendental perspective on this life still awaits us. Only then will it become really meaningful for us."[125] Looking at the world through the cold eye of Reason, Husserl would sadly agree; but with his other eye, an eye rooted in a passionate dream of enlightenment and a deeply felt compassion for the sufferings of humanity, he could not refrain from proclaiming too early—much too soon—the glorious perspective of a transcendental Reason already, despite an infinite task, triumphant.

The obligation therefore falls on the poet, T. S. Eliot, for example, to remind us, as he does in "The Hollow Men,"[126] through one of the countless voices denied to our hearing in the philosophical discourse of modernity, that—

> The eyes are not here
> There are no eyes here

Dying before the Holocaust, Husserl was spared the horror of men whose eyes reflected the absolute impossibility of vision. For looking and seeing are impossible without faith, hope, and love. No transcendental I, no eyes. Here.

3 The Glasses on Our Nose

Wittgenstein's Optics and the Illusions of Philosophy

Look for [*suche*] nothing behind phenomena: they themselves are
what is to be learned.
                          Johann Wolfgang von Goethe[1]

True philosophy consists in relearning to look at the world.
                          Maurice Merleau-Ponty[2]

No theory is kind to us that cheats us of seeing.
                          Henry James[3]

I have nothing to say, only to show.
                          Walter Benjamin[4]

To repeat: don't think, but look!
                          Ludwig Wittgenstein[5]

I

In Wittgenstein's *Philosophical Investigations*, there is a note in which the
philosopher remarks that "we find certain things about seeing puzzling, because we do not find the whole business of seeing puzzling enough."[6] This
note prompts me to ask about Wittgenstein's philosophical interest in vision. What was it about vision, about seeing and sight, that attracted his
philosophical attention? How come this philosopher, noted for his "linguistic turn," his *Sprachspiele*, advises us not to "think," but to look? What
does he mean? What does this advice tell us about Wittgenstein's relation
to the historical ocularcentrism of philosophical discourse?

In this chapter, I want to argue [1] that Wittgenstein's early work, the
Tractatus Logico-Philosophicus, was in a certain, very oblique way deeply
influenced by visualism—the visualism that, at least since the time of Plato,
if not indeed from the more archaic time of the mystic visionary cults,
has dominated our philosophical thought, and [2] that, in his later work,
Wittgenstein's intensive interest in vision, and the considerable attention
he gave to the function of visualism—the rhetoric, or metaphorics, of

94

vision—in the formulation of arguments and positions of epistemology, were a thoroughgoing repudiation of this influence, a radical attempt to free philosophical thought from this hegemony of vision and put an end to treacherous metaphors from the zone of vision, as well as to misleading assumptions about the nature of vision and dubious arguments in which the mischief of vision has somehow always figured.

With regard to the question of ocularcentrism—the hegemony of vision in our cultural paradigm of knowledge, truth, and reality—I think it fair to say that Wittgenstein distrusted and disliked, and explicitly rejected, the use of "grand narratives" in philosophizing, and that, although he never explicitly recognized ocularcentrism as such and never discussed it as such, this attitude, especially intense in the years following the publication of the *Tractatus*, unquestionably *implies* an opposition to ocularcentrism as an interpretation or explanation of the history of philosophy and the history of vision. For related reasons, the later Wittgenstein also rejected philosophical oversimplification and reductionism, thinking which assimilates all things (entities, phenomena, situations, experiences) to one *kind* of thing (entity, phenomenon, situation, experience), twentieth-century versions of the doctrine of immutable species. And this he did, as we know, explicitly. Wittgenstein would thus have had no use for Heidegger's interpretation of Western history, according to which modernity is "the age of the world picture," an epoch obsessed with representations, an epoch in the history of being—and the history of ontology—toward the pictorial, enframing character of which Western civilization was already disposed from the very beginning.

Nevertheless, even though Wittgenstein never attacked ocularcentrism as such, or by name, there can be no doubt, I think, that in the years following the *Tractatus* he articulated a powerful—and, I would say, overwhelmingly successful—critique of the pernicious operations and effects of ocularcentrism in the way that philosophers have thought about questions and problems in logic, the philosophy of mathematics, epistemology, aesthetics, and even ethics and religion. Thus, for example, a situation that Wittgenstein imagines in *On Certainty* shows us just how odd the typical philosopher's appeal to the evidence or testimony of the eyes—for, after all, "seeing is believing"—can be:

> If a blind man were to ask me "have you got two hands?" I should not make sure by looking. If I were to have any doubt of it, then I don't know why I should trust my eyes. For why shouldn't I test my *eyes* by looking to find out whether I see my two hands? *What* is to be tested by *what*? (Who decides *what* stands fast?)[7]

In the situation he describes, appealing to looking and seeing would be an absurd way to settle the philosophical question. And yet, it is a strategy that philosophers have tried. What did they think they were doing?

II

Some philosophers have argued that there is "next to nothing about vision or visibility in the *Tractatus*. 'Picture' or *Bild*, which sounds visual, always refers to representations or models viewed purely abstractly in terms of their isomorphism (or, in the case of *false* propositions, isomorphism-failure) with the reality they purport to picture."[8] To be sure, the relations that obtain between propositions and facts are purely logical; they are not (visible) causalities. In other words, the structural "space" of these relations is a strictly *logical* space, not a space of sensation and vision. Moreover, there is no viewing-point, no perspective, no positionality: although the logical structures are indeed visibly represented on the page for our eyes to see, they are intended for a purely *mental* eye, an abstract, disembodied eye—the godlike eye of the philosopher, whose vision takes place outside the world of time and space.

I want to argue, however, that, in spite of the fact that this work requires a purely logical interpretation, it is a text deeply influenced by, and belonging to, the tradition of ocularcentrism, because it can make sense only if read *first* as a work conceived by, and addressed to, a certain mental or intellectual vision. As a work which makes use of pictures, a work which supplements words with visual *representations* of logical structures, it assumes our mental capacity for picturing something to ourselves, assumes the work of vision, and assumes a long tradition of visually constituted epistemologies—epistemologies of disembodied insight and intuition, epistemologies of clear and distinct ideas, epistemologies which only a god's eye could propose and enjoy.

While denying any participation by the philosopher's gaze, the *Tractatus* nevertheless presupposes it. Thus, this work offers a theory of language, of meaning and truth generated by, and constructed out of, visual experience. That its affiliation with the ocularcentrism of the tradition consists in its being, rather like Spinoza's *Ethics* and Leibniz's *Monadology*, a purely *optical* work of thought absolutely detached from the world of bodies and causalities in no way diminishes its character as a work in this tradition—the tradition, above all, perhaps, of Plato, Descartes, and Husserl.

P. M. S. Hacker has argued that Wittgenstein's "pictoriality" does not mean more than "representationality."[9] But what, exactly, does *this* mean?

In what sense, or way, does "representationality" escape visualism—escape not only its substance but its rhetoric? And how can we understand "isomorphism," or "logical space," without in any way assuming a pictorial, visionlike, or image-producing mental activity? Could Wittgenstein have presented, formulated his theory *without* his optical demonstrations? Could he have completely explained the logic of the relationship between language and world, a relationship in which we are to "see" a certain "mirroring," without in any way depending on the optics of a mental eye? Was he not bewitched, in this work, by a certain visualism?

It might be useful to run through some of the *Tractatus* propositions, to see what, and how, Wittgenstein wants to say and show.

> [1.13] The facts in logical space are the world.
> [2.1] We picture facts to ourselves. [*Wir machen uns Bilder der Tasachen.*]
> [2.11] A picture [*Bild*] presents [*stellt dar*] a situation [*Sachlage*] in logical space, the existence and non-existence of states of affairs [*Sachverhalten*].
> [2.12] A picture is a model of reality.
> [2.13] In a picture, objects have the elements of the picture corresponding to them.
> [2.131] In a picture, the elements of the picture are the representatives [*vertreten*] of objects.
> [2.15] The fact that the elements of a picture are related to one another in a determinate way represents that things are related to one another in the same way. Let us call this connection of its elements the structure of the picture, and let us call the possibility of this structure the pictorial form of the picture.
> [2.151] Pictorial form is the possibility that things are related to one another in the same way as the elements of the picture.
> [2.1511] *That* is how a picture is attached to reality: it reaches out to it.
> [2.1512] It is laid against reality like a measure.
> [2.1514] The pictorial relationship [*abbildende Beziehung*] consists in the correlations of the picture's elements with things.
> [2.16] If a fact is to be a picture, it must have something in common with what it depicts.
> [2.18] What any picture . . . must have in common with reality, in order to be able to depict it—correctly or incorrectly—in any way at all, is logical form, i.e., the form [*Form*] of reality.
> [2.201] A picture depicts [*bildet*] reality by representing [*darstellt*] a possibility of the existence or non-existence of a state of affairs.
> [2.202] A picture represents a possible situation in logical space.
> [2.223] In order to tell whether or not a picture is true or false, we must compare it with reality.
> [3] A logical picture of facts is a thought.

[3.001] "A state of affairs is thinkable": what this means is that we can picture it to ourselves.

[4.01] A proposition is a picture of reality. A proposition is a model of reality as we imagine it [*so wie wir sie uns denken*].

[4.022] A proposition *shows* [*zeigt*] its sense.

[4.112] Philosophy aims at the logical clarification of thoughts. . . . Without philosophy, thoughts are, as it were, cloudy and indistinct: its task is to make them clear and to give them sharp boundaries.

[4.116] Everything that can be thought at all can be thought clearly. Everything that can be put into words can be put clearly.

[4.121] Propositions cannot represent logical form: it is mirrored [*spiegelt*] in them. What finds its reflection in language [*was sich in der Sprache spiegelt*], language cannot represent [*darstellen*].[10]

This extensive survey should suffice to support the argument I wish to make with regard to Wittgenstein's early work. How can we discount the visual rhetoric? If it could have been avoided, replaced by a neutral, non-visual vocabulary, why did Wittgenstein persist in relying on a vision-generated, vision-based language? Surely, if such language could have been avoided, then the fact of his persistence can only be regarded as the extreme of perversity. Why the visual metaphors in a discourse obliged to achieve as much clarity and distinctness as possible? How are we to understand the modeling, the mirroring, the reflecting, the showing, the depicting, the representing, without drawing on our experience with vision—and without presupposing a long history of ocularcentric discourse, ocularcentric thinking? And what *is* "logical space"? How can it be understood except by an analogy that makes it dependent on our experience with the space of vision, touch, and bodily movement? In spite of the references to "logical space" and "logical correlations," the *Tractatus* is a work dependent on the philosophical discourse of ocularcentrism, a work inextricably bound up in a way of thinking deeply indebted to our experience with vision and to a long history of philosophical assumptions and constructions concerning the evidence of vision, the objects of vision, and the way vision works in (picturing and representing) the world.

Later on, in the *Philosophical Investigations*, Wittgenstein would say, no doubt with, among other things, his *Tractatus* in mind, "A picture [*Bild*] held us captive" (PI, §115). What picture? What illusion? Describing the vision that once held him hostage, he says: "Thought, language, now appear to us as the unique correlate, picture, of the world" (PI, §96).

To loosen the hold, the spell, that this picture has on us, Wittgenstein, having liberated himself, adopts an aporetic style of thinking, relentlessly questioning us, relentlessly compelling us to question, to suppose, to imagine and elaborate, to experiment in thought. Again and again, he puts a mirror before our minds to reflect back our thought through a medium that reveals its queerness. Or he echoes our train of thought in a fragment of dialogue that alienates that thinking and amplifies its oddity. Our philosophical rendering of the familiar then suddenly appears uncanny, and as the illusions we constructed are gradually dispelled, we begin to feel amazed that we could ever have entertained such strange thoughts about our life-world, the all too familiar world of quotidian experience. As Heidegger observed, in *Being and Time,* we are farthest from ourselves: what is nearest is farthest, farthest from a true understanding.

III

Wittgenstein's philosophical manifesto, his credo, may be summed up in one of his notes: "To repeat: don't think, but look!" (PI, §66). This counsel is good; but I trust that I would not be judged too ungrateful if I call attention to its use of a visual rhetoric. Nor is it beside the point to call attention to the frequent use of this rhetoric throughout the *Philosophical Investigations* and other late writings. But of course, this use does not necessarily, and as such, indicate or betray any persistent entanglement in the ocularcentrism of the tradition. Indeed, as we shall see, Wittgenstein's visual rhetoric in the years following the *Tractatus* is in the service of a "linguistic turn" that revolts against the hegemony of vision and twists free of its domination.

"We want," he says, elsewhere, "to *understand* something that is already in plain view. For *this* is what we seem in some sense not to understand" (PI, §98). According to Wittgenstein, our way of philosophizing "is like [wearing] a pair of glasses on our nose through which we see whatever we look at. It never occurs to us to take them off" (PI, §103).

"Philosophy," as Wittgenstein would have it, "simply puts everything before us, and neither explains nor deduces anything.—Since everything lies open to view, there is nothing to explain. For what is hidden, for example, is of no interest to us" (PI, §126). "The aspects of things that are most important for us are hidden because of their simplicity and familiarity. (One is unable to notice something—because it is always before one's eyes)" (PI, §129).

"What we are supplying," he tells us, "are really remarks on the natural history of human beings; we are not contributing curiosities, however, but observations which no one has doubted, but which have escaped remark only because they are always before our eyes" (PI, §415). We philosophers need, then, to learn how to see, see what is before our very eyes. "A main source of our failure to understand is that we do not command a clear view [*übersehen*] of the use of our words. Our grammar is lacking in this sort of perspicacity [*Übersichtlichkeit*]" (PI, §122. But also see §133 on the impossibility of the philosopher's dream of a "complete clarity").

Like Goethe, like Nietzsche, Wittgenstein is not interested in what lies *behind* "appearances": reality is not something essentially hidden, something invisible, something inaccessible to knowledge; reality is all there, all to be seen. The problem, then, lies in the blindness of the philosopher: the innumerable ways in which philosophers think themselves into a certain epistemic, aesthetic, or moral blindness. Among the questions in his *Zettel*,[11] there is this: "What justifies the blind man in saying he cannot see?" (§265). The question is undoubtedly meant to provoke thought about our requirements for knowledge, the conditions under which we would consider a certain (type of) claim to be sufficiently justified, and the sorts of things—such as the man's visible bearing and comportment—that we should want to take into account. However, with a bold and surprising twist, the question may be turned around and directed at the philosopher, the blind man who says he cannot see what is plainly staring him in the face (see also op. cit., §§446–47 and 461). Wittgenstein wanted not only to cure the philosopher's peculiar forms of blindness, but also to alter the philosopher's way of seeing. In effect, he wanted to achieve the *discursive construction* of a different way of seeing. And, as we shall see, he also wanted to deconstruct discursively the ocularcentrism of epistemology while articulating for philosophical use a different *understanding* of vision.

IV

One of the ways in which he repudiated ocularcentrism—but, as I have said, without thinking of it as such—was by challenging a certain picture of the mind, a certain conception of the mind and mental activity: the conception, namely, according to which the mind is something like a private theater, an inner space, stage, or screen, that the representations, or pictures, produced by our mental activity traverse in a ceaseless show of meaning. "The concept of the 'inner picture' is misleading," he argued, "for this concept uses the 'outer' picture as a model" (PI, p. 196e). This picture of mind, of mental activity and its meaning, this picture of an inner picture, to which we alone, with the gaze of our mind's eye, enjoy access, is a temptation we must resist: "We should really like to see into his head. And yet we only mean what elsewhere we should mean by saying: we should like to know what he is thinking" (PI, §427). There are no objectlike "meanings" to be "seen" by one's mind in the privacy of the skull: "If God had looked into our minds, he would not have been able to see there whom we were speaking of" (PI, p. 217).

"What really comes before our mind," he asks, "when we *understand* a word?" Answering for the philosophers whose ocularcentric thinking he is subjecting to a subtle form of ridicule, he replies: "Isn't it something like a picture? Can't it *be* a picture?" (PI, §139. Also see §§140–41, 294–317, and 422–27). "This 'private exhibition' is," he declares, nothing but "an illusion" (PI, §311. Also see §305). "It is no more essential to the understanding of a proposition that one should imagine anything in connection with it, than that one should make a sketch from it" (PI, §396). But why are we tempted to think otherwise?

Wittgenstein acknowledges the appeal of the picture theory of meaning, but attempts to convince us that this picture, this picture of meaning as a picture in (before) the mind, is neither necessary nor sufficient: "There really are cases where someone has the sense of what he wants to say much more clearly in his mind than he can express in words. (This happens to me very often.) It is as though one had a dream image quite clearly before one's mind's eye, but could not describe it to someone else so as to let him see it too. As a matter of fact, for the writer (myself) it is often as though the image stays there behind the words, so that they *seem* to describe it *to me*."[12]

Without a diagnosis of the disease, there can be no cure; and, like Nietzsche a physician to philosophers, Wittgenstein attempts to provide both. "We fail to get away from the idea that using a sentence involves imagining something for every word. . . . It is as if one were to believe that a written order for a cow which someone is to hand over to me always had to be accompanied by an image of a cow, if the order was not to lose its meaning" (PI, §449).

Arguing against vision-generated conceptions of introspection, intuition, and reflection, Wittgenstein wrote this provocative note: "But what can it mean to speak of 'turning my attention onto my own consciousness'? This is surely the queerest thing there could be! It was a particular act of gazing that I called doing this. I stared fixedly in front of me—but *not* at any particular point or object. My eyes were wide open, the brows not contracted (as they mostly are when I am interested in a particular object). No such interest preceded this gazing. My glance was vacant; or again, like that of someone admiring the illumination of the sky and drinking in the light" (PI, §412. See also §413). Nor is there a meaning, a private inner picture, coming between my act of looking and the object of my gaze (PI, §§393–402).

Again and again, Wittgenstein questioned and problematized the way that vision, as paradigm of knowledge, truth, and reality, has tempted us to think: to think about attention (*Zettel*, §673: attention is not a gazing, not a *Hinstarren*), about remembering (*Zettel*, §662: remembering is not a seeing, not a *Sehen*), about intending and thinking (*Zettel*, §§231–47: these activities do not involve the entertainment of a picture or image), about imagining and anticipating (PI, §§393, 398–402). According to Wittgenstein, not even knowing what someone *looks like* requires the presence of a mental picture or image (PI, §450). And, in opposition to a long-established school of thought, he will argue against the *Wesensschau*, ventriloquizing the thought process of the philosophers he is challenging, for the first time saying out loud and in the public domain what they have never before been willing to say except to themselves: "I feel as though, if only I could fix my gaze absolutely sharply on this fact, get it in focus, I must grasp the essence of the matter" (PI, §113). Stated thus in the public domain, such a train of thought immediately betrays its oddity, its foolishness. We can tell at once how far-fetched such thinking is—how far removed it is from the "uncorrupted" understanding of people outside the philosophical conversation.

One of the more mischievous consequences of the visual paradigm can be found in the epistemological discourse concerning the existence of "other minds," other human beings. As Wittgenstein shows us, skepticism regarding the existence of others is greatly facilitated, if not even, indeed, made possible, by a certain—erroneous and misleading—understanding of the nature of seeing.

Do we actually, or really, *see* other people, or only infer their presence—hypothetically, probabilistically, and therefore problematically? "Our problem," he insists, "is not a causal but a conceptual one" (PI, p. 203e). Thus he asks: "Isn't it a misleading metaphor to say: 'My eyes give me the information that there is a chair over there?' " (PI, §356). A fortiori: "My attitude towards him is an attitude towards a soul. I am not of the *opinion* that he has a soul" (PI, p. 178). Knowing what I am looking at and what I see is not making an inference from a mental image, for there is no such image, no such representation, that could *eclipse* the object of my gaze (PI, §388). Moreover, "If I am *now* in doubt whether I have two hands, I need not believe my eyes either" (PI, p. 221).

" 'I cannot know what is going on in him' is above all a *picture*" (PI, p. 223). A "picture": that is to say, a philosophically constructed vision, an erroneous and misleading understanding of what it is to *see*, is responsible for the skeptical problematic. Whereas, in regard to the preceding matters (how to understand understanding, knowing, attention, meaning, intending, imagining, anticipating, remembering, and all the other "mental" processes), *ocularcentrism* as such was responsible in a significant way for the epistemological problems entangling them, here it is rather an erroneous and misleading *understanding* of vision that has been responsible for the problematic.

"If I see someone writhing in pain with evident cause, I do not think: all the same, his feelings are hidden from me" (PI, p. 223). "Just try—in a real case—," he suggests, "to doubt someone else's fear or pain" (PI, §303). " 'I believe that he is suffering'.—Do you also *believe* that he isn't an automaton?" (PI, p. 178e). "It would go against the grain," he adds, "to use the word in both connexions. (Or is it like this: I believe that he is suffering, but am certain that he is not an automaton? Nonsense!)" Continuing the thought-experiment, he writes this: "Suppose I say of a friend: 'He isn't an automaton.'—What information is conveyed by this, and to whom would it be information? To a *human being* who meets him in ordinary circumstances? What information *could* it give him? (At the very most, that this man always behaves like a human being, and not occasionally like a machine.)"[13]

"But can't I imagine," he asks, "that the people around me are automata, lack consciousness, even though they behave in the same way as usual?—If I imagine it now—alone in my room—I see people with fixed looks (as in a trance) going about their business—the idea is perhaps a little uncanny. But just try to keep hold of this idea in the midst of your ordinary intercourse with others, in the street, say! Say to yourself, for example: 'The children over there are mere automata; all their liveliness is mere automatism.' And you will either find these words becoming quite meaningless; or you will produce in yourself some kind of uncanny feeling, or something of the sort" (PI, §420). And then he comes to the lesson of the story: "Seeing a living human being as an automaton is analogous to seeing one figure as a limiting case or variant of another; the cross-pieces of a window as a swastika, for example."

The crucial point, here, is that the labyrinth of skepticism into which some philosophers find themselves inevitably drawn is in large part made possible by a very odd (*seltsam*) understanding of what it is to see. As I would state it, the principal oddity, the decisive mischief, consists in the error of at least three unacknowledged, unrecognized assumptions: [1] that seeing is a disembodied, purely intellectual act of "interpretation," and [2] that perception necessarily involves an inference, because [3] what we actually *see*, strictly speaking, is always only an internally produced image, copy, or representation, bearing the "meaning" of the perceptual act (PI, pp. 199–200).

Wittgenstein repeatedly ridicules the philosopher's predilection for generalized, abstract doubts, groundless doubts, a skepticism completely unmotivated by specific and unusual circumstances. That I am some-times—occasionally—deceived by what I see, sometimes—occasionally—mistaken about what I see, does not give me any reason to doubt my sight in general. Nor can my power to survey a field of things all of which are si-multaneously present (*vorhanden*) within the horizon, and thus my capac-ity to envision the world as a whole, entitle me to place the world *as such*, the world *itself*, within a phenomenological *epokhé*, as Edmund Husserl supposes is possible.[14] For, as Wittgenstein's *other* phenomenology reminds us, the world is the *background* for all figures of sight and insight: it is the very *ground* of doubt, the ground that makes all doubts possible in the first place. The world is *not* (just) the sum of all objects, the sum of all things. The grammatical role of the world is *different* from the grammatical role of the things we see *within* the world. With words that are echoed in Wittgenstein, Husserl summoned phenomenology to attend to "the things themselves": "*Zu den Sachen selbst!*" he cried. But, for Wittgenstein, the world is *not* a "thesis," *not* a "posit." To think of it as such is already to ex-change it for the object of a certain idealism. Only a tyrannical, unexam-ined ocularcentrism could have made a philosopher like Husserl forget, or overlook, the ground of vision, the background that no philosophical vision, regardless of its tuition, and regardless of its power, could ever hope to mas-ter, bracket, and contain.

In his later work, Wittgenstein deconstructed each of the three assump-tions about seeing which I noted in the paragraph immediately preceding the last. One needs to consider, for example, his discussions of the differ-ence between seeing and forming an image (*Zettel*, §621–46) and the dif-ference between seeing and interpreting (PI, p. 197). And also his questioning of sense data theories—in, for example, his *Remarks on Colour*, where we find him pondering the sort of simple statement about perception with which some of the philosophers he knew loved to work: " 'I see a tree,' as the expression of the visual impression,—is this the descrip-tion of a phenomenon? *What* phenomenon? How can I explain this to someone?"[15] And where we also find him exploring the logic of our dis-tinction between seeing and inferring: "Do I actually *see* the boy's hair blond in the [black-and-white] photograph?!—Do I see it grey?—Do I only *infer* that whatever looks *this way* in the picture, must in reality be blond?"

(*Remarks on Colour,* §271. Also consider §§63–64). Again and again, his imaginary dialogues, his little *Gedankenexperimente* reveal the unexamined assumptions, unacknowledged confusions, and odd epistemological renderings of "common sense" in the accounts of vision frequently found in philosophical texts.

Did Wittgenstein have, then, an ocularcentric interest—an especially strong, central interest in vision, an interest that would betray the hold of ocularcentrism even on his own later thinking? I would not say so. I think, rather, that the considerable attention he gave to seeing, observing, noticing, looking, seeming, and appearing, not only in the notes published under the title *Remarks on Colour,* but also in the *Zettel,* the notes of his *Philosophical Investigations,* and the other published notes, is an indication of the dimensions of visualism, the dimensions of its hegemony, not only as our current cultural paradigm of knowledge, truth, and reality, but also as the elective paradigm of knowledge, truth, and reality in the entire history of Western philosophy. In other words, Wittgenstein's attention to the philosophical discourse of vision is an index of the extent to which, far from being under the spell of this paradigm, he was attempting to problematize it—and ultimately, in fact, to demonstrate the need to shift paradigms. In the way he treats seeing, his shift to a grammatical—or, say, linguistic—paradigm is, I think, unquestionable.

Although I have argued that the *Tractatus* is a work under the spell of a certain visualism, or at the least a certain vision, it must be noted that Wittgenstein's diagram of the eye is not so much a point about our eyes and our sight as it is a way of illustrating, or showing, something that it is difficult to say about the (transcendental) conditions and limits of the knowable and the sayable. The context suggests that one should read the diagram as an illustrative supplement to his argument about the grammar of reflexive pronouns and the logic of our conception of the self. Even the musings and reflections in *Remarks on Colour* show that Wittgenstein was somewhat less interested in vision as such than he was in the epistemological questions and problems that arise from and surround the seeing of colors. The notes in this book are full of thoughts, many, typically, in the form of questions, concerning believing, intending, imagining, anticipating, knowing, recognizing, learning, understanding, feeling, describing, explaining, inferring, and justifying. These notes, as he says, are really explorations of the "logic of concepts" (§§22, 71–72, 106, 188), and an attempt to differentiate psychological, and more generally, empirical questions about experience from questions of conceptual grammar (§§4, 32, 114, 158, 211, 335).

"What does anyone tell me by saying, 'Now I see it as . . . ?' " (PI, p. 102). " 'Seeing as . . . ' is not part of perception. And for that reason it is like seeing and also *not* like seeing" (PI, p. 197). (In the chapter on Levinas, we are compelled to return to this matter, questioning what is involved in seeing another (being) *as* a *human* being. For the "as," here, is deeply perplexing: contrary to the moral imperative, it seems to subsume the individual under the categorial operations of an instrumental and objectifying approach. The logic of the "as"-structure is a logic, in this sense, of violence.) In the *Philosophical Investigations*, Wittgenstein gives a good deal of thought to the grammar, the language games, of "seeing . . . as," "noticing an aspect," and "the dawning of an aspect" (PI, §539; also pp. 193–215). Even here, though, it could be argued that Wittgenstein's interest was not in vision as such, nor even only in the contrast between [a] the grammar of our ordinary way of talking about seeing and its objects and [b] the logic of the accounts that philosophers have proposed, but rather more in [c] showing how proper respect for the grammar of the language we ordinarily use in talking about our experience with sight can dissolve our philosophical perplexities about larger, more central—or more general—epistemological problems, of which the philosophical accounts of seeing are merely instances, exemplifications, or heuristic illustrations. Thus, e.g., he examined the grammar (the language game) of "seeing . . . as" in order to demolish one of the ways in which philosophers have found themselves cornered in the web of idealism because they came to believe that all we ever see, or all we are ever entitled to claim we see, are visual sense data, color patches here-now, the immediate contents of our own private minds. ("Seeing . . . as" is a special language game with special motivations, rules, conditions.) Similarly, he examined the grammar of "seeing the dawning of an aspect" (PI, §539; pp. 193–215) as a way of shedding light on our epistemic criteria for cognitive processes such as recognizing, learning, and understanding; and he studied the grammar of "seeing what is common" (PI, §73) as a way of problematizing some of the major arguments in the history of philosophy claiming to establish essences, universals, and general ideas. A note in his *Philosophical Investigations* asks us to question "the idea that if you see this leaf as a sample of 'leaf shape in general', you *see* it differently from someone who regards it as, say, a sample of this particular shape." What *he* wants us to understand, and *see*, is that, "if you *see* the leaf in a particular way, you *use* it in such-and-such a way according to such-and-such rules" (PI, §74). It is, for him, a matter of use, of language games and other social practices, not a matter of "intellectual intuition," some special power of sight or insight.

On my reading, Wittgenstein's work in the wake of the *Tractatus* is a sustained challenge to the domination of vision and the rhetoric of vision in the history of philosophical thinking. Thus, as he shows in his *Philosophical Investigations*, the domination of the visual paradigm even distorts the way philosophers have understood our experience of *our own* feelings and emotions, tempting philosophers to think of such experience as a matter of self-observation. Wittgenstein shows, however, that, and also how, using observation as the model for interpreting this experience alienates us from ourselves and makes our otherwise normally understandable experience suddenly seem exceedingly strange, uncanny, and puzzling. In other words, the philosopher's peculiar optics is what creates a problem where before there was nothing at all problematic: "If you observe your own grief, which senses do you use to observe it? A particular sense; one that feels grief? Then do you feel it *differently* when you are observing it? And what is the grief you are observing—is it one which is there only while it is being observed?" (PI, p. 187).

V

In Wittgenstein's later writings, what changed most fundamentally, I think, was his conception of philosophy itself. Philosophy became a struggle against the "bewitchment" of our intelligence by means of language. The task of philosophy, therefore, is to clear away misunderstandings, assemble reminders for particular clarificatory purposes, and achieve a measure of perspicacity or *Übersichtlichkeit*. And its methods are like therapies, curing us of the confusions and temptations to err that afflict our thinking like diseases. Most of the misunderstandings that need to be cleared away are misunderstandings peculiar to philosophers: errors to which philosophers are singularly prone, since their thinking inevitably takes them *away* from the familiar terrain of "conventional wisdom."

Wittgenstein's so-called linguistic turn enabled him to deconstruct a framework with some very tenacious ideas and assumptions, dominant for a long time in the epistemological systems of both rationalism and empiricism, regarding the nature of seeing—ideas and assumptions that philosophical thought, departing from "common sense" and "ordinary" language usage, discursively constructed, and that have played a significant and rather impishly perverse role in the philosophical elaboration of theories claiming to account for knowledge, understanding, belief, deception, illusion, learning, and so forth. Although many of these ideas and assumptions that Wittgenstein disputes are clearly dependent on an ocularcentric way of thinking—the function of a vision-generated and vision-based logic—it seems that Wittgenstein never thematized, nor challenged, this logic as such. And yet, it must be acknowledged that, in his later writings, he singled out for especially sharp and sustained interrogation four of the major, vision-generated tenets that disfigure the epistemologies to which he was heir. In other words, without challenging ocularcentrism explicitly, he nevertheless challenged many of the philosophical constructions of vision—the predominant ways philosophers have interpreted, described, and explained vision—and unequivocally rejected the common philosophical uses of vision in the construction of theories of knowledge.

Above all, and in particular: [1] philosophies that rely on the psychology of introspection and intuition and model the activity of the mind on vision; [2] the picture theory of the mind, for which the mind is an inner theater or screen, mental activity a form of seeing, and ideas and meanings come in the form of images; [3] the assumption that self-knowledge is a form of self-observation, and that the justification of such knowledge follows the logic of third-person reports; and finally, [4] phenomenalism, the theory which holds that the perception of "external objects" is the outcome of a process of interpretation, an inference based on the direct and immediate perception of private intensional objects or "sense data."

Thus, however one interprets the *Tractatus*, there can be no question that, later, by the time of the *Philosophical Investigations*, Wittgenstein was a major advocate for what subsequently has been described as the "linguistic turn," and that this turn is, above all, a turn away from vision as the paradigm of knowledge, truth, and reality. But the historical significance of this shift in paradigms should not blind us to another of Wittgenstein's contributions: how, along the way, he reminded us to retrieve and restore a less epistemologically distorted, less metaphysically encumbered understanding of our experience with seeing. As he said, "a picture held us captive." What his brief dialogues and thought-experiments, with their relentless questioning, have repeatedly shown us is that the seeing which philosophers have been thinking about and making use of is an artifact of philosophical discourse, nothing, in the end, but an elaborate construction. It is easy to forget the extent to which, in the light of this revelation, we have been liberated from the tyranny, the spell, of such discursive construction and have accordingly been enabled to experience a seeing free of philosophical intrigues and to reflect on a world of things "in plain view."

Philosophers, he says, do entirely too much "thinking" and not nearly enough "looking." What do they overlook? To what are they blind? How could they justify what they claim to be able to see? How could they justify having overlooked what Wittgenstein shows them to have overlooked? What could justify them in saying that they cannot see what Wittgenstein has seen and shown?

VI

In *Remarks on Colour*, Wittgenstein asks: "But can I believe that I see and be blind, or believe that I'm blind and see?" (§85). And also this: "Can I teach the blind what seeing is, or can I teach this to the sighted?" (§319). Making fun of epistemologies that demand justification and rational reconstruction for all forms of knowledge, a note (§265) among those in his *Zettel* reads: "What justifies the blind man in saying he cannot see?"

As a philosopher, I must confess that I cannot find relief—nor indeed do I think I should—from the conviction that the most urgent philosophical questions with regard to vision concern ethics and morality. Wittgenstein's questions—the ones, for example, that we have just read—were doubtless intended to be understood as challenges to contemporary epistemology, contestations of its assumptions, its conceit, its invisible work of construction. But there is an uncanny ambiguity, or say duplicity, hidden within his questions. For what Derrida has called a "double reading," his questions seem readily to permit a certain transposition, a certain dislocation, removing them from a field of discourse where their meaning is clearly epistemological and abruptly situating them within the disquieting provocations of a discursive field where their sense and significance invoke the moral and call with urgency for an *ethical* response.

Have the glasses on the philosopher's nose, designed of course to improve the conditions of vision, instead caused a certain moral blindness? Wittgenstein examines the epistemology of color blindness with impressive subtlety. He asks us to think about red things and green things. But what about white skin and black skin? In a world deeply divided by racism, what can the philosopher say—what *should* the philosopher be saying—about discriminations based on the color of skin, and about the color blindness of an ideal justice?

For how long have philosophers overlooked the faces of poverty, the faces of crime, and the victims of violence? How long will the moral dimensions of vision, our capacity to see pain and suffering, hunger and spiritual destitution, continue to be neglected? As the ancient philosophers understood, skepticism is, first of all, and most urgently, the recognition of a moral tragedy, a question of our ethical responsibility for the other, and not a problem for the theory of knowledge.

Philosophers must learn how to see what is in plain view—and they must have the courage to say what they see. But not everything is visible, not everything in plain view. And so philosophers must also learn how to see that which is hidden—and how, then, to speak about this. For things are hidden for different reasons, different causes, and in different ways. Hidden, but not necessarily in the ways that Platonic and Kantian metaphysics had posited, namely, as an invisible reality behind ephemeral appearances. Such hiddenness was, for Wittgenstein, an illusion that his optics could dispel. But there are others ways for things to be hidden, other forms of hiddenness. Thus, there are times when philosophers must read between the lines, penetrate palimpsests, decipher traces, rummage through remnants, enter the darkness of crypts, dig among the ruins, and piece together puzzling fragments.

In a text unmistakably influenced by Benjamin, Adorno once argued that "philosophy is interpretation," the endless task of working with "fleeting disappearing traces" and "ciphers": "only in traces and ruins is it [philosophy] prepared to hope that it will ever come across correct and just reality."[16] His example: the commodity structure. "Like a source of light, the historical figure of commodity and exchange value may free the form of a reality, the hidden meaning of which remained closed to investigation of the thing-in-itself problem, because there is no hidden meaning which could be redeemable from its one-time and first-time historical appearance."[17] Is the connection between the ragpicker and the commodity structure of late capitalism in plain view? It is, in a sense, right before our eyes—if they are not shut.

There are times when philosophers must be willing to experience the dark night of the soul and bring to light what nobody wants to face. And there are times—times which Herakleitos understood—when philosophers must learn to hide, cover, and protect with a certain invisibility the truth that they see and love.

In a note written sometime in the year 1930, hence before the Holocaust, Wittgenstein consigned to paper, with words that call to mind the ninth of Benjamin's "Theses on the Philosophy of History,"[18] a dark vision, at once looking back to the past and forward, with apprehension, into the future: "I once said, perhaps rightly: The earlier culture will become a heap of rubble and finally a heap of ashes, but spirits will hover over the ashes."[19] Here we are engaged, I would say, by a vision entirely different from the one that figures in the rest of his philosophical discourse: this, after all, is not a vision of colors, not a vision of duck-rabbits, not a vision of ordinary objects, not a vision of human faces that picture the soul, but a vision seemingly capable of seeing the future—a prophetic, or apocalyptic vision. And yet, he does not talk about the vision *behind* his remark. Is this vision a question of seeing X as Y? Is it a question of seeing the dawning of an aspect? How could the philosopher argue for this way of looking at our civilization? What is to be said to someone who cannot see it this way?

The vision that is required of the philosopher has always been a difficult vision, immeasurably more ambiguous, immeasurably more paradoxical, than the seeing solicited by the picture of the duck-rabbit, which Wittgenstein deploys to show the reversal of an ambiguous figure-ground relationship and the dawning of a different figure. Could we think of the vision that this picture solicits as a counterexample to the doctrine that vision is *always* a matter of seeing what is in plain view? And can we see how a certain level of discomfiture in exercising the eyes' natural ability to reverse such figure-ground structures might be related to an inability—or, say, unwillingness—to tolerate and appropriately resolve a certain level of ambiguity, intricacy, and complexity in the moral questions asked of us by life? As Aristotle understood, morality is always to some extent a question of perception—a matter that always makes a certain claim on our capacity for (right) perception. If, as the Frankfurt School studies on fascism were the first to suggest, rigidity in perception could be a symptom of moral rigidity, a symptom of the rigidity of an authoritarian character, then seeing the dawning of a new aspect and seeing a figure-ground reversal are not only matters for the theory of knowledge: though seemingly insignificant, they are also, in fact, matters of the greatest ethical and moral significance. Considered in this light, seeing "the other" (Jews, blacks, aborigines, homosexuals) *as* "human" may still be a perception deeply corrupted, complicitous in a structure of violence.

Thus the questions of justification that Wittgenstein broaches in his meditations on seeing are not just questions for every theory of knowledge: they are also questions which can turn our thoughts about vision and blindness in the direction of compassion and justice. Wherever compassion and justice are at stake, what we see and what we fail to see are moral questions that call imperatively for a discourse of justification.

VII

I am not saying this as an accusation. One cannot accuse Wittgenstein of moral insensitivity, moral indifference, moral blindness. Both his life and his work bear witness to a most acute moral consciousness and an extreme spiritual anguish. Here was a man capable of deep sympathies and intense compassion, but who gazed upon the miseries of the world with eyes too clear-sighted, and possibly too inwardly reflective, for weeping. In the *Philosophical Investigations,* he wrote:

> If someone has a pain in his hand, . . . one does not comfort the hand, but the sufferer: One looks into his face. (p. 286)

It is of course always possible for philosophers to read this as nothing but a grammatical or an epistemological remark, the inner voice of which would be dry, impersonal, without affect; but with equal justification, one may also read it as a biting indictment of a long-dominant history of philosophical thought incapable of responding appropriately to the suffering of the other.

To form a sense of his way of looking at things, one should perhaps consider his tone and style: restrained, minimalist, ascetic—as if somehow purified, purged of the lower passions and interests, aphoristic, often seeming strangely elevated and oracular, the style and tone of a modern-day seer, a soothsayer with a morality play to write. Listen again to his words: "I once said, perhaps rightly: The earlier culture will become a heap of rubble and finally a heap of ashes, but spirits will hover over the ashes."

But the play is always deflationary. And if there be hints of elevated or prophetic vision, they are immediately reduced to brief flashes of insight and little illuminations of everyday life, reminding us to notice, to pay attention, to look again, but with greater care, so that we *see* what must be seen. Wittgenstein's words will always bring us down to the present, reminding us of the glasses on our nose—reminding us that our morality plays are nothing, after all, but long-enduring language games. Reminding us, though, to turn away from the speculative metaphysics we are absorbed in reading and begin paying attention to quite ordinary things.

Like the Israeli poet Yehuda Amichai, Wittgenstein can see a marvelous and extraordinary presence even in the most ordinary things. In "Tourists," one of Amichai's *Poems of Jerusalem,* the poet tells a story that exemplifies this way of looking and seeing:

> Once I sat on the steps by a gate at David's Tower, I placed my two heavy baskets at my side. A group of tourists was standing around their guide and I became their target marker. "You see that man with the baskets? Just right of his head there's an arch from the Roman period. Just to the right of his head." . . . I said to myself: redemption will come only if their guide tells them, "You see that arch from the Roman period? It's not important: but next to it, left and down a bit, there sits a man who's bought fruit and vegetables for his family."[20]

The Wittgenstein of my imagination would, perhaps, have appreciated the poet's location of the marvelous—and understood, too, that closure to the marvelous is at the same time insensitivity to the suffering of other beings. A question of the ethical disposition.

VIII

There is a logic or grammar to the use of our language for looking and seeing, and it is not difficult to imagine circumstances where following the rules of grammar could mean the difference between life and death—or justice and injustice. In any case, the logic or grammar that distinguishes "looking" and "seeing" and tells us how these words may (must) be used is more intricate than one might at first suppose. Four thought-provoking scenes:

> "The international commission *looked for* the remains of the bodies concealed by the death squads, but failed in their efforts and left *without seeing* [i.e., finding] them."
> "The international commission *looked for* the remains of the bodies concealed by the death squads, but, although they *saw* [i.e., found] them, they left *without looking at* them."
> "The international commission *looked into* the pit and in fact *looked right at* the remains, yet did not *really see* them."
> "The villagers *saw* the death squads murdering innocent women and children, but were afraid to *look at* them."

It is easy to overlook the significance for life—for perception—of grammatical intricacies. Which is why Wittgenstein tells philosophers to start looking. And maybe, if they were really to look, they would see things that have been escaping attention—and be able, as Benjamin urges, to *show* what needs to be seen. Like Nietzsche before him, whose critical remarks on the philosophical use of important words from everyday life were undoubtedly encouraging him, Wittgenstein undertakes what might be called a "phenomenology of language usage," not only to break the spell of an extravagant metaphysics and a tragic epistemology, but also in order to change the world—a world he saw with uncanny serenity and lucidity through eyes opened, I suspect, by the intensity of his own terrible suffering.

In a note written in 1948, Wittgenstein said: "When you are philosophizing, you have to descend into primeval Chaos [*ins alte Chaos*] and feel at home there [*sich dort wohlfühlen*]."[21] Wittgenstein's gaze called attention to the most ordinary things—"what lies in front of everyone's eyes."[22] But this gaze was always, in fact, rooted elsewhere, elsewhere at home. In the Chaos that ordinary things conceal. In the uncanniness (*Unheimlichkeit*) of the ordinary.

Destined to see the illuminated, not the light.
                    Johann Wolfgang von Goethe, "Pandora"

4 Gestalt Gestell Geviert
The Way of the Lighting

I, of whom I know nothing, I know my eyes are open, because of
the tears that pour from them unceasingly.
Samuel Beckett, The Unnameable[1]

Solange der Mensch im Gebiete der Natur weilt, ist er im
eigentlichen Sinne des Wortes, wie er über sich selbst *Herr* seyn
kann, *Herr* der Natur. Er weist die objektive Welt in ihre
bestimmte Schranken, über die sie nicht treten darf. Indem er das
Objekt sich *vorstellt,* indem er ihm Form und Bestand gibt,
beherrscht er es. . . . Aber sowie er die Schranken aufhebt, sowie
das Objekt nicht mehr *vorstellbar* ist, d.h. sowie er selbst über die
Grenzen der Vorstellung ausgeschweift ist, *sieht er sich selbst
verloren.*[2]
F. W. J. Schelling

I

In the phenomenology of perception, the formation and articulation of the
figure-ground structure (*Gestalt*) is the most elementary level of sensory
meaning (*Sinn*). At this level, the focused concentration of sensory, perceptive awareness articulates a figure of central interest, eliciting it, bringing
it out from the surrounding field. There is a logic, a λόγος, already inherent in this phenomenon: if we follow Heidegger's etymological interpretation of the ancient Greek words, according to which the verb form
corresponding to λόγος, namely λέγειν, originally meant gathering and
laying-down, perhaps we may say that the logic of the figure-ground formation is none other than a question of such a λέγειν, a gathering and
laying-down taking place at the most elementary sensuous level, corresponding to the gathering concentration of perceptive awareness and to its
momentary settling-down and staying awhile with that which is of passing
interest within the field of presencing.

In "Plato's Doctrine of Truth," Heidegger declared that "everything depends on the ὀρθότης, the correctness of the glance."[3] And yet, Heidegger
never pressed any critical encounter with the phenomenological account of
the perceptual *Gestalt.* But, perhaps in belated dialogue with Husserl, his

teacher, who elaborated a phenomenology of parts and wholes in his *Logical Investigations*, Heidegger does make explicit, e.g., in the lecture-essay on "Das Ge-Stell" (one of the 1949 Bremer *Vorträge*, bearing the general title "Einblick in das was ist," "Glance into What Is"), a crucial distinction between organic wholes and atomically constituted totalities. Implicit in this seemingly minor distinction is an entire critical history of the present: a hermeneutically reflexive phenomenology capable of remarking the changing configurations assumed by the *epokhé* across the epochs of Western history; an interpretative diagnosis, therefore, of our psychosocial and sociocultural pathology, instantiated as an inveterate tendency in the historically predominant character of our way of looking and seeing, which we shall articulate here phenomenologically in terms of the formative differentiation and stabilization of the perceptual figure and its ground. But also implicit here, I believe, is an allusion to a vision of redemption: a vision healed and made whole again through the "destruction" of our modern ontology and the historical emergence of a new figure-ground configuration.

For if, as Heidegger contends, we "belong" to being and can come into our own (*sich er-eignet*) as *Dasein* and thus fulfill (*vollbringe*) our highest vocation (*äusserste Bestimmung*) only *through* our relation to being,[4] and if, conversely, being may be said to "need" (*braucht*) us in order truly to presence (*damit es wese*), truly to take place (*ereignet*),[5] then this critical "destruction" of ontology would seem to require a certain unfolding of our naturally endowed capacities, capacities that could essentially fulfill themselves only to the extent that they learn how to respond appropriately to the presencing of being. Thus it would require some fundamental changes in our patterning of perceptual experience—for example, our ability to *see* the being of beings differently, to *envision* otherwise its presencing in and as the beings of our visible world—in so far as prevailing innerworldly conditions, now quite inimical, should permit.

In the second section of this chapter, I will argue, in an elaboration of a phenomenology I consider to be implicit in Heidegger's thinking, [1] that there is, in our ordinary, everyday way of looking and seeing, an inveterate tendency to totalize and reify the perceptual *Gestalt*, bringing its dynamics to a standstill, a state of permanence and availability for which Heidegger, possibly with Schelling's text in mind, used the term *Bestand*; [2] that this is a tendency which undoubtedly characterized even the vision of the early Greeks, but which has become increasingly pronounced since the beginning of the modern epoch inaugurated in the humanism of the Rinascimento; [3] that the reification and totalization of the perceptual *Gestalt*, a process that takes place through the subject's acts of re-presentation

(*Vor-stellung*) within the subject-object structure, is a manifestation, a primary site and instance, of what Heidegger calls the *Gestell* (enframing, or the universal imposition of a total grid of interpretation), effecting a certain disfiguration (*Verunstaltung*)[6] of the figure-ground formation; and finally [4] that, with the introduction, in his later thinking, of the concept of the *Geviert* (the fourfold of earth and sky, gods and mortals), Heidegger was attempting to articulate, at least in a provisional and preliminary way, the potential for a new historical *Gestalt* formation, a disclosive gathering and laying-down no longer disfigured by the perceptual processes operative in and as the enframing of *Gestell*.

This account will bring out into the open ways in which the ocular-centric discourse of metaphysics *reinforces* the false sociocultural reality—the unreconciled social condition of our own construction—that it nevertheless accurately reflects; but we will also discover that, in spite of its hegemony, this discourse is compelled to acknowledge experiences with vision that permit a breaching of its power and even the articulation, if only in its margins and interstices, of a different way of looking and seeing—a vision of different character.

In the third section, I will examine Heidegger's writings on the pre-Socratics, arguing that, in heeding the articulations of the phenomenon of the lighting, his rigorously hermeneutical phenomenology lets the claim (*Anspruch*) on our capacity for vision itself—a claim first laid down for our eyes by the presencing unconcealment, the giving and the givenness of the field of lighting—suggest and evoke the traits (*Grundzüge*) of an historically different way to look and see: somehow, even in these historically dark times, and in the face of the most extreme, most penetrating and pervasive sociocultural pressures, to receive nevertheless, in a receptively appropriate (*geeignet, geschickt*) way, and to whatever extent be possible, the gift (the *Es gibt*, i.e., both the giving and the givenness) of this lighting, that by grace of which alone a field of visibility, an open space delimited by its horizon and the concealments of the invisible, is first opened up and laid down for us. (My words "by grace of" are not at all meant to reinscribe vision in the myths of ontotheology, but rather to recognize that the lighting is something beneficent that we receive as given and take for granted, even if only in its ontically degraded and not in its ontologically engaged dimensionality.)

The most appropriate way to relate to the presencing of being is called, in Greek, the ὁμολογεῖν, and it is a deep, ontological, mimetic correspondence between the lighting of the visual field—that as which the being of beings presences for our vision—and our own way of looking, seeing, and making visible. This correspondence essentially requires the overcoming of the ontologically forgetful habitus of ordinary, everyday vision, a vision of restricted dimensionality (*Einschränkung*), and also, beyond this, the achievement of a radically different interactive relationship with the *ground* of perception—a relationship that might be described as *mimesis*, since it would bring forth an *isomorphism* or *correspondence* between our ontic vision and its ontological ground, the primordially disclosive opening-up, laying-down and gathering of the field itself, which is the gift of the lighting.

The isomorphism would take place when, through a process of recollection, we not only [i] realize that, in forming a figure-ground structure within the lighting, our way of looking, seeing, and making visible is itself—like the primordial lighting—an opening-up, laying-down, and gathering, and [ii] realise that our opening-up, laying-down, and gathering is derivative from and dependent on the primordial opening-up, laying-down, and gathering of the lighting, that by grace of which alone our looking and seeing are made possible, but also [iii] translate this understanding into our worldly comportment, looking, seeing, and making things visible in the clearings we ourselves open up, lay down, and gather in such a way that the lighting—which as ground withdraws from visibility into self-concealment—is nevertheless to some extent unconcealed in its presencing, made visible *as* the primordial opening-up, laying-down, and gathering of a field of visibility and invisibility, *as* the clearing within which vision as we know it first becomes possible. Thus, the ὁμολογεῖν would be an attempt to learn from the lighting another way of looking and seeing, another way of receiving the presencing of beings.

As a way of looking and seeing, this ὁμολογεῖν would thus be in a *hermeneutical* relationship to the interplay of concealment and unconcealment, manifesting as an interplay between the visible and the invisible. By calling the ὁμολογεῖν "hermeneutical," I mean that it would be a way of relating to that which is presencing which preserves and protects the interplay, preserves and protects the dimensionality of the invisible, caring for concealment. Here, then, we shall consider hermeneutics to be a discipline of interpretation that understands, respects, and protects the most deeply hidden, the ever-invisible, realizing in paradoxical principles both of theory and of practice that it is actually only through invisibility and concealment that the truth of perception is preserved and protected—from dogmatism, from captivity in enframing, and from the commodifications of the marketplace. This hermeneutical "as" is not just a strategy for reading texts; it is also precisely the "as" that is involved, for example, in the possibility of our seeing the lighting *as* the presencing of being; it is the "as" that is involved in seeing the figure-ground differentiation *as* an instance of the ontological difference between being and beings; and it is also the "as" that is involved in the imaginative effort to see the disfigured perceptual *Gestalt*, releasing the figure-ground structure which typically forms in the epoch of the *Gestell*, as a *Geviert* released from its metaphysical reifications, released into the gathering openness of its deepest, most redemptive, most reconciled truth. (This hermeneutical "as" figures also in Wittgenstein's "seeing as," as in our seeing the dawning of an aspect.)

Now, the gathering of re-collection, as a return to the opening ground, a *Rücknahme in den zu eröffnenden Grund*,[7] would be crucial to the transfiguration of the figure-ground *Gestalt:* its release from the disfigurements of enframing (*Gestell*) and its emergence and becoming as a gathering of the fourfold.[8] The opening, gathering, and laying-down that would take place in and as the ring of the *Geviert* is therefore to be understood as entering into a figure-ground formation, a *Gestalt*, that our looking and seeing would have opened up, gathered, and laid down by *virtue* of their being (or say by virtue of their *character* as) a hermeneutical re-collection of being, gathering the presencing of the lighting, the boundless giving-to-behold of the field, into the pain and the thankfulness of memory.

Finally, in the fourth section, a concluding section of this study, I will briefly take up some critical questions that still need to be considered—questions about recollection, world-disclosure, and a new historical beginning.

II

In *The Unnameable*, Beckett articulates, as an experience with vision, the pathology of enframing that holds sway in our time. He writes:

> My eyes being fixed always in the same direction I can only see, I shall not say clearly, but as clearly as the visibility permits, that which takes place immediately in front of me, that is to say, in the case before us, the collision, followed by the fall and disappearance. . . . In a word, I only see what appears immediately in front of me, I only see what appears close beside me, what I best see I see ill.[9]

What he describes, here, is the pathology in a reifying way of looking and seeing, eyes that can impose on what they see only that mode of being present which is reflected in what Heidegger has called the "frontal ontology" of traditional metaphysical discourse. In *Being and Time*, Heidegger reminds us that, "when we merely stare at something, our just-having-it-before-us lies before us *as a failure to understand it any more*."[10] Heidegger connects staring, as a way of looking and seeing, with an ontological attitude that posits what is there to be seen as *vorhanden*, as being present-at-hand. The history of the West is a story of the increasing reification of the perceptual *Gestalt*. Thus, in modernity, the *Gestalt* becomes a manifestation of *Gestell*.

In "Das Ge-Stell," a lecture-essay not yet published in an English translation, Heidegger, like Hegel, sees the diremptions that have shattered the modern world. And, like Benjamin, Heidegger sees the world constructed in the time of modernity as a world in ruins, a world in which only fragments and traces remain to tell the truth. In "Das Ge-Stell," then, he observes that, in the present epoch, our perceptivity has for the most part been subtly pressured into losing—or disengaging from—its original, spontaneously emergent sense of organic structural integrity, so that we experience the wholeness of structural wholes as mere collections of fragments, shards, splinters. He writes:

> The fragment [*Stück*] is something entirely other than the part [*der Teil*]. The part shares and imparts itself [*teilt sich mit*] with [by, as, in] parts in the organic whole [*das Ganze*]. It takes part in the whole, belongs to it. The fragment on the other hand is separated out and indeed is thus as fragment, as what it is, only as long as it is locked up in opposition to other fragments. It never shares and imparts itself in and as part of an organic whole.[11]

The importance of this passage lies, as I read it, in the crucial distinction between an organic whole and a collection of atomic parts—in effect the distinction between an oppressive, pathological figure-ground *Gestalt*, fragmented and disfigured by the enframing conditions operative in the epoch of *das Gestell*, and a radically different *Gestalt* released from such conditions. If we distinguish between a *totality* and a *whole*, we may say that, whereas the first is a closed totality, the second would be a whole precisely because of its openness, its consent to alterity, the passage of time, the endless justice of emerging and perishing.

In the same essay-lecture, Heidegger gives the "enframing" of *das Ge-Stell* further definition: "The *Ge-Stell*," he says there, "is universal in its imposition [*Stellen*]. It concerns everything that presences [*alles Anwesende*]."[12] For "in the *Ge-Stell* the presencing of everything that presences is placed at our disposal and made readily available [*zum Bestand*]."[13] Why is this dangerous? In "Die Gefahr" ("The Danger"), another one of the Bremer *Vorträge*, Heidegger asserts that, "according to its essence, the *Ge-Stell* does not protect [*wahrt nicht*] the truth of the thing as thing." In other words: "In the essence of the *Ge-Stell* it comes to pass that the thing loses its protection [*Verwahrlosung*] as thing."[14] The very being of the thing is at stake, here. But not only the being of the thing: Our "ownmost" being as human beings, who we are and who we could become—that also is at stake, as the passage from Schelling already suggested.

Although the ancient world was not subject to the rule of enframing, traces of a way of thinking that was already, without knowing it, preparing the ground for the distinctive, ever-increasing enframing of the modern world can sometimes be detected in its philosophical discourse. Thus Heidegger finds it necessary to ask a question which calls for the history of being: "In what sense and in what way is it manifest, [even] in the earliest moment of the coming to pass of being [*des Seinsgeschickes*], that in being, i.e., in [the Greek philosophers' conception of] φύσις, a [certain imposed] fixing-in-place is already taking place [*ein thesis-Charakter west*]?"[15] However, in spite of the evidence that a tendency to enframe the presencing of being has been operative, albeit in concealment, from the very beginning of our Western experience and thought, Heidegger insists that enframing is not a completely ordained fate: "Enframing is, though veiled, still glance, and no blind destiny in the sense of a completely ordained fate."[16] The little phrase "still glance" is crucial, but easily overlooked. The point here is that, even though the significance of enframing may not be readily apparent, it *is* manifest in and as the way we look and see—if only we would attend closely, thoughtfully, and questioningly to our experience with vision. And if we infuse this experience with awareness, we will come to understand that it is "no blind destiny," but rather a way of being-in-the-world, and more specifically a response-ability, that exhibits a certain historical unfolding and that therefore suggests the contingency of a future for which we must bear some responsibility—even if the coming-to-pass of a radically different world-disclosure (*Welterschliessung*) is not something that we can immediately and directly bring about simply by willing it and undertaking a course of historically effective action. (To be sure, such fundamental change can happen, and undoubtedly will; for change is happening all the time. Moreover, how we live our lives within the bounds of the present world-disclosedness can and will make a difference, can and will bring about change. But the point is that we are responsible for preparatory gestures, even though making the coming-to-pass of a radically different world-disclosedness, a radically different beginning, into the immediate object of our will and our action is simply not intelligible.)

Other statements in this text leave no room for misunderstanding: "If enframing is a destiny of the coming to presence of being itself, then we may venture to suppose that enframing, as one among being's modes of coming to presence, changes."[17] Thus he says that "another destining, yet veiled, is waiting."[18] But, he adds, "modern man must first and above all find his way back into the full breadth of the space proper to his essence."[19] I take this to include by implication the spacing of the perceptual *Gestalt:* it too must be allowed to presence, to emerge and take shape, in accordance with the logic (the λέγειν) of its full dimensionality; it too must be gathered and laid down in such a way that it is kept open to that as which the being of beings presences for our perceptual organs, namely, the deeper, more primordial opening-up, gathering, and laying-down—the deeper, more primordial Λέγειν—of the perceptual field as a whole. Mindful of the etymological connection between *Ereignis* and *Eräugnis*, a connection in which the event of being by which it comes into its own is encrypted in a word referring to the eyes, Heidegger gives this point an interpretation that explicitly makes a claim (*Anspruch*) on our capacity to see, our response-ability as beings gifted with vision: "Disclosing coming-to-pass [*Ereignis*] is a bringing to sight that brings into its own [*eignende Eräugnis*]."[20]

In his work on Nietzsche, Heidegger describes the will that emerges in the time of the *Gestell* in a way that enables us to translate the account into a description of the perceptual *Gestalt* distinctive of this time: the *Gestell* is manifest, he says, in "the will's surrounding itself with an encircling sphere of that which it can reliably grasp at, each time, as something beneath itself, in order on the basis of it to contend for its own security. That encircling sphere bounds off the constant reserve of what presences (οὐσία, in the everyday meaning of this term for the Greeks) that is immediately at the disposal of the will. This that is steadily constant, however, is transformed into the fixedly constant, i.e., becomes that which stands steadily at something's disposal, only in being brought to a stand through a setting in place."[21] Although the figure-ground *Gestalt* of our perception always takes the form of a ring, i.e., a figure at the center of focus surrounded by a recessive ground that fades away, at its horizon, into the invisible, in the epoch of the *Gestell,* this ring becomes a *willful* gathering of the ground that lays out the ground in reified, totalized form before (in front of) the ego-logical subject. Thus, if the ὑποκείμενον of Greek metaphysics is, as Heidegger puts it, "that-which-lies-before, which, as ground, gathers everything onto itself," then we must argue that it is not only the ego as subject which may be called ὑποκείμενον; for the *ground* of perception, being subject to the ego-logical will, before which it lies, is also a ὑποκείμενον: a background that is, paradoxically, at once reified as eternally present and yet, because it remains forgotten in this state, disconnected from the focal figure of the object, it is also eternally absent, simply nothing.[22] This disconnection between figure and ground in the typical experience of perception is a symptom that gives us fateful warning: the times in which we are living are indeed dangerously "out of joint" (*aus den Fugen*).[23]

In order to understand the perceptual *Gestalt* as a site and instance of enframing, it is necessary to reflect on perception as a process of articulation, a process of bringing-forth (*hervorbringen*). What is distinctive about the way that perception under the sway of enframing articulates and brings forth a figure-ground *Gestalt*? "Enframing," Heidegger says, "challenges forth into the frenziedness of ordering that blocks every view of the coming-to-pass of revealing and so radically endangers the relation [of human beings] to the essence [*Wesen*] of truth."[24] Although enframing "comes to pass as a destining of revealing," it is "a destining that gathers together into the revealing that challenges forth."[25] Although, under the spell of enframing, perception still takes part in a process of unconcealment and effects a certain bringing-forth, its interaction with the presencing of being tends to become a "challenging-forth into ordering," an "ordering of the real as standing reserve."[26] Such perception *is* of course disclosive, but it is also at the same time deeply forgetful, willfully concealing the openness of the ground, the gift (the *Es gibt*) of the field in which, and by grace of which, it takes place—and even repressing the fact of this willful concealment: "The Open [itself] becomes an object, and is thus twisted around toward human beings."[27]

Under the spell of enframing, then, perception is never far from violence; its knowledge, in fact, is a power that can come only from aggression and torture. The *Gestalt*, therefore, essentially undergoes a process that it would not be an exaggeration to describe as its disfigurement: "The original emergence and coming-to-be of energies, the φαίνεσθαι, . . . becomes a visibility of things that are already there. . . . The eye, the vision, becomes a mere looking-at or looking-over or gaping-at."[28] These words come from Heidegger's 1936 *Introduction to Metaphysics*. But it is clear that he already understood this point much earlier, because, in *Being and Time*, a work which leads us through a strenuous learning-process toward the achievement of a "moment of vision" (*Augenblick*), he called attention to our inveterate tendency to fall into "a fixed staring at something that is purely present-at-hand [*vorhanden*]."[29] Under the cold stare of the gaze, the φύσις, the spontaneously "emerging power" presencing in and as the *Gestalt* is "hardened" into a state of permanent presence, "deprived of the possibility of appearing spontaneously"—deprived, also, of its radiance, its *Schein*.[30]

With regard to the question of this dullness, this loss of radiance, perhaps it will suffice for the moment to note, here, just two decisive passages: [1] In *Being and Time*, Heidegger asserts that, "in 'setting down the subject', we dim entities down to focus."[31] [2] In "The Question Concerning Technology," Heidegger says that "Enframing blocks off the shining forth and holding sway of truth."[32] With regard to the "hardening into permanence," Heidegger argues, in *Basic Concepts*, that "presencing does not mean mere presence, but emerging and opening-up. . . . Mere presence, in the sense of the present-at-hand [*Vorhandene*], has already set a limit to presencing, emergence, and has thus given up presencing."[33] In elaborating this point, he observes that "what presences only presences in emerging and precisely not in the presence that has congealed into permanence." "It belongs," he says, "to the essence of presencing that its possible non-essence of hardening into something permanent is repelled in it."[34] All these assertions gain special significance when they are understood concretely as phenomenological observations referring to the emergence and dissolution of the figure-ground structures that form in the event of perception and depend on the way our looking and seeing let them emerge, bringing them, drawing them forth, out of the encompassing field of visibility.

Most in question, perhaps, and most at stake, is our attitude towards the ground: whether or not its dynamism, its openness, its dimensionality, is granted by the corresponding receptive openness of our perception—our willingness, for example, to let perception be decentered, drawn into abysses of invisibility, radically surprised. As an ontologically oriented capacity, perception calls upon one to "engage oneself with the open region and its openness [*das Offene und dessen Offenheit*] into which every being comes to stand."[35] Elaborating this point, with words ("not to lose myself") that echo Schelling's, quoted at the beginning of this study, Heidegger explains that:

> To engage oneself with the disclosedness [*Entborgenheit*] of beings is not to lose oneself in them; rather, such engagement withdraws in the face of beings in order that they might reveal themselves with respect to what and how they are and in order that presentative correspondence might *take its standard* from them.[36]

Moreover, this comportment requires an acceptance of concealment: "Letting-be," he says, "is intrinsically at the same time a concealing [*Das Seinlassen ist zugleich ein Verbergen*]. In the ek-sistent freedom of Dasein . . . there is concealment [*Verborgenheit*]."[37] We need to give thought to the social, political, and cultural significance of the disruptive and anarchic ontological "standard" or "measure" implicit in this engagement, this way of looking and seeing.

Gestalt psychology has demonstrated the organic interdependencies, the reciprocally altering interactions, that are constitutive of an undisturbed *Gestalt* formation process. Insisting that "a theory of perception must be a field theory,"[38] Köhler points out, for example, that "objects show a considerable change in size when they are located within a region which has been strongly influenced by a figure."[39] This means, he says, that the aftereffects of such figure-forming processes tend to *alter* given visual objects. "Prolonged inspection of any specific visual object tends," he notes, "to change its organization. Moreover, other objects which are afterwards shown in the same region of the field are also affected, namely displaced or distorted."[40] Consequently, as the fixation of a staring gaze, the enframing typical of the *Gestell* interrupts the figure-ground interplay and distorts *both* figure and ground. Instead of a dynamic, spontaneously flowing interaction between figure and ground, a looser, freer, softer differentiation between the periphery and the center of focus, deconstructing the metaphysical dualism that prioritizes the center, there is a "freezing" of the flow, interrupting the work of time—the emergence and dissolution of perceptual configurations. And when the figure is subject to such reifying intensity, it becomes detached from its ground, frozen in a state of permanent disfiguration. As for the ground, although it is the opening openness, the end-less origin of the figures that enframing brings forth, its presencing is either forgotten, suppressed, and neglected, or else it is submitted to the most extreme ontic reduction—as if it could be possessed by the egological subject as just another figure.

Herbert Guenther notes that the openness of the perceptual ground "is present in and actually presupposed by every determinate form. Every determinate entity evolves out of something indeterminate and to a certain extent maintains its connection with this indeterminacy; it is never completely isolated from it. Because the indeterminate entity is not isolated from the indeterminacy . . . , our attention can shift back and forth between one and the other."[41] The enframing gaze cannot, will not, let the ground be ground; it cannot, will not, tolerate its immeasurableness, its withdrawal from the grasp of perception, its refusal to be totalized, reified, possessed. Instead of a gaze that is softly focusing, gently hovering, open and receptive to the dynamics of change, open and receptive to the spontaneous emergence of new configurations taking place in the dimensions of the surrounding field; instead of a gaze that "withdraws in the face of beings in order that they might reveal themselves,"[42] in the epoch of enframing there is a tendency for the gaze to become aggressively dualistic—sharp, linear, and atomizing. This is the gaze that has installed—and continues to serve— a metaphysics of reified presence, a metaphysics of closure, violence, and mortification.[43]

This reification is a persistent theme in Heidegger's thought, something he clearly articulated in *Being and Time* and repeatedly emphasized in subsequent lectures and writings. In a 1941 course on Anaximander, for example, Heidegger declared that "permanence is contrary to the . . . essence of being, contrary to the ἀρχή, contrary to the ἄπειρον. . . . But what presences *essentially* and yet contrary to the essence is the *non-essence*. . . . To the extent that what respectively presences corresponds to the essence of presencing, it does not consist in and solidify into duration unto permanence."[44] What resists measure, limitation, finitude, what refuses the ordinance of time, that Anaximander regards as ἀδικία, injustice.

In the age we call "modernity," our sight has increasingly become a "line of sight" (*Blickbahn des Anblicks*), moving in the "predetermined perspective" (*schon bestimmten Vorblickbahn*) of an ego-logical subject.[45] The rise to power of this subject—more specifically a *bourgeois* subject, inseparable from the capital-driven economy and culture of the bourgeoisie—involves the reduction of the being of people and things to the reified condition of objects that are, as Heidegger puts it, "either to be beheld (view, image) or to be acted upon (product and calculation). The original world-making power, φύσις, degenerates into a prototype to be copied and imitated." To this he then adds the thought we quoted earlier: "The original emergence and coming-to-be of energies, the φαίνεσθαι, . . . becomes a visibility of things that are already-there. . . . The eye, the vision, becomes a mere looking at or looking-over or gaping at."[46]

According to Heidegger, in the world of Greek antiquity people did not relate to what is as to an inwardly conceived image (*Bild*) or representation (*Vorstellung*). For the Greeks, what is is what presences; and this experience with perception did not involve looking at what is and having a representation of it in the mind; nor did it involve making the one who is looking into a "subject" and making what is presencing into an "object" (*Gegenstand*). This construction is the distinctive mark of modernity. It is only in the modern period—the period beginning with the self-affirmation of "Man" in the humanism of the sixteenth century and with a way of looking at the world reinforced and carried forward, albeit in very different projects, by the Cartesianism and empiricism of the seventeenth and by the rationalism and romanticism of the eighteenth—that what is present is determined [1] as an ob-ject, [2] as being there *for* a subject, [3] as (re)presented by the subject to itself, [4] as placed (*gesetzt, gestellt*) to *lie before* the subject, and finally, therefore, [5] as present in the form of a representation. In and with this determination of what is present, the ever-increasing power of the *subject* is claimed and asserted. As Derrida correctly remarks in "Sending: On Representation," *Vorstellung* "marks the gesture which consists of placing, of causing to stand before one, of installing in front of oneself as available, of localizing ready-to-hand, within the availability of the preposition. . . . The subject is what can or believes it can offer itself representations, disposing them and disposing of them."[47]

Now, Heidegger argues that what is distinctive of modernity—and the cause of his concern—is not so much the fact that experience can be a process of representation as it is the fact that representation is universalized, that it becomes the sole medium for all experiencing, and that its way of relating to what is present encourages us in the attitude of domination. And this means it encourages us in an attitude that does violence to the background of perception, either by simply forgetting its way of presencing, or by gathering it into the *Gestalt* in a reified re-presentation of presencing.

In telling the history of philosophy, Heidegger attributes to Platonism the first major step towards the modern transformation of the world into an image or picture (*Bild*). Derrida nicely summarizes Heidegger's argument in "The Age of the World Picture":

> If for the Greeks, . . . the world is not essentially a *Bild*, an available image, a spectacular form offered to the gaze or to the perception of a subject; if the world was first of all presencing (*Anwesen*) which seizes man or attaches itself to him rather than being seen, intuited (*angeschaut*) by him; if it is rather man who is taken over and regarded by what is, it was nevertheless necessary for the world as *Bild*, and then as representation, to declare itself among the Greeks, and this was nothing less than Platonism. The determination of the being of what is as εἶδος is not yet its determination as *Bild*, but the εἶδος (aspect, look, visible figure) would be the distant condition, the presupposition, the secret mediation which would one day permit the world to become representation.[48]

And with the historical advent of representation, "Man" becomes in two senses the one who re-presents: it is *we human beings* who determine what is and how what is shall be. It is we who become the "representatives" of and for being, asserting the legitimacy of our domination as the ones sent by destiny, *das Geschick*, to watch over all of being.

Precisely because the modern gaze is driven by the will to power, and tends accordingly to assault the invisible, to round it up and hold it hostage in the camps of the totally visible, Heidegger felt compelled to argue, during his 1973 seminar in Zähringen, that phenomenology must be practiced as "a phenomenology of the nonappearing" (*eine Phänomenologie des Unscheinbaren*).[49] This hermeneutical rendering of phenomenology commits it to functioning as a practice of resistance, a practice that would challenge and subvert the metaphysics of unity, totality, and reification that circulates in and prevails in our present culture. In the field of our vision, this involves decentering the gaze, disrupting its tendency to exclude and deny what falls outside its narrow, frontal focus.

For Heidegger, the *Gestalt* is the site of the deepest strife. Thus, for example, in his discussion of "The Origin of the Work of Art," he maintains that

> the strife [*Streit*] that is brought into the rift [*Riß*] and thus set back into the earth and fixed in place [*festgestellte*] is the *Gestalt*. Createdness [*Geschaffensein*] of the work means: truth's being fixed in place in the figure [*Festgestelltsein der Wahrheit in die Gestalt*]. *Gestalt* is the structure [*das Gefüge*] in whose shape the rift composes and submits itself [*sich fügt*]. This composed rift [*Der gefügte Riß*] is the fitting or joining of the shining of truth [*die Füge des Scheinens der Wahrheit*]. What is here called *Gestalt* is always to be thought in terms of the particular placing and framing [*aus jenem Stellen und Ge-stell*], as which the work occurs [*west*] when it sets itself up and sets itself forth [*insofern es sich auf- und her-stellt*].[50]

Although this passage is about the Greek temple as a work of culture constructed within the Greek world to mediate the relation between this world and the earth upon which it stands, it may also be read hermeneutically as a deeply truthful comment on the *Gestalt* that is formed in perceptual experience—as a comment the truth of which requires of us that we think this *Gestalt* ontologically, i.e., in its ontological dimensionality. What the passage thus calls to our attention is the fact that, among other things, the perceptual *Gestalt* is always a site where the differentiation between figure and ground instances, manifests, the strife, the dynamic tension, inherent in the ontological difference. At the level of perception, the rift of ontological difference constitutes a certain necessary rending, a certain necessary tearing-apart, of the perceptual field: a figure is brought forth, and as it is being wrested, drawn away from the presencing ground and field, the ground and field withdraw, sometimes receding, however, only in correspondence to a violent, carelessly imposed oblivion. Whether or not the truth shines (*west*) in the perceptual *Gestalt* essentially depends, then, on the way in which the *Gestalt* is set up and set forth.

The poet René Char once said: "Je retirai aux choses l'illusion qu'elles produisent pour se préserver de nous et leur laisserai la part qu'elles nous concèdent." ("I shall take from things the illusion they produce to preserve themselves from us and leave them the part they concede to us."[51] These words, however, can be given (at least) two absolutely opposite interpretations. Thus they demand a double reading. According to one reading, the poet would be exemplifying and honoring the very will to power that Heidegger laments, seeing it manifest everywhere in our contemporary world; for the poet would be describing a relationship to things not at all different from the violent possessiveness prevailing in our time. We of today are all too familiar with commodification and the transformation of things into capital resources. So the truth involved here could not be the truth (*Wahrheit*) as Heidegger understands it; for Heidegger, as we know, the essence of truth—unconcealment—demands an attitude of caring, protecting, safeguarding, preserving, as his etymological reading of the German words *wahren, bewahren, verwahren,* and *gewähren* brings out.—"Dasein," he says in the *Beiträge,* is the "Wächter der Wahrheit," the guardian of truth, the "Wahrer" of the openness of truth, the one who lives in the care, the "Sorge" and "Wahrung" of being.[52] And such care demands the protection and preservation of the thing's dimensions of concealment and self-concealment. We must also bear in mind that, when Heidegger thinks about perception, he thinks from and with the German word, *Wahrnehmung,* which means not only taking-as-true, or taking-to-be-true, but also, if thought more etymologically, taking into one's care.

There is, then, a second possible reading of Char's words, quite the antithesis of the first. The violence that Heidegger laments in ordinary perception is the violence that is promoted by thinking—one-dimensionally— that the essence of truth lies in our certitude over correctness. But Heidegger learned from the ancient Greeks that there is another, very different violence in relation to the truth: the violence, namely, that comes from understanding that the possibility of such truth is always dependent on ἀλήθεια, unconcealment, the opening up of a field of disclosedness. For the ancient Greeks, "being comes to presence [*west*] out of unconcealment." Therefore Heidegger says that they "were perpetually compelled to wrest [*entreissen*] being from appearance [*Schein*] and preserve [*bewahren*] it against appearance."[53] The poet's words, read in this light, take on a radically other meaning. Char is speaking of his struggle for a deeper sense of truth, speaking of his struggle against the temptation to settle for mere correctness—the temptation to impose on things his own ready-made interpretation, defending against the deeper truth things might reveal, breaching the defenses of the common perception. Heeding the poet's call-ing, Char is attempting, against the pressures of the modern *Gestell*, to ex-perience the birth of things, the awesome event of unconcealment, the moment of opening, the very *giving* of the possibility of truth as we ordi-narily see it. The poet's violence is thus actually a recognition of the over-whelming power of concealment—and an expression of awe and wonder before the event of unconcealment. The poet's violence toward things is not the indifference, neglect, or assault common in our time; contrary to ap-pearances, it expresses the very deepest caring for the truth, wresting the phenomenon *out of* the reification of everyday experience and *returning* it to the interplay of concealment and unconcealment. This could not be more at odds with the attempt, common in our time, to wrest the phenomenon *out of* this interplay and *pull it into* the reification and dullness of the realm of everyday perception, everyday experience.

This, our second interpretation, is supported by a passage from *Being and Time.* Here is what Heidegger says:

> It is essential that Dasein should explicitly appropriate what has al-ready been uncovered, defend itself *against* semblance and disguise, and assure itself of its uncoveredness again and again. . . . The uncover-ing of anything new is never done on the basis of having something completely hidden, but takes its departure, rather, from uncoveredness. . . . *Truth (uncoveredness) is something that must al-ways first be wrested from entities.* Entities get snatched out of their hiddenness. The factical uncoveredness of anything is always, as it were, a kind of *robbery.* Is it accidental that when the Greeks express themselves as to the essence of truth, they use a *privative* expression—ἀ-λήθεια?[54]

Heidegger's point is that love for the truth requires that one resist the spell of conventionality (average everydayness), and that one be willing to fight for the truth, engaging those powerful, and sometimes overwhelming forces in the world which make it difficult, even dangerous, to reach and win it. The poet's violence (indicated by the word "wresting") is violence for the sake of openness to the event (*Ereignis*) of unconcealment, a poet-izing (*dichterisch*) violence intended to rescue the phenomenon from the captivity in which the culturally hegemonic paradigm of truth as correct-ness has been holding it.

In "What Are Poets For?," Heidegger is inspired by Rilke's poetry to make an observation with profound implications for our understanding of the psychology behind the ego's gaze. Calling attention, as would Freud, to the ego-subject's strategies of defense, strategies that often turn out to be self-defeating or self-destructive, he says: "Objectification blocks us off against the Open. The more venturesome daring does not produce a defense."[55] (Representation, in re-presenting to oneself, and on one's own terms, whatever presents itself, is thus always a defensive response. And in encounters with others, it will function as a structure of prejudice.) Practiced as Heidegger wants it, phenomenology draws the gaze outside and away from its center, its site of power, situating it instead in the ekstatic intertwining of the visible and the invisible—there where it is vulnerable to ἀλήθεια, the endless surprise of truth.

III

Commenting on a text attributed to Parmenides, one in which the philosopher broaches the question, "What does it mean to say and think that being is?," Heidegger proposes a reading that seems to direct the question toward our experience with perception, and most of all, with vision: according to Heidegger, the ancient Greeks (presumably, that is, the few and not the many, i.e., the great poets and philosophers, and not, or not necessarily, the people at large) experienced the *ground* of presencing as "a luminous appearance in the sense of illumined, radiant self-manifestation."[56] In "A Dialogue on Language," Heidegger holds that "The Greeks were the first to experience and think of φαίνομενα as phenomena. But in that experience it is thoroughly alien to the Greeks to press present beings into an opposing objectness; φαίνεσθαι means to them that a being assumes its radiance, and in that radiance appears. Thus, appearance is still the basic trait of the presence of all present beings, as they rise into unconcealment."[57] And since appearance—phenomenal presencing or unconcealment—is the truth (*Wesen*) of beings, only a hermeneutical phenomenology, letting what is present show itself from out of itself, can be true to appearance.

With enframing, there is, as we have noted, a fixating and dimming-down, not only of the lighting that constitutes the perceptual field, but also of whatever appears, whatever is visible, within its openness: the *Gestalt* that forms in conformity to the subject-object structures imposed by the conditions of modernity, is flattened out, rendered dull, no longer allowed the possibility of shining. As Heidegger states the point in "The Question Concerning Technology," enframing "blocks the shining-forth and holding-sway of truth."[58] Spelling this out phenomenologically more than he does, I would say that enframing so reduces the space within which appearance must take place that "the splendour of radiant appearing" is made virtually impossible.[59] Even before this lecture, indeed as early as *Being and*

Time, Heidegger observed that, "By looking at the world theoretically, we have already *dimmed it down* [*abgeblendet*] to the uniformity of what is purely present-at-hand, though admittedly this uniformity comprises a new abundance of things which can be discovered by simply characterizing them."[60] This means there is no more experience of *Schein* in the sense of radiance, and no more experience of *Schein* in the sense of powerfully dynamic appearing, emerging, coming to pass, presencing; there is only the experience of *Schein* as illusion. Of the awesome dynamic radiance of φύσις, the ever-emerging, ever-changing energy of "nature" as the ancient Greek poets and philosophers experienced it, only "a last glimmer and semblance" of its original presencing (*Wesen, Anwesen, Wesung*) has been preserved.[61] This dimming-down also takes place in the typical experience with (prosaic) predication: "In 'setting down the subject', we dim entities down to focus in 'that hammer there', so that by thus dimming them down we may let that which is manifest be seen *in* its own definite character as a character that can be determined."[62] Subsequently, when Heidegger turned his thought to the language of myth and poetry, the language, for example, of Pindar and Hölderlin, which he regarded as gloriously "radiant," it would seem that he wanted to exempt such language from this dimming-down, although I do not know of any text where he explicitly argues the point.

Be this as it may, in a later work, "The Turning," Heidegger speaks of a glance (*Blick, Einblick*) through which "the coming to presence of being enters into its own emitting light," a glance "which retrieves that which it catches sight of and brings it back into the brightness of its own looking." And he explains this by adding that, "in its giving of light, [the glance] simultaneously keeps safe the concealed darkness of its origin as the unlighted."[63] The emission of the lighting inscribes for our vision its radiant commission as an organ of being, laying down the fateful trajectory of its historical mission (*der Auftrag unserer Geschichte*)[64] and gathering all the restless motions of sight, of vision, in what we might call, drawing on Husserlian terminology, the "natural attitude," into the clearer composure of the lighting's conditional openness.

Anaximander is believed to have said, or thought something like this: that, "whence things have their origin, there they must also pass away according to necessity; for they must pay penalty and be judged for their injustice, according to the ordinance of time."[65] Heidegger's reading of Anaximander (e.g., in his 1946 study, "The Anaximander Fragment," which I shall be discussing here in some detail) gives careful thought to the way being has presenced, and the way being could presence, as and in the field of our vision.

Seeing the lighting, here, as opening up the field of vision and laying it down before us, Heidegger directs our attention to the fact of "being's primordial self-illumination," observing, however, that the "unconcealment of beings, the brightness granted them, obscures the light of being" and also that, "as it reveals itself in beings, being withdraws." "In this way," he adds, "by illuminating them, being sets beings adrift in errancy."[66]

Even when Heidegger's reading of the fragment is not explicitly concerned with the perceptual *Gestalt*, what is said lends itself strikingly well to an interpretation in terms of our perceptual experience. The γένεσις and φθορά about which Anaximander speaks are, says Heidegger, "ways of luminous rising and decline." Origination, γένεσις, is understood as "a movement which lets every emerging being abandon concealment and go forward into unconcealment," whilst φθορά, passing away, is understood as "a going which in turn abandons unconcealment, departing and withdrawing into concealment."[67] The figure-ground structures that are formed in perception are no exception to this law of nature: they are nothing, ultimately, but "ways of luminous rising and decline." And yet, since in the world of human beings, markedly contrasting with the world of the animals, the perceptual process is always mediated, always dominated, by the demands of ego-logical consciousness, this law of nature, the law ordaining the passing-away of all that comes into being, can be willfully resisted. Its effectiveness, its pressure may for a time be resisted and deferred; but it will never in the end be abrogated. Whenever such willful resistance takes place, what happens is that the figure-ground dynamics are temporarily petrified, as both figure and ground are subject to the disfigurements of enframing.

Heidegger holds that what presences in presencing is not "something over against a subject, but rather an open expanse [*Gegend*] of unconcealment, into which and within which whatever comes along lingers."[68] But the adult human being of the modern bourgeois world is an ego-logical subject, and the rise to power of this subject has meant the pervasive transformation of this open expanse, reducing it to the condition of being an object standing over against this subject.

According to Heidegger, whose thinking remains strongly committed, here, to a phenomenological method, "Presence within the lighting articulates all the human senses."[69] That is to say, our being—our living—within the gift (*Es gibt*) of this lighting is what gives an enabling field to our senses, which the lighting draws out into the world, into the interplay of concealment and unconcealment. Thus, to the extent that our way of perceiving is truly phenomenological, truly hermeneutical, i.e., to the extent that we let the phenomenon show itself from out of itself and do not resist its dynamics by imposing our will on it, one may say, with Heidegger, that, "if what is present stands in the forefront of vision, everything presences together: one brings the other with it, one lets the other go. What is presently present in unconcealment lingers in unconcealment as in an open expanse. Whatever lingers (or whiles) in the expanse proceeds to it from concealment and arrives in unconcealment."[70] Such perception is explicitly contrasted with the non-phenomenological, non-hermeneutical perception typical of our ordinary, everyday experience: "What is for the time being present, what presently is, comes to presence out of absence. This must be said precisely of whatever is truly present, *although our usual way of representing things would like to exclude from what is present all absence.*"[71]

In ordinary, everyday perception, "something is out of joint," something is (in Anaximander's terms) "unjust," for what is present—the being that figures in the center of perceptual focus—is separated from the ground of its concealment, and the ground no longer presences as an open reserve of spontaneously emerging and disappearing configurations. "How is what lingers awhile in presence unjust? What is unjust about it? Is it not the right of whatever is present that in each case it linger awhile, endure, and so fulfill its presencing?"[72] Of course. However:

> What has arrived [in presence] may even insist upon its while solely to remain more present, in the sense of perduring. That which lingers perseveres in its presencing. . . . It strikes the willful pose of persistence, no longer concerning itself with whatever else is present. It stiffens—as if this were the way to linger—and aims solely for continuance and subsistence.[73]

The injustice (ἀδικία) of our usual (*alltäglich*) way of looking and seeing consists in the fact that, "coming to presence in the jointure of the while, what is present *abandons* that jointure and is, in terms of what lingers awhile, in *dis*junction. Everything that lingers awhile stands in disjunction."[74] What, more precisely, then, is this "disjunction"? Heidegger's answer is that "the disjunction consists in the fact that whatever lingers awhile seeks to win for itself a while based solely on the [metaphysical] model of continuance. Lingering as persisting . . . is an insurrection on behalf of sheer endurance. . . . In this rebellious whiling, whatever lingers awhile insists upon sheer continuance."[75] It may be said, moreover, that "whatever lingers awhile is inconsiderate toward others, each dominated by what is implied in its lingering presence, namely, the craving to persist."[76]

And yet, in spite of its being split off from the dynamic interplay of concealment and unconcealment, whatever is present *owes its presence* to the non-present—indeed, *is* present only "insofar as it lets itself belong to the non-present."[77] Were the figure-ground structure formed in and by our perception to be instead (hermeneutically) phenomenological, then there would be order, justice, δικἡ: "present beings which linger awhile let order belong ἀλλἡλοις, to one another."[78]

There is, to be sure, a certain "injustice" inherent in the very nature of perception. Thus, for example, the things that are copresent within the spread of my visual field are necessarily arrayed in such a way that, relative to my point of view, some of them will block and hide other things. And if there is a strong source of lighting, it is natural that some things will be located within the shade or shadows that other things cast. But this is not what concerns Heidegger. What concerns him is rather the reification and totalization of presencing, the anxiety-driven, defensive, violent appropriation of the *Es gibt* of the ground:

> Presencing itself unnoticeably becomes something present. . . . As soon as presencing is named, it is represented as some present being. Ultimately, presencing as such is not distinguished from what is present. . . . The essence of presencing, and with it the distinction between presencing and what is present, remains forgotten. *The oblivion of being is the oblivion of the distinction between being and beings.*[79]

Reducing the presencing of the ground to the being-present of the figure, ordinary, everyday perception obliterates, annihilates the ontological difference between being and beings.

A critical account of the perception characteristic of late capitalist modernity can also be derived from a reading of Heidegger's 1951 study, "Logos (Heraclitus, Fragment B50)." The interpretation with which we shall be working here hinges on recognizing that the *Gestalt* formation is a concrete, material *instance* of the opening-up, laying-down, and in-gathering named by the Greek term, λέγειν. Commenting on Heraclitus, Heidegger writes: "Λέγειν properly means the laying-down and laying-before which *gathers* itself and others."[80] He then clarifies the character of this gathering, saying: "But gathering is more than mere amassing. To gathering belongs a collecting which brings under shelter."[81] This gathering, as Heidegger understands it, "is already included in laying. Every gathering is already a laying. Every laying is of itself gathering. . . . Laying brings to lie, in that it lets things lie together before us."[82] But is our perception not, in a certain important sense, a sense persistently ignored, the articulation of a preliminary λόγος, a *proto-logos*, a preliminary λέγειν? Does it not *articulate* our encounter with the world, laying down, for example, a field of visibility, gathering together all that is visible within the compass of this field and letting it all lie there before us? And does it not *depend* on the gift of the lighting, that by grace of which *our* laying-down of a field of visibility is first made possible? Heidegger writes: "The λόγος by itself brings that which appears and comes forward in its lying before us to appearance—to its luminous self-show-ing."[83] Then what must claim our thinking is the question whether the *way* in which we perceive, the way in which we look and see, listen and hear, forms a *Gestalt* "which brings under shelter": whether, in short, the figure-ground *Gestalt* that perception (*Wahr-nehmung*) articulates really is true to the essential nature, or say the potential, that is hermeneutically pro-jected by the (German) word itself. So we must ask: Is the *character* of our perception really a protecting, preserving, safeguarding caring? (In the *Beiträge*, Heidegger speaks of *Dasein* as devoted "zur Verwahrung des Seyns," the "Wahrer" and "Wächter der Wahrheit des Seyns.")[84] These questions call for heightened awareness and critical reflection, attentive to the *way* in which our habits of perception—our looking and seeing, for ex-ample—lay down and gather what we are given to experience into the hermeneutical interplay of a figure-ground formation. Is our perception an ontological re-collection, a hermeneutical remembering of the primordial Λόγος whose Λέγειν first opened up, laid down, and ingathered the field within which our perception takes place? And is our perception letting this Λέγειν actually be manifest in the world of our lives—letting it be mani-fest, but in a protective, caring, and therefore hermeneutical way that does not violate its immeasurable depths of withdrawal—*as* that on which the λεγειν of our own perception essentially depends? (Note: A capital Greek letter is used, here, when the reference is to the ontological and a small Greek letter is used when the reference is to the ontic.)

We can learn much from thinking about how, in his commentary on Heraclitus, Heidegger challenges our ordinary, everyday habits of listening and hearing. For what he has to say about listening and hearing easily translates into a radical challenge to our habits of looking and seeing—and to our willingness and capacity to realize the potential that comes to us in the gift of vision. With concern for our listening and hearing, Heidegger contends that "proper hearing" is a hearing that is appropriated by the tone set down by the Λόγος, a hearing that lets itself be determined, tuned, by this tone the Λόγος sets. Proper hearing, he says, "rests in the Laying that gathers, i.e., in the Λόγος."[85] Thus our way of looking and seeing would be-come a ὁμολογεῖν, were it to let itself become, like our way of listening and hearing, a "proper" looking and seeing, appropriated by, and accordingly appropriate to, the Λέγειν (articulation) of the Λόγος, presencing for our vision in and as the lighting of our visionary field.

Heidegger holds that "Laying [i.e., the Λέγειν of the Λόγος] secures everything present in its presencing, from which whatever lingers awhile in presence can be appropriately [*eigens*] collected and brought forward by mortal λέγειν."[86] Although Heidegger is still commenting, here, on words attributed to Heraclitus, and is therefore still speaking about our listening and hearing, what he has to say continues to be equally true of our looking and seeing. Indeed, unless this commentary is allowed to serve as a critical interpretation challenging all our habits of perception, it risks losing all significance. Thus I take this passage to explicate the ontological *conditions* that are laid down, not only for our listening and hearing, but also for our looking and seeing—conditions that lay down a certain claim on our capacity for seeing and stake out the nature of our responsibility as beings gifted with a potential for vision that we are free either to realize or to neglect.

"All disclosure," says Heidegger, "releases what is present from concealment. Disclosure needs concealment. . . . Λόγος is *in itself and at the same time* a revealing and a concealing. It is Ἀλήθεια."[87] If perception—looking and seeing, for example—must count as disclosure (*Welterschliessung*), as an articulation (λέγειν) of the world, and as an opening unto the possibility of truth (ἀλήθεια), then it must *need and acknowledge* concealment. And yet, the perception encouraged by the time in which we are living does *not* encourage the recognition of such a need. Not so much as a shadow is permitted to cross the field of vision prized by our culture of glittering commodities and disciplinary surveillance.

Concerned, in his commentary on Heraclitus, about our capacity for listening and hearing, Heidegger says there:

> If the ἀκούειν of mortals is directed to Λόγος alone, to the Laying-that-gathers, then mortal λέγειν is skillfully brought [*schicklich verlegt*] to the gathering [*das Gesamt*] of the Λόγος. It is destined [*Vom Geschick her*] to be appropriated [*er-eignet*] in ὁμολογεῖν. Thus it remains appropriated [*vereignet*] to the Λόγος. In this way, mortal λέγειν is fateful. But it is never Fate itself.[88]

The significance of this thought must not be restricted, however, to listening and hearing, even though it is with our capacity to hear the sound or tone set by the Λόγος that Heraclitus is concerned. For if, in its broadest meaning, Λόγος is opening articulation, the Laying-that-gathers, then what is said here about listening and hearing must also bear on our other perceptive capacities: no less than hearing, they too are organs of being.

Thus, for example, it is a question—indeed a most fateful question—of the appropriation of our capacity for looking and seeing. What is at stake is whether or not our capacity for looking and seeing, our capacity for vision, will *itself* become a laying-that-gathers by virtue of the way in which it lets the figure-ground *Gestalt* come into being, linger awhile, and pass away—and whether or not it will let the Laying-that-gathers, i.e., the gift of lighting, which alone has made vision possible and on which our vision depends, come to light, in the hermeneutic interplay of concealment and unconcealment, *as* that by grace of which its own laying-and-gathering, its own *Gestaltung*, is first made possible. It is a question of "submitting" ourselves to the "measurement" of the Λόγος—which means, in the case of sight, submitting to the assignment, the dispensation, the mission, that the coming-to-pass (*Ereignis*) of the lighting lays down through its emission.

Accordingly, in rendering our looking and seeing (or, for that matter, our listening, touching, handling, gesturing, and moving) ontologically hermeneutical in relation to the field of lighting first opened up for them, we must make four major steps: [1] our looking and seeing must become more fully what they already to some extent are, namely, a λέγειν; [2] our looking and seeing must "show" themselves *as* (let themselves be visible *as*) a λέγειν; [3] our looking and seeing must somehow "show" (make visible) that there is a more primordial Λέγειν; and [4] our looking and seeing must "show" themselves *as dependent on* this more primordial Λέγειν.

Heidegger's 1954 study, "Moira (Parmenides VIII, 34–41)," also bears on the hermeneutical task laid down for our vision. It is very much concerned with what Heidegger calls "the everyday perception of mortals."[89] He writes:

> Modern philosophy experiences beings as objects [*Gegenstände*]. It is through and for perception that the object comes to be a "standing against". As Leibniz clearly saw, *percipere* is like an appetite which seeks out the particular being and attacks it, in order to grasp it and wholly subsume it under a concept, relating this being's presence [*Präsenz*] back to the *percipere* (*repraesentare*). *Repraesentatio*, representation [*Vorstellung*], is defined as the perceptive self-presentation (to the self as ego) of what appears.[90]

This analysis of representation is an elaboration of the analysis that figures in his 1942–43 lectures on Parmenides, where he says: "Man is the living being that, by way of representation, fastens upon objects and thus looks upon what is objective, and, in looking, orders objects, and in this ordering posits back upon himself the ordered as something mastered, as his possession."[91] Since philosophy is not only a reflection *on* the experience of its time, but is always also—albeit to a greater or lesser extent—a reflection and reproduction *of* this experience, it should not be surprising that the modern age *sees* beings as objects, and that, in the culture of commodity capitalism, the light cast by the Leibnizian analysis of perception, extending beyond the borders of the philosophical text, should foreshadow a time in which vision becomes an instrument of the ego's will to power, an anxiety-driven mechanism, subordinating everything to its greed, its appetite, its concept of endless pleasure.

The more our vision commodifies, the more it reifies, splitting off the figure-ground configuration from the lighting of the field, the more, as Heidegger puts it, "the lighting of the being of beings, *as* a lighting, is concealed."[92] To be sure, we must agree with Heidegger that the "play of the calling, brightening, expanding light is not actually visible," if by "not visible" we understand him to mean that this lighting, which is the very presencing of being, is not visible, and does not allow itself to be made visible, *in the same way* that things like trees, birds and stones are visible. But this "not actually visible" does *not* mean "absolutely invisible," "transcending all conceivable forms of visibility," or "beyond the possibility of being seen by an appropriately ontological way of seeing." Thus, Heidegger continues, saying: "It shines imperceptibly, like morning light upon the quiet splendour of lilies in a field or roses in a garden."[93]

In thinking, with Parmenides, the meaning of "Moira" and the normative significance of its measurement for our lives in today's world-order, Heidegger asserts that "the essence of Ἀλήθεια [or say the dimensionality of the lighting] remains veiled." And he goes on to explain this crucial point by saying that "the visibility it bestows allows the presencing of what is present to arise as outer appearance [*Aussehen*] (εἶδος) and aspect [*Gesicht*] (ἰδέα). Consequently the perceptual relation to the presencing of what is present is defined as 'seeing' (εἰδέναι). Stamped with this character of *visio*, knowledge and the evidence of knowledge cannot renounce their essential derivation from luminous disclosure."[94] "Cannot renounce": and yet, of course, this is precisely what the modern way of looking and seeing has tried to accomplish. That this struggle to deny our dependency must inevitably fail does not mean, however, that we cannot for the most part conceal it from ourselves, shutting out the deep enlightenment—and the ground-shaking challenge to our ways—with which it might otherwise favor us.

"Mortals," Heidegger says, "accept . . . whatever is immediately, abruptly, and first of all offered to them. . . . They keep to what is unfolded [i.e., what is present] in the twofold [i.e., the ontological difference between being and beings], and attend only to that aspect which immediately makes a claim upon mortals; that is, they keep to what is present without considering presencing [i.e., the *giving* of the lighting that opens up and lays down the field of vision]."[95] Read in terms of the figure-ground *Gestalt* that is formed in vision, Heidegger would be saying, here, that our looking and seeing keep so narrowly focused on the figure of the object, the object that figures in their perceptual interest, that they pay no heed to the presencing of the lighting and the contextual ground that surrounds the focal object. This reading is supported by what Heidegger says next in his commentary on Parmenides:

> Where ordinary perception . . . encounters rise and fall, it is satisfied with the "as well as" of coming to be, γίγνεσθαι [*Entstehen*], and passing away, ὄλλυσθαι [*Vergehen*]. It never perceives place, τόπος, as an abode, as what the twofold [i.e., the spacing opened up by the ontological difference] offers as a home to the presencing of what is present. . . . Ordinary perception certainly moves within the lightedness of what is present and sees what is shining out, φανόν (VIII, 41), in colour, but is dazzled by changes in colour, ἀμείβειν, and pays no attention to the still light of the lighting that emanates from duality [i.e., from the spacing of the ontological difference].[96]

On my reading, "duality," here, may be taken to refer to the differentiation of figure-ground, a differentiation that instances in the perceptual field the hermeneutical effect of the ontological difference. Heidegger's words, then, contain both an ontologically grounded criticism of ordinary perception and also an implicit indication, a hint, pointing toward a *different* way of looking and seeing. (*Beiträge zur Philosophie:* "in dieser Lichtung warten zu können, bis die Winke kommen.")[97] For if paying no attention to the lighting that emanates from "duality"—from the differentiation of figure and ground—constitutes an errant, fallen way of looking and seeing, a way that deepens the oblivion of being, we may suppose that in a *more appropriate* way of looking and seeing, the lighting would be taken up into the protection and preservation of what I propose to call, keeping in mind Heidegger's remark that "die Wächterschaft des Menschen ist der Grund einer anderen Geschichte," a "guardian awareness."[98] Would this "other history" be one in which we would finally see a real reconciliation of the diremptions and contradictions that have defined our modern world?

In "Kaufmannsladen" ("Toy Shop"), a note in *Minima Moralia*, Adorno observes that

> disenchantment with the contemplated world is the sensorium's reaction to its objective role as a "commodity world". Only when purified of appropriation would things be colourful and useful at once: under universal compulsion the two cannot be reconciled.[99]

This critical, theoretically informed observation enables us to see what is missing from Heidegger's account. In a certain sense, Adorno and Heidegger have noticed the same phenomenon. But, unlike Adorno, Heidegger does not connect the phenomenon he sees and describes so well with a critical, theoretically informed analysis of the political economy. To this extent, he calls attention to the fact only to re-enchant it, throwing on it a light that is ultimately blinding.

The same themes—lighting and perceiving—are elaborated further in Heidegger's 1943 study, "Aletheia (Heraclitus, Fragment B16)." According to Heidegger, Heraclitus

> tells of the lighting whose shining he attempts to call forth into the language of thinking. Insofar as it illuminates, the lighting endures. We call its illumination the lighting [*die Lichtung*]. What belongs to it, and how and where it takes place, still remain to be considered. The word "light" means lustrous, beaming, brightening. Lighting bestows the shining, opens what shines to an appearance. The open is the realm of unconcealment and is governed by disclosure.[100]

Who is addressing us here? Whose voice is summoning us to think about the lighting? Whose words are we really reading? By telling us what "Heraclitus" is telling and attempting, isn't Heidegger *himself* telling and attempting the same? Isn't *he* trying to tell us of the lighting? Isn't *he* trying to call it forth, so that it may shine into the language of (his own) thinking? It would be a most perverse reading that insisted on denying to Heidegger the substance of thought here—as if he were merely a disinterested commentator, neutrally handing down as accurately as possible the thought of another. He turns to the thought of Heraclitus because he is drawn to it, attracted to it, finds it compelling. If he is putting words into Heraclitus's mouth, is that not because those words came to him under the spell of Heraclitus's thought? The incontestable fact of the matter is that Heidegger does not speak of the lighting only in texts where he is explicitly commenting on Heraclitus; he also speaks of it in contexts where one can only assume that it has become a major theme in Heidegger's own thought, carrying a significance essentially independent of Heraclitus. So we may say, then, that it is a question, here, of the relationship between the *Gestalt* and the lighting: how the *Gestalt* is formed; whether or not the figure-ground differentiation is articulated by our looking and seeing in a way that re-members (re-collects) the truth of the lighting and holds the structure of perception open to its play, its concealments and unconcealments.

Following the passage on the interpretation of which we have just been reflecting, Heidegger asks:

> Why is it that we stubbornly resist considering even once whether the belonging-together of subject and object does not arise from something that first imparts their nature to both the object and its objectivity, and the subject and its subjectivity, and hence is prior to the realm of their reciprocity?[101]

Carrying this question forward in the direction that Heidegger's preceding discussion would suggest, we are led to the thought that subject and object are gathered together and belong together in and by grace of the field of the lighting—that elemental presencing of being which opens up, lays down, and gathers a field of visibility. It is the lighting that first *joins* subject and object in a dialectic of differentiation; and it is the lighting that, in its configuration as ground, offers and submits itself to the conditions of perceptivity that rule in the life of a mortal. But in modern times, this "mortal" has become an ego-logical subject: someone who, constituting himself as a subject, focuses on what is present and turns it into an object, a figure *split off* from the dynamic ground, the surrounding contextual and referential field. If our time is "out of joint," so is the figure-ground *Gestalt*.

This splitting off, of subject from object, figure from ground, and the *Gestalt* itself from the presence of the lighting, is symptomatic of the antagonisms that persist in our deeply divided and still unreconciled society. And when we consider what this splitting means when the "object" of the gaze is another "subject"—when it is a question of how another "subject" is looked at, faced, seen, made to figure in the figure-ground *Gestell*—then we are approaching the root of the suffering, rage, and violence distinctive of the contemporary world. How different social relations would be if they could be deeply rooted, by virtue of an awareness (*Stimmung*) that does not presently form very often, in a felt sense of being gathered together into the underlying unity of the lighting, a felt sense of belonging together in the Laying-down-that-gathers—and of having always already belonged together, gathered through the gift of that lighting, in a dimension of being "prior to the realm of their reciprocity"! Stereotyped, reifying perceptions of the other, ways of looking at others that are inseparable from racism, nationalism, and ethnic hatreds, would be more difficult to sustain, if the awareness toward which Heidegger is gesturing were to be cultivated as the subsoil (Λέγειν) in which our vision needs to be well rooted.

To be sure, as Heidegger says, "the jointure thanks to which revealing and concealing are mutually joined must remain the invisible of all invisibles, since it [is that which] bestows shining on whatever appears."[102] It must certainly be protected from the will to total visibility, because if not properly cared for, its gift of light and darkness would fall into oblivion and negation, placed at the disposal of the dominant will to power; and the peoples of the world would eventually be left without any place to hide from totalitarian tyranny and terror. But this possibility, this danger, makes it all the more necessary that we not let the invisibility, the withdrawal of the jointure fall into total oblivion, absolute negation. We need to make this jointure *visible* in our world: visible, however, *as* the invisible of all invisibles. And this means that our looking and seeing must let themselves *be appropriated by* this invisibility, becoming, through their capacity for ontological recollection, its hermeneutic organ, protecting and preserving its necessary withdrawal.

This interpretation points toward the need for an historically different way of looking and seeing: a way of looking and seeing that obeys in care the way of the lighting. Heidegger continues:

> If we think it [i.e., the presencing of being] as lighting, this includes not only the brilliance, but also the openness wherein everything, especially the reciprocally related, comes into shining. Lighting is therefore more than illuminating, and also more than laying bare. Lighting is the meditatively gathering bringing-before into the open. It is the bestowal of presencing.[103]

According to Heidegger, "The event of lighting [*das Ereignis der Lichtung)* is the world. The meditatively gathering lighting which brings into the open is revealing; [but] it abides in self-concealing."[104] Thus it is necessary that, in virtue of our way of looking and seeing, we protect and preserve the self-concealment of the lighting, while at the same time opening to this "event" and letting it come into its own by gathering it into our way and making it visible hermeneutically *as* that which opens up our world.

Heidegger's discussion of the lighting is haunted, however, by deep— and well-founded—anxieties. What concerns him is the danger that, in spite of all his precautions, references to this lighting will be misunderstood. For the self-giving of the lighting both is and is not a lighting, a light we can see. Taking place within the realm of the visible, it can appear only as that which visibly withdraws from the reach of our vision. Thus, most of all, Heidegger is worried that the "event," the giving, of the lighting—the wonder of the gift, *that there is light*—will be degraded by a reduction to the physics and optics of light. "The lighting," he says, "is no mere brightening and lightening." And that is because what he is trying to get us to *see* is a "revealing-concealing lighting concerned with the presencing of what is present."[105] Appealing, in spite of the terrible dangers, to our capacity, our potential for vision, he tells us that "the lighting not only illuminates what is present, but *gathers it together* and secures it in advance in presencing."[106] Thus, were our own way of looking and seeing to become a recollection and mimetic repetition of this gift of lighting—or, in other words, were our way to become an ontologically appropriate, ontologically appropriated ὁμολογεῖν, it would, in its own way, become a gathering, a vision of the *Geviert*, gathering earth and sky, gods and mortals.

Because we are beings gifted with a capacity-to-see the potential of which still remains unrealized and unfulfilled, the gift of the lighting—the wonder that *Es gibt* lighting—makes a claim on us: a claim that burdens us with the responsibility to realize our great potential for vision, our capacity for responsiveness, our response-ability. Gods and men, says Heidegger,

> are not only illuminated in the lighting, but are also enlightened from it and toward it. Thus they can, in their own way, accomplish [*vollbringen*] the lighting (bringing it to the fullness of its essence) and thereby protect it. . . . [Moreover, because they receive this lighting and are dependent on it,] they are appropriated into the event of lighting, and are never concealed. On the contrary, they are revealed, thought in still another sense [i.e., in that the claim of this lighting on their responsiveness, e.g., on their responsibility for "using" their capacity to perceive it, puts them on trial]. Just as those who are far distant belong to the distance, so are the revealed—in the sense now to be thought—entrusted [*zugetraut*] to the lighting that keeps and shelters them.[107]

As beings of sight, we are dependent on the gift of the lighting, and therefore are entrusted *to* it. But we are also thereby entrusted *with* it, because the lighting can come into its own, or come back to itself "in the fullness of its essence" (as Heidegger puts it), only through the mediation of *our* way of looking and seeing. For it is only by (the) virtue of our looking and seeing that the lighting can be made visible hermeneutically, visible *as* the coming of the lighting which first makes our vision possible. Furthermore, the coming of the lighting, as the interplay of concealment and unconcealment within which all that is comes to presence, can be protected and preserved only by (the) virtue of a *way* of seeing and looking that [1] makes it visible *in its invisibility*, acknowledging our finitude, our limited horizons, and the immeasurable abyss of the invisible, and that thereby [2] *respects* the withdrawal and self-concealment of the lighting, protecting and preserving it, instead of violently penetrating its abodes of concealment with an insolent demand for total visibility, total clarity, total control. The lighting gives us light; but it also subverts that sovereignty of the gaze, leading it into the shadows, into the dark, into the realms of semblance and deception; obstructing its powers of penetration; compelling submission to the invisible beyond being. The lighting opens our eyes—to blindness.

Following Heraclitus, who was merciless in criticizing the ways of his contemporaries, Heidegger formulates his own criticism of the looking and seeing that predominates in the contemporary world. He writes:

> Mortals are irrevocably bound to the revealing-concealing gathering which lights everything present in its presencing. But they turn from the lighting, and turn only toward what is present, which is what immediately concerns them in their everyday commerce with each other. . . . They have no inkling of what they have been entrusted with: presencing, which in its lighting first allows what is present to come to appearance. Λόγος, in the lighting of which they come and go, remains concealed from them and forgotten.[108]

As Heidegger is quick to point out, however, the recollection of the lighting cannot take place in a perception, a way of looking and seeing, for example, that is grasping, possessive, driven by the will to power:

> the golden gleam of the lighting's invisible shining cannot be grasped, because it is not itself something grasping. Rather, it is the purely appropriating event [*das reine Ereignen*]. The invisible shining of the lighting streams from the wholesome self-keeping in the self-restraining preservation of destiny [*Geschick*].[109]

Whilst addressing "those who are enlightened in accordance with their essence, and who therefore hearken to and belong to the lighting in an exceptional way,"[110] Heidegger is also articulating, rather more for the benefit of those whose sight has fallen into a blind forgetfulness, what might be called the ontologically appropriate(d) way of looking and seeing: "Gods and men," he says, "belong in the lighting not only as lighted and viewed, but also as invisible, bringing the lighting with them and, in their own way, preserving it and handing it down in its endurance."[111]

Writing and lecturing about the lighting, Heidegger *is* handing it down; calling attention to its invisibility, its self-concealment, he *is* caring for its preservation—and letting us know that we too are entrusted with its preservation. Our response-ability is our responsibility. If we fail to live by the way of the lighting; if we fail to let our looking and seeing be guided by the nature of the lighting, then the more we press toward the power of total visibility, total domination over the *ground* of perception, the more we are in danger of falling into an abyss of darkness, an epoch of night, instead of enjoying—in a possible future—the openness of an ekstatic vision, a vision which gathers what is to be seen into a *Gestalt* without enframing the perceptual ground and denying beings the releasement of their presencing within the dynamic interplay of concealment and unconcealment.

Were there a looking and seeing that could "accomplish the lighting" and "bring it to the fullness of its essence," this would be a way of looking and seeing that, by virtue of its ὁμολογεῖν, [i] *releases* the figure-ground *Gestalt* which it gathers and lays down from pressures toward closure, keeping it ever *open* to the immeasurable openness of the ground and field, and correlatively [ii] *checks* its drive toward total graspability, total visibility, letting what presences be gathered into a *Gestalt* that opens out into the invisible and lets this invisible be gathered up hermeneutically, i.e., without violence to its being invisible. Were there such a looking and seeing, gathering and laying down in accordance with the ontological "normativity" of the methodological principles formulated in Heidegger's extremely radical conception of hermeneutical phenomenology, the *Gestalt* would become a *Geviert*, a gathering of the fourfold. But such a "moment of vision," such an *Augenblick*, as Heidegger calls it in *Being and Time*, is hardly more than thinkable in today's tragic world. For, however strong the passion and commitment of an individual in regard to the responsibility with which we are entrusted as beings gifted with a potential for vision that has not yet been realized, little can be accomplished without favorable social and cultural conditions. These conditions do not presently exist. But, of course, they cannot come to pass without our engagement, our preparations— which does not mean, however, that we can bring about the favorable conditions by imposing our will. For the will to power that holds sway in our time is a major factor in the modern *Gestell*, a major source of the oblivion of being into which our world has been cast. For this reason, when thinking about the possibility of a "new beginning," Heidegger speaks of the need to cultivate an attitude beyond the either-or dualism of the active and the passive—an attitude he calls "waiting," in which the modern will to power has been radically transformed. (Repeating a point I made earlier: We must be "able to wait in this lighting until the hints come." In this waiting, our guardian awareness is crucial, for, as Heidegger puts it in the *Beiträge*, "the guardian awareness of human beings is the ground of another history.")[112]

We will now turn to Heidegger's lectures on Parmenides (winter semester 1942–43), wherein we find the philosopher still struggling with the themes that occupied him in earlier works: truth and illusion, ἀλήθεια, concealment and unconcealment, the lighting and clearing, the gaze. "That the Greeks were visual, that they were 'eye-people', what does this contribute," he asks, "to an elucidation of the essence of truth as unconcealedness, openness, and clearing?" "It does not contribute anything," he replies, "because it cannot have the least significance. That fact cannot mean anything, because the factual functioning of the eyes does not give any information, and *cannot* give any information, about the relation of man to beings. What is just an 'eye' without the ability to see?"[113] Making the same point he makes in his study on Heraclitus, where he asserts that we do not hear because we have ears, but have ears because we hear,[114] he goes on to say: "We do not see *because* we have eyes, but we have eyes because we can 'see.' " "But what does it mean to 'see'?" he asks. "We understand it, in a very broad sense, as the foundation for all physical, physiological, and aesthetic 'optics': namely, it is what allows for an immediate encounter with beings, things, animals, and other people, in the light." This brings him to broach the question of our relationship, as beings gifted with a certain capacity, a certain *ontological* potential for vision, not only to visible beings, but also to the interplay of concealment and unconcealment, the conditions of visibility and invisibility, in which and as which being presences:

> Of what help . . . would any light be, no matter how luminous, and what could any optical instrument do, no matter how refined and accommodating, if the power to see did not itself *in advance* get a being in sight by means of the visual sense and the medium of the light? Just as the eye without the ability to see is nothing, so the ability to see, for its part, remains an "inability" if it does not come into play in an *already established relation* of man to visible beings. . . . And how could such a relation of man to beings as such hold sway if man did not *stand in* a relation to being? If man did not *already* have being in view, then he could not even think the nothing, let alone experience beings. . . . But what else is this relation of being to the essence of man than the clearing and the open which has lighted itself for the unconcealed? If such a clearing did not come into play as the open of being itself, then a human eye could never become and be what it is, namely, the way man looks at the . . . encountering being.[115]

The importance of these lectures on Parmenides—especially with regard to the question of our looking and seeing, and the question of the presencing of being in and as the opening of the lighting—cannot be overestimated. Thus, for example, nowhere in his later writings can we find such a clear and elaborate formulation of the strange and perplexing theme that is at the heart of "The Turning": the theme, namely, of a "turning" in the direction of the gaze in the historical unfolding of modernity. The historical significance of this theme demands our thought. In the course of our reflections on the text of these lectures, the strangeness of what Heidegger later has to say, for example in "The Turning," will become, I believe, more phenomenologically meaningful.

What is surely most uncanny in these lectures is the thought that being *looks:* "The look of being [*der Anblick des Seins*], which looks into beings [*der in das Seiende hereinblickt*]," he says, "is in Greek θέα" (p. 147 in English; p. 219 in GA 54). This is to be contrasted, he says there, with the "grasping look." "Night and day," Heidegger remarks, "take their essence from what conceals and discloses itself and is self-lighting" (p. 102 in English; p. 151 in GA 54). But prior to presencing in and as "what is visible and seeable," being (*Physis*) presences in and as the opening event of lighting. And, as such, it may be described as "looking into" and "seeing" what it lights up, all the beings it makes visible and all the beings it makes invisible, i.e., as being "what surveys [*überblickt*] everything that comes into the light and stays in it and lies in it, i.e., everything normal and ordinary, and it is what gazes into [*hereinblickt*] everything ordinary, indeed in such a way that it precisely appears in the ordinary itself and only in it and out of it" (p. 102 in English; pp. 151–52 in GA 54).

Delving into the etymology of the Greek words for looking and seeing, Heidegger points out that, for the ancient Greeks, looking and seeing (*Hinsehen, Zusehen*) did not mean a representing "by which man turns toward beings as 'objects' and grasps them" (p. 103 in English; p. 152 in GA 54). Instead, it is a question of a visionary communication "in which the one who looks [*das Blickende*] shows himself, appears, and 'is there.' " (p. 103 in English; p. 152 in GA 54). In other words, the one who is looking and seeing is merely an opening to that which appears. The one who is looking and seeing "emerges, as unconcealed, into the unconcealed" (p. 103 in English; p. 152 in GA 54). "Originally experienced," then, looking "is not the grasping of something but the self-showing in view of which there first becomes possible a looking that grasps something" (p. 103 in English; p. 152 in GA 54). This experience of looking (*Blicken*) could not be more different from the modern—a grasping, *erfassendes Blicken*. Indeed, the modern experience overturns, reverses, the ancient: "If [modern] man experiences looking only in terms of himself and understands looking precisely 'out of himself' as Ego and subject, then looking is a 'subjective' activity directed to objects. If, however, man does not experience his own looking, i.e., the human look, in 'reflection' on himself as the one who represents himself in looking, but if instead man experiences the look, in unreflected letting-be-encountered, as the looking at him of the person who is encountering him, then the look of the encountering person shows itself as that in which someone awaits the other as counter, i.e., appears to the other and is" (p. 103

in English; pp. 152–53 in GA 54). In this way, for the Greeks, we show *who* we are, we reveal the essence of our *character*, by the character of the way we engage in looking and seeing. The Greeks could accordingly judge people by the character of the way they make visible—and also how they relate to the invisible. Heidegger says: "The looking that awaits the other and the human look thus experienced disclose the encountering person himself in the ground of his essence" (p. 103 in English; p. 153 in GA 54).

"We moderns," Heidegger says, "have for a long time been so deflected that we understand looking exclusively as man's representational self-direction toward beings. But in this way looking does not at all come into sight; instead it is understood only as a self-accomplished 'activity', i.e., an act of re-presenting. To re-present means here to present before oneself, to bring before oneself and to master, to attack things" (p. 103 in English; p. 153 in GA 54). By contrast, "the Greeks experience looking at first and properly as the way man emerges and comes into presence. . . . Thinking [the Greek experience] as moderns and therefore insufficiently, but for us surely more understandably, we can say in short: the look, θέα, is not looking as activity and act of the 'subject' but is sight as the emerging of the 'object' and its coming to our encounter." Thus: "Looking is self-showing and indeed that self-showing in which the essence of the encountering person has gathered itself and in which the encountering person 'emerges' in the double sense that his essence is collected in the look, as the sum of his existence, and that this collectedness and simple totality of his essence opens itself to the look—opens itself at any rate in order to let come into presence in the unconcealed at the same time the concealment and the abyss of his essence" (pp. 103–4 in English; p. 153 in GA 54).

Because "our" looking and seeing are dependent on the lighting of being, the lighting in and as which being presences, showing itself for our looking and seeing, there is a sense—a sense that the Greek poets and philosophers seem to have understood—in which a perceptual interaction that we tend to think of as "ours," as centered in and coming from ourselves, in deeper truth "is not something human but belongs to the essence of being itself as belonging to appearance in the unconcealed" (p. 104 in English; pp. 153–54 in GA 54). Moreover, there is a consequent sense, again a sense the Greek poets and philosophers seem to have recognized, according to which the looking and seeing is accomplished by being itself, and is "not something human," in so far as the "event" that is the continuous giving of the lighting and "the showing of being itself" is experienced as a "look," the "glance" of being "looking" into the openness of the visual field and making visible what appears there. Indeed, according to Heidegger, the

Greeks—or at least the greatest of the Greek poets and philosophers—experienced their own looking and seeing as a disclosive shining-forth and lighting-up *only* because what they saw—namely the disclosive shining-forth that opens up a visual field and renders beings visible—they *saw as* the hermeneutical presencing of the gods, and more particularly, as *the gods'* way of looking into the world and holding the human beings dwelling there within the divine measure and beholdenness of their radiant beholding (see, e.g., p. 106 in English; pp. 156–57 in GA 54). "Being," Heidegger says, "is what in all beings shows itself and what looks out through them, the precise reason man can grasp beings as beings at all. That which looks into all that is ordinary, the uncanny as showing itself in advance [*Hervorblickende*], is the originally looking one in the eminent sense. . . . The so-called gods, the ones who look into the ordinary [*Hereinblickende*] and who everywhere look into the ordinary, are οἱ δαίμονες, the ones who point and give signs" (p. 104 in English; p. 154 in GA 54). Heidegger's interpretation of this experience continues:

> Because the god is, as god, the one who looks and who looks as the one emerging into presence, . . . the god is the [one] . . . that in the look presents himself as the unconcealed. The one who presents himself in looking is a god, because the ground of the uncanny, being itself, possesses the essence of self-disclosing appearance. But the uncanny appears in the ordinary and as the ordinary. The looking one appears in the sight and "outward look" of the ordinary, of beings. (P. 104 in English; p. 154 in GA 54)

But that "which *within* the ordinary comes to presence *by his own look* is man" (p. 104 in English; p. 154 in GA 54. Italics added). "Therefore," says Heidegger, "the sight of the god must gather itself within the ordinary, in the ambit of the essence of this human look, and must therein have its figure [*Gestalt*] set up" (p. 104 in English; pp. 154–55 in GA 54). Now, because the Greeks could *see* that their looking and seeing depended on the lighting—the look—of the gods shining into their world, Heidegger suggests that "man himself is that being that has the distinctive characteristic of *being addressed by being itself,* in such a way that in the self-showing of man, in his looking and in his sight, the uncanny itself, god, appears" (p. 104 in English; pp. 155–56 in GA 54. Italics added).

For Heidegger, "we who have come so late, however, can only experience the essence of the δαίμονες [the uncanny presencing of the gods] as shining into the ordinary and presenting themselves in beings and in that way pointing beings toward being, on the condition that we attain at least an incipient [hermeneutical] relation to the [hermeneutical] essence of ἀλήθεια, and thereby recognize that, for the Greeks, disclosure and emergence prevail in the essence of every originarily emergent being." And he goes on to say that, "insofar as being comes into presence out of ἀλήθεια, there belongs to it self-disclosing emergence. We name this the self-opening and the clearing" (p. 106 in English; p. 157 in GA 54).

Whence this "condition," that we attain some thoughtful relationship to the opening of the lighting, that "circumstance" as which being presences for our vision? "What shines is what shows itself to a looking. What appears to the looking is the sight that *solicits* man and *addresses* him, the look. The looking performed by man in relation to the appearing look [i.e., the lighting of being that shines into and through the world of the ordinary] *is already a response to the original look, which first elevates human looking into its essence*" (p. 107 in English; p. 158 in GA 54. Italics added). This point is crucial. According to Heidegger, the grasping look that is typical of us ego-logical moderns is our way of responding to that which appears. But this way is *not* primary; what is (pre)ontologically "first" is "the look of emerging into presence," the hermeneutical, truly phenomenological way of looking and seeing that lets the phenomenon show itself from out of itself (p. 107 in English; p. 158 in GA 54). The "look of the [modern] subject," Heidegger argues, "is the look of a being that advances by calculating, i.e., by conquering, outwitting, and attacking. The look of the modern subject is, as Spengler said, following Nietzsche, the look of the predatory animal: glaring [*das Spähen*]" (p. 108 in English; p. 159 in GA 54). Could reconnecting the gaze of the modern subject with the "ground" of the lighting alter this violent character? This is the principal question that motivates the inquiry in this chapter.

Of course, the Greeks also experienced looking as willful:

> The Greeks too experienced the look as an activity of man. But the basic feature of this grasping look is not glaring, by means of which beings are, so to say, impaled and become in this way first and foremost objects of conquest. For the Greeks, looking is the "perception" [*Vernehmen*] of beings *on the basis of a primordial consent* [*Einvernehmen*] given *to* being, which is why the Greeks do not even know the concept of object and never think being as objectivity. (P. 108 in English; pp. 159–60 in GA 54. Italics added to English translation.)

(In Merleau-Ponty's *Phenomenology of Perception*, this "primordial consent" is shown to be a prepersonal, prereflective dimension of our embodiment as visionary beings. The term he uses is "primordial contract": "To say that I have a visual field is to say that by reason of my position I have access to and an opening upon a system of beings, visible beings, that these are at the disposal of my gaze in virtue of a kind of primordial contract and through a gift of nature, with no effort on my part; from which it follows that vision is prepersonal [i.e., already taking place "beneath" the level of the ego-logical subject]."[116] I want accordingly to argue that it might be through a "return" to our prepersonal experience with the lighting that a new phase in moral enlightenment would first become possible.)

In "Language," Heidegger argues that it is language which speaks— meaning that it is language which first brings man about, brings him into existence. "Understood in this way," he says, human beings would not only speak; they would also "be bespoken" by language.[117] In the *Parmenides* lectures, Heidegger effects a similar reversal of our modern way of understanding looking and seeing. For Heidegger's Greeks, who experienced the presencing of being as a "primordial look," the uncanny truth that human beings are looked upon, are beheld, are held in the beholding of the gods' radiant vision, is much more significant than the obvious truth that human beings can look and see: "man, precisely as the looked upon [*der Angeblickte*], is first received and taken up into the relation of being to himself and is thus led to perception" (p. 108 in English; p. 160 in GA 54). Heidegger explains that "the Greeks experience man as the being whose being is determined through a relation of self-disclosing being itself to what, on the basis of this relation, we call 'man' " (p. 109 in English; p. 161 in GA 54). In other words, for the Greeks, we not only show ourselves in and by our looking and seeing; by grace of the lighting, the shining looking of the gods, we also are beheld, made visible, and thus revealed to ourselves, revealed precisely in regard to our visionary capacity. Experiencing themselves more as beheld, more as held in the uncanny beholding of the gods and δαίμονες than as engaged in looking and seeing, the Greeks felt themselves bound by virtue of their sight to carry a certain responsibility, recognizing a certain claim on their capacity for responsiveness, for a way of looking and seeing that would take into its care the presencing of the lighting, in and as which "the ones who shine into the ordinary," the "self-emergent looking ones" come to appearance "in this ordinary" and "as something ordinary" (pp. 109, 111 in English; pp. 161, 163–65 in GA 54).

What is involved in this taking into care? It is a question, Heidegger says, of saving, conserving, preserving, and protecting: "the saving and conserving of the un-concealed is necessarily in relation to concealment, understood as the withdrawal of what appears in its appearing. The conserving is grounded in a perpetual saving and preserving. This preserving of the unconcealed comes to pass in its pure essence when man strives freely for the unconcealed and does so incessantly throughout his mortal course on earth" (p. 124 in English; pp. 183–84 in GA 54). But it is not only a question of taking into care the unconcealed, and the unconcealedness of the unconcealed; if it is the essence of language to be a naming and calling that shelters presence in absence,[118] looking and seeing, experienced as emerging into the condition of being-beheld, and accordingly experienced as being-beholden, must also take *Entziehung*, withdrawal into concealment, and concealedness itself, into their care. For without their protection of the invisible, and of invisibility itself and as such, no visible being can be saved from the dangers of nihilism, from commodification, from reduction to mere means, from *das Gestell*.

But such care-taking (*Wächterschaft*) presupposes the guardian awareness of recollection (*Erinnerung* as a *Wiederholung*), a hermeneutical looking and seeing that do not forget, do not overlook, the gift of the "circumstance" of the lighting (p. 134 in English; pp. 199–200 in GA 54). As Heidegger points out, "appearance is founded in a pure shining, which we understand as a radiating light. The same appearance, however, is also a self-showing that meets a reception and a perception. Perception can now grasp what shows itself merely as what is perceived in the perceiving and can overlook as something incidental, and ultimately forget, the appearance that dwells in the self-showing, i.e., appearance in the sense of pure shining and radiating. The unconcealed is thus experienced more and more only in its relation to man and in terms of man, i.e., in its character as something encountered" (p. 136 in English; p. 203 in GA 54). But, he insists, "it is not thereby necessary that man, even if he thinks the relation of being to himself emphatically in terms of himself, should also posit himself as 'subject' in the modern sense and declare being to be his representation" (pp. 136–37 in English; p. 203 in GA 54).

Looking and seeing in a way that attempts to re-collect the *Lichtung*, the opening of the open, taking into care both concealment and unconcealment, thus becomes our highest ontological responsibility—but at the same time, this attempt is our openness to the "directive" that comes from the lighting itself: it is the channel, so to speak, through which the lighting, "the look of being," can communicate its "directive" to our vision and "model" the ontologically most appropriate(d) way of looking and seeing. The lighting of being, were it to be *seen* as glance, as look, could thereby become, as it was for the Greek poets and philosophers, the "model" (παράδειγμα) for our all-too-human sight—and the liberating "measure" of the extent to which we have realized the potential for vision latent in our natural endowment. Since the "light is the determining (*maßgebende*) radiance, the shining and appearing," our comportment as beings gifted with sight could thus be attuned (*bestimmt*) by the lighting: it could *become* the way of the lighting (p. 144 in English; p. 214 in GA 54). Here is Heidegger: "The open is that closest that we co-intend in the essence of unconcealedness, though [typically] without explicitly heeding it or genuinely considering it, let alone grasping its essence in advance, so that all our experience of beings could be *ordered and guided* [*beschickt und geleitet*] by the presence of this open" (p. 142 in English. Italics added, translation altered. p. 212 in GA 54).

But this "open" is no ordinary measure, norm, order, or guide: "The open and its extension into the vastness of the unlimited and limitless are zones without stopping places, where every sojourn loses itself in instability. The open provides no shelter or security. The open is rather the place where what is still undetermined and unresolved plays out, and therefore it is an occasion for erring and going astray" (pp. 143–44 in English; pp. 213–14 in GA 54). The open is "anarchic," preceding all human institutions of order. How, then, he asks, "can the open be essentially sheltering?" (p. 144 in English; p. 214 in GA 54). What the anarchic opening of the lighting shelters is—our freedom (p. 143 in English; pp. 213–14 in GA 54). "The lighting, understood as brightness, first bestows the possibility of the look and therewith the possibility of the encountering look as well as the grasping look" (p. 144 in English; p. 215 in GA 54). Furthermore: "In this context, the open is the light of the self-luminous. We name it 'the free' and its essence 'freedom' " (p. 148 in English; p. 221 in GA 54).

Our freedom lies in confronting these existential possibilities. And comporting ourselves appropriately. For Heidegger, this means: *letting* ourselves be appropriated, claimed, by what most calls for a thoughtful responsiveness, namely, the "circumstance" of the lighting itself and as such: for "perception of what emerges and is unconcealed is a perception of something shining in the light, i.e., it is seeing and looking. Only because looking is *claimed* in this way can the 'eye' receive a priority" (p. 146 in English; p. 218 in GA 54). This is why, by virtue of our looking and seeing, "the eye of man," as Heidegger puts it, "can become [i.e., has the free existential possibility of becoming] a *sign* for the relation of man to the unconcealed in general" (p. 146 in English; p. 218 in GA 54. Italics added).

According to Heidegger, "the Greeks could be visual only because it is ἀλήθεια that determines the relation of their humanity to being" (p. 147 in English; p. 218 in GA 54). As the lighting that opens up and maintains a visual field, ἀλήθεια (primordial unconcealment) is for our vision *maßgebend*, is measure-giving: "the open and lighted determines what appears therein and makes it comply with the essential form of the look that looks into the light. In correspondence to this appearing look, the disclosing perception and grasp of beings, i.e., knowledge, is conceived as a [correct] looking and a seeing" (p. 147 in English; p. 219 in GA 54. Italics added). But this "normativity," and the claim it makes against our ordinary, grasping way of looking and seeing, are ontological, and cannot directly prescribe for us the universally appropriate ontical correspondence. Thus Heidegger says: "Strictly speaking, the essence of the open reveals itself only to a thinking that attempts to think being itself in the way that it is presaged to our destiny in the history of the West as what is to be thought in the name and essence of ἀλήθεια" (p.149 in English; p. 222 in GA 54). And then he adds, most significantly, that "every person in history knows being immediately, though without acknowledging it as such" (ibid.).

Now, according to Heidegger, "to think being is very simple"; "but," he concedes, "that simple is for us the most arduous" (p. 149 in English; p. 222 in GA 54). To begin thinking and seeing the opening presencing of being, we must somehow begin to see "ekstatically," *doubling* our ordinary way of looking and seeing with a looking and seeing held open into the openness of the visual field, thereby *doubling*, through our own sight—through the λέγειν (gathering laying-down) of our own sight—the primordial Λέγειν of the "look (glance) of being." Heidegger says: "To think being does not require a solemn approach and the pretension of arcane erudition, nor the display of rare and exceptional states as in mystical raptures, reveries, and swoonings. All that is needed is simple wakefulness in the proximity of any random unobtrusive being, an awakening that all of a sudden *sees* that the being 'is' " (p. 149 in English; p. 222 in GA 54. Italics added).

What kind of experience (*Erfahrung*) is involved in such seeing? "The 'it is' of beings, being, shows itself, if it does show itself, in each case suddenly . . . the way that something irrupts into appearance, from non-appearance" (p. 149 in English; pp. 222–23 in GA 54). Indeed, since being "is not a ground but is the groundless," he maintains that "to think being requires in each instance a leap, a leap into the groundless from the habitual ground upon which for us beings always rest" (p. 150 in English; p. 223 in GA 54). Instead of this necessary "leap," however, we typically "seek a ground only in the form [figure] of a being, and hence never carry out the leap into [the openness of] being or leave the familiar landscape of the oblivion of being" (ibid.). In this way, we do not see, do not make visible, *as invisible*, the ontological difference, "the primordial decision by which being bestows on man unconcealedness, i.e., the truth of beings as a whole" (ibid.). This means that we do not see the figure-ground differentiation—and do not make it visible—*as* the invisible instancing of the "primordial decision." And this, in turn, means that we overlook the great potential latent in our experience with vision. Referring to this "primordial decision" (*Entscheid*), Heidegger says: "The character of this bestowal hides and secures the way historical man belongs within the bestowal of being, i.e., the way this order entitles him to acknowledge being and to be the only being among all beings [able] to see the open. Man, and only he, constantly sees into the open, in the sense of the free, by which the [lighting of the] 'it is' liberates each being to itself and on the basis of this liberation *looks at man in his guardianship of the open [Wächterschaft für das Offene]*" (pp. 150–51 in English; p. 224 in GA 54. Italics added). Dwelling in the lighting of being, we are not only made visible, and ourselves made able to make visible; we are also thereby "beheld" by this lighting, held in our beholdenness to the gift of the lighting: to us alone, as the only beings capable of responding hermeneutically, disclosingly, to this gift, comes the responsibility for receiving it and responding with a vision born of guardian awareness.

In his *Introduction to Metaphysics*, Heidegger defines the phenomenological attitude that would direct ontologically appropriate looking and seeing: "To apprehend [*Vernehmen*] . . . means to let something *come* to one, not merely accepting it, but taking a *receptive* attitude toward that which shows itself."[119] We are responsible for the character of our responsiveness to the phenomenon—to all that shows itself before our eyes. (The practice of phenomenology that Heidegger formulates in the "Introduction" to *Being and Time*, namely letting the phenomenon show itself from out of itself, could not be more radical; it is so uncompromisingly radical, so deeply respectful, I think, of presencing, that it can well serve as the formal conceptualization of an originary, ontologically appropriate ethics.) But are we willing to let the phenomenon presence (*west*), practicing the patience and restraint of what Adorno[120] once named the "long and tranquil gaze upon the object"? I continue our reading of the *Parmenides* lectures. Heidegger observes that

> although man and only he constantly sees into the open, i.e., encounters beings in the free of being, in order to be struck by them, yet he is not thereby already entitled to bring being itself explicitly into its ownmost, i.e., to bring it into the open (the free), i.e., to poetize being, to think it and to say it. Because only unconcealed beings can appear and do appear in the open of being, man adheres, at first unwittingly and then constantly, to these beings. He forgets being and in such forgetting learns nothing more than the overlooking of being and the alienation from the open. (P. 151 in English; pp. 224–25 in GA 54)

Although it is the opening lighting that dwells in ἀλήθεια which "first lets beings emerge and come to presence as beings" (p. 159 in English; p. 237 in GA 54), our relationship to this opening has been a blind seeing:

> Man alone sees this open. More specifically, man gets a glimpse of this open while comporting himself, as he always does, to beings, whether these beings are understood in the Greek sense as what emerges and comes to presence [i.e., as *physis*], or in the Christian sense as *ens creatum*, or in the modern sense as objects. In his comportment to beings, man in advance sees the open by dwelling within the opening and opened project of being. Without the open, which is how being itself comes to presence, beings could be neither unconcealed nor concealed. Man and he alone sees into the open—though without beholding it. *Only the essential sight of authentic thinking beholds being itself.* But even there the thinker can behold being only because he as man has already glimpsed it. (P. 159 in English; p. 237 in GA 54)

It is precisely toward such "essential sight" that we have been thinking in this chapter, interpreting it in relation to the presencing of the ground in the figure-ground *Gestalt* as an ekstatic way of looking and seeing, hermeneutically doubling the lighting of being—the "look of being"—through its "ownmost" (*eigenst*) guardian openness, its "ownmost" gathering and laying-down-before, embracing the openness of the ground, embracing it *with* openness, letting the ground show itself from out of itself, *as* ground, *as* open, *as* the ever-emerging, ever-becoming, ever-yielding.

The "look of being," i.e., the coming of the lighting into the field of vision it opens up, gathers, and lays down, is the guiding ontological "norm" for our vision; it is the "directive" in accordance (attunement) with which our vision could realize and fulfill its ontological *Geschick*, its pre-ontologically inscribed, or pre-ontologically endowed potential. To the extent that our looking and seeing are ontologically appropriate(d) in their relation to this lighting, this "look of being," they would be engaged in a hermeneutical *doubling* of the "look of being," for they would mimetically repeat, in a ὁμολογεῖν, the opening, gathering, and laying-down-before (i.e., the Λέγειν) of being, presencing in and as the field of lighting within which our vision takes place. Through this doubling, which would not only *repeat* the Λέγειν of the lighting, but hermeneutically let it show itself from out of itself in the field of our vision, the "look of being" would come into its own. Thus, the doubling achieved by our way of looking and seeing would also mean a doubling of the lighting as *Er-eignis:* our vision, *er-eignet*, would come into its own, realizing and fulfilling itself by virtue of its ὁμολογεῖν, whilst at the same time making it possible for the lighting itself, the very presencing of being as such, to come into its own, to the extent that our looking and seeing let it be visible as that on which they depend and therefore as that by grace of which alone they are first possible.[121]

But there must also take place a *second* gesture of doubling, for if the formation of a figure-ground *Gestalt* is ever to transform into a *Geviert*, it must become radically open to the openness of the ground—and that means radically open to the possible irruption, or supervenience, of a redemptive moment in which a new epoch, the beginning of a new order of world-disclosure, might (if ever) come to pass. Such radical openness, however, requires that our looking and seeing practice focusing on the figure of their "object," bringing it forth and making it stand out, whilst also, at the very same time, attending appropriately—and that means with a radically different approach—to the phenomenal, hermeneutical presencing of the perceptual ground. The doubleness, here, consists in a certain tension (*Streit*) between [1] a gaze that is required, in accordance with the modern conditions (*Be-ding-ungen*) of objectness, to be strongly centered and focused, concentrating on the articulation of an objective figure, and [2] a gaze that the unconcealment (ἀλήθεια) of being requires, in accordance with its radically different conditionality (*Be-dingt-sein*), to be ekstatically decentered, accomplished in softening its focused concentration, loosening its per-ceptive grasp, and freely hovering in the anarchic *dif-férance* between figure and ground, open to whatever might emerge, whatever might come forth from the immeasurable, abyssal depths of the ground.

This conflict between two ways of looking and seeing would, however, be transformed, to the extent that the concentrating gaze could overcome its inveterate drive, a compulsion characteristic of modernity, to objectify, i.e., to reduce the thing (*Ding*) to the state of an object (*Gegen-stand*). For, as Heidegger argues, drawing on the evidence of etymology, according to which the Old High German word for "thing" means a gathering, *if* the thing somehow were to be appropriately—and that means phenomenologically—experienced, i.e., as the *thing* that it is and not as an object, then it could perhaps become an uncanny, even awe-inspiring site for the gathering of the fourfold, a site where the perceptual *Gestalt* of the modern epoch could at last become, in a new beginning, a new epoch of world-disclosure, a *Wesensentfaltung seiner Wahrheit*,[122] a *different* gathering of the lighting: that open-grounded *Gestalt* which Heidegger calls by the name *das Geviert*.[123]

Our title for this chapter names in thought two permutations of the perceptual *Gestalt*. If *Gestalt* refers to a gathering for a while of the lighting, of the visible and the invisible, into a practical structure, *Gestell* names a gathering of the lighting, of the visible and the invisible, into the nihilism of a phantasmagoric reification, and *Geviert* attempts to think the historically new possibility of a gathering of the lighting into a configuration of the most dynamic openness. *Geviert* would thus be the name of a certain dream, the vision of another beginning, a time coming after the overcoming of the *Gestell,* when perception, assuming a radically different *Gestalt* configuration, would take place as a hermeneutical λέγειν, a gathering of earth and sky, mortals and gods, a gathering outside our present order of time and history, a gathering in which, because of our response-ability, our *Wahr-nehmung,* our care for the hermeneutics of truth as beings gifted with sight, it might somehow become possible for each of the four to become a realm of inconceivable disclosure, opening beyond the reach of representation into the depths of the invisible.—But is this a vision that could be "true" only as long as it remains absolutely impossible?

IV

For Heidegger, the question of being and the question of a "new beginning" are deeply intertwined. But I think that, in the texts of the later thinking, his vision of this "new beginning" hovers anxiously between an apocalyptic discourse of mysticism (where, for example, the transition is thought in terms of "waiting," "leap," and the coming of another god) and a more restrained discourse of diagnosis, critique, and recollection. Because of this ambiguity, Heidegger's discussions of world-disclosedness (*Welterschliessung*) have often been interpreted to mean or imply that we are absolutely caught, trapped, within our present framework of meaning and intelligibility, and that only another god, an apocalypse or catastrophe, something totally *outside* this framework, could ever get us out of its determinism.

But this interpretation does not correspond at all to Heidegger's view. [1] There is a crucial distinction between *Schicksal* (fate) and *Geschick* (destiny, dispensation). *Geschick* refers to the fact that we are thrown into a world of existential possibilities; what we make of these possibilities is up to us. [2] "World-disclosedness" must not be understood as an absolutely closed framework or system of interpretation. It is not a totally determinate grid, totally determining everything that takes place within its clearing, its purview. Such an understanding misses the whole point. The significance of Heidegger's term is precisely that it *denies* the possibility of systemic closure: what the term tells us is that it is always a question of concealment and unconcealment, and therefore we cannot split off dogmatically what appears within our world from that which is beyond or outside it. "World-disclosedness" signifies that our world-order, the world as we know it, the world-interpretation within which we live, is inherently, radically open—open to alterations coming both from the inside and from the outside. It is because validity-claims (the propositional truth of statements or assertions) take place within the openness of the dimension of world-disclosedness that totalitarian regimes cannot ultimately succeed in suppressing or otherwise controlling them.

[3] Earlier, we considered Heidegger's critical observations about staring. For Heidegger, the statement (*Satz*) or assertion (*Aussage*) is the linguistic equivalent of the stare, and his criticism of the one is similar, *mutatis mutandis*, to his criticism of the other. When Heidegger denies that the locus of truth is (solely) in the assertion or statement; when he argues against the correspondence theory of truth; and when he holds that assertoric truth, truth in the sense of correctness, is founded on, or derivative from, truth as ἀλήθεια, truth as unconcealment, this is not because he is attempting to downgrade it or restrict its power to challenge and disrupt the prevailing world-order. Quite the contrary! His critique of the tradition comes from a thoughtful caring for the truth, a deep concern to protect and preserve it from all forms of positivism, all forms of ideology, all forms of dogmatism—all forms of closure. For Heidegger, to locate truth exclusively in the dimension of the statement or assertion is precisely to reify it, to limit its referential and implicational field, and to restrict its vulnerability to contestation: unless assertions or statements are located in an interpretative context (a field of meanings, a field of enquiry, a universe of discourse), there is no way to account for uncertainty, the finitude of knowledge, the possibility of error and deception, processes of disconfirmation and revision, and challenges to the prevailing understanding. If it is only by contextualizing statements or assertions within the openness of a field of meaning and enquiry that we can understand, question, and do justice to their validity-claims, then Heidegger's argument for seeing truth (the truth of assertions or statements) as grounded in ἀλήθεια is an attempt to *rescue* such truth from a one-dimensionality that encourages, even shelters, dogmatism and positivism. Heidegger's insistence on situating truth not in propositions (statements or assertions) but rather in ἀλήθεια, unconcealedness, is an attempt to protect and preserve truth from the closure that totalitarian regimes always try to impose. To understand that propositional truth is grounded in and derived from ἀλήθεια, the interplay of concealment and unconcealment that is always open—open even

to the coming to pass of an inconceivably different interpretation of the world as a whole—is to see that totalitarian regimes can never dominate and dictate forever the truth of what is.

For Heidegger, this danger requires that we see truth taking place within the care (*Wahrnis*) of ἀλήθεια, the "primordial truth" of unconcealment. Ἀλήθεια protects the search for truth by holding it within the openness of its dimensions. Ἀλήθεια watches over the truth by reminding us that truth is surrounded by darkness, the invisible, the unknown; it reminds us that what we know is really very limited, inevitably fallible, and always subject to error and deception. And I surmise that it was only because he thought of ἀλήθεια in this way that he was tempted at first—with what unfortunate consequences he later realized—to describe ἀλήθεια as "primordial truth." Later, he realized that this description caused his argument to be terribly misunderstood—and he carefully withdrew it in an explicit analysis of the problem.[124]

Before any statement or assertion, any validity-claim can be posited, a field of meaningfulness, a field of referentiality, must be opened up; and it is through the field which has been opened up, gathered, and laid down that the claim of the statement or assertion is made intelligible and questionable. Ἀλήθεια names the opening up, gathering, and laying down of this field, names it in recognition of its inherent, ongoing openness—a dynamic openness that takes place at and in the interplay of concealment and unconcealment.

By situating the truth of statements or assertions within the dimensions of ἀλήθεια, Heidegger thinks this truth in all its fragility, vulnerability, and contestability. To think the truth of validity-claims as taking place within unconcealment is to think the truth within the dynamic interplay of concealment and unconcealment—within the forms of resistance and contestation that come from the presently unknown, whatever is beyond the present horizon. What is unconcealed is always still surrounded by a delimiting horizon; but the horizon has two faces, one of which faces into the openness beyond, the region of the concealing and the concealed. The boundary formed by the horizon is not a rigid barrier, but a place of metaphor: it is in the dimensions opened up through the interplay of concealment and unconcealment that learning and change take place.

In "On Truth and Lies in a Nonmoral Sense," Nietzsche asks, "What is truth?" Answering his question, he writes: "A movable host of metaphors, metonymies, and anthropomorphisms."[125] Bearing in mind the etymology of the word, *metaphor*, it may be said that ἀλήθεια is the *metaphoring* of statements of truth: it *metaphors* by carrying them into the space of questionability, uncertainty, and contestation, resisting closure, maintaining their openness to the unknown, the inconceivably other.

In the poem "On the Road Home," Wallace Stevens gives lucid expression to the difference between seeing things in their propositional truth and seeing things aletheically, i.e., in a way that is open to the dimensions of their unconcealment. Resisting reductionism, he is granted extraordinary aesthetic encounters, even with the most ordinary things:

> It was when I said,
> "There is no such thing as the truth,"
> That the grapes seemed fatter.
> The fox ran out of his hole.
>
> You . . . You said,
> "There are many truths,
> But they are not parts of a truth."
> Then the tree, at night, began to change.[126]

The visible beauty of things, their presencing as *scheinende Erscheinungen*, depends on whether or not they are approached aletheically—and given, thereby, a receptive space. Aesthetic experience is essentially metaphoric and aletheic.

[4] Heidegger spoke of "waiting" because he had to avoid the nihilism in visions of a new beginning dependent on the will to power. As he argued against Nietzsche, if the problem of nihilism can be traced to the will to power, then the will to power cannot save us from the danger. But he never meant by "waiting" that there is nothing we can do in response to this danger. On the contrary, there is much that we can do to prepare for a new epoch, a new beginning, a different world-disclosedness—so long as what we do does not perpetuate the will to power by actions and activities that continue the dualism of the activity-passivity scheme. Thus Heidegger repeatedly speaks of "preparatory steps," "preparatory gestures." Learning to look and see otherwise, for example, could be such a preparation. Learning to look and see differently could mean beginning to look and see a world that is otherwise than "being," otherwise than metaphysically reified, unified, and totalized presence.

[5] What, then, would it mean for us to dwell, by virtue of our looking and seeing, in what I am calling the way of the lighting? What difference would a recollection of the lighting (re-collection, *Erinnerung* as *Wiederholung*) make in the life of our world? I want to suggest, here, that what ἀλήθεια, unconcealment, could teach us is the radical ethics and aesthetics of phenomenology—letting the phenomenon, whatever is encountered in

the world of our dwelling, simply show itself from out of itself. The ethics and aesthetics of ἀλήθεια is openness to alterity. Grounding truth in ἀλήθεια is grounding "truth" in end-less questioning.

Recollection, for Heidegger, would not be just experiencing (once again, but also, for the first time) our belongingness *(Zugehörigkeit)* to being; it would also be experiencing, making contact with, our sense of the *loss* of being—what it is like to live in the abandonment of being *(Seinsverlassenheit)*, and in the loss of its protection of truth *(Verwahrlosung)*. Heidegger's discussion of recollection is a narrative of loss, of mourning; it is also narrative of suffering, pain, and need: a *Leidensgeschichte*, in the wake of our abandonment by being. These are, he argues, dark times, needful times. The gods have fled. And so he documents some dimensions of our cultural experience of this abandonment, attempting to understand the deepest, most ontological meaning of our experience. He looks, for example, into anxiety, dread in the face of nothing, boredom, depression, defensive aggression, lust and greed, the insatiable hunger for possessions, for power and domination.

One way to think this sense of abandonment is to reflect on how we look and see—and think in what way our looking and seeing could be otherwise. Heidegger's "narrative" of suffering, pain, and need, an essential dimension of meaning at the very heart of his reading of the history of philosophy, should be understood in this light: as an attempt to get us to look at our world and see its need, its pain, its suffering—see clearly to the point where we can even see how our looking and seeing are responsible for, have contributed to, this pain, this suffering, this need, forgetting the presencing of being and the consequences of such forgetting. Recollection is also, therefore, learning to look and see in a way that re-collects being. This is not waiting in the ordinary sense of doing nothing, but consists, rather, in preparatory steps and gestures *(Vorbereitungen)* toward another world-disclosedness, another beginning.

Recollection, returning perception to its ground, prepares for a different ontological grounding. At the heart of Heidegger's *Leidensgeschichte*, therefore, is a conviction that he shares—at least in its most abstract formulation—with Adorno, viz., that all reification is a forgetting. For Heidegger, reification is the forgetting of being, forgetting that being ready-to-hand and being present-at-hand—the predominant ways in which being has presenced in the history of our world-order—are not the only possible ways in which being can presence. Thus, the task of thinking must be a critique of reification and an attempt at a recollection (re-collection) of a different sense of presencing.

This study is intended as a contribution to this project, examining how reification is, and has been, at work in the figure-ground formation of our visual perception. But the implications of this examination—implications that, admittedly, Heidegger left insufficiently elaborated, especially in the social and political realms, are of the utmost significance for our daily lives—and for the prospect of changing their conditions. The reification of presencing—which is the betrayal of hermeneutical phenomenology—directly affects the way we look at and see other human beings. Hence its overcoming would be a decisive precondition for the gathering of the fourfold.

Closure to the perceptual ground means closure to other ways of looking and seeing. Such closure is manifest in the perceptual stereotyping, rigidity, and avoidance of ambiguity that are characteristic of the so-called authoritarian personality.[127] People whose way of looking and seeing fit this profile cannot tolerate figure-ground ambiguities; cannot easily see the intricacies and complexities of a moral situation; cannot easily assume hypothetically and theoretically the standpoints and viewpoints of others; cannot comfortably inhabit the reciprocity of points of view that is constitutive of moral development in its most mature stage.

Late in his lifetime, Horkheimer suggested that, at the very heart of critical social theory, there is a certain messianic "longing for the utterly Other" (a *Sehnsucht nach dem ganz Anderen*).[128] Although I do not want to suggest too much proximity between Heidegger and Horkheimer, I think one could say, nevertheless, that in Heidegger's concern for our recollection of the ground (for recollection as a *Rücknahme in den zu eröffnenden Grund,* as he formulates it in the *Beiträge*)[129] there was, most deeply, most essentially, most decisively, a concern for our openness to the inconceivably Other—thought through the figure, the trope, of a new beginning. Commenting, in the *Beiträge,* on his interpretation of Kant, Heidegger remarks that it is not intended to be historically accurate (*historisch*), but rather to be timely (*geschichtlich*), i.e., "drawn into the preparation of a future thinking, . . . a timely intimation of an utterly Other [*auf die Vorbereitung des künftigen Denkens and nur darauf bezogen, wesentlich, eine geschichtliche Anweisung auf ein ganz Anderes*]."[130] Later in this text, he explains that "the Other means that which, as sheltering of the truth of being, lets a being be [a] being" ("das Andere meint jenes, was als Bergung der Wahrheit des Seins Seiendes ein Seiendes sein lässt").[131] Since the being of the ground essentially consists in its openness, an openness that defies the logic of identity, I believe that, to the extent that we learn how to be open to the presencing of the ground—for example, in the way in which our looking and seeing relate to the ontological ground in the formation of a local figure-ground difference, we would inevitably find ourselves drawn into the immeasurable, abyssal dimensionality of the ground, drawn into the *openness* of the ground—and drawn, thereby, into the most extreme responsibility for our own openness to the inconceivably Other.

In the *Beiträge*, Heidegger argues that we must not overlook the "primordial depth and groundlessness" of ἀλήθεια.[132] He goes on to say that the "amplitude and indeterminateness of ἀλήθεια in its preplatonic usage also demanded a correspondingly indeterminate depth." However, in the subsequent discourse of philosophy, the opening granted by ἀλήθεια, lighting the way to (assertoric) truth, can no longer be seen. "All that remains," he says, is the faintest "recollection of the image of the lighting."[133] Even a glimpse of the openness of the ground fills us with dread. We can see this openness only as an abyss. But, says Heidegger: "the open of the abyss is not groundless. Abyss is not the No to every ground as groundlessness, but rather the Yes to the ground in its concealed broadness and farness."[134] We need to learn this entrustment—and responsibility—to the openness as which the ground presences. Only in this way can we learn what it means to be open—open even to the inconceivably Other. And only then might we be prepared for the coming-to-pass of another beginning.

However, the question of another beginning, considered through the question of the ground of being, is not something to be considered only in the discourse of metaphysics. It is also, and first of all, the most concrete, material question in and for our perception—our potential as beings gifted with the capacity to look and see. It is, in fact, a question that calls into question, concretely and materially, the way in which we are disposed to differentiate figure and ground, the way in which we relate to the presencing of the ground, in, for example, our looking and seeing. Heidegger knows this; nevertheless, he keeps his (post)metaphysical eye steadily focused on the metaphysical dimension of the problem—the entirely, inconceivably Other toward which the openness of the ground of being draws us. And with tragic consequences, because he loses sight of the ethical, moral, and political dimensions: the need for receptive openings that already haunts our experience of the ground of perception: openings, above all, I would say, to the face of the other, openings that are still struggling for recognition in the unreconciled ground of our visual formations. And yet, it is only in relation to being, to the question of being, that we can think the dimensionality of beings and repudiate programs that contribute to the reification, the commodification, the stereotyping of human beings and to the technological instrumentalization of animals and nature. To learn from the lighting a way of looking and seeing that would be more open to the openness of the ground, more open to whatever it might bring forth, would be at the same time to learn a way of looking and seeing that would be more open and responsive to the alterity of the other being—a way of looking and seeing that would recognize its responsibility to and for the other already binding it in the very ground of its possibility.

In "The Way Back into the Ground of Metaphysics," an introduction added in 1949 to *What Is Metaphysics?*, Heidegger observes that

> [metaphysics] thinks about beings. Whenever the question is asked what beings are, beings as such are in sight [*in der Sicht*]. Metaphysical representation owes this sight [*Sicht*] to the light of being [*dem Licht des Seins*]. The light itself, i.e., that which such thinking experiences as light, does not come within the purview [*in die Sicht*] of metaphysical thinking; for metaphysics always represents beings only as beings [*nur in der Hinsicht auf das Seiende*].[135]

How, then, could our looking and seeing ever find their way back to their grounding in the opening circumstance of the lighting, learning from the ways that it presences—learning from its great powers of revealing and concealing? There is, as Heidegger reminds us, pointing to the gods' appearance in the sky, "a disclosing that lets us see what conceals itself, but lets us see it not by seeking to wrest [*herauszureißen*] what is concealed out of its concealedness, but only by guarding the concealed in its self-concealment."[136]

In this regard, a sagacious remark by Nietzsche may be read as anticipating the thesis for which I have been arguing:

> Without this art [of masking, of concealment], we would be nothing but foreground and live entirely under the spell of that perspective which makes what is closest at hand and most vulgar appear as if it were vast, and like reality itself.[137]

v

In his *Logic*, Hegel declares that "thinking is always the negation of what we have immediately before us."[138] Our thinking, here, has been guided by this directive. But if we are to realize the negation of what we have immediately before us, we must also have some sense of that which is other, for the negation can be meaningful only when it is mediated by that which opposes it as its other. And yet, we can say very little—not nothing, but almost nothing—about this other still to come in a "new beginning." Thus, with Hegel no doubt in mind, Heidegger tells us, in the "Vorblick" (preview, anticipatory glance) which begins his *Beiträge zur Philosophie (Vom Ereignis)*, that "the time of 'systems' has gone by. The time for cultivating [*Erbauung*] the essential form [*Wesensgestalt*] of beings [i.e., for cultivating the *Gestalt* of their presencing, their *Wesen* and *Aufgehen*] out of the guardian truth [*Wahrheit*] of being [*des Seyns*] has not yet come."[139]

It would be difficult to disagree with the proposition that "no-one knows the *Gestalt* of the coming beings [*Seienden*]." But when Heidegger, appropriately eschewing the temptation to prophetic vision, speaks, in this text, of the future *Gestalt*, he is using a word from which I want to wrest a much more concrete meaning, a dimension of meaning we must presume that he did not explicitly intend or acknowledge. This is one of the ways in which it is possible to carry his thinking forward. Reading his words after the reflections in which we have here been engaged, reading them, now, in the context of a discourse on the formation of the figure-ground *Gestalt* in our looking and seeing, we should not be surprised to find that the words bring forth into unconcealment something we were not able to see before. Taking Heidegger's words to refer to the structuring of our perceptual experience brings out for further unfolding an existential dimension of the question of being—the question of the ground—that Heidegger's own thinking left for the most part unthought. Instead of letting this concrete dimension appear, Heidegger spells out the significance of the renunciation, remarking that, "without the already protective appeal [*behütenden Zuspruch*] of beings," every attempt to draw on the "truth of being" in order to imagine or produce a different *Gestalt* "would need other powers [*Kräfte*] of questioning and saying, projecting and bearing [*des Werfens und des Tragens*] than what the history of metaphysics has ever at any time before been able to bring forth."[140] Without forgetting this, however, we have attempted, here, to begin thinking toward, and into, a future still to come—a future, perhaps, that will always be still to come, cultivating as best we can (and as the "Vorbereitung des anderen Anfangs") the experience of a different *Wesensgestalt*.[141] The imaginary *Gestalt*, namely, that Heidegger calls *das Geviert*, that figure-ground structure in perception into which we may someday receive and welcome—without racism, nationalism, and other forms of hate, coercion, and exclusion—a truly free and open gathering of the fourfold.

In his essay "On Language as Such and on the Language of Man," Walter Benjamin recalls a poem by Friedrich Müller, "Adam's Awakening and First Blissful Nights": "Man of the earth step near, in gazing grow more perfect, more perfect through the word."[142] This vision is engaging. But as long as there is even one gaze that cannot—or will not—see the pain, suffering, and misery of another being; so long as there is even one gaze that cannot—or will not—see its own responsibility for the misery of another being, *these* words, the words of the poet, must continue calling and reminding our vision, recalling what the gaze has consigned to the insignificance of the background, gathering it eloquently toward the future configurations of a time of reconciliation.

Exposure to the openness of the ground, and thus to the inconceivable otherness that the ground holds in the reserve of its concealment, is absolutely meaningless, unless we take it to heart as a guide for ethical life, for *Sittlichkeit*—take it thus to imply the most demanding measure (*Maßstab*) of our comportment toward the unapproachable, ever-withdrawing dimensions of alterity that belong to all beings—but, above all, and in an absolutely singular way, to those beings in whom we must see, and acknowledge with tact and respect, the presence, the being, that is called "humanity."

The attempt at a re-collection of the ground must not perpetuate an abstract relationship to the being of beings. We need it to become engaged with a concrete, material re-collection—a re-collection, for example, of the ground that presences for our sight in the figure-ground *Gestalt*. Moreover, its ontological significance, as a gesture in the direction of openness to the absolutely Other, must be *supplemented* (in Derrida's sense of this term) by the imperative to respond with justice to the claims of all those whose suffering and misery have been marginalized or rendered invisible, thrust into the background and forgetfulness of our perception. As an effort to engage with the openness of the ground, an effort to respond to the absolutely Other, this re-collection of the ground must become, as Marcuse says, "a remembrance of what could be."[143] A remembrance with all the critical, disruptive force—and all the compassion—that this imperative has carried in the discourse of the Frankfurt School. A remembrance that is responsible to, and for, the mortals of Otherness whose suffering and injustice the prevailing *Gestalt* of perception is bent on overlooking.

5 The Field of Vision

Intersections of the Visible and the Invisible in Heidegger and Merleau-Ponty

All that is visible clings to the invisible. . . . Perhaps the thinkable to the unthinkable.

Novalis[1]

Every visible is invisible. . . . The invisible of the visible.
Maurice Merleau-Ponty, *The Visible and the Invisible*[2]

[Immanent critique] must dissolve the rigidity of the temporally and spatially-fixed object into a field of tension of the possible and the real.
Theodor Adorno, "Sociology and Empirical Research"[3]

All reification is a forgetting.
Max Horkheimer and Theodor Adorno,
Dialectic of Enlightenment[4]

I

We shall be giving thought, here, to perception: to the formation of the figure-ground *Gestalt*, the relationship among figure and ground, the field of perception, and the horizon that delimits it. In questioning our experience with vision, we will be working with a number of different texts, but will give special attention to two texts in which the nature—or, say, the character—of our sight, our capacity for vision, is the major topic of thought.[5] These two texts, each one in its own way a record of the boldest, most radical, and most unsettling thinking, are *Conversation on a Country Path*, a meditation on *Gelassenheit* (releasement) that Heidegger wrote down in 1944–45, and Merleau-Ponty's "Working Notes," fragmentary texts written near the end of his life and published posthumously in a collection bearing the title *The Visible and the Invisible*.[6]

In his *Phenomenology of Perception*, Merleau-Ponty wrote: "I am a field, an experience."[7] Later, in his 1959 "Notes de Travail," he wrote that, "the world is a field, and as such is always open."[8] "There are fields in intersection, in a field of fields, wherein the 'subjectivities' are integrated" (VIE 227, VIF 281). In fact: "Each field is a dimensionality, a being is dimensionality itself" (VIE 227, VIF 280). In Merleau-Ponty's phenomenological meditations on the logic of the perceptual field, Heidegger's "Feldwege," his "paths in the field," are given a needed hold on our experience with perception.

The question of the figure-ground *Gestalt* that is formed in perception is of much greater importance than it might at first seem. As this present study will demonstrate, reflection on this matter takes us right into the formulation of a radically hermeneutic phenomenology, and thus into illuminations of the attitude of *Gelassenheit*, a new approach to the problematic of ontology, and a far-reaching critique of metaphysics. Indeed, it might be argued that, in Heidegger's *Gelassenheit* essay, there is such a bold rethinking of the figure-ground formation and its field that the dialogue effects a decisive "Revolution der Ortschaft des Denkens" (a "revolution in the topology of thinking").[9]

There are, as both Heidegger and Merleau-Ponty understood, some quite surprising rewards for a path of thinking that attempts to deconstruct the elegant conception of the ground which has held sway in the discourse of metaphysics by returning to the more elementary experience of the ground in the structure of perception. Similarly, it can be useful to begin with a hermeneutic phenomenology of perception as one way (*Weg*) to think anew [i] the subject-object structure and the character of the relationship it involves, [ii] the reduction of the *presencing* of being (*die Anwesenheit des Anwesens*) to being ready-to-hand (*Zuhandensein*) and being present-at-hand (*Vorhandensein*), which are the only two *modes* of presencing we recognize in our time, and [iii] the reduction of the immeasurable dimensionality of being, of that which opens up the field or ground of the ontological difference between being and beings, to the ontic dimensions of beings.

Taking a position that agrees with Heidegger, the authors of the *Dialectic of Enlightenment* remark that "the loss of memory is a transcendental condition for science."[10] If, because of the increasing instrumentalization of reason, one may suspect an inner connection between the historical development of rationality in the West and the forgetting, or rather the suppression, of the potential for enlightenment inherent in our perceptual capacities, then our reflections here should be read as attempting a certain critical recollection, an *anamnesis* both of our still unrealized potential—an ontological normativity—and of the historical suffering for which this falling-short is responsible.

The project for philosophical thought involves two deeply related tasks: a recollection of the as yet undeveloped potential in nature's gift of perception and a recollection that brings to light the violence that is both cause and effect of our historically predominant way of looking and seeing. In what follows, I am suggesting that, in redeeming the immemorial depths of vision, both Heidegger and Merleau-Ponty made significant contributions to this project.

II

Consider two well-known examples of ambiguous, reversible *Gestalten:* the duck-rabbit, derived from Jastrow, that appears in Wittgenstein's *Philosophical Investigations*[11] and the equally familiar formation that can be seen either as a white vase in a black space or as the heads of two people— twins, in fact, since their silhouettes are isomorphic—directly facing one another across a white space.

These drawings attract and hold our attention because of their perceptual ambiguity: they invite us to *reverse* the figure-ground relation that we initially and spontaneously see. They invite us to shift our visual focus, seeing as figure what we had taken as ground and seeing as ground what we had taken as figure. They invite us to allow our eyes to *play* with the freely flowing interplay that is possible between figure and ground, to *soften* the dualism that typically differentiates figure and ground. The duplicity of these images makes them intriguing; it also makes them a source of visual pleasure. In their presence, one experiences a certain *jouissance*, a certain delight, a certain quite singular freedom: it is as if one were magically transported back in time—back to the innocent enchantments of early childhood. For, once upon a time, our vision knew nothing of the inhibitions, the constraints, the disciplinary regimes to which, in due time, it would be subjected. Once upon a time, our vision could move freely, spontaneously, back and forth, between dream and reality, fact and fantasy. For the child, *Gestalt* reversals were natural events, manifestations of a mimetic magic inherent in the visionary world. Why *shouldn't* a duck turn into a rabbit or a rabbit turn into a duck?

The *Gestalt* shift, reversing figure and ground, letting a different configuration emerge—Wittgenstein talks about the dawning of an aspect—is a prime example of a *hermeneutical* process: it is the hermeneutics that is inherently and spontaneously operative in the dynamics, the ekstatic interactions, intertwinings and intercrossings of the perceptual act, *in so far as* it be deeply, chiasmically, ontologically thought and re-membered.

In "On the Mimetic Faculty," an essay on a topic that assumed considerable importance in the thinking of the Frankfurt School philosophers—
especially Horkheimer, Adorno, and Marcuse—Benjamin wrote this:

> Nature creates similarities. One need only think of mimicry. The high-
> est capacity for producing similarities, however, is man's. His gift of
> seeing resemblances is nothing other than a rudiment of the powerful
> compulsion in former times to become and behave like something else.
> Perhaps there is none of his higher functions in which his mimetic fac-
> ulty does not play a decisive role.[12]

According to Benjamin,

> this faculty has a history in both the phylogenetic and the ontogenetic
> sense. As regards the latter, play is for many its school. Children's play
> is everywhere permeated by mimetic modes of behavior, and its realm
> is by no means limited to what one person can imitate in another. The
> child plays at being not only a shopkeeper or teacher but also a wind-
> mill and a train. (Ibid.)

And he follows this point with a question: "Of what use to him is this school-
ing of the mimetic faculty?" Of what use is the hermeneutic ability to see
something *as* something else? These "natural correspondences," he says,
"are given their true importance only if seen as stimulating and awakening
the mimetic faculty in man." Insisting that the "gift of producing similarities . . . and therefore also the gift of recognizing them, have changed with
historical development," Benjamin contends that the "direction of this
change seems definable as the increasing decay of the mimetic faculty. For
clearly, the observable world of modern man contains only minimal
residues of the magical correspondences and analogies that were familiar to
ancient peoples."[13] For him, "the question is whether we are concerned with
the decay of this faculty or with its transformation." Or again: "The question is whether this [faculty] can be developed and adapted to improved understanding."[14] Although we will not be concerned, here, with the "mimetic
faculty" as such, the question that Benjamin puts to history—the question,
namely, regarding its decline and the possibility of transformation, or, say,
a new beginning—will also be ours: ours, in particular, with regard to the
historical fixation (*Ge-stell*) that imposes itself in our time, our epoch, on
the structure (*Gestalt*) of figure and ground in our everyday perception.

For Heidegger, as we shall see, the question that Benjamin formulates
must become a question of being, an ontological question challenging the
history of metaphysics as a history of being. But perhaps a promising beginning for our present work of thought would be to reflect on the

phenomenology of the playfulness in the child's mimetic attitude, for it is surely such aesthetic playfulness that maintains figure and ground in a freely flowing interaction and lets the structure they form undergo a spontaneous reversal. In short, it is a question of a deconstructive, afformative movement, in perception, that can release the figure-ground structure from an inveterate tendency to reification that inhibits the free, spontaneous interaction between the focal figure and its dynamic ground.

It is inherent in the nature of the perceptual *Gestalt* that the being of the ground, the ontological event of its field-dimensional presencing, is radically *different* from the being of the figure—different from that (figurative being) which presences *within* its allowing. However, for both rationalism and empiricism, schools of thought which *re-present* perception as an act of *re*-presentation, the nature of the field or ground is either ignored, since its being, its presencing, cannot be mastered, cannot be totalized and reified, or else it is turned into another figure, another object, another (*vorhanden* or *zuhanden*) being. Interpreted in this way, perception is nothing but a transposition of the metaphysical re-presentation of the Absolute Ground of Reason, duplicating the repressive measures that such Reason imposes—recoiling in horror from its occasional glimpse into the abyss—on the ground it has made its own. "To think being," Heidegger says in his 1942–43 lectures on Parmenides, "requires in each instance a leap, a leap into the groundless from the habitual ground upon which for us beings always rest."[15] And he adds: "Being, however, is not a [graspable] ground but is [for the gaze that would grasp it] the groundless. . . . In fact, we surely fall into the abyss, we find no ground, *as long as* we know and seek a ground only in the form of *a being,* and hence never carry out the leap into being or leave the familiar landscape of the oblivion of being."

In terms of the problematic of the present study, viz., the phenomenon of the perceptual field and the differentiation of figure and ground, the post-metaphysical importance of Heidegger and Merleau-Ponty consists in the fact that, in their phenomenological articulations of perception, they both attempted, albeit each in his own way, to deconstruct these metaphysical re-presentations, subtly violent disfigurations of the ground—and to point in the direction of another way of experiencing the field of perception and its figure-ground formations. And, although neither said so explicitly, perhaps they had an intuitive sense that a different understanding of perception—a different *experience* with perception—might somehow, someday, make possible a new, post-metaphysical beginning for philosophical thought. The post-metaphysical question—question for a post-metaphysical phenomenology—is therefore: Can the perceptual field, the ground of perception, be *released* from our historical compulsion to represent it in a way that accommodates our will to power and its need to totalize and reify the presencing of being? In other words: Can the ground be experienced *as* ground? Can its hermeneutical way of presencing, i.e., as a dynamic interplay of concealment and unconcealment, be given *appropriate* respect in the receptivity of a perception that *lets itself* be *appropriated by* the ground and accordingly *lets* the phenomenon of the ground *be* what and how it is? Can the coming-to-pass of the ontological difference that is constitutive of all the local figure-ground differences taking place in our perceptual field be made visible hermeneutically, and thus without violence to its withdrawal into concealment? But the question concerning the constellation of figure and ground cannot be separated from the question concerning the structure of subject and object. Hence the possibility of a movement beyond metaphysics must also think the historical possibility of breaking out of this structure into the spacing of the ontological difference: *différance*, the primordial, sensuous, ekstatic *écart*. As Heidegger states it in his Parmenides lectures, it is a question of "the way historical man belongs within the bestowal of being (*Zufügung des Seins*), i.e., the way this order entitles him to acknowledge being and to be the only being among all beings to *see* the open" (PE 150, PG 223. Italics added). We might also say that it is a question of our response-ability, our capacity as beings gifted with vision, to measure up to the responsibility for perceptual responsiveness laid down for us in the "primordial de-cision" (*Entscheid*) of the ontological difference (ibid.). To recognize the operation of the ontological difference taking place in the figure-ground difference of the perceptual *Gestalt* is to recognize the ontological difference as the primordial *Riß*, the primordial *Ur-teil* underlying all our perceptual syntheses and judgments—and recognize, moreover, that this rift, *this* division, decision, and scission, an ekstatic *écart* underlying and gathering all our so-called acts of perception, is also the only "norm" (ἀρχή) by which our condition, our essential deciding and becoming as the ones who are gifted with sight, can ultimately be judged.

In a 1943 text, "On the Essence of Truth," Heidegger says:

> To engage oneself with the disclosedness of beings is not to lose oneself in them; rather, such engagement withdraws in the face of beings in order that they might reveal themselves with respect to what and how they are and in order that presentative correspondence [*vorstellende Angleichung*] might take its standard [*das Richtmaaß*] from them.[16]

Borrowing words from Foucault, who borrowed the thought from Georges Dumézil, I want to suggest that, in thinking about perception, we must look for "structured norms of experience, the scheme of which could be found with modifications on different levels."[17] This articulation of different structural and normative levels of experience is the major theme of Merleau-Ponty's early pre-phenomenological work, *The Structure of Comportment*, a critique of prevailing theories that set the stage for all his later, genuinely phenomenological work. The claim that we shall be considering here, then, is that there is in our perception an ontological norm; but if the configuration of such a norm takes place—and is—only in the breach, then we shall be compelled to acknowledge that the ordinary, everyday perception it solicits is summoned to endless transcendence—and thus to a certain transgression.

In *Phenomenology of Perception*, Merleau-Ponty renders the lighting visible as the worldly, ontic assignment and articulation of a normative level for vision: "The lighting," he says there, "directs my gaze." "We perceive in conformity with the light." "The lighting is . . . what we take as the norm" (PPE 310–11, PPF 358–59). But in "The Anaximander Fragment," Heidegger shows that there is also an *ontological* assignment of normativity, which the gift of the lighting articulates. "Presence within the lighting," he says there, "articulates [i.e., brings forth, gives an enabling field to] all the human senses."[18] The ontological norm, or measure, gift of the lighting, draws the gaze of the ego-logical subject into its abyssal dimensionality, into the depth of a ground and field that resists totalization and closure, denying the gaze its sovereignty, its lucidity and certainty, and calling into question the ontic compromises that would reduce the ontological dimensionality of the lighting to a mere level of illumination serving the sociocultural normalization of the gaze. The normativity of the lighting that Heidegger is attempting to bring into our recollection as that dispensation and assignment by which the character of our vision will ultimately be measured is a chiasmic intertwining of concealment and unconcealment, the presence and the absence of light, the anarchy of the deepest, most extreme night, which the lighting protects, and into which it endlessly withdraws. The lighting gives light; but it also brings opacities, false appearances, destabilizing shadows, and blinding darkness, reminders of our irremediable finitude. If the ontic normativity of the light can be made to serve any economy of perception, the ontological normativity of the lighting is an absolutely uncompromising measure, a measure beyond being, that submits all regimes of perception to the questioning of its deconstructive justice. Measured against the abyssal dimensionality of the lighting, the force-field of perception that has structured life in the modern world could begin, perhaps, to lose its enchanted hold.

III

In his *Phenomenology of Perception*, Merleau-Ponty asserts that "it is necessary to put our surroundings in abeyance the better to see the object, and to *lose* in background what one *gains* in focal figure, because to look at the object is to plunge oneself into it, and because objects form a system in which one cannot show itself without concealing others" (PPE 67, PPF 81–82. Italics added). According to this account, figure and ground are inevitably opposed to one another in a strict logic of equivalence: for every gain, there is an equal loss. In this logic, a logic that the modern bourgeoisie has institutionalized and embodied, the visibility of things always comes at a price; and the penalty is always a certain differential concealment. Such is the economic "justice" (δική) of perception.

In a later chapter, Merleau-Ponty essentially reiterates this point: "I have visual objects because I have a visual field in which richness and clarity are in *inverse proportion* to each other, and because these two demands, either of which, if taken separately, might be carried to infinity, when brought together, produce a certain culmination and optimal balance in the perceptual process" (PPE 318, PPF 367. Italics added). Is Merleau-Ponty right? Is there a compulsory, inevitable trade-off between richness (in the ground) and clarity (in the figure)? Must perception always involve such a strife, such a dualism? Is no other way of experiencing their interaction an historical possibility? What is in question here—and indeed at stake—is certainly *not* the differentiation of figure and ground as such, but rather the *way* in which this differentiation is constituted and maintained—or say held in our beholding. It is, then, a question of their interaction, and more specifically, the dynamics of their structural differentiation: whether there is an ongoing, free flow of "communication" between figure and ground, or, instead, a certain obstruction, a barrier, a fixation, a reification of the difference, inhibiting the spontaneity of this "communication." Could there be a *freely flowing interaction* between figure and ground, instead of a relation of gain and loss, fullness and emptiness, absolutized presence and totally negated absence? When the ground withdraws and a figure emerges, is it necessary that the gaze forget and deny the ever-emergent energies of the ground, its boundless wealth and generosity, its resourcefulness, its unlimited capacity to *bring forth* (*hervorbringen*) ever-new configurations of being?

We must ask whether this logic of gain and loss, this logic of equivalence, is a matter of essential necessity—or whether the dynamics of the perceptual *Gestalt* could be otherwise. It could be, for example, that the sway of this logic is to a certain extent a reflection of the political economy within which we live—a reflection of its character, the character it prizes and rewards. In any case, we must not immediately assume that it is entirely natural, that it is in no way an historical construction—hence, a contingency that could somehow be altered, provided that certain historical conditions were also to be altered. And we must not immediately take our normal, everyday habits of perception as establishing the ideal norm for perception. Its deepest implicit potentialities, its enlightenment, and its "promise of happiness" might call for perception with a radically different character.

IV

In "Plato's Doctrine of the Truth," Heidegger contends that "everything depends on the ὀρθότες, the correctness of the glance."[19] And he attempts to articulate a distinction between what we might call the glance of *correctness* (which sees truth statically as correspondence) and the gaze of ἀλήθεια (which sees truth ekstatically in the openness of the interplay between the visible and the invisible, concealment and unconcealment). Some scholars may take it that Heidegger could not possibly have in mind, here, our visual perception, our capacity for vision. However, even a cursory glance at his major early work, *Being and Time*, will show beyond reasonable controversy that Heidegger meant what he said and said what he meant. Here is a partial index of his references—enough, perhaps, to demonstrate that readings which interpret these words, references, and discussions as "mere" figures of speech or as "mere" metaphors, having nothing to do with our sight and our capacity for vision, are on very shaky ground: insight (83, 102), blindness (88), looking at (89), staring (88–89, 98, 104), circumspection (98–99), looking at things theoretically (98–99, 177), observation (99, 104), sight (99, 186–87), seeing (99, 186–87, 214–16), glimpse (102), beholding and intuition (129, 177), the "eternal observer" (140), foresight (191), focus (197), and the "moment of vision" (376, 387). Careful examination of other writings—not only the "Conversation on a Country Path," on which we shall presently be concentrating, but also "The Question Concerning Technology," "The Turning," "The Age of the World Picture," the still untranslated "Das Gestell," "Science and Reflection," and his texts on Anaximander, Parmenides, and Heraclitus—can only give weight to this reading.

In the "Conversation on a Country Path about Thinking," a scientist, a scholar, and a teacher, each representing a distinct point of view, converse while taking a walk on paths that traverse, and put them again in touch with, the fields of the countryside—*Feld-Wege*. They are gathered together on a path of thinking laid down by the question of being. They have allowed themselves to be claimed by what calls for thought. And what most calls for thought is thinking itself.

The scholar, representing a traditional philosophical point of view, remarks that "thinking, understood in the traditional way, as re-presenting, is a kind of willing. . . . To think is to will, and to will is to think."[20] This enables the teacher, representing Heidegger's most advanced stage of thinking, to go right to the heart of the matter: "I want non-willing," he says (DT 59, G 32). The scholar, however, like the one falling into the abyssal dialectic of despair that Kierkegaard diagnoses in *Sickness Unto Death*, can think "non-willing" only as another form of willing: "Non-willing means . . . willingly to renounce willing" (ibid.). What the three are attempting to think, rather, is a thinking *released* from willing altogether, a thinking, therefore, *beyond the duality of willing and non-willing*. (In the "Epistemo-Critical Prologue" to his essay on the *Trauerspiel*, Benjamin attempted, in a perhaps rather similar spirit, to disconnect truth as disclosure from the will of the subject: "Truth," he wrote, "is the death of intention.")[21]

Like some of Plato's dialogues—the *Lysis* and the *Phaedrus* come at once to mind—Heidegger's conversation takes place away from the city—on a country path. And, significantly, it continues into the evening, into the night. The only dialogue of Plato that takes place at night is the *Symposium*, on the topic of love. Perhaps it is, here too, a question of love—or say a certain caring, the love that manifests thinking. Be that as it may, the scientist, the least likely of the three, observes that the thought he just articulated was "not my doing but that of the night having set in, which without forcing, compels concentration" (DT 60, G 33). This "not my doing" indicates already a certain understanding of non-willing. And the reference to the night suggests an even deeper intuition. For, in the night, one cannot see—the invisible holds sway. The night is the time of sleep and dreaming. It is the time, also, of fantasies, haunting: in the night, one can feel more intensely the presence of what is absent. The night, moreover, is the time when the old and familiar boundaries, the very definition of things, cannot be counted on: there is, instead, confusion, interpenetration, chiasmic intertwining, a *deeper* unity. Though much of it was probably written at night, the discourse of traditional philosophy is a philosophy of the light, of the day. It is a discourse produced under the hegemony of daylight vision.

Heidegger's discourse, interrupting this hegemony, takes place at night, and, as the teacher says, "still far from human habitation" (DT 60, G 33).

Allowing himself to be drawn into the spirit of the conversation, and expressing, whether or not he realizes it, a certain experience of the "non-willing" they are seeking to understand, the scientist declares: "Ever more openly I am coming to trust in the inconspicuous guide who takes us by the hand—or better said, by the word—in this conversation" (ibid.). It is a question, they all agree, of somehow letting their capacity for releasement (*Gelassenheit*, letting-go, letting-be) be awakened. "Awakened": that is to say, it cannot be a question of *willing* releasement. Taking up this point, the scientist says: "You speak without letup of a letting-be and give the impression that what is meant is a kind of passivity. All the same, I think I understand that it is in no way a matter of weakly allowing things to slide and drift along" (DT 61, G 35). The three concur that what they are trying to think is "beyond the distinction between activity and passivity," because "releasement does *not* belong to the domain of the will" (ibid.). But, as they also agree, "releasement" cannot be identified with the traditional *theological* concept of a renunciatory non-willing (DT 62, G 36). As we shall see, releasement involves a certain *neutralization* of the will-to-see, so that the gaze relates to what it is given to see with composure and equanimity, letting it appear as it is. (One of Heidegger's words for this is *Erscheinenlassen*. He also will speak of a *Seinlassen*.)

The scientist then asks a crucial question, shifting the conversation to the problematic of re-presentation: "What has releasement to do with thinking?" (DT 62, G36). To this the teacher replies: "Nothing, if we conceive thinking in the traditional way as re-presenting." The scientist promptly confirms this, confessing that, "with the best of will, I cannot re-present to myself this nature of thinking [i.e., releasement]." This seems to lead them into a dilemma, an impasse: If releasement is not a matter of re-presentation, how can it be thought by a philosophical thinking that knows only the work of re-presentation? "What in the world am I to do?" asks the scientist. "We are to do nothing but wait," says the teacher. This, as the scientist is the first to admit, leaves them all very disoriented: "I hardly know any more who or where I am," he says (DT 62, G 37). This also shows just how radically the ontological question challenges ordinary and familiar experience: it even calls into question our sense of who and where we are. In *Being and Time*, published in 1929, Heidegger called upon us to think of ourselves as essentially *Da-sein*: being-there, ekstatically living in the openness of being. But who then, including Heidegger himself, fully understood what this interpretation meant, what new self-understanding it demanded of us? In his 1942–43 Parmenides lectures, Heidegger emphasizes that, for the pre-Socratic philosophers and poets, looking is "self-showing": "the human look thus experienced [accordingly] disclose[s] the encountering person himself in the ground of his essence" (PE 103, PG 153). How we see shows, reveals, betrays the *Grundzüge* of *who* we are—just as much as, if not more than, it places before us, within the openness of their unconcealment, the beings *at which* we are looking.

According to the story Heidegger wants to tell in his 1944–45 "Conversation on a Country Path," we are essentially ekstatically open beings, living in the immeasurably open dimension of being. But we are, virtually from the very beginning, closed to this dimensionality: virtually from the very beginning, our experience is foreclosed, inhibited, restricted, too bent on willful mastery, too keenly focused on objectification to be aware of it—or take it into our care. We are essentially ekstatic: but this essentiality is only given to us as a potential that needs to be realized, a capacity that needs to be developed. Thus it must be said that we are *always already* ("immer schon") *Da-sein*, beings *of* (belonging to) the openness—and yet also that we are *not yet* ("noch nicht") such beings, not yet *Da-sein* (see the teacher's comment, DT 72, G 50: "That [*before* being released by waiting into the openness of that-which regions,] we were [*outside* it], and yet we were not." Also see the exchange on DT 75, G 53).

If we go to "The Anaximander Fragment," we find Heidegger observing there that what is always presencing, together with the things that are visibly present, is not "something over against a subject, but is rather an open expanse [*Gegend*] of unconcealment, into which and within which whatever comes along lingers" (AXE 34, AXG 319). According to Heidegger, we do not notice the open expanse that the lighting gives us because our "vision is confused by habituation to the multiplicity of the ordinary."[22] Ordinary vision, the vision of *das Man*, of the anonymous anyone-and-everyone, attends to beings and overlooks being, sees what is visible and ignores the invisible, notices *what* is present but is unaware of presencing (the gift, or givenness, of the field) as such. Ordinary vision *empties* the contextual field of meaning: for ordinary perception, the ground is not significant. Although the ground is the *source* of the figures we see—as we are wont to say—"against" it, ordinary vision regards it as not sufficiently interesting, and it tends therefore to cut off the ground from the figures which engage its attention, thereby inhibiting a freely flowing interplay between them in a disfigurement that affects them both.

"But what else," Heidegger asks us in his Parmenides lectures, "is this relation of being to the essence of man than the clearing and the open which has lighted itself for the unconcealed?" (PE 146, PG 217). Heidegger claims, in other lectures on Parmenides, that the ancient Greek poets and philosophers experienced being, the immeasurable ground of presencing, the field laid down for vision, as "a luminous appearance in the sense of illumined, radiant self-manifestation."[23] For them, for their vision, being is ("is" in the sense of the Greek φύσις and the German *west*) a "self-disclosing emergence," the "self-opening" and "clearing" of a field of visibility; it is the dispensation (*Es gibt*) of "lighting"; it is "the light of the self-luminous" (PE 148, PG 221; also PE 150, PG 223) that surrounds beings, shining upon them and into them, lighting them up, making them visible (PE 106, PG 156). Moreover, he argues, "if such clearing did not come into play [*Weste nicht solche Lichtung*] as the open of being itself, then a human eye could never become and be what it is" (PE 146, PG 217). This suggests, according to Heidegger, that, essentially considered, *even we moderns* (always and already) dwell as visual beings in a radiant and *open* field; but ordinary vision, and especially the vision of our present time, is driven by the will to power, marked by an inveterate *tendency* to reduce the dimensionality of the field in a process of reification and totalization.

In the *Parmenides* lectures, Heidegger argues that "the open, to which every being is liberated as if to its freedom, is being itself" (PE 150, PG 224). And it is "the open," he says, that "first lets beings emerge and come to presence as beings" (PE 159, PG 237). "Man alone sees this open" and "gets a glimpse of this open while comporting himself, as he always does, to beings, whether these beings are understood in the Greek sense as what emerges and comes to presence, or in the Christian sense as *ens creatum*, or in the modern sense as objects" (ibid.). Indeed: "In his comportment to beings, man *in advance* sees the open by dwelling within the opening and opened project of being" (ibid.).

However, we see the opening of the open "without beholding it" (ibid.). "The Open [i.e., the ground itself] becomes an object, and is thus twisted around toward human beings."[24] As a predominant characteristic of our time, this objectifying tendency, reducing the dimensionality of the visual field, is called "enframing" (*das Gestell*), and, according to Heidegger, it effects a corresponding reduction (*Entschränkung*) in the lighting, the presencing of which first opened up a field for our vision: "Enframing blocks [*verstellt*] the shining-forth and holding sway of truth [i.e., the moment, or event, of aletheic unconcealment by grace of which there is a visual field]."[25] In his work on Nietzsche, Heidegger even asserts that, because of the enframing of the open dimensionality that takes place in the modern world, "the whole field of vision [*Gesichts-kreis*] has been wiped away."[26]

Enframing also, of course, affects the horizon of vision: "The horizon no longer emits light of itself. It is now nothing but the point of view posited in the value-positing of the will to power."[27] In another text, directing our attention to (what we might call) the *character* of our vision and to how this way of looking and seeing affects what is, what is present, to be seen, he observes that "the original emergence and coming-to-be of energies, the φαίνεσθαι, becomes a visibility of things that are already-there. . . . The eye, the vision, becomes a mere looking-at or looking-over or gaping-at."[28] In a certain sense, or to a certain extent, ordinary vision falls into an inveterate tendency—especially, he thinks, in our time—to stare.

There are, Heidegger contends, two ways of looking and seeing, two understandings: one, seeing in the "original sense," is "emergent self-presenting"; the other is "grasping" (PE 107–8, PG 158–59). The first is also described as "the look of being" (*der Anblick des Seins*) (PE 147, PG 219) and as "the essential sight of authentic thinking," beholding in the openness of the lighting the presencing unconcealment of being itself (PE 159, PG 237). It would be a soft, gently hovering gaze, softening, deconstructing the metaphysical division that separates figure from ground. But in a culture such as ours, driven by the will to power, vision tends to become, as Heidegger already phrased it in *Being and Time*, "a fixed staring at something that is purely present-at-hand."[29] (In his *Phenomenology of Perception* [PPE 54, PPF 66–67], Merleau-Ponty speaks of Western metaphysics as positing a "freezing of being.") Now, to be sure, Heidegger admits, "The Greeks were acquainted with the grasping look [*der erfassende Blicken*], just as, conversely, and in addition to such looking as an act of subjective representation, we also know the look of encounter [that lets presencing bring beings forth from out of itself]" (PE 107, PG 159). "But," he says, "the question is not whether both these essential forms of looking, the encountering and the grasping, are known or not. The issue is which one, the look of emerging into presence or the look of grasping, has the essential priority in the [experiencing and] interpretation of appearances and on what basis this rank is determined" (ibid.). The "look of the modern subject is the look of a being that advances by calculating, i.e., by conquering, outwitting, and attacking. The look of the modern subject is, as Spengler said, following Nietzsche, the look of the predatory animal: glaring [*das Spähen*]" (PE 108, PG 159). Of course—and this is most important for understanding Heidegger's reading of the Greeks and, more generally, his relationship to the history of Western civilization, which many commentators have taken to be driven by a certain nostalgia for the glorious past of ancient Greece—it must be acknowledged that "the Greeks too experienced the look as an activity of man.

But the basic feature of this grasping look is not glaring, by means of which beings are, so to say, impaled and become in this way first and foremost objects of conquest. For the Greeks, looking is the 'perception' ['*Vernehmen*'] of beings on the basis of a primordial consent [*Einvernehmen*] given to being, which is why the Greeks do not even know the concept of object and never think being as objectivity" (PE 108, PG 159–60).

The modern way of seeing is responsible for the historical fact that the gift of being, the presencing of being, which is open to many possible ways of being visible, gets to be seen in only *two* modes: being ready-to-hand and being present-at-hand. These, and these alone, corresponding to the two ways of looking and seeing, are the two historical ways in which being has presenced in the restricted dimensionality (*Entschränkung*) that enframes and conditions our modern world.[30]

To make this historical process more understandable, Heidegger always resorts to the telling of a narrative. Once upon a time, he says, in the world of the ancient Greek poets and philosophers, the field of vision was experienced as φύσις, a field of powerful energies, an inexhaustible source of lighting, an immeasurably deep ground, out of which ever-new configurations of visible being emerge, only to return after a while, to dissolve back into the energies of the ground. In ordinary perception, and especially in our own time, this φαίνεσθαι of the ground, the open field of visibility, that event, that dispensation (*Geschick*) by grace of which a field of lighting opens itself up for the activity of vision, becomes fixated, "hardening" into the objective condition of "permanent presence."[31] What Heidegger calls "the splendour of radiant appearing" thus turns dull, as the presencing of the field, the presencing of the ground, recedes into the oblivion of our forgetfulness, our *Seinsvergessenheit*. This reification of the presencing of the ground, closing off a "free field,"[32] an open space, means that the beings we see *within* the visual field are "deprived of the possibility of appearing spontaneously"—and that, being without an open, receptive space into which they can spread, extend, and radiate, they are deprived of a radiance (*Schein*) that they would otherwise display.[33]

The increasing dominance of a certain tendency in vision has increasingly produced a world different from the world of the ancient ones: a visually governed world that, moreover, reproduces and reinforces the increasing dominance of this tendency and, at the same time, the occlusion, or even indeed the suppression, of all other potentials. In the Greek world of antiquity, this type of vision, vision with this character, certainly existed; but, at least among poets and philosophers, a different way of looking and seeing could take place and shine forth.

In the *Parmenides* lectures, Heidegger attempts a description of the way poets and philosophers of Greek antiquity must have looked at the ordinary and self-reflectively experienced their looking. "By way of preparation," he writes, "we note that the uncanny, or the extraordinary, shines *throughout* the familiar ambience of the beings we deal with and know, beings we call ordinary. . . . In its essence [the uncanny] is the inconspicuous, the simple, the insignificant, which nevertheless shines in all beings" (PE 105, PG 156. Italics added. Translation altered). But the Greek poets and philosophers did not overlook this inconspicuous shining—and this way of looking at the ordinary things of their world was visibly reflected in the character of their comportment, showing who they were and who they thought themselves to be: "That which within the ordinary comes to presence by his own look is man. . . . Man himself is that being that has the distinctive characteristic of being addressed by being itself, in such a way that in the self-showing of man, in his looking and in his sight [*in seinem Blicken und seinem Anblick*], the uncanny itself, [which to Greeks eyes took the form of a] god, appears" (PE 105, PG 154–55).

Let us return, now, to the progress of the conversation on a country path. What, in our world and our time, would a receptive "openness," an "openness to the presencing of being," involve? And why should it matter? The scientist reflects that, "previously, we had come to see thinking in the form of transcendental-horizonal re-presenting" (DT 63, G 38). The scholar then comments: "This re-presenting, for instance, *places before us what is typical* of a tree, of a pitcher, of a bowl, of a stone, of plants, and of animals, as that view into which we look when one thing confronts us in the appearance of a tree, another thing in the appearance of a pitcher, this in the appearance of a bowl, various things in the appearance of stones, many in the appearance of plants, and many in the appearance of animals" (ibid. Italics added). In re-presentation, we see only "what is typical." In other words, re-presentation is a process of repetition, re-producing a typifying, reifying way of seeing that is normal, standard, and habitual. It is, we might say, a normalized pathology: a fixation on the same, a compulsion to see always the same, a way of patterning our experience, a way of receiving what we are given to see so (ontically) common that the (ontological dimension of the) pathology is not even recognized.[34]

In "What Are Poets For?," where Heidegger records thoughts suggested by his reading of Rilke, the philosopher is led to a crucial moment of recognition: "Objectification," he says, "blocks us off against the Open." And then he adds this: "The more venturesome daring does not produce a defense."[35] Instead of thinking, experiencing, perceiving in a way that is simply present, *openly* (ekstatically) present to (with) what is presencing—this would be the phenomenological attitude formulated in the "Introduction" to *Being and Time,* namely, letting the phenomenon show itself from out of itself—we think, experience and perceive as an act of will. But the action of the will is an essentially *aversive* intervention, aggressively establishing a (temporal and spatial) distance which delays, postpones, and pushes away. The prefix in the word "re-presentation" indicates this deferral, this willful, anxiety-driven refusal to let the phenomenon show itself from out of itself; and it points to the presence of what might well be called a repetition-compulsion, arising from a deep-seated anxiety—perhaps, as a defensive ego-logical response to the no-thingness of the openness as which being presences—and from the deeply pattern-forming need that it arouses: a need, namely, to master and dominate the presencing of what presences by re-presenting it to ourselves on our own ego-logical terms. And the words "places before us" betray the fact that this re-presentation is under the spell of modern metaphysical enframing—*das Gestell.* In German, the prefix is "vor," which bears both a temporal and a spatial sense of "before." The spatial sense connects especially clearly with the totalizing, typifying, reifying character of enframing: that which presences is *placed before one* in a *frontal* position that makes visual mastery and domination that much easier.

In his lectures on Parmenides, Heidegger gives a very blunt—and normatively charged—definition of re-presentation (*Vor-stellung*): "To represent means here to present before oneself, to bring before oneself and to master, to attack things" (PE 103, PG 153). And here, as elsewhere, he connects representation with the rise to power of the modern ego and its installment in a subject-object structure: "Metaphysically thought, the essence of the Ego consists rather in its making every other being something standing over against it, its object, its over-and-against, its pro-jected ob-ject. . . . Thereby the Ego proceeds to the totality of beings and presents this to itself as something to be mastered" (PE 137, PG 203–4). "Man," he adds later, in an analysis that was anticipated by Schelling,[36] "is the living being that, by way of re-presentation, fastens upon objects and thus looks upon what is objective, and, in looking, orders objects, and in this ordering posits back upon himself the ordered as something mastered, as his possession" (PE 156, PG 232). I think this analysis is correct, but it needs to be connected to a cultural analysis of the commodity structure, and of course the institutions of private property and capital.

Following a discussion of how representation typifies, how it patterns our responsiveness to the ordinary things that appear in our field of vision—commonplace things like trees, pitchers, and bowls, the friends' conversation (re)turns to the phenomenon of the ground or field. To the scholar's analysis of re-presentation, the scientist says: "You describe, once again, the horizon which encircles the view of a thing—the field of vision" (DT 63, G 38). "It goes," says the teacher, "beyond the appearance of the objects."—"Just as," adds the scholar, "transcendence passes beyond the perception of objects." The teacher follows this with a crucial observation: "Horizon and transcendence . . . are [normally] experienced and determined only relative to objects and our re-presenting them" (DT 64, G 38). In other words, the openness of the field and its horizon are subject to a process of reification: they are not experienced in releasement, i.e., not allowed to presence as they are. Thus the teacher adds that "what lets the horizon be what it is has not yet been encountered at all." And he explains what he means, by saying: "We say that we look into the horizon. Therefore the field of vision is something open; but its openness is *not due* to our looking" (italics added). Following the logic of this hermeneutic phenomenology, the scholar notes that, "likewise, we do not place the appearance of objects, which the view within a field of vision offers us, into this openness." The teacher then elaborates the phenomenon further: "What is evident of the horizon . . . is but the side facing us of an openness which surrounds us; an openness which is filled with views of the appearances of what to our re-presenting are objects."

This prompts the scientist to wonder what this openness is "as such," "if we disregard that it can also appear as the horizon of our re-presenting?" The teacher is ready with a response. Giving an answer that recalls the Anaximander fragment about which Heidegger was thinking, the teacher says: "It strikes me as something like a *region,* an enchanted region where everything belonging there returns to that in which it rests" (DT 65, G 40). But when the scholar requests clarification, he cannot say more—"if by 'understanding' you mean the capacity to re-present what is put before us as if sheltered amid the familiar and so secured." The problem is that re-presentation is inherently dualistically differentiating, hence foreclosing—as the prefix implicitly indicates; whereas what would be appropriate, given the openness, and what is called for—say releasement—is precisely *not* such closure. How, then, can the region and its horizon, together with the enchanted field within its bounds, be thought, experienced, seen with the openness and *Erscheinenlassen* of releasement?

Learning from the older form of the German word for "region," the three friends are led to think of the region as an "open expanse" which gathers and shelters, "resting in an abiding" (DT 66, G 41–42). It is "an abiding expanse which, gathering all, opens itself" and lets everything belong in its own resting. (In the essays on Heraclitus and Parmenides, Heidegger will say that the Λόγος, an early Greek word for being, is a laying-down and an ingathering—Λέγειν. Λόγος would therefore be a word one could use to name what here, in their conversation, the three friends are calling "die Gegnet," "that-which-regions.") The scientist, now, following the logic of the phenomenon with considerable care, carries forward their understanding of the region, saying that he "see[s] that-which-regions as *withdrawing* rather than coming to meet us" (DT 66, G 42). He thus sees the field of vision as a region that withdraws into concealment. But this is only part of the story, part of the event: the withdrawing or receding of the ground takes place "so that," as the scholar immediately notes, "things which appear in that-which-regions no longer have the character of objects." In other words, as the teacher explains, when the ground of vision (or of perception in general) is properly experienced in its withdrawing self-concealing, things will no longer be experienced as objects (*Gegen-stände*), as standing opposite us, or even, indeed, standing fixed at all (DT 67, G 42). Instead, things will simply lie before . . . , resting unconcealed in the field of their presencing, resting in the concealment with which the field embraces it.

At this point, the three friends find themselves saying more than they can understand—or more, anyway, than they can understand in the traditional sense of "re-present." "Probably," the scholar opines, "it can't be re-presented at all, in so far as in re-presenting, everything has become an object that stands opposite us within a horizon" (DT 67, G 43). "Any [traditional type of] description would reify it," as the teacher points out.

Re-presentation is a mode of relating to *things* that knows only how to experience them in their reduced and reified state, as *objects* for subjects. There are only two ways that things are allowed to presence (be present) for a subject bent on re-presenting them: either as being ready-to-hand (*zuhanden*) or else as being present-at-hand (*vorhanden*). That there could be any other historical possibility for things to be encountered is simply not conceivable within the framework of re-presentational thinking. Re-presentation essentially *refuses* the dynamic presence of the thing and will not consent to encountering the thing until it has re-presented that transcendent presence to itself on its own terms, viz., as a graspable, completely determinate ob-ject, something standing over against it, enframed, fixed, mastered, ever at our disposal in the dualistic structure of subject and object. A fortiori, re-presentation *also* must refuse the dynamic presencing of the *ground*, the field of perception as such. But, whereas things have allowed themselves to be reduced to objects for subjects, the presencing of the ground cannot be possessed in this way at all. The more one tries to grasp it, to objectify its dynamic presencing, the more it recedes, withdrawing into the elusiveness of its self-concealment. In fact, the more intensely one tries to grasp the ground (*Grund*) as an ob-ject, as a figure, the more intensely one will experience it instead in its disfigurement—as a groundless ground, an *Ab-grund*, an abyss (PE 150, PG 223).

And yet, as Hölderlin understood, thinking the abyssal nature of the ground not under the sign of nihilism but, on the contrary, under the sign of an inexhaustible sending or giving: "Vom Abgrund nemlich haben wir angefangen."[37] ("From the abyss, namely, we began.") The only appropriate attitude, therefore, is what the three friends agree to call "waiting," a *receptivity* that is very different from the "receptivity" described in Kant's *Critique of Pure Reason*, and in which "we leave open what we are waiting for" and let ourselves be released into openness (DT 68, G44). This is the only way to let the phenomenon of the ground show itself, from out of itself. Moreover, this attitude calls for a certain egolessness in their own discourse together: somewhat like the analysand freely associating words in the course of Freudian analysis, they must learn to "move freely in the realm of words" (DT 69, G 45), thinking with words released from the ego's censorship; and they must even learn to renounce the practice of identifying themselves with what they say (DT 71–72, G 49). Who speaks, and whose words are whose, does not matter.

Returning to a matter that still calls for thought, the friends let their attention be drawn to the presencing of the horizon. The teacher suggests that "the horizon is but the side of that-which-regions turned toward our representing. That-which-regions surrounds us and reveals itself to us as the horizon" (DT 72–73, G 50). But the horizon has another, darker face, for that-which-regions opens out into the incommensurable openness of the invisible, a field of presencing concealed behind the horizon, beyond the horizon that makes visible our limitations, our finitude. The three agree that, in one sense, we are *always already* within the horizon; but in another sense, we are *not* so long as we have *not yet* "released ourselves" from a "transcendental" (metaphysical) relation to the horizon (DT 73, G 51). But such releasement, they also agree, is not something they can "do" all by themselves (DT 71, 74; G 49, 53); and yet, this does not mean that there is nothing to be "done." What the three friends call "waiting," for instance, *is* a way of thoughtfully *preparing* ourselves for the historical-cultural moment when releasement becomes possible. In "waiting," we become aware of our "belonging" to that-which-regions and allow ourselves to be "appropriated" by the claim it makes on our capacity for an open mode of responsiveness—a mode of perceptivity that corresponds, by *virtue* of its openness, to the gift (*Es gibt*) of the opening openness of the field, the ground, that-which-regions (DT 73–75, G 51–53).

What is the relation, then, between releasement and that-which-regions? It is agreed that the relation is neither a connection of cause to effect (as in the objective thought of empiricism) nor a transcendental-horizonal connection (as in the subjective thought of rationalism). But it also "can be thought of neither as ontic nor as ontological": not the first, because it requires a turning-away from the "fallen" state of forgetfulness typical of ordinary, everyday experience; but not the second, in so far as "ontological" is to be understood in the pre-*Kehre* terms of the essential structures of *Dasein* (DT 76–77, G 55). No positive answer to this question comes to them at this point.

The three friends consequently return in an ever-deepening hermeneutical circle to question the thing: What about the relation of the thing to that-which-regions? (DT 77, G 56) The scientist suggests that the region "determines [*be-dingt*] the thing as thing." The scholar suggests that it would therefore be best to call the relation "determining." (He uses the word *Bedingnis.*) Retrieving the point they reached earlier in thinking about the relation between releasement and that-which-regions, the scientist replies: "But determining is not making and effecting; nor is it rendering possible in the sense of the transcendental." This leads to their thinking together about "the relation of man to the thing," the scientist reminding them that they earlier had begun to question "the relation between the ego and the object" (DT 77, G 57) and that, in this regard, they had come to the realization that the subject-object relation "is apparently only an *historical variation* [*eine geschichtliche Abwandlung*] of the relation of man to the thing, so far as things can become objects" (DT 77–78, G 57. Italics added). And it is clear that, with this recognition of historical contingency, a recognition that also figures prominently in Heidegger's lecture on "The Turning" (1949–50), they have taken a decisive and consequential step in preparation for thinking our historical emancipation from the dominance of the subject-object structure and the traditional re-presentation of the figure-ground formation.[38]

The teacher points out that things "have become objects [even] *before* they attained their [essential] nature as things" (DT 78, G 57). And the scholar suggests that "The same is true of the historical change of the human being to an ego" (ibid.). We human beings have become ego-logical subjects *before* ever having realized our true dignity—the wondrous gift of our great potential. We are more than, and other than, the philosophers' "rational animals" and "ego-logical subjects." But who are we? What *is* our nature, the becoming of our *Wesen?* The three friends are not ready to venture an answer; but they are quite sure that, in order to achieve, not just a new historical self-understanding, but rather an understanding that in some deep way is felt as more essentially fulfilling, we shall be required to learn a different way of seeing. And this, they believe, requires learning non-willing—and, in particular, "a relinquishing of the willing of a horizon [*ein Absehen vom Wollen des Horizontes*]" (DT 79–80, G 59). Such relinquishing is a precondition for "receiving" the regioning of that-which-regions in an attitude of releasement, an attitude of *ausdauernde Verhaltenheit,* "steadfast composure" (DT 81, G 61).

Nearing human habitation again, and consequently nearing the end of their conversation, the three friends give thought together to the nature of thinking itself, taking as the measure of their collaboration the deep connection between thinking and thanking. (Heidegger discusses this matter at greater length in the lectures of *What Is Called Thinking?*) With this, they approach a crucial question—one that might be called "the reception of the given"—or "the way of approaching the given." Although the reception of the given constitutes a fundamental problem for every theory of knowledge, every attempt to understand perception, it has never before been questioned with regard to thanking. And yet, we know well that the appropriate way to receive a gift is to give thanks. Why do we not think of the receptivity involved in perception as calling for an appropriate expression of thankfulness? How can we take the given for granted? In the objectivating discourses of empiricism—the discourses of Locke, Berkeley, and Hume, for example, the given plays a crucial role, but is reduced to atomic impressions, particulate sensations, punctual sense-data: it is never problematized as such; that there is anything at all given to us for our beholding, rather than nothing, is simply there for the taking, taken for granted. And in the subjectivizing discourses of rationalism—Kant's above all, perhaps—the given is always re-presented in such a way that its givenness, its having been given, is lost sight of in the subject's assumption of the power to give the given to itself: in Kant, the moment of receptivity is immediately concealed beneath the process of re-presentation.

In broaching the relation between thinking and thanking, the three friends are implicitly calling into question the way in which both philosophical schools have given the gift of thought to the perceptual given—and to the appropriateness of our reception. With this, we return to the question of releasement—the appropriate comportment toward that-which-regions, the field of perception, the ground of the figure-ground *Gestalt*. Although this comportment is not spelled out in much phenomenological detail, we can, I believe, gathering together the few fragments that shine and catch our eye, like splinters of broken glass, constellate a preliminary concept. As a way of receiving that which it is given us to behold, *Gelassenheit* calls for a composed, relaxed gaze, very alive and steady but not too sharply focused, hovering gently in a meditatively neutralized mode of engaged awareness, letting the phenomenon show itself from out of itself. It is a question of *neutralizing* the will, neither willing nor non-willing, learning how to "ground" one's capacity to see in the mood (*Stimmung*) of equanimity, letting the ontological attunement of this mood determine and direct the gaze. We should not be surprised to learn from this conversation that *Gelassenheit* is, in fact, the only attitude appropriate to the hermeneutics of the phenomenological method, as Heidegger already characterized it in *Being and Time*. Letting the phenomenon show itself from out of itself means, however, letting the ground, the field, that-which-regions, presence without needing to grasp it and objectify it in a mastered totality. And it means—as is suggested by the friends' discussion (DT 88–89, G 72) about the word attributed to Heraclitus, which they translate as *In-die-Nähe-hinein-sich-einlassen*, "letting-oneself-into-nearness"—letting the interaction between figure and ground—hence the interplay between the visible and the invisible, the present and the absent, the near and the far—take place freely, spontaneously. It means, therefore, that we must let go of our compulsion to impose our will on the flow of this interaction. Finally, it means developing a capacity for receptive openness that would radically alter our modern ego-logical identity—for as long as we continue to understand and comport ourselves as such subjects, we will continue to reduce to a state of objectivity and ready availability all the things we are given to behold, and even the immeasurable fields of visibility and invisibility that are gathered hermeneutically around them. (It needs, however, to be said here that the *Gelassenheit* of Heidegger's radically hermeneutical phenomenology, letting the phenomenon show itself from out of itself, does not mean an *uncritical and passive* reception. Since, as his discussion of the three senses of *Schein* in *Being and Time* and his even more elaborate, and almost baroque discussion of this word in the *Parmenides* lectures demonstrate, appearance can be illusory and deceptive as well as veridical, it is imperative that the method of phenomenology ensure a *double* movement, combining releasement with a shattering deconstruction of the phenomenon. This balancing of trust and suspicion, of course, only makes releasement all the more difficult and treacherous.)

In his 1935 *Introduction to Metaphysics*, Heidegger reiterates the conception of phenomenological method he formulated in *Being and Time*, holding that "to apprehend [*Vernehmen*] . . . means to let something come to one not merely *accepting* it, but taking a *receptive* attitude toward that which shows itself."[39] But this is not the attitude (*Einstellung, Verhalten*) of ordinary vision. Perhaps, as Heidegger seems to acknowledge in his Parmenides lectures, it never was, not even in the world of the ancient Greeks—except among a few extraordinary poets and philosophers whose thought has been passed down to us. Be this as it may, in any case this is not the attitude that prevails in our time. Moreover, if Heidegger's historical narrative makes sense and is at all convincing, it seems plausible to believe that, in modern times (i.e., since the emergence of humanism in the fifteenth century), a culture and economy driven by fantasies of domination have made this attitude an *increasingly* difficult one for anyone, even extraordinary poets and philosophers, to embody.

Now, according to Heidegger's discussion of the *Gestalt* in "The Origin of the Work of Art," where it is, of course, a question of the mighty strife (*Riß*) between earth and world, a strife that the Greek temple brings to heightened presence within its precincts, it must be concluded that the figure-ground *Gestalt* formed in perception is a local manifestation of this strife, and that therefore, wherever and whenever a visual *Gestalt* is formed, a vision *appropriated* by the presencing of being should see a local configuration where the ontological difference is taking place. To see this—to see the figure-ground *Gestalt* hermeneutically, *as* an ontological event of differentiation—would accordingly be the *most appropriate* way of seeing what is there (what *Es gibt*) to be beheld. In thinking about the work of art, Heidegger says: "The strife [*Streit*] that is brought into the rift [*Riß*] and thus set back into the earth [*zurückgestellte*] and fixed in place [*festgestellte*] is the *Gestalt*. Createdness of the work means: truth's being fixed in place in the figure [*Festgestelltsein der Wahrheit in die Gestalt*]. *Gestalt* is the structure [*das Gefüge*] in whose shape the rift composes and submits itself [*sich fügt*]. This composed rift [*Der gefügte Riß*] is the fitting or joining [*Fuge*] of the shining."[40] Only what we might call, drawing on the word Heidegger uses in "On the Essence of Truth,"[41] a radical deformation or undoing (*Verunstaltung*) of the *Gestell*—that form of the *Gestalt* formation of ordinary perception most distinctive of the modern world—could fit the hermeneutical attitude of the phenomenological method that Heidegger formulates in *Being and Time* and in this way be appropriate to the ontological difference constitutive of the perceptual *Gestalt* and presencing locally in its dynamic differentiation of figure and ground. (My word "dynamic," here, should be understood in a way that suggests the activity of overwhelmingly powerful energies, the spontaneous, uncontrollable emergings and recedings of φύσις, localized in the interactions between figure and ground, the visible and the invisible.)

In "The Turning," Heidegger draws on an etymological connection between *Eräugnis* and the German word for "eye" (*Augen*) to suggest a way of seeing and looking that lets itself be *appropriated by* the presencing of the ontological dimension of the perceptual ground and that thereby would be *appropriately* receptive and responsive to it: "Disclosing coming-to-pass [*Ereignis*] is bringing to sight that brings into its own [*eignende Eräugnis*]."[42] It is a question of our somehow learning the way of a "glance" (*Blicken*) through which—or say by virtue of which—"the coming to presence of being enters into its own emitting light," a hermeneutical way of looking and seeing "which retrieves that which it catches sight of and brings it back into the brightness of its own looking."[43] By *virtue* of its hermeneutical character, this way of looking vouchsafes a ring of invisibility and concealment to the field of light and visibility, letting the field open out into a dimensionality entirely beyond its grasp in the free reciprocating gesture of its *own* giving of light: "in its giving of light, [seeing] simultaneously keeps safe the concealed darkness of its origin as the unlighted."[44]

The lectures on Parmenides suggest, using some traditional phenomenological vocabulary, that as a way of seeing, *Gelassenheit* requires that we let the openness of the perceptual field—that clearing as which being comes to pass and presences for our vision—be our guide: "The open dwells in unconcealedness. The open is that [which is] closest [and] which we co-intend in the essence of unconcealedness, though without explicitly heeding it or genuinely considering it, let alone grasping its essence in advance, *so that the presence of this open could order and guide all our experience of beings*" (PE 142, PG 212. Italics added). In these lectures, Heidegger is attempting to draw a picture of ancient Greek life that will point to the *maßgebende* Leuchten, the determining or measure-giving radiance (PE 144, PG 214) of the lighting and will suggest that, when it is retrieved from forgetfulness and gathered up by re-collection (at PE 124, PG 184–85, Heidegger refers to Plato's doctrine of ἀνάμνησις), when it is saved and preserved in its unconcealedness, it may be seen as providing *the ontolog-*

ical norm by which our vision should be guided and directed. (On the lighting as normative for our vision, also see Merleau-Ponty, PPE 310–11, PPF 358–59.)

With regard to *beings*, figures emergent from the ground, Heidegger holds that "man can comport himself to beings as unconcealed only if he perpetually *directs* his thinking to the unconcealedness of the unconcealed . . . and in that way saves beings from withdrawal into concealment" (PE 124, PG 184–85). With regard to *being itself*, that is, with regard to the presencing of the field or ground within which beings figure and present themselves in various configurations, Heidegger suggests that *Gelassenheit*, as the ontologically appropriate way of looking and seeing, requires that our vision be *aletheic*, truly hermeneutical, re-collecting and thereby protecting that which *withdraws* in the coming to pass of beings (PE 102–10, PG 152–62). (In *Wahrnehmung*, the German word for perception, Heidegger's etymologically attuned ears hear not only the taking-as-true of ordinary, everyday perception, but also the preserving, protecting, caring of a perception deeply rooted in the guardian awareness of a recollection of being.) For that which withdraws from our totalizing grasp, concealing itself in its own immeasurable dimensionality in the very process of bringing beings forth into visibility and unconcealment, is what ultimately protects the being of beings from our will to power, preserving them in their transcendence. As a way of looking and seeing, *Gelassenheit* must serve concealment, the immemorial depths of the invisible, as much as, if not more than, it serves the cause of unconcealment. It is this that makes such a comportment "aletheic." It is this that accounts for the priority— and the uncanny freedom—of the gaze of releasement in relation to the gaze of the ordinary ego-logical subject.

(In anticipation of objections to a reading that introduces the concept of an ontological *norm*, I would argue that, in these lectures, as well as in many other writings, Heidegger speaks not only of being determined, guided and directed; he also speaks of compliance. Thus, in his phenomenological description of an ontologically appropriate understanding and way of seeing, he says (PE 147, PG 219): "The open and lighted *determines* what appears therein and makes it *comply* with the essential form of the look that looks into the light. In correspondence to this appearing look, the disclosing perception and grasp of beings, i.e., knowledge, is conceived as a looking and a seeing.")

The friends' conversation on the country path closes with a deepening sense of what it means to be open to the presencing of being, presencing for our vision in, and also as, the opening-up of a region of light, a field of visibility. The conversation also closes, therefore, with the articulation of a certain sense of enchantment, and a deeper understanding of what is involved in being appropriated (*vereignet, geeignet*) by "that from whence we are called"—called to a more thoughtful perceptivity, belonging whole-heartedly to that-which-regions.

But Rilke's fourth "Duino" elegy reminds us that the ego-logical subject, the bourgeois subject, does not easily renounce its will to power: It proclaims, "Ich bleibe dennoch. Es gibt immer Zuschaun." ("I remain nevertheless. There is always looking.") And adds, though perhaps with a certain anxiety, "Hab ich nicht recht?" ("Am I not right?")[45] Then to the extent that this deeper understanding which the three friends approached was a gift of the gathering night, perhaps neither we, nor they, should forget that, as Benjamin once put it, without meaning to be cynical, "the day dissolves what the night produced."[46]

v

In "Working Notes" dated January 1959, Merleau-Ponty wrote, echoing at once the concerns of both Husserl and Heidegger:

> Our state of non-philosophy—Never has the crisis been so radical—
> The dialectical "solutions"—either the "bad dialectic" that identifies
> the opposites, which is non-philosophy—or the "embalmed" dialectic,
> which is no longer dialectical. End of philosophy or rebirth? (VIE 165,
> VIF 219)

This note continues:

> Necessity of a return to ontology—the ontological questioning and its
> ramifications:
>
> the subject-object question
> the question of inter-subjectivity
> the question of Nature

> Outline of ontology projected as an ontology of brute Being—and of
> *logos*. . . . But the disclosure of this world, of this Being, remains a
> dead letter as long as we do not uproot "objective" philosophy
> (Husserl). (Ibid.)

Articulating in characteristically reticent language a divergence from Husserl that is surely an indication of the increasing influence of Heidegger's thought, Merleau-Ponty explained that, for him, "ontology would be the elaboration of the notions that have to replace that of transcendental

subjectivity, those of subject, object, meaning" (VIE 167, VIF 221). To begin with, he thinks, we must "deepen" the description of the perceived
world, by understanding perception as "spread [*écart*]" (VIE 168, VIF 222).
What this means, or involves, is something we will attempt in due course
to clarify.

Although I believe that his *Phenomenology of Perception* is far more
innovative, bold, and radical, in spite of its incomplete escape from the
philosophy of consciousness, than he gives himself credit for achieving,
by 1959, Merleau-Ponty wants to put his earlier thought at an unmistakably great distance from his later thinking, on which the influence
of Heidegger—not only *Being and Time*, but also the works that come
after the so-called turning—is unquestionably much more decisive.
Thus he wrote:

> Results of Ph.P.—Necessity of bringing them to ontological explicita-
> tion. . . . The problems that remained after this first description: they
> are due to the fact that in part I retained the philosophy of "conscious-
> ness." (VIE 183, VIF 237)

Five months later, in another note, he states: "The problems posed in Ph.P.
are insoluble because I start there from the 'consciousness'-'object' distinction" (VIE 200, VIF 253).

To be sure, the task of describing the figure-ground structure (*Gestalt*)
and the field-character of all experience is already begun in his *Phenomenology of Perception*, where we will find him asking, "What, ultimately, am
I?" and answering, "I am a field" (PPE 406, PPF 465). But later, he says, " 'To
be conscious' is here nothing but 'to belong to' " (PPE 424, PPF 485), which
betrays, we might say, a certain continuing obsession with "consciousness"
as the *point d'appui*, or say the point of departure for his philosophical reflections. And yet, does this statement not already attempt to articulate the
possibility of a truly radical transition, making belonging-to (*Zugehörigkeit*), or, say, the attunement (*Grundbestimmung*) of being-in-the-
world (*in-der-Welt-Sein*) the fundamental experience?

Be this as it may, in his "Working Notes," his thinking has certainly
achieved a much greater "Ortverlegung"; although even here he will write,
"To be conscious = to have a figure on a ground—one cannot go back any
further" (VIE 191, VIF 245). "The *Gestalt*," he is convinced, "contains the
key to the problem of the mind" (VIE 192, VIF 246). Therefore, as in his
earlier phenomenology, here also the concept of the field will play a crucial
role. But, whereas his earlier work perhaps stressed the field as contextual
delimitation, here he perhaps gives more attention to the openness of the

field, and frequently describes it using Heidegger's hermeneutical language of concealment and unconcealment. "The world," he says, "is a field, and as such is always open" (VIE 185, VIF 239).

"What," he asks, "is a *Gestalt*?" In his notes, he replies: "It is a principle of distribution, the pivot of a system of equivalencies . . . it has a certain weight that doubtless fixes it not in an objective sight and in a point of objective time, but in a *region*, a *domain*, which it dominates, where it reigns, where it is everywhere present without one ever being able to say: it is here. . . . It is a *double ground* of the lived" (VIE 204–5, VIF 258–59. Italics added). And he goes on to declare, as a point that significantly enriches the phenomenology of perception one finds in Heidegger: "My body [itself] *is* a *Gestalt* and it is co-present in every *Gestalt*" (VIE 205, VIF 259).

In a formulation that lets us discern in the figure-ground structure the involvement of the ontological difference, manifesting in the formation of our most primordial, sensuous experience, Merleau-Ponty observes that we need to "understand perception as differentiation, forgetting as undifferentiation" (VIE 197, VIF 250). And this means that we need to experience and think the perceptual formation as an *écart*, a separation—and thus, I would add, as a certain dimension of the experience of *ekstasis*. But, he is quick to point out, it is not a question of "making" or "allowing" it: "This is the night of forgetting. Understand that the 'to be conscious' = to have a figure on a ground, and that it disappears in disarticulation—the figure-ground distinction introduces a third term between the 'subject' and the 'object'. It is *that separation [écart]* first of all that is the perceptual *meaning*" (ibid.).

In a text published in *Signs*, Merleau-Ponty asserted the seemingly paradoxical proposition that "to see is as a matter of principle to see farther than one sees, to reach a being in latency."[47] But when the point is given an adequate experiential rendering, the paradox disappears, returning us to the hermeneutical nature of the perceptual field as a phenomenon. What he here calls its "latency" is elsewhere ("Working Notes") referred to as "pregnancy":

> *Pregnancy:* the psychologists forget that this means a power to break forth, productivity (*praegnans futuri*), fecundity—Secondarily: it means "typicality". It is the form that has arrived at itself, this *is itself,* that posits itself by its own means, is the equivalent of the cause of itself, is the *Wesen* that is because it *este*, auto-regulation . . . there is—
> —The pregnancy is what, in the visible, requires of me a *correct* focusing, defines its correctness. My body *obeys* the pregnancy, it "responds" to it. (VIE 208–9, VIF 262)[48]

(One should notice how the meaning of *Wesen* undergoes, here, a certain *glissage*, or slippage, from its original Husserlian sense to a philosophically new and unfamiliar sense that *makes* sense only in the light of Heidegger's articulation of its relation to φύσις.) "Pregnancy" introduces the interplay of concealment and unconcealment into our thought of the *Gestalt:* it *connects* the structure of figure-ground differentiation with this interplay.

Merleau-Ponty (VIE 206, VIF 259) contends that "the *Gestalt* implies the relation between a perceiving body and a sensible, i.e. transcendent, i.e. horizonal, i.e. vertical and not perspectival world." (In this context, his insistence that it is "not perspectival" is intended to remark his disagreement with the "sovereign vision" of idealism and intellectualism, schools of thought which posit an absolute position for their vision of the world.) And he explains the *Gestalt* further:

> It is a diacritical, oppositional, relative system whose pivot is the *etwas*, the thing, the world, and not the idea. . . . Every psychology that places the *Gestalt* back into the framework of "cognition" or "consciousness" misses the meaning of the *Gestalt*. (VIE 206, VIF 259)

Now, as we have already noted, the *Gestalt* forms and unfolds in a field, emerges from it and dissolves back into it. But, writing in the light of Heidegger's work, Merleau-Ponty carries this understanding of the phenomenon further: "Each field," he says, "is a dimensionality, and being is dimensionality itself" (VIE 227, VIF 280).

In an extremely significant note (January 1960), drawing his thinking into the ontological dimensionality, where concealment and unconcealment, visibility and invisibility, presence and absence are in play, Merleau-Ponty observes that:

> The invisible is *there* without being an object; it is pure transcendence, without an ontic mask. And the "visibles" themselves, in the last analysis, they too are only centered on a nucleus of absence. (VIE 229, VIF 282–83)

In a quite uncanny (*unheimlich*) way, Merleau-Ponty's thinking, here, approaches that of Heidegger—closer, perhaps, than he realizes—when he describes the figure-ground formation as a "dis-junction" (VIE 228, VIF 281). For this word moves in the proximity of Heidegger's post-*Kehre* constellation of words for the self-disclosive articulation (*Ereignis*) of being: *Fug, Fügung, Unfug*, difficult words that may be provisionally translated into English as "jointure," "fit," and "disjointure," or "being out of joint," "not fitting" (see, e.g., his 1943 essay, "Aletheia: Heraclitus, Fragment B 16").

In another note (May 1960), it becomes even clearer that, and also how, Merleau-Ponty wants to introduce Heidegger's hermeneutical phenomenology into his own philosophical project:

> I say that every visible: [1] involves a ground which is not visible in the sense that the figure is and [2] even in what is figural or figurative in it, [the visible] is not an objective *quale,* an in-Itself surveyed from above, but slips under the gaze or is swept over by the look, is born in silence under the gaze . . . —hence, if one means by the visible the *objective quale,* it is in this sense not visible, but *unverborgen.* When I say then that every visible is invisible, that perception is imperception, . . . that to see is always to see more than one sees . . . it must not be imagined that I add to the visible perfectly defined as in-Itself a non-visible (which would be only *objective* absence) (that is, objective presence *elsewhere* in-Itself)——One has to understand that it is *the visibility itself* that involves a non-visibility. (VIE 246–47, VIF 300. Italics added.)

The importance of this text is that, among other things, we can discern Merleau-Ponty's attempt to translate Heidegger's hermeneutics of the ground, in which the "ground" of the discourse of Reason is profoundly shaken and rendered abyssal, into a radically hermeneutical phenomenology of perception, in which the figure-ground structure, and hence too the subject-object structure, laid down by the "rational" vision of ocularcentric philosophies are given a hermeneutical reading and *mis en abîme.*

In the text titled "The Intertwining—The Chiasm," reflections published together with his "Working Notes" in *The Visible and the Invisible,* Merleau-Ponty brings this reading to bear on his phenomenological account of our experience of colors, arguing that color is first and foremost a field-phenomenon—that every appearance of color is really *to be seen as* "an ephemeral modulation" of the world, a "concretion of visibility," an accent that *emerges* from a less precise, more general color-tone (VIE 131–32, VIF 173–74).[49] As this perhaps suggests, his phenomenology of color, here, comes strikingly near to thinking what the Greeks called φύσις.

Following a reference to Heidegger, Merleau-Ponty's "Notes" say "that the visible is *pregnant* with the invisible, that to comprehend fully the visible relations (house) one must go unto the relation of the visible with the invisible" (VIE 216, VIF 269). Of course, Husserl, too, gave thought to the invisible—the invisible sides of the die and the house, for example. (See his *Cartesian Meditations.*) But Husserl could never tolerate the *mis en abîme* that must ultimately be recognized in the phenomenon of the invisible: he was always too strongly committed to rationalism, and to the transcendental idealism it required, to learn from the phenomena themselves the messages they could deliver from out of the deep.

"Interrogation and Dialectic," another text included in *The Visible and the Invisible,* challenges, not the hegemony of ocularcentrism in philosophical thinking, but rather the spell of the philosophical doctrine of "pure vision," the "aerial view" (*pensée de survol*), the "sovereign vision" that dominates the other (VIE 73, 77–78, 83, 88; VIF 104, 109, 115, 121). The "privilege of vision," he says, "is not to open *ex nihilo* upon a pure being *ad infinitum:* the vision too has a field, a range" (VIE 83, VIF 115). "Far from opening upon the blinding light of pure Being, or of the Objective, our life has, in the astronomical sense of the word, an atmosphere: it is constantly enshrouded by those mists we call the sensible world or history" (VIE 84, VIF 116).

Merleau-Ponty also comes near Heidegger's interpretation of the thing as a site for the gathering of the fourfold: "Things," he says in "The Intertwining—The Chiasm," "are structures, frameworks, the stars of our life"; things are "field beings," presences with different levels or dimensions of generality and specificity; they are not only situated *in* fields, not only *belonging to* or *inhering in* fields, but they also are themselves "fields of intersection," occupying "fields of fields" (VIE 227, VIF 281).

Like Heidegger, Merleau-Ponty uses phenomenology to contest the history of metaphysics, which has reduced the thing to an object, reduced human beings to subjects, and posited the object it has artificially constructed within a structure of re-presentation (*Vor-stellung*) that relates it to a disembodied subject outside time, history and indeed outside the life-world. "I open up access to a brute Being with which I would not be in the subject-and-object relation," he writes ("The Intertwining—The Chiasm," VIF 222, VIE 276). And, on the next page, he records his thinking about the way both empiricism and intellectualism have conceived the thing: "critique of the usual notion of the thing and its *properties*——critique of the logical notion of the subject . . . " (VIE 224, VIF 277). Later in this text, bringing out the psychopathology that is reflected in the doctrines of our Western metaphysics, he directly attacks the philosophical deployment of the concept of *Vorstellung* in the attempt to give an account of our experience (VIE 252–53, VIF 306–7).

Elaborating on the "intertwining," a new concept he has introduced into the discourse of phenomenology,[50] Merleau-Ponty observes that "the seer and the visible reciprocate one another and we no longer know which sees and which is seen" (VIE 139, VIF 183). He further declares that "there is no problem of the *alter ego* because it is not *I* who sees, not *he* who sees, because an anonymous visibility inhabits both of us, a vision in general" (VIE 142, VIF 187–88). This, we might say, interrupts the philosophical construction of the subject-object structure and begins to break it down, pointing—since it is also a question of a political economy and culture in which forms of (capital) possession and domination have become fundamental—towards the possibility of a radically new *cultural* experience of people and things.[51] (The way of looking and seeing toward which both Heidegger and Merleau-Ponty were moving is also, moreover, a way of looking and seeing that would inherently *resist* a totalitarian politics. Psychological research studies sponsored by the Frankfurt School and subsequently reported by Merleau-Ponty in "The Child's Relations with Others" indicate that the "authoritarian personality type" has a low tolerance for perceptual ambiguity and tends to pattern perceptual experience in extremely rigid, linear ways.)

An important note reads thus: "Show that since the *Gestalt* arises from polymorphism, this situates us entirely *outside* the philosophy of the subject and the object" (VIE 207, VIF 260. Also see VIE 137, VIF 180–81). For Merleau-Ponty, presencing is *chiasmic*, an immeasurably deep intertwining of presence and absence, concealment and unconcealment, visibility and invisibility that deconstructs the metaphysical doctrine of subject and object—and the cultural practices and habits with regard to people and things that this discourse reflects, reinforces, and presumes to make legitimate. In the texts of *The Visible and the Invisible*, Merleau-Ponty's radical phenomenology shows *how* the subject-object structure figures in a theory and culture of re-presentation—and *why* this re-presentation of people and things, together with a certain re-presentational reification of the figure-ground interaction, must actually be seen as an historical disfigurement.

In a note dated February 1959, the philosopher asks, "What is Philosophy?" His answer, an echo of Heidegger: "The domain of the *Verbergen*" (VIE 183, VIF 237). Following Heidegger, Merleau-Ponty challenges the philosophical tradition as a philosophy of consciousness that "disregards Being and prefers the object to it" (VIE 248, VIF 302). Phenomenology must assist us in returning in thought from the presence of the beings that are present to the presencing of being. And perhaps one of the consequences of such a returning would be a new ontology, interrupting the cultural reduction, now centuries old, that renders people as subjects and turns things into useful objects-at-our-disposal.

Calling into question the "ontological value" of the *Gegen-stand*, Merleau-Ponty writes:

> The reconquest of the *Lebenswelt* is the reconquest of a *dimension*, in which the objectifications of science themselves retain a meaning and

are to be understood as *true* (Heidegger himself says this: every *Seins-geschick* is true, is part of the *Seinsgeschichte.*) It's a question of bringing out what has been *"verdeckt"*: [1] the exigency to grasp the *Ursprung*——*Entdeckung* of the *Ursprung* and [2] the reduction of the *Gegenstand*, i.e., *Verdeckung* of the *Ursprung*. (VIE 182, VIF 236)

"*Ursprung*" may be taken to refer, here, to the ground or field of our perceptual experience.

Once again, then, the formation of the perceptual *Gestalt* is understood in terms of the intertwining or interplay of concealment and unconcealment. For reasons that by now should be obvious, this phenomenology of the *Gestalt* formation functions as a discursive subversion of the *Ge-stell*, the metaphysical ideology that favors re-presentation (*Vorstellung*) and the logic of identity that endlessly reproduces an ontology of domination.

A crucial development in Merleau-Ponty's thinking takes place with his introduction of the phenomenology of the "flesh" (VIE 130–275; VIF 172–329). The flesh, he says, is to be thought—and lived—as "an element of Being" (VIE 139, VIF 184). It completely unweaves the threadbare text of the body that has held our culture and its philosophical discourse spellbound and in thrall at least since the time of Platonism. The flesh is, he claims, an "essential notion for philosophy" (VIE 259, VIF 313), and is in fact "the place of emergence of a vision" (VIE 272, VIF 326). There is, he contends, just "one sole tissue" (VIE 253, VIF 307), just one elemental medium—a chiasmic flesh; and this medium is to be recognized as an "ontological tissue," a primordial Λέγειν gathering together, binding, and intertwining, all beings, present and absent, into destiny of a world. The flesh, "medium" of subject and object (VIE149, VIF 195), is "of the world" as much as it is "my own," because it is "a texture that returns to itself" (VIE 146, VIF 192). The concept of the flesh thus makes it possible to penetrate the "architectonics of the human body, [exposing for the first time] its ontological framework" (VIE 155, VIF 203). With the intertwinings of the flesh, Merleau-Ponty deftly unravels the philosophical text of the objective body and the subject-object structure—unravels it warp and woof.

"My flesh and that of the world involve," according to Merleau-Ponty,

clear zones, clearings, about which pivot their opaque zones, and the primary visibility, that of the *quale* and of the things, does not come without a second visibility, that of the lines of force and dimensions, the massive flesh without a rarified flesh, the momentary body without a glorified body. (VIE 148, VIF 195)

This passage on zones is reminiscent of Ralph Waldo Emerson's essay "Circles": "The eye," he says there, "is the first circle; the horizon which it forms is the second; and throughout nature this primary figure is repeated without end."[52] It also relates to Heidegger's own discussion of zones in his *Parmenides* lectures. This discussion moves to bring out the fact that the openness of the visual field "deconstructs" the ego-subject's defensive, anxiety-driven patterning of perceptual experience and implicitly explains thereby the ego-logical subject's anxiety in the face of this openness: "The free is the guarantee [*Bürgschaft*], the sheltering place [*die bergende Stätte*], for the being of beings. The open, the free, shelters and salvages being. We ordinarily think of the open, the free, and the vast as conditions of scattering, dispersion, and distraction. The open and its extension into the vastness of the unlimited and limitless are *zones* [*die Zone*] without stopping places, where every sojourn loses itself in instability [*ins Haltlose verliert*]. The open provides [our egos] no shelter or security" (PE 143–44, PG 213–14). In the last passage quoted, Merleau-Ponty is attempting to continue the translation of Heidegger's concept of a *Lichtung* into the elemental hermeneutics of his phenomenology of the flesh. Heidegger himself inaugurated this difficult translation, as our consideration of texts such as his *Conversation on a Country Path* clearly demonstrate; but unlike Merleau-Ponty, Heidegger always avoided the call to think through the problematic of embodiment—even though, in the course of his thinking, this problematic calls for thought with surprising frequency and urgency, and unquestionably arises from the immanent logic of his own deliberations.

The concentric circles, zones, and clearings surrounding the body are bounded, in our experience of the world, by the horizon, and Merleau-Ponty's phenomenology does not ignore this hermeneutic boundary:

> No more than are the sky or the earth is the *horizon* a collection of things held together, or a class name, or a logical possibility of conception, or a system of "potentiality of consciousness": it is a new type of being, a being by porosity, pregnancy, or generality, and he before whom the horizon opens is caught up, included in it. (VIE 148–49, VIF 195)

We participate bodily in the opening-up of the field-dimensions in which we live—"even beyond the horizon . . . unto the depths of being" (ibid.). Husserl, too, gave thought to the phenomenon of the horizon; but his commitment to the sovereign subjectivity of transcendental idealism and an imperative of systematic Reason that requires totality and completeness made it impossible for him to acknowledge appropriately the openness beyond the horizon. Thus, for example, in *Ideas* I, the world as a whole, the world as such, can be made into an *object* of theoretical doubt and contained within the phenomenological *epokhé* only because he thinks of the world as a "collection of things held together": he cannot see the world as the necessarily ungraspable ground, a field of unfathomable dimensions and a horizon that withdraws from approach. Like the philosophers of empiricism, he can see the world only as an object, a container of things—but still just one more thing. The world Husserl *sees* is the world of *thought*, the world *as* thought, as the posit (*Gestell*) of thought. But a phenomenology truly committed to letting the phenomenon show itself from out of itself must deny philosophical reifications of the horizon, renounce the possession of the world implicitly claimed by the transcendental *epokhé*, and insist on an experience of the world-ground that is *appropriately* respectful of its open, abyssal dimensionality. Vision is a question of exposure; phenomenology must not attempt to reduce this experience. As Heidegger puts the point, "modern man must first and above all find his way back into the full breadth of the space proper to his essence."[53]

In his *Phenomenology of Perception*, Merleau-Ponty asserted, albeit in a vocabulary that he would later indict because of its residual affiliation with the philosophy of consciousness, that "we must rediscover, as *anterior* to the ideas of subject and object, the fact of my subjectivity and the nascent object, that *primordial layer* at which both things and ideas come into being" (PPE 219, PPF 254). Thus we find that, in "The Intertwining— The Chiasm," Merleau-Ponty returns to a theme he demonstrated in his *Phenomenology of Perception*, again pointing out that our everyday perception—and all the philosophies of modernity that have emerged from it—have "forgotten" the existence of "latent intentionality," our prepersonal, prereflective engagements with the world, and imposed on perception a Euclidean interpretation that makes it difficult, if not virtually impossible, to break out of the subject-object structure and the *Gestalt* formation to which we have been accustomed.

A version of this "latent intentionality" (*fungierende Intentionalität*) also figures in Heidegger's *Being and Time*, although neither Heidegger nor Merleau-Ponty could recognize it in the concept of a pre-ontological understanding of being. But if there be, as Heidegger wants to maintain there, such a level of understanding, then there must be a level of intentionality—a dimension, we might add, of the chiasmic flesh—through the functioning of which a certain pre-ontological attunement to (and by) the presencing-field of being is constituted. Should we be surprised, then, to find Heidegger asking, in his commentary on Heraclitus, Fragment B16: "Why is it that we stubbornly resist considering even once whether the belonging-together of subject and object does not arise from something that first imparts their nature to both the object and its objectivity, and the subject and its subjectivity, and hence is prior to the realm of their reciprocity?"[54]

For Heidegger, that from which subject and object emerge—and that, therefore, which is the ground of their intertwining, their unity—is the ground or field of their presencing: the clearing and making-visible that is the gift of the lighting. But, in his *Parmenides* lectures, Heidegger turns a critical eye on the habits of ordinary seeing: "in the zeal of the ordinary seeing of sense perception [*im Eifer des gewöhnlichen Sehens der sinnlichen Wahrnehmung*], we overlook what holds good and serves under visible things and between them and our vision, the closest of all, namely brightness and its own proper transparency, through which the impatience of our seeing hurries and must hurry. . . . The closest [i.e., the self-emerging lighting that lays down the field for our vision] appears therefore as if it were nothing" (PE 135, PG 201). Bearing in mind that φαίνειν means "showing as letting appear," Heidegger elaborates his critical analysis: "The unconcealed, that which lies in the light of the day, is what appears from out of itself [*was von sich aus erscheint*], in appearing shows itself, and in this self-showing comes to presence (i.e., for the Greeks, 'is'). . . . Appearance [*Das Erscheinen*] is *founded* in a pure shining [*Scheinen*], which we understand as a radiating light [*aufgehende Leuchten*]. The same appearance, however, is *also* a self-showing that meets [both] a perception and a reception [*Vernehmen und Aufnehmen*]. Perception can now *grasp* what shows itself merely as what is perceived in the perceiving and can *overlook* as something incidental, and ultimately forget, the appearance [as] that [which] dwells in the self-showing, i.e., appearance in the sense of pure shining and radiating" (PE 136, PG 202–3).

This brings Heidegger's phenomenology very close to Merleau-Ponty's: they are both attempting to bring to light, to make visible, a dimension of our perceptual experience which underlies the subject-object structure. In the preceding quotation, Heidegger's distinction between "reception" and "perception" is crucial. There is a pre-ontological reception that is anterior to ontic perception; there is a pre-ontological openness to the lighting, to the field and ground of perception, that always comes *before* the grasping patterning of ontic perception and its subject-object structure. Heidegger's *hermeneutical* phenomenology brings out this underlying dimension of our perceptual experience, which we tend to forget or repress. Thus he also says in the *Parmenides* lectures that "because only unconcealed beings can appear and do appear in the open of being, man adheres [*hält sich der Mensch*], at first unwittingly and then constantly, to these beings. He forgets being and in such forgetting learns nothing more than the overlooking of being [*die Verkennung des Seins*] and alienation from the open" (PE 151, PG 225).

Both Heidegger and Merleau-Ponty seem to assume that the hermeneutical disclosure of the field-inherent dimension underlying perception could loosen the grip of this way of patterning our experience. Merleau-Ponty's phenomenology, even the earlier phenomenology of his *Phenomenology of Perception*, goes into this dimension, where we might say that a primordial "recollection of being" has always already taken place long before we have realized it, much more deeply than the accounts of perception proposed by other philosophers. Perhaps Merleau-Ponty was nearing this very recollection when he wrote, in *Phenomenology of Perception:* "When I turn toward perception, [I] find at work in my organs of perception a thought older than myself, of which those organs are merely a trace" (PPE 351; PPF 404. See also PPE 254, PPF 293–94).

Granting the sociocultural construction of perception, but insisting at the same time that this construction must acknowledge an irreducible nature beneath it, an order of being both determinate and yet always also further determinable—in certain partially predetermined ways, Merleau-Ponty proposes, in his last writings, a return to "wild" perception, a "descent" into "pregnancy" (VIE 212–13, VIF 265–67), into the dimension of our prepersonal, prereflective intentionality, arguing that it is in retrieving the figure-ground formations in our experience of this dimension that we will interrupt the metaphysics of our cultural life and begin to recollect the presencing of being in its primordial laying-down of the ontological difference.

Returning to the chiasmic element of the flesh means, for Merleau-Ponty, a return to the intertwining, and hence to the reversibility, of subject and object (VIE 263–65, 271–72; VIF 316–19, 324–26); it means, also, a return to an "ecstatic" experience of the figure-ground differentiation, and a movement (VIE 265, 271; VIF 318, 324) beyond the metaphysical dualism of the active and the passive. (In rationalism, the subject is active, the object passive; in empiricism, the subject is passive and the object active.) All this is decisively involved in what he calls, in "Interrogation and Dialectic," our "openness upon being" (VIE 88, VIF 122).

Although he does not take up for thought the ontologically appropriate attitude that Heidegger calls "Gelassenheit," his work brought him into its proximity. Thus, for example, in "Reflection and Interrogation," likewise a late writing collected in *The Visible and the Invisible*, he argues that we need to understand our "initial openness" to the world—"how there is openness" (VIE 28, VIF 49). But for him, much more than for Heidegger, this calls for phenomenological meditations on our "natal bond," *notre lien natal* (VIE 32, VIF 53–54) with the presencing of being—a bond we may always enjoy by grace of the elemental medium of the flesh.

A crucial point is reached, perhaps, with the realization that our seeing is, after all, a question of learning-to-see ("Reflection and Interrogation," VIE 4; VIF 18). But it is important to understand that such learning does not have to involve normalization, the imposition, in the name of *das Man*, of the ontologically blind vision of the anonymous anyone-and-everyone. This so-called normal vision, setting the norm for our cultural and spiritual life, is in fact, as Heidegger has shown, a vision that has recoiled before the openness of the field into which it has been thrown. Since this openness reveals to vision that it is thrown into groundlessness and nothingness, the normal reaction will be anxiety and closure—a need to control, master, and dominate.

However, the intertwinings and reversabilities that take place in Merleau-Ponty's phenomenology of the flesh suggest that there is a certain potential for overcoming and transcending our culturally invested pathology. Reading what is inscribed on the scrolls of flesh, Merleau-Ponty wrote a note which says "that it is being that speaks within us, and not we who speak of being" (VIE 194, VIF 247). Also: "It is not we who perceive, it is the thing that perceives itself yonder" (VIE 185, VIF 239). These experiences of intertwining and reversal, experiences that essentially involve a certain figure-ground reversal, a deconstruction of the normal structuring of perception, must surely be considered as necessary, if only preliminary steps on the path that would take us towards a vision of *Gelassenheit*.

Heidegger, too, articulates the need for a seer-seen, subject-object *reversal*, "re-turning" the perceptual relationship to a determination that he reads into the experience of the early Greek philosophers and poets: "In insight [*Einblick*]," he says, in "The Turning," "men are the ones who are caught sight of."[55] We become the beheld, held to account in our very beholding, by the field of vision in which we are situated and to which we belong. In "The Age of the World Picture," he maintains that "man is the one who is looked upon [*vom Seienden Angeschaute*] by that which is; he is the one who is . . . gathered toward presencing by that which opens itself. To be beheld by what is, to be included and maintained within its openness. . . . —that is the essence of man in the great age of the Greeks."[56] And, in his 1942–43 lectures on Parmenides, elaborating the same theme, he argues that, for the Greeks, the one who looks presents himself, shows himself, "in the sight of his essence, i.e., emerges as unconcealed, into the unconcealed" (PE 103, PG 152).

If, in the Parmenides lectures, Heidegger articulates a reversal of seer and seen, whereby the one who looks is the one disclosed, and indeed made visible not only in facticity, but also in essence, he also brings out a reversal of priority, whereby the ordinary, everyday act of looking is displaced and becomes secondary. The move he makes here is similar to the argument he makes with regard to what we ordinarily think of as "truth": Just as truth in the sense of correctness is displaced and becomes secondary and derivative in relation to ἀλήθεια, disclosedness, the opening-up and laying-down of a field of meaning within which the enquiry into the correctness of validity-claims can be undertaken, so too the looking we consider normal is displaced and shown to be secondary and derivative in relation to a seeing first made visible by the ancient Greeks, in which vision is open to the open: "The looking [*Das Er-blicken*] performed by man in relation to the appearing look is *already a response* to the original look [*ursprünglichen Blick*], which first elevates human looking into its essence" (PE 107, PG 158). He also claims that "the Greeks experience the grasping look as perception, because this look is *determined originally* on the basis of the encountering look [*das er-fassende Blicken*, i.e., the aletheic look that, by virtue of its openness, its appropriately hermeneutical relationship to the interplay of concealment and unconcealment, corresponds to the opening-up, laying-down, and ingathering of the field of lighting, as which being presences for our vision]. . . . In the ambit of this primordial look [*Im 'Gesichts'-kreis dieses anfänglichen Blickes*], man is 'only' the looked upon. This 'only', however, is so essential that man, precisely as the looked upon, is first received and taken up into the relation of being to himself and is thus led to perception" (PE 108, PG 160. Italics added). Ultimately, then, we may be brought to the possibility of a "repetition" of this inaugural perception in the way we look and see, the way we relate to the field or ground of perception, thereby interrupting the continuum of history in the realm of our perception and, with our own achievement of vision—a radically other vision—preparing ourselves to receive the first hints of a new beginning.

Heidegger thus calls our attention to the more ontological (dimension of) vision in words that have a certain affinity with Merleau-Ponty's phenomenological description, in the *Phenomenology of Perception*, of the prepersonal "natal bond," the "primordial contract," the bodily felt sensory connectedness that *precedes and secures* "perception" as we ordinarily think of it—perception, that is, as a relation between a subject and its object. In his *Phenomenology of Perception*, Merleau-Ponty comments, using language that is already very close to that of Heidegger: "To say that I have a visual field is to say that by reason of my position I have access to, and an opening upon, a system of beings, visible beings, that these are at the disposal of my gaze in virtue of a kind of *primordial contract* and through a gift of nature, with no effort made on my part; and from which it follows that vision is *prepersonal*" (PPE 216, PPF 250–51. Also see PPE 267, 327, 352 and PPF 309, 377–78, 405. Italics added). In the *Parmenides* lectures, Heidegger likewise points to the emergence of perception on the basis of *a* "primordial consent" (*anfänglichen Einvernehmen*) given to being (PE 108, PG 160). But the difference that the recognition of this originary moment could make hinges on the ability of our gaze to take up for thought a relation that takes hold of us at the prepersonal level of our experience (Merleau-Ponty) and of which we have a pre-ontological understanding—the relation, namely, between our gaze and the gift of lighting that lays out the perceptual field for its activity:

> Just as the eye without the ability to see is nothing, so the ability to see, for its part, remains an "inability" if it does not come into play in an *already established* relation of man to visible beings. And how could beings be supposed to appear to man, if man did not *already* relate in his essence to beings as beings? And how could such a relation of man to beings as such hold sway if man did not stand [already] in a relation to being? If man did not *already* have being in view, then he could not even think the nothing, let alone experience beings. And how is man supposed to stand in this relation to being if being itself does not address man and claim his essence for the relation to being? But what else is this relation of being to the essence of man than the clearing and the open which has lighted itself for the unconcealed? If such a clearing did not come into play [*Weste nicht solche Lichtung*] as the open of being itself, then a human eye could never become and be what it is, namely, the way man looks at . . . the being encountering him." (PE 146, PG 217. Italics added.)

It is because of this prior mode of "seeing" that Heidegger can write of "the having [always already] seen" of the "seer," both in his lectures on Parmenides (PE 111, PG 165) and in his short text on "The Anaximander Fragment." Man alone, as Heidegger says, is gifted with the capacity to see the open, that field of presencing "which first lets beings emerge and come to presence as beings" (PE 159, PG 237). Whether we realize it or not, by dwelling in the open, inhabiting it, belonging to it, and being attuned (*bestimmt*) by it, we have always already seen it. And yet, we must also say: not yet. Because "Man and he alone sees into the open—though without beholding it. Only the essential sight of authentic thinking beholds being itself. But even there the thinker can behold being only because he as man has *already* glimpsed it" (ibid. Italics added). Merleau-Ponty would agree, and would point out that his phenomenology brings to light a prepersonal bodily dimension that correlates both with the pre-ontological under- standing of being which Heidegger discusses in *Being and Time* and with the *Einvernehmen* of the *Parmenides* lectures. As early as his *Phenome- nology of Perception*, Merleau-Ponty was calling attention to our ekstatic embodiment, the hidden experiential fact of our primordial perceptual openness, which the hermeneutics of his phenomenology renders visible, perhaps for the first time: "Vision," he writes there, "is an action . . . in- wardly prepared only by my primordial opening upon a field of transcen- dence, that is, once again, by an *ekstase*" (PPE 377, PPF 432).

One of Merleau-Ponty's notes on the *Gestalt*, written for *The Visible and the Invisible*, reads as follows:

> To say that there is transcendence, being at a distance, is to say that be- ing (in the Sartrean sense) is thus inflated with non-being or with the possibility that it is not only *what it is*. The *Gestalthafte*, if one really wanted to define it, would be that. . . . And at the same time the *per- ception of* . . . the *Gestalt* cannot be a centrifugal *Sinngebung*, the imposition of an essence, a *vor-stellen*——One cannot distinguish *Empfindung* and *Empfundenes* here. It is *openness*—— (VIE 181, VIF 234–35)

This openness resists the labor of re-presentation, resists the deformation and disfigurement of the *Gestalt* that takes place under the rule of "en- framing," the *universal imposition* of order in the epoch Heidegger calls *Das Gestell*, And it is this same openness that receives the suffering, vio- lent gaze of everyday perception and bestows upon it the grace of an ele- mental ground from out of which configurations of being ceaselessly emerge in unconcealment, offering themselves to the gaze that is willing to let go of its inveterate tendencies and learn the beholding of *Gelassenheit*.

Thus, the task of phenomenology must be to lead our vision back to the openness of the lighting:[57]

> Presence in the lighting articulates [i.e., brings forth, gives an enabling field to] all the human senses. ("The Anaximander Fragment": AXE 36, AXG 322)
>
> Lighting bestows [*gewährt*] the shining, opens [*gibt . . . frei*] what shines to an appearance. The open [*Das Freie*] is the realm of uncon- cealment and is governed by disclosure. ("Aletheia: Heraclitus, Frag- ment B16": AE 103, AG 258)
>
> The lighting not only illuminates what is present, but gathers it to- gether and secures it in advance in presencing. ("Aletheia": AE 120, AG 278)

The lighting of the being of beings, as a lighting, is concealed. ("Moira: Parmenides VIII, 34–41": *Early Greek Thinking*, p. 87; *Vorträge und Aufsätze*, p. 241)

The event of lighting [*Das Ereignis der Lichtung*] *is* the world. The meditatively gathering [*sinnend-versammelnde*] lighting which brings into the open [*ins Freie*] is revealing; [but] it abides in self-concealing. ("Aletheia": AE 118, AG 276)

If we think it [i.e., the presencing of being] as lighting, this includes not only the brilliance [*die Helle*], but also the openness wherein everything, especially the reciprocally related [*das Gegenwendige*], comes into shining. Lighting is therefore more than illuminating, and also more than laying bare [*Freilegen*]. . . . It is the bestowal of presencing [*Gewähren von Anwesen*]. ("Aletheia": AE 118, AG 276)

Mortals are irrevocably bound to the revealing-concealing gathering which lights everything present in its presencing. But they turn from the lighting, and turn only towards what is present, which is what immediately concerns them in their everyday commerce with each other. . . . They have no inkling of what they have been entrusted [*zugetraut*] with: presencing, which in its lighting first allows what is present to come to appearance. Λόγος [as the gift of a laying-down and gathering of a field of illumination], in whose lighting they come and go, remains concealed from them and forgotten. ("Aletheia": AE 122, AG 281)

The play of the calling, brightening, expanding light is not actually visible. It shines imperceptibly, like morning light upon the quiet splendour of lilies in a field or roses in a garden. ("Moira": *Early Greek Thinking*, 96; *Vorträge und Aufsätze*, 251)

But I cannot resist pointing out that, after saying this lighting "is not actually visible," Heidegger draws an analogy that implies that the lighting *is* visible—or perhaps rather, *could* be visible, could be seen, if one were to give it the gift of one's responsive awareness. This point is supported by the sixth passage above and also by the next two quotations.

Ordinary perception [*Das gewohnte Vernehmen*] certainly moves within the lightedness of what is present and sees what is shining out . . . in colour; but it is dazzled by changes in colour . . . and pays no attention to the still light of the lighting that emanates from duality [*Zwiefalt*: from the spacing of the ontological difference, i.e., from the ground of being]. ("Moira": English 100, German 255)

The lighting, therefore, is no *mere* brightening and lightening [*kein bloßes* Erhellen und Belichten]. . . . [This is true because this lighting is a] revealing-concealing lighting concerned with the presencing of what is present [*das Anwesen des Anwesenden*]. ("Aletheia": AE 119, AG 277–78)

In view of these passages, passages that make no sense and serve no purpose if interpreted as "mere" metaphors, "mere" figures of speech, i.e., as without experiential reference, we shall, before we conclude our reflections on Merleau-Ponty, endeavor to read some passages on light and lighting that have been taken from his *Phenomenology of Perception* and to which we might want to give particular attention. Their affinity with the preceding passages from Heidegger is most striking. One is this:

> We perceive in conformity with the light, as we think in conformity with other people in verbal communication. (PPE 310, PPF 358)

Translating this passage into Heidegger's ontological discourse, I take it to be suggesting that being gives the lighting to perception as the ontological *norm* (or say *Anspruch*) for our vision, gives it as that gradient of illumination necessary for making beings visible, making them stand out as figures against a ground. The word "conformity" would then broach the question of the difference between *ontic* conformity, the "blind" and thoughtless conformity of *das Man* and the *ontological* conformity of a vision thoughtfully letting itself be appropriated by the normative claim of the lighting, the claim of the presencing of being, ultimately abyssal and anarchic, which continually questions the openness of our gaze—its responsiveness, its exposure to the disclosedness and alterity of beings.[58] A second, related passage reads thus:

> The lighting is not on the side of the object, it is what we assume, what we take as the *norm*, whereas the object lighted stands out before us and confronts us. The lighting is neither colour nor, in itself, even light; it is *anterior* to the distinction between colours and luminosities. (PPE 311, PPF 359. Italics added.)

A third especially significant passage is perhaps this:

> Lighting and reflection . . . play their part only if they remain *in the background* as discreet intermediaries, and *lead* our gaze instead of arresting it. (PPE 310, PPF 358. Italics added.)

In this third passage, Merleau-Ponty may be read as giving phenomenological articulation to the ontological difference between being and beings, rendering it concretely in terms of a field-organizing interplay of concealment and unconcealment: the way that the lighting, as the presencing of being, withdraws into the abyssal invisibility of the background, as the beings to which our attention is drawn come forward into configurations of visibility.

One final passage. Calling our attention to "a tension which fluctuates around a norm," Merleau-Ponty makes the following observation:

> For each object, as for each picture in an art gallery, there is an optimum distance from which it requires to be seen, a direction viewed from which it vouchsafes most of itself: at a shorter or greater distance we have merely a perception blurred through excess or deficiency. (PPE 302, PPF 348)

Here, the norm is articulated in terms of the percipient subject's bodily positionality in relation to the visibility of the object. But it is crucial to understand that it is the *field as a ground of difference* that lays down the ontological norm or condition for the subject. (Heidegger, "Aletheia": AE 120, AG 278: "Just as those who are far distant belong to the distance, so are the revealed—in the sense now to be thought—entrusted to the lighting that keeps and shelters them.") In this regard, re-presentation may be interpreted as an attempt on the part of the subject to appropriate the norm as a condition of its own making. Re-presentation would then be an act of insolence, a demonstration of the will to power, a refusal to acknowledge our responsibility for a comportment in perception that—through its thoughtful recollection—sees in the field of visibility the invisible presencing of being. Thus, as Heidegger states the point in his *Parmenides* lectures (PE 151, PG 224), it is ultimately a question of our caring, our "guardianship of the open": our "Wächterschaft für das Offene."

VI

In his "Working Notes," Merleau-Ponty wrote: "Each field [of perception] is a dimensionality, and being is dimensionality itself" (VIE 227, VIF 280). But in attempting to think in a way that would "measure up" to the claim on our vision—or say the extreme exposure—that the recognition of this dimensionality would imply, he was conscious of the resistance that would be encountered, and therefore called attention to the difficulties faced in discerning and overcoming the presence of a certain "blind spot" operating, as he put it, using the phenomenological grammar of the first-person singular, "at the center of my sovereign vision" (VIE 78, VIF 109). Bringing out the logic of the perceptual field and its dimensionality, he argued that we must give up our metaphysical illusions and learn a way of seeing that is informed by the concession that:

> every visible is invisible, . . . perception is imperception, consciousness has a *"punctum caecum"*, . . . [and] to see is always to see more than one sees. (VIE 247–48, VIF 300)

"Dimensionality" increasingly figured in Heidegger's thinking also. Thus, for example, in the very important 1962 lecture, "Zeit und Sein," he remarked that:

> Dimensionality consists in a reaching out that opens up [*lichtenden Reichen*], in which futural approaching brings about what has been, what has been brings about futural approaching, and the reciprocal relation of both brings about the opening up of openness [*die Lichtung des Offenen erbringt*].[59]

If, as this passage suggests, our entrance into this dimensionality depends on a "reciprocal relation," it must also be said that this relation can take place only at the chiasmic intersection of the visible and the invisible—that intersection where the mode of being which is called "the human being" exists in a dangerous condition of arrogance, blinded by the illusion of mastery over the invisible.

For both Heidegger and Merleau-Ponty, the phenomenology of perception is ultimately a questioning of the potential for enlightenment in "ordinary perception" ("Moira": English 99, German 254), "the everyday perception of mortals" ("Moira": English 99, German 253): whether, and to what extent, human beings "can in their own way accomplish [*vollbringen*] the lighting (bring it to the fullness of its essence) and thereby protect it" ("Aletheia": AE 120, AG 278). But their discourse is addressed, first of all, to those from whom it can receive a welcoming understanding: "those," in Heidegger's words, "who are [already somewhat] enlightened [*erlichtet*] in accordance with their essence, and who therefore hearken to and belong to the lighting in an exceptional way" (ibid.). For, as Heidegger says, the coming-to-pass of being encourages us to believe that "another destining [*Geschick*], yet veiled, is waiting."[60] In a double reading, this also says: Another destining is waiting for us—but perhaps only when we have learned, at the last, how to wait.

A character in Samuel Beckett's *Endgame* asks: "What in God's name could there be on the horizon?"[61] Perhaps only more of the same. Perhaps nothing—or nothing in the name of God. But it seems that for both Heidegger and Merleau-Ponty, the way to enlightenment is a path of vision that would eventually take them into the clearing and openness of fields unknown to the philosophers of traditional metaphysics. On the paths they followed, there would certainly be great trials, temptations, and dangers, as they well understood—but also, perhaps, in some of the commonest and most familiar places, the quiet joy of those unforeseeable enchantments that the great systems of metaphysics have, in their impatient will to power, again and again overlooked.

6   Outside the Subject
Merleau-Ponty's Chiasmic Vision

To understand and judge a society, one has to penetrate its basic
structure to the human bond upon which it is built.
Humanism and Terror[1]

[Vision] is that gift of nature which Spirit [*l'Esprit*] was called
upon to make use of beyond all hope.
Phenomenology of Perception[2]

With the first vision, . . . there is initiation, . . . the opening of a
dimension that can never again be closed.
The Visible and the Invisible[3]

We have to promote new forms of subjectivity through the refusal
of the kind of individuality imposed on us for several centuries.
Michel Foucault, "The Subject and Power"[4]

What do I bring to the problem of the same and the other? This:
that the same be the other than the other, and identity difference
of difference.
The Visible and the Invisible (VIE 264, VIF 318)

I. INHERITANCE

The inheritance of a philosopher's thought necessarily involves an intricately mediated reception. To inherit a philosopher's thought is always a
question of inhabiting its life, its nooks and crannies: questioning its hesi-
tations, its doubts, its intrigues, its excitement, its deepest silences—taking
up what remains unthought and carrying that forward. Inheritance is never
repetition, but the gratitude that consists in responding to the challenge of
its vision, and in assuming responsibility for that which remains unthought
within the matter that was most deeply engaged.

Here, then, we shall be continuing a certain phenomenological archaeology, not so much concerned to excavate more deeply, but rather to extend
dimensions of the site, uncovering, recovering a significance upon which
Merleau-Ponty only touched. It will be a question of making contact with
moral and spiritual sources, elaborating the moral significance of the

prepersonal dimension of perceptual experience that he brings to light when his phenomenology deconstructs the metaphysical narrative of subjectivity and breaches the defenses of the subject-object structure.

The premise of this chapter is that we need to return to the sources of moral vision carried in and by the body of felt experience. Merleau-Ponty's work makes it possible for us to understand this return as a process of making contact, through our experience of embodiment, with our participation in an elemental flesh, an intercorporeal flesh of intertwinings and reversibilities. Because of the moral predispositions already inscribed in the flesh, making contact with this dimension of our body of experience and recovering our felt sense of the flesh, of our being-flesh, could perhaps solicit a heightened sense of justice, of responsibility for the other—and motivate a different moral vision.

II. THE GROUNDING OF VISION OUTSIDE THE SUBJECT: AN ALTERNATIVE ETHICS

In "La Fausse Monnaie," a work that provoked Derrida to think about counterfeit money in *Donner le temps*, Charles Baudelaire depicts a scene in which a man and the woman he loves, seated in a café and conversing over drinks, suddenly find themselves the objects of six staring eyes, held tightly by the desperate, importunate beholding of an old beggar and his two weak and starving children. Shaken by this encounter with suffering, the man later discusses this experience with his friend:

> Not only was I moved by this family of eyes, but I felt a little ashamed of our glasses and decanters, too much for our thirst. I turned my gaze to look into yours, dear love, to read *my* thought in them; and as I plunged my eyes into yours, . . . you said to me: "Those people are insufferable with their eyes open wide as coachdoors! Couldn't you ask the proprietor to send them away?" So you see how difficult it is to understand one another, . . . and how incommunicable thought is, even between people who love each other.[5]

In this man's confession of shame before the suffering he sees and in the woman's attitude in response to what she is seeing, we can see the difference between a vision that is exposed, a vision that lets itself be exposed, to the destitution of the other and a way of looking and seeing that is ruled and motivated by pure egoism. Our concern with the reading of this passage is quite different from Derrida's, and yet, I trust and believe, not without a certain affinity. For it could be said that our concern is with the given in perception—and correspondingly, with the reception of the given. But here it will be a question, ultimately, of the spirit, the moral sensibility upon which the gift of our capacity to see would draw.

Baudelaire's narrative represents, as I said, two absolutely opposed ways of looking and seeing—looking at others, looking at the world, seeing. Two absolutely opposed responses, affirming two correspondingly different, even bitterly conflicting senses of responsibility: for others, for the poor, the homeless, the hungry, the Other.

I want to argue that no representation could better illustrate the difference between a way of seeing characteristic of the ego-logical subject—the classical bourgeois subject, that is, whose vision is conditioned by its inherence in the structure and exchange economy of subject and object—and that way of seeing, that peculiar vision, which becomes possible, for the first time, when the gaze originates in a prepersonal experience of intersubjectivity and remains rooted in this dimension, intact in its contact with this dimension, exposing itself to the Other in an experience that is outside the subject-object structure, alien to its economy, even as it accommodates itself to the historical expression of the instinct for self-preservation and the ego's entire social reality.

Of course, in order to elaborate this argument, it will be necessary to draw out, to elicit from our reading of the texts, a moral phenomenology that is at most fairly recessive. But it can be shown, I think, that Merleau-Ponty sets the stage for the realization that, at the very root of vision, there rules an absolute exposure and responsibility in relation to the Other. An exposure and responsibility, in fact, that ultimately extend, beyond the realm of being we call "human," to the world of nature—the winds, the seas, the earth, the forests, and all the animals.

In "The Child's Relations with Others," there is a section concerned with the correlation between psychological rigidity and perceptual rigidity—a correlation of consequence not only for our understanding of the child's social development, but also for our understanding of the so-called authoritarian personality and various forms of intolerance, prejudice, and hatred. Commenting on the research of Frenkel-Brunswik, Merleau-Ponty emphasizes the existence of a connection between the political issue and a way of looking and seeing:

> Frenkel-Brunswik does not propose that psychology *alone* is in a position to solve political problems. There are, in her view, subjects who are without social prejudices of any kind, who are perfectly "liberal" in the sense that they admit that all men are brothers, that one cannot con-

centrate all the characteristics of evil in Negroes, Jews, or any other mi-
nority and yet who, for all that, are rigid subjects because they refuse
to see among men even the most striking differences of *situation*—
differences which pertain to the collectivity in which they have lived
and received their initial training. There is an abstract or rigid liberalism which consists in thinking that all men are *identical*. There are
also liberals who are truly liberal, in the sense that they conceive very
well that there can be differences of historical situation among men
and different cultural environments. This does not prevent them from
treating each man (in so far as his situation permits him to be a man)
like any other. But the fundamental identity of men does not close
their eyes to the cultural differences which may develop and which
must be understood.[6]

It must be conceded, of course, that the chiasmic nature of our flesh, into
the depths of which we are about to enter, cannot by itself, automatically,
preclude a looking and seeing moved by prejudice and intolerance. For in
the normal course of socialization and ego-formation, our vision becomes
disconnected from the chiasm. But it will be argued that, to the extent that
we are able to achieve a chiasmic gaze, a vision completely *reconnected* with
our chiasmic nature, our vision would be radically altered by its exposure
to alterity and could not easily be moved by the attitudes that cause such
moral blindness.

With a progressively keener understanding of the possibility of a radical critique of the philosophies of the disembodied subject coming from
within phenomenology itself, and with a steadily more focused awareness of the ethical implications suggested by this critique, Merleau-Ponty
moved from the hermeneutical unconcealment of a prepersonal dimension
of embodied experience to the unconcealment of an ecstatic, chiasmic flesh,
a weave of elemental intertwinings intricately operative in every configuration of experience, whether between the subject and another subject or
between the subject and an object. Thus, by way, first, of a phenomenology
of perception and then, much later, a phenomenology of the flesh, he was
able to deconstruct the metaphysical claims of the ego-logical subject, the
cogito, and exhibit an intersubjectivity—in fact, an intercorporeality—not
only more "ancient" than this subject, but entitled to claim a certain ontological privilege. Moreover, he could show, first and foremost in the realm
of vision, that, and how, our corporeal intersubjectivity introduces substi-
tutions and reversibilities that are radically decentering, exposing the ego-
logical subject to radical problematizations of its identity and, correlatively,
its assumptions regarding alterity, it relationship to the other.

And yet, he gave only occasional passing recognition to the ethical normativity implied by this phenomenological demonstration of the ontological priority of an ecstatic, chiasmic flesh and its dialectics of intersubjectivity. This elaboration of the ethical was made difficult, I believe, by his strangely unresolved interpretation of the experience that his phenomenology recovered, oscillating without sufficient self-reflection between a logic of the same and a logic of alterity in his exhibition or representation of the subject's gaze. Thus, in the end, he leaves us with an unreconciled vision, a vision that has not reconciled or overcome the fundamental moral crisis in our contemporary culture of the individual: the crisis, namely, on which the conflict between the normative commitments or imperatives implicit in these two logics—and in the radically different social orders, the different political economies that might be said to correspond to them— challenges us to reflect. As we shall see, while the gaze that Merleau-Ponty exhibits in "The Child's Relations with Others" seems unequivocally to break the spell of the logic of identity, the very late manuscripts published under the title *The Visible and the Invisible* reveal the chiasmic reversibilities of vision only to interpret reversibility in terms of a narcissism of mirroring. This means that his phenomenology of vision remains under the spell of this terrible logic even as it recovers, "before" and "beneath" the anonymous and prepersonal dimension of perception, an even deeper dimension of experience—a dimension ruled by the alterity of the chiasmic.

Merleau-Ponty's claim regarding the narcissism of vision binds vision to this logic of identity at the very moment when his phenomenology has recovered in the reversibilities of mirroring a potential for deconstructing the narcissistic identity of the subject. This is significant, because it means that the very promising archaeology of the prepersonal dimension of embodied experience which his early phenomenological work recovered—an archaeology promising in its adumbrations of an ethical disposition, a corporeal schematism already assigned to the flesh—would not become the groundwork for an alternative ethics—an ethics outside the subject, outside the enchanted circle of the subject-object structure. However, the thesis of this chapter is that the work which Merleau-Ponty began enables us to envision the possibility of a phenomenological narrative that would indeed articulate in its decisive moments the moral development of a gaze no longer ruled by the ego-logical subject: a gaze the moral character of which would be normatively determined, instead, by the logic of alterity, by a reversibility that would put us in touch with the perspective of the other. Such a gaze, however, would inevitably constitute a site of resistance and subversion in relation to the prevailing social culture and its economy of egoism and exchange. Such a gaze would be strongly disposed, I believe, to disrupt the prevailing administration of our principles of justice, making visible the cruelties and injustices that normally escape notice, or anyway, appropriate recognition. It will be the purpose of this chapter, therefore, to trace, at least in their outlines, the different representations of the gaze in Merleau-Ponty's lifetime of work, collecting and then, as briefly as possible, examining the most important textual passages.

Everything will depend, however, on the recognition that perception—vision, for example—is nature's gift of a capacity, and therefore a potential, that can be developed through moral education. When, in "The Philosopher and His Shadow," Merleau-Ponty speaks of an "ontological rehabilitation of the sensible," referring to the reversibility that takes place between the touching and the touched when one of my hands touches the other, and to the consequent deconstruction of the subject-object structure, the rehabilitation that I have in mind is the one that takes place through the realization of the moral "destination" of the sensible. For example, in the moment when our vision, taken over by the ego-logical subject, once again makes contact with an affective dimension of experience "outside" this subject and lets itself be moved and guided by what this experience can communicate. In concluding his Preface to the *Phenomenology of Perception*, Merleau-Ponty asserts that "true philosophy consists in relearning to look at the world" (PPE xx, PPF xv). Just such relearning to see is what we are attempting to think here—think and undergo.

III. THE NATURE OF THE PREPERSONAL:
AN IDENTITY TRANSCENDING THE SUBJECT

Arguing in 1945, in his second major work, the *Phenomenology of Perception*, against the philosophical program he calls "objectivism," Merleau-Ponty remarks that the "function" of such a program is "to reduce all phenomena which bear witness to the union of subject and world, putting in their place the clear idea of the object as in itself and of the subject [as self-contained and self-originating]" (PPE 320, PPF 370). Thus, he says, it is the peculiar mode of reflection that philosophers have adopted, or perhaps the way that philosophers have understood the process of reflection, which objectifies lived experience to this effect, "whereas, when I perceive, I belong . . . to the world as a whole" (PPE 329, PPF 380).

Merleau-Ponty contends that what philosophers have termed "subject" and "object" are in reality "two abstract 'moments' of a unique structure which is presence" (PPE 430, PPF 492). This accordingly assigns phenomenology its task: it must "rediscover," as "anterior" to the structure of subject and object, that "primordial layer" out of which that structure first emerged (PPE 219, PPF 254). This means that phenomenology must excavate hermeneutically "beneath the relation of the knowing subject to the known object" (CRO 98, CROF 3); that it "must return to the *cogito* in search of a more fundamental *Logos* than that of objective thought" (PPE 365, PPF 419); and that it must learn, for example, as he states in "Eye and Mind," how to enter into "the immemorial depths of vision."[7]

Correlatively, his fidelity to the phenomena compelled him to argue with equal force against the programs of idealism and intellectualism: "I am borne into personal existence," he asserts, "by a time which I do not constitute" (PPE 347, PPF 399). And, in a passage that carries singular significance when read in the light of the "tracework" that distinguishes the Levinasian conception of the phenomenological task,[8] Merleau-Ponty observes:

> When I turn toward perception, [I] find at work in my organs of perception a thought older than myself, of which those organs are merely a trace. (PPE 351–52, PPF 404)

"My personal existence," he says,

> must be the resumption of a prepersonal tradition. There is, therefore, another subject beneath me, for whom a world exists before I am here, and who marks out my place in it. This captive or natural spirit is my body, not that momentary body which is the instrument of my personal choices and which fastens upon this or that world, but the system of anonymous "functions" which draw every particular focus into a general project. (PPE 254, PPF 294)

In other words, Merleau-Ponty brings to light, as *prior* to our personal, ego-logical experience, an anonymous and prepersonal existence, an anonymous and prepersonal subject. This dynamic, temporal schema may also be thought in structural terms. Thus Merleau-Ponty will also speak of recovering a dimension "beneath" this experience, because he holds that, in the course of the ego-logical subject's formation, this prepersonal experience is not entirely destroyed, lost, or forgotten, but merely, as it were, deeply sublimated or suppressed: surpassed, but still preserved, and therefore, at least in principle, always to some extent potentially recoverable (PPE 347, PPF 399). The shocking significance of this recovery is, I think, made clear with great force when the philosopher tells us that, "if I wanted to render the perceptual experience with more faithful precision, I ought to say that *one* perceives in me, not that I perceive" (PPE 215, PPF 249). In this formulation, we see Merleau-Ponty radically decentering, radically destabilizing the sovereign subject that has dominated the philosophical discourse of modernity.

Let us return, now, to the point that "when I perceive, I belong . . . to the world as a whole." The recovery of our prepersonal existence is also, for Merleau-Ponty, the recovery of "a communication with the world more ancient than thought" (PPE 254, PPF 294). Thus he also wants to say that, "in so far as I have sensory functions, a visual, auditory and tactile field, I am already in communication with others" (PPE 353, PPF 406). This is a level of "communication" that he describes by reference to a corporeal intentionality that does not recognize the ego-logical boundaries constitutive of our "normal" experience:

> My body . . . discovers in that other body a miraculous prolongation of my own intentions, a familiar way of dealing with the world. Henceforth, as the parts of my body together comprise a system, so my body and the other person's are one whole, two sides of one and the same phenomenon, and the anonymous existence of which my body is the ever-renewed trace henceforth inhabits both bodies simultaneously. (PPE 354, PPF 406)

As we shall see, this is a description that anticipates by many years Merleau-Ponty's introduction, in his last manuscripts, of the metaphorical concepts of "intertwining" and "chiasm." In another formulation of the prepersonal communicativeness at work in this intentionality, Merleau-Ponty says:

> The communication or comprehension of gestures comes about through the reciprocity of my intentions and the gestures of others, of my gestures and the intentions discernible in the conduct of other people. It is as if the other person's intention inhabited my body and mine his. (PPE 185, PPF 215. Also see PPE 320, PPF 370.)

This passage is significant, in part, because it introduces the concept of "reciprocity," again anticipating his last manuscripts. But it is also significant, of course, in that it intimates the existence of a certain moral disposition already orienting our bodily comportment—even if this moral "compass" is very rudimentary, preliminary, and pro-visional.

In other intriguing passages of note, Merleau-Ponty elaborates what we might call the "emotional essence" of this prepersonal dimension of communication, bringing to the fore, with particular attention to vision and touch, the intertwining of the different senses and their respective fields, and arguing that, in consequence, we can touch things from which we are distant with the tactile sensibility of our eyes and therefore that, correspondingly, we can be touched, affected, by what we behold from a certain distance (PPE 223, 229; PPF 258, 265. Also see VIE 134, VIF 177). Even in these descriptions, as we can see, the concept of "reversibility," which assumes much greater importance in his last writings, is clearly prefigured.

In making the phenomenological argument against solipsism in his *Phenomenology of Perception*, Merleau-Ponty commented that,

> the perception of other people and the intersubjective world are problematical only for adults. The child lives in a world which he unhesitatingly believes accessible all around him. He has no awareness of himself or of others as private subjectivities. (PPE 355, PPF 407)

In "The Child's Relations with Others," a text drawn from material discussed in 1960 in a series of courses he gave at the Collège de France, and in other texts he wrote during the last decade of his life, Merleau-Ponty elaborated this thought, showing its confirmation by empirical research into the psychology of child development. Although his principal concern seems to have been the phenomenological refutation of the presuppositions behind the argument for solipsism, the experiences to which he calls our attention and the vocabulary he uses to articulate them incontrovertibly imply that what is ultimately at stake is moral experience, and therefore that this argument against solipsism constitutes a phenomenology of moral experience, tracing its origin and development in the life of the child. It is greatly to be lamented, I think, that the scholars continuing his work have not given sufficient recognition to the significance of Merleau-Ponty's work for a phenomenology of moral experience.

In "The Concept of Nature" lecture course he gave at the Collège de France, Merleau-Ponty pointed to "an ideal community of embodied subjects, of intercorporeality."[9] But he left this intriguing thought quite undeveloped. "The Child's Relations with Others," however, begins to flesh out this extremely bold thought, pointing, for example, to the unmistakable evidence for a certain "pre-communication" and "postural impregnation" taking place between the infant and others (CRO 119, CROF 33). "I live," he says, "in the facial expressions of the other, as I feel him living in mine" (CRO 146, CROF 69). This, he thinks, argues for the view that such experience constitutes an "initial sympathy," and consequently even a certain "initial community" (CRO 118–20, CROF 31–34). Thus, in "The Child's Relations with Others," the anonymous, prepersonal dimension of experience excavated many years earlier in the *Phenomenology of Perception* is finally rendered in terms that explicitly bring out its significance for moral life and moral vision. Even here, however, he leaves the significance of this evidence for a phenomenology of moral experience surprisingly undeveloped. Of particular importance for our concerns is the fact that he does not explore the implications of this material for a radical critique of the egoism and individualism that prevail in modern culture and for the articulation, in the evocative language of his phenomenology, of a different moral vision, a different vision of morality.

The task which the resumption of this project would seem to suggest— or which certainly, in any case, one might profitably undertake—calls for reflecting on the transformative potential inherent in the phenomenological recovery (Merleau-Ponty's crucial words are "récupération" and "reprise") of this marvelous experience of prepersonal intercorporeality in the early life of the infant. What if the adult, instead of maintaining a gaze the character of which is solely determined by an ego-logical subjectivity— and consequently by an objectifying, instrumental rationality and a correspondingly ego-centered ethics—should undertake to ground the character of his or her gaze, his or her moral vision of the world, in the bodily felt sense that would emerge from the effort to recover something of the infant's experience, long suppressed, split off, forgotten, of intercorporeality, an ontologically significant prepersonal interconnectedness among all beings? What if the adult, instead of perpetuating a vision, a way of looking and seeing that has been complicitous for too long in an ontology and politics of violence, were to attempt to make contact with this prepersonal intercorporeality, with what, in "The Intertwining—The Chiasm" (VIE 137, VIF 181), Merleau-Ponty will call a "universal flesh," so that the character of the gaze would be normatively determined, would be more radically attuned, by the openness to alterity constitutive of the perceptual field as a whole? If the gaze that predominates in our time is a gaze that reflects the fragmentations, the diremptions, the reifications distinctive of modernity, is it not possible that a gaze in deeply felt contact with the affective-conative wholeness and openness of this field could emerge from this experience with a tact and intactness that would significantly alter its character? It would be a question of a vision, a way of looking and seeing, that is wholehearted, fully embodied, whole—not borne of the metaphysical dualisms that ushered in the age of modernity, most especially, those forms of splitting that set up irreconcilable oppositions between reason and feeling, mind and body, reason and imagination, meaningful thought and thoughtless perception, reality and appearance, ego and other.

In "Eye and Mind," Merleau-Ponty gives voice to a vision in touch with its sense of the dimensionality of the visual field:

> We must take literally what vision teaches us: namely, that through it we come into contact with the sun and the stars, that we are everywhere all at once. (EM 187)

Merleau-Ponty's "Working Notes," written during the last years of his life and published posthumously in *The Visible and the Invisible*, elaborate the radical significance of this dimensionality, bringing the question of vision back to my experience of the other person:

> There is . . . no problem of the *alter ego*, because it is not I who sees, not he who sees; because an anonymous visibility inhabits both of us, a vision in general, in virtue of that primordial property that belongs to flesh, of being here and now and of radiating everywhere and forever. (VIE 142, VIF 187–88)

This passage merits special attention, because the reference to an "anonymous visibility" resumes the phenomenological vocabulary of the much earlier work, the *Phenomenology of Perception*, while the reference to the "flesh," in which our vision is rooted, carries this work forward, formulating a more explicit, more audacious challenge to the subject-object structure within which the metaphysics of the modern age has persisted in thinking our moral relations with others—and indeed with everything in our world.

The boldness of some of the texts published posthumously in *The Visible and The Invisible* is really quite breathtaking. And yet, it is a boldness that continues the earlier work, excavating and recovering a deeper dimension of our experience with vision, rather than introducing a break in his project. In the reference, for example, to "a visibility older than my operations or my acts" (VIE 123, VIF 165), one may clearly hear echoes of passages in the *Phenomenology of Perception*. But in the later texts, our embodiment is figured in radically new terms, for he wanted, instead, to articulate a dimension that metaphysical discourse cannot possibly comprehend and appropriate. Thus, in *The Visible and the Invisible*, he brings to light a dimension not only (temporally) "prior to" and (structurally) "beneath" the personal or ego-logical structuring of experience, but even (temporally) "prior to" and (structurally) "beneath" the "initial sympathy" and "initial community" of the prepersonal. This deeper dimension he calls "flesh," drawing on mythopoetic language from the ancient beginning of philosophical thought: it is in terms of flesh, he says, that we must think "the formative medium of the object and the subject" (VIE 147, VIF 193). This way of thinking shows us that:

> my body is made of the same flesh as the world . . . and moreover, . . . this flesh of my body is shared by the world. (VIE 248, VIF 302)

But, he warns,

> we must not think the flesh starting from substances, from [the metaphysical splitting that opposes] body and spirit . . . but as an element, as the concrete emblem of a general manner of being. (VIE 147, VIF 193)

"The flesh," he says,

> is not matter, is not mind, is not substance. To designate it, we should need the old term "element," in the sense it was used to speak of a *general thing*. . . . The flesh is in this sense an "element of being." (VIE 139, VIF 183–84)

Thus, "my body sees only because it is a part of the visible in which it opens forth" (VIE 153–54, VIF 201). And being a "part," being "of" the visible, "of" its *partage,* and sharing in its fate—this means that "he who sees cannot possess the visible unless he is possessed by it" (VIE 134, VIF 177–78). In one stroke, this phenomenology succeeds in canceling the complicity of the philosopher's conception of vision in forms of domination and violence.

The figure of the flesh also enables Merleau-Ponty to introduce two other terms of decisive importance: "chiasm" and "intertwining." In his words, "by a sort of chiasm, we become the others and we become world" (VIE 160, VIF 212). And "things pass into us as well as we into things" (VIE 123, VIF 165). We need to recover, we need to see,

> the intertwining of my life with the lives of others, of my body with the visible things, by the intersection of my perceptual field with that of others. (VIE 49, VIF 74)

We need to recover this experience *for* our way of looking and seeing. We need to understand that,

> in reality, there is neither me nor the other as positive, positive subjectivities. There are . . . two opennesses, two stages where something will take place. (VIE 263, VIF 317)

And we need this understanding to serve as the "grounding" of our vision.

For Merleau-Ponty, the intertwinings, the chiasmic dynamics of the flesh, suggest that a certain *reversibility* takes place in the perceptual field:

> The chiasm, reversibility, is the idea that every perception is doubled with a counter-perception . . . one no longer knows who speaks and who listens. (VIE 264–65, VIF 318)

Nor, for that matter, who is the looking subject and who is the object seen.

But Merleau-Ponty further claims, repeating a point he made in "Eye and Mind" (EM 166), that this reversibility means that the flesh involves a certain process of "mirroring" (VIE 255, VIF 309) and that, in consequence, "the seer is caught up in what he sees, [so that] it is still himself he sees: there is a fundamental narcissism in all vision" (VIE 139, VIF 183). Elaborating the meaning of this claim, Merleau-Ponty continues, arguing that,

> for the same reason, the vision he exercises he also undergoes from the things, such that, as many painters have said, I feel myself looked at by the things, my activity is equally my passivity—which is the second and more profound sense of the narcissism: not to see in the outside, as others see it, the contour of the body one inhabits, but especially to be seen by the outside, to exist within it, to emigrate into it, to be seduced, captivated, alienated by the phantom, so that the seer and the visible reciprocate one another and we no longer know which sees and which is seen. (VIE 139, VIF 183)

In other words, as I have argued elsewhere at greater length than I shall be able to argue here, this is a "mirroring" which actually, in effect, double-crosses the reflective "narcissism" that Merleau-Ponty discerns.[10] This is not the narcissism of Descartes, Freud or Lacan: not at all the self-absorption or self-aggrandizement of a monadic ego, but rather the beginning, in fact, of a deconstruction of ego-logical subjectivity. For while it is true that the others whom I see reflect my bodily presence back to me through their eyes, so that, when I look at them, I am able to see myself, this passage of reflection through the gaze of others also obliges me to see myself in dispossession, in a condition of decenteredness: I recognize myself as another for an other, and I am obliged to acknowledge that there are other perspectives. In the eyes of others, I behold the truth that I belong to the "universal flesh" of the visible and the invisible. Looking into the eyes of others, I may see myself; but what I should see is that I am exposed, vulnerable, held in their beholding. Thus I am exposed to the possibility of being touched and moved by what I see reflected in or through their gaze. The reflective mirroring between myself and the other thus sets in motion a certain reversibility of our positions. As I have argued elsewhere, this reversibility in the structuring of the visual field radically subverts the narcissism of vision and its obedience to a logic of identity. Moreover, it constitutes an experience of the utmost importance for the formation of one's sense of justice: it is a preliminary experience, an intimation, of the responsibility commanded by justice; it is *already* an experience of the meaning of justice.[11]

Although Merleau-Ponty sees reversibility and reciprocity in the inter-twinings and reflections set in motion between my gaze and yours, and sees, when reflecting on the significance of research into the "psychology" of the child, what he terms an "initial sympathy" and an "initial commu-nity," his unfortunate willingness to continue describing the mirroring and reversibility of chiasmic vision as a "narcissism" suggests that he still could not clearly see in the exchange of gazes that he discusses in *The Visible and the Invisible* the most radical subversion of narcissism and its logic of iden-tity; nor does he seem to see any moral predisposition, any rudimentary or preliminary orientation toward the Good, toward Justice. And yet, he says that

> we will have to recognize an ideality that is not alien to the flesh, that gives it its axes, its depth, its dimensions. (VIE 152, VIF 199)

What I want, therefore, to argue is that we need to think of this "ideality" as the "inscription" of a certain moral predisposition or orientation. I want to say that the prepersonal experience with vision constitutes the hint of a promise: the promise, namely, of a potential the development of which is possible. Not teleologically predetermined, not in the least assured, but al-ways just possible—depending, in the case of children, on favorable social conditions, and in the case of adults, on their willingness to restore a felt connection between their vision and their prepersonal experience.

Returning to the *Phenomenology of Perception*, we find that Merleau-Ponty was already insisting there that

> our relationship to the social is, like our relationship to the world, deeper than any express perception or any judgement. . . . We must re-turn to the social with which we are in contact by the mere fact of ex-isting, and which we carry about inseparably with us before any objectification. . . . The social is already there when we come to know or judge it. . . . Prior to the process of becoming aware, the social exists obscurely and as a summons [*sourdement et comme sollicitation*]. (PPE 362, PPF 415–16)

This may be reassuring. But the argument sketched all too briefly in this chapter can easily be misunderstood. I certainly do not want to suggest that adults should undergo a regression to identity-confusion, regression to a mode of experiencing prior to the formation of ego-logical subjectivity, but rather that there is a need for vision to reestablish contact with chiasmic ex-perience, with the intertwining of gazes, with the "universal flesh" out of which it emerged, so that an historically new form of subjectivity and a different way of looking and seeing, neither that of the prepersonal nor that of the egoic, might—perhaps—come into being.[12]

What we need, here, is a narrative giving phenomenological articulation to a certain developmental process in regard to our capacity for vision. In *The Visible and the Invisible*, Merleau-Ponty implied such a narrative, maintaining that

> the stages passed through are not simply passed; they have called for or required the present stages. . . . The past stages continue therefore to be in the present stages—which also means that they are retroactively modified by them. (VIE 90, VIF 123)

We might begin the elaboration of this narrative by taking Merleau-Ponty's work to suggest a developmental schema showing, from a temporal and dynamic point of view, three phases or moments and, from a structural point of view, three dimensions or strata. [1] In the first phase, a phase we would identify with early childhood, there is a passive, anonymous, prepersonal experience with vision, an experience prior to thematic consciousness, prior to volition, and belonging to a time prior to the conventional, ego-logically constructed order of time, exposing the identity of the one who sees to the radical alterity of the chiasm, the intertwining and its reversibilities. Thus we might say that, in this phase, vision enacts the immediate responsiveness, or the immediately responsive responsibility, of a proto-moral self. [2] Stéphane Mallarmé once wrote these marvelous words, useful in introducing the second phase: "L'enfant abdique son extase. . . ."[13] In the second phase, a phase largely determined by the processes and conditions of socialization to which the child happens to be exposed, the experience of the first phase is *aufgehoben*, repressed and surpassed, but also to some extent still preserved, becoming a "tracework" dimension that continues to function "beneath" the formation of the ego-logical subject. Here vision belongs to—and serves—the self-centered ego-subject of a bourgeois modernity whose way of looking and seeing is predominantly motivated by self-preservation and self-interest. Here, vision, detached from its experience of a chiasmic alterity, reflects and manifests the familiar forms of conventional ego-logical morality. [3] Whereas the first phase is a vision whose proto-moral disposition is the gift of nature and the second phase is the destiny of a vision that has been socially constructed, the third phase, manifesting the vision of a truly moral self, is entirely contingent on the moral motivation of the subject. In other words, the possibility for this phase to come about is entirely dependent on a certain "practice of the self": the willingness of the ego-logical subject to work on itself and undertake a process of radical self-deconstruction, whereby it would return to make contact with and retrieve (if only in the form of a certain tracework) the prepersonal experience of chiasmic vision that was suppressed, alienated, and forgotten in the course of a necessary and inevitable socialization.

To the extent that the subject retrieves something of the infant's first-phase experience with vision, the "initial sympathy" normally constitutive of that phase could be taken up and developed, becoming a freely embraced, reflectively affirmed sympathy, while the first-phase participation of the infant's vision in the "syncretic sociability" of an "initial community" could become the adult citizen's participation in a deliberative community of principled sociability built on a true reciprocity of gazes—gazes which look with respect at one another and would be capable of reversing their point of view to identify it with that of the other. I want to speak, here, not of empathy, *Einfühlung*, but of sympathy, because the former is a concept that would inevitably inscribe the experience in question within the very metaphysics of subjectivity out of which Merleau-Ponty is trying to break. The prefix suggests the wrong picture: that of a solitary subject which must overcome its inwardness, its self-enclosure, to project and transfer its feelings into an other who is no less closed off from corporeal inter-subjectivity.—And perhaps we should also say that the prefix suggests a picture which is an all-too-accurate reflection and representation of the alienated world modernity has produced, but which we must unequivocally oppose in order to flesh out the possibility of a vision constitutive of a radically different moral and political order.

The recuperation of this vision, were it to be undertaken, would be the realization of a response-ability that has *always already* claimed us as beings gifted with the capacity to see, but which, without this difficult work of retrieval in consciousness and freedom, would not be confirmed as the identity-shattering ground of our visionary existence. According to this schema, vision is a capacity stretched between the "always already" and the "not yet." For the "moral self" is a never-ending, never-completed, ongoing project of exposure to the other, a difficult and, for some, a frightening process of self-deconstruction in responsiveness to the other. But perhaps we can find some measure of comfort after all in the thought that the moral vision which we have not yet realized has by a gift of nature always already been granted us as a possible destiny.

The hope which this argument represents, a hope the adumbrations of which Merleau-Ponty's work traces and to which he gives expression in the second of the quotations at the beginning of this chapter, but which he never spelled out, is that the tracework recovery of this chiasmic experience—the restoration of felt contact with its intertwining of subjectivities—could alter the moral character of the predominant gaze.

In "The War Has Taken Place," written at the close of the Second World War, Merleau-Ponty reflected on anti-Semitism as a way of looking and seeing:

> An anti-Semite could not stand to see Jews tortured if he really saw them, if he perceived that suffering and agony in an individual life— but this is just the point: he does not see Jews suffering; he is blinded by the myth of the Jew. He tortures and murders the Jew through these concrete beings; he struggles with dream figures, and his blows strike living faces. Anti-Semitic passion is not triggered by, nor does it aim at, concrete individuals.[14]

Perhaps. But does this reflection avoid confronting the question of radical evil? In any case, I believe that a looking and seeing in felt contact with what we might call, after Levinas, the asymmetry and heteronomy of its chiasmic dimension could not only, if it were engaged as a social practice, elevate the moral condition, the moral sense and sensibility of the human world; it could also, as some of the passages quoted earlier suggest, profoundly alter our relationship to nature, encouraging the development of a deeper sense of responsibility for the earth and the life it sustains—for its rivers and lakes, its forests, its animals.[15] If responsibility extends as far as our ability to be responsive, the emergence of a chiasmic vision would perhaps see with more feeling the injustices of our world and be moved by the very sight of so many threats to the inconceivable beauty of its life. Perhaps.

Vision is . . . that gift of nature which Spirit [*l'Esprit*] was called upon to make use of beyond all hope, to which it was to give a fundamentally new meaning, yet which was needed, not only to be incarnate, but in order to be at all.

Maurice Merleau-Ponty, *Phenomenology of Perception* (p. 127)

7 The Invisible Face of Humanity

Levinas on the Justice of the Gaze

They walked, and in their talk of the beauty of the earth do not notice the frail little beggar girl tripping after them.

> Anton Chekhov, "A Day in the Country"[1]

We tend to take the speech of a Chinese for inarticulate gurgling. Someone who understands Chinese will recognize *language* in what he hears. Similarly, I often cannot discern the *humanity* in a man.

> Ludwig Wittgenstein, *Culture and Value*[2]

Something happened there [at Auschwitz] that no-one could previously have thought even possible. It touched a deep layer of solidarity among all who have a human face. Until then—in spite of all the quasi-natural brutalities of world history—we had simply taken the integrity of this deep layer for granted.

> Jürgen Habermas, "Historical Consciousness and the Post-Traditional Identity"[3]

The possibility of pogroms is decided in the moment when the gaze of a fatally wounded animal falls on a human being. The defiance with which he repels this gaze—"after all, it's only an animal!"—reappears irresistibly in cruelties done to human beings, the perpetrators having again and again to reassure themselves that it is "only an animal."

> Theodor Adorno, *Minima Moralia*[4]

It might astonish some that—faced with so many unleashed forces, so many violent and voracious acts that fill our history, our societies and our souls—I should turn to the *I-Thou* or the responsibility of one person for the other to find the categories of the Human. . . . The humanity of the human—is this not, in the contranatural appearance of the ethical relation to the other man, the very crisis of being qua being?

> Emmanuel Levinas, "Apropos of Buber: Some Notes"[5]

Is it certain that the ultimate and proper meaning of the human signifies in its exhibition, in the manifestation of the manifested *for myself* (which is the way this meaning is thought), in guise of a thought revealing the truth of being? Is it so certain that man does not have his meaning beyond what he can be and what he can show himself? Does that meaning not show itself as meaning precisely as secret of the face?—open, that is, exposed, without defense? . . . A meaning, I say, beyond what man can be and show himself: the face is meaning of the beyond. Not sign or symbol of the beyond; the latter allows itself to be neither indicated nor symbolized without falling into the immanence of knowledge.

Emmanuel Levinas, "The Meaning of Meaning"[6]

[In] repressive society, the concept of man is itself a parody of divine likeness. The mechanism of 'pathic projection' determines that those in power perceive as human only their own reflected image, instead of reflecting back the human as precisely what is different.

Theodor Adorno, *Minima Moralia*[7]

The reconciled condition would not be the philosophical imperialism of annexing the alien. Instead, its happiness would lie in the fact that the alien, in the proximity it is granted, remains distant and different, beyond the heterogeneous and beyond that which is one's own.

Theodor Adorno, *Negative Dialectics*[8]

Could a greater miracle take place than for us to look through each other's eyes for an instant? We should live in all the ages of the world in an hour; ay, in all the worlds of the ages.

Henry David Thoreau, *Walden*[9]

All at once, / two millennia before that new creature / whom we enjoy when touching begins, / suddenly: faced with you, I am born, in the eye.

Rainer Maria Rilke, "Arrival"[10]

In the innermost sanctum of the divine truth, where man might expect all the world and himself to dwindle into likeness of that which he is to catch sight of there, he catches sight of none other than a countenance like his own. The Star of Redemption is become countenance which glances at me and out of which I glance. Not God become my mirror, but God's truth.

Franz Rosenzweig, *The Star of Redemption*[11]

Then his soul looked through the gate where appearance becomes an enigma and seeing becomes a presentiment.

Hermann Hesse, "Iris"[12]

PREFACE: IN THE DESTITUTION OF MEANING

What needs to be said, here, at the very beginning, and by way of a preface, although we will in any case, whether we broach the matter here or not, continue to be bewildered throughout the course of these reflections, is that Levinas's use of certain philosophical words, and his intricate engagement with certain conceptual formations on the mediation of which his own discourse still to some extent draws and depends, are marked by the traces of an effort to contest and interrupt some of our words and concepts, and introduce for further thought some radically new ones, double-crossing familiar, long-standing meanings, and leaving nothing but a trace of their former configurations. Every one of his crucial words, and every crucial word that we shall be using to elaborate what he is saying and carry it forward, must be read as if double-crossed, or written within scare-quotes. But this should not be regarded as an excuse to deny that, in some broad sense, his discourse is a thinking and questioning of (what we might still be able to call) our experience.

Levinas's rhetorical mode seems to speak somehow in two voices: corresponding (i.e., co-responding) to the unrepresentable ambiguity of the trace, the claim of alterity, its anarchic nonidentity oscillating interminably between presence and absence, the real and the imaginary, the virtual and the actual, his language seems to oscillate, to equivocate undecidably between the constative and the performative, between description and prescription, between the literal and the metaphorical, between a discourse that could be situated within a certain familiar phenomenology and a discourse that reads and sounds like moral exhortation, or sometimes like the inspirational invocations and evocations of deeply religious experience.[13] There is even a certain incantatory quality in his writing: frequent repetitions of words, phrases, even entire sentences. This quality, this doubled tonality, is neither due to inattention nor to an arbitrary, capricious, and self-indulgent will.[14] Rather, it is meant to address us, his readers, in a powerfully affective-conative modality, immediately affecting the moral experience from out of which we draw our thinking. It is, for him, a question of addressing us in a way that might enable us to form, in response, what might be called a "deep, bodily felt sense" of the experience that he is trying to communicate. Such a "felt sense" could not be more different from the conceptual formations with which we are accustomed to working.[15] And it seems that Levinas is indeed committed to the belief that a certain "return" to the body's deep, felt sense of the good, a "return" effected by phenomenology, responsive to the description of such a sense and thereby, in so far as this be possible, actually enacting contact with it, could perhaps be strongly motivating, encouraging and guiding the realization of the good in one's life.

I think the impression of a certain rhetorical equivocation is true; but its truth makes understanding his thought extremely difficult, even treacherous. I think that his discourse does indeed make use, often simultaneously, of rhetorical modes that philosophical thought, at least in modern times, has kept separate. But I also think that there is a discernible logic in the way he works with the equivocations, the dialectical ambiguities and tensions set in motion by his rhetorical modes. It is as if, for a while, we must let ourselves be exiled with him in the destitution of meaning—there where all meaning is subjected to the most radical alteration, becoming virtually unrecognizable, certainly beyond the familiar forms of philosophical representation and appropriation. We are being asked, I think, to listen into the equivocations and reverberations of sound and sense, to hear something that is coming to voice: something being said in, by, and as the very event of saying.

The peculiarities of his rhetoric, however, are of such a nature that many philosophers have even felt compelled to question whether his work can, or should, be regarded as (still) phenomenological. If we equate phenomenology with Husserl's transcendental phenomenology, we cannot read Levinas's work as phenomenological. Not only does Levinas refuse Husserl's transcendental reductions and the transcendental egology; but he rejects Husserl's conception of intentionality. Moreover, he is not at all disturbed by the fact that his "descriptions" do not fit our moral experience as we normally live it, for the "inadequation" makes manifest the extent of our moral depravity and the work on ourselves that we need to do.

The phenomenology that Levinas practices is also quite unlike what we find in Heidegger, even though, in Heidegger's radical formulation for the "Introduction" to *Being and Time*, the phenomenological attitude is said to require the most extreme openness to the phenomenon, just as it shows itself. And even though, in "The Essence of Truth," written a few years after *Being and Time*,[16] we find Heidegger thinking of the phenomenological attitude in terms of a certain "exposure," *Aus-setzung* and *ek-sistente Ausgesetztheit:* "exposure to the disclosedness of beings," to "beings as a whole." Of course, for Heidegger, this exposure is first and foremost a question concerning our relation to ontology, and not our ethical comportment.

Although Levinas cautiously embraces a certain version of phenomenology, he resists any accommodation with hermeneutics as he understands it, because, whereas phenomenology can be rescued from its initial idealism and essentialism, hermeneutics seems to offer no such promise. According to Levinas, its interpretation of all experience in terms of the "as-structure" constitutive of "knowledge" imposes a typification incapable of respecting the singularity of the individual's experience.[17] In other words, it refers all attempts to understand the meaning of an experience to the conditions of a preceding structure (*Vor-Struktur*) of understanding, thereby ruling out in advance any sense or meaning that cannot be correlated with a presently recognized possibility of understanding. This makes the method inherently arrogant, inherently complicitous in the violence of a logic that reduces the other to the same. However, when I have written of "hermeneutical phenomenology," I have not meant to bind phenomenology to the Gadamerian method, but rather to draw on the word's etymological and mythological history—most of all, its associations with Hermes the trickster, the god of wild meanings, surprising revelations, and bewildering concealments—in order to reinforce in our practice of phenomenology a radical exposure to alterity.

Briefly formulated, it is my contention that Levinas's discourse renounces the normally separate rhetorical modes (modes that Habermas and even Lyotard insist on keeping distinct), because what it states or describes is not ordinary, conventional experience, experience lived superficially, but rather the deeper structures of our moral experience—structures functioning in a dimension that is for the most part concealed from awareness, perhaps repressed or denied, and represented by schools of philosophical thinking that can only betray it. (Is it not threatening to our culture of egoism, this discourse that evokes our existential exposure, our moral subjection to the other?) As an approximation, we might say, in an older language, not ultimately fitting, that he is developing a method and vocabulary within phenomenology to call upon the normative transcendental structures that carry the deep potential neglected by our ordinary, conventional, and quite superficial moral experience—and indicate our further moral development, beyond the ordinary and conventional.[18] In order, however, for this work of articulation actually to make a difference in our lives, it must not only describe these deep, deeply repressed structures in constative form; it must also speak of them and to them in such a way that we are sensibly moved to make contact with them and to entrust and submit our conventional moral experience, judgment, and action to the authority, the commandment, of their more primordial disposition.

Levinas often shared his reflections regarding language, intensely aware of the difficulties that his own use of the philosophical words inherited from the tradition could not easily avoid. In "Language and Proximity," Levinas argues that what he terms "ethical language"

> does not proceed from a special moral experience, independent of the description developed until then. It comes from the very meaning of approach, which contrasts with knowledge, [and] of the face which contrasts with phenomena.

Thus, he says,

> Ethical language alone succeeds in being equal to the paradox in which phenomenology is abruptly thrown: starting from the neighbor, it reads this paradox in the midst of an absence which orders it as a face.[19]

Two statements in *Otherwise than Being* are perhaps even more illuminating:

> Ethical language, which phenomenology resorts to in order to make its own interruption, does not come from an ethical intervention laid out over descriptions. It is the very meaning of the approach which contrasts with knowing. . . . A description that at the beginning knows only *being* and *beyond being* turns [i.e., in order to serve, it is obliged to turn] into ethical language.[20]

For, according to Levinas, only

> The tropes of ethical language are found to be adequate for certain structures of the description: for the sense of the approach in its contrast with knowing, [for] the face in its contrast with a phenomenon. (OB 120, AE 155)

Only an evocative, invocative, exhortatory use of language, a metaphorical and poetizing use of language, a revelatory use of language, a rhetorical form that uses equivocation to speak on and to several different levels of experience at the same time, can function performatively, enacting what at the same time it describes, speaking with phenomenological fidelity of a deep truth that we have concealed from ourselves, speaking in a way that might radically interrupt and alter our conventional and superficial moral experience, our conventional moral sensibility and perception—perhaps even bringing about certain shifts without the mediation of deliberation and will.

What Levinas says is accordingly meant to be phenomenologically true: not, however, of conventional and superficial moral experience, but rather in regard to the deeper, more primordial (and thus pre-conventional) dispositions of our moral nature, the realization of which (in both senses of this term) would constitute a "post-conventional" moral experience, a sense of responsibility and obligation not only beyond the conventional, but even beyond the Kantian "Sollen" of moral autonomy, since, in its extreme urgency and exigency, the sense of obligation and responsibility [1] takes hold of us at a primordial level of our embodiment, prior to reflective judgment and even prior to volition, and [2] demands that we realize it in taking on a supererogatory responsibility that is possible only to the extent that we undergo a radical "sacrifice" of our ego-logical identity, subjecting its very existence to the welfare of the other. The moral demands that Levinas deciphers are unquestionably extreme. But we are self-interpreting beings; so it is not impossible that his efforts to invoke and awaken in us such a new self-understanding could actually motivate a process of self-transformation. Thus, for one to accept as true the deep phenomenological descriptions that Levinas formulates is to let oneself be correspondingly (i.e., co-respondingly) transformed by them. What Levinas says about our moral experience of the other is indeed, then, phenomenological, bringing-forth a certain latency, a certain suppressed or concealed potential. But this potential—certain primordial, proto-moral dispositions—is not an inert, already-made, fully formed implicit reality to which the truth of the phenomenological discourse needs only to be an adequately explicit correlation or correspondence, merely rendering descriptively explicit what was already there implicitly, merely describing without in any way affecting and altering—or say performing—the implicit dispositions.[21]

In order to avoid inertness, his discourse, his rhetoric, must be a saying the truth of which cannot be understood in terms of the correspondence theory of truth, because its truth exceeds the said. What the correspondence theory of truth misses, or rather conceals, is precisely the co-responding, the way certain descriptive language can engage with our experiencing, its evocative, affectively charged character setting in motion resonances and reverberations that can bring forth new configurations of meaning, of sense.

This is what Levinas means, I believe, when he insists that his thinking cannot be understood in terms of "disclosure." As saying, the truth that concerns him exceeds the said because it not only speaks descriptively about us to us, saying the *present* character of our experience, but it also speaks performatively, diachronically, diacritically, saying this present experience in a way that makes contact with—and brings out—its deeper, conventionally concealed moral disposition. Moreover—and this is a crucial moment in the excessiveness, the wildness, the diachronicity, of the saying, corresponding to the double tonality, the equivocal mode of the rhetoric—

saying continues to speak about them to us *while* they are undergoing the transformative process, working through the difference between the "always already" and the "not yet." For although our moral responsibility to and for the other has *always already* taken hold of us, subjecting us to its alterity, it has *not yet* been realized—in both senses of this term. Levinas addresses us, then, in such a way that the saying diachronically exceeds the said by virtue of its being able still to communicate with us, still to function with descriptive fidelity and revelatory power, in the articulation of the character of our moral experience even after our experience has undergone an alteration in response to the initial provocative invocation. Since the truth is in the saying and its enactments, its alterations of experience, the temporality of the saying must be diachronic: unlike the said, it can "have" something to say not only *before* the experiential shift that, with infinite respect and patience, it might provoke, but it can continue to speak, to resonate, *even after* the shift it has encouraged. Thus, Levinas refers to the work of his phenomenological discourse as "revelatory." I suggest that another word for this might perhaps be "performative." In any case, the crucial point for Levinas is that the way in which we think and say the sublimity of our moral experience must somehow avoid reifying and totalizing.

But this is possible for him only insofar as we understand his words—words referring, for example, to the face, the body, the flesh, and vision (i.e., sight, gaze, seeing, and looking)—as literal, rather than merely figurative, merely ornamental, "metaphorical" in *that* sense. Or if we want to read his words as metaphorical, then I think we should take them to be used in accordance with the Greek etymology of the word "metaphor," i.e., as used in a way that deeply moves us, carrying our experience forward into its transformation. But in *this* sense of the word "metaphor" his words are being used literally, but in such a way that they may *alter* that to which they are referring in the very process of referring. In this way, we can understand his words as quite "properly" phenomenological, albeit truthful only to that dimension of our experience that they bring out from its ordinary, conventional concealment. And therefore also as disturbing and disruptive—quite improper—in relation to the ordinary meanings we give to the words. Levinas's words effect a certain erasure, a certain *Aufhebung*, a sublation not strictly Hegelian, that always brings the old context of meanings with it, but only in a process that radically alters their sense. (And what we take to be "what was" implicit *is* not what was implicit, but rather what *becomes* what was implicit only now, in the present process of making explicit.) But ultimately, the dimensions of the moral experience that

Levinas describes and explicates are such that they must be understood to unfold within a temporality beyond being: the temporality, namely, of an immemorial "always already" that is also an infinitely deferred "not yet." Thus, in a passivity prior to consciousness, prior to volition, prior to freedom, we are always already claimed by and for a supererogatory responsibility to and for the other: an obligation to and for the other has always already taken hold of us—through our very flesh. However, this responsibility has not yet been consciously enacted. It is up to us to realize it in the exercise of our freedom.

In "The Other of Justice,"[22] Axel Honneth expressed an uncertainty that many of Levinas's readers share regarding the face-to-face ethical relation: Is it primarily visual or is it primarily a matter of conversation? In his discussion of this study,[23] Simon Critchley holds—and I think that he is right—that the ethical relation can, as it were, "fulfill" itself only in conversation; but I think that it would be a mistake to exclude the visual dimension altogether, because that would then ignore a crucial dimension of our sensibility: what I am calling the deeply elemental "bodily felt sense" that may (come to) be formed through the *exposure* constitutive of the immediacy of visual relation. But it is difficult to resolve all the perplexities surrounding this question. It seems to me that what is needed to carry Levinas's thinking forward is a "thicker," more narrative phenomenology, bringing out the phases and dimensions of moral development, concentrating through its double tonality on the articulation of the deeper dispositions of our bodily sensibility, making contact with the proto-moral nature of our primordial, pre-conventional embodiment.

Levinas speaks of the face, of the "I" looking and seeing the face of the other; yet he denies that it is a question of perception (EaI 85–87). How can this be? Should we take him to be withdrawing the face altogether from the realm of the visible? Then his words—"face," "looking," "seeing"—could only assume a metaphorical meaning, or rather, as I would prefer to say, a metaphorical use, where by "metaphorical use" we would be compelled to admit that we could make no connections with, and draw no implications for, our moral experience of the (face of the) other. In answer, for example, to the question, whether the face is something given in intuition, Levinas replies in the negative. But that is only because he holds that, in what the philosophical tradition *represents* with the concept of "intuition"—and also, for that matter, in what philosophical thought has always represented with the concept of "perception," there is a strong, virtually irresistible tendency to possess and appropriate, to reify and totalize, reducing the other to the same, whereas the deep experience of the face that he wants to solicit and elicit, or invoke and evoke, must constitute an *absolute* relation to the face, letting the other's way of presenting herself to me exceed the idea of the other in me. Furthermore, by the same logic, a logic that "respects" the immeasurable and incomparable dimensionality, the withdrawal and absence of the face, the face is not to be described as a "phenomenon," because this word cannot easily be separated from the ontological discourse of disclosure, of correlations in the realm of knowledge, in which it has figured since Kant, and Levinas is attempting to articulate a radically different experience with the face of the other. (In the preceding sentence, I have placed the word "respect" between scare-quotes in order to indicate that it must be understood differently, because as used in that sentence it no longer belongs to the discourse of moral symmetry and equivalence.) Nor is it a question of the "physical" face, the face as (i.e., reduced to or totally identified with) its merely physical being.[24] For the face can no more be reduced to the physical than can the meaning of our humanity. But this must not be taken to mean a total withdrawal of the face from the physical—as if the face could manifest without physical incarnation. Nor should we draw the conclusion that, if Levinas is not referring to the face in its physicality, is not referring to "the physical face," he must be using words in a "merely metaphorical" sense.

To conclude that, whatever Levinas may mean by the "face," there can be no connection with the face in its physicality, the face as a physical manifestation, the face of our incarnate experience, would be a tragic error. It would subtract from the introduction of the face-to-face relation the promise of a new way of thinking about our moral experience. Levinas's attempt to think the ethical relation in terms of the face-to-face seems to promise new possibilities for thought and experience; but this promise is annulled when the face is not thought literally, as bearing on our experience. Likewise, when he denies that our relation to the face is "perception," it would be quite perverse to conclude that the relation is instead to be conceived, or represented, as purely "spiritual," "mental," "cognitive," "intellectual," or "linguistic." I read Levinas's denial as a forceful way of saying that we need radically to rethink what "perception" is in the light of our experience of the other in the face-to-face relation. His way of saying this is exaggerated, paradoxical, in order to break through prevailing habits of thought. The deep, culturally concealed experience of the face-to-face ethical relation that Levinas is pointing towards both is and is not faithfully rendered, both is and is not appropriately contacted, by the philosophical concept of "perception." But it is necessary for us to insist that, through this concept, we can at least glimpse a trace of the dimensionality of the moral experience that Levinas wants to evoke.

Similar comments must be made with regard to Levinas's invocations of the body, the flesh, and vision. They are all to be understood as pointing to an elemental experience which is beyond essence, beyond the ontology of our philosophical representations, "merely" the traces—tracings—of the physical, of what is understood in conventional morality. But they are not mere metaphors: he means to be referring to our embodiment, our flesh, our ways of touching others, our ways of looking at people and seeing their humanity. But since his hope is to communicate in a way that might enable us to undergo profound alterations in our experience, his mode of discourse is compelled to assume a certain doubleness, addressing "what is" in a way that solicits what could be otherwise.[25] And yet, out of the deepest solicitude for our moral singularity and alterity, he lets us respond to the possibilities that his discourse evokes according to our own rhythm, our own inner necessity. (The communicative problem that we are attempting to understand, here, is not, I think, altogether different from the problem about which Kierkegaard wrote in his *Concluding Unscientific Postscript.*[26] There, too, it was a question of an experience-altering communication that truly respects the moral singularity and otherness of the other.) He means at one and the same time both our seeing as we understand it and our seeing otherwise. With the same words, he addresses us simultaneously in terms of our present (presently recognized) conventional experience and also in terms of a (perhaps presently unrecognized) pre-conventional dimension of our experience, with which we could be moved to make some meaningful bodily felt contact, and in contactful relation to which our present conventional experience could (perhaps) undergo a radical alteration. Only a diachronic rhetorical mode would be able to work this way, exceeding the spellbinding logic of the same.[27]

Because of our nature as reflective, self-interpreting beings, the phenomenological description that emerges from our self-reflection can set in motion, can motivate, can enact a process of deep self-transformation. Thus, when one wholeheartedly accepts as true a deep phenomenological description, one is already to some extent undergoing a co-responding process of self-transformation. Levinas uses the constative, descriptive mode of language in ways that enable it to touch and move us, enacting, bringing into being, that of which it speaks. What I think that his *descriptions* attempt to articulate are the primordial *inscriptions* of moral responsibility, the traces of our primordial subjection to moral obligation, that are registered in the

depths of our flesh; and it is in the struggle to make the impossible connection between description and inscription and bring it into our felt awareness that his descriptions assume their *prescriptive* force. But in suggesting
the word "prescriptive" here, I of course do not mean to imply that Levinas
is trying to dictate or impose how we should live our lives, but rather—if I
may anticipate here what is to come—that his phenomenological descriptions refer, in a paradoxical, diachronic temporality, to an inscription of responsibility that takes hold of us bodily long before its moral assignment
can be consciously realized and taken up by our freedom. The prefix in my
use of the word "prescription" is accordingly meant to carry the sense of
"before," referring to the "always already" of an "event" of inscription that
(must have) preceded consciousness, preceded ego, and comes to heightened
consciousness through the struggle for its recuperation in phenomenological description.

I. LIGHT AND POWER:
AN ANCIENT CLANDESTINE FRIENDSHIP

In "Diachrony and Representation" (1985), we find Levinas still engaging the question of vision, giving thought to the ocularcentrism of our
civilization:

> The sphere of intelligibility—the reasonable [*du sensé*]—in which
> everyday life as well as the tradition of our philosophic and scientific
> thought maintains itself, is characterized by vision. The structure of a
> *seeing* having the *seen* for its object and theme—the so-called inten-
> tional structure—is found in all the modes of sensibility having access
> to things. . . . But it is apparent that it is also found in the company hu-
> man beings keep among themselves, between beings who speak to one
> another, and of whom it is said that they 'see one another' ['*qu'ils se
> voient*']. Thus the priority of knowledge [*connaître*] is announced.[28]

For Levinas, as we shall see, it will always be the sociality or ethics of the
gaze, and in particular, the relation between my gaze and the presence of
the other (*autrui*), that constitutes the problematic which thought must engage. "We must," as he says in *Totality and Infinity*, a much earlier work,
"analyze more closely the privilege of vision" (TaI 189, TeI 163). Thinking
of Heidegger's account, according to which (on Levinas's reading) the gift
of the light is the opening or clearing of an openness for vision to take place,
Levinas argues, as if registering what must be an objection to such an account, that "a being comes as though from nothingness" (ibid.). And he

concludes his remarks on vision by saying that "we find this scheme of vision from Aristotle to Heidegger" (ibid.). The problem, for Levinas, is thus clear: "in the light of a generality which does not exist is established the relation with the individual" (ibid.).

According to Jacques Derrida, Levinas was the first philosopher to give thought to "the ancient clandestine friendship between light and power, the ancient complicity between theoretical objectivity and technico-political possession."[29] On Derrida's reading, Levinas was already formulating an argument against the hegemony of vision in his *Théorie de l'Intuition dans la Phénoménologie de Husserl*. In that very early work, Levinas argues against the imperialism of *theoria*, the primacy of theoretical consciousness and its theoretical glance. For Levinas, even transcendental phenomenology, Husserl's method for rescuing the phenomenon, experience, from the violence of a philosophical thought that would betray it by requiring it to satisfy the ideal of objectivity, intelligibility, transparency, and lucidity, is ultimately guilty of intrigues with violence, reducing the radically other (*autrui*) to the same. For Levinas, the entire history of philosophy—its humanism and its Enlightenment—can only be a history of its commitment to light: the "violence of light." (In fact, even the *word* "history" derives from a root which refers to sight. History consists of the stories that are told by those who were eyewitnesses to the events in question. But does this necessarily mean, as Giorgio Agamben implies,[30] that in overcoming the metaphysics of presence, this original experience of history, seemingly bound to the authority of the gaze, must be also be overcome?) However, as we shall see, Derrida is surely right in maintaining that Levinas did not, and perhaps could not, overcome the authority of the gaze and liberate his ethics from the vision-generated, vision-centered rhetoric out of which philosophical thought has always been constructed. "How," Derrida asks, "will the metaphysics of the face as the *epiphany* of the other free itself of light?"[31] "What language will ever escape it?"[32] On my reading, however, Levinas already understood this point of difficulty. In any case, it must, I think, be acknowledged that Levinas, without twisting free altogether of the ocular language—as he says in *Totality and Infinity*,[33] "Ethics is the spiritual optics"—succeeded nevertheless in suggesting, albeit, perhaps, with too much equivocation or discretion, a significant challenge to the dominant way of understanding (re-presenting) vision, questioning the historical inevitability of the subject-object structure and stressing the primacy of being sensibly affected over against the sovereignty claimed by cognition and theoretical contemplation.[34]

In an essay on Samuel Beckett's *Endgame,* Adorno observes that "Ontology comes into its own as the pathogenesis of the false life."[35] Throughout his work, Levinas associates the historically dominant concepts of ontology—truth, knowledge, reason, reflection, objectivity, and certainty— with a philosophical discourse saturated by the power of light and the violence of a logic of the same.[36] This association constitutes the grounds for his relentless and unsparing critique of the "ontological imperialism" (TaI 44, TeI 15) inherent in all these concepts peculiar to our philosophical tradition:

> The light that permits encountering something other than the self makes it encountered as if this thing came from the ego. The light, brightness, is intelligibility itself; making everything come from me, it reduces every experience to an element of reminiscence. Reason is solitary. And in this sense, knowledge never encounters anything truly other in the world.[37]

Knowledge, the bringing of light, is always only an instrument of egological power, ego-logical mastery:

> To know amounts to grasping being out of nothing or reducing it to nothing, removing from it its alterity. This result is obtained from the moment of the first ray of light. To illuminate is to remove from being its resistance, because light opens a horizon and empties space— delivers being out of nothingness. . . . The ideal of Socratic truth rests on the essential self-sufficiency of the same, its identification in ipseity, its egoism. Philosophy is an egology. (TaI 44, TeI 14)

The hermeneutical glance, seeing the other person *as* something, inevitably subjects the other to the violence of classificaiton, a system of categories. Hermeneutics too must therefore be repudiated, insofar as it consists in a showing, a making-present, a bringing-to-light, that assume the possibility of a complete convergence, a total correlation, between the subject and the object of knowledge, or that assume "revelation" to bring a totally determinate "essence" to light, in both cases reducing the other to the same. Reason, which is the demand for universality of knowledge, favors "the unlimitedness of light and the impossibility for anything to be on the outside" (TO 65, TA 48). Light, servant of a totalizing Reason that encompasses everything within its universality, reduces transcendence to the immediate presence of "evidence," its most lucid immanence. Light and Reason are allies because Reason demands total lucidity, total transparency, total visibility. Charging Heidegger—but, I think, inaccurately, unfairly—with an "ontological imperialism" driven by the metaphorics of light, Levinas contends that, for Heidegger,

> what commands the non-coinciding of thought with the existent . . . is a phosphorescence, a luminosity, a generous effulgence. The existing of the existent is converted into intelligibility; its independence is a surrender in radiation. . . . Reason seizes upon the existent through the void and nothingness of existing—wholly light and phosphorescence. Approached from being, from the luminous horizon where it has its silhouette, but has lost its face, the existent is the very appeal that is addressed to comprehension. (TaI 45, TeI 15)

Taking truth out of this metaphorics, Levinas accordingly asserts that, "If truth arises in the *absolute experience* in which being gleams with its own light, then truth is produced only in veritable conversation or in justice" (TaI 71, TeI 43). This, it could be said, is the point where one must locate Levinas's "linguistic turn": until we are situated in language, we cannot "know" what we are seeing—we may not really *see* until conversation with others makes us (able to) see.[38] But justice may still depend on seeing— although it must, according to liberal constitutions, be *blind* to some consequential differences.

There are instructive affinities in this regard with Walter Benjamin, who was likewise compelled to begin his thinking with the recognition that, as he worded it, "The gaze [*Blick*] is the natural propensity [*Neige*] of the human being."[39] Derrida might say that this propensity is precisely our phototropism. It is also our cognitive and volitional directedness, our intentionality. Thus, another affinity between Levinas and Benjamin: they both challenge intentionality because of its inherent willfulness, its egoity, its reduction of radical transcendence, its refusal of exposure. For example, in the Preface to *Totality and Infinity*, unfortunately ignoring Husserl's late manuscripts, where the *Stimmung* of a primordial, corporeal intentionality, a *fungierende Intentionalität*, is brought to articulation, Levinas writes: "intentionality, where thought remains an *adequation* with the object, does not define consciousness at its fundamental level. All knowing, as intentionality, already presupposes the idea of infinity, which is preëminently *non-adequation*." (TaI 27, TeI xv. Also see OB 23–59, AE 29–76. But also note TaI 23, TeI xii, where he broaches the intriguing thought of a radically different vision, a wholly different way of looking and seeing, and where, correspondingly, instead of rejecting intentionality altogether, he suggests the possibility of a different intentionality, "bereft of the synoptic and totalizing virtues of [normal, modern] vision, a relation or an intentionality of a wholly different type." It is toward the elaboration of such a vision, a vision of radically different character, that my reflections on Levinas, here, may indicate the way.) As for Benjamin, it is in his "Epistemo-Critical Prologue" to *The Origin of German Tragic Drama*, that we find his strongest argument against intentionality:

> Truth does not enter into relationships, particularly intentional ones. The object of knowledge, determined as it is by the intention inherent in the concept, is not the truth. Truth is an intentionless state of being, made up of ideas. The proper approach to it [*Das ihr gemäße* Verhalten] is not therefore one of intention and knowledge, but rather a total immersion and absorption [*Eingehen und Verschwinden*] in it. Truth is the death of intention [*Die Wahrheit ist der Tod der Intention*].[40]

If the gaze is the ultimate manifestation of willful directedness, of phototropic intentionality, it is also, as Benjamin's carefully chosen word, *Neige*, suggests, not only our natural propensity, but also our decline, our fall into the dregs.

"We contest vision its primacy in being." For Levinas, it seems, vision—and its accomplice, the light that makes vision possible—inevitably effectuate a "suppression of the other" (TaI 302, TeI 279). "Transcendence," he insists, cannot be understood in terms of a vision of the Other, but only in terms of a primordial "donation." A "sacrifice" (TaI 174, TeI 149). "Vision," he says, "is not a transcendence. . . . It opens nothing that, beyond the same, would be absolutely other, that is, in itself. Light conditions the relations between data; it makes possible the signification of objects that border one another. It does not enable one to approach them face to face" (TaI 191, TeI 165–66). One might suppose that, with the concession that vision takes place within a field, and that this field is bounded by a horizon that opens out into the invisible—an account of vision that we find in Heidegger and Merleau-Ponty, Levinas would admit the transcendence in vision. Instead, he argues, against Heidegger, that

> to see is always to see on the horizon. The vision that apprehends on the horizon does not encounter a being out of what is beyond all being. Vision is a forgetting of the *there is* [*il y a*] because of the essential satisfaction, the agreeableness [*agrément*] of sensibility, enjoyment, contentment with the finite without concern for the infinite. (TaI 191, TeI 166)

Levinas articulates well, here, Heidegger's critique of a "fallen" vision. But Heidegger draws a crucial distinction between the "forgetful" vision of everyday life and a vision that is grounded in ontological recollection. Levinas does not seem to recognize this distinction—at least not in this text.

Here, his sweeping indictment sees no alternative potential: the fault in vision is hopelessly essentialized. In a later writing, however, while still arguing against vision, he suggests a very different experience with vision,
one in which its "passivity," its "subjectivity," "subjectivity" in the sense of
"subjection," and not its outwardly directed intentionality, its assertive
willfulness, comes to light:

> Sight is, to be sure, an openness, a consciousness, and all sensibility,
> opening as a consciousness, is called vision; but [even] in its subordina-
> tion to cognition, sight [still] maintains contact and proximity. The visi-
> ble caresses the eye. One sees and hears like one touches.[41]

This experience of the "caress" is a significant concession, because it follows
Merleau-Ponty in suggesting that there is, or could be, a gaze that is not
bent on domination, not driven by the need to reduce the other to the same:
a gaze, therefore, "beyond being," beyond ontology. And, as we shall see, it
also has implications for the extension of the ethical relation into the political context of justice.

Levinas's attitude toward vision is actually quite complicated, because,
even in *Totality and Infinity*, where there are passages in which he condemns vision in a seemingly sweeping indictment, there are also passages
where (in an unfair misreading) he attacks what he takes to be Heidegger's
fatalism and hints at the possibility of an interruption in the history of a
totalizing and reifying vision:

> [the] interpretation of experience on the basis of vision and touch is not
> due to chance and can accordingly expand into a civilization. It is incon-
> testable that objectification operates in the gaze in a privileged way;
> [but] it is not certain that its tendency to inform every experience is in-
> scribed, and unequivocally so, in being. (TaI 188, TeI 163)

Indeed, in the Preface to this work, in addition to the remark (already cited)
about a radically different "type" of vision, he even seems to recognize for
vision an emancipatory and redemptive service:

> We oppose to the objectivism of war a subjectivity born from the es-
> chatological vision. (TaI 25, TeI xiv)

This radically different way of seeing—but is it really a question of seeing
with the eyes, or should this reference to "vision" be read as "merely"
metaphorical?—is even recognized to be crucial for the emergence of a radically different form of subjectivity—a subjectivity "founded in the idea of
the infinite," a subjectivity, therefore, in which the ethical vocation would
be taken to heart. (A major concern of Levinas's work consists in articulating and bringing forth an experience and conception of the subjectivity of

the subject that would be radically different from, and indeed an uncompromising repudiation of, its entire historical formation as represented and produced by the culture of modernity. Briefly stated, the difference is between the subject as an ego-logical center of power, an origin of activity for the sake of its self-preservation and self-interest, and the subject as subjected by way of flesh and sensibility to the categorical moral imperative embodied in the other person.)

There is a passage in *Totality and Infinity* (TaI 89, TeI 61) where Levinas speaks of "seeing in justice and injustice." So it might seem that he is ready at least in principle to trust our eyes, to entrust the difference between justice and injustice to the capacity of our eyes for *seeing* the difference. But there are persistent equivocations in his discussions of seeing, of vision—equivocations, for example, that make many of his readers think it uncertain whether he is actually referring to our experience with vision or whether, instead, he is speaking "merely" metaphorically, and whether he is recognizing the possibility of a different way of seeing, or instead merely calling for the end of an ocularcentric ethics, morality, and politics.

I will argue that Levinas's references to vision are not "merely" metaphorical, but that their strangeness and peculiarity are due to the fact that he wants to "withdraw" from vision as it is commonly realized in our culture and correspondingly represented by reflection in philosophical thought, and that he wants, moreover, not only to disturb, to question, to interrupt such vision, but to evoke in us a radically different vision. I think it also true, however, that to some extent, the perplexing ambiguities surrounding vision in *Totality and Infinity* are due to the fact that his thinking was undergoing a transition in that work from an account of the ethical relation in terms of the gaze to an account in which what he calls "saying" becomes the crucial medium for evoking the deep experience of the ethical relation toward which he is directing us.

For the most part, however, both in his early and in his late writings, Levinas regards vision—and the hegemony of vision as paradigm of knowledge, truth and reality in the thinking of philosophy—with unqualified suspicion. Examining "the formal logic of the gaze" (TaI 289, TeI 265), he concludes that it is a "panoramic look" (TaI 220, TeI 195; also see TaI 294, TeI 270–71) inherently blind to manifestations of infinity and allied with the forces of totality: the gaze, he says, "totalizes the multiple" (TaI 292, TeI 268; also see TaI 305, TeI 282). And it imposes a reified presence on all the beings that it encounters.[42] Formulating his disagreement with Husserl, and thus, a fortiori, with all versions of transcendental idealism, Levinas argues that vision "is essentially an *adequation* of exteriority [otherness] with interiority [i.e., the conditions of sameness imposed by ego-logical subjectivity]: in it exteriority is reabsorbed in the contemplative soul and, as an *adequate idea*, revealed to be a priori, the result of a *Sinngebung*. The exteriority of discourse cannot be converted into interiority [as idealism always tries to do]" (TaI 295, TeI 271. See also *Ethics and Infinity* 87). An equally offensive adequation can be found, *mutatis mutandis*, in the gaze that operates in the discourse of empiricism, for its objectivism is a requirement, a condition, that the "subject" imposes on the field of its gaze. But in this indictment of vision, is he not essentializing it? Is he not assuming the impossibility of altering it?[43]

In *Totality and Infinity*, Levinas attempts to counter the domination of vision and its supposedly insurmountable epistemo-ontological norm of *adequatio* by reminding us of the invisible, the limits of our vision and comprehension, and the desire of the spirit for a recognition of that which exceeds the presence of the given:

> Invisibility does not denote an absence of relation; it implies relations with what is not given, of which there is no idea. Vision is an adequation of the idea with the thing, a comprehension that encompasses. Non-adequation does not denote a simple negation or an obscurity of the idea, but—beyond the light and the night, beyond the knowledge measuring beings—the inordinateness of Desire. Desire is desire for the absolutely other. (TaI 34, TeI 4)

It is a question of a "metaphysics" that, in opposition to the totalizing and reifying effects of "ontology," "desires the other beyond satisfactions," which therefore "understands the remoteness, the alterity, and the exteriority of the other. For Desire, this alterity, non-adequate to the idea, has a meaning. It is understood as the alterity of the Other and of the Most-High" (ibid.). In a strikingly similar spirit, Max Horkheimer, in a 1970 conversation with Helmut Gumnior, evoked what he called our "Sehnsucht nach dem ganz Anderen" (longing for the wholly other).[44] But for Horkheimer, traumatized by the Holocaust, resorting to this evocation is an admission that philosophical thought is powerless and hopeless in the face of a future he sees continuing the totalitarian exclusion of the radically other. Levinas is perhaps able to sustain a deeper faith in the promise of redemption; but his faith is constantly exposed to suffering. The promise, the eschatological vision—nothing more, now, than the trace of a passing trace—is endlessly deferred.

Longing for the wholly other. But how is the wholly other to be seen? How is the gaze to relate to the invisible? How can one put the wholly other into images? Levinas partially answers these questions by defining a difference between "disclosure" (*dévoilement*) and "revelation" (*révélation*), correlating disclosure with vision and revelation with speech:

> To put speech at the origin of truth is to abandon the thesis that disclosure, which implies the solitude of vision, is the first work of truth.
> (TaI 99, TeI 72)

"To disclose a thing is," he says, "to clarify it by forms: to find for it a place in the totality" (TaI 74, TeI 47). Benjamin is helpful here, because he, like Levinas, wants to distinguish between a "revelation" of truth and its totalizing, reifying "exposure." Thus, in the "Epistemo-Critical Prologue" to the *Trauerspiel* essay, he states that "truth is not a process of exposure [*Enthüllung*] which destroys the secret, but a revelation [*Offenbarung*] which does justice to it."[45] To do justice to the truth is to protect and preserve its dimensionality of concealment, its reach into the invisible. Only in this way is the truth saved from dogmatism, pretensions to absolutism, authoritarian and totalitarian regimes of power. Only in this way are the limits of human reason, shattered and left in ruins when it attempts to exceed its horizons, its conditions of possibility, recognized and granted their measure. But why does Levinas think that placing the origin of truth in speech gives it more protection from reification than vision? Or is it a matter of protection? If speech is the origin of truth, that is because it is communication. But speech can deceive—and a wink, a glance, a look can speak, sometimes, more plainly, more revealingly, more consolingly, than words.

Unfortunately, there are times when Levinas connects disclosure in an essentializing way not only with vision, but also with phenomenology, the method for thinking about the dimensions of our experience as lived that he inherited from Husserl, often associating the method—as if in an essential way—with vision, light, knowledge, and disclosure; but sometimes he also recognizes that phenomenology can bring us to the *limits* of disclosure, where an experience of transcendence could breach the ego's cognitive defenses and leave us exposed and vulnerable. I would argue that, radically conceived, phenomenology can no longer be contained within disclosure and the correspondence theory of truth. Nor must vision be limited to disclosure, to a truth by correspondence and adequation. Against disclosure—and phenomenology as disclosure, Levinas writes:

> The welcoming of the face and the work of justice—which condition the birth of truth itself—are not interpretable in terms of disclosure.
> (TaI 28, TeI, xvi)

Phenomenology, here understood as "the comprehension effected through a bringing to light," is accordingly identified with and limited to disclosure, correlation, equivalence:

> [it] does not constitute the ultimate event of being itself. The relation between the same and the other is not always reducible to knowledge of the other by the same, nor even to the *revelation* of the other to the same, which is fundamentally different from disclosure. (Ibid.)

It may be possible to articulate knowledge of *things* in terms of a phenomenology of disclosure; but what concerns Levinas is our experience of other people, and this, he believes, since it involves a relation to the transcendent, the infinite, the invisible, cannot be comprehended within such a phenomenology. The other is *not* a "phenomenon," not an "appearance"—or at least not, I want to add, in the Husserlian sense:

> contrary to all the conditions for the visibility of objects, the being is not placed in the light of another, but presents itself in the manifestation that should announce it; it is present as directing this very manifestation—present before the manifestation, which only manifests it. The absolute experience is not disclosure but revelation: a coinciding of the expressed with him who expresses, which is the privileged manifestation of the Other, the manifestation of a face over and above form. (TaI 65–66, TeI 37)

But could there be a different phenomenology, a phenomenology that would be obedient to revelation, a phenomenology that would, by virtue of its openness, its exposure to the other, assist the other in living beyond essence, beyond typologies, "otherwise than being"? Why couldn't Heidegger's radical conception of phenomenology, as formulated at the beginning of *Being and Time* (letting what is, what is presencing, show itself from out of itself), in which he profoundly alters Husserl's conception, manifest the morally imperative recognition, respect, and care for the other? Why does Levinas equate phenomenology with Husserl's transcendental version? This is, I think, just what he does when he argues that

> consciousness does not consist in equaling being with representation, in tending to the full light in which this adequation is to be sought, but rather in overflowing this play of light—this phenomenology—and in accomplishing events whose ultimate signification . . . does not lie in disclosing. (TaI 27–28, TeI xvi)

Disclosing requires of the other, or imposes on the other, a fixed identity; revelation welcomes, is receptive to, the other's deepest identity-transcending, essence-transcending needs. Levinas accordingly believes that, in the presence of an other human being, vision is confronted with a dimensionality, an invisibility, that it cannot possibly comprehend. Faced with this alterity, the composure of the gaze, its indifferent serenity, is irrevocably shattered:

> Behold vision turning back into non-vision, into the refutation of vision within the sight's center, into that of which vision is but a forgetfulness and re-presentation.[46]

Non-vision, the invisible, the impossibly visible, subverts the discourse of ontology and the pretensions of a rationality, a knowledge, that depends on totalizability and possession.

"Western philosophy," according to Levinas, "has most often been an ontology: a reduction of the other to the same . . . that ensures the comprehension of being" (TaI 43, TeI 13). Thus, Levinas will argue that our ontology has been, and still is, "a philosophy of injustice":

> Ontology as first philosophy is a philosophy of power. It issues in the State and in the non-violence of the totality, without securing itself against the violence from which this non-violence lives, and which appears in the tyranny of the State. Truth, which should reconcile persons, here exists anonymously. Universality presents itself as impersonal; and this is another inhumanity. (TaI 46, TeI 16)

Consistent with this analysis, Levinas tends to regard the world-disclosure constitutive of "knowledge," of "com-prehension," as the principal objective of a systematic, *instrumental* rationality: "we disclose," he says, "only with respect to a project" (TaI 64, TeI 36).

But, although he certainly does not condemn knowledge as such, does not even condemn instrumental rationality as such, he often seems not to allow or recognize any other form of rationality. In "L'Ontologie Est-elle Fondamentale?," for example, he seems to be suggesting that "the rational reduces to power over the object."[47] (In this regard, his critique of reason is quite similar to the critique that Horkheimer and Adorno make in *Dialectic of Enlightenment*. And this suggests that it may be charged with similar objections. Thus, it might be argued, against all three, that the violence is not in reason as such but rather in its abuse, or in its inadequate and one-sided development.) Nor is there recognition of a *knowledge* appropriate to the ethical relation, because all knowledge, for him, reduces the other to the same, the equal:

> Knowledge is always an adequation between thought and what it thinks. . . . Knowledge has always been interpreted as assimilation. Even the most surprising discoveries end by being absorbed,

comprehended with all that there is of "prehending" in "comprehending." The most audacious and remote knowledge does not put us in communion with the truly other; it does not take the place of sociality; it is still always a solitude.[48]

The inherent tendency of knowledge is always, it seems, "the suppression of alterity" and "a thought of the equal" (EaI 66, 91; EeI 71, 96).

Maintaining, moreover, that the "original ethical impulse" is always already violated once it is understood in the neutral impersonal light of reason, Levinas often appears to leave no room for a "public use of reason" on the side of justice—a justice of reason that would side with the different, the other, the stranger, the poor, the widow, the orphan. This is a question that still needs to be worked out within the compass of Levinas's thought.

Justice for the other, justice to the other: Levinas shows us that there are many more dimensions to justice—but also that justice is more aporetic—than philosophical thinking has recognized. Thus he shows that even the conception of consciousness that defines it in terms of intentionality bears on the possibility of a moral and political order in which the other can receive justice. Near the beginning of *Totality and Infinity*, Levinas distances his thinking from that of Husserl. He writes that

> this book will present subjectivity as welcoming the Other [*l'Autrui*], as hospitality; in it the idea of infinity is consummated. Hence, intentionality, where thought remains an adequation with the object, does not define consciousness at its most fundamental level. (TaI 27, TeI xv)

This is his principal argument against intentionality.[49] But he does not want to abandon phenomenology. What he therefore attempts to work out is the phenomenology of a relation to the other that precedes the emergence of intentionality as he understands it—in other words, without intentionality—a phenomenology that does not begin from consciousness. We are not compelled to read this as a denial that there is a legitimate application for the concept of intentionality; it may be read as saying only that, before the symmetry and velleity of the subject-object (noesis-noema) correlation, the subject is always already passively engaged by a more primordial relation with the other: a relation that takes place, as we shall see, in a radically different way.

This means, however, that there is, for Levinas, a radically different subject, a subject whose existence and life the philosophical discourse of modernity has not been willing to acknowledge. In the bourgeois philosophies of modernity, the subject is understood as a self-made ego-logical individual, a solitary monad, confidently defined by its self-containedness, its self-sufficiency, its self-groundedness, and its resourcefulness in self-preservation. The glorious essence of this subject is freedom: a life measured by its enjoyment of independence and autonomy.[50] According to the prevailing ideological narrative, this subject desires to be in absolute possession and control of whatever it encounters: its freedom, its autonomy, consists in the pursuit of private interests and pleasures. But, paradoxically, its will to power requires, at the same time, a strong system of ego-logical defenses, ensuring its impenetrability, marking its closure: in order to avoid losing control, this subject must *receive* nothing. Nor can it *give* without conditions that would inscribe the gesture in an exchange economy ruled by the logic of equivalence. Thus, the ultimate project of the modern subject's freedom can only lie in a contradiction:

> in [guaranteeing] this permanence of the same, which is reason. Cognition is the deployment of this identity; it is freedom. That reason in the last analysis would be the manifestation of a freedom, neutralizing the other and encompassing him, can come as no surprise once it was laid down that sovereign reason knows only itself, that nothing limits it. The neutralization of the other which becomes theme or object—appearing, that is, taking its place in the light—is precisely its reduction to the same. (TaI 43, TeI 14)

For Levinas, this critique of philosophical vision—of its ontology, its cognition, its intentionality, its reason, and the modern bourgeois subject—must somehow be translated into an effective interruption of history, of historical construction:

> The breach in totality . . . can be maintained against an inevitably totalizing and synoptic thought only if thought finds itself *faced* with an other refractory to categories. Rather than constituting a totality with this other as with an object, *thought consists in speaking.* (TaI 40, TeI 10)

Already announced near the beginning of *Totality and Infinity,* Levinas's hope for a breach in the continuity of history draws its inspiration, not from vision, but from speech, the binding of the divine breath that is given to all mortals:

> The claim to know and to reach the other [*l'autre*] is realized in the relationship with the Other [*l'Autrui*] that is cast in the relation of language, where the essential is the interpellation, the vocative. The other is maintained and confirmed in his heterogeneity as soon as one calls upon him, be it only to say to him that one cannot speak to him. . . . The invoked is not what I comprehend: *he is not under a category.* He is the one to whom I speak. . . . The interpellated one is called upon to speak; his speech consists in "coming to the assistance" of his word—in being *present.* (TaI 69, TeI 41)

This passage demonstrates, I believe, that Levinas is attempting to think the breaching of totality and the possibility of an historical opening for transcendence in terms of a fundamental paradigm shift in our prevailing culture, especially with regard to the way we experience others. What is at stake emerges from the difference between seeing and speaking, gaze and voice, knowledge and acknowledgment. In the relationship borne of speaking, borne of language, visibility is not determinative, not essential. In fact, for Levinas, authentic speech is possible only on condition that the one who speaks recognizes in the other a dimensionality that is inherently invisible.

For Levinas, as for Rilke, the invisible is of the utmost significance. So much weight is given to the invisible that even a utopian imagination, with its images of a more perfect justice, is accused of a certain complicity in violence. For any images that we might produce could only reproduce the same system of repressions; they could never be sufficiently different, sufficiently otherwise. There can be no image or representation of the just and equal society, the "kingdom of ends" where it is the face of the Other that commands unconditionally (TaI 215–17, TeI 190–92). (In this regard, there is a point of convergence between Levinas and Adorno: seeing the danger, a repetition of the same, they both give heed to the ancient prohibition of images of God in Judaic law.) "There is," Levinas concedes, "a utopian moment in what I say; [but] it is the recognition of something that cannot be realized, but which, ultimately, guides all moral action."[51] "What counts," he says, "is the idea of the overflowing of objectifying thought by a forgotten experience from which it lives" (TaI 28, TeI xvii). Images, however, can function only on behalf of objectifying thought: they belong to a system of controls; they obey what Adorno would call "the logic of identity."[52] And their origin in spontaneity, in freedom, means that, regardless of contrary appearances, they will always be in the service of the ego and its interests. "I have just refused the notion of vision to describe the authentic relation with the Other [*l'Autrui*]; it is discourse, and more exactly, response or responsibility, which is this authentic relationship" (EaI 87–88). This "refusal" of vision is also, for Levinas, a refusal of the image, of representation—and of the sovereignty of the visible, which cannot possibly, even when seen as bounded by a two-faced horizon, give way to the transcendence of objectifying thought. "The metaphysical relation," by which Levinas means our relation to the transcendent, the invisible infinite, "cannot be properly speaking a representation, for the other would therein dissolve into the same: every representation is essentially interpretable as a transcendental constitution [i.e., an effect of the intentionality or will of the ego-logical subject]" (TaI 38, TeI 8). Thus he argues that, "The shimmer of infinity, the face, can no longer be stated in terms of consciousness, in metaphors referring to light and the sensible" (TaI 207, TeI 182). What matters is not visible.

Not visible. Not an appearance, not something that can "come to light"—not a phenomenon to which any of the methods of phenomenology could possibly do justice. And yet, he speaks of the "shimmer" of infinity. Is this "mere" metaphor? If so, what significance can it carry for our experience? What does it actually mean? Why continue to use a metaphor drawn from vision, referring to something normally visible? Why not concede the visibility of the shimmer, the visibility of the infinite in, or through, or as the shimmer? Why could it not be argued, instead, that the shimmer of the infinite is sensible, is visible—only not for ordinary vision, the way of looking and seeing, namely, that typically issues from the modern (bourgeois) ego-subject? What could his words possibly mean, if the shimmer really could not be seen—not ever, or not at least, say, by the one who wrote those words? If no shimmer of infinity was seen, from where do his words draw their authority? Does Levinas risk more than paradox, more than he supposes, when he withdraws infinity absolutely from the visible—when, for the sake of the ethical relation, he takes the "metaphysical" experience of the other entirely out of the visible, out of sight, rather than extending it from the visible into the invisible?

Far from directing us toward easily settled answers, these questions, provoked by the assumption that the language of vision and light is only metaphorical—but also, even as mere metaphor, entirely in the service of a totalizing immanence, only give rise to more questions, including questions about his turn to the mediations of language, and the way he understands his own work.

In the Preface to *Totality and Infinity*, Levinas writes:

> Peace is produced as the aptitude for speech. The eschatological vision breaks with the totality of wars and empires in which one does not speak. It does not envisage the end of history within being understood as a totality, but institutes a relation with the infinity of being which exceeds the totality. . . . The experience of morality does not proceed from this vision—it consummates this vision; ethics is an optics. But it is a "vision" without image, bereft of the synoptic and totalizing, objectifying virtues of vision, a relation or an intentionality of a wholly different type—which this work seeks to describe. (TaI 23, TeI xii. Also see TaI 29, TeI xvii, where he repeats his claim that ethics is an optics.)

The equivocations in this passage are intriguing. Ethics is, he says, an optics. This suggests that it is the consummation of a certain vision, though, to be sure, it is a "wholly different type" of vision: an extra-ordinary vision, perhaps an eschatological vision, but without (utopian) images. And yet, however different, it maintains the ethical within the realm of vision. So a way of seeing—our ordinary way of seeing—is at stake, subjected to the most radical questioning. Furthermore, this ordinary way of seeing, described as a way that imposes silence, is indicted in the name of, and for the sake of, a way of seeing that welcomes speech, welcomes conversation and debate. Here there is not even a hint of hostility to vision as such. Rather, there is a carefully drawn *difference* between a way of looking and seeing that is allied with the forces of war and violence and a radically different way of looking and seeing. And although the radically other way gives way to speaking, it is not a minor matter that it is in and as an "eschatological vision" that the difference is drawn—and the experience of morality is "consummated." Thus, one might seem justified in complaining that Levinas does not spell out the new "optics," does not elaborate the "phenomenology" of this extra-ordinary vision, does not tell us very much—almost nothing—about the ethical *character* of this other vision, other way of looking and seeing.

In a later chapter, he writes—possibly falling into the same metaphysics of presence he elsewhere so vehemently rejects—that "Speech refuses vision, because the speaker does not deliver images of himself only, but is personally present in his speech, absolutely exterior to every image he would leave" (TaI 296, TeI 273). But is this not a rather peculiar, or at the very least, a peculiarly limited conception of how vision figures in the speech situation? Is the gaze always driven by narcissism? Is narcissism absolutely unavoidable? When I am in conversation with others, is my looking at them, my seeing them, necessarily or primarily a matter of producing and communicating images? Speech might well refuse such an interaction; but the gaze cannot be reduced to this function. Between mother and infant, between two people in love, between two close friends, a glance, a wink, a look may suffice to console, to assuage some suffering—may be worth a thousand words. Levinas here idealizes speech; but speech, as he knows, can be deceitful, mean-spirited, malicious, cruel. The briefest of looks could enable the hunchback one passes on the street to experience the true height of his dignity.

In "Diachrony and Representation," Levinas asks a question that introduces yet other dimensions of ambiguity in his relation to vision and language:

> Does not the "seeing one another" [*le "se voir entre humains"*]—that
> is to say, clearly, language—revert, in its turn, to a seeing, and thus to
> the egological significance of intentionality, . . . the gathering of all al-
> terity into presence, and the synchrony of representation?[53]

Here, in this passage, "seeing one another" is not really seeing, but only a metaphor for language, and real seeing, seeing properly so called, is not allowed to be otherwise than ego-logical, turned and directed by a seemingly unalterable obsession with reducing the alterity of the other to the same.

And yet, taking advantage of a double meaning that the French language makes possible, namely the fact that the phrase "il me regarde" means both "he looks at me" (or "he sees me") and "he concerns me" (or "he is of concern to me"), Levinas comments that

> qu'il me regarde ou non, "il me regarde."⁵⁴

The text continues, explaining his understanding of the visible and invisible dimensions of the face of the other which confronts my looking:

> I call face [*visage*] what, thereby, in the other [*en autrui*], looks at me [*regarde le moi*]—concerns me [*me regarde*]—in recalling . . . his abandon, his defenselessness [*son sans-défense*] and his mortality, and his summons [*appel*] to my ancient responsibility.

In another text, "The Rights of Man and the Rights of the Other," Levinas works with the double meaning to say that

> the other "looks at me" ["*me regarde*"], not in order to "perceive" me, but in [the sense of] "concerning me," in "mattering to me as someone for whom I am answerable."⁵⁵

Here, however, he sets the double reading in motion only, it would seem, to deny one of the interpretations: the interpretation that remains would, quite paradoxically, entirely withdraw the matter—and the mattering—from the realm of perception, the realm where two gazes would meet. But this withdrawal, if understood straightforwardly, would not be without consequence. The other is supposed to matter to me, to be of concern to me: But how? In what way? Since I and the other are both made of flesh, do we not encounter one another with meaningful eyes, ears, gestures? And do I not therefore need to know from Levinas how my responsibility for the other is embodied, revealed, communicated? Can the need for a phenomenological narrative be ignored? How do my eyes look at the other when I fail to realize this answerability and remain indifferent to my responsibility? How would my eyes look at the other once they are bound by my primordial responsibility? How would the ethical relation be embodied in and as looking and seeing? These questions suggest that perhaps Levinas's objection is not to the ethical involvement of the gaze as such, but only to the way it is conceptualized in philosophical discourse, namely, as ordinary "perception." What he would be arguing, then, is that, as ordinary "perception," the gaze of the "I" can only be a violation of the other's alterity, and that it needs to be experienced otherwise. Which means that the "I," the subject of the gaze, must itself become otherwise.

In *Otherwise Than Being*, Levinas touches on this problematic, but leaves it without providing any phenomenological narrative that would be instructive for the vision of the eyes. "Who is looking?" he inquires. And he replies:

> the question asks that "the looker" be identified with one of the beings already known, even if the answer to the question "Who is looking?" should be stated in the monosyllabic "Me."[56]

The question for Levinas is whether or not the looking and seeing of the gaze can be withdrawn from being: whether or not it can escape ontologizing, reifying, totalizing, the violence of ego-logical drives and self-interest. Perhaps Levinas introduces the idea of a "listening eye" to provoke philosophical thinking beyond the ordinary answers (OB 30, 37; AE 38, 48). But, in *Difficult Freedom*, he evokes a moment that it would certainly be wrong to read as "merely" metaphorical, i.e., "merely" figurative, rather than as an attempt to think about our looking and seeing in "straightforwardly" phenomenological terms:

> when I really gaze, with a straightforwardness devoid of trickery or evasion, into unguarded, absolutely unprotected eyes . . . [57]

Well, what will I see? And does the *character* of my gaze, here, live up to the eyes' "ethical" responsibility? In "On Jewish Philosophy," an interview in *In the Time of Nations*, Levinas declares that the face "appeals to responsibility before appearing to the eye," drawing a contrast between the appeal and the appearing that would seem to suggest that the appeal initially takes hold of us at a "preconscious" and therefore "bodily felt" level.[58]

In *Totality and Infinity*, Levinas, describing the everyday situation, observes that, "The Other measures me with a gaze incomparable to the gaze by which I discover him" (TaI 86, TeI 59). In other words, it is inherent in the exposure of my visibility that I experience myself in judgment before the gaze of the other, that I see this judgment reflected in the other's eyes; but I cannot, or rather, ought not, return the judgment, for this would commit the offense of treating the other according to a principle of symmetry and equivalence. But is Levinas's sentence to be read as "merely" metaphorical or is it to be taken to heart as an attempt to articulate an ethical *experience* with vision in the face of strong ego-logical defenses and strategies of resistance?

Reading Levinas, we often cannot decide with any confidence what the reference of his words is supposed to be. If his words are not to be taken literally, to what, then, do they refer? Isn't Levinas attempting to articulate in phenomenological terms—and that means in terms of our experience—the ethical character of a vision, a way of looking and seeing, that would be radically different from the character of vision that today is prevailing? If so, his discourse is a phenomenology describing with normative and performative force.

In *Totality and Infinity,* Levinas speaks of "seeing in justice and injustice a primordial access to the Other [*l'Autrui*] beyond all ontology" (TaI 89, TeI 61). If his use of the word "seeing," here, is not "merely" metaphorical, not a "merely rhetorical" phototropism, then it would constitute an attempt to articulate a *normative ideal* for our sight, our capacity to see—and also an attempt to instruct, to teach, to speak appealingly to our *capacity* for vision, our capacity to bring forth a different way of looking and seeing.

Levinas's writing holds us in an unsettling suspension: always suspended between "seeing" literally understood as experience and "seeing" understood as a figure of speech; between a phenomenology describing the present historical actuality and a normatively inspired phenomenology describing a radically different future; between, as we shall see, the visible face (the face-to-face) as an actual or possible ethical experience and the invisible face as trope for a certain conception of justice. When these crucial terms cross one another, they may *seem* to cross each other out. What is gained, what lost, in these undecidable rhetorical ambiguities, these double-crossings?

II. THE FACE BENEATH THE SURFACE

In Levinas's work, it is the human face that is perhaps given the greatest gift of thought. "The true essence of man," he explains, "is presented in his face" (TaI 290, TeI 266). But what is a face? Faced with the horrors of regional wars and the breakdown of institutions to maintain law and order, Montaigne sometimes resisted a cultivated disposition to skepticism and ignored his affirmation of tolerance and open-mindedness, writing, in his *Essays,* that "Truth must have one face, the same and universal."[59] For him, though, it was a question of affirming a morality and justice grounded, not in nature, not in customs, not in the fortunes of power, and not even in the positivism of law, but rather in what he took to be the rule of reason:

> What then will philosophy tell us in this our need? To follow the laws of our country—that is to say, the undulating sea of the opinions of a people or a prince, which will paint me justice in as many colors, and refashion it into as many faces as there are changes of passion in those men? I cannot have my judgment so flexible.[60]

But truth and justice must also be responsible to and for the singularity of the concrete individual: in their universality, they must also, somehow, recognize the incomparable existence, the exigent face, the absolute claims, of the singular. On this, Levinas has something—but not enough—to say.

To begin our consideration of Levinas's thought concerning the face, we should note that he tells us, in a late essay, that "It is necessary to say that, considering the way I am using the word *face*, it should not be understood in a narrow way [*d'une manière étroite*]."[61] That this is an accurate observation will, I believe, be confirmed by our reading of his works. That this introduces certain difficulties—or at the very least provokes some questions not easily settled—is one of the important matters to which we will be attending in this section of the chapter. As we shall see, it compels us to situate our thinking about the face in the equivocations and tensions of a semantic field where there can be no certitude with regard to a literal or figurative reading, and where, therefore, the connection between the "I" and the other in the face-to-face ethical relation and the connection between the "I" and all others in the moral-political relation, where it is a question of coming in judgment before the face of justice, become extremely problematic. For the moment, perhaps it will be sufficient to read what he says in the interview titled *Ethics and Infinity*: speaking there of the face of the other, he describes it as "the expressive in the other," and adds, in parentheses, that "the whole human body is in this sense more or less face" (EaI 97). This is an intriguing and promising thought, but nowhere can I find any further elaboration.

Now, "proximity" is a key word in Levinas's thinking about the ethical dimension of interpersonal relationships. This "proximity" would seem to be, for him, a phenomenological concept referring to *experienced* closeness. Thus it would not be a question of objectively measurable distance. Indeed, it must be noted that, if authentically felt, this closeness not only would not *preclude* a certain experience of distance (Benjamin's "aura," which he defines as surrounding anything that returns my gaze); but on the contrary, one who experiences such "proximity" would actually be compelled to undergo an experience of distance—the distance, namely, of awe and enchantment, the overwhelming distance of moral respect—as if in the presence of a revelation.[62] For Levinas, the infinite distance of the other *in his very proximity* shows itself above all in the face: "The way in which the other presents himself, [even] exceeding the idea of the other in me, we here name face" (TaI 50, TeI 21).

Levinas's phenomenology of the face introduces into ethical discourse a surprising new theme, one that immediately seems to promise a radically different way of thinking about the ethical relation. But this new theme is not without its perplexities. Whilst with one hand, he writes of the face in a vocabulary that assumes, or even seems to require, its visibility and points in a promising way to an ethical moment in our experience with sight, with the other hand he erases the assumption of visibility and double-crosses this relation to sight, seemingly withdrawing it entirely from the realm of our experience with vision. But doesn't this withdrawal of the face from visibility and sight also risk withdrawing from ethics all that might have been gained for it by introducing the face and the face-to-face relation into the discussion? Does the denial of the face's "phenomenality" necessarily mean that the face must be denied to phenomenological articulation? I suggest that one possible answer might be that the *sense* of this denial could constitute the very substance of the phenomenological treatment.

When, in "The Pact," Levinas meditates on the ceremony of the Covenant and shifts from a discussion of the face-to-face visibility, the visible co-presence of the other that is possible in a small community where everyone is *literally* visible to everyone else, to a discussion of the abstract universality of justice, he still invokes the face of the other, formulating the universal obligations of justice with regard to people who are strangers, literally invisible, literally beyond the range of any possible face-to-face relation.[63] But this shift is not immediately comprehensible, since it radically destabilizes the way we should understand the face in the phenomenology of the singular ethical relation: in reading this phenomenology, we are initially disposed to understand his references to the face to be literal; but when the face also figures in his discourse on justice, it seems that, because of the invisibility of the face when it is a question of universal justice, we must regard these references to the face as "merely" metaphorical. And this compels us to rethink the sense of *all* his references to the face in the discourse concerning the ethical relation. Indeed, it can seem that we are left with an undecidable dilemma threatening the philosophical weight of his thought.

Thus I have been strongly tempted to think that his extension of the question of the face beyond the ethical relation of the face-to-face, i.e., beyond a situation where, in an important, if only preliminary sense, the face of the other is literally visible, to the question of justice, where, in an equally important, if no less preliminary sense, the face of the other does not belong to the visible (either because the other inhabits a distant life-world or because, as it is said, the judgment of justice, assuming the theoretical perspective of universality, must be blind), could only purport (if I may be excused for relying, here, on a vocabulary frequently complicitous in the violence of the logic of commodity exchange) the "loss" of that deepening of our understanding and our experience of the singular ethical relation which the phenomenological concreteness of the face and the face-to-face seemed initially to promise.[64]

But further thought brings out a significant connection between the face of the face-to-face ethical relation and the face of justice: in the (normatively ideal) experience of the ethical relation, there is (is to be) a deep, deeply felt sense of the other's withdrawal into unfathomable invisibility. If (even) the face of the other in the face-to-face relation is, in a sense that bears imperative moral force, invisible, might we not see the invisibility essential to the institutions of justice as already prefigured in the invisibility of the singular ethical relation? The tensions in our dilemma can be resolved, I think, only dialectically: starting out with a phenomenology that describes the visibility of the face, Levinas can register the spiritual infinity, the transcendence of the other in the realm of the visible only indirectly, through (à travers) a certain negation of the visible.

Thus, arguing against Heidegger, Levinas asks whether "the sight of a face" takes place "in the light of being" (OB 18, AE 22). He asks this question because, for him, sight is allied with light as a force that is primarily oppressive and violent: "Is not sight here immediately a taking charge?" (ibid.). Conscious of the paradox, Levinas introduces invisibility even into the face-to-face relation of neighbors, insisting that, in truth, the human face is "not seen," is actually, in a morally crucial sense, never seen: "meeting the face is not of the order of pure and simple perception, of the intentionality which goes toward adequation" (EaI 86, 96). We must carefully consider this argument about the face never really being seen, never really being visible, because it certainly disturbs our settled convictions and assumptions about what is taking place in our face-to-face relations with others—and, more generally, what it means for something to be visible or invisible. But undoubtedly, the whole point of the argument, leading us into the labyrinth of a paradox, is, as much as possible, to unsettle our experience of faces, casting them into an abyssal phenomenality, an abyssal "presence" where they can only haunt us, resistant to the point of anarchy in relation to our conventionally sedimented experience.

In our experience of the face, a crucial feature, for Levinas, is its exposedness, its vulnerability to the natural aggression of our gaze:

> The nakedness of the face is not what is presented to me because I disclose it, what would therefore be presented to me, to my powers, to my eyes, to my perceptions, in a light exterior to it. The face has turned to me—and this is its very nudity. It *is* by itself, and not by reference to a system. (TaI 74–75, TeI 47)

In an interpretation that we will be connecting with an experience narrated by Rilke, he argues that, through the face,

> the human being is exposed to the point of losing the skin which protects him, a skin which has completely become a face, as if a being, centered about his core, experienced a removal of this core, and losing it, was "for the other" before any dialogue.[65]

"The face," he says, "rends the visible" (TaI 198, TeI 172). It "is not a form offered to serene perception."[66] (We may agree. But why must perception be understood as serene, or contemplative? There is no textual support for thinking that this is how perception is understood in the phenomenologies of Heidegger and Merleau-Ponty.) Working with certain assumptions about perception that it would be terribly unfair to attribute to Heidegger and Merleau-Ponty, and that in any case are quite debatable, he maintains, without attempting to diminish the appearance of paradox, that the face "is neither seen nor touched—for in visual or tactile sensation, the identity of the I envelops the alterity of the object" (TaI 194, TeI 168). But perhaps the appearance of paradox would vanish, were it to be explained that Levinas is not withdrawing the ethical relationship from the world of flesh and blood, the visible and tangible world, but is instead denying the ways being seen and being touched have been interpreted in the philosophical discourses of idealism, empiricism, and naturalism, as well as the ways they are understood and experienced in a culture—ours—that degrades human relations and violates the moral dignity, the moral presence, of the other, reducing moral presence to a merely physical, objective matter and subjecting it to all kinds of exploitation. Explaining how our perception of the face needs to be understood instead, he writes: "Immediately it summons me, claims me, recalls me to a responsibility I incurred."[67]

Levinas's repudiation of perception is so strong, so unequivocal, that it might easily suggest that it is not at all a question of "experience," of what

we see or fail to see—or that it would be inappropriate, or even worse, a betrayal, a moral offense, to speak of the face in terms of such experience. But
Levinas does not in fact press his argument that far: my relation with the
other *is*, he says, a question of "experience"—only not "objective" experience (TaI 25, TeI xiii). And in fact he does not at all hesitate to depend on
that word throughout his lifetime of writings. (I suggest that the seemingly
paradoxical way that words work in Levinas's assertion that the face does
not figure in perception is similar to the seemingly paradoxical way they
work in Foucault's assertion in *The Order of Things* that before humanism
and the Enlightenment, "Man" did not exist, and the way they work in Derrida's argument against Husserl in *Speech and Phenomena*,[68] asserting that
perception, if thought as "full and simple presence," does not exist.)

Is it possible, then, to call Levinas's writings on the face—writings that
seem to offer descriptions of a possible way of experiencing the face—
contributions to the discourse of phenomenology? The answer must be in
the negative, if [1] phenomenology must be, as he says in the interview of
Ethics and Infinity, a method that "describes what appears"—a "look
turned toward the face," and if [2] "the look is knowledge, perception," i.e.,
an adequation between the looking and the face of the other (EaI 85). But
Levinas himself frequently refers to his work by calling it phenomenology.
And there really is no compelling reason to deny that phenomenology can
be the description of the face as revelation. For Levinas, our experience of
the face of the other is not (should not be?) an experience of disclosure.
Here is how he defines "disclosure":

> To recognize truth to be disclosure is to refer it to the horizon of him
> who discloses. . . . The disclosed being is relative to us and not *kath'
> auto*. . . . According to the modern terminology, we disclose only with
> respect to a project. (TaI 64, TeI 36)

Here, now, is how he describes the face's "revelation," or "manifestation
kath' auto":

> Here, contrary to all the conditions for the visibility of objects [i.e.,
> contrary to conditions for disclosure], the being is not placed in the
> light of another but presents itself in the manifestation that should
> only announce; it is present as directing this manifestation—present
> before the manifestation, which only manifests it. (TaI 65, TeI 37)

It could be useful at this point briefly to consider Heidegger's approach
to this problematic. Although Heidegger's hermeneutical phenomenology
is sometimes characterized in terms of disclosure, it is really a question
of what Levinas calls "revelation." For Heidegger argues that truth as

adequation, as correspondence, as correctness—that which Levinas calls "dévoilement"—is founded upon and derived from the experience of a more primordial event: *aletheia*. The recognition of *aletheia* is crucial: to situate truth as correctness *within* the openness of *aletheia* is the only way to *care* for the truth, for truth as correctness, because situating truth-claims in the interplay of concealment and unconcealment constitutive of this field of openness denies them any dogmatic authority, any right to claim completeness, absoluteness, finality, certitude. And this turns out to be, in spite of Levinas's disavowals, very much in keeping with the Levinasian conception of revelation. Heidegger refrains from using that word, however, because he fears that it would reinscribe his radical phenomenology within the metaphysics of ontotheological discourse. But he is very clear in arguing that to care for the truth requires preserving and protecting the dimension of its concealment. Otherwise, we surrender truth to positivism. As he says in "The Origin of the Work of Art," implicitly deconstructing the conception of the acting subject and the character of its action that has prevailed in modern culture at the same time that he challenges all our cultural assumptions, and all our complacent self-assurance, regarding "what is": "The resoluteness intended in *Being and Time* is not the deliberate action of a subject but the opening up of human being, *out of its captivity in that which is*, to the openness of Being."[69] Could this openness to being imply a possibility that is otherwise than being?

In a 1986 interview, Levinas reiterates that the face is otherwise than being: "the face does not give itself to be seen. It is not a vision. The face is not that which is seen . . . is not an object of knowledge."[70] (Not an object of knowledge, of course, in Levinas's quite narrow and one-sided conception of "knowledge.") And when pressed on the question of phenomenology, he replies: "it is very difficult to give it [the face] an exact phenomenological description. The phenomenology of the face is very often negative."[71] But this reply is certainly not a repudiation of phenomenology. Quite the contrary. That it is difficult for him is clear. Nevertheless, his use of the phenomenological method, broadly conceived, makes a significant approach. The difficulty, as he puts it, is that he is "not at all sure that the face is a phenomenon. A phenomenon is what appears. Appearance is not the mode of being of the face."[72] The face withdraws from the reach of the Husserlian "reduction," and it is with this in mind that Levinas denies that the face is an appearance, a phenomenon. For the "reduction" subjects the other person to the primacy of a method for establishing self-evidence. As an ethical relation, this of course can only be an offense. Perhaps the matter also hinges on whether or not the appearing of the appearance must be construed in terms of the traditional subject-object structure. In any case, the face, for Levinas, is not (but I would prefer to say "not only") an "object of knowledge," but a "commandment," a "demand" that "has authority, but not force."[73]

Moreover, the face is not an image or representation: "Because it is the presence of exteriority [i.e., radical alterity or transcendence], the face never becomes an image or an intuition" (TaI 297, TeI 273). Nor is the face a symbol, because a symbol always in the end imposes a logic of sameness on the other with which it makes a connection: its recognition of alterity is always conditional, for it "still brings the symbolized back to the world in which it appears."[74] Nor is the face a mask, for a mask hides, but always also indicates—and betrays—what it hides.[75] We will be returning to the question of the face and the mask later in this section.

For the moment, the point to be considered is the transcendence that constitutes the face, a transcendence that, in spite of all the indictments of vision and light, and in spite of the availability of alternative vocabularies, Levinas nevertheless describes by choosing the vision-related word "gleam":

> without philosophically "demonstrating" eschatological "truths," we can proceed from the experience of totality back to a situation where totality breaks up, a situation that conditions the totality itself. Such a situation is the gleam of exteriority or of transcendence in the face of the Other [le visage d'autrui]. (TaI 24–25, TeI xiii)

And he informs his readers that

> the rigorously developed concept of this transcendence is expressed by the term infinity.

From the face's presence as a transcendence into infinity, it follows that

> the face resists possession, resists my powers. In its epiphany, in expression, the sensible, still graspable, turns into total resistance to the grasp. This . . . can occur only by the opening of a new dimension. (TaI 197, TeI 172)

So the face is in the sensible, is—in some sense—to be seen. But is the gaze necessarily, essentially grasping and possessive? Is it condemned, like the gaze of the Medusa, to turn whatever it sees into a petrified phenomenon, an object for a subject obsessed by possession? Levinas seems to assume here, first of all, what he elsewhere would be committed to challenging as a perpetuation of the "imperialism of the same," viz., that there is such a "thing" as an essential nature; second, that, in the case of looking and seeing, its character is totally determined by an essential nature; and third, that, in the case of looking and seeing, this essential nature is to be grasping and possessive. "This new dimension," he tells us, "opens in the sensible appearance of the face" (TaI 198, TeI 172). But if vision is inherently grasping and possessive, how would Levinas be able to say, to tell us, how the face reveals itself *in* the sensible? How could he attest to the truth of the face's epiphany, to its resistance to the grasp, to its opening up of a new dimension? Must he not have *seen* it with his own two eyes? If not, from where would his authority, his right to speak, be coming?

In *Ethics and Infinity*, conversations with Philippe Nemo, Levinas continues the familiar refrain:

> the face is meaning all by itself. You are you. In this sense, one can say that the face is not "seen." It is what cannot become a content which your thought would embrace; it is uncontainable, it leads you beyond. It is in this that the signification of the face makes its escape from being, as a correlate of knowing. Vision, to the contrary, is a search for adequation; it is what par excellence absorbs being. But the relation to the face is straightaway ethical. (86–87)

For Levinas, "the infinite comes in the signifyingness of the face. The face signifies the infinite" (EaI 105). But is signification possible only through language? Can it not also take place through the visibility of the face? Levinas tells Nemo that, "When in the presence of the other, I say 'Here I am!' this 'Here I am!' is the place through which the infinite enters into language, but without giving itself to be seen" (EaI 106). But if the infinite cannot be seen, if it is in no way sensible, would it not also, on the same grounds, be inaudible, not giving itself to be heard?

Even when writing on Merleau-Ponty, whose phenomenology unquestionably articulates a way of seeing radically different from the vision that Levinas accuses, Levinas maintains his animadversions, implicitly against *all* forms of vision:

> Behold vision turning back into non-vision, into insinuation of a face, into the refutation of vision within sight's center, into that of which vision . . . is but a forgetfulness and re-presentation.[76]

What, for Levinas, obstructs our vision, turning it back into non-vision, is the invisibility of the other's face:

> It is [a question of] a relationship with the In-visible, where invisibility results not from some incapacity of human knowledge, but from the inaptitude of knowledge as such—from its inadequation—to the infinity of the absolutely other. . . . This impossibility of coinciding and this inadequation are not simply negative notions, but have a meaning in the *phenomenon* of non-coincidence *given* in the diachrony of time. (TO, 32, TA 10)

But why must vision be bound, as if by fate, to adequation and coincidence? Why could it not be an encounter with the invisible that *lets it be* the invisible beyond being? Why non-vision, rather than a *different kind* of vision? (Consider the way of looking and seeing suggested by Heidegger in his *Conversations on a Country Path*.) Perhaps, at times, Levinas is tempted to think a different vision, a "metaphysical" vision no longer the captive of an ontological need to dominate. Here, for example, he describes the gaze of the other:

> [In the] gaze that supplicates and demands, that can supplicate only because it demands, . . . and which one recognizes in giving . . . is precisely the epiphany of the face as a face. The nakedness of the face is destituteness. . . . To recognize the Other [*l'Autrui*] is to give. But it is to give to . . . him whom one approaches as "You" [*Vous*] in a dimension of height. (TaI 75, TeI 48)

One reason why this passage is important is that the gaze described here defies the essentializing that Levinas elsewhere imposes on it.

Levinas tells us that, "The dimension of the divine opens forth from the human face" (TaI 78, TeI 50). How does he experience this? (I deliberately avoid asking, here, "How does he know this?") Is this not something that many in our civilization have claimed to see? According to the Scriptures, when Moses descended from Mount Sinai after his communion with God, his face was shining with such an awesome radiance that, when the Israelites saw it, they fled in mortal dread. Why should we deny that this radiance was a real experience—something that the Israelites actually saw? "Absolute experience," says Levinas,

> is not disclosure [*dévoilement*]; to disclose, on the basis of a subjective horizon, is already to miss the noumenon. (TaI 67, TeI 39)

Agreed. But despite his criticisms and suspicions of vision, we find Levinas frequently characterizing the face in terms of the gaze and what it sees: in addition to describing the face as an "epiphany," he writes, for example of the other's "defenceless eyes," "the absolute frankness of his gaze," "this gaze which forbids me my conquest"; and he observes that "his gaze must come to me from a dimension of the ideal," that I must learn to "catch sight of the dimension of height and the ideal in the gaze of him to whom justice is due."[77] But then, separated by no more than the time of a blink, he writes: "The epiphany of a face is wholly language." Thus, rather than abandoning vision altogether, Levinas makes a surprising move: he turns vision into speech. If we may attribute any virtue to the eyes, it is that they can speak:

> The face is a living presence. . . . The face speaks. The manifestation of the face is already discourse. (TaI 66, TeI 37)

When the other one speaks to me, her face "undoes" whatever form I may have imposed on her—whatever form would have made her "adequate to the same" (ibid.). "This presence," he then declares,

> affirmed in the presence of the image as the focus of the gaze that is fixed on you, is said. (Ibid.)

The presence of the face that speaks, that expresses itself in meaningful language ("signification") cannot be reduced to my "evidence," to my way of seeing. Nevertheless, this presence, an irreducible otherness, can also come by way of vision. For he says, in no uncertain terms, that

> the eyes [of the other] break through the mask—the language of the eyes, impossible to dissemble. *The eye does not shine; it speaks.* (TaI 66, TeI 38. Italics added.)

Finally, vision vanishes, mysteriously sublated, inscribed by some sleight of hand into the phrase "listening and word":

> The vision of the face is no more vision, but listening and word.[78]

For Levinas, the encounter with the face is not only an experience with language; what makes this experience fundamentally significant is that it is also an ethical experience: "the encounter with the face—that is to say, moral conscience."[79] More specifically, though without any argument or any phenomenological "demonstration":

> since the Other looks at me, I am responsible for him, without even having *taken on* responsibilities in his regard; his responsibility is *incumbent on me*. . . . I say in *Otherwise Than Being*, that responsibility is initially a *for the Other*. This means that I am responsible for his very responsibility. (EaI 96)

A face, therefore, "obsesses us" (OB 158, AE 201) with its strange duality, hovering between the visible and the invisible, "as if the face of this other, though invisible, *continued my own face* and kept me awake by its very invisibility."[80] And because the face of the other can have this hold on me, awakening my conscience, Levinas asserts that "formal reason" is necessary only for a being "who does not have the strength to suppose that, under the visible that is history, there is the invisible that is judgement"

(TaI 246, TeI 225). But we human beings are not angels; few of us have this strength. For us, then, the deontology of "formal reason," incorporated in the institutions of the state, becomes a necessary moral compass.

We will return to the question of reason. For the moment, however, I want to persist in the questioning of Levinas's engagement with the phenomenology of vision. It is important to note, at this point, that Levinas has explicitly stated that he regards his writings on the experience of the face of the other as contributions to phenomenology:

> I have attempted a "phenomenology" of sociality starting from the face of the other person—from proximity—by understanding in its rectitude a voice that commands.[81]

Levinas can alter the phenomenology he inherited in many ways, can question some of its principal assumptions, even radically change its "approach" to the subject and introduce new normative concepts to guide this approach; but he cannot renounce it entirely. Because phenomenology is the only method for approaching the human—approaching the face of the other— that is uncompromisingly committed to *respecting* the articulation of experience just as it is actually lived—in contrast to methods which involve approaches to a subject's experience from an objective point of view that is external to, or independent of, this experience, and that therefore can never entirely avoid being impositional, oppressive. Thus he emphasizes that "This 'beyond' the totality . . . is reflected *within* the totality and history, *within* experience" (TaI 23, TeI xi–xii). In other words, the "beyond" that happens in one's encounter with another face-to-face is not at all beyond experience, not therefore beyond the approach of a certain ethically responsive, ethically responsible phenomenology. (Must we not therefore be able to *see* this beyond that is within?) But the beyond is, to be sure, explicitly introduced as an "eschatological" or messianic concept, which, "as the 'beyond' of history, draws beings out of the jurisdiction of history and the future; it arouses them and calls them forth to their full [timeless] responsibility" (ibid.). Within worldly time, within history, yet also rooted beyond the totality of these orders because of its absolute deontological force, the face can be the site, the medium, of divine judgment. The visible face of the other binds me in (and to) its concrete singularity: I am beholden to you. But it also binds me in (and to) its abstract universality: beholding your humanity, our kinship, I am beholden to everyone and committed thereby to the calling, the work of justice. This binding takes place below the level of consciousness, below "intentionality" as Levinas understands it. Some people may therefore deny its truth as a description of their experience. The task of his phenomenology would accordingly be a transformative one: through the responsibility of self-critical reflection, to put us in touch (once again) with this dimension of our experience and raise it into moral consciousness. Levinas's phenomenology is obliged to be both descriptive and normative, both constative and performative, both statement and evocative exhortation. It must speak with moral force, by a saying that exceeds what is said.[82]

In some respects like the face of the angel of history that Benjamin reads into Klee's drawing,[83] the face that Levinas wants us to see is a face,

> Submitting history as a whole to judgement, . . . it restores to each instant its full signification in that very instant: all the causes are ready to be heard. (TaI 23, TeI xi–xii)

This face whose character Levinas is here describing: Must he not *have seen* it? What would such a "seeing" involve? In "Meaning and Sense," he explains this uncanny "presence" of the face by observing that, in the experience of the

> extra-ordinary visitation and epiphany of the face, there is an ethics *prior to and independent of* culture and history [and] it is on this basis that one is able to judge civilizations.[84]

Before recognition in full consciousness, I have always already responded to the presence, the face, of the other—responded in a way that implicitly acknowledges my responsibility for her and to her. The face is like an overwhelming force that erupts into the order of private lives and social history, breaching its defensive causal continuity to command our responsibility and pass the judgment of "divine" justice on each of us.

In many respects, Levinas's thinking does not undergo great changes between his early and late writings—as he himself remarks. However, there is a significant shift in the way he describes the "presence" of the face: whereas, in *Totality and Infinity*, it is said to be "beyond" in the sense that it is an *excessive presence*, in *Otherwise Than Being*, it is "beyond" as an *irretrievable absence*. But even in the earlier work, there are passages where he is already emphasizing a certain dimension of absence rather than a "full" or "excessive" (and therefore conceptually ungraspable) presence:

> The relation with the face is not an object-cognition [i.e., not disclosure]. The transcendence of the face is at the same time its absence from this world into which it enters, the exiling [*dépaysement*] of a being, his condition of being stranger, destitute, or proletarian.
> (TaI 74–75, TeI 47)

But in order, in the later work, to put additional stress on the "beyond" as absence, he begins to speak about the face of the other as "lit up" by the passing trace, more past than past, of an invisible infinity (OB 12, 91; AE 14, 116). The ethical "presence" of the other is not an ontological presence; nor does it belong to the order of passing "appearances," in accordance with which the trace of transcendence would have to show itself in terms of an objective chain of causality. Coming from the immemorial beyond— beyond the world of time and memory, the face in its brief passage through the world "expresses" its moral presence in an absolute, absolutely irretrievable absence. (This phenomenology of the "immemorial" is prefigured by Merleau-Ponty in his *Phenomenology of Perception,* where he speaks of finding "at work in my organs of perception a thought older than myself of which those organs are merely the trace."[85] It is a question, for him, of a prepersonal existence belonging to "a past which has never been a present."[86] "I am borne into personal existence," he writes there,[87] "by a time which I do not constitute.") The "presence" of this face is not that of an ontological presence, not the presence of a being, "because it transcends the present in which it commands me" (OB 12, AE 15). It is not even a residue of presence—only the advent of an "unrepresentable trace" (OB 116, AE 149), "the trace of the utterly bygone, the utterly past absent."[88] But it is also, he soon remarks,[89] a trace of hope. For every face, invisible even when facing me, bespeaks its kinship with all other human beings, however distant from me, however invisible to me, and thereby invokes a future justice, a justice to-come: *à-venir.*

Elaborating his description of the face, Levinas introduces an element that, as we shall see, draws a connection between his ethics of the face-to-face, an ethics between singular persons, and his theory of justice, a morality and politics of the social universal:

The beyond from which a face comes is in the third person.[90]

That is to say that the face of the other brings before me the justice of the witness, and not only the claims of an absolute singularity. We will return to this question of the third person (*le tiers*). For the present, I want to continue thinking about the face, considering some of the phenomenological constellations introduced in his late work, *Otherwise Than Being:*

A face is not an appearance or sign of some reality. . . . A face does not function in proximity as a *sign* of a hidden God who would impose the neighbor on me. It is a trace of itself, a trace in the trace of an abandon. . . . [Thus, it is] an invitation to the fine risk of approach qua approach, to the exposure of one to the other, . . . the expression of exposure, saying. (OB 93, AE 118)

Two further traits figure in the phenomenological description here: the exposure of the face, i.e., vulnerability and injurability, and the saying that comes from the depths of immeasurable suffering. This saying, taking place in the silence that always comes *before* speech, is my command: yet, because of its singular temporality, it is not the same as the Kantian "Sollen" (ibid.). But when Levinas speaks of this commanding "presence" of the face, he states in no uncertain terms that

> the mode in which a face indicates its own absence in my responsibility requires a description that can be formed only in ethical language. (Ibid.)

The problem, for him, thus becomes the formulation of a philosophical task, viz., to learn, somehow, patiently, how to speak of all this, how to say it in new, absolutely different words, words that would not end up reinscribing the experience in the vocabulary and context of an ethical discourse that, however well intentioned, could only abuse it, violate it, injure it, imposing on it the injustice of an identitarian, totalitarian logic.

Finding a way to speak about the face of the other poses, for Levinas, the most intractable and interminable difficulties. These difficulties are due in large measure to what Levinas calls the "trace," a trope that refers to the non-identity of the other's face—a non-identity that makes it impossible for me to grasp it in an act of perception and knowledge; a non-identity, moreover, that also invades my own experience, withdrawing it from my self-possession and even shattering my own identity as a "subject." (We are, of course, taking this term in its paradigmatically modern, i.e., essentially Cartesian or Kantian sense.) How can phenomenology as a "descriptive" enterprise overcome or escape its identity-logic? This is the question with which Levinas struggles.[91] The trace is at the very heart of this struggle, since in a most uncanny way it resists articulation within the architecture of phenomenology—and yet it seems that only a certain phenomenology could possibly recognize it.

It is only in *Otherwise Than Being*, a late work, that the face is figured, above all, as nothing but a trace—cipher of the claim of alterity. In *Totality and Infinity*, a much earlier work, the face is described as an absolute singularity, infinitely transcendent, beyond essence, beyond being, beyond the positivity of presence: absence from the world. But in the later work, this absence, this radical alterity, mark of nonidentity, is brought into language in the figure of the trace, emphasizing its withdrawal from being, its absolute, uncompromising irretrievability (OB 166, AE 211). And yet, the "reading" of the trace, the trace of the other that subjects me to its claim, must continue to be the principal concern of his phenomenology. Thus, in effect, his phenomenology becomes what I have elsewhere[92] called a "tracework": an approach to the unapproachable, which withdraws itself from every approach; an attempt to describe the indescribable, the unrepresentable—an attempt to decipher the tracework of alterity in the very topography of the flesh. But how can there be a phenomenology of the indescribable, the inapparent? How can we *see* a spectral visibility? How can we say anything about an alterity that haunts me, a trace that can be located, properly speaking, neither "in" me nor "in" the other—a trace that manifests my subjection to the other but operates somehow in the between-us that is otherwise than being? How can we say anything at all about a trace that is supposed to be a nonidentity, "less than nothing," when anything we might say cannot avoid describing it and attributing an identity? Is the trace nothing but a "dialectical illusion"? We cannot avoid reflecting on the trace here. But it will also be necessary to consider the provocations of the trace, its paradoxical, aporetic relation to visibility and legibility, in the next section.

My experience of the other's face is not that of a presence reducible to the present; the encounter is said to happen in a paradoxical spatiality and an equally paradoxical temporality: for in my face-to-face encounter with the other, my experience is subject to the moral law, which has left a trace of its primordial inscription in my flesh. The trace belongs to a time "before the present, older than the time of consciousness [ego] that is accessible to [ego-logical] memory (OB 93, 106; AE 118, 134–35). Even before the time of my first "actual" encounter with another—in an immemorial time before any order of time we can conventionally calculate, I have already been deeply touched and marked by, and prepared for, the encounter: inhabiting my flesh, there is, thus, before any actual encounter, the "trace of a passage" (OB 91, AE 116) that is also the passage of a trace. In other words, I have been touched and marked by the moral law.

I would like to suggest that we might think of the trace that is in question here as virtually nothing—*unless we make something of it*. The significance of this formulation, however, will perhaps be intelligible only when it is thought—despite Levinas's resistance—in terms of a reflexive process of moral development. For Levinas, a mere trace of a trace is all that remains to carry the assignment of a moral responsibility, a responsibility already inherent in my capacity to be responsive to the "presence" of the other and already importuning me even before I am able to recognize its claim on my existence. It is as if I were being touched and moved from afar by the categorical force of a moral imperative: a claim coming from "an immemorial past, a past that was never present" (OB 88, AE 112). But this past is not entirely lost, for it haunts the moral sense, which imagines it as preserved in the intricate tracework of the flesh, in the intrigue of an archi-writing.

This is not mysticism; not "dialectical illusion." Nor is it in the conventional sense mere metaphor. What I think he means is that obligation first takes hold of us bodily—in the flesh—in a time that is, at each and every moment, i.e., both synchronically and diachronically, prior to thematizing consciousness, prior to reflective cognition, and therefore prior to the ego's construction of a worldly temporal order. Morality, for him, is not—or not first of all—an obligation mediated, as for Kant, by the formal and procedural universalization of maxims; nor is it grounded in appeals to "good conscience" constructed through processes of socialization. Instead, morality is first of all a *bodily carried* sense of obligation, an imperative sense of responsibility immediately, but not consciously felt in the flesh: a bodily responsiveness that, unless severely damaged by the brutality of early life experiences, the "I" cannot avoid undergoing—at least to some extent—when face-to-face with the other. Even *before* beholding the other, the "I," as a "being" of flesh, is already rendered beholden; thus, at least in the normal case, when the "I" actually beholds another face-to-face, the "I"'s felt sense of beholdenness will be to some extent immediately awakened. But not necessarily awakened enough to motivate moral comportment. And it is through this sense of beholdenness that the "humanity" of the other, and eventually the universal claims of justice, are in the first instance recognized.

Thus, in spite of the impossibility of thematizing, representing, or narrating the "pre-history" of the traces of the other's claims on me, on my responsibility and obligation, Levinas nevertheless undertakes to *describe* the register of these traces. But can we tell whether these "traces" are discoveries or fabulations? Is it possible that they are nothing but the wishful projections of certain norms, values, and ideals, cast onto "human nature" in order to give them the force of nature? What kind of "reality" is to be ascribed to them? If neither discoveries nor inventions, could they be, ambiguously, paradoxically, both and neither? Are they figures of the moral imagination schematizing an ideal of moral relationships in terms of a deep topography of the intersubjective body? Could it be said that the traces of the other's claims on me have no reality other than the role they play in my tracework itself—the tropological staging of my self-development as a moral subject, provocatively figured as a reflexive turn, or rather return, to retrieve, or attempt to retrieve, traces of motivation and guidance from the gift of a primordial incarnation, a body imagined as already graced with a moral predisposition? In this case, it is not that traces of the moral inscription are (in some straightforward way, synchronically) already there, present in the flesh, simply awaiting the time of a reading, but rather that they are a tropological production, markings on a fabulous topography of the body, legible, if at all, only in and as the very movement that would make the flesh reveal its moral assignment—legible, as it were, only by the heart that seeks them as signposts of encouragement along the stages of its moral journey. (This points beyond the bounds of the present chapter, but we will be returning to the question of moral development in the next section.) References to originary traces of alterity, traces of the other's absolute claims on my ability to be responsive, would thus represent, in effect, a way of turning the goal of moral maturity into an origin and positing the origin as the goal. Or perhaps we can say only that, in the philosopher's obsession with tracework, there is a response to the suffering of the other that would remind us, for the sake of this other, of the need to keep a terrible vigilance—that, namely, as Levinas testifies, of a certain inconsolable, irremediable insomnia. Perhaps the trace, alterity taking hold of the flesh, can only be thought in terms of a "hauntology."

There is, in his phenomenological attempts to say the ethical and theologico-political signification of the face, an intriguing remark, intricately reconfiguring its presence:

> A trace lost in a trace, less than nothing in the trace of an excessive, but always ambiguous trace of itself (possibly a mask, in a void, possibly nothingness or "pure form of the sensibility"), the face of the neighbor obsesses me with his destitution. (OB 93, AE 118)

Possibly a mask. . . . In our world, says Levinas at another time and in another place, "faces are masks."[93] But this, for Levinas, is a condition of disgrace: the face disfigured by ego-logical investments. The face of one who has fallen away from the fully human. A later passage in the same text is instructive in this regard:

> The face as the desensibilization, the dematerialization of the sense datum, completes the movement, still caught up in the figures of mythological monsters, by which the animal body or half-body let an evanescent expression break through on the face of the human head they bore.[94]

We are never very far away from the possibility of reverting to cruelties and monstrosities that deny our experience of the face of the other. The mask that represents a human face, attached to the body of a mythological monster, is a reminder of the persistent entanglement of myth and Enlightenment and a warning against the illusions of total disenchantment. We may "have" faces; but we are still, in a certain sense, bound to the condition of the animals.

The mask is a significant trope in *Otherwise Than Being*, sharpening Levinas's phenomenology of the face as a critical hauntology and transformative appeal. The "I," he says there, is at first a "no-one, clothed with purely borrowed being, which masks its nameless singularity by conferring on it a role" (OB 106, AE 135). Under the "borrowed mask of being" (OB 106, AE 134–35), there is the dimension of our humanity—not only our nakedness, our destitution, our exposedness and vulnerability, but also our felt responsiveness to others:

> Prior to the play of being, before the present, older than the time of consciousness that is accessible in memory, in its "deep yore, never remote enough," the oneself is exposed as a hypostasis, of which the being it is as an entity is but a mask. (AE 134–35, OB 106)

The socialized gloss is a "comic mask" (OB 107, AE 136), concealing from ourselves and from others the painfulness of existence. Attempting to formulate the emergence of the moral self as a process whereby one "returns" to the felt sense haunting that hypostasis and retrieves it for moral life, he again speaks of the mask, carefully distinguishing the process with which he is concerned from prevailing conceptions of the self's formation:

> The recurrence in the subject is thus neither freedom of possession of self by self in reflection, nor the freedom of play where I take myself for this or that, traversing avatars under the carnival masks of history. (OB 125, AE 161)

If the first of these conceptions of freedom may be identified as "modern," the second may perhaps be identified as "postmodern." (But in terms of Marx's analysis of the historical evolution of capitalism, both conceptions would represent mere masks of freedom: "A definite social relation between people which has assumed the phantasmagoric form of a relation between things.")[95] In any case, the process toward which Levinas's phenomenology is pointing is radically different. For him, the formation of the moral self involves tearing off the masks, returning to one's exposedness, making felt contact with that existential condition and living from out of that, without the mediation of the masks. From an ego-logical point of view, this

exposure of the face to the face of the other would be the unspeakable terror of self-effacement, the most extreme deconstruction of the identity of
the "self" as the culture of modernity has conceived it. There is no telling
what identity-shattering effect this exposure of the face behind the mask
could have on the eyewitness, the one who sees it—as Rilke's narrative,
which we will soon be reading, certainly suggests.

In a major series of lectures gathered under the title *What Is Called
Thinking?*, Heidegger reflects on the mode of perception that Levinas excludes from the ethical relation, observing that

> man is the beast endowed with reason. Reason is the perception of what
> is, which always means also what can be and ought to be. To perceive
> implies, in ascending order: to welcome and take in; to accept and take
> in the encounter; to take up face to face; to undertake and see
> through—and this means to talk through. . . . [A]*nimal rationale* is the
> animal which lives by perceiving what is. . . . The perception that pre-
> vails within reason produces and adduces purposes, establishes rules,
> provides means and ways, and attunes reason to the modes of action.
> Reason's perception unfolds as this manifold providing, which is first of
> all and always a confrontation, a face-to-face presentation. Thus one
> might also say . . . [that] man is the animal that confronts face to face.
> A mere animal, such as a dog, never confronts anything, it can never
> confront anything *to its face;* to do so, the animal would have to per-
> ceive *itself.* It cannot say "I", it cannot talk at all.[96]

Continuing this thought, he reminds us that "*Persona* means the actor's
mask through which his dramatic tale is sounded." And he therefore contends that, "Since man is the percipient who perceives what is, we can think
of him as the *persona,* the mask, of being."[97] Called to a thinking that recalls the Holocaust, but perhaps is too shattered to see beyond it, Max
Horkheimer sees a different truth behind the mask: "The narrow-minded
and cunning creatures that call themselves men will someday be seen as
caricatures, evil masks behind which a better possibility decays. In order to
penetrate those masks, the imagination would need powers of which fascism has already divested it. The force of imagination is absorbed in the
struggle every individual must wage in order to live."[98]

In one of his lectures, a Talmudic commentary published in *Nine Talmudic Readings,* Levinas writes to remind us of the

> essential manner in which the human being is exposed to the point of
> losing the skin which protects him, a skin which has completely become
> a face, as if a being, centered about his core, experienced a removal of
> this core and, losing it, was "for the other" before any dialogue![99]

This passage comes so close to describing an experience about which Rilke writes that one should not be surprised to discover some day that Levinas actually had it in mind when he wrote that passage. There are, near the beginning of Rilke's *Notebooks of Malte Laurids Brigge,* two frightening sets of notes, all the more frightening because of the peculiar detachment and lightness of their tone: notes about learning to see—or rather, more specifically, learning to see faces. This is indeed a question of imagination, a question with which it must struggle—and not without questioning itself. For what occupies the imagination—the production of images—is not without its risks, its dangers. As the Jewish prohibition against making images of the divine face would remind us.

> I am learning to see. I don't know why it is, but everything penetrates more deeply into me and does not stop at the place where until now it always used to finish. I have an inner self of which I was ignorant. Everything goes thither now. What happens there I do not know. . . .
>
> . . . I am learning to see. . . . To think, for instance, that I have never been aware before how many faces there are. There are quantities of human beings, but there are many more faces, for each person has several. There are people who wear the same face for years; naturally it wears out, it gets dirty, it splits at the folds, it stretches, like gloves one has worn on a journey. These are thrifty, simple people; they do not change their face; they never even have it cleaned. It is good enough, they say, and who can prove to them the contrary? The question of course arises, since they have several faces, what do they do with the others? They store them up. Their children wear them. But sometimes, too, it happens that their dogs go out with them on. And why not? A face is a face. . . .
>
> Other people put their faces on, one after the other, with uncanny rapidity and wear them out. At first it seems to them they are provided for always; but they scarcely reach forty—and they have come to the last. This naturally has something tragic. They are not accustomed to taking care of faces, their last is worn through in a week, has holes, and in many places is thin as paper; and then little by little the under layer, the no-face, comes through, and they go about with that.
>
> But the woman, the woman; she had completely collapsed into herself, forward into her hands. It was at the corner of rue Notre-Dame-des-Champs. I began to walk softly as soon as I saw her. . . .
>
> . . . The woman startled and pulled away too quickly out of herself, too violently, so that her face remained in her two hands. I could see it lying in them, its hollow form. It cost me indescribable effort to stay with those hands and not to look at what had torn itself out of them. I shuddered to see a face from the inside, but still I was much more afraid of the naked flayed head without a face.[100]

This text gives many things to be thought. Here, however, I will limit myself to some brief comments. The notes are initially about faces, and not the face: they are about surfaces, about the faces we present to the world outside ourselves, the masks that we adopt, at once concealing and revealing ourselves in the multiplicity of roles we play, and play out, on the stages of life's way. But with the appearance of "the woman," these notes take a frightening turn, as we are confronted with "a face from the inside," and compelled to imagine a human being *without* one of these faces. What, then, would we be facing? A woman, of course, without her repertoire of social faces. (What is the significance of the fact that "the other," here, is a woman?) And yet, I want to say, this woman would *still* have a face: *the* face, namely, of a human being. However deformed, however disfigured, she would still have the face of her humanity. This, I take it, is the face of ethical experience towards which Levinas wants to draw us—the invisible face, the face of our humanity, the one that is, in a certain sense, hidden from view, beneath, or behind, the faces we present, the masks we play, to the world. This, the naked and exposed face, the face that is other than these faces, is the one that we need to *learn* how to see.

The notes suggest a certain phenomenology; they abandon a customary discretion to touch, to reach into an experience that could turn our thoughts in the direction of the coming-into-visibility, the "epiphany," of this invisible face, the face that Levinas describes as "naked," the face that he says speaks in its silence of the other's utter "destitution." The first note begins with an acknowledgment of learning: "I am learning to see." The author then says: "I don't know why it is, but everything penetrates more deeply into me and does not stop at the place where until now it always used to finish." This experience of being "penetrated" is crucial for learning to see the face of the other. (This "penetration" is what Levinas is referring to when he writes about our subjection to the other, our exposure to the moral imperative embodied in the presence of the other.) Anyone and everyone can see the superficial masks, the social faces that people wear; but it sometimes takes a certain moral education, a certain learning, to see the deeper, more invisible face of humanity in the other. Even though, in a sense that Levinas wants us to see, everyone has always already witnessed, beheld, and been held in beholdenness by, this invisible face. Even though, in an important sense, one that we need to think through very carefully, this face of ethical communion is pre-eminently visible, is "in plain view," right in front of us, right there to be seen. Always already—and yet, not yet. Or perhaps even, in another sense, never.

This "true" face of the other comes to the surface in interaction with my responsiveness, but comes as the immeasurably deep. It is my responsiveness to the other that solicits this face, that welcomes it and brings it to the surface, making it to some extent visible. The face is not a face, not a mask on the surface: it is the immeasurable, impenetrable depth of the other; it is the most intimate distance of the other. It is the "presence" of the other for a "me" which is responsive in a dimension of my being itself so deep that, until I have been tutored and have given it some thought, I am not even conscious of its happening. Thus the author says: "I have an inner self of which I was ignorant. Everything goes thither now. What happens there I do not know."

The face is a paradoxical presence, an imperative at once absolutely singular and absolutely universal. For every face is absolutely unique, expressing and manifesting the individual; and yet, the face is also that through which, most of all, our "common" humanity is most undeniably in evidence, most visibly demonstrated. But the face of the individual, the face as singular, can betray its universal humanity—just as, conversely, the presence of the universal can betray the singularity of the face. And if both dimensions of the face are vulnerable to imposed invisibility, they are equally vulnerable to imposed visibility.

The face that the poet writes of seeing in the woman's hands is in a certain sense *not* her face: her face is rather what remains behind, naked, flayed, without describable traits, withdrawn therefore from all description, all narrative, all representation, all thematization and knowledge (OB 96–97, AE 122–24). What the poet sees left behind is the absolute withdrawal of the woman's humanity—her real face—from all rationally constituted systems of meaning: "the anarchy," as Levinas puts it, "of what has never been present" (OB 97, AE 124). What the poet imagines he sees fills him with horror: for it is (again in Levinas's words) "as if the face of this other, although invisible, continued my own face and kept me awake by its very invisibility, by the unpredictability that it threatens."[101]

Reflecting on Fewkoombey in Berthold Brecht's *Threepenny Novel*, Walter Benjamin speaks of "a new face, or rather, scarcely a face but 'transparent and faceless', like the millions who fill barracks and basement apartments."[102] According to one way of reading the *Notebooks*, the woman whom Rilke observes *loses* her face; she thus becomes faceless. She loses not only her individuality, but perhaps also, if only for the common eye, her humanity. For it would be precisely the lost social face that manifested, that insisted, on her singular representation of humanity. Without such a face, she would become less than human: something terrible, an inhuman monster.

Is the face, then, merely a mask, merely a surface? Is our *humanity* merely mask and surface, only skin deep? Is it in the skin that covers the face?

In "Ethics as First Philosophy," Levinas articulates with a powerful phenomenological lucidity the experience of the moment of unmasking that is crucial to the formation of the moral self. What he wants us to see is that the unmasking of *my* face occurs in the face-to-face, precisely when I find myself deeply affected by what I see as the vulnerability, the mortality of the other:

> From the very beginning, there is a face to face steadfast in its exposure to invisible death, to a mysterious forsakenness. Beyond the visibility of whatever is unveiled, and prior to any knowledge of death, mortality lies in the Other. . . . But in its expression, in its mortality, the face before me summons me, calls for me, begs for me, as if the invisible death that must be faced by the Other, pure otherness, separated, in some way, from any whole, were my business. It is as if that invisible death, ignored by the Other, whom already it concerns by the nakedness of its face, were already "regarding me" prior to confronting me, and becoming the death that stares me in the face.[103]

It is through the face of the other that I am able to unmask myself, for it is the face of the other, showing me death, that compels me, that enables me, to touch my own death—and thereby to tear off the mask that seals me into an egotism even more terrible.

As if understanding Levinas's thought that "the face summons me to my obligations and judges me" (TaI 215, TeI 190), Nathaniel Hawthorne was tormented by such matters. In his "Preface" to *Mosses from an Old Manse*, he says: "So far as I am a man of really individual attributes, I veil my face."[104] Precisely this is in question in "The Minister's Black Veil" (1836), in which Hawthorne tells the story of a minister who covers his face with a black veil that he never allows himself to remove, not even when at home by himself, not even as he lies dying. Although the minister's services, and the man himself, are welcomed by all, the cause and motive behind this strange comportment soon become the topic, of course, of endless speculation within the community. The black veil is a monstrous defacement, a monstrous disfigurement; and it becomes an uncanny presence, a haunting obsession, among the faithful parishioners, in whom it creates terrible anxieties and crises of conscience.[105] In some respects, its effects of meaning are like those suggested by Gyges's ring,[106] about which Levinas writes with obsessive frequency:

> Gyges's ring symbolizes separation. Gyges plays a double game, a presence to the others and an absence, speaking to "others" and evading

speech; Gyges is the very condition of man, the possibility of injustice and radical egoism, the possibility of accepting the rules of the game, but cheating. (TaI 173, TeI 148)

What egoism, what injustice, what dark sin, what evil, could the minister be hiding? Is the veil intended to make all those he encounters finally come face-to-face with their own egoism, their own injustice, their own sin and evil? Is the minister, stubbornly resisting the community's pressures to remove his disquieting veil, refusing to play by the rules of the game—by rules that permit people to live in comfortable self-deception, without conscience, without guilt, without exposure? Is the veil a confession of "the shame that freedom feels for itself" (TaI 86, TeI 58–59) and a reminder of conscience to others? (See also TaI 82–85, 100; TeI 54–55, TeI 74.)

There is a provocative remark by Nietzsche in *Beyond Good and Evil* that would seem to bear on these questions, perhaps penetrating the mystery of the minister's veil:

> A man whose sense of shame has some profundity encounters his destinies and difficult decisions on paths which few ever reach and of whose mere existence his closest intimates must not know: his mortal danger is concealed from their eyes, and so is his regained sureness of life. Such a concealed man who instinctively needs speech for silence and for burial in silence and who is inexhaustible in his evasion of communication, *wants* and sees to it that a mask of him roams in his place through the hearts and heads of his friends. And supposing he did not want it, he would still realize some day that in spite of that a mask of him is there. . . . Every profound spirit needs a mask: even more, around every profound spirit a mask is growing continually, owing to the constantly false, namely *shallow* interpretations of every word, every step, every sign of life he gives.[107]

Might not this description interpret the deep shame, the trauma, the wound, that the minister nurses deep in the flesh of his psyche?

Never removed, the minister's veil *becomes*, in effect, his surrogate face. But if the face is itself only a veil, a front, what lies behind it? Confronted with this uncanny phenomenon, can we continue to assume that behind every face there is a soul, a spiritual presence, a transcendental ego? Can we assume that there is an essential truth behind the incomprehensible appearance? Or is the veil precisely an epiphany of the face, the face showing itself in its nudity, its destitution, its confession of the flesh, of moral weakness and spiritual sin? In *Elective Affinities*, Goethe observed that

> any peculiarly unhappy person, even if he is blameless, is marked in a terrible way. His presence excites a sort of horror whenever he is seen

and noticed. Everyone searches his appearance for traces of the monstrous fate which has been laid upon him; everyone is curious and at the same time fearful.[108]

This could easily be imagined as an observation reflecting on the minister's black veil. Is the veil the visible manifestation of a deep and inescapable unhappiness: the shame of human sinfulness? the compassionate suffering of one who has taken upon himself an impossible responsibility for others? the unhappiness of one who feels the sufferings of all God's sentient creatures? the pain of one who cannot turn away from or shut his eyes to the injustices that divide and destroy?

Levinas struggles with difficult moral questions, drawing us through the face into the realm of death. The face, he says, is a living "that is still not arrested in the absolute immobility of a death mask" (OB 90, AE 115). But, in its living, it nevertheless always "signifies mortality"[109] and calls the ego, "hostage of the other person," to answer for this death, or death in life, "to which the face of the other person is exposed."[110] In *Totality and Infinity*, an earlier work, he wrote:

> We have attempted to expose the epiphany of the face as the origin of exteriority [i.e., my moral subjection to the other]. The primary phenomenon of signification coincides with exteriority; exteriority is signifyingness itself. And only the face in its morality is exterior. In this epiphany the face is not resplendent as a form clothing a content, as an *image*, but as the nudity of the principle, behind which there is nothing further. The dead face becomes a form, a mortuary mask; it is shown instead of letting see—but precisely thus no longer appears as a face. (TaI 261–62, TeI 239)

Not even in death can the face be known; because, in death, what is there before me is no longer a face. That other whom I would like to possess with my gaze and know in Levinas's sense of "know," integrating it into a worldly totality, is other than the infinitely other (TaI 55, TeI 26). Thus I remain claimed by the other, "hostage" to the other, responsible to and for the other, even beyond the other's death.

The "hermeneutic" speculation into which the sight of the minister's veil draws us ends in failure, in a resigned acceptance of the withholding or withdrawing of all meaning. Levinas would certainly understand this:

> The notion of the face . . . brings us to a notion of meaning prior to my *Sinngebung* and thus independent of my initiative and my power. (TaI 51, TeI 22)

The veil, the face's "supplement," intensifies the experience of a failure in the fulfillment of meaning-giving intentionality. We cannot see what we want to see, cannot know what we want to know: our seeing and knowing are frustrated, denied fulfillment. Unlike things, which *give* themselves to me,

> the face is present in its refusal to be contained. In this sense, it cannot be comprehended, that is, encompassed. It is neither seen nor touched—for in visual and tactile sensation the identity of the I envelops the alterity of the object, which becomes precisely a content. (TaI 194, TeI 168)

If the face is a bar to the ego's bestowing of meaning and to the ego's enjoyment of meaning-fulfillment, so too is the minister's black veil. Precisely as such a bar, however, the veil compels us to question ourselves: it exposes us in our nakedness; it *subjects* us to its questioning.

Perhaps the minister shrouds his face in order to symbolize a commitment to God that spells his death to the world. Perhaps he sacrifices his own face in order to let the invisible face of God be seen, or at least felt: the veil would then be like the face of a mirror, an instrument of divine judgment, compelling all those who look at it to look deeply into themselves and examine their sins with the presence of divine judgment in their hearts. The black veil, assuming the exteriority of the face hidden behind it, arrests the gaze, denying it any representation of the face, returning the gaze to its source; it throws people into abysses of shame and guilt; it confronts people with reminders of death. The minister's veil is perhaps the face's way of appealing to responsibility "before appearing to the eye."[111]

Hooper's last words perhaps suggest that the face itself is only a veil, and that what it conceals is the mystery of life and death. In any event, Hooper's veil causes fear and trembling, for to look at it is to be drawn into its abyssal blackness, its annihilation of face, and turned, through its mirror-like inversions, into a corpse or a ghost. The veil is, in effect, a mask of death, a death's head, an exemplary display of divine justice. A revelation that conceals what it reveals, a concealment that reveals concealment.

The veil is not only a bar to contact and open dialogue, not only a bar to sympathy and consolation; it is also a bar to meaning, to the fulfillment of presence.[112] It announces the time of Apocalypse, but continually defers the promise of ultimate meaning, the promise of redemption. Not even in death is the minister's veil withdrawn and the promise of revelation kept.

If, as Benjamin argues, "Truth is not an unveiling that destroys the mystery, but rather a revelation that does it justice,"[113] then the minister's black veil is indeed an instrument of truth, compelling those who encounter it to face the most demanding truth. For this most demanding truth, what is required is not an unveiling of the face, but, on the contrary, a veiling that serves revelation: "The absolute experience," as Levinas says, "is not disclosure but revelation."[114]

What is revealed? The suffering, the destitution of the other. And to the extent that this suffering, this destitution, is a consequence of the face that we have, whether wittingly or unwittingly, immediately or mediately, imposed on the other, it commands us to "unmake" it. "The face," says Levinas, "is unmade": "Le visage est défait."[115] In "Facies Hippocratica," Rebecca Comay comments, with regard to this sentence, that "The 'unmaking' of the face is the only way to 'save' a face already defaced by its inscription in the world of exchange and measure—the world as such."[116] Perhaps the minister's veil, unmaking his face and signifying his spiritual death to the world, may also be read as a protest against the disfigurements of a world in which the moral dimension of face-to-face relationships is reduced to the measures of an equivalence economy. Perhaps the veil withdraws the face from this disfigurement, withdraws it from the totalizing system of calculative rationality and calculative justice, withdraws it into the invisible realm where a divine justice may judge it.

"When we look at someone," says Benjamin, "there is the expectation that the recipient of the gaze will return our look. When this expectation is met, there is the experience of aura in its fullness. . . . To experience the aura of a phenomenon means to invest it [*belehnen*] with the ability to look at us in return."[117] The minister's black veil is a refusal to return the gaze, a refusal, therefore, of the auratic. But precisely because it denies the gaze of the other, it holds the other in its spell. According to Benjamin,

> the deeper the remoteness that a glance has to overcome, the stronger will be the spell that is apt to emanate from the gaze. In eyes that mirror, the absence of the looker remains complete. It is precisely for this reason that such eyes know nothing of distance.[118]

For Benjamin, the question of distance is crucial to the logic of symbol and allegory—and nowhere, perhaps, more compelling than with regard to the allegorical significance of the baroque image of the death's head (*Totenkopf*).[119] Examining the different effects of symbol and allegory, he takes us into the "abyss of allegory" (*Abgrund der Allegorie*),[120] arguing that,

> whereas in the symbol destruction is idealized and the transfigured face of nature [*das transfigurierte Antlitz der Natur*] is fleetingly revealed in the light of redemption [*im Lichte der Erlösung*], in allegory the observer is confronted with the *facies hippocratica* of history as a petrified, primordial landscape. Everything about history that, from the

very beginning, has been untimely, sorrowful, unsuccessful, is expressed in a face—or rather in a death's head. And although such a thing lacks all "symbolic" freedom of expression, all classical proportion, all humanity—nevertheless, this is the form in which man's subjection to nature is most obvious and it significantly gives rise not only to the enigmatic question of the nature of human existence as such, but also of the biographical historicity of the individual. This is the heart of the allegorical way of seeing, of the baroque, secular explanation of history as the Passion of the world [*Leidensgeschichte*]; its importance resides solely in the stations of its decline. The greater the significance, the greater the subjection to death, because death digs most deeply the jagged line of demarcation between physical nature and significance. But if nature has always been subject to the power of death, it is also true that it has always been allegorical. Nature and death both come to fruition in historical development, just as they are closely linked as seeds in the creature's graceless state of sin.[121]

Quoting a passage from Daniel Casper von Lohenstein's *Hyacinthen* ("Yea, when the Highest comes to bring in the harvest from the graveyard, so will I, a death's-head, become an angel's countenance"),[122] Benjamin provokes the thought that if the black-veiled face should be seen as a death's-head, it could also evoke the countenance of an angel, the angel, perhaps, of divine justice. But not far from these allegorical images the logic of elective affinities turns the death's-head into the monstrous, many-eyed head of a Medusa, the monster whose sight petrifies all those who are unfortunate enough to have received the looks it casts.[123] (For Merleau-Ponty, the gaze becomes "inhuman" when it withdraws from, and does not experience itself as, "communication" and "communion.")[124] Like the face of Medusa, with so many eyes that one can never hide from its terrible judgment, the black-veiled face, the death's-head, will frighten all those who see it, compelling them to face the imperative truth of divine justice. Until the time of redemption, the truth that we must face is the legible truth of suffering, a *Leidensgeschichte* etched into the flesh of faces: in particular, a history of the injustices that indifference and hatred in regard to those who are seen as our other, our enemy, have traced in a writing still invisible to many.

In his *Phenomenology of Perception*, Merleau-Ponty began a lifetime of reflection on the phenomenology of our perception of others, correctly recognizing that questions of morality and political justice are already at stake in the very earliest moments of perception. He shows that

> our relationship to the social is, like our relationship to the world,
> *deeper* than any express perception or any judgement. It is as false to

place ourselves in society as an object among other objects as it is to place society within ourselves as an object of thought, and in both cases the mistake lies in treating the social as an object. We must return to the social with which we are in contact by the mere fact of existing, and which we carry about inseparably with us before any objectification.[125]

There is, he points out, an "anonymous," "pre-personal" subject, a subject radically different from the Cartesian and Kantian subjects, that precedes the *cogito*, the ego-logical subject of perception and knowledge.[126] This subject is indeed a subject—but not, or not first and foremost, in the egological sense traditionally understood by empiricism and intellectualism. Rather, we must recognize the presence of a subject because of our original *exposure* to the solicitations of the other.[127] Even before we are actively engaged with others at the level of perception, we have already, according to Merleau-Ponty, been "passively" responsive to their presence: it is, in fact, a question, as Levinas has so beautifully described it, of "a passivity more passive than passive." (With his elaboration of this moment, it is clear that Levinas is pursuing, both beyond and against Husserl, Husserl's own phenomenology of a corporeal intentionality he described as "passive synthesis.") I would argue, and have done so elsewhere, that it is the experience of exposure peculiar to this original subject, always already responsively subject to the other, and not only the reflexively critical experience of the subsequently achieved ego-logical subject, which we must retrieve and the development of which we must nurture if there is to be any real hope for the sociocultural construction of a truly *universal* subject—a subject, namely, that would hold itself responsible for the extension of justice, beyond visibility, beyond the possibility of discursive, face-to-face relations, to all sentient beings.

In "Juliette, or Enlightenment and Morality," a chapter of *Dialectic of Enlightenment* that seems to have been written by Max Horkheimer, we are reminded, however, of the limitations on the "exposure" and "compassion" of the original subject, reminded that the "universal subject" necessary for the rule of justice will not emerge from the course of nature without social mediation. Indeed, according to the argument of this chapter:

> there is an aspect of compassion which conflicts with justice, to which of course Nietzsche allies it. It confirms the rule of inhumanity by the exception which it practises. By reserving the cancellation of injustice to fortuitous love of one's neighbour, compassion accepts that the law of universal alienation—which it would mitigate—is unalterable. Certainly, as an individual, the compassionate man represents the claim of the individual—that is, to live—against the generality, against nature and society, which deny it. But that unity with the universal, as with

the heart, which the individual displays, is shown to be deceptive in his own weakness. It is not the softness but the restrictive element in pity, which makes it questionable; for compassion is always inadequate.[128]

I think this is correct. To end injustice, social policy cannot, and must not, depend on the velleities and vicissitudes of compassion, or on the contingencies of philanthropic gestures. But Horkheimer and Adorno do not recognize, here, that the potential for compassion can come from a much deeper dimension of individual experience and that our social practices— including practices that construct the ways of our perception—can draw on this potential, work with it, and develop it, making it a much stronger, more reliable source for the moral energies that are needed to build a more just social order.

By calling attention to the primordiality of exposure, passivity, and vulnerability in our being with others, and articulating it phenomenologically as a dimension of our embodied experience, our experience as beings of a spiritual flesh, Levinas is able to connect responsibility for social justice to the facticity of a responsiveness to the other that precedes the voluntarism of the ego-logical subject, taking hold of us, binding us, through the compassion of the deeper, more primordial dimension of our incarnation. Through the very nature of our embodiment, our flesh, which is far deeper, infinitely deeper, than our conventional experience of the body would ever concede, we are always already being moved, whether we realize it or not, by a deep compassion for the other. (And this is presumably true even of the man who takes pleasure in torture or commits murder. Investigating the childhood of such men, one always uncovers stories of abuse that severely damaged or virtually destroyed this dimension of their embodiment. Behind the evil deeds of Auschwitz, one may also find a "thoughtlessness" that disconnects the agent from the bodily felt sense of his acts. Evil is possible only as a radical alienation and uprootedness in our embodiment.)

Read in conjunction with the phenomenological narrative of moral formation elaborated by Merleau-Ponty, Levinas's account makes a contribution of incalculable significance. Modern theories of justice forgot the wisdom in ancient Greek culture that Plato and Aristotle attempted, albeit not unproblematically, to pass on in their discussions of moral education, and in particular, the best way to approach and draw on the inherently proto-moral order already implicit in the earliest natural experiences of infancy and childhood, so as to give them, in their maturity, the desired moral form. However, Levinas does not provide an adequate account of the *developmental* stages through which the experience of exposure and responsiveness, of subjection to the other, must pass in order to become the responsibility for justice that is morally required of the adult as citizen of a democratic state and member of a planetary community. Nor does he sufficiently register the importance of socialization and the importance of social-political institutions in making possible the step, the transition, from the ethical, where it is a question of seeing in the other person an absolute singularity, to the moral-political, where it is a question of recognizing all others according to the justice of an abstract universality. Thus he does not sufficiently explain the essential and decisive *connection* between the "ethical" experience to which he calls our attention—the face-to-face responsibility for the concrete, singular other—and the problematic of justice, in which it is a question of responsibility for all others, abstract others—including those who are invisible and unknown, those who are deceased and those not yet born.

But this is not merely a limitation charged against Levinas, nor is it merely a problematic for philosophers to work on. Rather, it is first and foremost a question and a challenge confronting everyone who is endowed by nature with a capacity to feel, to see and hear, to engage in discourse, to be responsive. It is a question of our responsibility for the universal extension of justice to all sentient beings: how we are to respond to the absolutely irrecusable, singular claims on our humanity asserted by the very existence of all the other sentient beings—beings whose faces we cannot see, cannot ourselves face—passing for a time through the world.

In *Otherwise Than Being,* Levinas denounces the "freedom" that a certain modern bourgeois liberalism, now a politics of egoism and ruthless capitalism, has always prized: not even the "carnival masks of history" (OB 125, AE 161) can succeed in masking the suffering wrought by such freedom, always enjoyed at the expense of the other. This, I think, is what Benjamin was pointing to when he wrote, in his *Trauerspiel* book:

> Everything about history that from the beginning has been untimely, sorrowful, unsuccessful, is expressed in a face—no, in a skull.[129]

History until now is a story of oppression and violence, a story also, therefore, of untold suffering. For the gaze rooted in compassion, rooted in a *sense* of justice defying the tales of the victors, who would make this suffering, for which they are the cause, totally invisible, history therefore can present itself only as the death or mortification of the face—as a death's-head or skull. The face of history is a skull that faces the living with the face of death, the face of injustice: a face of death *due* to injustice. But if the face of history is even today, in a time of destitution amidst abundance, nothing but a grinning skull, or rather, as in the killing fields of Cambodia, a pyramid of skulls, why must we tolerate it remaining in this state until the time of redemption, until the end of time and history as we have known them, when the radiance, the *Schein*, of the face of God—another god?—might burn through the chains of the historical continuum? Must it be that only the angel of history, an angel sent in a time beyond time by the god of the time of redemption, will give to the suffering human face its longed-for justice?

In the maturity of the moral self posited by Habermas, the face becomes a mask of discursive reason. Is it possible that there is, paradoxically, and contrary to his unquestionably admirable intentions, a monstrous inhumanity in the face this mask both conceals and reveals? Whether it conceals or reveals, the mask always betrays!

In our time, the persistence of injustice, of institutionalized forms of violence against the oppressed, has created a new kind of mask: the mask of the terrorist who resorts to violence as the only remaining weapon in the struggle against the greater violence of injustice. In *Die Maßnahme*, Berthold Brecht wrote of revolutionaries whose faces, visible for all to see, were reduced to "empty pages on which the revolution may write its orders."[130] This reading of their faces may itself be an injustice; but in any case, today's most extreme revolutionaries wear masks to conceal the reading of their faces. In a series of interviews, Subcomandante Marcos, leader of the native peoples of Chiapas, Mexico, reflected on the significance of the ski masks he and his army are forced to wear. The masks are not only necessary for their survival; they are also emblematic, hermeneutical, and allegorical, hiding faces behind multiple layers of meaning. Whereas the duplicitous enemies of the people have "double faces," faces that conceal their indifference to the suffering of the poor behind faces that are really faceless masks of bureaucratic design, the oppressed cover their faces with masks of facelessness to fight against a regime of injustice in which they are treated and seen as "faceless." The masks of the guerrillas demonstrate this reality, expressing the condition that makes it necessary for them to engage in a struggle to give back to the native people their true faces. The struggle of the Zapatista National Liberation Army is very much a struggle *for* the truth, a struggle *over* the truth. The masks thus speak the monstrous truth: the truth, namely, that the truth is concealed as long as injustice prevails. Masks must conceal their faces, then—until that moment when the struggle for truth is ended in a lasting victory for the oppressed and the faces of the people, shining with the beauty of a *recognized* dignity, the *invisible* face of their humanity, can be seen and heard wherever justice is at stake.[131] It is very much a question, as Rilke's story says, of "taking care of faces." But in a time, as

Adorno points out in writing about Beckett's *Endgame*, when it can some-. times seem that "the only face left is the one whose tears have dried up."[132]

III. THE HUMANITY OF THE OTHER:
A QUESTION FOR VISION

In *Totality and Infinity* (TeI 188, TaI 213), Levinas observes that, "in the eyes that look at me," there shines "the whole of humanity." At the same time that Levinas wants to insist on "our" uniqueness and singularity (each of us must be seen and made visible as "the only one of his kind"), he also wants to say that each of us "belongs to humanity" (*au genre humain*). It is easy for us to say something like this, for, in a sense, the experience in question is very familiar. So familiar, in fact, that we may not at once real- ize how perplexing, how uncanny it actually is. How is it possible for the universal—humanity—to shine forth in and from the singular? How can the singularity of the other reflect the universal? Why is it absolutely im- perative that I see the other in his or her singularity if I am ever to see the other's humanity, the other's universality? And how can we escape from the hermeneutical "seeing as," a form of language which seems to impose itself on us at the very moment when we are trying to say something that withdraws the singular from typification?

Reflection on our experience with vision in the constitution of the ethical relation can compel our exposure, beyond the possibility of meta- physical resolution, to the inalterably aporetic logic of the relation between the universal and the singular in the revelation of humanity that takes place through the "presence" of the other. Seeing the humanity *of* the singular other, seeing humanity *in* the singular other: seeing the other *as* human. The hermeneutical grammar of the "as," hidden in the first two locutions, is more paradoxical than it may seem. For the experience in question radi- cally exceeds the possibility of representation within the logic, the cate- gories, of universal and singular, in terms of which metaphysics has always attempted to represent it. This is, ultimately, what I want to show in the course of our hopeless struggle, here, to understand, to make sense, of this experience with sight within the framework of our metaphysical heritage.

In *Difficult Freedom*, Levinas makes two assertions which, if thought to- gether, could almost be read as suggesting completion in the form of a prac- tical syllogism:

[1] "The face of man is the medium through which the invisible in him becomes visible and enters into commerce with us."

[2] "It is in economic justice that man glimpses the face of man."[133]

The first proposition is important because, as I will show, it suggests that it is the visibility of an invisible dimension to the face that mediates the transition from the ethical relation to the relation required by justice. The second proposition is also important, because it could be thought to challenge the distinction Levinas makes between the ethical and the political and the priority he asserts for the ethical. It certainly seems to recognize that conditions of economic justice are as crucial for an ethical experience of the other person's humanity as the ethical experience is necessary for realizing the need to work for economic justice. Seeing humanity in and as the face of the other is not an experience that phenomenology can easily articulate; not even Levinas's greatly altered method is sufficiently responsive to the intricacies and mediations of this experience.

In his *Critique of Instrumental Reason,* Max Horkheimer wrote with concern of his impression that "the capacity for experience that transcends the immediate situation is being atrophied."[134] There is support for this observation in a passage in *Otherwise Than Being,* where Levinas condemns the withdrawal from social concern that he discerns among the intellectuals who are his contemporaries. He remarks that

> one can call it utopian, yet it is the exact situation of men, at least in our time, when intellectuals feel themselves to be hostages for destitute masses unconscious of their wretchedness. Intellectuals are today mistrustful of a philosophy of the one keeper of his brother, the one-for-the-other . . . : they would scornfully call it humanist or even hagiographical. (OB 166, AE 211)

Levinas is not afraid of appearing to be uncompromisingly utopian; he will not abandon the cause of justice for those who are needy and destitute. To this end, he gives a radically different interpretation to the ethics of responsibility for the other—and ultimately articulates, albeit differently from Habermas, a discursive conception of justice that he believes can alone protect and preserve the infinite otherness of the other. His conception is grounded in our experience of ourselves as hostage to the other. It is, however, as we shall see, a conception that rejects humanism for its failure to do justice to the other.

What is involved in the shift from the perspective of the ethical relation, in which the "I" sees the absolute singularity, the absolute uniqueness of the other, to the perspective of the moral-political relation, where it is a question of the normative universality of justice, requiring a symmetrical relation involving comparisons, equivalences, and calculations of reciprocity? Has the discourse of humanism failed to see and make visible what matters here? And if it has, what would account for its failure? What

298 / *The Philosophers*

alteration in the gaze would correspond to, or even perhaps make possible, the shift from the ethical to the moral-political relation? Would the shift ultimately depend, not merely on a fundamental alteration in the gaze, but even more on a shift from a relation happening in the light of perception to a relation happening in speech? Then does Levinas in fact attempt to withdraw *both* relations from vision, light, and the ontological commitments of vision and light, in order to "return" them to the speaking and listening? Does Levinas ultimately need, therefore, to withdraw the face of the other, and the relations through which the humanity of the singular other is to be revealed, not only from the discourse of humanism, but also from the discourse of the Enlightenment?

"Je est un autre."[135] Levinas admired and often repeated these words. All his philosophical works could be read as an elaboration of the experience condensed into these words. When René Char wrote that the poet is a "guardian of the infinite faces of the living,"[136] he understood that the vision of the poet, unlike that of the paradigmatic Western philosopher, is a vision rooted in feeling—and that it is first of all through feeling that one sees humanity in the faces of others. All of us (but I, as Levinas would say, most of all) need to learn the seeing that is rooted in feeling, in sensibility. This is the seeing that can "recognize the gaze of the stranger, the widow, the orphan" (TaI 7).

We live, says Levinas, in a world "where no being looks at the face of the other" (TaI 302, TeI 278). Robert Coles tells a story that exemplifies this moral blindness. In "Children as Moral Observers," he reports what a black child of eleven, a child living in Soweto, South Africa, told him in the summer of 1979, fourteen years before the final, official end to apartheid:

> One day, I'm ready to go die for my people. It's that bad. We are treated like dogs. . . . When I go to Joburg [Johannesburg], I look at the white people, and there is fear in their faces. They can't see us, but we see them. They don't want to see us, but we have to see them! I hope, some day, God helps us settle this; He will have to come down here again, and open a lot of eyes![137]

For this child, in whose face, as Levinas would say,[138] traces of God's presence are to be seen, the intrigues between vision and domination, vision and violence, seeing as friendliness, welcoming the neighbor, and seeing as discrimination, denying the humanity of the other, could not be more visible—nor more intelligible.[139] It is crucial that the child attempts to *return* the gaze that looks at him without seeing him: he understands that the day must come when there is, between blacks and whites, a symmetry, a reciprocity of gazes.[140]

In Jean-Paul Sartre's *Nausea*, the narrator, Roquentin, reports and comments on a thought-provoking conversation with someone whom he calls the Self-Taught Man. As we enter this conversation, the Self-Taught Man is speaking:

> "But Monsieur, . . . how can you judge a man by his face? A face, Monsieur, tells nothing when it is at rest."
>
> [Roquentin replies] "Blind humanists! This face is so outspoken, so frank—but their tender, abstract soul will never let itself be touched by the sense of a face."
>
> "How can you," the Self-Taught Man says, misunderstanding, but making a cruicial point, "*stop* a man, say he *is* this or that? Who can empty a man? Who can know the resources of a man?"[141]

Instead of the abstractions of humanism, Sartre, taking the side of Roquentin, wants an existential morality drawing on the truth of concrete experience—the experience, for example, of being touched and moved by the presence of an other's face. The Self-Taught Man, however, can think this concreteness only in terms of an oppressive positivism, imposing on the other the logic of a reified identity. He can think the gaze in its concreteness only as the gaze of a Medusa, turning the other to stone. That we should *see* the other's humanity, *see* humanity in the other, seeing in touch with feeling, is to him incomprehensible. (For different reasons, this would also be problematic for Roquentin, who in this respect cannot be identified with Sartre.) There is a certain blindness in the vision of humanism. Is it then merely a question of "further enlightenment"?

Perhaps, as Levinas says, there is, in the experience of a human face, "a reasonable significance which Reason does not know."[142] I have suggested that it is precisely this significance that Levinas's phenomenological ethics elicits and articulates: a moral experience of the other, face-to-face, that takes hold of me in a dimension of my incarnation that *precedes* the formation of the ego-logical structure and *continues to function*, whether or not I am conscious of it, even after the ego-logical identity is formed; a moral experience that *continues to function*, in each and every moment, always the prior—an acknowledgment of the other's humanity that, in relation to any and every moment of thematized, reflectively explicit cognition, has (will have) always already taken hold of me. Diachronically preceding the formation of the ego, and remaining to some extent synchronically operative, "beneath" the level of consciousness, this acknowledgment of the other's humanity precedes the ego's construction of a worldly temporal order, precedes the order, the measure, the reckoning of the ego's timing. It is in this sense that Levinas will say that it is a question of the "immemorial," an experience "more ancient," to use Merleau-Ponty's felicitous phrase, "than thought" (Merleau-Ponty, PhP 242). But how can this "immediate" experience of the humanity of the other serve as the grounding for the moral-political concern for justice?

In an interview near the end of his life, Michel Foucault hinted at a conception of the political that would, in effect, move him much closer to the conception of rights and justice in the ideal speech situation of Jürgen Habermas's theory of deliberative democracy; but he expressed this conception with words that move him closer to Levinas as well, declaring that forms of rationality "rest upon a foundation of human practices and human faces."[143] But how strong is the foundation laid down by the experience of face-to-face encounter? How can there be what Levinas calls the "maieutic awakening of a common reason" in the face-to-face relationship?[144] How can the face-to-face encounter be incorporated into a moral and political rationality, a moral and political justice?[145] What is it about the face that makes it capable of bearing this rationality, this justice? What do we see in the face? What can we, what *will* we see? What do we *refuse* to see? To what do we shut our eyes? How much truth, how much humanity, can we face?

To see humanity in the face of the other. To see the other's humanity. To see the other *as* human. What does this mean? What does it involve? How is it to be taught? How is it to be learned? Is it, after all, something teachable, learnable? Is it an experience that involves social mediations? What social practices could alter our cultural habits of perception? Levinas devoted a life-time of thought to this problematic. In *Totality and Infinity*, he broached the problem in a challenge to those who would depend solely on the institutions of an abstract, formal universality of Reason to establish a society in which this recognition of the other's humanity would be assured:

> If . . . the first rationality gleams forth in the opposition of the face to face; if the first intelligible, the first signification, is the infinity of the intelligence that presents itself (that is, speaks to me) in the face; if reason is defined by signification rather than signification being defined by the impersonal structures of reason; if sociality precedes the apparition of these impersonal structures; *if universality reigns as the presence of humanity in the eyes that look at me;* if, finally, we recall that this look appeals to my responsibility and consecrates my freedom as responsibility and gift of self—then the pluralism of society could not disappear in the elevation of reason, but would be its condition. It is not the impersonal in me that Reason would establish, but an I myself capable of society. (TaI 208, TeI 183–84. Italics added.)

In this passage, Levinas articulates the problem that his phenomenology must face, if it is to succeed in arguing for such a "first rationality." This is a problem that the words in italics call to our attention. But we also will need to consider very carefully what is said about the "gift of self" and about the role of "Reason" in establishing an "I" that would be truly "capable of society." (Before we think about the problem, however, we must consider how difficult it would be to read his reference to the eyes, here, as "merely" metaphorical.) If, as Levinas has argued, to look at the face of the other is to see an irreducibly singular, absolutely unique being, how can I also see in this face the other's humanity—if seeing this humanity means seeing something universal, something common to both of us? Would this not be reducing the alterity of the other to the same, the incomparable to the comparable?

According to Levinas, each of us lives out a life "visible" to others: " 'He is looking at me'—everything in him looks at me; nothing is indifferent to me" (OB 93, AE 118). But is this "visibility" literal or metaphoric? In this remark, the sense in which I am "visible" to the other, "seen" by the other, is that I am "seen" by the other, whether or not another person is actually present, because I experience myself always called before the tribunal of conscience, always taken hold of by obligation, responsibility, and a concern for justice. Thus, it would seem that a literal sense of visibility and being seen is not intended. And yet, the literal sense cannot be denied without jeopardizing the "metaphorical" extension. Levinas does not in fact ignore the literal. When I am face-to-face with another person, I can, according to Levinas, actually *see* the humanity of this person in the very shining of the face, in the very gaze of the eyes.[146] And, when he says this, it seems clear that he *means* "see" in the literal sense. But what is it that I see in this shining? Nothing could be easier than to understand how I may be said to see *you*. But it is not so clear what it could mean to say that I see *your humanity*. And yet, the momentous transition from the concrete singularity of a face-to-face ethical relation to the abstract, normative universality of the moral-political perspective, where it becomes a question of justice (a justice that necessarily concerns everyone, and that therefore is not limited to the concrete immediacy of face-to-face presence), would seem to *depend* on our ability to see humanity in the concretely present other—or say, see the other's humanity. (Is this the same thing as seeing *that* you are a human being?)

The face, he says, is both the concrete other who is or could be facing me here and now, and also the abstract other, witness for humanity: "both the neighbor and the face of faces, visage and visible" (OB 160, AE 204). "The neighbor that obsesses me is already a face, both comparable and incomparable, a unique face and [yet also] in relationship with [all other] faces, which are visible in the concern for justice" (OB 158, AE 201). In other words, the face is both the concrete, visible presencing of this absolutely unique, absolutely singular, incomparable person, infinitely other, and *also* the uncanny, visibly *invisible* presencing of a certain undeniable abstract (mediated) universality. The paradox, here, if that is what it should be called, is that the face-to-face relation which the "I" shares with the other somehow connects me to the whole of humanity: somehow, the personal relation that engages the "I" is at some heightened level a *manifestation* of a shared humanity. This is how we might imagine it. Thus it is in this experience that the deontological sense of justice, the concern for justice, is first aroused. In order to clarify how the connection between the "I" and the concrete other becomes a concern for justice, a universal justice for "the whole of humanity," Levinas points to the presence of "the third party":

> [1] The presence of the face, the infinity of the other, is a destituteness, a presence of the third party (that is, the whole of humanity which looks at us), and a command. (TaI 213, TeI 188)
> [2] [The] third party, the whole of humanity, [is present] in the eyes that look at me. (Ibid.)

The witness in the third party (*le tiers*) figures not only in *Totality and Infinity*, his most important early work, but also in *Otherwise Than Being*, his most important late work.[147] And in both works, it is the perspective in terms of which Levinas attempts to think the question of justice. Here is a passage from *Totality and Infinity* that lays out the significance of the third party, who is also the witness:

> The third party [implicitly, therefore, the whole of humanity] looks at me in the eyes of the Other—language is justice. It is not that there first would be the face, and then the being it manifests or expresses would concern himself with justice; the epiphany of the face qua face opens humanity. The face in its nakedness as a face presents to me the destitution of the poor one and the stranger. . . . The poor one, the stranger, presents himself as an equal. His equality within this essential poverty consists in referring to the third party, thus present at the encounter, whom in the midst of his destitution the Other already serves. (TaI 213, TeI 187–88)

Although the figure of the third party is certainly useful in elaborating the *connection* between the concrete face-to-face ethical relationship and the impersonal, abstract, institutionally mediated relationships at stake in matters of justice, as well as the *transition* from the concreteness and singularity of the ethical to the abstractness and universality of the moral-political, I want to argue, in agreement with Derrida, that the transition from the asymmetry of the face-to-face relation to the symmetry and equality of the relation defined by justice is not as straightforward as he supposes.[148] More specifically, I want to argue that Levinas makes the concept of the third party carry more of a burden than it can bear and that its entrance on the scene cannot entirely resolve the perplexing, seemingly paradoxical contradiction involved in the double signification of the face. In a late interview, Levinas tells us that "the moment of objectivity motivated by justice" requires that we "efface" the singular, concrete face in order to let the "universality" claimed for justice shine forth:

> [We] must, out of respect for the categorical imperative or the other's right as expressed in his face, un-face [*dé-visager*] human beings, sternly reducing each one's uniqueness to his individuality in the unity of the genre, and let universality rule.[149]

What is involved in the transition from the "facing" of the other in the face-to-face ethical relation to the "un-facing" that is required by the moral-political perspective? The transition to the perspective of justice requires that we turn away from feelings and actions in relation to a visible, concrete singularity (a singularity, however, whose "own" moral dimensionality extends into the invisible), and assume the abstract, universal perspective of a *different* invisibility—this time the blindness of impartiality and universalizability that is required by the principles of justice, as well as the extension of moral responsibility beyond the possibility of face-to-face relations. But what is involved in this transition from the ethical relation to the perspective of justice? How is it "motivated" by the claims made against our vision in the realm of the visible—in the context of what the visible calls upon us to see?

In part, our problem lies, I think, in Levinas's insufficiently elaborated introduction of the third party—above all, in the fact that it has to represent more than one function in soliciting and bringing about this crucial transition. It is crucial to understand how the presence of the "third party," a "presence" even when actually absent, is supposed to account for the way that my experience of the other's humanity is "corrected" or "adjusted," to become a moral-political recognition of universal claims for justice—a bond, an obligation, a responsibility, and commitment that is connected at once with the visible and with the invisible, the present and the absent. One thing we may say, I think, is that it stands for the gaze returned in accusation. For the gaze of the third party affirms equality and reciprocity: as

Merleau-Ponty says, the "I" not only sees; the "I" is also visible, seen, and in being seen, or being visible—the price it must pay in order to see—it finds that its gaze is necessarily returned. This gaze returned, almost impossible to escape, subjects the "I" to the reflective judgment of an ever-present humanity, a gaze looking at us and calling us to account from every material, sensuous surface. The third party is a witness who judges.

But I would argue that the presence of what Levinas calls "the third party," representing—even when not actually present—the absolute demand for the symmetry and reciprocity promised by the principle of universal justice, must be understood as more than, and other than, simply a necessary "correction" or "adjustment" to the asymmetry—the privileging of the concrete other—in the face-to-face ethical relation. Levinas himself says that "the pluralism of society could not disappear in the elevation of Reason, but would be its condition" and that it is Reason—by which I take him to mean the social and cultural institutions incorporating Reason—that will establish an "I" "capable of society" (see TaI 208, TeI 183–84, quoted at length a few pages earlier). The third party, whose "objective gaze" introduces the normative perspective of moral-political universality, must be understood, for example, as representing, or standing in for, all the social mediations—the larger processes of socialization and moral education, including the sociocultural practices involved in the formation of perception and sensibility. It must therefore be understood as representing the social-political institutions of civil society and state that serve to interpret, maintain, and protect the work of justice by ensuring the necessary social conditions for the singularity of the face-to-face ethical relation—the relation that Levinas holds to be primary and foundational for the moral and political order of justice. And yet, the third party also serves to remind us of the inescapable aporia, the inescapable injustice, and even violence, involved in seeing the other *as* other in order to do justice to this other.

We need a story about the "movements" that are required of the gaze in the transition from the ethical relation to the perspective of justice. In "The Other of Justice," Axel Honneth defends Levinas, observing that "The moral point of view of equal treatment . . . requires continuous correction and supplementation by a viewpoint indebted to our concrete obligation to individual subjects in need of help."[150] I wholeheartedly agree. With admirable clarity, Levinas sees that, and also how, the ethical relation is necessary for the perspective of justice; he also sees that the perspective of justice is necessary for social life. And what he sees he shows with admirable rhetorical force. But I question his assertion that the face-to-face relation is primary, is the *foundation* for the perspective of justice. We thus need to see that, and also how, the incorporation of the impartial perspective of justice in the institutions of civil society and state must be regarded as not merely necessary for social life, but more particularly, as itself a necessary condition for the ethical relation. To spell out the argument for this point here would take us beyond the horizons of our present topic; but perhaps it will suffice to say that we need to see that, and how, the institutions of civil society and state interpret, maintain, and protect the perspective of justice indirectly as well as directly—for example, by establishing favorable conditions for socialization, so that the ethical relation can be taught, maintained, protected, realized. By "favorable conditions," I mean to envision conditions of social justice that would, for example, forever end the reproduction of poverty and cruelty in family life. The function of the perspective of justice represented by the third party is not, as Levinas suggests, merely to "correct" the priority and privilege accorded to the singular other—the other one—in the ethical relation. We cannot simply look to altering face-to-face relations through "raising consciousness" in the individual. We cannot ignore the task of altering the social conditions, political institutions, and the cultural life-world within which the face-to-face relation takes place. The ethical and the moral-political are interdependent, equally dependent on the other.

Levinas has a phenomenological story to tell in regard to our acknowledgment of the other's humanity; but I submit that a compelling story would hinge on a more differentiated conception of the presence of the third party in order to explain how I am bound to experience the humanity of the other as a universal normative claim and am thereby elevated to a vision of justice. In any case, however, Levinas sees that the first chapter of this story requires an understanding of the nature of the moral claim: its taking hold through the visibility of the ethical relation, against the elemental sensibility of the flesh, and registering its first meaning as a sense of responsibility, obligation, and justice carried by the body, carried by the flesh. He sees that we need a phenomenology of embodied moral experience, an account that avoids both rationalism and empiricism, both idealism and realism, revealing how this experience goes beyond Kantian deontologism in the rigorousness of its claim.

But how can the ethical be understood as incarnate, without reducing it to the objectivity of the merely physical or the subjectivity of ego-logical immanence? How can the flesh that embodies the ethical be at once material and spiritual—or rather, beyond such metaphysical duality? And how can Levinas's "return" to the embodiment of moral experience reveal an obligation, a responsibility that exceeds that required of us by the categorical imperative? In his review of Honneth's paper on "The Other of Justice," Thomas McCarthy rightly argues that Honneth fails to make sufficiently clear—and I would argue that Levinas does not either—"just how and in which respects it [what McCarthy calls "the care perspective" of justice] goes beyond the bounds of a Kantian doctrine of virtue in which benevolence and beneficence figure centrally."[151] And he argues that,

> if loving concern for concrete individuals is meant as a general but indeterminate (Kant would say "imperfect") obligation, it might be accommodated by discourse ethics along the lines that Habermas sketched in his earlier discussion of Carol Gilligan's ethics of care. If not, he will need some justification for such determinate *moral* obligations. How, when, and why do "asymmetrical", "unilateral" and "nonreciprocal" moral obligations arise?

A completely satisfying account in answer to all these questions is more than I can hope to provide here. But in the context of our concerns, I will say, as part of the answer, that the obligation constitutive of the ethical in Levinas's thought exceeds the Kantian not only because the asymmetry of its demand on us makes the demand supererogatory, infinitely more exacting, more exigent, but also because its binding *precedes* critical reflection, *precedes* judgment, being a binding and urging, first of all, of the flesh. In the phenomenology of moral experience that Levinas sketches, it is—and must be—a question of the role of embodiment, the "first nature" of flesh, of sense and sensibility, always already attuned in a rudimentary way to the moral dimension of sociality, the role of this "first nature" in the formation of the moral perspective demanded of our "second nature." On my reading, Levinas was attempting to articulate his conception of an *embodied* ethics, in which practical reason would finally be recognized in its embodiment—in our gestures, our listening, our looking and seeing. What Levinas's phenomenology shows us is that moral obligation cannot be understood without understanding how, in a time before memory, it takes hold of our flesh, our embodiment, and how, unless first damaged by the brutal conditions of early life, it emerges in response to the presence of the other.

Looking at other persons and seeing their humanity—thus also the whole of humanity somehow present in the singular—must therefore be, for Levinas, a distinctive mode of looking and seeing. It is not a question of an intellectual or cognitive act—not a deduction or inference, not a judgment of analogy. Seeing the other's humanity cannot be a matter of seeing that the other is *like* me, nor can it be seeing that I am *like* the other. For seeing resemblances (analogical reasoning) can only be a reduction to the (symmetry of the) same—and consequently an act of violence (ibid.). Thus, it also cannot be a question—though Levinas sometimes seems to suggest otherwise—of seeing the other *as* human. What must be insisted on is that I simply *see* the other's humanity! At all costs, Levinas wants to resist both an idealism that would entirely withdraw the humanity of the other from the visible and an empiricism that would reduce the visible reality of the other to an ontology that denies the dimension of transcendence. He will therefore insist that the face-to-face relation cannot be abstractly represented, and even that it cannot be adequately comprehended by one of the subjects involved in the relation. Nor, a fortiori, considering the way representation works, can the humanity of the other be represented by any external agent—not even the "third party."

To move beyond the conceptual dilemmas, the aporia, which the humanity visibly manifest in the face of the other constitutes, philosophical thought is obliged to find a new way to recognize and articulate the face-to-face experience. And this is just what Levinas attempts. In struggling to think this experience otherwise than in terms of being, i.e., otherwise than in terms that would inevitably force it to obey the logic of identity, reducing the other to the same, he attempts to effect a fundamental alteration in our approach to the other. The "appearance in being of these 'ethical peculiarities'—the humanity of man," requires, he says, "a rupture of being" (EaI 87). Therefore, it is useless to turn for inspiration to the discourse of humanism, because this discourse is entirely woven out of the violence of an essentialism belonging to the age-old framework of Western ontology. With words that are reminiscent of one of Nietzsche's notes, published in book 1 of *The Will to Power*,[152] and some of Heidegger's thoughts in his 1947 "Letter on Humanism,"[153] Levinas writes: "Humanism has to be denounced only because it is not sufficiently human" (OB 127–28; AE 164).

In place of the discourse of humanism, Levinas offers a discourse that attempts to articulate, to bring out, or say solicit, a certain normative experience. Using, as always, a mode of discourse that appears to reverberate between the descriptive and the prescriptive (since, as phenomenological description, not everyone would or could accept it as true), he says:

> It is my responsibility before a face looking at me . . . that constitutes the original fact of fraternity. (TaI 214, TeI 189)

(I will not undertake, here, a critique of Levinas's reduction of the other to the gender of "fraternity," since Derrida has already initiated such a critique, examining the textual repercussions of this surprising blind spot. Suffice it to say that Levinas's support for traditional gender identities and roles represents a terrible disfigurement.) It is in and through the responsibility that has taken hold of my flesh, the flesh of my vision, that I find myself compelled to see the other person "as" another human being. According to Levinas,

> fraternity *precedes* the commonness of a genus. My relationship with the other as neighbor gives meaning to my relations with all the others. All human relations as human proceed from disinterestedness. The one-for-the-other of proximity is not a deforming abstraction. In it, justice is shown *from the first*. (OB 159, AE 202. Italics added.)

Elaborating on this point, Levinas draws our attention to how we are sensibly affected by the presence of others (OB 101, AE 127) and he observes that, in the ethical relation of proximity, others "do not *affect* me as examples of the same genus united with my neighbor by resemblance or common nature, individuations of the human race, or chips off the same block, like stones metamorphosed into men" (OB 159, AE 202). This also means that

> humanity, to which proximity properly so called refers, must then not be first understood as consciousness, that is, as the identity of an ego endowed with knowledge or . . . with powers. Proximity does not resolve into the consciousness a being would have of another being that it would judge to be near inasmuch as the other would be under one's eyes or within one's reach, and inasmuch as it would be possible for one to take hold of that being, hold on to it or converse with it, in the reciprocity of handshakes, caresses, struggles, collaboration, commerce, conversation. (OB 83, AE 104)

If it be true, as is often said, that I will tend to see a reflection of myself mirrored in the eyes of the other, it must also be said, I think, that this mirroring, instead of encouraging narcissism, most often double-crosses it, enabling me to contact what Kant in *The Doctrine of Virtue* referred to— but without appreciating the aporia—as "the humanity in my own person"; and that, when our gaze is *rooted* in this contact and *comes from* this contact, we may accordingly see—may be able to behold—the humanity of the other.[154] In other words, the humanity of the other is something that becomes most visible—is given in luminous visibility—only to those most in touch with their own humanity. For Levinas, "The [idea and ideal of the] unity of the human race is in fact *posterior* to fraternity. Proximity is a difference, a non-coinciding, an arrhythmia in time, a diachrony refractory to thematization" (OB 166, AE 21l). The other can be thematized only as beyond thematization, represented only as beyond representation: "he loses his face as a neighbor [when inscribed] in narration. The relationship with him is indescribable in the literal sense of the term, unconvertible into a history, irreducible to the simultaneousness of writing, the eternal present of a writing that records or presents results" (ibid.).

Compelling us to make a momentous alteration in our thinking, he shows, in what he calls a "prehistory of the ego" (OB 117, AE 150), that the experience of the humanity of the other which is visible in the face is first of all a question of our exposure to the other, an immediate, bodily felt response, taking place in a passive bodily disposition *before* all ego-logical consciousness, before all intentionality, knowledge, and volition: a bodily disposition that registers in a very deep level as obligation and responsibility in view of the command, at once singular and universal, that visibly issues from the face of the other.[155] But because of what is left unsaid, there is a certain uncertainty or equivocation in what Levinas says regarding the way in which this responsibility, this ethical disposition is related to the visibility of the face of the other. As I understand him, he wants to say that this responsibility takes hold of me prior to any and every actual face-to-face encounter with another person—a thesis that only makes sense to me if it means that this responsibility takes hold of my flesh, becoming a bodily carried disposition—but that actual face-to-face encounters can be occasions for the awakening and realization of this originary responsibility. A "direct optics."[156]

We still need a phenomenological account of the "moments" involved in the transition from the perspective of the concrete singular other to the perspective of the abstract universal other. This task, however, requires that we first of all clearly distinguish the ethical from the moral-political, the "good"—that which constitutes the individual's conception of happiness in a good life—from the "right" and the "just"—that which would be equally good for everyone. For many years, Levinas made this task more difficult than it otherwise would have been because he used "the ethical" to refer to *both* dimensions of our life with others: both the ethical, which cocerns the good (conceptions of the good life, conceptions of happiness), and the moral-political, which concerns what is right and just, equally good for all. He eventually attempted to "correct" the semantic dimension of this confusion in his thinking.[157] But he left unchanged his association of "the Good" with moral-political obligation, denying himself any way to recognize that there can be different, equally moral conceptions of the good life and making it seem as if the categorical imperative of moral obligation imposes on all people the same conception of happiness, the same conception of the good life.

Be this as it may, in Levinas's account, the ethical relation constitutes the very structure of subjective experience: it is the subject's exposure to the other which makes the subject a subject: "The exposure *precedes* the initiative a voluntary subject would take to expose itself" (OB 180, AE 227). What defines the ethical subject, for Levinas, is not, therefore, freedom and autonomy, but rather its "pre-logical subjection,"[158] its "involuntary election" by "the Good" (OB 15, AE 19): "the Good is not presented to freedom; it has chosen me before I have chosen it. No one is good voluntarily" (OB 11, AE 13. Also see OB 18, AE 22). But Levinas would not deny that I am always free to refuse this "election." Moral character is thus a question of *what I make* of this initial disposition—what I make of the fact that I have already been taken hold of by "the Good," or what I would prefer to call the right and the just. In words addressed to "The Youth of Israel," he says:

> Attachment to the Good precedes the choosing of this Good. How indeed to choose the Good? The Good is good precisely because it chooses you and grips you before you have had the time to raise your eyes to it.[159]

The "Good" is thus, in Levinas's special sense, "anarchical," that is to say, more ancient than any thematized moral principle, and more ancient than, radically other than, and irreducible to, any conventional, socially constructed normative order—even older than any transcendental "origin" posited by "morality." Indeed, the force of the Good as a reflective principle depends on the prior hold it has on our embodiment. Unfortunately, Levinas does not sufficiently flesh out in a phenomenology of moral experience how this "involuntary election" by "the Good" takes place and how it connects with our freedom—not only our capacity and desire to make existential choices in regard to happiness and the good life, but also our moral obligation to make the choices that justice requires of us. But I take it that it is first and foremost a question of the elemental flesh, a question of our embodiment. If it is felt at all, the moral universality is felt first of all in and as a certain *bodily* sense of obligation. (But I think we must recognize that often only the embodiment of a saint or a bodhisattva would be sufficiently developed for this felt sense to take form. And indeed it often seems that the moral experience of obligation and responsibility which Levinas is "describing" could only be that of the saint or bodhisattva. But then he would be describing a comportment that he is also attempting performatively to bring forth.)

This embodied dimension explains how there can be an obligation that Levinas describes as coming *before* cognition and volition. It is "an order which, beyond representation, *affects me* unbeknownst to myself, 'slipping into me like a thief'. . . . It is the coming of an order to which I am subjected before hearing it, or which I hear in my own saying. It is an august command, but one that does not constrain or dominate" (OB 150, AE 191. Italics added). (Would it be possible to connect this account to Habermas's claim that there are normative presuppositions implicit in speech as a social practice?)

Returning moral experience to its sources, Levinas calls attention to the "passive" quality of this bodily felt sense. But he contends that it is a question of "a passivity more passive than passivity," because the conventional sense of "passivity" understands it in terms of an ontological dualism, as the opposite of activity, hence as a *willed* passivity. Whereas the passivity to which Levinas is calling our attention is not a passivity that originates in the ego. It is rather an existential condition into which, as it were, we are thrown. Or it is as if our ability to see the Good were in the very nature of things.

Crucial, then, to Levinas's way out of the dilemma, the paradox, in the "I"'s experience of the other's simultaneous singularity and universality is the exposition of a radically different conception of the "I," the subject who looks and sees. Everything hinges on this reconfiguration of the beholding subject, bringing out, I believe, what Merleau-Ponty calls the "prepersonal" dimension of its experience of the other, showing that this experience is not self-assertion, but rather subjection [*l'assujettissement*], the experience of being held, through the gaze, in beholdenness to the other: before the face I cannot simply remain there contemplating it, I have *always already* responded to it. "I can recognize [see] the gaze of the stranger, the widow and the orphan," he says, but "only in giving or refusing" (TaI 77, TeI 49). And yet, justice requires that we always also concede that the response has *not yet* taken place, that the responsibility has *not yet* been realized—and that the justice that the other's moral existence commands is in a time to come.

According to classical liberalism, the bourgeois subject should enjoy a will free of all influences, "une volonté soustraite à toute influence."[160] But Levinas wants to point to a condition of subjectivity that precedes this voluntarism: he thinks that, prior to becoming an autonomous ego, I am a subject of flesh and bones already subjected to the wisdom of the moral imperative, the normativity of the good and the right deeply inscribed in my flesh and bones (OB 164; AE 208, 209). Inscribed not by torture, as in Kafka's story "The Penal Colony," but, as it were, by the grace of nature. We need to give thought to this nature.

In "Substitution," one of the most important chapters in *Otherwise Than Being,* his last major work, Levinas comments that,

> for the philosophical tradition of the West, all spirituality lies in consciousness, thematic exposition of being, knowing. In starting with sensibility interpreted not as a knowing but as proximity, in seeking, through language, contact and sensibility, . . . we have endeavored to describe subjectivity as irreducible to consciousness and thematization. (OB 99–100, AE 126)

This attention to sensibility is a major innovation in moral theory, promising even more than Levinas might have suspected. The fact of "incarnation," he says, elaborating his phenomenology of moral experience,

> far from thickening and tumefying the soul, . . . exposes it naked to the other, to the point of making the subject expose its very exposedness. . . . The concept of the incarnate subject is not a biological concept. The schema that corporeality outlines submits the biological itself to a higher structure. (OB 109, AE 139)

Somewhat later, he explicitly introduces the question of the categorical imperative into our thought of embodiment:

> The fact that immortality and theology could not determine the categorical imperative signifies the novelty of the Copernican revolution: a sense that is not measured by being or not being; but on the contrary, being is determined on the basis of sense. (OB 129, AE 166)

Levinas is calling our attention, here, to "a pre-original reason that does not proceed from any initiative of the subject, an an-archic reason" (OB 166, AE 211–12). It is, he says, "a reason before the beginning, before any present, because my responsibility for the other commands me before any decision, before any deliberation" (ibid.). "This recurrence" to an incarnate reason, he argues,

> would be *the ultimate secret* of the incarnation of the subject; prior to all reflection, prior to every positing, an indebtedness before any loan, not assumed, anarchical, subjectivity of a bottomless passivity, made out of assignation, like the echo of a sound that would precede the resounding of this sound. (OB 112, AE 142)

The peculiar "presence" of this Levinasian categorical imperative, taking hold of us "beneath the level of prime matter" (OB 110, AE 140), transforms the very substance of our bodies from "matter" into "flesh":

> The incarnation of the [moral] self [must be understood as] a passivity prior to all passivity at the bottom of matter becoming flesh [*la matière se faisant chair*]. (OB 196, AE 150)

(This suggests an interpretation that would connect it with Merleau-Ponty's thought, in *The Visible and the Invisible*, of "a glorified body," "un corps glorieux,"[161] and of "an ideality that is not alien to the flesh, that gives it its axes, its depth, its dimensions."[162] For me, this "ideality" includes the moral "inscription" of the flesh. In one of his working notes,[163] the philosopher writes, intriguingly, that "my flesh itself is one of the sensibles in which an inscription [*inscription*] of all the others is made. . . . " I find Merleau-Ponty's use of this word "inscription" charged with significance, since that same word plays a major role in Levinas's tracework phenomenology of moral experience.) As "passivity incarnate" (OB 112, AE 142), the flesh of our bodies receives an assignation, "an extremely urgent assignation" (OB 101, AE 127), an "exigency" (OB 112–13, AE 143–44) that takes hold of our vision, our beholding, and makes us correspondingly beholden, facing the other in a condition of subjection, "hostage" to the other, responsible to and for the other. If from the hands of family and neighbors, the child has not suffered traumatic cruelties in the early years of its passage through the world, but on the contrary has been recognized and appropriately nurtured, this categorical imperative, our incarnate moral assignment, can give crucial support and guidance to moral deliberation, moving and disposing us according to its commandment:

> The *logos* that informs prime matter in calling it to order is an accusation, or a category. But [the] obsession [that takes hold of us in the form of a moral predisposition] is anarchical; it accuses me beneath the level of prime matter. . . . Western philosophy, which perhaps is reification itself, remains faithful to the order of things and does not know the absolute passivity, beneath the level [that traditional thought describes in terms of the dualism] of activity and passivity. (OB 110, AE 140. We should again consider the use of the structural and topographic words "level" and "beneath," which suggest a diachronic sublation, somehow preserving what is nevertheless surpassed.)

But the embodiment of the categorical imperative cannot be understood, therefore, until our way of thinking about the body undergoes a radical revision. Thus he says:

> The body is neither an obstacle opposed to the soul, nor a tomb that imprisons it, but that by which the self is susceptibility itself. Incarnation is an extreme passivity, . . . exposed to compassion, and, as a self, to the gift that costs. (OB 195, AE 139)

Crucial for our understanding of embodiment is, then, the "proximity" of the face-to-face ethical relation that takes place between the "I" and an other:

> The relationship of proximity cannot be reduced to any modality of distance or geometrical contiguity, nor to the simple "representation" of a neighbor; it is already an assignation, an extremely urgent assignation—an obligation, anachronously prior to any commitment. This anteriority is "older" than the a priori. This formula expresses a way of being affected [*affecté*] without the source of the affection becoming a theme of representation. We have called this relationship irreducible to consciousness [by the word] "obsession." (OB 100–1, AE 127)

I want to call attention to Levinas's word, "assignation," here, because it already assigns to the body, in the form of a certain "sign," the inscription of a moral obligation, the urgent claims of the moral law. Thus it is not surprising to find a passage where this inscription in the flesh, this moral *logos* (OB 121, AE 156) is actually made explicit. In the ethical relation set in motion by the "approach" or "proximity" of the other,

> there is inscribed or written [*s'inscrit ou s'écrit*] the trace of infinity, the trace of a departure, but trace of what is inordinate, does not enter into the present, and inverts the *arkhé* into an-archy, that there may be . . . responsibility and a [morally disposed] self. (OB 117, AE 149)

This turn in Levinas's phenomenology may seem queer, but it is only in fact an elaboration of Numbers 15:31, which reads—in so far as it gives itself to a reading—as follows: "One who has broken God's commandment is one who profanes the covenant inscribed in the flesh." In his essay "On the Mimetic Faculty," Benjamin writes about the attempt "To read what was never written."[164] This is the paradox into which Levinas's phenomenology draws us. The marking of the inscription, impossible as a metaphysical presence, nevertheless leaves a trace in withdrawing from presence and effacing itself. And it will only be through the deconstruction of our ego-logical identity that, in a process of moral transformation, what was never written, a double erasure, a double effacement, may indeed be retraced, read—and be thereby, finally, written. This is what Levinas refers to as the "posteriority of the anterior" (TaI 54, TeI 25). A question, therefore, of performative remembering.

Levinas speaks of the inscription, an inscription that underwrites the claims of the other, prescribing our responsibility, as nothing more than a "trace," or rather a mere trace of a trace, virtually illegible, because we cannot possibly return to the original moment of the inscription, and in any case, even if, *per impossibile*, we could, we still would not get at it, since it belongs to a past that never was fully present to itself. A phantom, a spectral remnant, the trace requires that we learn from its spectral visibility a different way of looking and seeing—a way that would be infinitely responsible for the other, whose visible presence before us is otherwise than being. But the moral imperative, having first of all taken hold of us through the very nature of the flesh, is nevertheless always already predisposing us in certain ways prior to the time when we are able to become conscious of its functioning—though it does not at all constitute a determinism of moral comportment, which always remains a question of the exercise of our freedom and depends on our willingness to engage in a process of recuperation, retrieving some sense of direction and motivation from the originary moral disposition. But if the attempt to retrieve or decipher the trace is impossible, why expend so much effort in tracework? For Levinas, what ultimately matters—what constitutes, let us say, the very possibility of virtue—is not the retrieval or deciphering of the trace—a metaphysically impossible task—but the *character* of the effort, the exertion, one's devotion to the task. It is by the character of this effort, this devotion that we are ultimately measured. For the mere facticity of this moral inscription determines absolutely nothing: everything depends on whether and how the "gift" of responsibility carried by our flesh is received for the *second* time. In other words, everything depends on whether and how the *recuperation* of this tracework disposition is made the highest concern of my moral life:

> Responsibility for my neighbor dates from before my freedom in an immemorial past, an unrepresentable past that was never present and is more ancient than consciousness. . . . [T]his anarchic responsibility, which summons me from nowhere into a present time, is perhaps the measure . . . of an immemorial freedom that is even older than being, or decisions, or deeds.[165]

Thus, as Alphonso Lingis notes, the dimension in which the sensuous material is laid out is "already extended by the sense of alterity."[166] (And yet, it is never extended enough, for the sense of alterity will always continue calling to be recognized, retrieved, and realized in our lives.) As Levinas expresses the point: "Sensibility is exposedness to the other" (OB 75, AE 94). Accordingly, it is also, as he will later demonstrate, using a description which recognizes that what is involved is an event that precedes one's social initiation into a thematic recognition of the moral order, exposure to the "anarchy of the Good," an ordering of our embodiment that precedes the cultural order of moral education. This means that

> the subjectivity of sensibility, taken as incarnation, is an abandon without return, [in fact], . . . a body suffering for another, the body as passivity and renouncement, a pure undergoing. (OB 79, AE 100)

Emphasizing his difference from Kant, Levinas describes this moral experience as "heteronomy" (OB 124, AE 160). But of course, this heteronomy is the most extreme antithesis of the heteronomy which, in Kant's moral system, *precedes* the stages of moral enlightenment or maturity (*Mündigkeit*) that are called "autonomy": as Levinas uses the term, it is a way of expressing the fact that, prior even to the heteronomy that Kant ascribes to a life determined solely by custom and convention, shame or fear of punishment—hence anarchically prior to the normative *arkhé* of the discursive social order, I am always already bodily claimed and bound, or say appropriated, by the moral law, a law subjecting me to the welfare of the other. But of course, as Adriaan Peperzak correctly points out, Kant "knew very well that, before I become aware of it, I am not able to establish the moral law by which I discover myself to be [already] ruled."[167]

In describing the "heteronomy" by which the moral law takes hold of me, Levinas deepens the "pathos" of Kant's moral philosophy, because the moral predisposition inscribed in the flesh is in conflict with desires of the flesh that are also inscribed from time immemorial and that are not (yet) bound to the moral law: its assignment is thus not assured an easy or automatic victory in this conflict. This is, I suggest, why Levinas emphatically uses words such as "persecution," "accusation," "wound," "trauma," "sacrifice," "hostage," "obsession," and even "violence" to describe the experience of responsibility and obligation that one feels—or should be able to feel—in seeing another human being. These terms may seem at first quite perplexing.[168] But I think that they can be explained once we take into account Levinas's distinction between *the ego* and *the moral self*, and understand the terms to be, first of all, accurate phenomenological descriptions of the ego's point of view with regard to the moral experience of the other. For whom would the embodied experience of the moral relation be ap-

propriately described as "persecution," "wound," "accusation," "violence"?
Would this not be the experience of the ego? The ego would "naturally"
experience the assignation of the moral law in these terms because the
moral law, inscribed in the flesh but ruling nevertheless "against nature,"
or rather, against a certain propensity of nature, would constrain its ego-
serving desires. But in fact the moral self could *also* use these terms to describe its experience of the moral relation. However, the grounds for its use
of these terms, and therefore what it would mean by these terms, would be
the very opposite of the ego's. Let us see why.

In *Difficult Freedom,* the persecution involved in responsibility is described as "an invisible universality."[169] What does this mean? I suggest
that the invisibility of the persecution, the wound, the trauma is a function
of the fact that, after having taken hold of the universality of the flesh in a
time before ego-logical memory, the event's significance nevertheless requires recognition and recuperation—an elective realization. Precisely this
realization would be the difficult work of freedom that overcomes the ego
and constitutes the moral self. Something that Freud remarked in *Civilization and Its Discontents* may clarify this question. He comments that

> the more virtuous a man is, the more severe and distrustful is his con-
> science, so that ultimately it is precisely those people who carried saint-
> liness furthest who reproach themselves with the deepest sinfulness.[170]

So the extreme terms that Levinas uses could also be used to describe the
experience of the moral self, troubled to the point of anguish and trauma
by a heightened moral conscience, aware that its response to the other is always too late and always too little.

In *Difficult Freedom,* Levinas says that the more just we are, the more
harshly we are judged. Judged not only by others, but by ourselves, by the
sense of our own conscience.[171] According to Levinas,

> Persecution is the precise moment in which the subject is reached or
> touched without the mediation of the logos. (OB 121, AE 154–55)

The ego is therefore, first of all, in the accusative (*accusé*), called upon to be
responsive to the other—"me voici!"—before there is an "I" existing in the
nominative:

> in the form of an ego unable to conceive what is 'touching' it, the as-
> cendency of the other is exercised upon the same to the point of inter-
> rupting it, leaving it speechless. . . . [Persecution] designates the form in
> which the ego is affected. (OB 101, AE 127–28)

318 / *The Philosophers*

For Levinas, I am bound in responsibility to and for the other, put radically into question by the irreducible alterity of the other, even "before the appearing of the other in sensibility" (OB 75, AE 95). The rigor of Levinas's ethics is extreme, not easily, not comfortably to be understood, especially when the face-to-face relation is thought to take place within the hell, the non-place, that was Auschwitz. But, according to Levinas, I am responsible even "for the persecution with which, before any intention, he [the other] persecutes me" (OB 166, AE 212). "Only the persecuted one must answer," he says, "for everyone, even for his persecutor."[172] (In Part IV, we will question the victim's responsibility for the persecution. It is certainly a controversial point.)

Calling attention to the tracework of a rudimentary and preliminary moral predisposition, illegible as such, but which nevertheless gives some initial moral direction and motivation, Levinas asserts that

> in the "prehistory" of the ego posited for itself there speaks a responsibility. The self is through and through a hostage, older than the ego, prior to principles. (OB 117, AE 150)

What Levinas calls the "self" is thus both earlier than and later than the ego—although the earlier and the later are also, by virtue of the sociocultural mediations and the thematic consciousness that separate them, irreducibly different. As I read this passage, it suggests that the moral "self" appears in two distinct phases or faces: a *pre-egological* phase or face which is immemorially earlier than the (personal) ego, and in which the flesh, a phantom tracework of moral inscriptions recorded like lacerations, is already touched, already "wounded" by the claims of the other, already responsive to the alterity of the other; and second, much later, a *post-egological* stage or phase, which, however, is only an existential or "elective" possibility, and which always depends on the commitment of the (personal) ego for its realization—depends, that is, on the ego's personal assumption of responsibility for *the developing transformation* of our initial or originary capacity to be responsive to the other. It would thus be a question of the emergence of a moral self from the traces of a prepersonal responsiveness to the registers of alterity, a moral self rooted in, and remaining in good contact with, a vital sense of this responsiveness.

If this reading be admissible, it would suggest that Levinas was engaged in a certain tracework, in a return to the primordial body of experience, for the sake of a calling to attempt, in the tropological language of phenomenology, the retrieval for present living of the original assignment of "motivations." Such tracework would begin to make visible, beyond the ego-logical stage or face, the very height of our moral development. But we need, at this point, something that Levinas does not give us: a phenomenological narrative that would articulate his moral vision in terms of a process of moral transformation, translating his provocative, but extremely abstract concepts into a much more concrete and intricately experiential language, a tracework truly capable of directing our attention to the transformative potential—and the logic of transformative phases—constitutive of our moral experience as beings wrought of a deeply spiritual flesh. Within the limits of this chapter, we shall attempt to adumbrate the main features of this narrative, emphasizing the paradoxical diachronicity of the recuperative effort.

It should, however, be noted here that, if we are inclined to think of the tracework as (re)marking a potential for the developing transformation of a deeply inscribed moral disposition, we must be prepared to concede that it can register its "accusation" of the flesh only by way of a certain radical dis-positioning or dis-placing of the presumed topography, for the dispositional tracework could never become legible except obscurely, marginally, and with the greatest of difficulty within the purview of the subject-object, subject-subject, and ego-alter structures recognized by the discourse of ontologies. Indeed, if the trace eludes the objection that it is a "dialetical illusion," that is because such an objection can be sustained only within a metaphysics determined by "presence."

In *Otherwise Than Being*, the struggle to think the face of the other—the ethical relation—within the architecture of phenomenology centers on the trace. We cannot linger, here, over this problematic, which I have discussed at some length elsewhere.[173] Perhaps it will suffice for the time being to say that we must at least attempt to think the trace—the presence of an absence, the absence of a presence—as a site of provocation *outside* of all ontologies. Since the passive reception of the moral commandment holding us responsible for the other takes place, for Levinas, in a past that never was, and never could be, (fully) present, in a time before the ego's conventionally constructed order of time, and consequently before ego-logical memory; and since the phenomenological attempt to recuperate that originary event, by which our responsibility for the other took hold of our flesh and founded our identity on a radical alterity, can never hope to return to that event as it was, the most that phenomenology can retrieve is, as Levinas says, just a trace of a trace. This means, of course, that hermeneutics, as traditionally conceived, must be avoided. Even so, however, the attempt to use our freedom to retrieve this trace from its spectral visibility is of the utmost importance for our developing transformation as moral selves: it can make all the difference in the world.

The peculiar tracework of the categorical imperative, legislating responsibility by way of a certain preliminary moral predisposition, a certain immediacy of responsiveness that is borne in and as our embodiment, functions "without the mediation of any principle, any ideality" (OB 100, AE 127). Hence the "anarchy" of this "assignation," recurrently antinomian—hence also, since it has never been present as such, the impossibility of representing it in standard concepts (OB 97, AE 123–24). Nevertheless, in Levinas's phenomenology, provocative traces of this assignation, virtually indecipherable, can be indicated, hinted at, by a certain evocative use of language. The relation between language and experience, especially with regard to the retrieval of the trace, constitutes what is unquestionably the most intractable and interminable problematic in Levinas's moral phenomenology. It is thus a matter we cannot avoid, even though our principal concern with regard to his moral phenomenology is the character of the gaze in the face-to-face of the ethical relation—the question, therefore, of the visible and the invisible. But if traces of the primordial moral law are at least to some extent retrievable, decipherable, legible, in spite of their nonidentity, their paradoxical ontological status, that will be possible only, as he says, by the most extreme abuse of language, double-crossing whatever descriptions may be ventured, casting doubt on every claim to retrieve, to see and read:

> If the anarchical were not signalled in consciousness, it would reign in its own way. The anarchical is possible only when contested by language, which betrays, but also conveys, its anarchy, without abolishing it, by an abuse of language. (OB 194, AE 127)

According to Levinas, the Good has always already given me an assignment by the time I become aware of its hold on my embodiment, my senses, my sensibility, my perception. I am beholden to the Good even before I behold its presence in the world. The assignment of the Good is, in fact, what first enables me to "catch sight of and conceive of value" (OB 122–23, AE 157–59). It is what gives what we might call the "naturally formed" ego, whose nature is to some extent otherwise disposed, the initial challenge and the initial opportunity to become a moral self. For Levinas, however, the fact that the moral law is already inscribed in the "nature" of the flesh should not be interpreted as an argument for moral naturalism—or at least not in the sense of "moral naturalism" for which philosophies of moral naturalism have always argued. He is not pointing to or arguing for "a natural benevolence, as in the moral philosophies of feeling." On the contrary, the moral disposition is "against nature," or rather, against the natural inclinations that the formation of the ego tends to favor. Levinas says, simply: "It is against nature, non-voluntary, inseparable from the possible persecution to which no consent is thinkable, anarchic" (OB 197, AE 157). Responsibility for others, he says, "could never mean altruistic will, instinct of 'natural benevolence', or love" (OB 111–12, AE 142).

And yet, if the moral law is an inscription that primordially informs the flesh, there must be a sense in which compassion, benevolence, responsibility for the other, and a vision of the Good are also natural. Why does Levinas want to emphasize that they are "contrary to nature"? I suggest that what he means is that there is a veritable abyss—an abyss, say, of legibility—between the assignation inscribed in the flesh by the categorical imperative and our comportment in the world. But I would argue that this is an abyss that could be bridged only by appropriate sociocultural mediations, processes of moral transformation, *Bildungsprozesse* which would undertake the decipherment of some of the traces of the secret, encrypted message inscribed in the nature of the body. It would be, then, the urgent function of such interactional social processes to encourage and enable us to *construct* our moral lives on the basis of the "secret gift" that is hidden in the body. (I would refer the reader again to TaI 208, TeI 183–84, quoted earlier at length, where Levinas writes of the "gift of self," but makes it clear that, in a crucial sense, the gift is received without realization.) Of course, Levinas's claim that I am "chosen" by the Good in this way should not be understood to deny that I can perversely chose to ignore this "election," that I can, for one reason or another, one cause or another, "misquote" the moral law to myself, and that I can also, due to the impoverished or brutal conditions in which I have grown up and in which I am living, entirely fail to experience, or say read, any sense of the moral law.

That Levinas's critique of moral naturalism is designed to open up the possibility of another way of experiencing "human nature" and the "nature" of embodiment, and that it thereby suggests a radically different way to conceive the kernel of truth distortedly represented in historical versions of moral naturalism, may be gleaned from a passage in which he argues that responsibility for the other comes to us from a time that is, as he expresses it,

> prior to all memory and all recollection. It was made in an irrecuperable time which the present, represented in recollection, does not equal, in a time of birth or creation of which nature or creation retains a trace, unconvertible into a memory. (OB 104–5, AE 133)

As I have already suggested, we might think of the moral assignment that is registered in the flesh as a "gift of nature." But it can only be a question, here, of a gift that is not, that cannot possibly be, fully or totally received, fully or totally retrieved—a gift, moreover, that does not in any way diminish the fact that the assignment is "against nature" (OB 197, AE 157): against nature in the sense that, whilst the obligation comes over us, is given to us, and takes hold of us only by grace of the very nature of the flesh, it nevertheless makes the most rigorous, most impossible demands on us, calling on us from a time before consciousness, before memory, before time itself, and before volition, to resist the temptations of desire that easily possess us in the time of our egoism.

It might be useful, at this point, to consider another contemporary formulation of the idea of a bodily felt categorical imperative. The formulation appears in Adorno's *Negative Dialectics:*

> A new categorical imperative has been imposed by Hitler upon unfree mankind: to arrange their thoughts and actions so that Auschwitz will not repeat itself, so that nothing similar will happen. When we want to find reasons for it, this imperative is as refractory as the given one of Kant was once upon a time. Dealing discursively with it would be an outrage, for the new imperative gives us a bodily felt sense of the moral supplement—bodily, because it is now the practical abhorrence of the unbearable physical agony to which individuals are exposed even with individuality about to vanish as a form of mental reflection.[174]

And he goes on to explain his thinking:

> The course of history forces materialism upon metaphysics, traditionally the direct antithesis of materialism. What the mind once boasted of defining or construing as its like moves in the direction of what is unlike the mind, in the direction of that which eludes the rules of the mind and yet manifests that rule as absolute evil. The *somatic, unmeaningful stratum of life* is the stage of suffering, of the suffering which, in the [Nazi extermination] camps, without any consolation, burned every soothing feature out of the mind, and out of culture, the mind's objectification.

I would certainly welcome the thought of a categorical imperative inscribed from time immemorial in the very flesh of our bodies. But Adorno damages it beyond mending when he attributes its origin to Hitler's imposition, when he reduces it to the physical, a materiality inimical to the spirit, and when he denies it discursivity and meaningfulness. To be sure, the hell realm of the extermination camps was designed to reduce human beings to animal bodies—and often almost succeeded. But even in the smallest measure of the "almost," there is a world of difference. And the difference is to be measured by the judgment of the moral law, peering out from eyes sunk into their sockets. The voices of this categorical imperative, the expressions of the body's *felt sense* of righteousness and justice, must be recognized. Unfortunately, Adorno could think this bodily carried imperative only as imposed, only in terms of the objective, physical body, and only, therefore, as mute, unable to speak, to articulate its sense of the moral. Perpetuating the old metaphysical dualisms that suppress recognition of the body-as-lived, the body of experience, he could not think the obligation phenomenologically in terms of the embodied subject's own *experience* of embodiment. What inmates and survivors of Auschwitz would have conceded that for the voice of the categorical imperative within them, they were indebted to Hitler?

But here we must acknowledge a disturbing, haunting question. In thinking such a categorical imperative in terms of embodiment, we must not avoid meditating on a point made by Habermas in "Historical Consciousness and Post-Traditional Identity." (The reader is referred to the third quotation that appears at the very beginning of this chapter.) But Habermas does not suggest, in this passage, that the Holocaust compels us to question the *existence as such* of a "deep layer of solidarity." Rather, he is suggesting that we need to reflect on the possibility that it can suffer irreparable trauma and destruction. And he implies that we must not ever take it for granted. If, however, there be no such "deep layer," or if the Holocaust could make us lose faith in this "deep layer," lose our trust in the very possibility of forming a bodily felt sense of its moral "presence," then Levinas's phenomenology of moral experience—and mine also—would suffer a truly irremediable catastrophe. Such a conclusion is difficult to avoid if we take this phenomenology to be deciphering a primordial inscription of the moral law encoded into the very nature of our flesh—and if, as I think ultimately we must, we take the logic of Habermas's reference to a "deep layer of solidarity" to be pointing toward some primordial endowment of proto-moral dispositions.

To give a truly satisfying answer to the problematic that Habermas broaches in this regard is not something that could be accomplished in the context of this already lengthy chapter. However, his remark is much too important to remain without at least some preliminary and provisional comment. But I think that what took place in Auschwitz, in the Holocaust, certainly shows that it is possible for evil to overwhelm the integrity of this "deep layer" and cause our bodily felt sense of the moral law to disintegrate; and thus I think that we must strive never to take its moral guidance for granted. In other words, since the moral development of this "gift of nature" can never be more than a contingent possibility, the "inscription" of a "prescription" that is in no sense preordained, in no sense predetermined, it must be recognized that the cruelty and brutality of social conditions—conditions produced in large measure by enduring injustices—can penetrate the flesh so deeply and alienate individuals from this first nature to such an extent that the moral development of their humanity may be permanently stunted and the gaze which, once upon a time, was directed by its contact with this potential may become horribly distorted, monstrously bent toward an evil it desperately embraces. But this means that we are obliged to question the validity of the Levinasian thesis that the ethical relation is the absolute foundation for justice.

In his *Trauerspiel* essay, Benjamin makes a point that I think bears on the problematic we are considering here:

> The sanctity of what is written is inextricably bound up with the idea of its strict codification. . . . So it is that . . . the script of sacred complexes . . . take the form of hieroglyphics. The desire to guarantee the sacred character of any script—there will always be a conflict between sacred standing and profane comprehensibility—leads to complexes, to hieroglyphics.[175]

We must assume that the primordial inscription of the moral law is hermeneutically encrypted in and as our incarnation: written, so to speak, in the form of hieroglyphics that require decoding, a reading that is possible only, I would say, through the collaboration of freedom, *Bildungsprozesse*, and the right sociocultural conditions.

There is, in Derrida's *Of Grammatology*, an explanation of arche-writing, this primordial inscription, that usefully brings out its ethical significance:

> The arche-writing is the origin of morality as of immorality. The nonethical opening of ethics. A violent opening.[176]

The tracework inscription is nothing but an opening, a beginning, preceding ethical consciousness, an inscription of the moral law that attempts to restrain uncivilized desire, but does not at all preclude evil. Evil is always possible. For this arche-writing is not the imposition of fate, but only the uncertain destiny, always at risk, of a promise kept in reserve.

And much can go wrong. Fully to understand how evil is possible, in spite of the gift of this primordial inscription, we would need to examine the origin of evil. This is an extremely difficult task that we cannot undertake here. I will simply assert, for now, that evil can exist, despite the primordial inscription, because the destiny that is encoded into the flesh is not a teleology, not a determinism: it is only a "reserved" promise, an entrustment, a message of hope, an invocation that must respect the subject's freedom. This will have to suffice, for the time being, as the beginning of a possible answer to the problematic which the quotations from Habermas, Benjamin, and Adorno force us to think through.

Let us now return to Levinas's radical revision of the categorical imperative. We note that it involves a radical rethinking of the conception of the subject, especially with regard to the way free individuals are represented in classical bourgeois liberalism. In contrast to the conception realized in liberalism, the other in Levinas's conception "does not limit but promotes my freedom, by arousing my goodness" (TaI 200, TeI 175). For Levinas, we are not—or should not be—autonomous monads exercising our freedom in the pursuit of self-interests that inevitably set us in motion against one another. We must recognize that, as subjects, we are not only needfully dependent on one another, but moreover elevated to goodness only by grace of the other, the one who brings us to a consciousness of our primordial subjection to the Good. The subject is not first of all, as classical liberalism insists, a free agent, but is a subject by grace of subjection to the Good: what Levinas calls "the condition of being hostage" (OB 117, AE 150). And it is through this condition, this experience of subjection that there can be eyes moved to tears by the distant suffering of others—"that there can be in the world pity, compassion, pardon and proximity—even the little there is, even the simple 'After you, sir' " (ibid.).

But it is extremely difficult for Levinas to make his phenomenological narrative of the face-to-face relation convincing, because it immediately encounters the strongest imaginable resistance from our culturally hegemonic self-understanding, compelled as it is to make use of a philosophical vocabulary that inevitably betrays it, and challenging as it does all our late-modern convictions—about freedom, autonomy, the identity of the subject, what it means to be human, the role of reason in ethical life, the origin of obligation and responsibility, the being of values, the ground of ethical relations, and even what it is that we see when we look at another person. Levinas understands the resistance well enough to analyze it and diagnose its pathology. Thus, he argues that the ego-logical subject of modern bourgeois culture knows of nothing prior to its freedom or outside of the necessity which runs up against this freedom. This is a crucial point, because the "obligation" and "responsibility" to which Levinas is calling our attention do not come from freedom, but from an immediate bodily responsiveness, an exposure and beholdenness which are constitutive of human nature as an elemental, chiasmic flesh, a flesh intricately and inextricably intertwined with the flesh of the other (OB 122, AE 157).

We are now ready to return to the problem with which we began this section, viz., seeing the other's humanity, or seeing humanity in and through the other: a problem that takes us to the very heart of the transition from the concrete singularity of the ethical relation to the abstract universality of justice. What is the relation between the experience of seeing the concrete and singular other and the experience constituted by the abstract, impartial, "blind" perspective of universal justice—justice for the invisible other of humanity? How does the asymmetrical ethical relation, in which I am face-to-face with a concrete and singular other, become the symmetrical moral-political relation—a relation to the invisible, abstract other whose call for justice concerns me, a relation in which I take on a certain responsibility for the whole of humanity? I would like to suggest that it would be useful to think about these questions in terms of what we will call, following Levinas, a process of individuation. Levinas mentions individuation, but never tells us about the process in which it takes place. He offers no narrative of developmental transformation, no story about the formation ego and self, and no account of how processes of individuation and processes of socialization, *Bildungsprozesse,* are diachronically intertwined. But what else could possibly be at stake when he says, in the long passage quoted earlier, that Reason establishes an "I" that is "capable of society" (TaI 208, TeI 183–84), if it is not a question of socialization and self-developing transformation? I will accordingly attempt to show something of the logic of these processes, explicating the transformations in terms of its phenomenological moments. The analysis that I am proposing is, I believe, implicit in Levinas's work, although it is never formulated in his work as I shall formulate it here. Here, then, with brief commentary, is a selection of three textual passages in relation to which I think the logic of the process can be clearly articulated:

[1] The unlimited initial responsibility, which justifies this concern for justice, . . . can be forgotten. In this forgetting, consciousness is a pure egoism. But egoism is neither first nor last. (OB 128, AE 165)

I would argue that this articulates the three phases or moments of the process: first, a primordial responsibility always already borne by the flesh, but not yet retrieved, thematized and freely developed; second, the pure egoism of consciousness, in which this primordial responsibility tends to be suppressed and "forgotten"; and third, the moment of return, in which there is a certain recovery of this responsibility, transforming it into a moral life of supererogatory responsibility for the other. This analytic explains why egoism is neither first nor last, but precisely in the middle, between the proto-moral self we receive and the self-developed moral self we are called upon to become. (See TaI 208, TeI 183–84 on "the gift of self": a gift suspended between the "always already" and the "not yet.")

> [2] . . . it is in the course of the individuation of the ego in me that is realized the elevation in which the ego is for the neighbor, summoned to answer for him. (OB 126, AE 162)

It is in the process of individuation that the self, the "elevated" dimension of the ego (the "moi" of the "me voici!") is realized. The articulation of the three phases or moments is implicit in this formulation of the ego's "individuation."

> [3] Without [experiencing a deep sense of] persecution, the ego raises its head and covers over the self. Everything is from the start in the accusative. . . . The more I return to myself, the more I divest myself, under the traumatic effect of persecution, of my freedom as a constituted, willful, imperialist subject, the more I discover myself to be responsible. (OB 112, AE 143)

According to the schema offered here, the moral self is both first and third; but, in its first phase or moment, it functions in a certain passive receptivity, not fully conscious of itself, whereas, in its third moment, it would voluntarily begin a process transcending the ways of the ego and its culture, retrieving in "recollection" at least the tracework of alterity in the flesh's primordial inscription, in order to become a self motivated by the "knowledge" of justice, a knowledge specifically mediated by the impersonal and "objective" perspective, or gaze, of the "third party" (*le tiers*). Thus we must look to the institutions of "Reason," representing the third party, to establish an "I," a self truly "capable," as Levinas phrases it, "of society" (again the reference is to TaI 208, TeI 183–84). What Levinas calls my "return to myself" and my "discovery" of my being already responsible is what we are here interpreting as a process of breaking through the ego's defensive constructs and retrieving the tracework of a supererogatory moral assignment, calling me to a radical responsibility for the other.

Drawing on the interpretation introduced into the chapter on Merleau-Ponty, we might think of Levinas's phenomenology as offering a narrative of developing moral transformation with regard to our capacity for vision; and we might conceptualize this narrative in terms of a temporal schema which articulates the body of moral experience in two different but interdependent readings, one of them diachronic, the other synchronic: [a] a diachronic representation concerned with the phases and faces of our embodiment in a *diachronic process* of moral development, and [b] a synchronic representation, topographic or structural (e.g., OB 110, AE 140), articulating the *synchronic dimensions* of this embodiment that are surpassed but nevertheless preserved in a certain tracework of memory and imagination, whenever a new phase of development emerges to carry forward and leave beneath it, as a latency that at any moment can involuntarily manifest or be to some extent reflectively retrieved, the remnants of the preceding phase. It seems to me that Levinas's moral phenomenology is very much in need of such a narrative.

Here, then, but only in its briefest and most schematic form, hovering undecidably between what can be remembered and what is imagined, is the narrative I want to suggest:

[1] *The proto-moral self of infancy:* that prepersonal, anonymous phase and dimension of our embodiment in which is registered, in a passivity of the flesh prior to consciousness, memory, and volition, a responsiveness to the other that is also the taking-hold of an absolute responsibility for the other, exposing me in the most radical way to the judgment of the other. To this extent, but only to this extent, I am always already a moral self. And yet, of course, it must also be recognized that, in this phase, I am not yet a moral self. But the assignment will have been registered.

[2] *The ego-logical subject:* As the infant grows up, the proto-moral experience is surpassed, yet traces of its alterity seem in some way to be preserved in a bodily memory beneath the formation of the ego-logical subject, who is strongly self-centered, lives in the self-absorbed pursuit of its own well-being, and believes itself to be self-contained, self-possessed, and self-grounded. The morality of this subject is at best conventional and, in Kant's sense, heteronomous.

[3] *The moral self:* This phase and dimension is merely a possibility, dependent on the ego's willingness to undergo a certain deconstruction and reconstruction of its identity by returning to retrieve the responsiveness and responsibility that it imagines originally took hold of the flesh in the time of its infancy. It is a question of returning to retrieve, in so far as possible, a dimension of our experience that—as we imagine it—continues to function "beneath" the ego-logical structure of the adult and continues, therefore, to obsess and haunt it. The moral self, a never-ending, never-completed project of exposure to the other, receives its gift of freedom only in submission to the responsibility that has already bound it to the other. In the radically altered intersubjectivity of the moral self, the involuntary mimetic reversibility of the first phase, in which the alterity of substitution—Levinas will also speak of the "I" as "hostage" to the other—makes one infant take over the suffering of another, and also the interest-

driven interchangeability of the second, ego-logical phase, would be transformed, to become, whatever the sacrifice, a truly selfless commitment to the welfare and justice of others. Thus, in this third phase, the moral self receives what is, in effect, a new face—and the anonymity that is possible only if one has a proper name to sacrifice. No longer anonymous, as in the first phase, no longer assuming the name that corresponds to the destiny of egotism, the moral self would act, as we say, with selflessness, in the name of a higher anonymity, a higher namelessness, a higher heteronomy, giving to others while remaining in self-concealment, self-effacement.

The transition that can take place in the third phase or moment of vision—the transition, that is, from the experience of the concrete other (whom I see facing me in the asymmetry of the face-to-face ethical relation) to the abstract, impartial, "blind" perspective of universal justice (where the other is an abstract other always invisible, and a figure for the whole of humanity), involves a process that may itself be articulated for analytic purposes in terms of three phenomenological moments. [3a] The first moment takes place when, by way of the deeply felt, bodily felt sense of beholdenness, of being touched and moved in spontaneous responsiveness to the visible presence of the singular and concrete other, we are made to feel very deeply our kindredness, our solidarity with the other in the very event of seeing. [3b] The second moment would be a moment of recognition, soliciting a deeply felt sense of responsibility for this other. Now the face of this other would visibly manifest an invisible dimension: this is "the face of the other's humanity." But this revelation is still in a sense limited: the "face of humanity" is seen only in and as the face of the singular and concrete other. But seeing the invisibility of the other would make possible a reflectively thematized transition to the next moment, when vision would properly become a question of justice. (This transitional moment is suggested, I think, by Levinas's assertion that "the face of man is the medium through which the invisible in him becomes visible and enters into commerce with us.")[177] [3c] This is the socioculturally mediated moment that Levinas (TaI 208, TeI 183–84) would call "knowledge," "reason," and "justice," in which the experience with vision would now be extended, generalized, reaching out even beyond the invisibility of the concrete other to behold the abstract and universal other, the whole of humanity: reaching out beyond all those visibly present, our eyes would now behold in the justice of the invisible all those who cannot be made concretely visible—all the living, all the dead, and all those of the future, generations who are not yet born. In the moment of reason and justice, the face of the other becomes an abstraction from vision, doubly invisible, not only because it is the face of others who are, or must be regarded as, beyond the horizons of my eye-sight, but because the dimensionality of the face is a revelation that is always, for Levinas, infinite and immeasurable.

It is crucial to see that, although we are endowed with a pre-originary predisposition to be affected by others, the capacity to respond depends for its actualization on our actually being affected by the other in face-to-face encounters which solicit, provoke, and awaken a certain "remembrance" of the inscription carried by the very flesh of our eyes—a moral imperative secretly commanding us to assume responsibility for the other that took hold of us in an immemorial past preceding the emergence of intentionality, ego-logical consciousness, and volition. The face of the other is an epiphany, an illumination that provokes this corporeal recollection, this *mémoire involontaire*, by communicating immediately with our primordial sensibility at a level entirely beneath intentionality, beneath consciousness. This is what happens in the third phase, in the moral transformation of the ego.

The narrative that we are schematizing thus gives us a way of thinking about the questions that introduced this section. The transition from the concrete, face-to-face ethical relation, in which the "I" can see humanity in the face of the concrete, singular other, to the moral-political relation, the abstract relation demanded by justice, in which the "I" recognizes the humanity of all others, is made possible by a certain mediating experience: the experience, namely, of seeing in the face of the concrete, singular other an *invisible and unfathomable* dimension, a dimension already withdrawing itself from visibility. For if even the face of the one who actually faces me is already seen to be invisible, already seen to be infinite, then my seeing *this* invisibility and being drawn into its withdrawal, drawn into its absolute alterity, would prepare me for the blindness that must be borne by a vision of the invisible humanity which looks back at us from the abstract face of justice, the invisible faces of the abstract other.

But everything hinges, here, if only at a certain point, and for a brief moment, on the redeeming character of our vision. Just as Levinas distinguishes, in *Totality and Infinity*, between touch, or contact, which denies transcendence for the sake of truth-as-disclosure, and the caress which brings out and reveals transcendence, so his critique of vision should have distinguished between the vision that is rooted in a primordial, deeply felt, bodily felt sense of exposure and enthrallment, responsiveness and responsibility, and the superficial, unfeeling vision that is promoted by an alienated, indifferent world. The deeper vision, a vision rooted in the primordial disposition of the flesh, would be the accomplishment of a post-conventional, revelatory vision, a vision no longer obedient to the merely conventional, still (in the Kantian sense) heteronomous determination of the moral. A vision obedient to the invisible, to that which can never appear, the imperative of a moral law more rigorous than the Kantian. A vision disenchanted, released from ontological idolatry, from the phantasmagoria of today's capitalism, from the production of images that destroy memory and imagination alike. However, it must be conceded that, in spite of the experience of the invisible even in the ethical relation, the face-to-face relation with a concrete other, there remains an unbridgeable gap between the recognition of the other in the ethical relation and the recognition of the other in the matter of justice: a transition from the ethical to the moral-political that only the urgent appeal for justice spoken by those who have suffered its absence can possibly overcome.

I also want to emphasize, here, in disagreement with Levinas, that the ethical relation cannot be the *foundation* for relations of justice, because *every* dimension of the experience depends on the intactness of the flesh, bearer of the primordial inscription of the moral sense; and every one of the moments depends upon certain favorable sociocultural conditions—a factor which cannot be adequately conceptualized and addressed simply by introducing the "third party." But if everything depends on favorable sociocultural conditions, then the ethical relation that Levinas regards as primary already depends on a certain minimum of social justice. Levinas himself seems, in fact, to realize this when he says, in *Difficult Freedom*, that "it is in economic justice that man glimpses the face of man."[178] The violence in the urban ghettos and Native American reservations, endlessly reproducing the effects of the hopeless poverty that persistent racism, inequality, and social injustice continue to produce, should by now be sufficient to demonstrate this point. The face-to-face experience of the ethical relation cannot be taken for granted. It is all too easily destroyed by degradation, brutal passion, senseless cruelty. But can we—a "we" the constitution of which Levinas's concept of the "third party" can at most only begin to theorize—then ignore the extent to which the conditions of living caused by systemic injustice are complicitous in such destructiveness? Is the connection not plainly visible?

IV. WHAT IF THE OTHER IS THE OPPRESSOR?

In Merleau-Ponty's phenomenological narrative, the beginning of moral consciousness in the child is an experience of intercorporeality that he brings to articulation by saying that "I live in the facial expressions of the other, as I feel him living in mine."[179] In another text, he explains his project as follows:

> We are interrogating our experience precisely in order to know how it opens us to what is not ourselves. This does not even exclude the possibility that we find in our experience a movement toward what could not in any event be present to us in the original and whose irremediable absence would thus count among our originating experiences.[180]

In thinking about the self's relationship with others as an interaction that first engages the self as a being of flesh, we must consider whether Levinas somehow forgets the dialectic of lord and bondsman in Hegel's *Phenomenology of Spirit*. We know that Merleau-Ponty follows the Lacanian account of the ego's specular formation and describes the interaction as an "encroachment," "transgression," and "alienation," while Levinas will use terms such as "wound," "persecution," "possession," "obsession," and "hostage" to characterize the ego's bodily felt experience of a primordial responsibility for the other, and will even refer to this primordial experience of obligation as "subjection." For Levinas, it is necessary to see that the formation of the self, the moral subject, is a process of subjection—subjection not in the sense of being under domination, of course, but in the sense of bearing responsibility for the other.

But what if the other is motivated by prejudice, intolerance of difference? What if the other is always, at least to some extent, as Foucault has argued very compellingly, a force that imposes normalization? What if the other is always, to some extent, the self's oppressor, the enemy of the self, unable or unwilling to recognize and accept the identity that would most deeply fulfill the self's social existence? Foucault's argument, drawing heavily, of course, on Freud, is that the subject's very identity and existence are dependent on processes of subjection, configurations of social power that are not merely effects imposed from outside, but, as internalized norms and ideals working within the economy of the psyche, become formative and constitutive of the subject's very being.[181] This implies a different sense of alienation, transgression, encroachment; a different sense of wounding, trauma, persecution, and hostage: a sense that is rendered even more disturbing when one considers to what torments, nightmares, and horrors these words must bear witness when taken to refer to the victims of racism, gender discrimination, homophobia, and other forms of normalizing oppression. In a society where such oppression is pervasive, the subject's experience of living in the facial expressions of the other and feeling the other living in "its own" can be irremediably devastating, identity-shattering, even, sometimes, annihilating—the very antithesis of a good beginning for the moral relation and the possibility of justice.

In this regard, the possibility of justice requires us, if only briefly, to reflect on one of Levinas's most difficult arguments. According to Levinas, the moral self is responsible even for its persecutors, responsible even for their responsibility. This is, of course, an exceedingly difficult moral demand; but the demand is rendered even more difficult to accept because of his moral discretion. Respecting our freedom, he will not state exactly what this might mean, what it might require of us. How, then, might the oppressed— the homeless and the hungry, the victims of racism, ethnic hatreds, and nationalism—be responsible for their persecutors and oppressors? Surely they cannot be held responsible for actions and circumstances over which they could have no control. But perhaps they may at the least be held to account in that they are responsible for keeping alive, as a lesson for future generations, the memory of their persecution. And perhaps they are responsible for finding within the unfathomable depths of their heart some way to grant, in time, the blessing of forgiveness. Indeed a difficult freedom.

Much hinges on what we can see—what we are open to seeing—in one another's faces. There can be no justice until we are all able to *see* how subjection causes pain and suffering in the differently treated other—and until each one who suffers the denial of recognition necessary for identity and social existence feels free at last to make such injustice visible in the realm of discursive reason. Thus the gaze must also become voice—a democracy of voices—in another Enlightenment, another history.[182]

V. JUSTICE: A PRESENTIMENT OF SEEING

So that a justice that can never come may nevertheless come, come now, we are called to the greatest vigilance, held responsible for the other in the very act of beholding, held hostage by way of the gaze, the face of the Other, moral "subjects" only by virtue of our being subject to the other through a sense of responsibility that is always already taking hold of us by the time our vision becomes conscious of itself in the act of perception. But what, then, are the radical, transformative potentialities inherent in the nature of perception and, more generally, in our embodiment, with regard to the development of moral character? If the order of justice is our concern, we need to learn an altered, radically transfigured vision, a vision rooted in a deeply felt sense of our interconnectedness with other sentient beings, a vision rooted in the moral disposition, the "categorical imperative" that nature gives us through our embodiment and that it is the duty of society to protect and realize in mature, post-conventional moral comportment. We need this vision. But because this "nature" has been terribly violated, corrupted; because the social conditions created by injustice do not care for, do not solicit and appropriately develop its originary disposition, we need a society radically different from ours: a society that can cultivate our capacity for vision and make it serve what Levinas calls "moral knowledge," the ideal of a reconciled society in which there is justice and equality for all, the ideal of a non-repressive society—a society no longer dominated by the *counterfeit* symmetries of the gaze blinded by the enchantments of self-interest and its calculative rationality.

In "The Authoritarian State," Horkheimer wrote: "The other is always in danger."[183] But to understand and see this, we must see that we ourselves are always already an other. Only then, perhaps, can we truly hearken to Levinas's words: "C'est l'heure de la justice!"[184] But that is a time which cannot be identified—it must not!—with any time present or foreseeable. Nor can the justice of the hour be anything more than forever provisional. Only those who understand why they cannot see the face of justice see it in the other.

Those are pearls that were his eyes.

The Tempest, Barnet, 1.2.394

What are eyes, if they can become precious stones? Once upon a time, the justice of nature transformed a mortal's eyes into pearls, revealing the great beauty that the eyes are capable of giving to the world. But the time of this sea change belongs to the realm of sacrifice and death.

8   Justice in the Seer's Eyes

Benjamin and Heidegger on a Vision out of Time and Memory

That things remain as they are: it is that which is the catastrophe.

Walter Benjamin[1]

What would happiness be that was not measured by the immeasurable grief at what is?

Theodor Adorno[2]

The resoluteness intended in *Being and Time* is not the deliberate action of a subject [*die decidierte Aktion eines Subjekts*], but the opening up of human being, out of its captivity in that which is, to the openness of being.

Martin Heidegger[3]

[Bourgeois idealism] contains not only the justification of the established form of existence, but also the pain of its establishment: not only quiescence about what is, but also remembrance of what could be.

Herbert Marcuse[4]

That which is not subjected to the process of difference is the *present*. The present is that from which we believe we are able to think time, effacing the inverse necessity: to think the present from time as difference.

Jacques Derrida[5]

I. PROBLEMATIC

In question and at stake, here, will be the gaze, or the glance, perhaps just a glimpse, of justice: "of justice" in both the subjective and objective senses. In a preliminary and provisional way, we shall be reflecting on the temporality, historicity, and violence of this connection.

In particular, we will undertake an initial reading of Heidegger's portrait of Kalchas the seer in his essay on "The Anaximander Fragment," in the hope of educing the peculiar logic, the dialectical spirit, that is at work in the seer's gaze. Benjamin's allegorical and dialectical modes of looking at the world will serve not only as a normative point of reference but also as a compelling conceptual force in the unfolding of the narrative, enabling us to think, beyond Heidegger, and otherwise than as being, as reification, the historical intervention, the justice and temporality, of the seer's gaze.

But a semblance of paradox surrounds this gaze. As we shall see, its futural, prophetic "intentionality" depends on a certain ἀνάμνησις, a process of recollection or remembrance, suspending the seer in the anguish of a time between the "always already" and the "not yet," the anguish of a justice that always comes "too soon" and always "too late," and the violence of a responsibility that must keep one eye for the signs of catastrophe and the other eye for the signs of redemption. For both Benjamin and Heidegger, the question of the end of history and the prospect of a new beginning requires vision. But the vision that is needed must look back in order to look ahead and look ahead in order to look back. Also in question, therefore, is what we might call the politics of memory and imagination.

We should not miss the significance of the fact that Heidegger introduces a discussion of the seer into his essay on Anaximander, suggesting, if not implying, that he sees a crucial connection between Δική, the topic of the Anaximander fragment, and the vision, the foresight, of the seer.

According, as Heidegger says, to the generally accepted text, the fragment, in English translation, reads:

> Whence things have their origin, there they must also pass away according to necessity; for they must pay penalty and be judged for their injustice, according to the ordinance of time.[6]

After examining the hermeneutical anxieties and difficulties involved in understanding and translating the fragment, questioning, above all, the equation of justice and the payment of penalty, expiation, or revenge, Heidegger turns to the question of our historical situation:

> Are we latecomers [*die Spätlinge*] in a history now racing towards its end, an end which in its increasingly sterile order of uniformity brings everything to an end? Or does there lie concealed in the historic and chronological remoteness of the fragment the historical proximity of something unsaid, something that will speak out in times to come? (AX 16, H 300)

The text continues:

> Do we stand in the very twilight of the most monstrous transformation our planet has ever undergone, the twilight of that epoch in which earth itself hangs suspended? Do we confront the evening of a night which heralds another dawn? . . . *Are* we the latecomers we are? But

are we also at the same time precursors of the dawn of an altogether different age, which has already left our historiological representations of history behind? (AX 17, H 300)

And, since historiography manifests the way we have situated ourselves in time and history, he remarks, critically, arguing a point with which Benjamin and Adorno could certainly agree, that

all historiography predicts what is to come [*errechnet das Kommende*] from images of the past determined by the present [*durch die Gegenwart*]. It systematically destroys the future and our historic relation to the advent of destiny. (AX 17, H 301)

"Can we nevertheless," he asks, "portray and represent the dawn of an age in ways different from those of historiography?" It is in part, for Heidegger, a question of seeing, of envisioning otherwise—and of a way of seeing that would come from the recognition of a need to prepare itself for an appropriate relationship to the "eschatology," the fateful dispensations of being (AX 18, H 301–2). This requires forming our images of the past in such a way that we retrieve, for the sake of a future we are preparing in the present, possibilities for justice concealed in what the past gives the present.

Writing of the "destiny of man" and the epochal dispensations of being, which he understands in terms of an interplay between unconcealment and concealment, the visible and the invisible, Heidegger turns to the rhetoric of light and vision, observing, for example, that "Man's inability to see himself [*das Sichversehen des Menschen*] corresponds to the self-concealing of the light of being" (AX 26, H 311). Contending that "little depends on what we represent and portray of the past [as such]," he stresses that "much depends on the way we are mindful [*eingedenk*: a word that Benjamin also uses] of what is destined" (AX 27, H 312). "Can we ever be mindful," he asks, "without thinking?" If thinking is to occur, however, then we will have to "abandon all claims of shortsighted opinion and open ourselves to the claim of destiny" (ibid.). It is crucial to keep in mind that Heidegger distinguishes between "fate" and "destiny," using "Schicksal" to refer to fate, a predetermined chain of events, and "Geschick" to refer to destiny, a future that can come to pass only if our appropriation of the past prepares for its arrival. So, then, does the "claim of destiny" speak in the early saying of Anaximander? In answering this question, Heidegger says:

We are not sure whether its claim speaks to our essential being. It remains to ask whether in our relation to the truth of being the glance of being [*der Blick des Seins*], and this means lightning [*der Blitz*] (Heraclitus, fr. 64), strikes; or whether in our knowledge of the past only the faintest glimmers of a storm long flown casts a pale semblance of light. (Ibid.)

It is in the midst of a struggle to understand the archaic words, words that he translates into a discourse on "being," that Heidegger thinks of Homer's *Iliad*, and refers to the story of Kalchas the seer, whom Achilles asks to interpret the wrath of the god. Homer writes, there, of Kalchas, "who knew all that is, is to be, or once was." And Heidegger comments:

> Before he lets Kalchas speak, Homer designates him as the seer [*der Seher*]. Whoever belongs in the realm of seers is such a one ὃς ἤδη . . . "who knew . . . "; ἤδη is the pluperfect of the perfect οἶδεν, "he has seen." Only when a man has seen does he truly see. To see is to have seen. What is seen has arrived and remains for him in sight. A seer has always already [*immer schon*] seen. Having seen in advance, he sees into the future. He sees the future tense out of the perfect. . . . What is it that the seer has seen in advance? Obviously, only what becomes present in the lighting that penetrates his sight. What is seen in such a seeing can only be what comes to presence in unconcealment. But what becomes present? (AX 33–34, H 318–19)

According to Heidegger,

> what is past and what is to come also become present, namely as outside the expanse of unconcealment. What presents itself as non-present is what is absent. . . . Even what is absent is something present, for *as* absent from the expanse [of unconcealment], it presents itself in unconcealment. What is past and what is to come are also ἐόντα [what is present]. (AX 35, H 320)

"The seer," he says,

> stands in sight of what is present, in its unconcealment, which has at the same time cast light on the concealment of what is absent as being absent. The seer sees inasmuch as he has [always already] seen everything *as present*. (Ibid. Italics added.)

In other words: "The seer is the one who has already seen the whole of what is present in its presencing." (AX 36, H 321. Here, and in subsequent quotations from this text, I have substituted the open "whole" for the closed "totality" as the translation for "das Ganze.") Thus, according to Heidegger,

> all things present and absent are gathered and preserved in *one* presencing for the seer. . . . The seer speaks from the preserve [*Wahr*] of what is present. He is the sooth-sayer [*Wahr-Sager*]. (AX 36, H 321)

Indeed, "the seer, as the one who has seen, is himself one who makes-present and belongs in an exceptional sense to the whole of what is present" (AX 38, H 323).

But what is involved in the seer's gathering and preserving? What does this mean? In particular, does it mean that the seer's vision is bound to the past, or to a metaphysical present, and that it cannot envision a radical break with the past? How does the seer belong to the whole? Does the gathering and preserving serve a metaphysics of presence? Should Heidegger be understood, here, as suggesting a metaphysics of history that would repress contingency, interruption, and difference? It is crucial to bear in mind, here, that, according to Heidegger, "seeing is determined, not by the eye, but by the lighting of being" (AX 36, H 322). Consequently Heidegger's commentary proceeds to a repudiation of "our usual way of representing things," since representation would "exclude from what is present all absence" (AX 37, H 323). This gives us an indication of the way we must answer our questions: Heidegger believes that the seer's vision gathers the absent, the invisible only if it is open to a future of radically new historical possibilities. Indeed, it gathers the absent not in order to reduce it to the order of the same, but precisely in order to see the present put in question by a temporality radically open to new historical possibilities.

In keeping with this approach, Heidegger will not assume in advance that he understands the "fundamental words" of the Anaximander fragment; thus, he translates these words in a way that respects their historical originality and acknowledges our great distance, the extremity of our difficulty in trying to understand them. Working towards a preliminary interpretation, he translates Anaximander's word Δικη not as *Gerechtigkeit*, the standard German word for "justice," but rather with the words related to *Fug*, suggesting the "rightness" of an overpowering jointure or enjoining:

> The fragment clearly says that what is present is in ἀδικία, i.e., is out of joint [*aus der Fuge*]. However, that cannot mean that things no longer come to presence. But neither does it say that what is present is only occasionally, or perhaps only with respect to some of its properties, out of joint. The fragment says: what is present as such, being what it is, is out of joint. . . . What is present is that which lingers awhile. The while occurs essentially as the transitional arrival in departure: the while comes to presence between approach and withdrawal. Between the twofold absence the presencing of all that lingers occurs. In this "between" whatever lingers awhile is joined, from its emergence here to its departure away from here. The presencing of whatever lingers obtrudes into the "here" of its coming, as into the "away" of its going. In both directions, presencing is conjointly disposed toward absence. (AX 41, H 327)

The commentary continues:

> Whatever lingers awhile [*Das Je-Weilige*] becomes present as it lingers
> in the jointure [*in der Fuge*] which arranges presencing jointly between
> a twofold absence. Still, as what is present [*als das Anwesende*], what-
> ever lingers awhile—and only it—can stay the length of its while.
> What has arrived may even insist upon its while [*auf seine Weile
> bestehen*] solely to remain more present, in the sense of perduring.
> That which lingers perseveres in its presencing [*beharrt auf seinem
> Anwesen*]. In this way, it extricates itself from its transitory while. It
> strikes the willful pose of persistence [*den Eigensinn des Beharrens*], no
> longer concerning itself with whatever else is present [or disposed to
> become present in some way]. It stiffens—as if this were the way to
> linger—and aims solely for continuance and subsistence. (AX 42,
> H 327–28)

So it is in the persistence of a being beyond the ordinance of time, beyond
and in defiance of its assignment or allotment of time, that ἀδικία, injustice, disjunction, consists:

> The disjunction [*die Un-Fuge*] consists in the fact that whatever lingers
> awhile seeks to win for itself a while based solely on the model of con-
> tinuance. Lingering as persistence, considered with respect to the join-
> ture of the while, is an insurrection [*Aufstand*] on behalf of sheer
> endurance [*bloße Andauern*]. . . . In this rebellious whiling [*dieses Auf-
> ständische der Weile*] whatever lingers awhile insists upon sheer con-
> tinuance. (AX 43, H 328)

It is, then, a question of domination—the violence and injustice of relations
of domination and subordination within the realm of beings:

> But in this way everything that lingers awhile strikes a haughty pose
> [*spreizt sich*] toward every other of its kind. None heeds the lingering
> presence of the others. Whatever lingers awhile is inconsiderate [*rück-
> sichtslos*] toward others, each dominated by what is implied in its lin-
> gering presence, namely, the craving to persist. (AX 45–46, H 331)

But there is an ontological dimension to this domination in the realm of beings: obliteration of the "ontological difference" between beings and the being of beings, or between what is present and presencing as such (AX 50–51,
H 335–36). "Perhaps," Heidegger therefore suggests,

> only when we experience historically what has not been thought—the
> oblivion of being—as what is to be thought, and only when we have for
> the longest time pondered what we have long experienced in terms of
> the destiny of being, may the early word speak in our contemporary
> recollection. (AX 51, H 337)

At the end of the essay, Heidegger returns to reflect on our contemporary situation and makes very clear the connection he sees between this situation and the ἀδικία of Anaximander's fragment:

> Man has already begun to overwhelm the entire earth and its atmosphere, to arrogate to himself in forms of energy the concealed powers of nature, and to submit future history to the planning and ordering of a world government. This same defiant man is utterly at a loss simply to say what *is*, to say *what* this *is*—that a thing *is*. (AX 57, H 343)

"The totality of beings," he says, "is the singular object of a singular will to conquer" (ibid. Here it is crucial to retain the word "totality"). "What mortal," he wonders, "can fathom the abyss of this confusion [*den Abgrund dieser Wirrnis*]?" (ibid.). His reply, reminiscent of Nietzsche, is unequivocal: "He may try to shut his eyes before this abyss. He may entertain one delusion after another. The abyss does not vanish" (ibid.). Thus, it becomes necessary, as a first gesture in recognition of the need for justice and the possibility of restitution and redemption, to think the abyss: necessary, in fact, to *recollect* the abyss, looking without blinking into the gaping abyss— to *see* it. Only such a vision could see the destruction of history and make it visible as a foreseeable end.

Could it be that it is precisely by virtue of an "abyssal" vision, a vision that recollects the abyss of being, that the seer is granted uncanny "foresight"? Could it be, paradoxical though it might seem, that it is only in and as a recollection of the *being* of beings, a recollection of the ordinance and assignment of time, that such "foresight" is first rendered possible? And could it be that it is precisely in and as this recollection that the seer's vision becomes a vision of justice, a vision that sees, with and through the ordinance and assignment of time, the ending of injustice, the ending of history as a history of unspeakable cruelty and suffering, perhaps the possibility of a new beginning? Could it be that, through a certain process of recollection, we might be granted a vision that not only sees this, but also serves what it sees, an organ and instrument of what we might perhaps call, with one eye on Benjamin, divine justice, divine judgment?

Heidegger leaves largely unthought the connection between the seer's peculiar "foresight" and the problematic of justice and restitution spoken of in the fragment. Likewise obscure in his essay is the connection between the seer's "foresight" and the need for a recollection of being, the lighting of the being of beings, an interplay between concealment and unconcealment within which beings come into being, into presence, stay a while, and then perish, even if driven by a disposition to persist. In order to work through these questions, we shall leave Heidegger for the time being and turn to Benjamin, whose writings are the product of a certain visionary thinking at once very like and very unlike that of Heidegger's seer.

What are the affinities and the differences between Heidegger's "recollection" (a process of hermeneutical *Erinnerung* and *Wiederholung* which in late works he also described using the word *Andenken*)[7] and Benjamin's "remembrance" (*Eingedenken*), and how do they figure in relation to the question of the continuation or ending of history? How are their respective textual practices of recollection and reminiscence related to their visions of justice? Reflecting, first, on the allegorical and dialectical modes of seeing that figure in Benjamin's work, we may be able, perhaps, to return to Heidegger and, thinking the two together, formulate some thoughts that carry forward into a very radical political perspective a difficult meditation concerning what I have called the seer's vision of justice.[8]

Benjamin left no doubt that he could see only irreconcilable differences between his thought and that of Heidegger. In a letter to Gershom Scholem, he wrote: "It is there that I shall find Heidegger on my path, and I expect some sparks to fly from the clash [*l'entre-choc*] of our two very different ways of viewing history."[9] Nevertheless, I would argue that there are—or anyway seem to be—many similarities and affinities between them. But the correlations are quite intricate and treacherous. From a certain angle, this is what one might see: Both saw a world of suffering and were moved by what they saw to consecrate their thinking to what they regarded an appropriate response. Both saw the historical departure from the origin, the beginning of history, as in some sense a degeneration; and neither thought the continuation of this decline inevitable and irreversible. Both saw in the decline a loss of memory and saw redemptive hope in the overcoming of forgetfulness. Both turned their philosophical gaze in the direction of history and the writing of history as they struggled to think the possibility of a radical transformation, a new beginning. Both thought it necessary to think this possibility as beyond time and history as we have known them, unequivocally rejecting the causal chain of history, the continuum of historical progress, and the conventional experience of the "now," the time of the "present." Both conceived the interruption of historical time in terms of a sudden flash of lightning, the absolutely unexpected gift of illumination, bringing insight, a moment of vision. Both regarded this vision as in some crucial sense "involuntary." Both drew a sharp distinction between such revelation or unconcealment and the evidence or disclosure of truth in an adequation between subject and object.[10] Both employed the figure of the seer, the visionary, to articulate the revolutionary substance of their thinking. Both believed that the vision and imagination of the seer must be grounded in a work of memory. Both thought of the interruption of historical time as manifesting the anarchy and violence of a world-transcending, or, say, divine dispensation of justice. And finally, therefore, both men turned to an allegorical mode of vision in order to think, in relation to time and history, what they could not avoid seeing as the decay and destructiveness in modern experience, and to wrest from the present a way of reading the signs of another beginning.

But there is, in spite of these apparent points of convergence, at least one striking difference—a difference that cuts very deeply, separating them beyond all possibility of reconciliation. Heidegger's vision of justice is first and foremost ontological: it is the Δική of the Anaximander fragment, the preserve of anarchy underlying the establishment of all ontic orders; it is the dispensation of finite temporality and the withdrawal of absolute grounding in relation to everything belonging to the ontic realm.[11] By contrast, Benjamin's vision of justice is first and foremost political: it is explicitly dedicated to remembering the victims of oppression and somehow redeeming the vision for which they died—or the vision the absence of which constituted the conditions that brought about their suffering, their destitution, their death. For Heidegger, the question of suffering is never formulated in relation to the politics of justice for the oppressed, as it always is for Benjamin. Thus, for Heidegger, the justice of anarchy, or the anarchy of justice, will essentially be, following Anaximander, a question of the coming-to-be, staying, and perishing of all finite beings, and, more specifically, a question of man's acknowledgment of the limits—the right measure—imposed by this cosmological order; whereas, for Benjamin, as we can see from a reading of his "Critique of Violence," what is at stake is the immediate end of domination and oppression.

Even when Heidegger interprets the "persistence of being" about which the fragment speaks, calling it ἀδικία, the injustice of domination, the imposition of the will to power, it may seem that he does not attempt to think the political dimension of justice, the implications for the politics of power that might correspond to the mythic and cosmological dimension which claims Anaximander's thought. Indeed, Heidegger explicitly warns against giving Δική and ἀδικία a moral, political, or juridical interpretation. But, as we shall see, Heidegger shows that these words implicitly carry political significance even if they do not immediately refer to our moral, political, and juridical life. For his warning was meant to prevent any reduction of

Δική to the justice of worldly institutional orders. It was not meant to prevent us from thinking critically about the latter in the light of the former. Indeed, according to the reading I am suggesting here—a reading in which, I am sure, Heidegger himself would have found much he could not agree to—the Anaximander text, somewhat like Benjamin's "Critique of Violence," makes it at least theoretically possible to formulate a standpoint from which, regardless of the standpoint one must attribute to Heidegger himself, one could perhaps begin to articulate, in the name of an absolutely uncompromising dispensation of justice, and in opposition to every institutional regime of law and justice constructed on this earth, the most extreme critical resistance, anarchic, excessive, and deconstructive, to bring to an end whatever forms of injustice the prevailing regime has produced.

The formulation of such a standpoint might begin by insisting that no juridical and moral institutions established here on earth can ever claim to represent the perfection of justice. But Heidegger's text also seems to allow the possibility of a very strong critical position with regard, in particular, to one historically powerful conception of justice, when he not only emphasizes (AX 41, H 327) that we must resist interpreting Anaximander's words, Δίκη and ἀδικία, in terms of our juridical and moral notions, but argues at some length (AX 42, H 328) against interpreting διδόναι δίκην and τίσιν as concerned with a payment of debt, recompense, or penalty. Moreover, he finishes this argument by declaring—unfortunately without elaboration—that, in particular, we must avoid the assumption that justice must be equated with retribution and revenge. Thus, his struggle to interpret these words very differently, viz., as a "giving [which] lets something belong to another which properly belongs to him" (AX 43, H 329), might be read—regardless of his actual intentions—as clearing the way for a repudiation of the ancient "justice" of retribution and revenge, and the no less ancient "justice" of the victors, in the name of, and for the sake of, a justice not reducible to any of its juridical and moral realizations in history—a justice that would, first of all, strive to be decisively other than the endless repetition of revenge and the "justice" of the victors.

The standpoint that this reading of Heidegger is suggesting, with regard to a different worldly institution of justice, is defined with great lucidity in a text by Adorno. In writing "On the Classicism of Goethe's *Iphigenie*," he comments that:

> Humanness requires that the law of an eye for an eye, a quid pro quo, be brought to an end; that the infamous exchange of equivalents, in which age-old myth is recapitulated in rational economics, cease. The process, however, has its dialectical crux in the requirement that what

rises above exchange not fall back behind it; that the suspension of exchange not once again cost human beings, as the objects of order, the full fruits of their labor. The abolition of the exchange of equivalents would be its fulfillment; as long as equality reigns as law, the individual is cheated of equality.[12]

Levinas wants to see an ethical relation no longer determined by symmetry, by equivalence, conceding the appropriateness of such measures only in the sphere of justice; Adorno wants to see economies of equivalence abolished even in the sphere of justice. How might we work toward the realization of a justice that, after Levinas, we might describe as always for the other, always giving beyond compare, beyond measure? Our imperative question. But it must be said, here, that the question of justice never was of great urgency for Heidegger: one would search his writings in vain for any satisfying philosophical response to the injustices of his time and any unequivocal recognition of a justice giving beyond what is due—a justice wholly for the other. But he does oppose relations of domination.

As for Benjamin, I would say that in every one of his writings matters of justice are at stake. This is the case even in the early (1924–25) essay on the *Trauerspiel*, the German mourning-play, where, because these matters are registered in a discourse on German baroque theater and rendered in allegorical forms, represented, as in the Anaximander fragment, in terms of the destructiveness of time and the corruptions of natural history, the bearing of the text on questions of justice has become highly mediated. But, in a text that conjures up images of a stage strewn with corpses and skulls, questions of justice can hardly be kept deeply buried.

That the stage was indeed already set, in that work, for sustained reflection on a certain narrative regarding justice is something that one can readily deduce from the "Epistemo-Critical Prologue" that introduces his *Trauerspiel* study: we can retrieve it not only from his discussion, there, of "natural history," but also from his treatment of "representation," "truth," and "knowledge." Moreover, the intention to engage in a relentless, unremitting questioning of modern liberal and conservative conceptions of right, duty, and justice is already implicitly manifest in the dialogue that Benjamin chose to abstract from the first act of the baroque drama "Ernelinde Oder Die Viermahl Braut," and placed at the very beginning of his first chapter.

Although the nostalgic, melancholy mood of this remark could not be more different from the mood of Heidegger's essay, its sense of "natural history," of a cosmological or ontological justice—the justice that metes out the destiny of transience to all finite beings—would seem to bring him into the proximity of the thought that Heidegger wants to read into the Anaximander fragment. But the immediacy of Benjamin's concern for political justice is manifestly at the very heart of the "Critique of Violence" (1921), and it is paramount in all his later writings—for example, Konvolut N, reflecting on "The Theory of Knowledge, Theory of Progress" (begun in 1927) and the "Theses on the Philosophy of History" (1940).

As we shall see, this difference between Heidegger and Benjamin with regard to the question of justice ultimately alters in some quite intricate ways even the similarities and affinities alluded to earlier. And yet, it must be said that, if Heidegger's critique of modern political institutions seems to offer only an abstract negation, a negation dangerously close, sometimes, to the mythical, and to be severely weakened by its inability to think outside the political alternatives of national socialism, on the one side, and, on the other side, the equally undesirable politics of Russian communism and American capitalism, Benjamin's *Critique of Violence* likewise seems to be unable to offer more than an abstract mythic negation of the present and to be hopelessly bound to a representation of the alternatives in which we must ultimately choose between fascism and communism. Of course, as we know, Heidegger chose the hope in Hitler's national socialism and Benjamin chose the hope in communism. And both these systems came to an end, exchanging the hope invested in them for the violence of totalitarian rule.

II. BENJAMIN'S DIALECTIC OF CATASTROPHE AND REDEMPTION

Hope is not memory held fast but the return of what has been forgotten.

Theodor Adorno, "On the Final Scene of Faust"[13]

The historian is a prophet facing backwards.

Friedrich Schlegel,
Athenaeum Fragments[14]

The future-oriented gaze is directed from the present into a past that is connected as *prehistory* with our present, as by the chain of continual destiny.

Jürgen Habermas,
The Philosophical Discourse of Modernity[15]

Many people have spirit or feeling or imagination. But because singly these qualities can only manifest themselves as fleeting, airy shapes, nature has taken care to bond them chemically to some common earthly matter. To discover this bond is the unremitting task of those who have the greatest capacity for sympathy, but it requires a great deal of practice in intellectual chemistry as well. The man who could discover an infallible reagent for every beautiful quality in human nature would reveal to us a new world. As in the vision of the prophet, the endless field of broken and dismembered humanity would suddenly spring into life.

Friedrich Schlegel, *Athenaeum Fragments*[16]

Prophecy is an occurrence in the moral world. What the prophet sees in advance [*voraussieht*] are the criminal courts of justice [*Strafgerichte*].

Walter Benjamin, "Rückblick auf Stefan George"[17]

§1

In "Le Prix du Progrès," Adorno wrote: "All reification is a forgetting."[18] It could be argued that Heidegger frequently expressed the same thought, although we would also have to recognize that there are certain major, even fundamental divergences between them with regard to the political implications of this thought.[19] And yet, the similarities are neither minor nor inconsequential. For Heidegger, reification is a consequence of our forgetting the opening of being; for Adorno, reification is a consequence of the forgetting of social conditions. In any case, like Heidegger, like Benjamin,[20] Adorno warns that there is in our culture an increasingly dangerous destruction of "memory, time, and recollection":

> The spectre [*Schreckbild*] of man without memory . . . is more than an aspect of decline—it is necessarily linked with the principle of progress in bourgeois society. [. . .] Economists and sociologists such as Werner Sombart and Max Weber correlated the principle of tradition to feudal, and that of rationality to bourgeois, forms of society. This means no less than that the advancing bourgeois society liquidates Memory, Time, Recollection [*Erinnerung, Zeit, Gedächtnis*] as irrational remains of the past.[21]

Loss of memory can be as dangerous as the foreclosing of foresight. Perhaps even more so. For Benjamin, forgetting is reification because, without a memory of the traces of paradise haunting childhood experience and cultural artifacts, there can be no dialectical opposition to the present—and consequently, no way out of its endless repetition. Benjamin's remembrance is therefore not in the conventional sense "conservative." It is very much a memory in the service of a Nietzschean forgetting, a forgetting that is intended to free us from enslavement to the past, from the weight of tradition—precisely so that we can experience the past as if for the first time, this time in terms of the needs of the present, and "remember" the image of a past the retrieval of which could at last, perhaps, in an explosion of revolutionary energies, break the spell, the grip, of a seemingly endless history of oppression and suffering.

It is fitting that, in writing about Proust, Benjamin describes his thinking as "the Penelope-work of remembrance" (*die Penelopearbeit des Einge-denkens*),[22] indicating the dialectical tensions, the antinomies and paradoxes, inherent in the process: although it is as impossible to recover memory-images of paradise as it is to imagine and foresee the end of history and the inception of a Messianic afterlife, the memory-work in question is the making present of a past, an origin, that actually never was present; but it is also a making-present that is meant to *unmake* the present. Moreover, since there is, in the very struggle to overcome forgetfulness, an intensified consciousness of the futility of the effort and a heightened sense that there is no possibility of retrieving the original experience intact and in its original redemptive immediacy, the work of remembrance suffers incurably from a vigilance of consciousness which continually deconstructs the work the more it struggles to succeed. Thus this work of memory is compelled to resign itself to being an inaugural repetition, a repetition that, in the crucial sense, fails to be the redeeming repetition.

Like Heidegger, Benjamin gives thought to the "soothsayer." Also like Heidegger, he returns the gaze of the soothsayer to the past, asking it to do the work of remembering, without which the promise of the future would be lost. In his "Theses on the Philosophy of History," he says:

> The soothsayer [*Wahrsager*] who found out from time what it had in store certainly did not experience time as either homogeneous or empty. Anyone who keeps this in mind will perhaps get an idea of how past times were experienced in remembrance [*Eingedenken*]—namely, in just the same way. We know that the Jews were forbidden to investigate the future. The Torah and the prayers, on the other hand, instruct them in remembrance. This stripped the future of its magic, to which all those succumb who turn to the soothsayers for enlightenment. This does not imply, however, that for the Jews, the future turned into homogeneous, empty time. For every second of time was the straight gate through which the Messiah might enter. (IL 264, S 506)

Contrary to conventional thinking, the vision of the seer, the soothsayer, is not a gaze of predictive foresight directed straightforwardly into the future;

it is, rather, a vision that derives its revelatory capacity entirely from a work of memory—a work of memory, however, that must also be a forgetting, a deconstruction of the past as a determining force of fate. An image is eventually produced. But the image, he tells us, is "not seen before being remembered."[23] Memory is therefore primary.

What, then, is the role of the seer's imagination? Intensely conscious of the Judaic prohibition against images of God, and thus of the redemption promised only for the end of time and history, Benjamin's political thought nevertheless depends on the revelatory power, the "weak messianic power" (*schwache messianische Kraft*),[24] of images—especially the images granted by virtue of the work of memory.[25] Benjamin attempts to draw a very sharp distinction between "prophetic vision" and the vision at work in imagination, the faculty that produces images, but in the final analysis he requires them to work antagonistically, dialectically, together. In a short text on the imagination, he asserts that the vision of imagination is deformative, or, say, deconstructive; whereas the vision of prophecy claims to see the forms of the future—although perhaps it is actually only inventing them. Contrary to the traditional way of understanding imagination, namely, as the faculty that produces or constructs images, Benjamin asserts that

> imagination has nothing to do with forms or formations
> [*Gestaltungen*]. . . . It does indeed take its manifestations
> from them, but the connection between them and the imagi-
> nation is so far from being inexorable that we might rather
> describe the manifestations of the imagination as the
> de-formation [*Entstaltung*] of what has been formed.[26]

The argument continues, clarifying his way of thinking about the soothsayer's prophetic vision:

> The exact opposite of imagination is prophetic vision. . . . Prophetic vi-
> sion is the ability to perceive the forms of the future; imagination is the
> awareness of the de- formations of the future. Prophecy is genius for
> premonition; imagination is the genius for forgetting. . . . The imagina-
> tion knows only constantly changing transitions.[27]

"Pure imagination," he adds, "is concerned exclusively with nature. It creates no new nature. Pure imagination, therefore, is not an inventive power."

The text accordingly expresses Benjamin's Judaic suspicion of both forms of vision and insists on maintaining a necessary dialectical tension between a purely deconstructive use of the imagination and its more inventive use in prophetic vision: a tension which will always threaten to undo the images produced by the prophetic mode.

At the heart of Benjamin's thought, however, is the conviction that the vision that matters most is a vision that comes from historical memory. When genuine, such historical memory consists in "messianic contacts" between the present and certain moments of the past. Although there is a sense in which this memory of the past follows the coming of an image, it is hoped that the work of memory will nevertheless eventuate in the coming of memorative images—for example, the "image of enslaved ancestors, rather than that of liberated grandchildren."[28] Images remembering the victims of history are, though not able to redeem their fate, at least able to accord their names some belated honor.[29]

In Benjamin's work, memory—Mnemosyne—divided into two "archaic" forms: *Gedächtnis* (let us call it recollection) and *Eingedenken* (let us call it remembrance). And in each of them, as Irving Wohlfarth points out, "Benjamin discovers a messianic potential at the very moment when they are threatened with final extinction—namely, at the beginning of the Second World War."[30] As the two German prefixes suggest, *Gedächtnis* is a form of memory that gathers and recollects many different events and episodes, weaving them together into a comprehensive narrative; by contrast, *Eingedenken* is a much more intense, more focused form of memory, concentrating its care on a singular historical constellation. *Gedächtnis* is also commemoration, a community's remembering together. In "The Storyteller," it is a question primarily of the former; in his "Theses on the Philosophy of History," it is primarily a question of the latter. In both texts, however, Benjamin is concerned above all to rescue the two functions of memory from the obliteration that threatens them. In "The Storyteller," Benjamin explains the difference between the two forms of memory:

> *Memory* creates the chain of tradition which hands events down from generation to generation. . . . It . . . encompasses the varieties of the epic. First among these is the one embodied by the storyteller. It ultimately establishes a whole web of interrelated stories. The next one starts where the last left off, as the great storytellers, especially the Oriental ones, always wanted to show. . . . Such is epic memory [*Gedächtnis*] and the storyteller's Muse. Against it should be set another principle, the Muse of the novel, which initially . . . lies concealed, not yet differentiated from that of the story. In epics, it can at most be occasionally divined, particularly at such solemn Homeric moments as the initial invocations of the Muse. What these passages announce is the perpetuating [*verewigend*] memory of the novelist as opposed to the short-lived [*kurzweilig*] reminiscences of the storyteller. The former is dedicated to the *one* hero, the *one* odyssey or the *one* struggle; the latter, to the *many* scattered [*zerstreut*] occurrences. It is, in

other words, *remembrance* [*Eingedenken*] that, as the novelist's Muse, joins memory [*Gedächtnis*], the storyteller's, their original unity having come apart with the disintegration of the epic.[31]

Whereas epic memory, recollection, and storytelling retrieve the past and bring with it the unchanging sameness of the chronological time-order, there is a type of memory that would attempt, however vainly, to rescue the past from this very order.

But if the origin is, as it must be, both within and external to the history that it inaugurates; if the philosopher's remembrance is the making-present of a past that has actually never been fully present; and if remembrance therefore cannot really be a retrieval, a repetition, of the origin, but at most, as Levinas would say, a trace of a trace, in what sense is it true memory—or a memory of truth? Here it is necessary to distinguish, as Benjamin does, between truth as "revelation" and truth as "exposure," as the correspondence, or *adequatio*, between thought and reality: the truth of *Eingedenken* is revelation, which is perhaps why, inspired by the use of "mémoire involontaire" in Proust's great novel, Benjamin can think of it as a form of memory disconnected from intentionality: an *unwillkürliches Eingedenken* (UDT 418).

Explaining, in the "Prologue" to his *Trauerspiel* essay, the distinction he wants to make between the revelation of truth and its totalizing, reifying exposure, Benjamin says:

> truth is not a process of exposure [*Enthüllung*] which destroys the secret, but a revelation which does it justice [*Offenbarung, die ihm gerecht wird*]. (OGT 31, UDT 146. Also see OGT 35–36 and UDT 150–51.)

This distinction is similar to Levinas's distinction between "disclosure" (*dévoilement*) and "revelation" (*révélation*),[32] and derives from kindred concerns: in drawing the distinction, Levinas intimates that "disclosure" is always injustice, that "the work of justice" requires "revelation."[33] It is also important to recall, here, Heidegger's distinction between "truth," understood according to the tradition as the correspondence between a proposition of thought and a state of reality, and "unconcealment" (*Unverborgenheit*), the necessary condition for the very possibility of "truth."[34] Benjamin's distinction would permit us to draw a corresponding distinction between memory as a repetition of that which is endlessly the same and memory as a repetition that, by virtue of its relation to the creative and renewing resources of the origin, makes a radical difference, a new beginning. Given the transcendence of the inception, neither form of repetition could actually return to the origin and bring it back to the present intact and as it was; and moreover, even if, *per impossibile,* repetition could go back and retrieve it "just as it was," what would be retrieved could only be a moment that, as origin, never was, and never could have been, totally and fully present to itself. But in any case, the distinction that Benjamin makes remains crucial: whereas the former repetition could produce only a betrayal of the promise, degeneration and destruction of its potential, the latter would let itself be inspired by the revolutionary energies set in motion through its very efforts, however vain, to retrieve the origin. As we shall see, both Benjamin and Heidegger depend on a revelatory memory that attempts the second kind of repetition in relation to the imagined origin of history.

In his early writings, and especially in the *Trauerspiel* essay, Benjamin's relation to the tradition is more sympathetic, tinged with a certain deep ambivalence: on the one hand, appreciation and longing for the wisdom buried in the tradition; on the other hand, not only the belief that it can be passed on only in a way that inevitably betrays it, but moreover the conviction that no authentic relation to tradition is possible *within* the order of tradition, and that the only authentic way to relate to tradition, the only way to receive it, is to destroy it and make way for the radically different. Thus, like Heidegger, Benjamin sees the need for a radical break from tradition. In fact, they both are moved to call for its "destruction." It follows that they would both be extremely critical of historicism in historiography, in historical memory, and in historical writing. For Benjamin, modern historiography is a devastating betrayal of the responsibility carried by memory. It ignores "every reverberation of 'lament' " in history and substitutes false consolations, the idols and fetishes of the marketplace. Thus he argues, with words that it would be easy to imagine finding in *Being and Time* (especially chapter 5 of the second division), that "in every era the attempt must be made anew to wrest tradition away from a conformism that is about to overpower it.[35] Remembrance of tradition *must* be catastrophic in all senses of the word "must":

> Historical materialism wishes to retain that image of the past as it appears unexpectedly to an historical subject at a moment of danger. The danger affects both the continued existence [*Bestand*] of the tradition and those who receive it. The danger is the same for both: that of becoming a tool of the ruling classes. In every era the attempt must be made anew to wrest tradition away from a conformism about to overpower it. (GS, vol. I, part 2, Konvolut N, p. 695)

354 / The Philosophers

"Tradition" is therefore not, as such, the enemy: "Tradition," that is, "as the discontinuity of the past as opposed to history as the continuum of events" (GS, vol. I, part 3, p. 1236). To make history, then, is not to record the passage of time, but the ability to "read" the images of the tradition that could interrupt this continuum. According to a note in the *Passagenwerk*, past and future are (to be) related not in terms of the passage of time, but through the "legibility" of the images that could indicate a radically new order of time and history (GS, vol. V, part 1, pp. 577–78).

But in the *Trauerspiel* essay, the attempt to appropriate history, to retrieve it through remembrance, could *only* be catastrophic, completely shattering, fragmenting, whatever meaningfulness lay buried in history: the reception of tradition could *only* be a process in which the constructions of meaning it bears are left in ruins. Consequently, the site where tradition would be gathered could not be located in a present with its past and future, a present now-time belonging to the same order of time as the tradition itself; it could be located only in a deferred future, a future, moreover, that would not belong to our present order of time and history. The remembrance that could redeem the past must belong to another time, another history. In question is the imaginative power of a remembrance that could awaken a past that never was and see it shatter the petrified solidity of the present "reality."

Historical remembrance is a dialectical experience of the catastrophic in four different senses: (i) it is fated to a certain failure in retrieving the redeeming origin; (ii) it cannot receive the past and hand it down without destroying it; (iii) since the present is a continuation, a repetition of an empty past severed from the origin, the work of remembrance must be *for the sake of* a violent, catastrophic destruction of the present; and finally, (iv) the past that it sees, with a vision already at odds with conventional optics, is a past that already lies in ruins. Thus, in his "Theses on the Philosophy of History," Benjamin uses the figure of the "Angel of History," the *Angelus Novus*, to comment that

> where we perceive a chain of events, he sees one single catastrophe.[36]

Here the dialectics of the seeing sets in motion a very different constellation of the three temporal moments—past, present, and future.

Howard Caygill holds that "for Heidegger, such ruination is potentially, but not necessarily, the issue of tradition, since for him the excessive moment of origin not only destroys but can also gather; it can allow things and events to be revealed."[37] This is only partly correct. I cannot agree that, for Heidegger, the future which memory serves must and should remain a future of this present. Nor can I accept the opposition that Caygill implies between gathering and destroying; for the "gathering" that figures in Heidegger's thought is a gathering, through recollection, of the *Es gibt*, and that means the *groundlessness of what is*. So a certain deconstruction of "what is" is already at work in the gathering of memory; it is not at all a gathering of memory under the spell of the metaphysics of presence. (The "ontological" in Heidegger is no longer "the essential." For the metaphysical tradition, Heidegger's "Wesen" can only be an *Unwesen*, an undoing of the traditional essence.) But Caygill continues the drawing of a difference:

> For Benjamin, the moment of origin or "handing over" is characterised by confusion and indecision—in the act of "handing over" there is no community or subject to give or receive, for the subject is indeed ruined by tradition. For Heidegger, the moment of origin is potentially a moment of clarity and resolute decision, one which enables a subject, be it a "hero" or a "people," to decide . . . "who they are and who they are not". This moment of origin is one of historical decision, enabling *Dasein* to choose as a subject its own destiny. For Benjamin such a choice of destiny is characteristic of tragedy, which always ends with a decision, while *Trauerspiel* ends with indecision and uncathartic catastrophe. Heidegger's moment of origin can be a moment of decision, resoluteness unto death, while Benjamin's origin provokes sadness and mourning for the death it brings about.

What Caygill says about Benjamin is certainly correct, at least with regard to the text in question: his seer is one who is lost in a lament over the ruination of historical meaning. But what he says about Heidegger is not the whole story. Even in *Being and Time*, the reception of tradition and its meaning is more of a struggle *against* historicism and *against* its preservation of tradition than Caygill recognizes. And, in light of Heidegger's critique of the traditional and modern conceptions of the subject, it can hardly be said that tradition is handed down and received by the traditional subject. Nor can it be said that, for him, the handing-down and the reception is a straightforward process without questions and problems. Moreover, the existential "moment of resoluteness" (*Entschlossenheit*) that figures in *Being and Time* is already an attitude in which the intentionality of the will has been to some extent deconstructed, turned inside out, a question, already, of a certain openness and exposure. Already attempting to think beyond the historicity of this intentionality, Heidegger himself is careful to point out that, in using the word *Entschlossenheit*, he is radically contesting the traditional way of thinking about resoluteness and historical action. And in his later writings, after the so-called *Kehre*, all investments of the will to power still holding sway in this attitude undergo further alteration, eventually assuming, in relation to history as the history of being, the radical ontological exposure of "letting be." And coming with this alteration, there is audible, I think, a certain tone of mourning, not entirely unlike Benjamin's, and no less equivocal, a lamentation over loss—the loss handed down in tradition and history *as* history and tradition—that reverberates through many of his later writings. Finally, one should note the extent to which, as early as *Being and Time,* Heidegger was already struggling to think the vision of historical recollection outside of the conventional constructions of time and memory.

According to Benjamin (Konvolut N 3, 1), "Heidegger seeks in vain to rescue history for phenomenology through the abstraction of 'historicality,' " whereas what "differentiates [dialectical] images from the 'essentiality' of phenomenology is their historical index" (GS, vol. V, part 1, p. 577). But is Benjamin's criticism justified? In the *Entschlossenheit* (resolute openness) of *Being and Time,* as in the *Vorbereitungen* (preparatory steps) of the later writings, we see that the seer's "moment of vision" is not, for Heidegger, as Benjamin claims, a merely abstract negation of history. Nor can it be said that Heidegger's practice of phenomenology perpetuates the traditional concept of "essentiality," which is of course under the spell of the metaphysics of presence. It must also be noted that most of Heidegger's discussions of the history of metaphysics are contextualized very concretely in critical reflections on contemporary life (on technology, environmental pollution, nuclear energy, commodification, the culture of narcissism, a false individualism, the destruction of experience, alienated labor) and in attempts to think the possibility of an end to history as we know it.

Be these matters as they may, I would argue that it is perhaps in the *Trauerspiel* essay that Benjamin's vision comes closest to the vision of the Anaximander fragment which Heidegger was attempting to understand. Influenced no doubt by the critical categories that Nietzsche deploys in *The Uses and Disadvantages of History for Life,* Benjamin's "Epistemo-Critical Prologue" to the *Trauerspiel* essay asserts that

> origin [*Ursprung*], although an entirely historical category, has, nevertheless, nothing to do with genesis [*Entstehung*]. The term origin is not intended to describe the *process* by which the existent came into being [*Werden der Entsprungenen*], but rather to describe *that which emerges from* the process of becoming and disappearance [*Werden und Vergehen des Entspringendes*]. (OGT 45, UDT 161. Italics added.)

What emerges, then, is not a celebration of progress, nor even an untroubled sense that the past can be taken over for future use in a constructive way, but only, rather, a profound sense of loss, ruin, destruction, catastrophe. What meaning emerges from tradition, what meaning comes to us from the past, is from the time of its very inception already fated to perish, to disappear: as Caygill says, in the *Trauerspiel* essay, Benjamin certainly thought that "the site of tradition is not a place where past, present and future are gathered together for resolute action, but one where the present is haunted not only by its past but also by its future of becoming past. It is a place of mourning. Here origin and its objects can never attain authenticity, but are always indebted to something which does not disclose itself."[38] But in later writings, it is important to discern provocative indications of a different relation, no longer in the attitude of a virtually inconsolable mourning, to origin, to the handing down and reception of the past, to present and future. There are incontrovertible differences, here, between Benjamin and Heidegger. But here, too, Caygill exaggerates. For Benjamin, too, was concerned with decision and action. Moreoever, having relinquished intentionality, his own approach risks falling into decisionism—the same danger that Heidegger is often accused of approaching.

Nonetheless, it is essential to keep in mind that the mood of sadness into which the soothsayer, the seer, of the *Trauerspiel* is fallen comes from his being moved by the sight of so much human suffering, whereas in the Anaximander fragment, what the seer sees is the endless passing away of nature, the fate that is immanent in the very nature of all things. In the one case, a *Leidensgeschichte,* in the other, a *Naturgeschichte.* But even if the object of Heidegger's seer is a "natural history," it is not solely a question of fate, since what the seer realizes is the *Geschick,* the destiny hidden in the image of fate, that constitutes a claim on our capacity to interrupt the present course of history.

By the time Benjamin wrote his "Theses on the Philosophy of History," his visionary was moved by a different attitude, at once more defiant and less willful, less intentional. And the perspective or field of vision (*Blickfeld*) correspondingly changed its character.[39] Benjamin became increasingly clear that what is needed is not merely a break with history as a chronicle of progress, a break with history as monument to the victors. The writing of history must be dedicated to the stories of the defeated, the victims: it must be a history that belongs to the other. But moreover, the historian must renounce the panoramic vision, the God's-eye perspective that claims to see a universal history. The historian's philosophical gaze must settle into the material of history, keeping eyes open for the ciphers of a "messianic force," however weak.

§2

There is, in Benjamin's writings, what might be called a "typology" of ways of seeing, each way embodied in a different figure. Perhaps the major figures are the collector, the flaneur, the melancholy brooder, the allegorist, and the dialectician of historical materialism and messianic remembrance. In what follows, we shall consider each of these figures in turn. As we shall see, despite their differences, all these figures embody a vision that involves a memorative image.

In the text marked "H," Benjamin suggests a portrait of the collector. The optics or gaze (*Blick*) of the collector is of a peculiarly dispassionate nature, a "disinterested observation" (*interesselose Betrachtung*)[40] not at all creative (*kein erschöpfender Blick*),[41] abstracting things from the "functional" order of production and consumption, making them useless, but precisely thereby especially "promising" as sites for the awakening of an "incomparable glimpse"[42] into otherwise invisible meanings, arousing memory-images, adumbrating the possibility of a world redeemed and made whole. Benjamin compares the collector's visual experience (*Schauen*) to that of a magician.[43] But the magic is not without struggle and self-sacrifice: struggle against the dissemination of meaning, against the haunting proximity of the invisible; the sacrifice of intentionality, of an excessive subjectivity, for the sake of an order yet to become visible. Benjamin writes:

> Perhaps the most hidden motive of the collector can be described thus: he takes up the struggle [*Kampf*] against destruction [*Zerstreuung*].[44]

Collecting always involves classifying; and classifying always involves recontextualizing. In collecting, the objects gathered are released from all their original functions in order to be recontextualized in the closest possible relation to similar things.[45] The hope is that this imposed classification, ordering things according to an "astonishing," seemingly "incomprehensible" network of relationships, will somehow release a certain *Tiefsinn*, a deeply concealed meaningfulness that otherwise could not be discerned.[46] The collector collects things, then, in order to collect memories—and collect through the medium of memories: "he vanishes in the world of memory."[47] The collector's effort to remember and see, or see and remember, is a constant "struggle against dispersion,"[48] against the spell of forgetfulness. The collector's vision, deeply absorbed, immersed in its objects, is grounded in the principle, the discipline, of gathering and recollecting. And the virtue of the gaze lies in this discipline. But it is, by its very nature, an extremely limited praxis. And it takes place indoors.

Very different is the gaze of the flaneur, the one who leaves the collector's bourgeois interiors and takes to the city streets, drifting anonymously through the urban crowds, temporarily playing the part of a disinterested spectator, seeking asylum in the crowds but never overcoming the feeling of marginality, remaining a resident alien, a stranger, a man in exile. The flaneur, strolling along the boulevards, meandering through the parks and gardens, making his way through the commodity displays of the arcades, whiling away hours in the sidewalk cafés, visiting the special meeting-places of the night, gives free play to well-disciplined eyes, ready for whatever might appear before them in some striking form, quietly and patiently observant, but sometimes looking about with a special vigilance, a certain *Aufmerksamkeit*, as if he were a detective on secret assignment. In manuscript "M" of the *Passagen-Werk*,[49] the *Pariser Passagen*[50] and "On Some Motifs in Baudelaire,"[51] Benjamin conveys a portrait of this figure, emphasizing points of view, ways of looking and seeing, a dialectical optics.

§3

Of great importance for Benjamin were the figures of the brooder (*der Grübler*) and the allegorist (*der Allegoriker*), to the character of whose distinctive gazes he devoted considerable thought. The principal text for these intimately related, yet quite distinct figures is the *Trauerspiel* essay. In describing the melancholy mood of the baroque allegorist, Benjamin says:

> For it was only rarely that the eye [*der Blick*] was able to find satisfaction in the object itself. (OGT 181, UDT 305)

Commenting on what he called "the peculiar imagistic quality of Benjamin's speculation," Adorno suggested that it had "its origin in his melancholy gaze, under which the historical is transformed into nature by the strength of its own fragility, and everything natural is transformed into a fragment of the history of creation."[52] The figure of the melancholy brooder, totally absorbed in the intense contemplation of fragments, remnants, and ruins, haunts Benjamin's work—especially the early work of the 1920s. Perhaps it is with this work in mind that Derrida was moved to write, in "Force of Law: The 'Mystical Foundation of Authority,' " that he (Derrida) does "not see ruin as a negative thing." And he confesses that he would like to write on the "love of ruins." "What else," he asks, "is there to love, anyway?" And he explains:

> One cannot love a monument, . . . an instrument as such except in an experience itself precarious in its fragility: it hasn't always been there, it will not always be there, it is finite. And for this very reason I love it

as a mortal, through its birth and its death, through the ghost or silhouette of its ruin, of my own—which it already is or prefigures. How
can we love except in this finitude? Where else would the right to love,
indeed the love of right, come from?[53]

Although the mood of this passage is different from the mood registered
by Heidegger's reading of the Anaximander fragment, there is a certain
proximity in the thought—a proximity that includes, in both cases, a connection between justice and the ruination, the passing, of all things finite,
according to the ordinance of time. In any case, Derrida undoubtedly cap-
tures, here, something of Benjamin's relation to ruins—a relation which
also connects the latter, I think, to the fragment of pre-Socratic thought.

In the *Trauerspiel* essay, Benjamin contends that "in the field of allegorical intuition, the image is a fragment, a rune." But he immediately adds,
with the characteristically conflicted emotions of the allegorist, torn between sadness and joy in seeing the destruction of a past that, for all its false
promises, nevertheless had for a time such a beautiful appearance (*Schein*):

> Its beauty as a symbol evaporates when the light of divine learning
> falls upon it. The false appearance of totality is extinguished. For the
> *eidos* disappears, the simile ceases to exist, and the cosmos it contains
> shrivels up. The dry rebuses which remain contain an insight, which is
> still available to the brooder [*Grübler*]. (OGT 176, UDT 300)

It may be assumed that, when he wrote this, Benjamin had in mind the fact
that *Schein*, in German, carries three meanings: radiance, appearance, and
illusion.

Somewhat later in the text Benjamin takes us into the very "heart" of
the allegorical way of seeing, into its negative dialectics:

> Whereas in the symbol, destruction is idealized and the transfigured
> face of nature is fleetingly revealed in the light of redemption, in alle-
> gory the observer is confronted with the *facies hyppocratica* of history
> as a petrified, primordial landscape. Everything about history that,
> from the very beginning, has been untimely, sorrowful, unsuccessful, is
> expressed in a face—or rather, in a death's head. And although such a
> thing lacks all "symbolic" freedom of expression, . . . all humanity—
> nevertheless, this is the form in which man's subjection to nature is
> most obvious and it gives rise not only to the enigmatic question of the
> nature of human existence as such, but also to the question of the bio-
> graphical historicity of the individual. This is the heart of the allegori-
> cal way of seeing, of the baroque, secular explanation of history as the
> Passion of the world; its importance resides solely in the stations of its
> decline. (OGT 166, UDT, 289)

Here, though, the brooder's mourning and melancholy hardly overcome, through the allegorical way of seeing, the catastrophe that has befallen meaning: history is revived, but only as dead, bereft of any meaning for the living.

There can be no doubt that the *Trauerspiel* text is, as Benjamin himself says, an invention and demonstration of his "own particular way of looking at things" (his *eigenen Betrachtungsart der Dinge*), refracted through the figures of the brooder and the allegorist (OGT 180, UDT 304). As Max Pensky argues with considerable insight, there is a certain distinction between the melancholy brooder and the allegorist; but Benjamin's work suggests that the dialectical logic inherent in the experience of the melancholy brooder is such that it prefigures, and gradually becomes, the experience of the allegorist.[54] Thus, for example, the melancholy vision of the brooder is a vision that is rooted in an experience of extreme alienation from a world that is seen as "a petrified, primordial landscape." It is a vision rooted in a bodily felt sense of suffering, a suffering that "corresponds" to the human condition with sympathy and compassion for all suffering beings; it is a vision rooted in lamentation, a devastating, deeply felt sense of loss, unforgettable yet irretrievable and irredeemable, of loss so great that it exceeds memory and representation.[55] It is a vision rooted at once in hope and despair, hopelessly resigned to a loss it cannot forget, reminded despite everything that even catastrophe must carry a secret promise of meaning. It is a vision hopelessly sunk in what Horkheimer once described as "die Sehnsucht nach dem ganz Anderen," a "longing for the radically other."[56]

In writing about Baudelaire, Benjamin gives us an easily recognizable portrait of the brooder. Unfortunately, the translation cannot pretend to preserve his multiple dimensions of meaning:

> What fundamentally distinguishes the brooder [*den Grübler*] from the thinker is that he does not meditate [*nachsinnt*] on something only with his mind, but also with his senses [*seinem Sinnen*]. The case [*Fall*] of the brooder is that of a man who, having found the solution to a major problem, immediately forgets it. And now he broods, not so much over the matter itself as over the passing of his meditations [*Nachsinnen*] on them.[57]

And he adds:

> The thinking of the brooder stands therefore under the sign of memory [*Erinnerung*]. Brooder and allegorist are made of the *one and the same* substance [*aus* einem *Holz*].

The memory of the brooder, he says, "presides over the unordered mass of dead knowledge. In it human knowledge has become fragmented [*Stückwerk*] in an especially pregnant sense, namely: as the heap of deliberately cut-up pieces out of which one constructs a puzzle."[58] But, he notes, times are not any longer favorable (abhold) for brooding. Consequently, in response to the puzzling disjointedness of the times, the crisis of meaning, the peculiar gaze of the allegorist is solicited and aroused, responsive to the need. That the times are out of joint is reflected in the art of the allegorist, who struggles with the pieces of the puzzle in order to turn melancholy experience into narrative and image: since there can be no eschatology "by which all earthly things could be gathered and exalted before being consigned to their end," the allegorist can only immerse himself in expressions of mourning mingled with desperate hope, a hope against hope, if not directly for redemption, then at least for some revelation of existential meaning in "catastrophic violence" (OGT 66, UDT 184): "The authentic experience of allegory, holding fast to fragments, is that of the perpetual past."[59]

But unlike the melancholy brooder, who is resigned to the conditions of fate, the allegorist assumes a more "active" role, at once more destructive and more hopeful. Obsessed by a faint sense that somehow the fragments could be joined together in a meaningful construction, the allegorist surrenders himself to searching for the still missing clue to the arrangement which would suddenly make visible, if only in the form of barely visible ciphers, the redeeming glow of a lost significance. The hope of the allegorist lies in the possibility that there is a dialectical way of seeing that could educe an otherwise invisible Tiefsinn from its engagement with the fragmented cultural material. But as the hope remains unfulfilled, forever deferred, the allegorist's gaze (allegorische Tiefblick) remains, in the end, in spite of all efforts, a Blick der Melancholie (OGT 176, 183; UDT 300, 308).

There is in this disappointment, moreover, a certain dialectical necessity. Because the allegorist's immersion and absorption in the subjectivity of mourning, his desperate commitment to the meaningfulness inherent in the experience of loss, virtually guarantees disappointment.[60] Unlike the intention involved in the gaze of the "Theses on the Philosophy of History," the gaze that draws on dialectical materialism and messianic hermeneutics, the melancholy gaze of the allegorist can yield no completely satisfying or redeeming memory-image:

> The intention which underlies allegory is . . . opposed to that which is concerned with the discovery of truth. (OGT 229, UDT 354)

The allegorist's treatment, spellbound within the contradictions of allegorical subjectivity, thus inevitably "betrays and devalues" (verrät und entwertet) the things he takes up at the same time that he "exalts" them by looking for traces of redemption. Thus the allegorical way of looking at things and handling them, rather than immediately restoring them to meaningful life, initially causes only their "mortification," bringing out the secret, invisible "justice" in ruination, destruction, and death (OGT 182, 177ff; UDT 306, 301ff). But, whereas the brooder loses himself in mourning, the allegorist attempts, by an exercise of will, of intention, to pass beyond this phase through a dialectic of destruction—although he knows with a painfully acute consciousness that revelatory truth ultimately requires of him the very "death" of intention.[61] The objects that the allegorist rescues from invisibility, from oblivion, are saved—but only as images empty of meaning, as illegible fragments of sense: the process of "restoration is haunted by the idea of catastrophe" (OGT 66, UDT 183). And yet, it is precisely such degradation and fragmentation, all the traces of catastrophe, that enable the allegorist to see in the objects that capture his attention the possibility of assigning an allegorical meaning, thereby reconstructing the object outside the illusoriness of the mythic world, within which it had for a passing moment appeared to be a meaningful and beautiful whole (OGT 174–75, UDT 298). The dialectical tension in the destructive phase of the allegorical art of seeing is evident in this passage from Benjamin's "Paris: Capital of the 19th Century":

> Dialectical thinking is the organ of historical awakening. Every epoch not only dreams the next, but also, in dreaming, it strives toward the moment of waking. . . . In the convulsions of the commodity economy we begin to recognize the monuments of the bourgeoisie as ruins, even before they have crumbled.[62]

Here we see an extremely intricate interweaving of hopeful intention (the monuments of the bourgeoisie deserve to be destroyed, reduced to ruins by the catastrophic violence of justice) and visionary perception (the monuments are seen as *already* in ruins).

Adorno was therefore correct in his description of the allegorical art of seeing, but perhaps still too captivated himself by its hopeless narcissism, when he said, in his very Benjaminian book on Kierkegaard, that,

> No truer image of hope can be imagined than that of ciphers, readable as traces, dissolving in history, disappearing in front of overflowing eyes, indeed confirmed in lamentation. In these tears of despair, the ciphers appear as incandescent figures, dialectically, as compassion, comfort, hope.[63]

Although, as Pensky shows, there is a real difference between the melancholy of the brooder and that of the allegorist, the latter is never very far from brooding subjectivity. As Pensky formulates the difference, it consists in the fact that, while the brooder "is capable of recognizing, however dimly, that the fragments, which in one sense remain meaningless, also begin to radiate meaning,"[64] he is not able to reconstruct this meaning, and risks falling into a state of despair, mourning the loss of meaning. There is a certain affinity, then, as Pensky notes, with what Benjamin calls "the destructive character."[65] The allegorist, however, attempts nevertheless to fit the fragments together, constructing by forceful intention a narrative of memory that might point toward the possibility of a messianic significance. But the melancholy dialectic does not escape the allegorist's extremely sensitive consciousness: aware that the construction is a product of his own arbitrary intentionality, he cannot deny that the hoped-for meaningfulness is ruined in and by the very act of constructing it. All that the allegorist can see, when his work is done and its conditions—its finitude, its mortal touch—are incontrovertible, is a faintly visible glow, a faintly visible trace, of originary meaning, bearing the objective memory of the paradise that seems irretrievably lost—or forever deferred. And yet, the destructive moment ultimately reveals the limits of this phase, showing that it cannot be identified with the end:

> As those who lose their footing turn somersaults in their fall, so would the allegorical intention fall from emblem to emblem down into the dizziness of its bottomless depths, were it not that, even in the most extreme of them, it had so to turn about that all its darkness, vainglory, and godlessness seems to be nothing but self-delusion. For it is to misunderstand the allegorical entirely if we make a distinction between the store of images, in which this about-turn into salvation and redemption takes place, and that grim store which signifies death and damnation. For it is precisely visions of the frenzy of destruction [*Visionen des Vernichtungsrausches*], in which all earthly things collapse into a heap of ruins, which reveal [*enthüllt sich*] the limit set upon allegorical contemplation [*allegorischen Versenkung*], rather than its ideal quality. (OGT 232, UDT 357)

Thus, even the faintest glimmer is sufficient to intimate a dialectical reversal:

> ultimately, the intention does not faithfully rest in the gaze at bones, but leaps faithlessly to the Resurrection. (OGT 233, UDT, 358)

As a reward for the allegorist's violent, destructive intentionality, the phase of destruction and mourning—the phase from out of which the melancholy brooder cannot escape—thus recurs to a phase where traces of the promise of redemption finally become visible. Nevertheless, it cannot be denied that the allegorical vision has little to offer to those who see injustice in the realm of the political.

§4

After the *Trauerspiel,* Benjamin's allegorical gaze underwent a certain transformation, a certain "education." Briefly stated, it became a way of seeing in which he attempted to bring historical materialism and messianic hermeneutics together in the form of explicitly dialectical images. Although the melancholy gaze and the gaze of the allegorist are also, of course, dialectical, we shall hereafter refer to this new way of seeing by calling it a "dialectical" gaze, a "dialectical" vision. And correlatively, we shall hereafter refer to the images that this way of seeing solicits by calling them "dialectical images." In this section, then, we will examine Benjamin's dialectical way of seeing, bringing out what might be termed the "anarchic" logic of its politics.

Adorno's description of the Benjaminian art is once again useful for introducing the change. What struck him in the course of reading Benjamin's later productions was the emergence of what he called "his Medusan glance":

> Before his Medusan glance, man turns into the stage on which an objective process unfolds. For this reason, Benjamin's philosophy is no less a source of terror, than a promise of happiness.[66]

The task for Benjamin was to translate this "glance," this "gaze," into the materiality and concreteness of images that would be useful for a revolutionary historiography and philosophy. In one of his notes for the *Passagen-Werk,* Benjamin wrote this:

> Sketch the history of the Arcades Project as it has developed. Its truly problematic component: to give up claim to nothing, to demonstrate that the materialistic presentation of history is imagistic in a higher sense than traditional historiography.[67]

Struggling to conceive the appropriate method, a synthesis, somehow, of dialectical materialism and messianic hermeneutics, bringing about the formation of concrete dialectical images and translating them into effective discourse, he declared that "history breaks down into images, not into stories" (B 67; GS V, 1, pp. 595–96). And he noted that there is:

> a central problem of historical materialism, which ought finally to be seen: must the Marxist understanding of history necessarily come at the cost of graphicness [*Anschaulichkeit*]? Or: by what route is it possible to attain a heightened graphicness combined with a realization of the Marxist method. The first stop along this path will be to carry the montage principle over into history. That is, to build up the large constructions out of the smallest, precisely fashioned structural elements. Indeed, to detect the crystal of the total event in the analysis of the

small, individual moment. To break, then, with the vulgar naturalism of historicism. To grasp the construction of history as such. In the structure of commentary. *Trash of history* [*Abfall der Geschichte*]. (B 48; GS V, 1, p. 575)

Defending Breton's *Manifestos* on Surrealism, texts with which he felt considerable immediate sympathy, but also, at the same time, with which he had points of serious disagreement, Benjamin said:

The revolutionary energies that appear in the "out of date," in the first iron constructions, the first factory buildings, the earliest photographs, the objects that are beginning to die out, grand pianos in the salons, the dresses of five years ago, trendy night spots when the vogue begins to recede from them. How these things relate to the revolution—no-one could have a more exact concept than these authors. Before these seers and sign-readers, no-one perceived how poverty, . . . the poverty of interiors, of enslaved and enslaving things, can transpose itself into revolutionary nihilism.[68]

Searching for texts in which he could perhaps discern some ideas for use in developing the dialectical way of seeing, Benjamin also turned to Grillparzer, whose comment, briefly touching on both prophetic and retrospective vision, gave him an opportunity to formulate an important point in this regard:

To contrast the theory of history with Grillparzer's comment: "To read into the future is difficult, but to see *purely* into the past is even more so: I say *purely*, meaning without clouding that retrospective gaze with everything that has happened in the meantime."

After this quotation, Benjamin wrote: "The 'purity' of the gaze [*des Blickes*] is not so much difficult as impossible to attain" (B 59; GS V, 1, p. 587).

Of major importance for the conceptualization of what, in *Angelus Novus,* he calls the "dialectical optic" is the question of intentionality. After discussing this question in his essay on the genre of the mourning play, Benjamin takes it up again (in 1923) in a short text bearing the title "On the Topic of Individual Disciplines and Philosophy":

Our gaze must strike the object in such a way that it awakens something within it that springs up to meet the intention. Whereas the reporter who adopts the stance of the banal philosopher and specialized scientist indulges himself in lengthy descriptions of the object at which his gaze is directed, the intensive observer finds that something leaps out at him from the object, enters into him, takes possession of him, and something different—namely the non-intentional truth—speaks from out of the philosopher.[69]

He goes on to say that this speech, this discursive gaze, "possesses author-ity," the authority of an objectivity that "stands in opposition to the con-ventional concept of objectivity, because its validity, that of the non-intentional truth, is historical—that is to say, anything but timeless; it is bound to a particular historical base and changes with history." According to Benjamin, then, the truth "leaps into existence as the result of an im-mersion of the object in itself provoked by the external gaze." Thus, while there is a sense in which the truth that becomes visible may be said to be non-intentional and objective, its manifestation is nonetheless *dependent* on a procedure that does involve intentionality: the solicitous intentional-ity of the gaze, interacting with the object that has caught its attention in such a way that the object's entire pre-history and post-history as a com-modity may quite suddenly be revealed.

Here there is an entire problematic that Benjamin, and all subsequent commentators, have left in the dark. It would seem necessary to draft a dis-tinction between the visionary moment of revelation, sudden and shocking, in which no intentionality is involved, and the deliberate, intentionality-driven procedures that must precede this moment, preparing the conditions that would make such a moment possible. Both the allegorical image and the dialectical image are sudden revelations, utterly unanticipated, beyond in-tentionality, impossible to correlate with reality in terms of the correspon-dence theory of truth. In this regard they are quite similar. But there are certain differences in the processes that precede their manifestation: differ-ences that neither Benjamin nor his commentators have sufficiently, I think, elucidated. In the case of the allegorical image, as well as in the case of the image or *Tiefsinn* that sometimes rewards the collector, the process is a slow, deliberate, painstaking "destruction," a willful, even violent, destruction of the object—very much a question of intentionality. In the case of the di-alectical image, there is no such procedure, although even here, it is a ques-tion of a certain preparedness, a certain vigilance, a certain openness to experience—the paradoxical curiosity of the flaneur, for example, which is at once intense and restrained, disinterestedly interested, interestedly dis-interested, practicing a critical alertness heightened by virtue of its alien-ation, its self-restraint, its rigorous *epokhé*. The "seer" who haunts the Paris arcades looks indiscriminately at everything: the hands of shopkeepers, the faces of shoppers, the gestures of pedestrians passing by, the commodities on display in the shopwindows, the mannequins dressed up in the latest fashions, the advertisements on billboards, the ragpickers, and the street-sweepers. Anything ready-to-hand, anything at all, might catch the mater-ial interest of his methodically disinterested, concretely "objective" gaze.

The dialectical image that comes in such circumstances manifests an objective, material truth—a truth that cannot be reduced to the intentionality of the gaze. But it cannot be denied that even the gaze of the flaneur, seemingly without purpose, without direction, seemingly free of material conditions, material worries, is informed by a wealth of background knowledge, intensely conscious of the social and cultural significance of the things that catch his eye: not at all an "innocent" gaze.

This "time of truth," when truth is "loaded to the bursting point with time" (B 50; GS V,1, p. 578), is a "profane illumination,"[70] an experience with vision that Benjamin describes as like a flash of lightning:

> It is not that the past casts its light on the present, or the present on the past; rather, the image is that in which that which has been [*das Gewesene*] enters, like lightning, into a constellation with the Now [*das Jetzt*]. (Ibid.)

"The dialectical image," he says, "is a lightning flash," *ein aufblitzendes Bild*:

> The Then [*das Gewesene*] must be held fast as it flashes its lightning image in the Now of recognizability [*Erkennbarkeit*]. The rescue that is thus—and only thus—effected, can only take place for that which, in the next moment [*im nächsten Augenblick*], is irretrievably lost. Cf., the metaphoric passage from the introduction to Jochmann on the prophet's gaze [*Sehblick*], which catches fire from the summits of the past. (B 64; GS V, 1, pp. 591–92)

If there is a way in which the images brought forth by the allegorical gaze slowly make their appearance, emerging only at the end of a laborious alchemical process of destruction and construction, the images brought forth by the dialectical gaze are, by contrast, instantaneous epiphanies, shocking eruptions, momentary awakenings from the mythic dream-time—the terrible phantasmagoria and enchantments—of capitalism. Arguing, in his "Theses on the Philosophy of History," that "the past can be seized only as an image which flashes up [*aufblitzt*] at the instant when it can be recognized and never seen again," he tells us that this "instant," the "Jetztzeit," can occur only "at a moment of danger."[71] Because of their historicality, the images that flash up in this way are not at all the timeless "essences" of transcendental phenomenology (B 50; GS V, 1, p. 577). Nor are they the "archaic" images of myth (ibid.). In no sense do they represent a pre-established harmony of meaning underlying the historical order. But the dialectical image does interrupt, does arrest, if only for an instant, the temporal continuum out of which it arose. And, as "the involuntary memory of a *redeemed* humanity,"[72] as an image "shot through" with "splinters"

(*Splitter*) of light from a "messianic time,"[73] it does leap out of this continuum, belonging not to the order of history, but to the "visual space" (*Bildraum*) of anarchy,[74] the avenging anarchy of a messianic justice yet to come:

> image is dialectics at a standstill [*Dialektik im Stillstand*]. For while the relation of the present to the past is a purely temporal, continuous one, the relation of the Then to the Now is dialectical: not of a temporal, but of an imagistic nature. (Ibid.)

This is the critical function of the dialectical image, a memory-image deployed in keeping with Benjamin's conception of dialectical materialism:

> The materialist presentation of history leads the past to place the present in a critical condition. (B 60; GS V, 1, 588)

The alienation-effect that the image achieves demonstrates this critical condition. As such, the image must avoid inducing sentimentality and empathy; it must be compelling entirely on "objective" or "material" grounds:

> For the materialist historian, it is important to distinguish the construction of a historical state of affairs very rigorously from what one generally calls its "reconstruction". "Reconstruction" by means of empathy is one-sided. "Construction" presupposes "destruction." (B 60; GS V, 1, p. 587)

The dialectical character of the image to be achieved creates within the discourse of history—a discourse that for too long has been seen as the unfolding of an immanent but invisible teleology of reason—what Benjamin calls a "forcefield" (*Kraftfeld*), drawing historical evidence into violent conflict between a "fore-history" and an "after-history" (ibid.). It is, therefore, not correct to read Benjamin, against Heidegger, as disregarding the futural dimension: were he to have done this, he would have been arresting the dialectic in a conflict between the past and a Now-time with no redemptive prospect, however deferred.

The decisive thing is, as he says, "the unique property of dialectical experience to dissipate the appearance of things always being the same" (B 63; GS V, 1, p. 591). This is why Benjamin emphasizes that "the concept of progress should be grounded in the idea of catastrophe. That things 'just keep on going' *is* the catastrophe" (B 64; GS V, 1, p. 592). As an aftereffect of the dialectical image, therefore, there is a crucial moment:

> the pastness [*das Gewesene*] of a particular epoch is always also "things as they have always been" [*das "Von-jeher-Gewesene"*]. As such, though, at times it comes into view [*vor Augen*] only at a very specific epoch: that is, the epoch in which humanity, rubbing its eyes, suddenly

370 / The Philosophers

recognizes the dream image as such. It is at that point [*In diesem Augenblick*] that the historian takes on the task of dream interpretation. (B 52; GS V, 1, p. 580)

As we shall see, Benjamin's chosen word for this critical, history-stopping moment, *Augenblick*, is the same word that Heidegger uses for the crucial moment—the so-called moment of vision—in his own critical reworking of our relation to history and historiography. And it would be difficult to deny that the proximity ends with the same word. In any case, Benjamin argues that the method at work in the dialectical image may be compared to the "splitting of the atom," because the sudden arising of the image "releases the enormous energy of history that lies bonded in the 'Once upon a time' of classical historical narrative" (B 51; GS V, 1, p. 578).

For the dialectical gaze, whose destructive moment Benjamin embodied, for a time, in the figure of the "Angel of History,"

Historical materialism has to abandon the epic element in history. It blasts the epoch out of the reified "continuity of history." But it also blasts open the homogeneity of the epoch. (B 65; GS V, 1, pp. 592–93)

But the dialectical gaze sees hope for redemption—"or, put differently, a revolutionary chance for the fight for the oppressed past"—concealed within catastrophe and destruction:

History is the subject of a structure whose site is not homogeneous, empty time, but time filled by the presence of the Now [*Jetztzeit*]. (I 263, 261; Sch 505, 502)

To rescue the past is at the same time to rescue the present, to salvage that in the present which can be an instrument for the undoing of its complicity with death, with the brutalities of injustice. But the present cannot be transformed "until all of the past has been brought into the present in a historic apocatastasis" (B 46; GS V, 1, p. 573). In this way, therefore, the dialectic image is, after all, involved in a process that might be called a "gathering." One reason why this passage is significant for us is that it does not seem to fit very easily into the interpretive framework within which Howard Caygill attempts to demonstrate that one of the principal the differences between Heidegger and Benjamin lies in the fact that for Heidegger, the "moment of vision" is a conservative gathering of historical time into the metaphysical structure of the present, a present, moreover, that is embodied in the temporally structured transcendental unity of the historical "subject," whereas he thinks that, for Benjamin, the "moment of vision" is radically dissociative and disseminative, and is made possible only by virtue of the most radical self-effacement of the traditional subject, sacrificing its intentionality and even its unity as the site for a gathering-in of the three dimensions of historical time.[75] But Caygill is right when he points to Benjamin's insistence that "for a fragment of the past to be struck by the contemporary, there must be no continuity between them" (B 60; GS V, 1, p. 587). This implies that the process of "gathering" does not necessarily function to preserve and perpetuate the continuum: instead, it may be the surest way to induce a violent clash. This in fact is the way I suggest that we understand the gathering of memory in the context of Heidegger's critique of historiography and his critical phenomenology of historical experience: the recollection of being is a gathering that throws all beings into a groundlessness that robs them of all their metaphysical attributes. Heidegger's "recollection" of the historical forms through which being presences does not gather in obedience to the so-called metaphysics of presence. On the contrary, it gathers into a vision of interruption and dispersion, into the unrealized possibilities of an originary temporality.

Be this as it may, the task of the dialectical gaze—its *Augenblick*—is, for Benjamin, not just to break off the "progress" of the historical continuum, but also to rescue the tracework of messianic hope that may be concealed within the familiar things of the profane world. If there be an after-history, an afterlife, for things that have been reduced to commodities, to the spellbinding fetishes of late capitalism, then the task of the dialectical gaze must be to retrieve their secrets in the form of images that can be used to construct them anew—in a different image, and with a different after-history:

> If the historical object is to be blasted out [*herausgesprengt*] of the continuum of the historical process, it is because the monadological structure of the object demands it. This structure only becomes evident once the object has been blasted free. And it becomes evident precisely in the form of the historical argument [*Auseinandersetzung*] which makes up the inside . . . of the historical object, and into which all the forces and interests of history enter on a reduced scale. The historical object, by virtue of its monadological structure, discovers within itself its own fore-history and after-history. (B 66; GS V, 1, p. 594)

Sifting through the "trash of history" (*Abfall der Geschichte*), the remnants of things, objects discarded as useless and worthless (B 48; GS V, 1, p. 575), and all the things that capitalism has shrouded in an invisible aura of false value, Benjamin's dialectical materialist is always vigilant, looking with a deeply penetrating gaze into the contradictory structure of these historical objects:

> Thinking involves both thoughts in motion and thoughts at rest. When thinking reaches a standstill in a constellation saturated with tensions, the dialectical image appears. . . . In short, it is to be found wherever the tension between dialectical oppositions is greatest. The dialectical image is, accordingly, the very object constructed in the materialist presentation of history [*materialistischen Geschichtsdarstellung*]. It is identical with the historical object: it justifies its being blasted out of the continuum of the historical process. (B 67; GS V, 1, p. 595)

§5

In the concluding paragraph of "Surrealism: The Last Snapshot of the European Intelligentsia," Benjamin alludes to a "dialectical justice," a "dialectical annihilation."[76] This is perhaps the most fitting description of the dialectical gaze, at once a "profane illumination" and a newly messianic hermeneutics, revealing the way to see the world in the light of redemption. But the justice of this gaze is more than an innerworldly justice; it is (to borrow a word from Derrida) "supplemented" by a justice that comes from the messianic dimension: it is an annihilating justice, effecting its judgment with an eye to what, in the "Critique of Violence," is called a "pure violence." And it is an anarchic justice, "anarchic" in a sense that Levinas, possibly inspired by this text of Benjamin's, defines with admirable lucidity in a note to the "Substitution" chapter of *Otherwise Than Being, or Beyond Essence*:

> The notion of anarchy we are introducing here has a meaning prior to the political (or anti-political) meaning currently attributed to it. It would be self-contradictory to set it up as a principle (in the sense that anarchists understand it). Anarchy cannot be sovereign, like the ἀρχή. [In the context of his "Critique of Violence," Benjamin would say: it cannot be law-positing or law-preserving.] It can only disturb the State—but in a radical way, making possible moments of negation *without* any affirmation. The State cannot therefore set itself up as a totality [*en Tout*].[77]

Anarchy cannot reign: that means, for Levinas, that it "remains in ambiguity, in enigma, and leaves a trace which speech, in the pain of expression, seeks to state. But there is only a trace."[78] The dialectical gaze is the defiant gaze of the philosopher engaged in an approximation to pure resistance, the justice of endless deconstruction; it is the gaze of the justice in anarchy, making visible for all to see the historical truth concealed by all political institutions: that their authority and legitimacy are groundless; that their origin in history is indebted to the violence of law-making, a violence concealed by myth and justifiable, if at all, only retrospectively, after the State has been founded; that however powerful they may be, their endurance is nevertheless marked by radical contingency; and that, as Anaximander is telling us, they are fated, like all things that come into being, to remain for a while and pass away. Belonging, in the end, to the fate of "natural history," all our political institutions are already in ruins. This is what the dialectical gaze can see. This is what it can make visible for others to see. This is its negative dialectics—an annihilating justice waiting for redemption.

In Konvolut N, Benjamin cites a letter from Max Horkheimer dated March 16, 1937, taking up the question of the incompleteness of history. The part of the letter that he quotes reads as follows:

> The assertion of incompleteness is idealistic, if completeness isn't included in it. Past injustice has occurred and is done with. The murdered are really murdered . . . If one takes incompleteness completely seriously, one has to believe in the Last Judgement. . . . Perhaps there's a difference with regard to incompleteness between the positive and the negative, such that only injustice, terror, and the pain of the past are irreparable. Application of justice, joy, works, all relate differently to time, because their positive character is largely negated by transience. This is primarily true of individual existence, in which sadness rather than happiness is sealed by death.

To which Benjamin replies:

> The corrective to this line of thought lies in the reflection that history is not just a science but also a form of memoration [*eine Form des Eingedenkens*]. What science has "established," memoration can modify. Memoration can make the incomplete (happiness) into something complete, and the complete (suffering) into something incomplete. That is theology; but in memoration we discover the experience [*Erfahrung*] that forbids us to conceive of history as thoroughly a-theological, even though we barely dare not attempt to write it according to literally theological concepts. (B 61; GS V, 1, pp. 588–89)

As an organ of justice, the dialectical gaze cannot disregard the future as the origin from which the universal light of redemption will come: "For the materialist historian, every epoch with which he occupies himself is only a fore-history of the one that really concerns him" (B 65; GS V, 1, p. 593). The materialist historian and philosopher cannot, like the Angel of History, turn his back on the future and look only into the past. In spite of textual passages where Benjamin would seem to suggest or imply this, it cannot simply be assumed to represent his complete or final position. And we must also take into account somehow the statement that Benjamin makes in concluding his "Critique of Violence," where he says: "A gaze directed [*Ein gerichteter Blick*] only at what is close at hand can at most perceive [*gewahren*] a dialectical rising and falling in the law-making and law-preserving formations of violence."[79] The German phrasing here reminds one that, for Benjamin, the philosopher's gaze is always to be directed by its concern for justice. But this justice is always, in his thinking, as in Kafka's, still to come—to come with the coming of the Messiah, to come as the "pure" catastrophic violence that would inaugurate a new beginning for humanity.

We must return, therefore, to the statement cited at the beginning of our discussion of Benjamin: "What the prophet sees in advance are the criminal courts of justice." There is an unsettled indeterminacy with regard to how the prophetic foresight, the seeing-in-advance, is to be understood—though in any case, it would certainly be contrary to all of Benjamin's thinking to read it as a predictive vision, as "prophetic" in this cheapened sense. And there is also an unsettling ambiguity, no doubt deliberate, certainly reminiscent of Kafka, in this solemn reference to the courts. Are they the courts of the political revolution that must take place here on earth—or are they the infinitely higher courts of the Last Judgment?

Disregarding the Judaic prohibition on images presenting that which pertains to the divine and continuing, despite his critique of the Enlightenment, the rhetoric, the metaphorics of light, Benjamin occasionally allowed himself to turn away from the past and think with the trope of the prophetic gaze, facing the light of the future and a justice still to come:

> The light cast by the messianic age would no longer be the lightning
> flash of an intermittent "dialectical image" but the unending illumina-
> tion of an "eternal lamp."[80]

Because it is, after all, only from the redemption to come that humanity can receive the fullness of its past—and most of all, the justice for which the righteous have been waiting. But before the coming of this justice that reason demands, the institutions of the present must be reduced to rubble. Sifting through this rubble, it is possible that we will find hints of the dreams that built the very institutions which repressed them. In "The Actuality of Philosophy," Adorno succinctly expresses this thought, echoing his friend Benjamin:

> Only in traces and ruins is it [philosophy] prepared to hope that it will
> come across correct and just reality.[81]

III. HEIDEGGER'S SEER IN THE MOMENT OF VISION

What is important is only whether the contemporary *Dasein*, in keeping with its existential possibility, is original enough still to *see* on its own the world that is always already unveiled with its existence, to bring it to words, and thereby to make it expressly visible for others.

Martin Heidegger, *The Fundamental Problems of Phenomenology*[82]

No transformation [*Wandel*] comes without an anticipatory escort [*vorausgleitendes Geleit*]. But how does an escort draw near unless there takes place an opening illumination [*wenn nicht das Ereignis sich lichtet*] which, calling, needing, envisions [*er-äugnet*] human being, that is, sees [*er-blickt*] and in this seeing [*Erblicken*], brings mortals to the path of thinking, poetizing building.

Martin Heidegger, "Overcoming Metaphysics"[83]

§1

In his book on Hegel, Charles Taylor explains Hegel's glorious vision, his way of seeing the phenomenology of the Spirit, arguing that,

> if we contemplate the succession of finite things where each passes and is succeeded by another, we are eventually forced to shift our central point of reference from the particular, finite, ephemeral things to the continuing process which goes on through their coming to be and passing away. This is the identity in difference. But the locus of this process is not any particular finite thing, but the whole system of limited ephemeral things.[84]

All finite beings are, as Hegel sees them, marked by inherent contradiction: contradiction internal to their very being, contradiction in their external relations to all other beings. As finite embodiments of the infinite, all finite beings must go under, submitting to the perishing that is inscribed from the very beginning as their fate. Moreover, every entity can be only by reference to another which it is not; hence it is related to an other which negates it and tends to suppress it.[85] Hegel's vision is in some ways quite similar to the vision that Heidegger attributes to Anaximander. But there are also some crucial differences between Hegel's vision and the vision that Heidegger constructs for himself in the process of reading and interpreting Anaximander. Because, for Heidegger, the philosopher's gaze must be directed by the question of Δικἠ, the ontological dimension of justice. As a vision of the ontological dimension of justice, the philosopher's gaze must eventually get involved, involved to the point of intervention, in the question of the continuation or interruption of history. For this question ultimately bears on the philosopher's position with regard to the repetition and reproduction of injustice, the perpetuation of domination and suffering, in the ontic realm of history.

Before we concentrate on Heidegger's reference to the seer in his commentary on the Anaximander fragment, it would be useful, I think, to consider in some detail Heidegger's discussion of the "moment of vision" (*Augenblick*) in division II of *Being and Time.* It is in this second division that he formulates critical questions and reflections with regard to fate and destiny; authentic and inauthentic ways of experiencing the orders of time, history, and tradition; the historical significance of our cultural forgetfulness of being; the need for a culture of memory; the need in our time for a radical break with the past and a repetition of the inception, the possibilities granted us in and as the origin of historical time; and the urgent need for foresight, a radically different understanding and vision of the future. Although at first it might seem that there is no significant connection between the resolute "moment of vision" and the experience that Heidegger attributes to the seer in his commentary on the Anaximander fragment— and that there is even less of a connection between the "moment of vision" and the "vision" that is involved in what Anaximander has to say in the fragment, we will see, by way of a reading of *Being and Time,* as well as some other texts, that such an interpretation would need to be corrected. There are, in fact, deep and significant connections to be seen.

§2

We will begin, as we did with Benjamin, by taking up, but only briefly, the question of memory in Heidegger's thinking. This we must do, not only because memory—recollection—is at the very heart of his thinking, but because, as I have already suggested and will here be arguing, it is, contrary to what might at first seem most obvious, the work of recollection and not prophetic foresight which constitutes the vision of the seer, both in the Anaximander fragment itself and in Heidegger's discussion of it.

Looking over the history of Western civilization, Heidegger, like Nietzsche before him, saw the ever-increasing manifestations of nihilism: a nihilism that he interpreted to be the signs and symptoms of the oblivion of being. And in particular, as he read deeply in the history of metaphysics, he discovered that the question of being is no sooner posed than the possibility of a thinking truly open to the claim of this question—truly open to being opened by it—is immediately foreclosed by ontically reduced interpretations, and moreover, that the traces of this foreclosure continue to go unnoticed. Heidegger also sees (writings 1936–46) that this "decline" from the opening moment that takes place in the history of metaphysics corresponds to an increasing "desolation of the earth" (*Verwüstung der Erde*).[86] Seeing this, he is moved to ask: "Can the extreme measure of suffering still bring a transformation here?"[87]

How can a philosopher respond to such a question—and to the need of which it speaks? For his part, Heidegger conceived the task of what he called "thinking" to be, first and foremost, the overcoming (*Überwindung*) of this "extreme blindness" (*aüßerste Verblendung*), this extreme "forgetfulness of being" (*Seinsvergessenheit*) within the discourse of metaphysics, by a process of recollection that would accompany the critical reading of the history of this discourse and by a corresponding critical analysis of the prevailing cultural conceptions of time, history, tradition, and historiography. What this work of recollection would demonstrate, with clear and incontrovertible textual evidence, is that every one of the major concepts that figured in the thinking which inaugurated the history of metaphysics underwent what can now, in retrospect, be seen as a process of increasing reduction and reification: it is now possible to see that, and also how, in the process of being handed down from generation to generation, the principal concepts were unknowingly being altered according to a concealed logic of totalization and reification: a process of "de-generation" separating these concepts from the creative power of their originary moment. This degeneration or ruination is made strikingly clear in such texts as "Overcoming Metaphysics," "Recollection in Metaphysics," and "The End of Philosophy and the Task of Thinking." The argument, in fact, is so strikingly clear that, when one first actually *sees* this logic of closure, the effect can resemble what Benjamin calls a shock of recognition.

"Our age rages," he said (lecture series 1951–52), "in a mad, steadily growing craving to conceive history in terms of universal history, as an occurrence."[88] For him, world history is rather "the destiny whereby a world lays claim to us."[89] There can be no recollection of being without the overcoming of the prevailing cultural conceptions that would, in effect, appropriate it for their own designs and ends. What is needed is a recollection that returns to think the "origin" which was posited in the history of being: a recollection that would release the hermeneutical significance of the "first inception," the opening "event" of being. In "Recollection in Metaphysics" (1941), Heidegger says:

> Recollection [*Erinnerung*] in the history of being is a thinking ahead to the inception [*Vordenken in den Anfang*], and belongs to being itself. The opening event [*Das Ereignis*] grants the time from which history

378 / The Philosophers

takes the granting [*die Gewähr*] of an epoch. But that time span when being gives itself to openness can never be found in historically calculated time or with its measures. The time span granted shows itself only to a reflection which is already able to glimpse [*zu ahnen vermag*] the history of being, even if this succeeds only in the form of an essential need.[90]

Such recollection, such thinking, would be the overcoming of "philosophy" as we have known it; and it would be, perhaps, a preliminary preparation for what might be called "another beginning": "But with the end of philosophy, thinking is not also at its end, but in transition to another beginning."[91]

The "first inception" belongs to a past that, while present, was never present to itself—nor, a fortiori, has it ever been present to itself *as* past. The first inception, the origin, depends on a future time to bring about a certain reflectively constructed presence to itself that it did not have—and could not have had. But just as, for Benjamin, the philosopher as historical materialist who brings the past into the present must struggle against the temptation simply to consign it to the past as nothing but ruination and catastrophe, so for Heidegger, the thinker who undertakes a process of recollection might be strongly tempted to see in the history of metaphysics nothing but an irredeemable decline. Resisting the Spenglerian narrative, however, Heidegger was able to (fore)see in the end of "philosophy" a "gathering into the most extreme possibilities" (*Versammlung in die aüßersten Möglichkeiten*).[92] The task of thinking, then, is to "gather" into recollection some of these still unrealized possibilities from their concealment in the original opening, the first inception of Western thinking. For Heidegger, the Anaximander fragment that we are considering in this chapter is an incipient saying of being.[93] And that means not only that we of today should read and think it in its incipience, its continuing originality and generativity, but that we must recognize in the saying the vision of a seer who has in an extremely significant sense already seen what is still to come. Not the ordinary events of the future, of course, but the revelation of something ontologically significant—or say a presently still concealed dimension of the history of being.

To some extent, the seer's "moment of vision," that moment in which the seer lets the work of Δικη, a "critique of the 'present,' " always untimely, always out of order, be seen, resembles the vision of the historian whose historiography Heidegger describes as "authentic": what is needed, he says, is a historiography that articulates a critique of the "present" and discloses "the quiet force of the possible" (BT 446, 449; SZ 394, 397). But it is not a question of prophecy, not a question of predictions about the future. Like Kant, neither Benjamin nor Heidegger wanted to encourage a "schwärmerische Vision," a vision with exalted pretensions.[94] The seer's vision can disclose the possible only if it takes responsibility for a recollection of the epochal presencing of being.

The temporality of this recollection (*Erinnerung*), however, is radically different from that of ordinary memory, because, whereas ordinary memory is straightforwardly concerned with the past, recollection is concerned with the generative event of an inception that has been, but still presents us with regenerative possibilities for a new beginning. As Heidegger expresses it in his 1941 *Grundbegriffe:*

> The inception is certainly something that has been, but [it is] not something past. What is past is always a no-longer being, but what has been is being that still presences but is concealed in its incipience.[95]

The past, of course, is past, and ordinary memory relates to it accordingly:

> Everything past is only something that has passed away. But the passing away of beings occurs in the essential realm of being. This does not, of course, "subsist" somewhere "in itself", but is what is properly historical in the past, the imperishable, and that means it is an incipiently having been and an incipiently presencing again.[96]

Recollection is concerned with an inception which, in one sense, bears the temporality of that which has already been, but which, in another sense, bears the temporality of that which has not yet been, not yet come to pass. Recollection is a return not to the past but to the originary temporality of inception, to gather up that which could still generate the truly new:

> According to the historiological reckoning of time, the earliest is indeed the oldest, and, in the estimation of ordinary understanding, also the most antiquated. The earliest, however, can also be the first according to rank and wealth, according to originality and bindingness for our history and impending historical decisions. . . . We name this "earliest" *the incipient* [*das Anfängliche*]. From it comes an exhortation, in relation to which the opining of the individual and the many fails to hear, and misconstrues its essential power, unaware of the unique opportunity: that recollection of the incipience can transport us into the essential.[97]

Thus, for the historian,

> everything earlier is something past, by means of which he can illuminate what comes later and what pertains to him according to his needs. Here the earlier has no power of decision because it is no longer experienced as the incipient in history.[98]

But for the thinker, the inception of metaphysics, as the discourse of being, is not consigned to the past:

> The inception, however, can only be experienced as an inception when we ourselves think inceptively and essentially. This inception is not the past, but rather, because it has decided in advance everything to come, it is constantly of the future. We must think about inception this way.[99]

Recollection into the first inception of Western thinking is therefore "a fore-thinking": "a forethinking into the more incipient inception."[100] It is a process that requires fore-sight and anticipation, preparations in thought that might indicate the way to another inception. But Heidegger emphasizes that we must understand these preparations appropriately:

> The word anticipation should show us the way to consider that what should be brought to knowing here cannot be produced from man by his own choice. Anticipation means grasping something that comes upon us, whose coming has long held sway, except that we overlook it. . . . Thinking in anticipation and for anticipation is essentially more rigorous and exacting than any formal-conceptual cleverness in whatever sector of the calculable.[101]

And he adds, most importantly, that

> to attain anticipatory knowing we must practice such knowing. . . . The fundamental condition [for such practice] is readiness to make ourselves free for the essential.

In other words, words that he used earlier, in his 1927 work, *Being and Time,* we must learn the attitude of *Entschlossenheit:* a kind of resolute openness or resolute preparedness, a steadfast, firmly committed anticipatory openness for what might still come from the first inception, if we think with care towards its recollection.

In an early text (1915), "The Concept of Time in the Science of History," Heidegger argues for a process of cultural creation (*Kulturschaffen*) that is mindful of tradition and "gathers what is past." But in the course of making this argument, he says that philosophical thought should undertake this creative cultural recollection "in order to work it through further, or to combat it."[102] The intriguing word, here, is of course the little word "or." In this phase of his thinking, Heidegger was just beginning to recognize the need for a very radical break with tradition—or perhaps, rather, with the way in which tradition has been received and handed down. Thus he was also beginning to realize that this break cannot be understood as straightforward, because there are, in the tradition, traces of a truth that must be preserved. But mere continuation of the inception—repetition in this sense—can only be de-generation. By the time he wrote *Being and Time*, he would take the "combat" a step further, not hesitating to speak of the need for a thinking that is willing to resort to argumentative "violence" (*Gewaltsamkeit*),[103] and indeed arguing that

> the question of being does not achieve its true concreteness until we have carried through the process of destroying the ontological tradition. (BT 49, SZ 26)

Since, as he says in *Being and Time*, "in the field of ontology, any 'springing-from' is degeneration," recollection of the inception, the inaugural opening, can only mean the *destruction* of the prevailing ways of experiencing and conceptualizing time, history, and tradition, ruled as they are by the assumptions of reifying ontology (BT 383, SZ 334). But he was also beginning, there, to articulate this "destruction" as an intricate hermeneutical process, a deconstructive process, destroying tradition precisely in order to rescue from the ruins what he will later refer to as the thought of the "first inception." It is necessary, he says,

> [to] destroy the traditional content of ancient ontology until we arrive at those primordial experiences in which we achieved our first ways of determining the nature of being. (BT 44, SZ 22)

The destruction must consequently be carried out with the understanding that it is part of a process of construction—a vision of another inception, seeing unrealized possibilities in a past that never was.

§3

As we shall now see, Heidegger later, in "The Turning" (1941), gives to the formulation of this destruction a surprising concreteness. "The Turning" ("Die Kehre") is a text of singular importance because, as its title indicates, it names what in retrospect can be seen as the most radical development in Heidegger's thinking: nothing less than a bold reversal of the way he had, in *Being and Time*, been attempting to receive and work with the opening question of metaphysics, the question, namely, of being. He effected this reversal after realizing that the analytic of Dasein, which immediately follows his radical formulation of the phenomenological method in the "Introduction" to *Being and Time*, is actually a terrible betrayal of this method, perpetuating the traditional foreclosure that already takes place in the very framing of the question of being—the question that is supposed to open and inaugurate the discourse of metaphysics. Radicalizing the

Husserlian formulation, Heidegger defines the phenomenological method as a hermeneutical procedure, a process that takes place in the interplay between concealment and unconcealment, a process of subjective self-restraint or self-effacement yielding to the presencing of what presents itself, letting the phenomenon show itself from out of itself.

In "The Turning," Heidegger argues, against the pressures of the metaphysical tradition, that

> we locate history in the realm of happening, instead of thinking history in accordance with its essential origin from out of destining.[104]

"Only," he says,

> when man, in the disclosing coming-to-pass of the insight [*im Ereignis des Einblickes*] by which he himself is beheld [*von diesem Erblickte*], renounces human "self-will" [*menschlichen Eigensinn*] and projects himself toward that insight [*Einblick*], away from himself, does he correspond [*entspricht*] in his essence to the claim of that insight [*Einblickes*].[105]

We are, he believes, in a time of grave danger; but he refuses hopelessness and turns his gaze into the inception, the opening, in order to foresee the possibility of a different future: "another destining, yet veiled, is waiting," he tells us.[106] But, he asks, ascribing—strangely—a visual presence to being:

> Will we, as the ones caught sight of [*als die Erblickten*], be so brought home into the essential glance of being [*in den Wesensblick des Seins*] that we will no longer elude it? Will insight into that which is bring itself disclosingly to pass? Will we correspond to that insight [*Einblick*], through a looking [*Blicken*] that looks [*blickt*] into the essence of technology . . . ? Will we see the lightning-flash of being in the essence of technology? [*Sehen wir den Blitz des Seins im Wesen der Technik?*][107]

This passage shows the strangeness of the text. But it is perhaps only fitting, after all, that a text intended to mark at once the most radical turning point in his own thinking and the possibility of a turning point in the unfolding decline of the history of being should turn to a hermeneutical phenomenology of the uncanny. With the trope of the "lightning-flash," absolutely shattering and bursting open the subject-object structure of traditional metaphysics, a structure within which we have been all too complacently comfortable, Heidegger is attempting to think in the most extreme visionary terms both the catastrophic-redemptive "turning of the danger" and the intense experience of the reversal that shattered and transformed his own thinking. With regard to the first aspect, he says: " The turning of the danger comes to pass suddenly." There is a "sudden self-lighting," a "lightning-flash" (*das Blitzen*) in which "the truth of be-ing flashes."[108] With regard to the second: "Insight into that which is [*Ein-blick in das was ist*]—thus do we name the sudden flash of the truth of being into [the realm of] truthless being."[109] "When insight comes disclos-ingly to pass, then we are the ones who are struck in their essence by the flashing [light] of being. In insight, men are the ones caught sight of. [*Die Menschen sind die im Einblick Erblickten*]."[110] Heidegger attempts to ex-plain the experience in question, but without mitigating the uncanniness of its ontic-ontological doubling:

> To flash [*blitzen*], in terms both of its derivation and of what it desig-nates, is "to glance". [Heidegger's word, here, is *blicken*, which can also mean "to look" or "to gaze at."] In the flashing glance and as that glance, the essence, the coming to presence, of being enters into its own emitting of light. Moving through the element of its own shining [*seines Leuchtens*], the flashing glance [*der Blick*] retrieves that which it catches sight of and brings it back into the brightness of its own look-ing [*birgt der Blick sein Erblicktes in das Blicken zurück*]. And yet that glancing, in its very giving of light, simultaneously also keeps safe the concealed darkness of its origin as the unlighted [*das Ungelichtete*]. The in-turning that is the lightning-flash of the truth of being [*Einkehr des Blitzes der Wahrheit des Seins*] is the entering, flashing glance—insight [*Einblick*].[111]

It would seem to be a question, here, of the possibility of a "glance" or "look," a "glance" or "look" *of* being and coming *from* being, doubled by the possibility of a *corresponding* look or glance on the part of appropri-ately thoughtful human beings. (This strange thought, however, also ap-pears in the 1942–43 lectures on Parmenides, wherein Heidegger under-takes a critical examination of our ordinary and habitual way of looking and seeing, and pursues the logic of this critique in a preparatory meditation on another, radically different way of looking and seeing.[112] Reflecting on the Greek word θεά, which he translates as "the look of being" that "looks into beings," he turns it into a trope for the argument that our looking is always already "claimed" by the presence of being, the opening up and clearing of a field of light by grace of which we are enabled to see.)

There is, of course, a strong temptation to give this text a "merely" metaphorical interpretation. I have repeatedly argued against reading Heidegger this way, if this designation opposes the "metaphoral" to the "literal" in a way that effectively denies the text any meaningful, transfor-mative relation to experience. What such a text calls for is not a blunt-ing of its power to shatter and burst open—its power to transform our experiencing and thinking, but instead an effort to take it seriously, take it to heart, and work with it in and as an experience of thinking.

Like Benjamin, Heidegger thinks the interruption of the continuum of history as a lightning-flash. It is at least possible—conceivable—that with the unexpected suddenness of a bolt of lightning, another inception could take place. But only, as Heidegger repeatedly insists, if we are in readiness: only if we have undertaken the necessary "preparations." Such "preparations" would not necessarily be followed by a new inception. But without our preparations, there can be no reason for hope.

In "The Turning," this most strange and disturbing text, which scholars have consistently neglected, undoubtedly because they are puzzled by what appears to be the "personifying" of being and cannot see how to give it an interpretation that is other than mythological or metaphorical, Heidegger is attempting to think such anticipatory preparations in terms of our experience as beings who have been given the capacity to see. In keeping with the image of lightning to designate the catastrophic intensity of the turning point, the abruptness and unexpectedness of the interruption in the historical unfolding of being, and the moment when the possibility of another inception first becomes manifest, he spells out what is required of us in preparation, proposing to think our historical task as calling for a response to the "glance of being" that would correspond appropriately to the claim made on our capacity for vision by this phenomenon. The "look of being" is therefore simply a provocative way to formulate the ontological claim on our visionary capacity. If, as he says in this text, we are always "seen," always "beheld" by the "look of being," this is because—or this is to say that—in beholding, we are always beholden, always held, always bound, in a certain ontological beholdenness: what, in *Being and Time,* Heidegger would call our *Schuldig-sein.* We are beholden, because the visibility of the world, the gift of the lighting that makes beings visible, makes a claim (*Anspruch*) on our capacity to look and see. In "The Turning," it is suggested that this claim calls on us to look and see with a thoughtfulness that would *correspond* to the manifestation of the possibility of a new inception in signs of hope—signs never more than flashes of light, instantaneous, puzzling, beyond the possibility of expectation. In question is the character of our gaze: whether it will respond to these signs with a looking and seeing that corresponds to the revelatory moment with appropriate thoughtfulness. In his meditations on Heraclitus, Heidegger would use the word ὁμολογεῖν to name this possibility of a correspondence between [a] *our* looking and seeing, as events and sites where both beings and the being of beings as a whole are brought into a certain moment of disclosedness or unconcealment, and [b] the event, the *Es gibt*, of being, as the disclosure or unconcealment that grants the field of lighting within which our world-disclosures take place. Are we capable of a vision, a looking and seeing, that could be described as "of being"? "Of being": that is to say, it would be a question of a looking and seeing that understand themselves to be involved in the unconcealment of being, a looking and seeing gathered, out of time, into originary temporality.

"The Turning" is very much, then, an allegorical text. The lightning-flash, rending the sky, effecting a decisive scission in the night, renders for all to see a visible reminder that the crisis of nihilism calls for a decisive response: a resolute commitment to the task of anticipatory thinking—thinking into the possibility of another inception. And with the differentiating scission that it articulates in the openness of the sky, it evokes the ontological difference between being and beings, representing it in the realm of the visible as a critical moment of "decision" in the history of being and the history of metaphysics. Thus it represents that opening moment of inception when the difference between being and beings was first brought forth. But the possibility of another inception is to be glimpsed in the space opened up by the rendering of the ontological difference. For it is into the space of this difference, into the immeasurable dimensionality of this difference, that originary presencing, while giving finite beings unconcealment, itself withdraws into concealment and thereby preserves historical possibilities for new forms of presencing from the nihilistic reductions of what might be called a certain ontological historicism. I mean by that the historical reductions of ontological possibilities to the presently prevailing modes of presencing.

Articulating a decisive difference, the lightning-bolt intimates at once the *Geschick*, the sending or decision of being, the fateful assignations of presencing which inaugurated the unfolding of its epochal history, and the resolute commitment, the decision to give thought to the *Geschick*, by which we human beings would be enjoined to correspond in appropriate ways to the calling of our time. As a flash of light illuminating the enveloping darkness, the lightning suddenly appears at the darkest, most hopeless moment—a messenger of hope, perhaps, intimating at least the possibility of a saving enlightenment.

§4

In chapters 4 to 6 of division II of *Being and Time*, the work to which we shall now give thought, Heidegger uses his existential phenomenology to formulate critical arguments against the conceptions of time, history, and tradition that have figured prominently in the history of Western philosophy and Western cultural life.

However strange it may seem, the fact is that the trope of the philosopher's gaze plays a major role in these chapters, continuing his attention to vision in the preceding division. In chapter 3, division I, Heidegger suggests that "in its projective character, understanding goes to make up existentially what we call Dasein's *'sight'* [*Sicht*]" (BT 186, SZ 146). He then names the disclosive forms that such sight can assume: the "circumspection of concern" (*Umsicht*); the "considerateness of solicitude" (*Rücksicht*); "a sight that is directed upon being as such" (*Sicht auf das Sein als solches*), "for the sake of which any Dasein is as it is"; and the sight of "transparency" (*Durchsichtigkeit*), of "self-knowledge," the "sight which is related primarily and on the whole to existence" (ibid.). After introducing this nomenclature, Heidegger comments:

> We must, to be sure, guard against a misunderstanding of the expression "sight". It corresponds to the "clearedness" [*Gelichtetheit*] which we took as characterizing the disclosedness of the "there". "Seeing" does not mean just perceiving with the bodily eyes; but neither does it mean a pure non-sensory awareness of something present-at-hand in its presence-at-hand. In giving an existential signification to "sight," we have merely drawn upon the peculiar feature of seeing, that it lets entities which are accessible to it be encountered unconcealedly in themselves. Of course, every "sense" does this within that domain of discovery which is genuinely its own. But from the beginning onwards, the tradition of philosophy has been oriented primarily towards "seeing" as a way of access to entities *and to being*. To keep the connection with this tradition, we may formalize "sight" and "seeing" enough to obtain therewith a universal term for characterizing any access to entities or to being, as access in general. (BT 187, SZ 147. See also BT 397, SZ 346.)

Soon after this passage, in regard to which we must forbear the extensive critical commentary its extremely questionable position calls for, Heidegger introduces "fore-sight" (*Vorsicht*) as one of the three background dimensions of existential understanding. But as he uses this term, it does not mean a prophetic power, an ability to make shrewd or valid predictions about the future, but refers, rather, to the fact that, as he formulates it,

> when something is understood but is still veiled, it becomes unveiled by an act of appropriation, and this is always done under the guidance of a point of view, which determines that with regard to which what is understood is to be interpreted. In every case, interpretation is grounded in *something we see in advance*—in a *fore-sight*. . . . Any-

thing understood which is held in our fore-having and towards which we set our sights "fore-sightedly", becomes conceptualizable through the interpretation. (BT 191, SZ 150)

In both the first and second divisions, Heidegger's frequent references to different ways of looking and seeing bear out his claim that "a Dasein can, in existing, develop the different possibilities of sight, of looking around [*Sichumsehens*], and of just looking" (BT 385, SZ 336. Also see BT 397, SZ 346). What concerns him in division II is that singular "potentiality-for-seeing" which he calls "der Augenblick": "the moment of vision." It is in terms of an experience with vision—but is it a look, a glance, a glimpse?—that, like Benjamin, he attempts to articulate a radically different relationship to time, history, and tradition.

Holding that there are authentic and inauthentic ways of being in time, being historical, receiving and handing down tradition, Heidegger lays out a phenomenology of these different ways, showing how there is a certain "pathology" in what we consider "ordinary" and "normal." Thus, for example, he shows that there are two very different ways of anticipating and awaiting (BT 386ff, 397–99; SZ 336ff, 346–48). Anticipation and awaiting, he argues, are ordinarily, normally, dominated by "curiosity," an often overwhelming impatience that cannot tolerate waiting and cannot benefit from it, that refuses to wait, or can only wait if it reduces the future to "what is coming next." As ways of inhabiting and structuring time, anticipating and awaiting can be either deeply felt experiences, rich and enriching, or they can be experienced in distraction, totally bent on a reifying making-present. According to Heidegger, we are living in an age, a time, in which there is less and less tolerance for deferral, for the postponement of gratification, less and less acceptance of waiting, less and less appreciation for the secret gifts in the experience of anticipating and awaiting. And this means that the structure and the dimensionality of the "time" in which we live are correspondingly reduced. This bears on the experience of fore-sight; and it explains why the vision of the seer can be understood, today, only in its degenerate form, viz., as the power to see and predict a determinate future.

With correlatively similar phenomenological analyses, Heidegger shows that there are two ways of experiencing the present: an inauthentic way, commonplace and normal, and an authentic way, much more difficult to achieve:

The ordinary way of characterizing time as an endless, irreversible sequence of "nows" which passes away, arises from the temporality of falling Dasein. (BT 478, SZ 426)

The ordinary way of experiencing time divides it into a series of present-at-hand now-points. Experienced in this way, the now-time (*Jetzt-Zeit*) is totally emptied of meaning, rendered homogeneous, repetitive, one-dimensional: it becomes a decayed version of Plato's "image of eternity," a form of endless suffering, dull and meaningless, bereft of radical hope (BT 425–26, 474–79; SZ 373–74, 421–27). Heidegger argues that neither the authentic "will be" nor the authentic "having-been" can be understood in terms of such a series of "now-times." Thus, just as there is a fallen, pathological experience of the future and the present, so too there is a fallen, pathological memory-experience of the past: a way of remembering that is really, when more deeply experienced, a kind of forgetting; a way of relating to what is past which is incapable of receiving it in a way that is open to what it bears—the unrealized "potentialities-for-being," the possible "destinies," that the past always carries forward. Dasein's "has-been" is not a reified past, exhausted and final, but that out of which futures are yet to be made (BT 432–37, SZ 380–85).

According to Heidegger (BT 394, SZ 344), it is in authentic resoluteness (*Entschlossenheit*) that the "moment of vision" (*der Augenblick*) takes place (BT 387, SZ 338). In *Die Grundbegriffe der Metaphysik: Welt, Endlichkeit, Einsamkeit* (lecture course, 1929–30), Heidegger credits Kierkegaard for suggesting his conception of the "moment of vision":

> What we are calling the Moment was in fact conceived by Kierkegaard for the very first time in philosophy. The conception launches the *possibility* of a completely new epoch of philosophy ever since antiquity.[113]

This "moment of vision" is to be understood, then, in terms of the way in which an historical Dasein chooses itself in relation to the existential possibilities inherent in its historical temporality. More to the point, it would constitute the most radical restructuring conceivable of the temporality and historicality within which Dasein could dwell. Temporalizing itself in authentic resoluteness, the "moment of vision" would be the "awakening" of "Dasein's capacity for being disclosive" (BT 384, SZ 335). Resoluteness, Heidegger says, is "the disclosive projection and determination of what is factically possible at the time" (BT 345, SZ 298). In relation to the "having-been" of history, it essentially involves "holding oneself open" (*sich freihalten*) for new historical possibilities (BT 355, SZ 307–8).

This is a rigorously hermeneutical process. The resoluteness at stake here cannot be understood, therefore, in terms of the ordinary concepts of historical decision and action. Nor can it be inserted into the linear time-structure of present-at-hand now-points:

> The moment of vision is a phenomenon which *in principle* can *not* be clarified in terms of the "now" [*dem Jetzt*]. . . . In the "moment of vision" nothing can occur; but as an authentic present or waiting-towards, the moment of vision permits us *to encounter for the first time* what can be "in a time" as ready-to-hand or present-at- hand. (BT 387–88, SZ 338)

(We shall need to return to this passage when we resume our consideration of Heidegger's commentary on the Anaximander fragment.) The word Heidegger uses to describe the "moment of vision"—and the way he uses the word—make this visionary disruption of the now-time clear. *Entschlossenheit* names a decisive commitment to a deep, ontologically responsible *openness* in relation to history and tradition. (According to Theodor Kisiel, "Entschlossenheit" first appears in Heidegger's writings in October 1922, introduced in relation to the "ability to unlock." And in 1924, it is discussed as a translation of Aristotle's προαίρεσις.)[114] It is the opposite of the "closing-off" (*sich verschliessen*) of a forgetting in which Dasein loses contact with its having-been, and is thereby cut off from its *futural* potentiality-for-being (BT 388–89, 448; SZ 339, 396): "Resoluteness," he says, "brings Dasein back to its ownmost potentiality-for-being-itself." Back, in other words, not to a fixed, totally determinate past, consigned to what has simply gone by, but to a "having-been" that is (still) full of possibilities: possibilities that could be retrieved only in a present that carries them forward (BT 354, SZ 307). "The character of 'having been,' " he says, "arises, in a certain way, from the future" (BT 373, SZ 326). It is the futurality of what has been (*das Gewesene*) that will "awaken" the present (BT 378, SZ 329). Thus Heidegger will also emphasize the futural dimension of resoluteness, explicating the hermeneutical phenomenology of its "anticipatory" (*vorlaufende*) structure (BT 314, 343–48; SZ 270, 297–301), while at the same time showing how "even a phenomenon like hope, which seems to be wholly founded upon the future," must be interpreted in a way that brings out its structural relation to the "having-been": "what is decisive for the structure of hope as a phenomenon is not so much the 'futural' character of that *to which* it relates itself, but rather the existential meaning of *hoping itself*" (BT 395–96, SZ 345). Hoping is only intelligible against a background of what has been. Hoping looks forward while remaining rooted understandingly in its critical appropriation of the past.

According to Heidegger, the "moment of vision" that is prepared by resoluteness is not at all an abstraction from historical situatedness. On the contrary: it must be thought as an "event" taking place in, and with regard to, a particular historical situation. But its way of being historically situated is to look for a perspective on the historicity of the present situation that would enable it to be seen and understood in terms of a "more original" (*ursprünglich*) temporality—a temporality from within which we might be liberated from the oppressive fatalism of the ordinary, degraded experience of time and history and might catch sight of radically new possibilities for historical life (BT 370–80, SZ 323–31). The moment of vision "brings existence into the situation and discloses the authentic 'there'" (BT 398, SZ 347. Also see BT 376, SZ 328). The "moment of vision" belongs, therefore, not so much to an individual, but rather more to a cultural community. In resoluteness,

> the present is not only brought back from distraction . . . , but it gets held in the future and in having-been. That present which is held in authentic temporality and which is thus authentic itself, we call the "moment of vision." (BT 387, SZ 338)

For Dasein to be in the "moment of vision" for its time is for it to see how a cultural community might be able to "take over" its destiny (*Geschick*) as the having-been of historical possibilities that it can in the present still work with creatively for the sake of its future (BT 436–37, SZ 384–85). In the resoluteness of the "moment of vision," Dasein can at least glimpse a way to turn what had seemed past, seemed an inevitable fate, into the future of a potential that has already been granted.

As an historical "event," the "moment of vision" cannot be correctly understood apart from Heidegger's critique of historiography (historiology) and the prevailing conception of tradition and history. According to Heidegger,

> authentic historiology becomes a way in which the "today" gets deprived of its character as present. . . . [As authentic, historiology] is necessarily a critique of the "present." (BT 449, SZ 397)

The appropriate object of historiography, for Heidegger, should be:

> neither that which has happened just once for all nor something universal that floats above it, but the possibility which has been factically existent [*die faktisch existent gewesene Möglichkeit*]. . . . Only by a historiology which is factical and authentic can the history of what-has-been-there, as settled fate [*entschlossenes Schicksal*], be shown to be otherwise, so that, in repetition, the "force" of the possible gets struck home into one's factical existence. (BT 447, SZ 395)

Struggling, very much like Benjamin, to liberate the cultural experience of historicity, and the historiography to which it gives rise, from their degradation, from a pursuit of the new that is in reality nothing but fate, an endlessly empty repetition of the same, Heidegger argues that

> in inauthentic historicality, . . . the way in which fate [*des Schicksals*] has been primordially stretched along has been hidden. With the inconstancy of the they-self [*als Man-selbst:* as anyone-and-everyone], Dasein makes present its "today". In awaiting the next new thing, it has already forgotten the old one. The "they" [*das Man*] evades choice. Blind for possibilities, it cannot authentically repeat what has been, but only retains and receives the "actual" that is left over, the world-history that has been, the leavings [*die Überbleibsel*] and the information about them that is present-at-hand [*die vorhandene Kunde*]. Lost in the making-present of the "today," it understands the "past" in terms of the [inauthentic] "present". On the other hand, the temporality of authentic historicality, as the moment of vision of anticipatory repetition [*vorlaufend-wiederholender Augenblick*], deprives the "today" of its character as present [*eine Entgegenwärtigung des Heute*], and weans one from the conventionalities of the "they". When, however, one's existence is inauthentically historical, it is loaded down with the legacy of a "past" which has become unrecognizable, and it seeks the modern. But when historicality is authentic, it understands history as the "recurrence" [*Wiederkehr*] of the possible, and knows that a possibility will recur [*wiederkehrt*] only if existence is open for it fatefully, in a moment of vision, in resolute repetition [*wenn die Existenz schicksalhaft-augenblicklich für sie in der entschlossenen Wiederholung offen ist*]. (BT 443–44, SZ 391–92)

The resoluteness of the "moment of vision" is not only the taking-up of an historically unseen possibility; it is also "at the same time a *disavowal* [*der Widerruf*] of that which in the 'today', is working itself out [only] as the 'past' " (BT 438, SZ 386). The "moment of vision" is possible, therefore, only when there is a decisive break with the fatalism of the past—with an experience and understanding of history and tradition that consigns the vision of the inception that is still carried within them to a continuum of now-times that are absolutely, irretrievably in the past. As resolute openness, *Entschlossenheit*, the "moment of vision" is a "disavowal," a "critique of the present" that *opens up* a space (*Spielraum*)[115] of difference, a space, in effect, of freedom, in relation to the past, to tradition, to history as we have known it, and to the prevailing, totally illusory enchantments of the latest "new" and the latest "modern." The disavowal is a crucial moment in the dialectical struggle against history and tradition, making possible the hermeneutical moment that Heidegger calls "repetition." This "repetition" is not at all a reactionary conservatism. It is not a sentimental attempt to revive a perishing tradition. It is not a glorification or celebration of the past as a demonstration of historical progress. As he conceives it, "repetition" is for the sake of the possible:

> The repeating of that which is possible does not bring again [*wieder-bringen*] something that is "past," nor does it bind the "present" back to that which has already been "outstripped." (BT 437, SZ 385–86)

The repetition that takes place in the "moment of vision" is thus not a repetition in anything like the ordinary sense:

> [It] does not abandon itself to that which is past; nor does it aim at progress. In the moment of vision, authentic existence is indifferent to both these alternatives. (Ibid.)

"We characterize repetition," he says,

> as a mode of resoluteness which hands itself down—the mode by which Dasein exists explicitly as destiny. But if destiny constitutes the primordial historicality of Dasein, then history has its essential importance neither in what is past nor in the "today" and its connection with what is past, but in that authentic historicizing of existence which arises from Dasein's future. (Ibid.)

The "moment of vision" is a hermeneutical repetition, not of the (finished) "past," but of the (still unfinished) "having-been." (This distinction between the "past" and the "having-been" is crucial: without it, Heidegger's position in *Being and Time* is totally misrepresented.) The "moment of vision" is, like the lightning-flash in Heidegger's essay on "The Turning" and Benjamin's "Theses on the Philosophy of History," the lighting up of inceptive possibilities in an historical "forcefield." It is the "repetition of a possibility of existence that has come down to us" (BT 437, SZ 385), a repetition of the inceptive "energies" of the origin, a way of *receiving* these "energies" and handing them down—in, as, and for the "destruction" of the past and a radically new beginning. Thus, although Heidegger—carefully avoiding the conceit of the predictive seer who would claim to "know in advance"—does not commit himself to saying what inceptive possibilities he thinks tradition is secretly handing down to us nor what possibilities he thinks we "ought" to be retrieving, he insists on his conviction that authentic repetition must be "rooted in the future" (BT 438–39, SZ 386–87).

However, while the "moment of vision" is described as looking into, or rather towards the future, it is not to be thought miraculously free of the repetition that perpetuates the historical continuum—the empty, homogeneous time-series in which the creatively explosive potential in the inception remains lost in oblivion, concealed by the injustice of "that which is." In a passage that has been ignored by the scholars, Heidegger writes:

> In everydayness, Dasein can undergo dull "suffering", sink away in the dullness of it, and evade it by seeking new ways in which its dispersion in its affairs may be further dispersed. In the moment of vision [*Augenblick*], indeed, and often just "for that moment" [*Augenblick*], existence can even gain the mastery over the "everyday"; but it can never extinguish it. (BT 422, SZ 371)

The seer's achievement of a "moment of vision" is not, for Heidegger, the absolute end of the history of suffering. Heidegger refuses to celebrate it as the inauguration of another beginning. While thinking of it as a moment of hope, he refuses to make it a false victory over time and tradition. The weight of tradition and the pull of the past can never be totally overcome. And perhaps this is not entirely regrettable.

Is there a decisive and unequivocal difference, then, as Caygill wants to argue, between Benjamin and Heidegger with regard to redemptive fulfillment? It certainly can be argued that "Heidegger keeps open the possibility that historical time may be a suitable vehicle for authenticity, [whereas this is] an option which Benjamin refuses to entertain."[116] But the distinction that he wants to draw, namely, between fulfillment *in* historical time (Heidegger) and the fulfillment *of* historical time (Benjamin), is easily thrown in question by the decisive openness of Heidegger's "moment of vision," that lightning-flash of insightful seeing which, by corresponding to the inceptive disclosiveness of the "look of being," suspends historical time as we have known it within the radically different order of primordial temporality, the temporality of the inception. What can be said with some confidence, however, as the last quotation from *Being and Time* shows, is that Heidegger does not attribute to the "moment of vision" any miraculous powers to break the spellbinding hold on us of a historicity inextricably bound up with the causes of our suffering. But there is a strong suggestion in Heidegger's work that nothing less than a total interruption of the prevailing temporal order, bringing to an end the historical as we have known it and making way for a new inception, would make such redemption possible.

§5

To know means to have seen, in the widest sense of seeing, which means to apprehend [*vernehmen*] what is present [*das Anwesenden*], as such.

Martin Heidegger,
"The Origin of the Work of Art"[117]

What is "present as such"? And what is involved in the "having (already) seen," which Heidegger emphasizes in "The Origin of the Work of Art" (1935–36) and again later (1946) in his discussion of the seer in "The Anaximander Fragment"? When Heidegger, retrieving Greek etymology, emphasizes that to see is to have already seen, that (as he says in his commentary on the fragment) a seer is one who "has always already seen," should we understand him to be attributing to the seer a predictive foresight, a "making-present" of the future? Or is it not, rather, a question of the seer's ability to see what is overlooked, though it is already in view? This gets at part of what is involved; but there are other dimensions. "Having already seen" registers the fact that the beholding of the seer is a capacity which comes from his realization that seeing is a gift, a dispensation (*Geschick*), and that it must be exercised in a way that acknowledges the debt that is owed—the beholdenness that *precedes* the seeing, *precedes* the beholding. "Having already seen" may thus be said to record the seer's recognition of being held in that beholdenness, always already responsible for seeing what he sees.

What, in the "moment of vision," in the seer's having-always-already-seen, is then "present as such"? In what way or sense is the future made present, seen "in advance"? In "The Anaximander Fragment," Heidegger says:

[1] "The seer sees inasmuch as he has seen everything as present [*als Anwesendes*]" (AX 35, H 320).

[2] "All things present and absent are gathered and preserved in *one* presencing for the seer" (AX 36, H 321).

[3] "The seer is the one who has already seen the whole [*das All*] of what is present in its presencing" (AX 36, H 321).

[4] The seer is "the one who has seen, is himself one who makes-present [*ein Anwesender ist*] and belongs in an exceptional sense to the whole of what is present [*in das Ganze des Anwesenden gehört*]. On the other hand, it does not mean that what is present is nothing but an object entirely dependent upon the seer's subjectivity" (AX 38, H 323).

[5] In question is the developing and exercising of our capacity to be "present" (*anwesend*) in the world in a way that would be "illuminating, apprehending, and thus gathering," "present" in a way that "lets what is present as such become present in unconcealment [*in der Unverborgenheit wesen läßt*]" (AX 38, H 323).

In arguing for a significant difference between Benjamin and Heidegger, Caygill points to the fact that Heidegger emphasizes the seer's "gathering" and "preserving," the seer's "making-present." He seems to think that this commits Heidegger to a metaphysical fetishization of the past, making it "present" in a present that continues our bondage to history. But what is it that the seer gathers and preserves? Casting her gaze into the world with a keen awareness of its entering the visible as a site of unconcealment that belongs to an interplay between the visible and the invisible, the seer gathers and preserves by letting be not just what is present, but also what is absent. Moreover, the seer makes them "present," gathers and preserves them, not in a now-present (the *Jetzt-Zeit* of history into which primordial temporality has degenerated), but rather in presencing as such. That is to say, the seer's vision dislodges things from their placement in the conventional time-continuum of history and gathers everything into the "preserve" of *primordial temporality*, surrendering all things to the deconstructive interplay (the "Spielraum") of concealment and unconcealment. But Caygill's argument depends on failing to recognize Heidegger's crucial distinction between "making present" in the sense of a *Gegenwärtigung* and "making present" in the sense of *das Anwesene*. The "gathering" and "preserving" that Heidegger's seer achieves thus actually *destroys* the spell of the reified timing of history, gathering all beings, beings both present and absent, into the possibility-field, the open "preserve," of a radically other time-order: "The seer speaks from the preserve [*die Wahr*] of what is present. He is the soothsayer [*der Wahr-Sager*]" (AX 36, H 321). What is this "preserve"? It is, for Heidegger, an abyssal dimension which exposes the contingency and transience of all historical formations. In a sense, then, the gathering is a gathering into the anarchy of temporal dispersal and dissemination—the radical *ekstasis* of primordial temporality, wherein the prevailing order of time and history is exposed to the violence, at once creative and destructive, of the inception.

In the abrupt declaration which marks the end of his "Theologico-Political Fragment," Benjamin connects his concept of revolutionary political action with the concept of "Naturgeschichte," suggesting that the destructive act would be a *mimesis* learned from nature:

> For nature is Messianic by reason of its eternal and total passing
> away. To strive after such passing, even for those stages of man
> that are nature, is the task of world politics, whose method must be
> called nihilism.[118]

(It may be that politics is always a form of violence, but this attraction to a redeeming violence that would put an end to all the violence of politics runs the risk of corruption and repetition, becoming itself just another sequence in the violence of that politics. But is Benjamin's nihilism the only politics one can derive from the concept of natural history?)

Gathering everything into the preserve of primordial temporality, into the interplay of concealment and unconcealment, the seer's way of looking and seeing returns everything, as Anaximander's fragment might be read as saying, to their "natural history": the process of coming into being, staying awhile, and perishing. Thus it may be said to return the established institutions and regimes of time and history to the deconstructive work of primordial temporality.

A crucial passage in this regard, one that we have already cited, clarifies both the character of the "moment of vision" and the character of its resoluteness:

> The moment of vision is a phenomenon which *in principle* can *not* be clarified in terms of the "now". The "now" is a temporal phenomenon which belongs to time as within-time-ness: the "now" "in which" something arises, passes away, or is present-at-hand. In "the moment of vision" *nothing can occur;* but as an authentic present or waiting-towards, the moment of vision permits us to encounter for the first time what can be "in a time" as ready-to-hand or present-at-hand. (BT 387–88, SZ 338)

"Nothing can occur": this tells against the common interpretation of "resoluteness," which takes it to be decision and action without reasons, beyond justification, and totally arbitrary: Heidegger's fall into the politics of irrationalism. Nothing, however, could be further from the truth. The "moment of vision" does not belong to a now-present in the prevailing order of time and history; nor, a fortiori, does it gather past, present, and future into the present of such an order. The "moment of vision" belongs, rather, to the "transcendental field" of possibility, the force-field of competing possibilities contained at the "origin" wherein the prevailing order of time and history arises. "Nothing can occur": Benjamin's dialectics in standstill?

The passage from *Being and Time* that we have just considered should be thought in connection with a passage from "The Origin of the Work of Art": the one, in fact, that was quoted at the very beginning of this chapter, and in which Heidegger comments, some eight or nine years later, on the way he understood "resoluteness" in the earlier work. Heidegger says there, in no uncertain terms, that

> the resoluteness intended in *Being and Time* is not the deliberate action of a subject, but the opening up of human being, out of its captivity in that which is, to the openness of being.

Critics and scholars have not given sufficient thought to the phrase "not the deliberate action of a subject." I take it that Heidegger is thereby locating "resoluteness" in the ontological, or, say, "transcendental" dimension: as the openness that recollects being, recollects presencing, it is actually a name for what he will later call "Gelassenheit." According to Heidegger, it was only at first that the word *Entscheidung,* meaning "decision," was used to signify an "act of man": in the course of his thinking, he soon wanted to understand it ontologically, i.e., as the "essence" of human being, whereby "man" is returned to the dimensionality of being as such and the chains of anthropologism are thrown off.[119] As we must learn from Heidegger's discussion of the lightning-flash in "The Turning," the resoluteness of the "moment of vision" is a moment when the way things have been is decisively and radically interrupted. Resoluteness may be called "action," but only in a very special sense. Heidegger says: "As resolute, Dasein is already taking action [*Als entschlossenes handelt das Dasein schon*]" (BT 347, SZ 300). The "already" is crucial here. Resoluteness is *always already* action because it is the transcendental condition for "action" in the standard sense of the term. It is the attitudinal "orientation" necessary for authentic action. If it seems to be arbitrary and irrational, that is due to the fact that it is being interpreted as decision and action in the standard sense, rather than as the transcendental condition, or the ontological orientation, for the very possibility of authentic action. Thus, contrary to the interpretation of his critics, Heidegger is not at all defining authenticity in terms of decisions and actions for which it would be wrong or inappropriate to ask for justifying reasons. (In "On the Essence of Truth," and in many other writings where he discusses freedom, Heidegger explicitly repudiates conceptions of freedom which think of it in egocentric terms, as an arbitrary, capricious, and irrational exercise of the will.)

Radically understood, the "decision" constitutive of *Entschlossenheit* is an ontologically drafted scission, a decisive break with the temporality of *das Man,* the causal continuum of history. It is a decisive break with history as a reifying forgetting of being. What is in question, as Heidegger expresses it in "The Anaximander Fragment," is the possibility of a "decisive turn [*entscheidende Wende*] in the destiny of being" (AX 57, H 342). The break consists in the decision to *alter the ground* for historical decision and action—to shift, as it were, to a radically *different* ground. This alteration takes place by virtue of a resolute *openness* to the presencing of being, the being of beings. Resolute openness to the presencing of being is the necessary condition for the possibility of authentic historical action. Thus, in Heidegger's later work, this *Entschlossenheit* becomes a question of the recollection of being—a deconstructive hermeneutics of memory that must struggle against the overwhelming force of illusory appearance, to make the frightening ruination (*Verderb*), the "untimely" work of Δικὴ, the never-seen, appear in a flash before the eyes of mortals.[120]

The "moment of vision" is the moment of resoluteness because it is that moment when there is a recollection of being and a corresponding openness that gathers all beings into the anarchic temporality and history of being, into the abyssal withdrawal of grounding principles where all the prevailing worldly institutions and regimes of time and history are subjected to what Derrida would call "the justice of deconstruction" and granted other possibilities of generation and construction. It is in this anarchic dimension of justice that resoluteness roots the "moment of vision." And therefore it is ultimately in this anarchic justice alone that authentic action can—and must—be "grounded." (See in this regard "The Anaximander Fragment," where Heidegger refers to what "arises from the abyss of that relation by which being has appropriated the essence of Western man.")[121]

What the seer has always already seen are not specific objects and events belonging to the conventional future: such a "predictive" vision is nothing but a cheap, fetishized simulacrum of the seer's art. When Heidegger says that the seer has "always already seen" (*immer schon gesehen*), what he means is that, by virtue of a recollection of being, the seer sees the ontological dimension of time and history, sees the conditions of possibility for historical ruptures and radically new beginnings, sees the decisive "justice" of the ontological difference, through which primordial temporality—Anaximander's "ordinance of time"—metes out the timing of beings (AX 54, H 339). What the seer "foresees" are not the ontic futures of specific objects and events, but rather the ontological, abyssal fate of all beings: the law, the "divine justice" that has always already decided their fate: their coming-into-being, their staying awhile, and the inevitability of their perishing. This fate, as already decided, sentencing all our institutions to the condition of being in ruins, is thus a future that is already past—and yet, of course, not yet. And it is *this* future, this already past future, that the seer sees. Always already—and yet, not yet. The seer must maintain these two temporal perspectives in a paradoxical moment of vision.

IV. JUSTICE IN THE SEER'S EYES

Thinking about Sophocles's *Antigone* in the course of some lectures that he gave in the years 1936–37, subsequently published under the title *Einführung in die Metaphysik*, Heidegger briefly touches on the question

of Δικὴ, giving thought to its significance as a fundamental question
not only for Greek tragedy, but also for the pre-Socratic philosophers—
Anaximander, Parmenides, and Heraclitus. Here we see him struggling to
translate the word into German, already convinced at this time that it must
not be understood in the familiar juridical, moral, or political sense.[122] The
translations that he finally proposes are *fügender Fug* (overwhelming order, governing order) and *fügende Gefüge* (governing structure): Δικὴ is
that fundamental framework of order which, as a decree or directive that
the overpowering (*das Überwältigende*) imposes on its rule (*Walten*), en-
joins or compels adaptation (*Einfügung*) and compliance (*Sichfügen*).[123]
Δικὴ is thus closely related to Μοῖρα, which is allotment, assignment, dispensation, and of course Νόμος, about which Heidegger says, in another
text, that it is "not only law, but more originally the assignment contained
in the dispensation of being."[124]

Δικὴ also emerges as a crucial question in Heidegger's discussion of
Nietzsche's statements concerning justice. Here Heidegger says that "Δικὴ
is a metaphysical concept, not originally one of morality. It names being
with reference to the essentially appropriate articulation of all beings [*hin-
sichtlich der wesensmäßigen* Fügung alles Seienden]."[125] But this is not to
be understood as implying that there is no connection between the metaphysical and the realms of the moral, the juridical, and the political. Indeed,
inasmuch as the metaphysical is concerned with being, it must carry
significance for these realms of life. There is further support for this interpretation to be found in Heidegger's comments on Plato's *Politeia*, immediately preceding the passage we just quoted:

> this tremendous dialogue in its entire structure and movement aims
> to show that the sustaining ground and determining essence of all po-
> litical being consists in nothing less than the "theoretical", that is, in
> essential knowledge of δικὴ and δικαιοσύνη. . . . Knowledge of δικὴ,
> of the articulating laws [*Fügungsgesetzen*] of the being of beings,
> is philosophy.[126]

If one puts the last two passages together, it is clear that, for Heidegger,
Δικὴ is the overpowering structure that underlies and rules over all political orders. What Anaximander says in the fragment we have been considering is that he sees how Δικὴ rules, sees in what way its assignment, its
decree, its enjoinment, holds sway over all political orders. And what he
says in the fragment is an attempt to make this overpowering (*Überwältige*)
ordinance visible *as* the overpowering—even to those whose capacity for
vision is less thoughtfully determined. What the seer has always already

seen, then, would be the "judgment" or "measure" of Διϰή, passing its sentence over all political regimes of power according to the ordinance of time, of primordial temporality. (Nietzsche's Zarathustra would perhaps speak here of the "revenge" of time.)

It is perhaps most of all, then, in his proximity to Anaximander's saying that Heidegger also comes closest to Benjamin. As I have tried to show, there are concerns that occupy Heidegger in his commentary on Anaximander which are also legible in Benjamin's *Trauerspiel* essay, his "Critique of Violence," and his "Theses on the Philosophy of History." On Heidegger's reading, the Anaximander fragment would speak of domination and violence in the realm of beings; of the fact that, in their persistence (*das Beharren*), all ontic orders are inherently violent, inherently unjust, excluding or annihilating other possible orders. It would speak of the anarchy of radical justice and the justice of radical anarchy, all too well concealed, a frightening dimension of justice that underlies all finite orders and their institutions of so-called justice. And it would speak of "restitution" for injustice. For the vision that speaks in this fragment, all political orders, all regimes of power, and all socially mediated relations in our time involve domination and are therefore inherently violent, inherently unjust.[127]

What Heidegger's reading of the Anaximander fragment suggests is that the seer's vision penetrates the world of appearances to see what the world would deny: making Διϰή visible, the seer introduces a radically transcendent perspective from which it can be seen, and said, that all our legal and juridical institutions are unjust, since they always fall short of absolute justice, the Διϰή of being. Moreover, every institution we may construct here on earth is already condemned to the "justice" of eventual decay and ruination. Every institution—including all our metaphysically authorized and socially binding meaning-systems. The justice which the seer sees and attempts to make visible is a justice that ultimately must call into question systems of meaning that have become ideologically reified, frozen in time, repressive.

The seer who speaks through the fragment attributed to Anaximander discerns Διϰή (divine justice) in the fact that what comes into being is granted only a certain limited time before it is sentenced to perish. But the seer's vision of divine justice is *itself* a work of justice. There is justice in the seer's eyes in both these senses. The seer discerns Διϰή because the gaze itself *belongs* to divine justice, is rooted in the most radical—the justice of anarchy and the anarchy of justice. Rooted in its recollection of the presencing of being questioned by the history of metaphysics, rooted accordingly in the *Ereignis*, the opening inaugural event in the history of being, the seer's gaze affirms the most radical justice and anarchy—endings and new beginnings—wherever it looks. It foresees and ruins in advance, pronouncing in advance—already—the ruination and end of all finite histories, all finite beginnings. Before the fact, it has already seen the violence (*Gewaltsamkeit*) of divine justice at work and in the name of that justice, it repeats the judgment of Δική, sentencing everything mortals build to an end in the order of time.

We are accustomed to thinking of law as inaugurating the necessary condition of the possibility of justice. But Benjamin suggests that, because of its irremediable violence, law is also the condition that makes of justice an infinite, end-less impossibility. In Heidegger's reading of Anaximander, Δική is an anarchic justice, a justice *before* justice; it is justice as the very de-limitation of the political. In other words, the Δική seen and foreseen by the seer is the anarchic origin of politics, the very deconstruction of its origin—and thus also of its narrative of origin, revealing the order of our political institutions as an order of violence, an order, as Benjamin's "Critique of Violence" argues, that began in violence and that only violence can preserve. But it is only in a vision serving the work of a different kind of memory that this anarchic origin will come to light.

To control the "justice" of time, metaphysics reduces the passage of time to presence and restricts historical memory to the reproduction of the causal continuum. Consequently, its vision of justice is in reality an affirmation of the domination of man by man, offering no hope for real change. Anaximander's vision, or the vision that Heidegger educes from the fragment, sees a *different* justice: not the reification of historical time in presence and domination, but the interruption of the violence in this regime of historical time. The fragment of Anaximander's thought that time has preserved and bequeathed to us is important for Heidegger because, when he reflects on the condition of our present world, what he sees is that we no longer have any sense of our proper limits, our proper place in the cosmological order: we are driven by a will to power that acknowledges no limits, that defies what Anaximander thought of as divine justice. What he sees is a world "out of joint": the tragedy of forgetfulness and the need for a recollection of the radical justice of primordial temporality. For it could only be out of the destructiveness, the abyssal violence of this temporality that another inception, a time of redemptive justice, might reveal its dawning light.

This violence, however, is not the Holocaust in which Jews, gypsies, homosexuals, the physically and mentally disabled, and the deformed were systematically gathered into death camps, tortured, and exterminated.

Unlike many others, Heidegger failed to see the evil in the Nazi movement, failed to foresee where its violent hatreds would end. To the reality of fascism, plainly visible for all to see, Heidegger shut his eyes. He who thought deeply about the vision of the seer, about epochal endings and new beginnings, somehow could not see—or did not want to see—that the brutal fascism to which, at least for a time, he gave his passionate support could only end in an exterminating conflagration. How shall we understand this philosopher's blindness? What good are philosophical meditations on the justice of time's ordinance, meditations on the ontological anarchy that awaits all political orders, when they do not enable the philosopher to see in the Nazi gatherings the triumph of evil?

V. JUSTICE WITHOUT VIOLENCE?

I would agree that we have, as Adorno says, undoubtedly thinking of Benjamin's "Theses," an imperative responsibility to "contemplate all things as they would present themselves from the standpoint of redemption": an obligation to envision—and make visible in a negative dialectic—perspectives "that displace and estrange the world, reveal it to be, with its rifts and crevices, as indigent and distorted as it will appear one day in the messianic light."[128] But will we, can we, know the difference between messianic visions of justice and the false visions against which Benjamin warns us—the visions, namely, of "seers whose visions appear to them over corpses"?[129]

Heidegger refuses to exclude absence from the realm of what is recognized and seen as present (AX 37, H 323). This may be read as an implicit call for justice. But he nevertheless questions the standard way of interpreting and translating Anaximander's word, τίσις, arguing that

> we usually translate τίσις by "penalty". This leads us to translate διδόναι as "to pay". Whatever lingers awhile in presence pays penalty; it expends this as its punishment (δική).

And then he remarks, assuming first an ironic tone, then a more serious tone:

> The court of justice [*Der Gerichtshof*] is complete. It lacks nothing, not even injustice—though of course no one rightly knows what might constitute injustice. (AX 45, H 330)

If one juxtaposes Benjamin's sentence about the seer's prophetic vision of the "criminal courts of justice," quoted at the beginning of our reflections on his thought, and these last two sentences of Heidegger, where he turns his gaze from Δική, the radical dimension of justice and injustice, to the courts of justice in our world, a certain provocative and intriguing *entre-choc* might be said to occur. Yet, in the end, both want to call into question not only the conventional institutions of justice, problematizing the claims of those who believe that they know very well what justice and injustice are, but also all the utopian visions of justice that have been handed down by the philosophers in useless and dangerous enthusiasms.

Of course, it must be noted that Δικη, the ontological dimension of justice, is indifferent to our distinctions between good and evil, better and worse institutions. Thus there is a certain truth in Benjamin's claim that Heidegger's phenomenology ends in an evil abstractness remote from the struggles of the oppressed, the victims of history. But I have tried to show that the perspective constituted by this ontological justice encourages the critical examination of our institutions and reveals them, in the light of their "natural history," to be mere constructions of sand. This unconcealment is not inconsequential: it denies our institutions their fateful necessity, submitting them to a condition of radical alterity.

Speaking of the confusion that has accompanied the oblivion of being, Heidegger asks: "What mortal can fathom the abyss [*Abgrund*] of this confusion?" And he follows this question with an apocalyptic warning reminiscent of Nietzsche:

> We may try to shut our eyes before this abyss. We may entertain one delusion after another. The abyss does not vanish. (AX 57, H 343)

For Heidegger, then, our institutions of justice must be held in suspense over the abyss—and the greatest danger comes from forgetting the radical anarchy, the more radical justice, that must be allowed to pass sentence on them from out of its reserve. Just as truth as correctness is "grounded" in the deconstructive, totality-defying anarchy of ἀλήθεια, ensuring that all claims to know the truth will remain an open question, so are all our moral-juridical institutions of justice "grounded" in the groundlessness, the anarchy of Δικη, the deconstructive justice of time, which destines all that comes into being to a time of perishing and calls into question thereby the nature of our claims to realize the imperatives of justice.

But it is when our eyes turn back to the immediate injustices of the world, after gazing into the fragments of Western civilization, looking for the revealing traces that might spell a secret of hope for the coming of a redeeming justice; or when our eyes turn back to the world after a "moment of vision" that has already seen the ruin of all political institutions spelled out in the Δικη of time's ordinance, already seen the fate reserved in presencing for all that presences—it is when our eyes turn back to "what is," to the world and its history of suffering, that the extreme difference between Heidegger and Benjamin is most pronounced. When it comes to the political meaning of the justice their respective gazes would make visible, there is ultimately no way that I can see to mediate and reconcile their visions. Both philosophers attempted to think, and themselves see with, a vision released from the historical time and memory of a metaphysics complicitous in the repetitions of violence that rage within the social world. And yet, as Caygill has argued with compelling logic, despite the abstractness that sometimes weakens Benjamin's own dialectical perspectives, it would be difficult to deny that his constellations of memory-images are "awakening" and "motivating" in a way that Heidegger's attempts at a visionary recollection which would release us from the spell of our captivity in the present have neither conceived nor desired.

It is Adorno's conviction that "to gain such perspectives without velleity or violence, entirely from felt contact with its objects . . . is alone the task of thought."[130] It may be easy to concur with this suggestion. But will we ever learn to see justice purely, as what Benjamin once wanted to call pure mediacy—without violence?

Even if we hold, with Heidegger, that Δικἠ is the ontically indifferent justice of time, a justice always untimely, always out of order, and irrevocably denying to all our institutions the justification and authority of an ultimate grounding, a perfect justice; even if we hold, with Benjamin, that the only true justice is "divine" justice, the endless, endlessly deferred intervention of messianic judgment, there is nevertheless an urgent question that it remains for us to answer here and now: what is our own responsibility for the dispensation of justice right now, while we are waiting to see the passing of its eternal sentence, the evidence of its incorruptible, transcendent jurisdiction?

One can imagine Benjamin taking up this question by returning to Anaximander's words and finding in them, as Heidegger did, the first moment of an extremely difficult meditation on justice—a moment of thought described with exquisite precision by Novalis, Friedrich von Hardenberg, when he wrote, in *Heinrich von Ofterdingen*, that

> *das Chaos muß in jeder Dichtung durch den regelmäßigen Flor der Ordnung schimmern* [in each poetic statement, chaos must shimmer through the veil of regular order].[131]

Doesn't the chaos of an impossible, but absolutely imperative sentence of justice persistently shimmer through the words of Anaximander's saying? But the question that puts us in question returns, returning again and again, for the justice of fate can never abrogate or efface the justice of our responsibility. At stake is our responsibility, as Heidegger and Benjamin understood, for a justice no longer hostage to the serial orders of time and history that have served relations of domination among beings: a justice which can only belong to messianic time. At stake, then, is the possibility of our return to the paradoxical experience of an originary temporality outside conventional time, other than eschatological time, gathering before the gaze its barely visible indications, its oldest promise, of a justice so long denied—the justice of a past that has never been present, a future that has already happened, a present always still to come. This is what we need somehow to see. Justice for the other in the ruins of domination. Justice for the other in the ruins of revenge. Untimely justice. Right now!

For there is no Enlightenment other than the one [still] to
be thought.

Jacques Derrida, *Politics of Friendship*

The Vanity of Compassion

How can one still have ideals when there are so many blind, deaf, and mad people in the world? How can I without remorse enjoy the light another cannot see or the sound another cannot hear? I feel like a thief of light. Have we not stolen light from the blind and sound from the deaf? Isn't our very lucidity responsible for the madman's darkness?

Emil Cioran, On the Heights of Despair

9 Shadows
Reflections on the Enlightenment and Modernity

The human gaze has a power of conferring value on things; but it makes them cost more too.

> Ludwig Wittgenstein, *Culture and Value*[1]

Yet no truer image of hope can be imagined than that of ciphers, readable as traces, dissolving in history, disappearing in front of overflowing eyes, indeed confirmed in lamentation. In these tears of despair the ciphers appear as incandescent figures, dialectically, as compassion, comfort, and hope.

> Theodor Adorno, *Kierkegaard: Construction of the Aesthetic*[2]

PRELUDE I. CRUDE FOYER

Over the centuries, many philosophers, from Plato to the men of the Enlightenment, have offered the world their great visions promising eternal happiness. In "Crude Foyer," Wallace Stevens questions the truth in these visions.[3] But, since there is always more to a poem than the prose of reason can possibly articulate, it is necessary to read the poet's own words:

Thought is false happiness: the idea
That merely by thinking one can,
Or may, penetrate, not may,
But can, that one is sure to be able—

That there lies at the end of thought
A foyer of the spirit in a landscape
Of the mind, in which we sit
And wear humanity's bleak crown;

In which we read the critique of paradise
And say it is the work
Of a comedian, this critique;
In which we sit and breathe

An innocence of an absolute,
False happiness, since we know that we use
Only the eye as faculty, that the mind
Is the eye, and that this landscape of the mind

Is a landscape only of the eyes; and that
We are ignorant men incapable
Of the least, minor, vital metaphor, content,
At last, there, when it turns out to be here.

I read this as a poem in which the *promesse de bonheur* represented by the great utopian visions of the philosophers—those, anyway, who, like Plato, like Augustine, like Kant, would posit in thought a paradise purely of the spirit, purified somehow of everything material, sensuous, aesthetic—is declared to be a "false happiness." And not only that, but also a trompe l'oeil perpetrated by the philosophical intellect, which would like to forget, to deny its "crude" origins, and trick the eye into accepting its pale mental substitute. Defending a worldliness that many philosophers have considered illusory, Stevens observes that more ordinary people would be quite content with a little more dream-fulfillment nowhere but here. The poem is thus a celebration of the possibilities for an earthly vision of happiness, a gentle reminder that the realization of the Enlightenment vision of a lucid reason cannot overlook the sensuous eye that alone can make it possible.

Although Stevens does not touch, here, on the darker dimensions of the false vision, I want to argue that, in what the poet calls the "landscape of the mind," there is an ideal of reason which has sacrificed all that is human. The enlightened happiness that is promised in the name of the spirit can all too easily turn out—as we only now, perhaps, can agree—to be not only an instrument of freedom, but also an instrument of our oppression. What kind of vision of happiness is it that would suppress the eye, requiring the renunciation of its sensuous materiality, its natural pleasures, and its image-making powers?

"Thoughts are the shadows of our sensations," said Nietzsche, "always darker, emptier, simpler than they."[4] Philosophers who would banish shadows from the very definition of their utopia, who would refuse to admit them into the foyer of their mind, must also look upon all forms of play with disapproving eyes, unable to enjoy even the most innocent transactions of metaphor. The poet must write in defense of shadows, challenging the life-denying visions of such philosophers, for in the very being of the shadow, the poetic eye will always recognize the aesthetic play of metaphor—and the sublime freedom of the imagination.

PRELUDE II. CITY LIGHTS

Dieu avait trop puissament vécu parmi nous. Nous ne savions plus
nous lever et partir. Les étoiles sont mortes dans nos yeux, qui
furent souveraines dans son regard.

René Char, "Pour un Prométhée Saxifrage:
En Touchant la Main éolienne de Hölderlin"[5]

In "Types of Lighting," Walter Benjamin calls attention to the fact that,
soon after the invention of electricity, there were numerous projects for city
lighting based on the eighteenth-century "idea of universal illumination";
and he recalls how, as early as 1836, Jacques Fabien warned against the effects of an "overabundance of light."[6] Needless to say, this warning has
been completely ignored. Our cities, today, are flooded by the lights of artificially produced electricity.

In the *Critique of Practical Reason,* there is a passage where, in the most
moving words, Immanuel Kant, the philosopher most identified with the
idea of universal enlightenment, interrupts an extremely abstract, theoretical, impersonal discourse to tell us of his own experience:

> Two things fill the mind with ever new and increasing admiration and
> awe, the oftener and more steadily we reflect on them: the starry heav-
> ens above me and the moral law within me. I do not merely conjecture
> them and seek them as though obscured in darkness or in the transcen-
> dent region beyond my horizon: I see them before me, and I associate
> them directly with the consciousness of my own existence.[7]

Today, however, as more and more people crowd into the cities, the conditions of possibility for this moral experience are vanishing. Bright, artificial lights deny to the populations of the modern city the awesome sight
of the starry skies. Dazzling city lights make it virtually impossible for
city residents to experience themselves, their lives, their world, in relation to the infinitely vast dimensions of the night's sky. What modern
city residents lose, what they are deprived of, is the Pascalian experience,
which Kant also knew. Filled with fear and trembling as he gazed up into
the dark and silent heavens, Pascal wrote: "Les espaces infinies m'ef-
fraient."[8] The loss of this perspective on human life—the perspective, so
to speak, of the immeasurable, of eternity and infinity—means the loss of
anything transcendent by which to take the measure of our lives. "Man"
finally becomes the only measure. This disconnection from a measure
that would require us to go out of ourselves and judge our lives from the
standpoint of eternity, the standpoint of universality, has brought about, I
believe, untold consequences for our moral life. Living out our lives

within a space that city lights enclose, we are left without the moral compass in nature's ciphers.

I take the star-concealing brightness of our city lights today as an indication of our historical distance from Kant's time—and as a factor contributing to our moral confusion. Is there a connection—an essential connection—between the human experience of moral law and the visibility of sky and horizon? Must we first be denied an experience of the stars in the night sky in order to realize, belatedly, the significance of the connection that Kant, though unable to foresee future implications, thinks it important to make and make known? Reflecting on Kant's text, Georg Lukács commented that "Kant's starry firmament now shines only in the dark night of pure cognition."[9]

In the political economy of late capitalism, the stars of the night sky have been pulled down to earth, reduced to shining in the artificial lights of the city and in the wealth of new merchandise on display in shop windows, carefully laid out to bedazzle and enchant the eyes of every passerby. Showing off their glittering surfaces, these commodities—our new stars, the only stars that can still be seen—cast a powerful spell over the city and alter even the most resistant consciousness, reversing the sense of what really matters, what is truly valuable, turning what is less into more, what is more into less. One's eye for the moral law is not merely bedazzled—it will often be rendered blind, capable of seeing only the idols of a market economy. For the eyes of a human being, this spiritual blindness is an infinitely worse fate than their merely physical disability.

In *City Lights*, Charlie Chaplin, appearing as a tramp in the writing of light on the silver screen, gives his life savings to a blind flower girl, so that she can undergo the surgery that will restore her sight. After the successful operation, with her sight regained, she returns to her flowers and sees the tramp. Not realizing at first sight that this is the man who sacrificed his own dreams for the future to give her the gift of vision, her eyes visibly express the conventional attitude towards tramps: a feeling of pity that is genuine, but mixed with judgment, and perhaps also a sense of moral superiority. But when, as she gives him a coin, their hands touch, she recognizes him at once as the man who made possible the restoration of her sight. Her mysterious benefactor is not a rich man, as she thought, but a tramp! And now, as they exchange gazes, her eyes are opened in a different way—opened by the sight, the revelation, of human kindness and unselfish generosity; opened by the moral height and dignity of a man whom the dominant class of people, morally blinded, can see only as a worthless tramp.

In a note for his Arcades Project, Benjamin wrote: "As long as there is even one beggar, just that long will there still be myth."[10] One might also say that, as long as there is even one beggar, the shadows that follow us as our double will speak in the haunting language of conscience of the presence of an other—an other who is in another sense our double—denied the justice of recognition.

THOUGHT WITHOUT SHADOWS: PLATO AND DESCARTES

To him who looks at the world rationally, the world looks rational in return.

> G. W. F. Hegel, *Introduction to the Philosophy of History*[11]

Ils prennent pour de la clarté le rire des ténèbres.

> René Char, "Mirage des Aiguilles"[12]

In Book V of Plato's *Republic*, Glaucon asks Socrates: "Who then are the true philosophers?" And Socrates replies: "Those who are lovers of the vision of truth."[13] Later on, Socrates tells Adeimantus about the disciplined character of the philosopher's gaze: "For he, Adeimantus, whose mind is fixed upon true being has surely no time to look down upon the affairs of earth, or to be filled with malice and envy, contending against men; his eye is ever directed toward things fixed and immutable."[14] In Book VII, Socrates tells a story, the "allegory of the cave," inviting Glaucon to imagine a society of people living since their childhood in a huge cave. According to Socrates, the people in this cave are chained by leg and neck, so that they cannot move and can see only what is in front of them. At some distance higher up is the light of a fire burning behind them; and between the fire and the prisoners—therefore behind them—there is a track with a parapet built along it, like the screen of a puppet show, which hides the performers while they show their puppets over the top. And behind the parapet, we are to imagine persons carrying various artificial objects which project over the parapet. Because of their chains, the prisoners would not be able to see any of these objects; but they would see the shadows of these things constantly thrown by the firelight on the wall of the cave facing them.

For Plato, this allegory describes the human condition, the condition of "the many," prisoners of their own ignorance, happily embracing the illusions of this state. All they can see are the shadows cast on the wall of the cave. For Plato, shadows belong to the world of illusion; they have no reality, no truth; and they therefore can yield no knowledge. The task of the philosopher must accordingly be to liberate these people from their cognitive confusion, making them see through the shadows to which they are attached and teaching them to desire true knowledge—knowledge of the Good.[15] But such knowledge requires turning the eyes toward that which shines most brightly. And eyes accustomed to the darkness of the cave would at first be so blinded by this brightness that they could catch a glimpse of the Good only in between their blinking. For most people, the light of the Good is unbearable; living in the dark, living in the midst of shadows and reflections is much easier. Only those destined to serve as philosophers have the strength of character to live in the light of the Good and in accordance with its guidance.

This brings us to a crucial moment in the telling of the allegory—a moment that commentators overlook—which concerns the responsibility of those who have succeeded in leaving the cave. According to Plato, those who have seen the light of the Good must return to the lower world: they must descend into the darkness of the cave to help others liberate themselves from ignorance and deception. However, in order for the philosopher to accomplish this task, he must be able to see in the dark. But why does Plato leave this unsaid? Was he perhaps afraid of the challenges to his way of thinking that the capacity to see in the dark would entail?

But if we no longer believe that there is a supersensible realm, a realm of ideal Forms more real than the world in which we go about our daily lives, we need to take another look at shadows. To be sure, the shadows of things are not the things themselves: shadows can never be satisfactory substitutes for the things that cast them. And yet, in the world of our perception, only things that are real cast shadows. What is without a shadow is without reality. And, whereas for Plato, shadows can never be objects of knowledge, nor can they ever lead us in the direction of knowledge, the phenomenology of perception, giving the gift of thought to the presence of the shadow, reveals the crucial role that shadows play in the acquisition of knowledge and the determination of our sense of reality.

The shadow that a thing casts is an essential factor in our taking the reality of that thing for granted. Moreover, once we understand the way shadows appear—understand the logic of their relation to the things that cast them—we see that they can provide reliable information about the things to which they are related. The shadow on the sundial tells us the time of day. From the shadow of the tree, we can tell that there is an oak, not a maple, nearby. Shadows fore-shadow knowledge, fore-shadow the possible visibility of whatever beings cast them. Before I see my friend, I see approaching me the shadow of a profile, a silhouette, that I immediately recognize as that of my friend. What would our world be like without shadows? We cannot even imagine it. But, even if we could, might we not feel that such a world would be that much poorer, bereft of the playful presence of shadows? Would we not feel the absence of the shadow that so often accompanies us on our passage through life as a certain quite immeasurable loss?

Plato's aversion to shadows figures centuries later in Christian theology—for example, in the way that St. Augustine thinks of the perfection of vision. Thus, in *De Trinitate* IX, he wrote:

> But we gaze upon the indestructible truth by reason of which we may
> define what the mind of man should be according to the eternal reason.

To be sure, Augustine does not explicitly refer to shadows. But it cannot be denied that in this conception, there is no receptive space for the play and work of shadows—no tolerance for, and certainly no pleasure in, the presence of shadows. It is not until Nietzsche that the presence of shadows, adumbrations, and foreshadowings will be received with an appropriate regard for the subversive truth they announce.

Descartes, writing at the beginning of the modern age, had no use for shadows. For him, the task of philosophy must be to establish a foundation for the building of our knowledge in an immediate, intuitive lucidity and absolutely unquestionable certainty. Shadows may not be avoidable in the real world; but they can have no place in the realm of clear and distinct ideas, the realm where knowledge of truth is to be possessed. When Descartes puts into effect his *epokhé*, suspending belief in the external world of the senses, shadows are put out of play, denied any role in the achievement of knowledge and the determination of truth. Nor is there any admission of shades of meaning, those purely intellectual versions of the shadow. The Cartesian method requires clear and distinct meanings, meanings without ambiguities, absolutely transparent. Such meanings, of course, must be contained in the chambers of the mind, because, as soon as they are expressed—inscribed, for example, on paper, they must forfeit their absolute determinacy, their immutability, their clarity and distinctness. The written word, the idea turned into configurations of black ink on white paper, is nothing, after all, but a shadow of the idea—its history traced on the surface of paper. Like the shadow, the words Descartes writes are, as words, two-dimensional, mere surface phenomena without material depth, without thickness. And, like shadows, his written words are subject to vicissitudes of interpretation, to confusions and misunderstandings, although he remained steadfast in believing that the "pure" cognitive meaning, completely formed by the internal operations of the mind, will be exempt from

all deformative alterations at least while it stays within the controlled totality, the inner space, of the mind. But as soon as the *cogito* writes, its
meaning is hopelessly lost in the shadows.

Perhaps one of the reasons for the contemporary attraction to shadows
is that, unlike Descartes and more like Montaigne, we no longer feel a need
for absolute certainty, and therefore do not need to defend our thought by
insisting on the ideal of totality, systematic closure. And perhaps there is
another reason of equal importance, a reason intricately connected, moreover, with the first: no longer under the influence of religious asceticism
and a theological dualism that regards the flesh as the mortal enemy of the
spirit, we no longer look upon the senses, the medium of the flesh, with con-
tempt and distrust.

At the end of the twentieth century, the end of the millennium, we look
for enlightenment even in the shadows. Perhaps because we are able to see
in them, and in their passing, a certain beauty and value; also, I think, because we can now recognize and tolerate—even, perhaps, enjoy—the role
of shadows in the very structure of knowledge. I think we know, now, that
we can *learn* from shadows. Thought without shadows cannot touch our
world. Nor can it be touched by it. We have finally cast metaphysics into
the shadows, letting their play double—and double-cross—the substantial,
essentialized identities of our cultural order that metaphysics was committed to defending.

It was as a lover of shadows, of their endlessly surprising poetry, that
René Char once wrote:

à voir de proche en proche une ombre mettre au monde une ombre par
le biais d'un trait lumineux, et à la scruter.[16]

ENLIGHTENMENT IN THE SHADOWS OF MODERNITY

The eclipse, the pessimistic coloring, comes necessarily in the wake
of the Enlightenment.

Friedrich Nietzsche, *The Will to Power*[17]

The brooding thinker [*Der Grübler*], whose glance, startled
[*aufgeschreckt*], falls on the fragments in his hands, becomes a
writer of allegories.

Walter Benjamin, *Zentralpark*[18]

For the philosophers of the Age of Enlightenment, the light of nature shines
most brightly in the theoretical activity of the intellect: it is in human reason that the light of nature finally attains its fulfillment. Reason is called a
natural light. This expresses the fact that, for the philosophers, nature was

to be seen as essentially rational, and Reason was to be exercised as the highest formation of nature, justified accordingly in its visions of domination, imposing its conception of order on a nature eternally mute.

But that was in the early days of modernity. Today, after Auschwitz, those visions of Reason awake have produced monsters far worse than the ones produced whilst Reason was sunk in sleep. Our modernity comes in the wake of the Enlightenment: it is a form of consciousness, a reflexivity, that finds itself awakening amidst the dark shadows that were cast by an Age of Reason which ended, not in a beautiful utopia, but in the horrors of an instrumental rationality gone mad. Thus we see that, in the unfolding story of modernity, dark shadows finally begin to appear, crisscrossing the pages of history and double-crossing the powerful light of Reason that for a time brought forth some glorious moral, political, and cultural changes. Like the very shadows it once banished from view, the Enlightenment itself now can seem a terrible shadow over the world it created, haunting a modernity that has been forced to confront the insanity and brutality of a technologized, totalizing Reason and has lost its faith in the power of Reason alone to illuminate the Right and the Good. Enlightenment must now be found concealed in the splinters of remaining light, in the ghostly shadows: for the philosopher thinking after metaphysics, there is at least as much to be learned from the presence of shadows as there is from the presence of light.

MODERNITY IN THE SHADOWS OF THE ENLIGHTENMENT

> . . . light for shade, shade for light . . .
> Walter Benjamin,
> *Gesammelte Schriften*[19]

Our modernity looks into the shadows that the Enlightenment overlooked. Judged from the perspective of the Enlightenment, with all its certainties, its self-confidence, its faith in the progressive triumph of Reason, our moment in the continuing unfolding of modernity can sometimes look like a time of terrible confusion, bewilderment, and blind errancy. Are we of today lost in the shadows? What is correct in the judgment made from the Enlightenment perspective is that we are engaged in defining who we are by looking into the shadows of the Enlightenment, working through the darker implications of the Enlightenment vision. This vision has caused suffering in three different ways, namely: because in many respects the normative imperatives of Enlightenment Reason are still far from being fully realized; because, in spite of noble intentions, it has sometimes been wrongly interpreted and actualized; and finally, because it has been knowingly betrayed and misused by those with evil intentions. Whereas the philosophers of the Enlightenment could see only simplicity, unity, clarity, and systematic totality; whereas they could assume complete control over meaning, and hence totally determinate, totally transparent meaning; whereas they could confidently ignore adumbrations of the marginal, the peripheral, and the implicit, we of today are obliged to give a more critical thought to these assumptions, cannot ignore intricacies, complexities, ambiguities, conflicts of interpretation, the breaches and caesurae in supposedly closed systems, and cannot overlook what philosophers of earlier times could comfortably overlook. We of today, heirs responsible for the present future of the Enlightenment project, are obliged to be allegorical thinkers, finding adumbrations of our destined roles among its cast of shadows.

Shadows: at once something and nothing, the very marks of negation traversing the force-fields of perception, negated by a metaphysics that refuses to acknowledge in its empire a negation of the nothingness which haunts its assumption of lucidity and the world it claims to illuminate; crossing and double-crossing the things of the world, touching their surfaces without leaving so much as a trace of their brief passage, but nevertheless assigning to the things the fate that conquers all materiality; following us insistently into the strongest light, precisely there where we would most have hoped to abolish all signs of our fallibility, our finitude, our struggle with mortality. As long as there is metaphysics, the play of shadows, inscriptions of difference, will haunt its violent rule, casting doubt on the substantiality of its "substances," mocking its belief in a realm of ontotheological transcendence, a ghostly reminder of the death that awaits us—and an early hint of the death of a metaphysics in which and from which we have for too long sought in vain an impossible, final Enlightenment.

METAPHYSICAL TOTALITIES AND TOTALITARIAN POLITICS

Nous ne pouvons vivre que dans l'entrouvert, exactement sur la ligne hermétique de partage de l'ombre et de la lumière.

René Char, "Dans la Marche"[20]

To train our image-making faculty to look stereoscopically and dimensionally into the depths of the shadows of history.

Rudolf Borchardt,
"Epilegomena zu Dante"[21]

The philosopher sits writing at her desk, bent over the white paper. Coming from behind her, the lighting is interrupted, bent by her hand. The gesture of writing, inscribing words in black ink, thus becomes, at the same time, the inscription of a shadow, temporarily obscuring some of the words. Unlike the metaphysicians of the past, this philosopher chases after the shadow, remarking an influence, a condition, that casts doubt on all metaphysical pretensions. Without substantial identity, inherently allegorical since it is not (quite) itself, but always of an other, the shadow mocks the very logic of identity, forever making a difference without leaving a trace of its presence. Shadows remark a presence that is always already an absence, an absence that is always already a presence. And wherever they figure, they cast a magic spell: without the attributes of objectivity, shadows have great power over the objects of our world: in an instant of caprice free of strife, they can suddenly return objects to the vicissitudes of concealment. Thus it might be said that, being one of the ways in which one thing hides another, shadows instance for our perception the ἀδικία, the "injustice" of which Anaximander speaks in the only fragment of philosophical writing that we may attribute to him. But it might also be said that, because of their peculiar dialectical negativity, shadows also foreshadow the visible inscription that would announce the coming of justice.

With the recognition of shadows, with their inclusion in the field of vision laid down by the discourse of metaphysics, the complicity of the philosophical gaze in totalitarian politics would at long last be silently contested. Inscribing traces of absence into the very weave of the metaphysical text, obscuring its claims to a perfect lucidity, shadows breach the laws of the system, which always assumes its achievement of absolute totality. In a philosophical discourse crisscrossed by shadows, hospitable to multiple shades of meaning, to mere adumbrations of thought, it would not be quite so easy to argue for a totalitarian politics.

There is a certain affinity between shadows and ashes. Like ashes, shadows are traces that can speak of evil—but also of the precariousness, the contingency, the fatal hidden doubt, of all our hopes. Philosophers with total visions of hope must be careful: those who avoid or deny the tracework presence of shadows are likely to end up, in Benjamin's words, as "seers whose visions appear over dead bodies," forever haunted by shadows that will relentlessly pursue them—shadows cast in ghostly forms from the realm of death.[22] On friendly terms with death, indeed its messengers, shadows silently move through the world, touching things lightly and without violence—as if to remind us that accounts are due in the time of justice.

10 Where the Beauty of Truth Lies

The perception of beauty is a moral test.
  Henry David Thoreau, *Journals*[1]

I

In ancient Greece, truth was not only a property of statements; it could also be attributed to the world of perception. With the beginning of modernity, there was a momentous change in the logic of truth: the site of truth was reduced to the constative sentence or proposition. Truth could lie only in the sentence or proposition. But in this conception, the beauty of truth is absent: it vanishes virtually without a trace. What if this modern turn is reversed? What if we could return to a conception of truth that would make it possible for us to see and think, once again, the beauty of truth? Could truth also lie, once again, in the realm of perception—in the care of those perceptions to which the beauty of things entrusted their revelation? Would not the beauty of truth be made visible thereby? And would not the truth about a thing lay claim to the visible in and as the most beautiful appearance of the thing in question?

I would like to give thought, here, to the relationship between truth and beauty.[2] In particular, what will concern us is the way that this relationship engages our vision in the interplay between the visible and the invisible. The immediate provocation will be a poem by Wallace Stevens in which the poet gives thought to this relationship.[3] In question are two irreconcilably opposed theories of the truth, theories that I suggest it might be useful to think of as Platonism and Nietzschean perspectivism; two correspondingly opposed philosophies concerning mind and reality, which we might in all brevity call idealism and realism; and, with the same oppositional symmetry, two conceptions of the site of the beautiful, the one seeing it shining in the supersensuous, the other seeing it in

419

the marvelous transformations of the sensuous. The poem bears the title "On the Road Home":

> It was when I said,
> "There is no such thing as the truth,"
> That the grapes seemed fatter.
> The fox ran out of his hole.
>
> You . . . You said,
> "There are many truths,
> But they are not parts of a truth."
> Then the tree, at night, began to change,
>
> Smoking through green and smoking blue.
> We were two figures in a wood.
> We said we stood alone.
>
> It was when I said,
> "Words are not forms of a single word.
> In the sum of the parts, there are only the parts.
> The world must be measured by eye";
>
> It was when you said,
> "The idols have seen lots of poverty,
> Snakes and gold and lice,
> But not the truth";
>
> It was at that time, that the silence was largest
> And longest, the night was roundest,
> The fragrance of the autumn warmest,
> Closest and strongest.

II

As many philosophers have noted, in the German language, the word *Schein* bears three distinct meanings:

(i) shining, radiance, luminosity
(ii) manifesting, phenomenal appearing, showing itself, coming to light
(iii) illusion, deception, semblance, "mere" appearance

In the Greek language of Plato's thought, the first two meanings were bound together by their etymology. But Plato's metaphysics, drawing a line of irreconcilable separation between the reality of a higher realm of pure Ideas and the illusoriness of a lower realm consisting of sensuous appearances, exhibits a logic that he saw connecting inextricably all three of these seemingly unconnected meanings.

In *The Republic* (475), Glaucon asks who the true philosophers are. And Socrates replies that true philosophers are lovers of the vision of truth.[4] Unlike ordinary people, the philosopher keeps his eye ever directed toward things fixed and immutable[5] (500). But what is this "eye"? For Plato, it is not the physical eye, but the eye of the soul, the eye of reason and intellect. In order for the soul or intellect to "see" the truth, it must in fact renounce and abandon the use of sight and the other senses[6] (537). Even so, Plato maintains that the soul is *like* the eye: "when resting upon that on which truth and beauty shine, the soul perceives and understands, and is radiant with intelligence; but when turned toward the twilight of becoming and perishing, then she has opinion only, and goes blinking about . . . "[7] (508). In order to see the truth—or see the essential beauty of truth, the vision of mortals must turn away from objects of earthly beauty; it must become a "science" of ideal forms[8] (532, 537). It must, as it were, look away from the things here on earth, gazing upwards, ascending an ontological hierarchy to behold the nonsensuous, supersensible truth, the Ideas that, being unchanging and eternal, forever stand above, and are thus "higher" than, the sensuous appearances.

In the *Symposium*,[9] Socrates describes the dialectical moments of this process, calling it love. Love is the vehicle whereby the initial attraction to sensuous beauty, the initial seduction, is transformed into a purely intellectual vision and knowledge of the essence of beauty as such. Although it is a sensuous love that sets this dialectic in motion, the beauty that seduces this love and draws it into its spell awakens a higher love in the "recollection" of the infinitely more truthful beauty of the Idea. In the *Phaedrus,* a dialogue that is also concerned with love, Socrates explains at length how, through "recollection," this transformation or sublimation takes place: the attraction to sensuous beauty becomes the occasion for an awakening of the soul's longing for a lost vision of beauty; and this awakening brings about a recollection of the "true beauty" it saw and knew, once upon a time, before being entombed in a material body[10] (249–50).

For Plato, there is beauty in that which shines: radiance is beautiful; and the beautiful always shines, always scintillates. But what is most beautiful, for him, is the truth. Thus, the beauty of truth lies in its shining: shining in a dazzling radiance is how truth in its beauty appears. But if truth cannot be seen by the physical eye, then neither can the beauty of its shining. The beauty of its shining must be a purely intellectual beauty, a beauty visible, visible as intelligible, only to the soul; it must be absolutely separated from the realm of the sensuous. For Plato, the visible beauty of that which shines in the realm of the sensuous can only be a deceptive beauty and an illusory truth. There is nothing on earth that can compare with the incomparable beauty, the most radiant appearing, τò ἐϰφανέστατον, of the truth of the forms, the eternal and immutable Ideas visible only to the theoretical vision of the rational soul. In Plato's thought, the beauty of truth shines only in the realm of the supersensible. The truth of beauty—its radiant shining—is visible only for a soul which has ascended to this realm.

III

In his "Epistemo-Critical Prologue" to *Ursprung des deutschen Trauerspiels*, Benjamin takes up the question of truth and beauty in Plato's *Symposium*. As he notes, for Plato, truth, the realm of Ideas, is the essential content of beauty: truth is not only thought beautiful; it is the most beautiful, exceeding nothing in its beauty. Benjamin argues, therefore, that, "if truth is described as beautiful, this must be understood in the context of the *Symposium* with its description of the stages of erotic desire."[11] And he points out that the beauty of truth in question in that dialogue is not so much beautiful in itself, as it is for Eros. "Likewise," he says, for truth: "it is not so much beautiful in itself, as for whomsoever seeks it" (ibid.). Although this might seem to imply that beauty must be subject to a certain relativism, Benjamin tells a story in order to suggest that beauty can take refuge in truth—in the "representational impulse" in truth—because "the assertion of the beauty of truth can never be devalued" (ibid.). Within the "preserve" of truth (Heidegger would speak here of *die Wahr* and *die Wahrnis*), beauty can be saved—but only as long as it is truthful, faithful to the truth that lies within its shining.[12] This is the price it must pay. But what is it for beauty to be truthful, faithful to its truth? Benjamin says:

> This representational impulse in truth is the refuge of beauty as such, for beauty remains brilliant and palpable as long as it freely admits to being so. (Ibid.)

Eros, he says, will follow beauty in its flight, its innocent withdrawal into the preserve of truth—but "only as its lover, not as its pursuer."[13] Despite the devoted attentions of Eros, however, beauty will not easily give itself to the lover—favoring the lover only a little more than the intellect, which despite its better judgment is attracted by the brilliance and cannot resist pursuing it: "for the sake of its outward appearance, beauty will always flee: in dread before the intellect, in fear before the lover" (ibid.). It is at this point in his narrative that Benjamin makes his most important argument, intimating that it may be only in the beauty of truth, only in and as the beautiful, that truth is a revelation that does not destroy the secret:

> only the latter [the lover] can bear witness to the fact that truth is not a process of exposure [*Enthüllung*] which destroys the secret, but a revelation [*Offenbarung*] which does justice to it. (Ibid.)

And then he asks the crucial question, "the innermost question of the *Symposium*": "But can truth do justice to beauty?"

Plato's answer, he says, is to make beauty the preserve of truth. Truth, accordingly, becomes the import or content of beauty: *das Gehalt des Schönen.* But how is this import, this content, to be seen? Benjamin's answer is that

> [it] does not appear by being exposed; rather it is revealed in a process which might be described metaphorically as the burning up of the husk [*Hülle*] as it enters the realm of ideas, that is to say, as a destruction of the work in which its external form achieves its most brilliant degree of illumination [*Leuchtkraft*]. (Ibid.)

In other words, the truth (the essential truth-content) of beauty is revealed when the beauty of truth—its work, its "salvation of phenomena in the realm of ideas"—is revealed.[14] Benjamin's thought, here, is intricately enigmatic. It may at least be assumed, however, that he does not mean to agree with Plato's metaphysical dualism. Sensuous beauty flees from the intellect because the intellect, caring only for the knowledge, would deny it, would will its destruction. But it also flees from the lover because the lover, caring only for its own immediate satisfaction, would try to possess it, to master it. In the end, the lover, too, would only destroy it. So Benjamin's thinking, here, is an attempt to rescue the radiant appearing of beauty from its degradation in systems of knowledge—but only by showing how its secret essence, beyond the grasp of ordinary knowledge, is revealed precisely at the moment when it is—or appears to be—sacrificed for the sake of a supersensuous and invisible truth. The truth of sensuous beauty appears in all its radiance, and is most visible, at the very moment when sensuous beauty effaces itself, destroys itself, revealing the truth-content that it sheltered and defended from the possessive claims of knowledge within the sensuous realm. In the very moment of its self-destruction, its self-effacement for the sake of what was thought to be the beauty of a supersensible truth—in that very moment, the sensuous "husk" of appearances, which in Platonism is thought to be protecting and preserving this supersensible truth, becomes a dazzling blaze of fire, revealing for a luminous knowledge the marvelous truth of beauty—the beauty of a truth that is truly nothing other than its most radiant sensuous appearances. If the beauty of radiance is the "evidence" of truth, then the truth of Platonism will have been visibly displaced: no longer will it lie in the supersensuous, but henceforth it will lie without degradation solely in the realm of sensuous appearances.

In "Credences of Summer," Wallace Stevens invokes the fire of sight, a fire that reduces to ashes all but the thing in the truth and beauty of its sensuous presence; invokes the truth of the most demanding beauty in a revelation of fire that spares—for such is its justice—only that which is absolutely essential: the thing to be seen in the uncanny presence of its thingliness.[15] Stevens says:

> Let's see the very thing and nothing else.
> Let's see it with the hottest fire of sight.
> Burn everything not part of it to ash.

IV

In order to begin his discussion of Nietzsche's attempt, in "The Will to Power as Art," at a final "twisting free" (*Herausdrehung*) of Platonism, Heidegger first returns to Plato, whose hierarchy of the sensuous and the supersensuous, subordinating the sensuous to the purely rational, Nietzsche wants to overturn and abolish. Heidegger's reading of Plato, and in particular, Plato's *Phaedrus,* is, I think, a compelling interpretation, keeping our thinking concentrated on the question of being, which he takes to become visible, for Plato, in the "Ideas." Thus, on Heidegger's reading, the Ideas constitute the being of beings, and are themselves the true beings, the true.[16] According to Heidegger,

> that Plato's question concerning art marks the beginning of "aesthetics" does not have its grounds in the fact that it is generally "theoretical," which is to say, that it springs from the interpretation of being; it results from the fact that the "theoretical," as a grasp of the being of beings, is based on a *particular* interpretation of being. The *idea*, the envisioned outward appearance, characterizes being precisely for the kind of vision which recognizes, in the visible as such, pure presence. (NA 167, NK 195)

The question that this leaves me with, and that it provokes me to ask, is: Just what kind of vision is this, which can discern the "pure presence" of being in the visible as such? What can be said, by way of a hermeneutical phenomenology, about the gaze capable of such a vision? Heidegger points to the fact that Plato (*Phaedrus* 250d) regards the gaze as coming from love:

> What is most loved and longed for in *eros* . . . is what at the same time appears and radiates most brilliantly. The *erasmiotaton* [the most loved, the most lovely], which at the same time is *ekphanestaton* [the most radiant, that which appears most luminous], proves to be the *idea tou kalou*, the Idea of the beautiful, beauty. (NA 167, NK 195)

What is radiant and in that sense beautiful is what brings to view, in the immediately passing sensuous appearances of things, their relation to the eternally unchanging Idea. But this event of revelation can take place only if there is, to begin with, an initial attraction to the beauty, the loveliness, of the appearances: there must be a certain predisposition to be attracted by and to them, a predisposition to be drawn—and drawn out (of oneself)—by and to them. This predisposition is none other than love (NA 194–95, NK 226–27).

Like Benjamin's discussion of truth and beauty, Heidegger's commentary focuses on *Phaedrus* 250d, which he translates as follows:

> But to beauty alone has the role been allotted (i.e., in the essential order of being's illumination [*die Wesensordnung des Aufleuchtens des Seins*]) to be the most radiant [*das Hervorscheinendste*] but also the most enchanting [*das Entrückendste*]. (NA 196, NK 227–28. The phrase in parentheses is Heidegger's interpolation.)

Interpretive commentary follows:

> The beautiful is what advances most directly upon us and captivates us. While encountering us as a being, however, it at the same time liberates us to the view [*Blick*] upon being. The beautiful . . . grants entry into immediate sensuous appearances and yet at the same time soars after being; it is both captivating and liberating. Hence it is the beautiful that snatches us from the oblivion of being and grants the view upon being. (Ibid.)

Thus the beautiful, as that which most brightly shines and glistens, is granted to us by way of the most luminous mode of perception with which we have been endowed and of which we are capable. And Heidegger reminds us that θεά, the Greek word for a goddess, is related in Greek to θεάομαι, the word for extraordinary viewing, a gaze granted the privilege

of a deity's revelation. Making as explicit as possible the ontological significance of this visionary experience, Heidegger says:

> The look reaches as far as the highest and farthest remoteness of
> being; simultaneously, it penetrates the nearest and brightest prox-
> imity of fleeting appearances. . . . The more radiantly and brightly
> fleeting appearances are apprehended as such, the more brightly
> does that of which they are appearances come to the fore—Being.
> (NA 196, NK 228)

So the beautiful draws us into what it initially shows us, and if we are appropriately disposed, it draws us through and beyond itself, to grant an unveiling
of being as such. According to Heidegger, the truth that beauty shows us, the
truth to which it transports us, is the "openedness" (Eröffnung) of being. The
truth of beauty, the beauty of truth, is given, therefore, to what he calls der
Seinsblick, the sight of being (NA 198, NK 230). However, for Plato, being is
not at all sensuous, not at all sensible. This means, correspondingly, that the radiance which constitutes its singular and extraordinary beauty must not, cannot be sensuous. Plato locates the truth of beauty and the beauty of truth in the
absolutely supersensuous (das Übersinnliche) which the sensuous only temporarily contains and puts at our disposition. There is, then, in the separation
(Entzweiung, Zwiespalt) between truth and beauty, the supersensuous and the
sensuous, not an unmitigated strife or conflict (Entsetzen), but instead what
Heidegger calls a "felicitous [beglückender] discordance" (ibid.).

Giving further articulation to the character of this relationship, Heidegger observes that

> both beauty and truth are related to being, indeed by way of unveiling
> [Enthüllung] the being of beings. Truth is the immediate way in which
> being is revealed [Seinsenthüllung] in the thought of philosophy; it
> does not enter into the sensuous, but from the outset is averted
> [abrückende] from it. Juxtaposed to it is beauty, penetrating [einrück-
> ende] the sensuous and moving beyond it, liberating in the direction of
> being [berückende Entrückung zum Sein]. (NA 200, NK 231)

Explaining the character of the love, the desire, the attraction that underlies, and is awakened from, the ontological oblivion of our natural disposition, Heidegger brings out the axiological hierarchy towards which Plato's
aesthetics are attempting to guide us:

> For Plato, the supersensuous is the true world. It stands over all, as
> what sets the standard [das Maßgebende]. The sensuous lies below,
> as the world of appearances. What stands over all is alone and from
> the start what sets the standard; it is therefore what is [most] desired.
> (NA 201, NK 232)

Heidegger is quite sympathetic to Nietzsche's attempt to overturn and abolish this hierarchy, sympathetic even to his affirmation of the sensuous, and correctly brings out the fact that this can be accomplished only insofar as the sensuous is no longer treated, no longer seen, as the realm of the "merely" apparent. There is still "semblance" (*Schein* in the sense of semblance); but it is now understood in terms of perspective, and is accordingly affirmed as proper to the very essence of the real. Of course, reality itself thereby becomes, in a sense, equivocal and indeterminate—a matter entirely of the perspective in question. Thus, for Nietzsche, no appearance can claim to be definitive; no perspectival appearance is a *mere* appearance in contrast to some higher, fixed reality (NA 213–15, NK 245–47). And therefore, the only error, the only illusion (*Schein* in this sense), is the vision which claims to see a reality that is constant, fixed, eternal, and definitive. So the radiance that Nietzsche sees is the luminous splendor, the beauty, of a shattered truth, an absolute truth broken, at last, into scintillating splinters of light, perspective appearances beyond number, endlessly transforming, endlessly becoming. The "truth" that Plato (thinks he) sees is, for Nietzsche, an illusion: just a fixation of appearing (*Festmachen eines Anscheins*), and one, indeed, which it is tempting to interpret not only as an attitude with ontological, epistemological, and axiological dimensions, but also as an attitude with what might be called a "psychological" dimension. This is an interpretation that is perhaps intimated, or in any case given some measure of support, by Heidegger's observation, in "What Are Poets For?," that

> objectification . . . blocks us off against the Open. The more venturesome daring does not produce a defense. But it creates a safety, a secureness for us. . . . We are secure where we neither reckon with the unprotected nor count on a defense erected within willing. A [true] safety exists only outside the objectifying turning away from the Open.[17]

If Heidegger's reference to a defense should provoke one to think of Freud's psychoanalytic studies, perhaps it is not after all beside the point to remind ourselves, as Heidegger reminds himself, that it was precisely during the time of Nietzsche's attempt to overturn Platonism and twist free of it that madness (*Wahn-sinn*) befell him! (But I am afraid that, to avoid some egregious misprisions, I must state unequivocally, here, that in turning to Freud for clarification, we must not tolerate psychoanalytic reductionism. If we avoid this common temptation, we can make use of psychoanalysis to elaborate an ontological interpretation of the "defense.")

Although Heidegger points out the temporal correlation, he does not venture any interpretation. Brevity requires that we forego, here, any lengthy consideration of the defensiveness I would like, under Heidegger's provocation, to put most radically into question. For the time being, perhaps it will suffice to say that it is in the re-presentation (*Vor-stellung*) of that which presences (that which is present) that the reification or objectification of presencing-as-such takes place. If on the one hand, the madness can be the divine madness of an ecstatic "rapture" that exposes itself to the openness, or the madness of a love of the beautiful that makes one ecstatically "beside oneself" with joy at the sight of dazzling sensuous radiance, on the other hand, as exposure and vulnerability, madness can also be an experience of terror and dread that necessitates a defense, shielding from the openness, blocking off its illumination, blocking off the radiant splendor of the sensuous. Objectification is visible: according to Heidegger, it is manifest as a dimming-down.[18]

v

In "Twisting Free—Being to an Extent Sensible," John Sallis returns to Plato's *Phaedrus* in order to question Heidegger's reading of Nietzsche with regard to the realm of the aesthetic. His attention, in this text, is given over primarily to Plato's hierarchical separation of the sensuous and the supersensuous, subordinating the sensible to a supposedly more intelligible meaning; Nietzsche's attempt to overturn the hierarchy and ultimately abolish the separation; and Heidegger's critical meditation on the success and significance of Nietzsche's attempt. The thesis for which Sallis wants to argue is, as his title suggests, that being is "to an extent" sensible, but that, in order for this to be seen, it is necessary to "free the sensible from the grid of presence."[19] Sallis says:

> What I've tried to show elsewhere, in a reading of that passage [250d] in the *Phaedrus,* is that τὸ καλόν has the character of a shining-forth of being in the midst of the sensible; that τὸ καλόν is, as it were, the name of the shining-forth of being in the midst of the sensible. (TF 19)

Sallis returns to this problematic in order, as he expresses it,

> to recover, within the Heideggerian project, such a shining-forth of being within the sensible; a shining, if you will, that pertains to the very being of the sensible. (Ibid.)

"But," he adds,

> I am trying to do so in a way that resists, certainly more than the *Phaedrus* and, it seems to me, more than Heidegger himself, the tendency to withdraw the shining from the sensible and to make it ultimately the shining of an εἶδος, the shining of something within the midst of the sensible that is in some sense readily detachable. (Ibid.)

Sallis argues that when Heidegger shifts his analysis from the present-at-hand, a mode of being that he regards as founded and derivative, to the ready-to-hand in its referential context, which he regards as the primary and therefore basic mode in terms of which, in our epoch, being presences, he

> draws the focus away from anything that could be regarded as just sensibly present, as simply there to behold, whether as form or content. It is a matter of leaving out of account everything about things that would pertain to them as present-at-hand, everything that could be apprehended by a gaze not involved in the [practical] complex of references. (TF 11)

Thus, if the beholding of sensuous beauty—of the sensuousness of the beautiful and the beauty of the sensuous—involves a certain disengagement from the ready-to-hand modality of the practical world, Heidegger's privileging or prioritizing of the ready-to-hand makes it difficult for him to do justice to the way in which sensuous beauty would be manifest. In other words, the mode of being in and as which the sensuous would appear in all its beauty is not given the phenomenological attention it requires.

Sallis therefore contends that it is necessary to articulate, with absolutely rigorous fidelity to the phenomenon, i.e., in terms of the hermeneutical phenomenology formulated at the beginning of *Being and Time*,

> how in the shining of the sensible a certain spacing operates so as to draw that shining out into a profiling and a horizonality that is irreducible to presence. (TF 16)

That is, it must also be shown that the shining of the sensible is a phenomenon that can no more be reduced to the present-at-hand of purely theoretical being than it can be reduced to, or eclipsed by, the practical ready-to-hand. In neither of these modes of being, modes of presencing, can the philosopher think the truth of beauty and the beauty of truth with due regard for the sensuous radiance of the phenomenon.

Plato, and to some extent, even Heidegger, subordinate the sensuousness of the sensible to the intelligibility of the essence, so that the sensible is always viewed as a "perpetually incomplete presence" in contrast to the theoretically held εἶδος, which is totally present in its fixed position before the contemplative gaze of the rational mind.

I support the thesis that Sallis expounds and find his argument to be compelling. Thus, in the next section, I would like to elaborate on his point about what he calls "a certain spacing." Further phenomenological attention to this spacing, bringing out its receptivity to the hermeneutical interplay of concealment and unconcealment, may perhaps make it somewhat easier to behold the radiant splendor of the sensuous in its appearance as such—the beauty of truth, the truth of beauty. The possibility of articulating this spacing depends, I believe, on the distinction that Heidegger draws between truth and ἀλήθεια. Without this distinction, and all that must come with it, the radiant beauty of truth will remain a mere Idea, a mere conceit, embellishing the philosopher's discourse.

VI

Over the years, Heidegger assigns many words to describe the disclosive visibility of beauty. His words, rendered in English translation, include, for example: shining, shimmering, glimmering, glowing, glistening, gleaming, dazzling, flashing, scintillating, sparkling, splendid, splendorous, radiant, luminous, illuminating. But who can see these revelations? Who can experience things in such transfigurations of the lighting? What is required of our vision? What must the aesthetic character of the gaze become, if it is to be appropriately responsive to such modes of presencing?

In the poem by Wallace Stevens, there is a magical transfiguration that takes place when things are released from the objectifying grasp of a gaze unable or unwilling to see them from multiple perspectives and points of view, a gaze unable or unwilling to play with the truth, unable or unwilling to see things in the interplay of concealment and unconcealment. Once the metaphysical separation of appearance and reality is abolished, even the properties of impermanence and mutability, attributed since ancient times to the sensuous appearances, undergo a profound alteration of sense: they are no longer to be thought as terms of degradation; they become, instead, terms of celebration, articulating the material of an aesthetic pleasure. Impermanence and mutability can now be seen as manifesting the metaphorical presencing of things—the beauty of their metaphoricity, their metaphorical truth. The poet says: "The grapes seemed fatter. . . . The tree, at night, began to change." Released from a gaze that is fixated on grasping only the absolute truth of an essence, as if there could be only one truth, one true perspective, the grapes and the tree undergo wondrous transformations. Even the most ordinary things are suddenly revealing themselves in a most extraordinary light.

For a gaze bound to the theory of truth as adequate correspondence, reflecting or mirroring that fixation, nothing can come to light, shining in the beauty of its truth and the truth of its beauty. Driven by its need for unity, totality, and identity, deeply committed to a hypostatizing essentialism, such a gaze will miss the fleeting shadows and reflections, the sensuous beauty of things as they appear in the light of different perspectives. Turning the world into a sum of objects conforming to predetermined categories of recognition, such a gaze will not see the revelation in and as which things give themselves to us: the subtle iridescence, the prismatic play of light and shadow on the surfaces of things, the delicate shimmering, the faint and quiet glow, the rich vibrancy of the colors: it will be denied an experience of the radiant splendor of appearing, of endless becoming. Resisting the *ekstasis* that would actually permit a phenomenon to reveal itself, to show itself from out of itself and be what and as it gives itself to be, the gaze is instead given a spectacle that corresponds to its own closure, its own avoidance of exposure: a dull, motionless world without vibrancy, untouched by the presence of inconceivable possibilities for transformation, visibly bereft of grace, of revelation, the uncanny light of redemption that is visibly invisible, but also invisibly visible.

The poem tells us that, with regard to the visible world, the beauty of truth lies—or say dwells and rests—in the sensuousness of appearances. And it tells us that this beauty lies—or, say, is present—in the exploration of different perspectives, in their proliferation: in the openness of an unforeseeable number of perspectives. Thus, it would tell us that, in another sense of "lies," what we take to be the beauty of truth is nothing but a lie, a simulacrum of truth and beauty, deceiving and tricking us, when it is seen only in terms of a single or dominant point of view: when something is made visible in a perspective and a lighting that claim to present its one and only truth, the absolute truth, the true reality, the truth that alone corresponds to the definition of the thing, the claim of truth lies.

VII

Rejecting the modern conception of truth which locates truth in constative sentences or propositions,[20] Heidegger argues, in "The Origin of the Work of Art" that "beauty is one way in which the truth occurs as disclosedness."[21] But this beautiful occurrence of truth is a shining that depends on certain conditions. As Heidegger observes in "The End of Philosophy and the Task of Thinking":

> Outward appearance is a manner of presence. No outward appearance without light—Plato already knew this. But there is no light and no brightness without the opening.[22]

Light "presupposes openness" (BW 386, SD 74). It can "radiate" only if a perceptual field of openness has already been granted. "The beam of light does not first create the opening, openness; it only traverses it" (BW 385, SD 73). Thus, as Heidegger notes in his essay on the work of art, "the Open brings beings to shine and ring out" (PLT 72, H 60). In his essay "On the Essence of Truth," Heidegger gathers these points together, arguing that the appearing of truth can shine in all its beauty only if there is an open region laid out to receive it.[23] The comportment of the gaze—a question of its character—must therefore be appropriately attuned to the opening, since "in that opening rests possible radiance, that is, the possible presencing of presence itself" (BW 387, SD 75). But, he argues,

> philosophy knows nothing of the opening. Philosophy does speak about the light of reason, but it does not heed the opening of being. (BW 386, SD 73)

Returning to the philosophical discourse of ancient Greece, Heidegger finds in the word ἀλήθεια a way of articulating this inaugural event of opening in relation to the experience of the beauty of truth:

> Opening is named with *aletheia*, unconcealment, but not [yet] thought as such. (BW 389, SD 77)

As the poetry of Pindar enables us to see, there was a time long ago when the truth could be revealed in all its beauty, brought forth through the struggles of art and craft into the "splendor of radiant appearing [*den Glanz des Scheinenden*]."[24] But in the modern world, truth is no longer granted this beautiful appearance: once, as Heidegger says, certainty becomes "the modern form of truth,"[25] a closure inimical to openness and radiance is imposed on truth. There is no more interplay between concealment and unconcealment, since this interplay introduces the play of uncertainty and surprise.

What defines the modern world, according to Heidegger, is the fact that the being of beings is subject to a powerful "enframing": it is reduced to presencing only in terms of reifying and totalizing representations. This "enframing" affects the way we can see things in their truth:

> Enframing blocks the shining-forth and holding sway of truth. [*Das Gestell verstellt das Scheinen und Walten der Wahrheit.*][26]

Heidegger's struggle to retrieve the Greek experience of the beauty of truth is therefore an attempt to resist and overcome this modern enframing of the truth. This struggle against the enframing of truth is already set in motion in *Being and Time* (especially §§33–34 and §44), wherein he challenges two fundamental assumptions of modern thought: the assumption that the sole locus of truth is the assertion and the correlative assumption that truth is a correspondence between reality and what is being asserted about it: a correspondence which is thought to be possible without any recognition of the moment when the opening-up of a perceptual field takes place, and without any recognition of the interplay of concealment and unconcealment, the founding moment of disclosure which necessarily precedes the determination of a truth—and, in fact, first makes truth possible.

In effect, the correspondence theory of truth rules out the possibility of an aesthetic experience of truth—a vision of its beauty, since it restricts the experience to the dimension of the adequation, where it gets set in a fixed relation. An aesthetic experience with truth is possible only when the realm of the sensuous is not entirely separated from the realm of intelligible meaning—and not degraded in relation to the latter. Moreover, it is only possible when the gaze lets it shine. And that means, when the gaze renounces its willful grasp, its desire to possess the truth, and lets the truth of the thing be disclosed within the openness of the perceptual field. Only then will the gaze be granted the beauty of truth: the thing in its moment of unconcealment, the event in which the thing is revealed in the intricate interplay of concealment and unconcealment. Here we come to the aesthetic significance of ἀλήθεια, the implications of this concept for the experience of the beauty of truth and the truth of beauty: ἀλήθεια remembers the spacing that is necessary for the radiance of appearing; it preserves the play of the interplay, the intricate hermeneutics of concealment and unconcealment; it reminds the philosopher's gaze to look for the event of unconcealment that precedes the positing of truth. To see the truth only in the moment when it is deposited in a proposition may be quite satisfactory for the purposes of science or the practical interests of everyday life; but it will entirely miss the aesthetic moment.

The aesthetic moment, the hermeneutic moment of ἀλήθεια, requires a gaze of divine madness, a gaze that has freed itself from the rituals and conventions of everyday life, a gaze appropriately prepared for the extraordinary revelations of truth, the metaphorical transformations of truth, that can happen only in the unconditional granting of openness in the very midst of the ordinary.

VIII

Can truth, then, do justice to beauty? Perhaps, if truth is no longer held hostage to the prevailing picture of "reality"; if truth becomes exposure to whatever this picture denies. But in his *Philosophie der neuen Musik,* Adorno asserted that truth can have "all its beauty [only] in denying itself the semblance of beauty."[27] Must we not concede this? But now, inverting Benjamin's question, I also want to ask: Can beauty alone do justice to truth? How can the truth be purely beautiful when there is still so much suffering in the world? And how can beauty be wholly truthful? Where does the beauty of truth lie?

As I meditate on these questions, the words of a poet who suffered deeply come to mind. There is much to think about in the fact that the poet—Rainer Maria Rilke—who wrote, in the final strophe of "The Turning" ("Die Wende"),[28]

> Work of seeing is done,
> now practise heart-work
> upon those images captive within you; for you
> overpowered them only: but now do not know them.

would also write, in the first of his "Duino Elegies,"[29]

> For the beautiful is nothing
> but the beginning of the terrifying. . . .

Notes

BLINDNESS, VIOLENCE, COMPASSION?

1. T. S. Eliot, "Eyes that last I saw in tears," in *Collected Poems* 1909–1962 (New York: Harcourt Brace Jovanovich, 1963), p. 55.

2. Denis Diderot, "Lettre sur les Aveugles à l'Usage de Ceux Qui Voient," in André Billy (ed.), *Oeuvres*, (Paris: Gallimard, 1951), p. 817; trans. by Derek Coltman, with the title "Letter on the Blind, for the Use of Those Who See," in *Diderot's Selected Writings* (New York: Macmillan, 1966), p. 15.

3. Eduardo Galeano, *Memory of Fire*, vol. 3: *Century of the Wind* (New York: Pantheon, 1988), p. 67.

MINIMA MORALIA

1. Theodor Adorno, *Minima Moralia: Reflections from Damaged Life* (London: New Left Books, Verso Editions, 1978), p. 247.

THE DISCURSIVE CONSTRUCTION
OF THE PHILOSOPHICAL GAZE

1. Plato, *The Dialogues of Plato*, trans. by Benjamin Jowett (New York: Random House, 1937), vol. 2, pp. 483–84. Translation modified.

2. Ibid.

3. Charles Taylor, *Sources of the Self* (Cambridge: Harvard University Press, 1989), p. 123.

4. Immanuel Kant, *The Critique of Practical Reason* (New York: Library of Liberal Arts, 1956), p. 166.

5. Edmund Husserl, "Philosophy and the Crisis of European Man," in Q. Lauer (ed.), *Phenomenology and the Crisis of Philosophy* (New York: Harper & Row, 1965), p. 172.

6. Plato, *Dialogues*, Jowett trans., vol. 1, p. 351.

7. Michel Foucault, "Questions of Method," in K. Baynes, J. Bohman, and T. McCarthy (eds.), *After Philosophy: End or Transformation?* (Cambridge, MA: MIT Press, 1987), p. 112.

8. Foucault, *The History of Sexuality*, vol. 3: *The Use of Pleasure* (New York: Pantheon, 1985), p. 8.

9. Baruch Spinoza, *Ethics* (New York: Hafner Publishing Co., 1947), book 4, prop. 27, p. 249.

10. G. W. F. Hegel, "Inaugural Address," in *Lectures on the Philosophy of History* (New York: The Humanities Press, 1955), vol. 1, p. xiii.

11. Jean-Jacques Rousseau, *The Social Contract*, book 1, ch. 7, and book 2, ch. 6.

12. Theodor Adorno, *Minima Moralia: Reflections from Damaged Life* (London: Verso, New Left Books, 1978), p. 151. Italics added.

13. Karl Marx, *Economic and Philosophical Manuscripts*, in Erich Fromm, *Marx's Concept of Man* (New York: Frederick Ungar, 1961), p. 134.

14. Ibid.

15. Jürgen Habermas, *Knowledge and Human Interests* (Boston: Beacon Press, 1971), pp. 314–15.

16. Friedrich Schiller, *On the Aesthetic Education of Man* (New York: Frederick Ungar, 1974), p. 71. See Letter 13.

THE IMPORTANCE OF PHENOMENOLOGY

1. Walter Benjamin, "The Storyteller," in *Illuminations* (New York: Schocken, 1969), p. 84.

2. Theodor Adorno, *Notes to Literature*, vol. 2 (New York: Columbia University Press, 1992), p. 101.

3. Giorgio Agamben, *Infancy and History: Essays on the Destruction of Experience* (London: New Left Books, Verso Edition, 1993), p. 13.

4. See Martin Jay, "Experience without a Subject: Walter Benjamin and the Novel," in *New Formations*, vol. 20 (summer 1995), pp. 28–45; "The Limits of Limit-Experience: Bataille and Foucault," in *Constellations*, vol. 2, no. 2 (1995), pp. 155–74; and "The Crisis of 'Experience' in a Post-Subjective Age," a workshop paper presented May 19, 1997, at the Alice Berline Kaplan Center for the Humanities, Northwestern University.

5. Adorno, "Subject and Object," in A. Arato and E. Gebhardt (eds.), *The Essential Frankfurt School Reader* (New York: Continuum, 1987), p. 503; "Zu Subjekt und Objekt," *Gesammelte Schriften* (Frankfurt am Main: Suhrkamp, 1977), vol. 10, part 2, p. 749.

6. Vladimir Jankélévitch, *Le Je-ne-sais-quoi et le Presque-rien* (Paris: Seuil, 1980), p. 12.

CHAPTER 1. DESCARTES'S WINDOW

1. Friedrich Nietzsche, *The Will to Power* (New York: Vintage Books, 1968), §410, p. 221.

2. Martin Heidegger, *The Basic Problems of Phenomenology* (Bloomington: Indiana University Press, 1982), p. 301; *Gesamtausgabe* (Frankfurt: Vittorio Klostermann, 1975), vol. 24, pp. 427–28.

3. Theodor Adorno, *Sören Kierkegaard: The Construction of the Aesthetic* (Minneapolis: University of Minnesota Press, 1989), p. 65.

4. Wallace Stevens, "Of the Surface of Things," in *The Collected Poems of Wallace Stevens* (New York: Alfred Knopf, 1961), p. 57.

5. Franz Kafka, *The Complete Stories* (New York: Schocken, 1971), p. 387.

6. Ibid., p. 384.

7. Joel Kovel, *History and Spirit: An Inquiry into the Philosophy of Liberation* (Boston: Beacon Press, 1991), p. 42.

8. René Descartes, *Méditations Métaphysiques*, in *Oeuvres de Descartes*, vol. 1 (Paris: F. G. Levrault, 1824), p. 259.

9. See Robert Romanyshyn, *Technology as Symptom and Dream* (New York: Routledge, Chapman & Hall, 1989).

10. Descartes, *Meditations on First Philosophy*, in *Philosophical Works*, vol. 1, trans. and ed. by E. S. Haldane and G. R. T. Ross (New York: Dover Publications, 1955), p. 155.

11. Edmund Husserl, "The Crisis of European Man," in Quentin Lauer (ed.), *Phenomenology and the Crisis of Philosophy* (New York: Harper & Row, 1965), p. 172. Also see his *Cartesian Meditations* (The Hague: Martinus Nijhoff, 1960), pp. 35 and 37: the transcendental ego must establish itself as "disinterested onlooker," in a position "above the naively interested ego"; in order to think philosophically—for example, about ourselves and others—we must learn the role of "non-participant onlooker," relating in this way even towards ourselves.

12. Concerning the philosophical gaze in ancient Greece, and its historical permutations, see Heidegger, "The Age of the World Picture," in *The Question Concerning Technology and Other Essays* (New York: Harper & Row, 1977), especially pp. 143 and 163. *Theoria*, in Aristotle, is a "pure beholding." Heidegger explains that "*theorein* comes from the coalescing of two root words, *thea* and *horao. Thea* (cf. theatre) is the outward look, the aspect, in which something shows itself, the outward appearance in which it offers itself. Plato names this aspect in which what presences shows what it is, *eidos*. To have seen this aspect, *eidenai*, is to know [*wissen*]. The second root word in *theorein*, namely *horao*, means: to look at something attentively, to look it over, to view it closely. Thus it follows that *theorein* is . . . to look attentively on the outward appearance, wherein what presences becomes visible and, through such sight—seeing—to linger with it." This archaeology enables us to measure just how far, and in what ways, our culture of vision has evolved. And it enables us, therefore, to reflect in a critical way, with some perspective on our cultural habits and practices, on the vision we take for granted.

13. Heidegger, "The Age of the World Picture," in *Question Concerning Technology*, pp. 165–67.

14. Descartes, *Rules for the Direction of the Mind*, in *Philosophical Works*, vol. 1, p. 3.

15. Ibid., pp. 7, 9, 34, 8, and 7, respectively.

16. Ibid., p. 7.

17. Ibid., p. 9.

18. Ibid., p. 29.

19. Ibid., p. 14.

20. Ibid., p. 28.

21. See, for example, Husserl, *Ideas: General Introduction to Pure Phenomenology*, vol. 1 (New York: Macmillan, 1931), pp. 223, 246, and 314.

22. Max Horkheimer, "The Problem of Truth," in *Between Philosophy and Social Science: Selected Early Writings* (Cambridge, MA: MIT Press, 1993), p. 333.

23. Descartes, *Discourse on the Method of Rightly Conducting the Reason and Seeking for Truth in the Sciences*, in *Philosophical Works*, vol. 1, p. 82.

24. Ibid., p. 99.

25. Ibid., pp. 87–88. Italics added.

26. Ibid., p. 87.

27. Ibid., p. 116.

28. Ibid.

29. Descartes, *Meditations on First Philosophy*, in *Philosophical Works*, vol. 1, p. 145.

30. Ibid.

31. See Romanyshyn, *Psychological Life: From Science to Metaphor* (Austin: University of Texas Press, 1982), and "The Despotic Eye," in David M. Levin (ed.), *Modernity and the Hegemony of Vision* (Los Angeles: University of California Press, 1993), pp. 339–60.

32. Descartes, *Meditations on First Philosophy*, p. 148.

33. Charles Taylor, *Sources of the Self: The Making of the Modern Identity* (Cambridge, MA: Harvard University Press, 1989), p. 161.

34. Descartes, *Meditations on First Philosophy*, p. 149.

35. Ibid., p. 156.

36. Ludwig Wittgenstein, *Philosophical Investigations* (London: Macmillan, 1953), p. 221.

37. Ibid., p. 187.

38. Descartes, *Meditations on First Philosophy*, in *Philosophical Works*, vol. 1, p. 188.

39. Ibid., p. 195.

40. Ibid., p. 196.

41. Ibid., p. 187.

42. Ibid., p. 192.

43. Wittgenstein, *Philosophical Investigations*, p. 178.

44. Ibid.

45. Ibid., §303, p. 102.

46. Ibid., p. 223.

47. Ibid., p. 203.

48. Ibid., p. 178.

49. Ibid., §420.

50. Adorno, *Minima Moralia: Reflections from a Damaged Life* (London: New Left Books, 1988), p. 105.

51. Maurice Merleau-Ponty, "The Child's Relations with Others," in *The Primacy of Perception* (Evanston, IL: Northwestern University Press, 1964), p. 155.

52. Ibid.

53. See in this regard Merleau-Ponty, *Phenomenology of Perception* (London: Routledge & Kegan Paul, 1962), pp. 346–65, 375, 405.

54. Ibid., p. 374.

55. Merleau-Ponty, "The Child's Relations with Others," in *Primacy of Perception*, p. 118.

56. Ibid., p. 116.

57. Wittgenstein, *Philosophical Investigations*, p. 223.

58. Ibid., p. 217.

59. See Merleau-Ponty, "The Child's Relations with Others," in *Primacy of Perception*, p. 155, and my discussion of narcissism in vision in chapter 6.

60. Merleau-Ponty, *Phenomenology of Perception*, p. 361.

61. Ibid.

62. Ibid., p. 362.

63. Ibid., p. 353.

64. Ibid., p. 354. The "normal" situation is lucidly exemplified in *L'Età Breve*, a novel by Corrado Alvaro (Arnoldo Mondadori Editore, 1976, p. 86), in which the author describes the experience of a lonely young boy in boarding school who sees a young girl pass by outside his window and suddenly realizes how, by this sighting, he is connected to her, but also how this very connection means that his happiness must escape his possession: "Così egli si trovò legato a un filo invisibile, non più solo, con una felicità che possedeva e che tuttavia gli sfuggiva di continuo . . . e nello stesso tempo col senso di avere perduto qualche cosa . . . e lo ritrovava all'improvviso." What the boy thought he lost and then discovered, discovered again, is the prepersonal corporeal intentionality to which Merleau-Ponty calls our attention, an intentionality that he himself describes with words such as "threads" and "lacework."

65. Merleau-Ponty, *Phenomenology of Perception*, p. 353.

66. Merleau-Ponty, "Interrogation and Dialectic," in *The Visible and the Invisible*, (Evanston, IL: Northwestern University Press, 1964), p. 78.

67. Ibid., p. 80.

68. See Merleau-Ponty, *Phenomenology of Perception*, pp. 93–94, 184, 198, and 346–65, and "The Child's Relations with Others," in *Primacy of Perception*, pp. 114–16.

69. Merleau-Ponty, "The Child's Relations with Others," in *Primacy of Perception*, p. 115.

70. Ibid., pp. 115–16. Italics added.

71. Ibid., p. 117.

72. Ibid., p. 124.

73. Ibid., p. 120.

74. Adorno, *Minima Moralia*, p. 105.

75. Heidegger, "The Age of the World Picture," in *Question Concerning Technology*, p. 127. Also see Dalia Judovitz, *Subjectivity and Representation in Descartes: The Origins of Modernity* (Cambridge: Cambridge University Press, 1988), an excellent contribution to our understanding of these issues.

76. Ibid., p. 128.

77. Ibid., p. 130.

78. Ibid., p. 129.

79. Ibid., p. 130.

80. Ibid., p. 117.

81. Ibid., p. 131.

82. See ibid., p. 147.

83. Ibid., p. 131.

84. Ibid.

85. Ibid.

86. Ibid.

87. Heidegger, *Being and Time* (New York: Harper & Row, 1962), p. 88. Also see ibid., pp. 68–69; the appendix to "The Age of the World Picture," in *Question Concerning Technology*, pp. 165–67; and my large work on vision, *The Opening of Vision: Nihilism and the Postmodern Situation* (London: Routledge, 1988), pp. 51–340, and 438–40.

88. Heidegger, "The Age of the World Picture," in *Question Concerning Technology*, p. 133.

89. Ibid., p. 139.

90. Ibid., p. 140.

91. Heidegger, "The Question Concerning Technology," in *Question Concerning Technology*, p. 33.

92. I am pleased to find this point argued by Taylor in *Sources of the Self*, pp. 163–64.

93. Merleau-Ponty, "Interrogation and Dialectic," in *The Visible and the Invisible*, (Evanston, IL: Northwestern University Press, 1964), p. 77.

94. Vision and crying were discussed by Hegel in the *Zusatz* to §401, part 3, of his *Encyclopaedia of the Philosophical Sciences*. See J. N. Findlay (ed.), *Hegel's Philosophy of Mind* (Oxford: Clarendon Press, 1971), pp. 75–88.

95. This is the principal thesis of my 1988 book, *The Opening of Vision*— and also its source, its origin. As a scholar, I cannot refrain from pointing out that this book, the first draft of which was completed in the summer of 1980, preceded by some ten years Jacques Derrida's *Mémoires d'Aveugle: L'Autoportrait et Autres Ruines* (Paris: Éditions de la Réunion des Musées Nationaux, 1990), in which he touches on the fact that the eyes are the site for both seeing and weeping, and concludes quoting Andrew Marvell's poem "Eyes and Tears,"

in which the poet observes "How wisely Nature did decree, / With the same eyes to weep and see!" But Derrida does little more than call attention to a connection. He does not attempt to explore its significance—a fact which perhaps suggests that, for him, the significance is merely metaphorical, merely rhetorical. A preliminary sketch of the account eventually elaborated in my book first appeared under the title, "The Opening of Vision: Seeing through the Veil of Tears," in *Review of Existential Psychology and Psychiatry*, vol. 16, nos. 1–3 (1978–79), pp. 113–46. In this sketch, I began my reflections on the significance of the connection.

96. See Romanyshyn, "The Despotic Eye," in D. M. Levin (ed.), *Modernity and the Hegemony of Vision*, pp. 339–60.

97. T. S. Eliot, "Eyes that I last saw in tears," in *Collected Poems 1909–1962* (New York: Harcourt Brace Jovanovich, 1964), p. 55.

98. Merleau-Ponty, *Phenomenology of Perception*, p. 171n.

99. Maurice Blanchot, *The Infinite Conversation* (Minneapolis: University of Minnesota Press, 1992), p. 21.

100. See J. Brown (ed.), *The Sacred Pipe: Black Elk's Account of the Seven Rites of the Oglala Sioux* (New York: Penguin, 1971).

101. Ralph Waldo Emerson, *Journals*, ed. by Joel Porte (Cambridge, MA: Harvard University Press, 1982), p. 160.

CHAPTER 2. HUSSERL'S TRANSCENDENTAL GAZE

1. Ralph Waldo Emerson, "Experience," in *Essays and Lectures* (New York: New American Library, 1983), p. 476.

2. Emmanuel Levinas, "No Identity," in Robert Bernasconi (ed.), *Collected Philosophical Papers* (Dordrecht: Martinus Nijhoff, 1987), p. 148; "Sans Identité," *L'Humanisme de l'Autre Homme* (Paris: Fata Morgana, 1972), p. 95. Also see his book *Autrement Qu'Être ou au delà de l'Essence* (The Hague: Martinus Nijhoff, 1974), p. 10, where he spells out a similar indictment: "A la réduction transcendentale de Husserl une mise entre parenthèses suffit-elle? Une façon d'écrire, de se commettre avec le monde qui colle comme l'encre aux mains qui l'écartent?"

3. Wallace Stevens, "Notes toward a Supreme Fiction," in *The Collected Poems* (New York: Alfred A. Knopf, 1954), I, ll. 5–6.

4. René Char, "Feuillets d'Hypnos," *Oeuvres Complètes* (Paris: Gallimard, 1983), p. 216.

5. Char, "Aversions," *La Nu Perdu, Oeuvres Complètes*, p. 473.

6. Walter Benjamin, *Ursprung des Deutschen Trauerspiels*, in Rolf Tiedemann and Hermann Schweppenhäuser (eds.), *Gesammelte Schriften* (Frankfurt: Suhrkamp Verlag, 1972), vol. 1, p. 330.

7. Edmund Husserl, *The Crisis of European Sciences and Transcendental Philosophy* (Evanston, IL: Northwestern University Press, 1970), p. 265. Hereafter this text will be designated by the abbreviation *Crisis*. For the original German, see *Die*

Krisis der Europäischen Wissenschaften und die Transzendentale Phänomenologie, Gesammelte Werke, vol. 6, ed. by Walter Biemel (The Hague: Martinus Nijhoff, 1962), p. 269. Hereafter, this text will be designated by the word *Krisis.*

8. Ibid., p. 290 in the English, p. 337 in the original German.

9. Husserl, "The Vienna Lecture," in *Crisis,* p. 277. For the German, see "Krisis," *Gesammelte Werke,* vol. 6, p. 322.

10. Husserl, "The Vienna Lecture," *Crisis,* p. 297. For the German, see *Krisis,* pp. 345–46.

11. Husserl, *Crisis,* p. 341; *Krisis,* p. 275.

12. Husserl, *Crisis,* p. 338; *Krisis,* p. 272.

13. Husserl, "The Vienna Lecture," in *Crisis,* p. 298; pp. 346 in the German.

14. Husserl, *Crisis,* p. 151; *Krisis,* p. 154.

15. Husserl, "The Vienna Lecture," in *Crisis,* p. 285; pp. 331–32 in the German.

16. Husserl, *Crisis,* p. 56; *Krisis,* p. 57.

17. Husserl, *Cartesian Meditations* (The Hague: Martinus Nijhoff, 1969), §15, p. 35. Also see §15, p. 37, where Husserl speaks of a "non-participant onlooker." This text will hereafter be designated by the abbreviation "CM."

18. Ibid., §2, p. 6, and §1, p. 2.

19. Theodor Adorno, *Against Epistemology: A Metacritique* (Oxford: Basil Blackwell, 1982). For the German, see *Zur Metakritik der Erkenntnistheorie: Studien über Husserl und die Phänomenologischen Antinomien* (Frankfurt am Main: Suhrkamp Verlag, 1972). See also his dialectically intricate analysis in "Subject and Object," in A. Arato and E. Gebhardt(eds.), *The Frankfurt School Reader* (New York: Continuum, 1987), pp. 497–511.

20. Adorno, *Against Epistemology,* p. 133.

21. Ibid., p. 134.

22. Adorno, "Husserl and the Problem of Idealism," in *Vermischte Scriften* (Frankfurt am Main: Suhrkamp Verlag, 1986), vol. 20, part 1, p. 124.

23. Ibid.

24. Ibid., p. 121. In *Otherwise Than Being, or Beyond Essence,* (Boston: Kluwer, 1991), Levinas also challenges Husserl along these same lines, referring (p. 29) to Husserl's assumption of an "immobile eternity."

25. Husserl, "Prolegomena zur reinen Logik," *Logische Untersuchungen,* vol. 1 (Halle: Niemeyer, 1922, 1928), p. 64.

26. Adorno, *Against Epistemology,* p. 197; *Zur Metakritik der Erkenntnistheorie,* p. 200.

27. Adorno, *Against Epistemology,* pp. 144–45; *Zur Metakritik der Erkenntnistheorie,* pp. 149–50.

28. Ibid.

29. Adorno, *Minima Moralia: Reflections from a Damaged Life* (London: New Left Books, Verso Editions, 1978), p. 247; *Minima Moralia: Reflexionen aus dem Beschädigten Leben, Gesammelte Schriften* (Frankfurt am Main: Suhrkamp, 1951), vol. 4, p. 281.

30. Husserl, *Ideas I: General Introduction to Pure Phenomenology,* trans. by W. R. Boyce-Gibson (London: Collier-Macmillan, 1969), p. 39.

31. Husserl, CM, p. 68.

32. Husserl, *Ideas*, §19, pp. 75–76.

33. Ibid., §33, p. 102.

34. Jacques Derrida, "Force and Signification," in *Writing and Difference* (Chicago: University of Chicago Press, 1978), p. 28.

35. Stephane Mallarmé, "Quant au Livre," *Oeuvres Complètes* (Paris: Editions Gallimard, 1945), p. 386: "Les mots, d'eux-mêmes, s'exaltent à mainte facette reconnue la plus rare ou valant pour l'esprit, centre de suspens vibratoire; qui les perçoit indépendamment de la suite ordinaire, projetés, en parois de grotte, tant que dure leur mobilité ou principe, étant ce qui ne se dit pas du discours: prompts tous, avant extinction, à une réciprocité de feux distante ou présentée de biais comme contingence."

36. Levinas, *Time and the Other* (Pittsburgh: Duquesne University Press, 1987), p. 64; *Le Temps et l'Autre* (Paris: Fata Morgana, Presses Universitaires de France, 1979), p. 92.

37. Ibid.

38. Adorno, *Against Epistemology*, p. 45; *Zur Metakritik der Erkenntnistheories*, p. 52.

39. Levinas, *Otherwise Than Being*, p. 20; *Autrement Qu'être*, pp. 24–25.

40. See Husserl, CM, §44, p. 96; *Ideas*, §33, p. 102, and §124, p. 320.

41. Husserl, *Ideas*, §92, p. 246.

42. Ibid., §124, p. 320.

43. Ibid. Also see Husserl, *Ideas* §66, pp. 175–76 (on "Faithful Expression of the Clearly Given: Unambiguous Terms"), and §84, pp. 224–26 ("Note on Terminology").

44. Derrida, "Force and Signification," in *Writing and Difference*, p. 27.

45. Ibid.

46. Derrida, " 'Genesis and Structure' and Phenomenology," in *Writing and Difference*, pp. 154–68.

47. Adorno, *Against Epistemology*, p. 152; *Zur Metakritik der Erkenntnistheories*, p. 157.

48. Levinas, *En Découvrant l'Existence avec Husserl et Heidegger* (Paris: Vrin, 1949).

49. Husserl, *Ideas*, §92, p. 248.

50. Husserl, "Second Investigation," in *Logical Investigations* (New York: Humanities Press, 1970), vol. 1, §15, p. 368. Also see his *Ideas*, §43, pp. 122–24.

51. Husserl, "First Investigation," in *Logical Investigations*, vol. 1, §17, p. 300. Husserl's attack on the picture theory of meaning is mainly located in §17–§23, pp. 299–311.

52. Husserl, "First Investigation," in *Logical Investigations*, vol. 1, §19, p. 304.

53. Husserl, "Sixth Investigation," in *Logical Investigations*, vol. 2, §4, p. 680.

54. Husserl, "Fifth Investigation," in *Logical Investigations*, vol. 2, §11, p. 559. Also see §12–§14 and other parts of §11, pp. 557–69.

55. Husserl, CM, §38, p. 79.

56. Adorno, *Against Epistemology*, p. 136; *Zur Metakritik der Erkenntnnistheorie*, p. 141. Also see p. 143 in the English translation and p. 148 in the original German text.

57. Stevens, "Tatoo," *The Collected Poems*, p. 81.

58. Levinas, "Diachrony and Representation," in *Time and the Other*, p. 99; *Le Temps et l'Autre*, p. 92.

59. Ibid.

60. Martin Heidegger, *An Introduction to Metaphysics* (New York: Doubleday, 1961), p. 99. Italics added.

61. Husserl, "Fifth Investigation," in *Logical Investigations*, vol. 2, §38, p. 640.

62. Levinas, *Le Temps et l'Autre*, p. 11; *Time and the Other*, p. 33.

63. For a more elaborate discussion of this matter, see my *The Opening of Vision: Nihilism and the Postmodern Situation* (New York: Routledge, 1988).

64. Adorno, *Against Epistemology*, p. 196; *Zur Metakritik der Erkenntnnistheorie*, p. 199. The phrase also appears on p. 216 in the English edition and on p. 219 in the German.

65. Emerson, "Circles," in *Essays and Lectures*, p. 403.

66. Emerson, "Nature," in *Essays and Lectures*, p. 9.

67. Husserl, "Second Investigation," in *Logical Investigations*, §21, p. 380.

68. Adorno, *Minima Moralia*, §98, p. 151.

69. Adorno, *Against Epistemology*, p. 151; *Zur Metakritik der Erkenntnistheorie*, p. 156.

70. Levinas broaches a similar criticism, puzzling over the "shining forth" of signification. See Levinas, *Otherwise Than Being*, p. 66; *Autrement Qu'être*, p. 83.

71. Husserl, "Third Investigation," in *Logical Investigations*, vol. 2, §6, p. 445.

72. Husserl, *Ideas*, §31, p. 97.

73. Husserl, "Prolegomenon," in *Logical Investigations*, vol. 1, §50, p. 191.

74. Husserl, *Ideas*, §46, p. 132.

75. Ibid.

76. Husserl, *Ideas*, §78, p. 204. For Adorno's discussion of Husserlian "evidence," see *Against Epistemology*, pp. 56–57; *Zur Metakritik*, pp. 62–64.

77. Husserl, *Logical Investigations*, vol. 1, §6, p. 61.

78. Ibid., §51, p. 195.

79. Ibid., §62, p. 226. Also see his CM, §4, p. 10, and §5, pp. 12 and 14.

80. Husserl, *Ideas*, §88, p. 240.

81. Husserl, CM, §27, p. 60.

82. Ibid., §5, p. 12.

83. Husserl, *Ideas*, §24, p. 83; *Ideen*, p. 43. For Adorno's discussion of this principle, see *Against Epistemology*, pp. 136–37; *Zur Metakritik*, pp. 141–42.

84. Husserl, CM, §15, p. 36.

85. Ibid., §15, p. 35.

86. See Husserl, *Ideas*, §42, p. 121: "Ein Erlebnis schattet sich nicht ab." ("Lived experience is without any shadows.")

87. Ibid., §6, pp. 15–16. On apodeictic evidence, see also "Third Investigation," in *Logical Investigations*, vol. 2, §6, pp. 444–46.

88. Husserl, "Prolegomenon to Pure Logic," in *Logical Investigations,* vol. 1, §63, p. 227.

89. On conflicts in what is seen, see Husserl, "Sixth Investigation," in *Logical Investigations,* vol. 2, §38–§39, pp. 764–70, and the appendix to this investigation, pp. 864–67. Also see *Ideas,* §19, p. 76.

90. Husserl, "Prolegomenon to Pure Logic," in *Logical Investigations,* vol. 1, §51, p. 196.

91. Ibid., §40, p. 159. Also see §49, pp. 187–88; §50, pp. 189–93; and §51, pp. 193–96.

92. Adorno, *Against Epistemology,* p. 100; *Zur Metakritik,* pp. 106–7.

93. Levinas, *Otherwise Than Being,* p. 38; *Autrement Qu'être,* p. 49. Also see, on the logic of the intricate interconnections among intentionality, truth, time, memory, and representation, p. 29 in the English translation and p. 36 in the original French.

94. Levinas, *Otherwise Than Being,* pp. 132–33; *Autrement Qu'être,* pp. 169–70.

95. Levinas, *Otherwise Than Being,* p. 133; *Autrement Qu'être,* pp. 169–70.

96. Husserl, "Preface," in *Logical Investigations,* vol. 1, p. xv. Also see p. 49.

97. Husserl, *Ideas,* §3, p. 50.

98. Husserl, CM, §34, pp. 70–71. Also see p. 72. Also see *Ideas,* §4, pp. 50–51. Adorno discusses eidetic variation in *Against Epistemology,* pp. 49, 117–23; *Zur Metakritik,* pp. 56, 123–29.

99. Husserl, *Ideas,* §70, p. 184; *Ideen zu einer reinen Phänomenologie und Phänomenologische Philosophie,* erstes Buch: *Allgemeine Einführung in die reine Phänomenologie, Gesammelte Werke,* vol. 3 (The Hague: Martinus Nijhoff, 1950), p. 132.

100. Adorno, *Against Epistemology,* p. 207; *Zur Metakritik,* p. 210.

101. Adorno, *Against Epistemology,* p. 150; *Zur Metakritik,* p. 155.

102. Adorno, *Against Epistemology,* p. 190; *Zur Metakritik,* p. 193.

103. Ibid.

104. Adorno, *Against Epistemology,* p. 189; *Zur Metakritik,* p. 193.

105. Levinas, *Otherwise Than Being,* p. 37; *Autrement Qu'être,* pp. 47–48.

106. Levinas, *Otherwise Than Being,* p. 30; *Autrement Qu'être,* p. 38.

107. Husserl, *Ideas,* §121, p. 314.

108. Husserl, CM, §8, pp. 18–19.

109. Ibid., §11, p. 25. Italics added.

110. Ibid., §44, p. 98. Italics added.

111. Levinas, *Otherwise Than Being,* p. 63; *Autrement Qu'être,* p. 86.

112. Levinas, *Otherwise Than Being,* p. 101; *Autrement Qu'être,* pp. 128–29.

113. Husserl, *Ideas,* §37, p. 111.

114. Ibid., §27, p. 93.

115. Ibid., §121, p. 314.

116. Husserl, "Fifth Investigation," *Logical Investigations,* vol. 2, §27, pp. 609–10.

117. See my chapter, in this book, on "Gestalt, Gestell, Geviert" (chapter 4).

118. Salvatore S. Nigro, "The Secretary," in Rosario Villari (ed.), *Baroque Personae* (Chicago: University of Chicago Press, 12995), p. 94.

119. Husserl, CM, §44, p. 94.

120. Husserl, *Ideas,* §137, p. 353.

121. Adorno, *Against Epistemology,* p. 61; *Zur Metakritik,* p. 68.

122. Adorno, *Against Epistemology,* p. 83; *Zur Metakritik,* p. 90.

123. Husserl, CM, §54, p. 118. Also see §50, pp. 108 and 111, and §55, p. 124

124. Maurice Merleau-Ponty, *The Visible and the Invisible* (Evanston, IL: Northwestern University Press, 1968), p. 248; *Le visible et L'invisible* (Paris: Gallimard, 1964), p. 301.

125. Novalis, Fragment 285, in Friedrich Schlegel, *Philosophical Fragments* (Minneapolis: University of Minnesota Press, 1991), p. 58.

126. T. S. Eliot, "The Hollow Men," in *Collected Poems 1909–1962* (New York: Harcourt Brace & World, Inc., 1963), p. 81.

CHAPTER 3. THE GLASSES ON OUR NOSE

1. Johann Wolfgang von Goethe, *Sämtliche Werke,* bd. 17: *Maximen und Reflexionen,* ed. by von Gonthier-Louis Fink, Gerhardt Baumann, and Johannes John (Munich: Carl Hanser Verlag, 1991), note 575, p. 824.

2. Maurice Merleau-Ponty, *Phenomenology of Perception* (New York: Routledge & Kegan Paul, 1962), p. xx; *Phénoménologie de la Perception* (Paris: Gallimard, 1945), p. xvi.

3. Henry James, letter to Robert Louis Stevenson (January 12, 1891), in Leon Edel (ed.), *Henry James: Selected Letters* (Cambridge: Harvard University Press, 1974), p. 242.

4. Walter Benjamin, *Gesammelte Schriften,* vol. 5: *Das Passagenwerk* (Frankfurt am Main: Suhrkamp Verlag, 1982), p. 574 (N1a, 8). See also Susan Buck-Morss, *The Dialectics of Seeing: Walter Benjamin and the Arcades Project* (Cambridge, MA: MIT Press, 1989).

5. Ludwig Wittgenstein, *Philosophical Investigations* (New York: Macmillan Co., 1953), §66. References to this text will hereafter be designated by the initials "PI."

6. PI, p. 212e.

7. Wittgenstein, *On Certainty* (Oxford: Basil Blackwell, 1969), §125.

8. See William J. Earle, "Ducks and Rabbits: Visuality in Wittgenstein," in David M. Levin (ed.), *Sites of Vision: The Discursive Construction of Sight in the History of Philosophy* (Cambridge, MA: MIT Press, 1997), pp. 293–314.

9. See P. M. S. Hacker, "The Rise and Fall of the Picture Theory," in *Perspectives on the Philosophy of Wittgenstein* (Cambridge, MA: MIT Press, 1981), p. 195.

10. Wittgenstein, *Tractatus Logico-Philosophicus,* trans. by D. F. Pears and B. F. McGuiness (London: Routledge & Kegan Paul, 1961).

11. Wittgenstein, *Zettel* (Los Angeles: University of California Press, 1970), §265, p. 49e.

12. Wittgenstein, *Culture and Value* (Chicago: University of Chicago Press, 1980), p. 79e.

13. On showing and exhibiting sensations and feelings, e.g., pain; on making one's sensations and feelings, e.g., pain, visible to others; on how to tell whether someone is in pain, and what it is to *see* another's pain, consult PI, §§283–317.

14. See Edmund Husserl, *Ideas: General Introduction to a Pure Phenomenology* (London: Collier-Macmillan, 1931), ch. 3, esp. §46.

15. Wittgenstein, *Remarks on Colour* (Los Angeles: University of California Press, 1978), §323, p. 60.

16. Theodor Adorno, "The Actuality of Philosophy," *Telos*, vol. 31 (spring 1974), pp. 120, 126. Also see his *Gesammelte Schriften*, vol. 1: *Philosophische Frühschriften* (Frankfurt am Main: Suhrkamp Verlag, 1973).

17. Ibid., p. 128.

18. Benjamin, "Theses on the Philosophy of History," in *Illuminations* (New York: Schocken, 1969), p. 257. I am referring, here, to Benjamin's interpretation of Paul Klee's *Angelus Novus* as the "angel of history."

19. Wittgenstein, *Culture and Value*, p. 3e.

20. Yehuda Amichai, *Poems of Jerusalem* (New York: Harper & Row, 1988), p.32.

21. Wittgenstein, *Culture and Value*, p. 65e.

22. Ibid., p. 63e.

CHAPTER 4. GESTALT GESTELL GEVIERT

1. Samuel Beckett, *The Unnameable* (New York: Grove Press, 1970), p. 22.

2. F. W. J. Schelling, *Schriften von 1794–1798* (Darmstadt: Wissenschaftliche Buchgesellschaft, 1980), p. 217. In the original, the last five words were not italicized. Translation: "As long as the human being remains within the domain of nature, he is in the true sense of the word *master* over nature as he is *master* over himself. He puts the objective world within its defined boundaries, over which it may not step. By *representing* the object, by giving it form and consistency, he masters it. . . . But as soon as he oversteps these boundaries, as soon as the object is no longer *representable*, that is, as soon as he himself has transgressed the limits of representation, *he sees himself lost.*"

3. Martin Heidegger, "Plato's Doctrine of Truth," in Henry Aiken and William Barrett (eds.), *Philosophy in the Twentieth Century* (New York: Random House, 1962), vol. 3, p. 265. Also see pp. 261 and 267. For the German, see *Platons Lehre von der Wahrheit* (Bern: Verlag A. Francke, 1947), p. 41. Heidegger's phrase is "Richtigkeit des Blickens."

4. Heidegger, *Beiträge zur Philosophie (Vom Ereignis)*, *Gesamtausgabe* (Frankfurt am Main: Vittorio Klostermann, 1989), vol. 65, p. 251.

5. Ibid., p. 251. Also see p. 260: Making an ontologically decisive distinction, Heidegger writes: "Das Seyn west; das Seiende ist. Seyn west als Ereignis."

6. I draw this word from Heidegger, *Vom Wesen der Wahrheit* (Frankfurt am Main: Vittorio Klostermann, 1949), p. 20. English translation: "On the Essence of Truth," in David F. Krell (ed.), *Martin Heidegger: Basic Writings* (New York: Harper & Row, revised edition, 1993), p. 132.

7. Heidegger, *Beiträge zur Philosophie*, p. 306. I translate: a "recuperative return to the opening ground."

8. In "Le Prix du Progrès," one of the notes included in *Dialectic of Enlightenment* (New York: Continuum, 1986), Theodor Adorno laments "the loss of memory" in our modern culture. And he ends this note with the assertion that "all reification is a forgetting" (ibid., p. 230). Although there are major irreconcilable differences between Adorno and Heidegger with regard to how they think *from* this point of convergence, they at least agree, albeit abstractly, that remembrance, or recollection, is crucial to the overcoming of a reifying metaphysics and culture. They also agree that this recollection is the telling of the history of our suffering, a *Leidensgeschichte*, rescuing, if not redeeming, the victims of evil. But, beyond this, what is it that needs to be remembered, if reification is to be subverted? Here, of course, their differences begin. First and foremost, the difference is this: for Adorno, the object of remembrance is the suffering of the victims of oppression and violence, whereas for Heidegger, the object of recollection as a history of suffering is our "ontological need" in the conditions imposed through the abandonment of being. In *Negative Dialectics*, Adorno articulated a very sharp criticism of this concern for our "ontological need," reading it as a heartless abstraction which conceals the plight of the poor, the oppressed, the needy. This criticism, alas, carries the sting of truth. I broach this matter, however, as a way of setting in motion a useful dialogue on the role of recollection in transforming the conditions of a deeply suffering, deeply needful society.

9. Beckett, *The Unnameable*, pp. 11–12.

10. Heidegger, *Being and Time*, (New York: Harper & Row, 1962), p. 190. This is one of several passages in which he refers to staring (in German, *das schlichte Sehen*). The others are on pp. 88, 98, and 104. For the German, see *Sein und Zeit* (Halle: Max Niemeyer Verlag, 1941), p. 149. Heidegger uses other words to make the same point. See note 28 below.

11. Heidegger, "Das Ge-stell," *Gesamtausgabe*, bd. 79 (Frankfurt am Main: Vittorio Klostermann, 1994), p. 36.

12. Ibid., p. 44.

13. Ibid., p. 32.

14. Heidegger, "Die Gefahr," *Gesamtausgabe*, bd. 79, pp. 46–47.

15. Ibid., p. 63.

16. Heidegger, "The Turning," in *The Question Concerning Technology and Other Essays* (New York: Harper & Row, 1977), p. 47. For the German, see "Die Kehre," in *Die Technik und die Kehre* (Pfullingen: Günther Neske, 1962), p. 45: "Das Gestell ist, obzwar verschleiert, noch Blick, kein blindes Geschick im Sinne eines völlig verhangenen Verhängnisses."

17. Heidegger, "The Turning," in *Question Concerning Technology*, p. 37; "Die Kehre," op. cit., p. 37.

18. Ibid.

19. Heidegger, "The Turning," in *Question Concerning Technology*, p. 39; "Die Kehre," op. cit., p. 39: " . . . muß der neuzeitliche Mensch zuvor allererst in die Weite seines Wesensraumes zurückfinden."

20. Heidegger, "The Turning," in *Question Concerning Technology*, p. 45; "Die Kehre," op. cit., p. 44.

21. Heidegger, "The Word of Nietzsche: God Is Dead," in *The Question Concerning Technology and Other Essays*, pp. 83–84. For the German, see "Nietzsches Wort: 'Gott ist tot,' " *Holzwege* (Frankfurt am Main: Vittorio Klostermann, 1950), p. 221.

22. See Heidegger, "The Age of the World Picture," in *Question Concerning Technology*, p. 128. For the German, see "Die Zeit des Weltbildes," *Holzwege*, p. 81.

23. Heidegger, "Der Spruch des Anaximander," *Holzwege* (Frankfurt am Main: Vittorio Klostermann, 1950), p. 323. In English, see "The Anaximander Fragment," *Early Greek Thinking* (New York: Harper & Row, 1975), p. 4. Hereafter, "EGT" will be substituted for the English title.

24. Heidegger, "The Question Concerning Technology," in *Question Concerning Technology*, p. 33. For the original German, see "Die Frage nach der Technik," *Die Technik und die Kehre* (Pfullingen: Günther Neske, 1962), p. 33: "Einmal fordert das Ge-stell in das Rasende des Bestellens heraus, das jedem Blick in das Ereignis der Entbergung verstellt und so den Bezug zum Wesen der Wahrheit von Grund auf gefährdet."

25. Heidegger, "The Question Concerning Technology," in *Question Concerning Technology*, p. 31. For the German, see "Die Frage nach der Technik," op. cit., p. 31: "Denn das Ge-stell ist doch nach allem Gesagten ein Geschick, das in die herausfordernde Entbergung versammelt."

26. Heidegger, "The Question Concerning Technology," in *Question Concerning Technology*, pp. 24, 31. For the German, see "Die Frage nach der Technik," op. cit., p. 31: Heidegger speaks there of "das Herausfordern in das Bestellen des Wirklichen als Bestand."

27. Heidegger, "What Are Poets For?," in A. Hofstadter (ed.), *Poetry, Language, Thought* (New York: Harper & Row, 1971), p. 110. For the German, see "Wozu Dichter?," *Holzwege*, p. 266: "Das Offene wird zum Gegenstand und so auf das Menschenwesen zu-gedreht."

28. Heidegger, *Introduction to Metaphysics* (New York: Doubleday, 1961), p. 52. For the German, see *Einführung in die Metaphysik* (Tübingen: Max Niemeyer Verlag, 1953), p. 48: "Das ursprünglich aufgehende Sichaufrichten der Gewalten des Waltenden, das *phainesthai*, als Erscheinen im großen Sinne der Epiphanie einer Welt, wird jetzt zur herzeigbaren Sichtbarkeit vorhandener Dinge. Das Auge, das Sehen, das ursprünglich Schauend einstmals in das Walten erst den Entwurf hineinschaute, hineinsehend das Werk her-stellte, wird jetzt zum bloßen Ansehen und Besehen und Begaffen."

29. Heidegger, *Being and Time*, p. 88. In *Sein und Zeit*, p. 61, Heidegger writes of "ein starres Begaffen eines puren Vorhandenen." Also see note 10 above.

30. Heidegger, *Basic Concepts* (Bloomington: Indiana University Press, 1993), p. 98; *Grundbegriffe* (Frankfurt am Main: Vittorio Klostermann, 1981), §23, pp. 112–15. Also see Heidegger, *Introduction to Metaphysics*, pp. 159–61; *Einführung der Metaphysik*, pp. 145–47. Heidegger speaks here of "Vorhandenheit" and a certain "ständige Anwesenheit."

31. Heidegger, *Being and Time*, pp. 196–97. For the German, see *Sein und Zeit*, p. 155: "die 'Subjektsetzung' blendet das Seiende ab." One might say that it is a question of the *grammar* of our perceptual experience—that when our experience is structured by the subject-object polarization, our looking and seeing do not let things come into the clearing and lighting in a way that would grant them *space* for shimmering and radiant shining.

32. Heidegger, "The Question Concerning Technology," in *Question Concerning Technology*, p. 28. For the German, see "Die Frage nach der Technik," p. 27: "Das Ge-stell verstellt das Scheinen und Walten der Wahrheit."

33. Heidegger, *Basic Concepts*, §23, p. 97. For the German, see *Grundbegriffe*, §23, p. 113.

34. Ibid., §23, p. 98. Also see §24, p. 102. For the German, see *Grundbegriffe*, §23, pp. 113–14.

35. Heidegger, "On the Essence of Truth," in *Basic Writings*, p. 125; *Vom Wesen der Wahrheit*, p. 14. Also see Heidegger, *Introduction to Metaphysics*, pp. 52–53, 57–61, 79; *Einführung der Metaphysik*, pp. 48–56, 71.

36. Heidegger, "On the Essence of Truth," in *Basic Writings*, p. 125. Italics added. For the German, see *Vom Wesen der Wahrheit*, p. 15: "Das Sicheinlassen auf die Entborgenheit des Seienden verliert sich nicht in dieser, sondern entfaltet sich zu einem Zurücktreten vor dem Seienden, damit dieses in dem, was es ist und wie es ist, sich offenbare und die vorstellende Angleichung aus ihm das Richtmaaß nehme."

37. Heidegger, "On the Essence of Truth," in *Basic Writings*, p. 130; *Vom Wesen der Wahrheit*, p. 19.

38. Wolfgang Köhler, *Dynamics in Psychology* (New York: Washington Square Press, 1965), p. 61.

39. Ibid., p. 102.

40. Ibid., p. 101n.

41. Herbert V. Guenther, *The Dawn of Tantra* (Berkeley: Shambhala Publishing Co., 1975), p. 27.

42. Heidegger, "On the Essence of Truth," in *Basic Writings*, p. 125; *Vom Wesen der Wahrheit*, p. 14. As already indicated, it is a question of a "Zurücktreten vor dem Seiende, damit dieses in dem, was es ist und wie es ist, sich offenbare."

43. There are many fascinating parallels between Heidegger's critique of the subject-object structure and the critique formulated by Adorno in his "Subject and Object," in Andrew Arato and Eike Gebhardt (eds.), *The Essential Frankfurt School Reader* (New York: Continuum, 1987), pp. 497–511. Of course, there are also enormous differences as well, for Adorno connects this critique

with an analysis of the bourgeoisie and brings out the intricate dialectic that turns the discourses of metaphysics into a concealed reflection of bourgeois ideology.

44. Heidegger, *Basic Concepts*, §24, p. 102; *Grundbegriffe*, §24, p. 119.

45. Heidegger, *Introduction to Metaphysics*, p. 99; *Einführung in die Metaphysik*, p. 89.

46. Heidegger, *Introduction to Metaphysics*, p. 52; *Einführung in die Metaphysik*, p. 48: "Das Auge, das Sehen, . . . wird zum bloßen Ansehen und Besehen und Begaffen."

47. Jacques Derrida, "Sending: On Representation," in *Social Research*, vol. 49 (1982), p. 309.

48. Ibid., p. 312.

49. Heidegger, *Seminar in Zähringen* 1973, Gesamtausgabe (Frankfurt am Main: Vittorio Klostermann, 1986), bd. 15, p. 399.

50. Heidegger, "The Origin of the Work of Art," in *Poetry, Language, Thought*, p. 64. For the original German text, see "Der Ursprung des Kunstwerkes," *Holzwege*, p. 52.

51. René Char, "Suzerain," *Le Poème Pulvérisé, Oeuvres Complètes* (Paris: Gallimard, 1983), p. 261. This line is quoted by Michel Foucault in *Folie et Déraison. Histoire de la Folie à l'Âge Classique* (Paris: Plon, 1961), p. x. For Foucault, this articulates "the most urgent and restrained definition of truth." Foucault's use of the word "restrained" suggests that he does not read Char's sentence to be describing an *assault* on things, an *attack* such as is characteristic, and indeed—according to Heidegger—definitive of our modern age. For a quick first reading, Char seems to be describing a very aggressive relation to things: the poet would *take away* from things the illusion that protects them from us, thereby exposing them, leaving them defenseless and vulnerable to our will to power; and he would *give* them, or let them keep, what they have granted us to behold. In short, he would *refuse* the appearance as which things give themselves to us. This would thus place perception and the love of truth within the *Gestell* of the most extreme will to power: the poet would have them completely determined by the violence inherent in re-presentation. But the poet's sentence is much more complex, much more subtle. In his perception, which in German is said to be a *Wahr-nehmung*, literally, a "taking-of-truth," a "taking-to-be-true," the poet, recognizing appearance (the *Schein* of the *Erscheinung*) *as* appearance, is attempting to break out of the spell of ordinary perceptual habits and wrest from things the deeper truth of their appearance—the truth, namely, of unconcealment. Foucault is right to speak, here, of "restraint," because the violent struggle is *for the sake of* the phenomenological *epokhé*, the restraint that lets the thing maintain its grounding in the interplay of concealment and unconcealment. There are other passages in Char's *oeuvre* which bear on these matters: "Faire un poème, c'est prendre possession d'un au-delà; nuptial qui se trouve bien dans cette vie, très rattaché à elle, et cependant à proximité des urnes de la mort" ("Nous Avons," p. 409, *Oeuvres Complètes*). "Le poète ne retient pas ce qu'il découvre; l'ayant transcrit, le perd bientôt."

("La bibliothèque en feu," ibid., p. 409). "La moindre clarté naît d'un acte violent, même une allumette que vous craquez, un phare d'auto que vous allumez. La Poèsie aime cette violence écumante et sa double saveur qui écoute aux portes du langage." ("Sous ma casquette amarante," ibid., p. 858). "L'imagination jouit surtout de ce qui ne lui est pas accordé, car elle seule possède l'éphémère en totalité" ("Moulin premier," *Le Marteau sans Maître,* ibid., p. 70). "Ces notes marquent la résistance d'un humanisme conscient de ses devoirs, discret sur ses vertus, désirant réserver *l'inaccessible* champ libre à la fantasie de ses soleils, et décidé à payer le *prix* pour cela." (*Feuillets d'Hypnos,* ibid., p. 173).

52. Heidegger, *Beiträge zur Philosophie,* pp. 296–97, 301–2.

53. Heidegger, *Introduction to Metaphysics,* p. 105. For the German, see *Einführung in der Metaphysik* (Tübingen: Max Niemeyer Verlag, 1953), p. 113.

54. Heidegger, *Being and Time,* p. 265. In German, see *Sein und Zeit,* p. 222: "Daher muß das Dasein wesenhaft das auch schon Entdeckte *gegen* den Schein und die Verstellung ausdrücklich zueignen und sich der Entdecktheit immer wieder versichern . . . Seiendes sieht so aus wie . . . , d.h. es ist in gewisser Weise schon entdeckt und doch nicht verstellt. Die Wahrheit (Entdecktheit) muß dem Seienden immer erst abgerungen werden. Das Seiende wird der Verborgenheit entrissen. Die jeweilige faktische Entdecktheit ist gleichsam immer ein Raub. Ist es Zufall, daß die Griechen sich über das Wesen der Wahrheit in einem privativen Ausdruck (*a-letheia*) aussprechen?"

55. Heidegger, "What are Poets For?," in *Poetry, Language, Thought,* p. 120. For the German, see "Wozu Dichter?," *Holzwege,* p. 275: Production (*Herstellen*) "ist nur in der Vergegenständlichung möglich. Sie sperrt uns jedoch gegen das Offene ab. Das wagende Wagen stellt keinen Schutz her."

56. Heidegger, *What Is Called Thinking?* (New York: Harper & Row, 1968), p. 237. For the original German, see *Was Heisst Denken?* (Tübingen: Max Niemeyer Verlag, 1954), p. 144: "Solches Weilen erfahren die Griechen als Scheinen im Sinne des gelichteten leuchtenden Sichzeigens."

57. Heidegger, "A Dialogue on Language," in *On the Way to Language* (New York: Harper & Row, 1971), p. 38. For the German, see "Aus einem Gespräch von der Sprache," *Unterwegs zur Sprache* (Pfullingen: Günther Neske, 1959), p. 132.

58. Heidegger, "The Question Concerning Technology," in *Question Concerning Technology,* p. 28, cited earlier. For the German original, see "Die Frage nach der Technik," op. cit., p. 27.

59. Heidegger, "The Question Concerning Technology," in *Question Concerning Technology,* p. 34. For the German, see "Die Frage nach der Technik," op. cit., p.34. Heidegger's phrase, here, is "Glanz des Scheinenden."

60. Heidegger, *Being and Time,* p. 177. Italics added. In *Sein und Zeit,* p. 138.

61. Heidegger, *Introduction to Metaphysics,* pp. 153, 159. In *Einführung in die Metaphysik,* p. 145: "ein letzter Schein und Schimmer."

62. Heidegger, *Being and Time,* p. 197; *Sein und Zeit,* p. 155.

63. Heidegger, "The Turning," in *Question Concerning Technology,* p. 45. Also see p. 49. For the German, see "Die Kehre," *Die Technik und die Kehre,*

p. 43: "Im Blick und als Blick tritt das Wesen in sein eigenes Leuchten. Durch das Element seines Leuchtens hindurch birgt der Blick sein Erblicktes in das Blicken zurück. Das Blicken aber wahrt im Leuchten zugleich das verborgene Dunkel seiner Herkunft als das Ungelichtete." See also op. cit., pp. 46–47.

64. Heidegger, *Beiträge zur Philosophie*, p. 11.

65. Heidegger, "The Anaximander Fragment," in EGT, p. 13. This is an English translation of Nietzsche's 1873 translation from the Greek, a translation he proposed in his *Philosophy in the Tragic Age of the Greeks*. For the original German, see "Der Spruch des Anaximander," *Holzwege*, 4th edition (Frankfurt am Main: Vittorio Klostermann, 1963), p. 296.

66. Heidegger, "The Anaximander Fragment," in EGT, p. 26. Here and throughout the chapter, I have reduced to a small "b" the capital "B" in the English translation of "Sein." For the German, see "Der Spruch des Anaximander," op. cit., p. 310: "Das Seiende selbst tritt nicht in dieses Licht des Seins. Die Unverborgenheit des Seienden, die ihm gewährte Helle, verdunkelt das Licht des Seins." "Das Sein entzieht sich, indem es sich in das Seiende entbirgt." "Dergestalt beirrt das Sein, es lichtend, das Seiende mit der Irre."

67. Heidegger, "The Anaximander Fragment," in EGT, p. 30. In the German text, p. 315: With regard to the "Weisen des sich lichtenden Auf- und Untergehen," the ways of luminous rising and decline, Heidegger writes of "das Gehen das dem Unverborgenen wieder ent-steht und in das Verborgene weg- und abgeht."

68. Heidegger, "The Anaximander Fragment," in EGT, p. 34. For the German, see "Der Spruch des Anaximander," op. cit., p. 319: "Das 'gegen' in gegenwärtig meint nicht das Gegenüber zu einem Subjekt, sondern die offene Gegend der Unverborgenheit, in die herein und innerhalb welcher das Beigekommene verweilt."

69. Heidegger, "The Anaximander Fragment," in EGT, p. 36. For the German, see "Der Spruch des Anaximander," op. cit., p. 322: "Die Inständigkeit in ihr [die Lichtung] ist das Gefüge aller menschliche Sinne."

70. Heidegger, "The Anaximander Fragment," in EGT p. 37. For the German, see "Der Spruch des Anaximander," op. cit., p. 322: "Wenn das Anwesende im vorhinein in der Sicht steht, west alles zusammen, eines bringt das andere mit sich, eines läßt das andere fahren. Das gegenwärtig in der Unverborgenheit Anwesende weilt in ihr als der offenen Gegend. Das gegenwärtig in die Gegend Weilende (Weilige) kommt in sie aus der Verborgenheit hervor und kommt in der Unverborgenheit an."

71. Heidegger, "The Anaximander Fragment," in EGT, p. 37. Italics added. For the German, see "Der Spruch des Anaximander," op. cit., p. 323: "Das jeweilige Anwesende, das Gegenwärtige, west aus dem Abwesen. Dies ist gerade vom eigentlich Anwesenden zu sagen, das unser gewöhnliches Vorstellen von allem Abwesen ausscheiden möchte."

72. Heidegger, "The Anaximander Fragment," in EGT, p. 41. For the German, see "Der Spruch des Anaximander," op. cit., p. 326: "Inwiefern ist das jeweilig Anwesende in der Ungerechtigkeit? Was ist am Anwesenden unrecht?

Ist es nicht das Rechte des Anwesenden, daß es je und je weilt und verweilt und so sein Anwesen erfüllt?"

73. Heidegger, "The Anaximander Fragment," in EGT, p. 42. For the German, see "Der Spruch des Anaximander," op. cit., pp. 327–28: "Das Angekommene kann gar auf seiner Weile bestehen, einzig um dadurch anwesender zu bleiben im Sinne des Beständigen. Das Je-Weilige beharrt auf seinem Anwesen. Dergestalt nimmt es sich aus seiner übergänglichen Weile heraus. Es spreizt sich in den Eigensinn des Beharrens auf. Es kehrt sich nicht mehr an das andere Anwesende. Es versteift sich, als sei dies das Verweilen, auf die Beständigkeit des Fortbestehens."

74. Heidegger, "The Anaximander Fragment," in EGT, p. 42. "Der Spruch des Anaximander," op. cit., p. 328: "In der Fuge der Weile wesend, geht das Anwesende aus ihr und ist als das Je-Weilige in der Un-Fuge. Alles Je-Weilige steht in der Un-Fuge."

75. Heidegger, "The Anaximander Fragment," in EGT, p. 43. "Der Spruch des Anaximander," op. cit., p. 328: "Die Un-Fuge besteht darin, daß das Je-Weilige sich auf die Weile im Sinne des nur beständigen zu versteifen sucht. Das Weilen als Beharren ist, von der Fuge der Weile hergedacht, der Aufstand in das bloße Andauern. Im Anwesen selbst, das je das Anwesende in die Gegend der Unverborgenheit ver-weilt, steht die Beständigung auf. Durch dieses Aufständische der Weile besteht das Je-Weilige auf der bloßen Beständigkeit."

76. Heidegger, "The Anaximander Fragment," in EGT, p. 46. "Der Spruch des Anaximander," op. cit., p. 331: "Doch dadurch spreizt sich auch schon jedes Weilige auf gegen das Andere. Keines achtet auf das Weilige Wesen des Anderen. Die Je-Weiligen sind gegen einander rücksichtslos, jedes je aus der im weilenden Anwesen selbst waltenden und von ihm nahegelegten Sucht des Beharrens."

77. Heidegger, "The Anaximander Fragment," in EGT, p. 44. "Der Spruch des Anaximander," op. cit., p. 329: "Insofern es in das Ungegenwärtige sich gehören läßt."

78. Heidegger, "The Anaximander Fragment," in EGT, p. 45. "Der Spruch des Anaximander," op. cit., p. 330: "Die je-weilig Anwesenden lassen Fug gehören *allélois*, einander."

79. Heidegger, "The Anaximander Fragment," in EGT, p. 50. Italics in the original. "Der Spruch des Anaximander," op. cit., pp. 335–36: "Unversehens wird das Anwesen und das Anwesende je etwas für sich. Vom Anwesenden her vorgestellt, wird es zu dem über alles Anwesende her und so zum höchsten Anwesenden. Wenn das Anwesen genannt wird, ist schon Anwesendes vorgestellt. Im Grunde wird das Anwesen als ein solches gegen das Anwesende nicht unterschieden. Es gilt nur als das Allgemeinste und Höchste des Anwesenden und somit als ein solches. Das Wesen des Anwesens und mit ihm der Unterschied des Anwesens zum Anwesenden bleibt vergessen. *Die Seinsvergessenheit ist die Vergessenheit des Unterschiedes des Seins zum Seienden.*"

80. Heidegger, "Logos (Heraclitus, Fragment B50)," in EGT, p. 60. For the original German, see *Vorträge und Aufsätze*, 3rd edition (Pfullingen: Günther

Neske, 1967), p. 208: "Eigentlich bedeutet *legein* das sich und anderes sammel-
nde Nieder- und Vorlegen." In future references to the German book in which
this text appears, the abbreviation "VA" will be used.

81. Heidegger, "Logos (Heraclitus, Fragment B50)," in EGT, p. 61. For the
German, see VA, p. 209: "Sammeln ist jedoch mehr als bloßes Anhäufen. Zum
Sammeln gehört das einholende Einbringen."

82. Heidegger, "Logos (Heraclitus, Fragment B50)," in EGT, p. 62. For the
German, see VA, p. 210: "Vielmehr ist das Lesen schon dem Legen eingelegt.
Jedes Lesen ist schon Legen. Alles Legen ist von sich her lesend. . . . Das Legen
bringt zum Liegen, indem es beisammen-vor-liegen läßt."

83. Heidegger, "Logos (Heraclitus, Fragment B50)," in EGT, p. 64. For the
German, see VA, 213: "Der *Logos* bringt das Erscheinende, das ins Vorliegen her-
vor-Kommende, von ihm selbst her zum Scheinen, zum gelichteten Sichzeigen."

84. Heidegger, *Beiträge zur Philosophie*, pp. 17 and 243.

85. Heidegger, "Logos (Heraclitus, Fragment B50)," in EGT, p. 67. Also see
pp. 64–68 and 74–75. For the German, see VA, p. 217: "in der lesenden Lege, im
Logos, beruht."

86. Heidegger, "Logos (Heraclitus, Fragment B50)," in EGT, p. 70. For the
German, see VA, p. 220: "Das Legen ist ein Bergen. Es birgt alles Anwesende in
sein Anwesen, aus dem es eigens als das jeweilige Anwesende durch das
sterbliche *legein* ein- und her-vor-geholt werden kann."

87. Heidegger, "Logos (Heraclitus, Fragment B50)," in EGT, p. 71. For the
German, see VA, p. 220: "Alles Entbergen enthebt Anwesendes der Verborgenheit. Das Entbergen braucht die Verborgenheit. Die *A-letheia* ruht in der *Lethé*,
schöpft aus dieser, legt vor, was durch diese hinterlegt bleibt. Der *Logos* ist *in
sich zumal* ein Entbergen und Verbergen. Er ist dies *Aletheia*."

88. Heidegger, "Logos (Heraclitus, Fragment B50)," in EGT, p. 74. For the
German, see VA, p. 224: "Wenn dem *akouein* der Sterblichen einzig am *Logos*,
an der lesenden Lege, gelegen ist, dann hat sich das sterbliche *legein* in das
Gesamt des *Logos* schicklich verlegt. Das sterbliche *legein* liegt im *Logos* gebor-
gen. Vom Geschick her ist es in das *homologein* er-eignet. So bleibt es dem *Logos* vereignet. Auf solche Weise ist das sterbliche *legein* geschicklich. Aber es
ist nie das *Geschick* selbst."

89. Heidegger, "Moira (Parmenides VIII, 34–41)," in *Early Greek Thinking*
(hereafter abbreviated "EGT"), p. 99. For the German, see *Vorträge und Aufsätze* (VA), p. 253: Heidegger's term, here, is *das alltägliches Vernehmen*, which
refers to apprehension generally, and not necessarily to perception as such.

90. Heidegger, "Moira (Parmenides VIII, 34–41)," in EGT, p. 82. For the German, see VA, p. 234: "Die neuzeitliche Philosophie erfährt das Seiende als den
Gegenstand. Es kommt zu seinem Entgegenstehen durch die Perception und für
sie. Das *percipere* greift, was Leibniz deutlicher sah, als appetitus nach dem
Seienden aus, greift es an, um es durch greifend im Begriff an sich zu bringen
und seine Präsenz auf das *percipere* zurück zu beziehen (*repraesentare*). Die
repraesentatio, die Vorstellung, bestimmt sich als das percipierende auf sich
(das Ich) Zu-Stellen dessen, was erscheint."

91. Heidegger, *Parmenides* (Bloomington: Indiana University Press, 1992), p. 156. For the original German, see the *Gesamtausgabe*, II. Abteilung: *Vorlesungen 1923–44*, vol. 54 (Frankfurt am Main: Vittorio Klostermann, 1982), p. 232.

92. Heidegger, "Moira," in EGT, p. 87. For the German, see VA, p. 241: "daß sich die Lichtung des Seins des Seienden als Lichtung verbirgt."

93. Heidegger, "Moira," in EGT, p. 96. For the German, see VA, p. 251: "Das Spiel des rufenden, entfaltenden und wachstümlichen Lichtes wird nicht eigens sichtbar. Es scheint so unscheinbar wie das Morgenlicht in der stillen Pracht der Lilien auf dem Felde und der Rosen im Garten."

94. Heidegger, "Moira," in EGT, p. 97. For the German, see VA, p. 252: "Das Wesen der *Aletheia* bleibt verhüllt. Die von ihr gewährte Sichtbarkeit läßt das Anwesen des Anwesenden als "Aussehen" (*eidos*) und als 'Gesicht' (*idea*) aufgehen. Demgemäß bestimmt sich die vernehmende Beziehung zum Anwesen des Anwesenden als ein Sehen (*eidenai*). Das von der *visio* her geprägte Wissen und dessen Evidenz können auch dort ihre Wesensherkunft aus der lichtenden Entbergung nicht verleugnen."

95. Heidegger, "Moira," in EGT, p. 99. For the German, see VA, pp. 253–54: "Diese [Sterblichen] nehmen auf . . . was sich ihnen unmittelbar, sogleich und zunächst, darbietet . . . Sie halten sich an das in ihr Entfaltete und zwar an jenes, was die Sterblichen unmittelbar beansprucht: an das Anwesende ohne Rücksicht auf das Anwesen."

96. Heidegger, "Moira," in EGT, pp. 99–100. For the German, see VA, pp. 254–55: "Und wo das gewohnte, aus den Wörtern sprechende Vernehmen das Aufgehen und Untergehen antrifft, begnügt es sich mit dem Sowohl-als auch des Entstehens, *gignesthai*, und Vergehens, *hollusthai*. . . . Das gewohnte Vernehmen bewegt sich zwar im Gelichteten des Anwesenden, sieht Scheinendes, *phanon* (VIII, 41), in der Farbe, aber tummelt sich in ihrem wechsel, *ameibein*, achtet nicht das stillen Lichtes der Lichtung, die aus der Entfaltung der Zwiefalt kommt."

97. Heidegger, *Beiträge zur Philosophie*, p. 242. I translate: "to be able to wait in this lighting, until the hints come."

98. Ibid., p. 240. I translate: "the protective watchfulness of humanity is the ground of another history."

99. Theodor Adorno, *Minima Moralia: Reflections from Damaged Life* (London: Verso, New Left Books, 1978), pp. 227–28. For the original German, see *Gesammelte Schriften*, vol. 4 (Frankfurt am Main: Suhrkamp, 1951), pp. 257–59.

100. Heidegger, "Aletheia (Heraclitus, Fragment B16)," in EGT, p. 103. For the original German, see VA, p. 258: "Denn er [Heraklit] sagt das Lichtend, indem er versucht, dessen Scheinen in die Sprache des Denkens hervorzurufen. Das Lichtende währt, insofern es lichtet. Wir nennen sein Lichten die Lichtung. Was zu ihr gehört, wie sie geschieht, und wo, bleibt zu bedenken. Das Wort 'licht' bedeutet: leuchtend, strahlend, hellend. Das Lichten gewährt das Scheinen, gibt Scheinendes in ein Erscheinen frei. Das Freie ist der Bereich der Unverborgenheit. Ihn verwaltet das Entbergen."

101. Ibid. The German reads as follows: "Wie kommt es, daß man auch dann, wenn man das Zusammengehören beider vermerkt, dieses von einer der beiden Seiten her zu erklären versucht oder aber ein drittes bezieht, was Objekt und Subjekt zusammengreifen soll?"

102. Heidegger, "Aletheia," in EGT, p. 115. For the German, see VA, p. 272: "Die Fuge, dank deren sich Entbergen und Verbergen gegenwendig ineinanderfügen, das Unscheinbare alles Unscheinbaren bleiben muß, da es jedem Erscheinenden des Scheinen schenkt."

103. Heidegger, "Aletheia," in EGT, p. 118. For the German, see VA, p. 276: "Denken wir es [das Weltfeuer] als das reine Lichten, dann bringt dieses nicht nur die Helle, sondern zugleich das Freie, worin alles, zumal das Gegenwendige, ins Scheinen kommt. Lichten ist somit mehr als nur Erhellen, mehr auch als Freilegen. Lichten ist das sinnend-versammelnde Vorbringen ins Freie, ist Gewähren von Anwesen."

104. Ibid. My italics. The German reads as follows: "Das Ereignis der Lichtung ist die Welt. Das sinnend-versammelnde, ins Freie bringende Lichten ist Entbergen und beruht im Sichverbergen."

105. Heidegger, "Aletheia," in EGT, p. 119. For the German, see VA, pp. 277–78: "Demgemäß ist das Lichten kein bloßes Erhellen und Belichten. Weil Anwesen heißt: aus der Verbergung her in die Entbergung vor währen, deshalb betrifft das entbergend-verbergende Lichten das Anwesen des Anwesenden."

106. Heidegger, "Aletheia," in EGT, p. 120. My italics. For the German, see VA, p. 278: "Die Lichtung beleuchtet Anwesendes nicht nur, sondern sie versammelt und birgt es zuvor ins Anwesen."

107. Heidegger, "Aletheia," in EGT, p. 119. For the German, see VA, pp. 278–79: "Sie sind in der Lichtung nicht nur beleuchtet, sondern aus ihr zu ihr er-leuchtet. So vermögen sie es denn auf *ihre* Weise, das Lichten zu vollbringen (ins Volle seines Wesens bringen) und dadurch die Lichtung zu hüten. Götter und Menschen sind nicht nur von einem Licht, und sei dies auch ein übersinnliches, belichtet, sodaß sie sich vor ihm nie in das Finstere verstecken können. Sie sind in ihrem Wesen gelichtet. Sie sind er-lichtet: in das Ereignis der Lichtung vereignet, darum nie verborgen, sondern ent-borgen, dies noch in einem anderen Sinne gedacht. Wie die Entfernten der Ferne gehören, so sind die indem jetzt zu denkenden Sinne Entborgenen der bergenden, sie haltenden und verhaltenden Lichtung zugetraut."

108. Heidegger, "Aletheia," in EGT, p. 122. For the German, see VA, p. 281: "Die Sterblichen sind unablässig dem entbergend-bergenden Versammeln zugekehrt, das alles Anwesende in sein Anwesen lichtet. Doch sie kehren sich dabei ab von der Lichtung und kehren sich nur an das Anwesende, das sie im alltäglichen Verkehr mit allem und jedem unmittelbar antreffen. Sie meinen, dieser Verkehr mit dem Anwesenden verschaffe ihnen wie von selbst die gemäße Vertrautheit. Und dennoch bleibt es ihnen fremd. Denn sie ahnen nichts von jenem, dem sie zugetraut sind: vom Anwesen, das lichtend jeweils erst Anwesendes zum Vorschein kommen läßt. Der *Logos*, in dessen Lichtung sie gehen und stehen, bleibt ihnen verborgen, ist für sie vergessen."

109. Heidegger, "Aletheia," in EGT, p. 123. For the German, see VA, p. 281: "Aber das Goldene des unscheinbaren Scheinens der Lichtung läßt sich nicht greifen, weil es selbst kein Greifendes, sondern das reine Ereignen ist. Das unscheinbare Scheinen der Lichtung entströmt dem heilen Sichbergen in der ansichhaltenden Verwahrnis des Geschickes."

110. Heidegger, "Aletheia," in EGT, p. 120. For the German, see VA, p. 279: "[jene] ihrem Wesen nach Erlichtete und so in einem ausgezeichneten Sinne der Lichtung Zu-hörende und Zugehörige sind."

111. Heidegger, "Aletheia," in EGT, p. 121. For the German, see VA, p.270: "diese [Götter und Menschen] nicht nur als Belichtete und Angeschaute in der Lichtung gehören, sondern as jene Unscheinbaren, die auf ihre Weise das Lichten mitbringen und es in seinem Währen verwahren und überliefern."

112. Heidegger, *Beiträge zur Philosophie*, pp. 240 and 242.

113. Heidegger, *Parmenides*, pp. 145–46. For the German, see the *Gesamtausgabe*, vol. 54, pp. 216–17. This German text will hereafter be referred to as "GA 54."

114. Heidegger, "Logos (Heraclitus, Fragment B50)," in EGT, p. 65. For the German, see VA, p. 215.

115. Heidegger, *Parmenides*, p. 146. Italics added. For the German, see GA 54, p. 217.

116. Maurice Merleau-Ponty, *Phenomenology of Perception* (London: Routledge & Kegan Paul, 1962), p. 216. In French: *Phénomenologie de la Perception* (Paris: Librairie Gallimard, 1945), p. 251.

117. Heidegger, "Language," in Hofstadter, *Poetry, Language, Thought*, p. 192. For the German, see "Die Sprache," *Unterwegs zur Sprache* (Pfullingen: Günther Neske, 1959), p. 14: "Die Sprache erwirkt und er-gibt erst den Menschen. So gedacht wäre der Mensch ein Versprechen der Sprache."

118. Heidegger, "Language," op. cit., p. 199. For the German, see "Die Sprache," op. cit., p. 22.

119. Heidegger, *Introduction to Metaphysics*, p. 116. For the German, see *Einführung in die Metaphysik*, p. 105: "Vernehmen meint einmal: hinnehmen, auf einen Zukommenlassen, nämlich das, was sich zeigt, erscheint."

120. Adorno, "Anmerkungen zum philosophischen Denken," in *Stichworte*, *Gesammelte Werke* (Frankfurt am Main: Suhrkamp Verlag, vol. 10, part 2, p. 602.

121. Heidegger, *Beiträge zur Philosophie*, p. 256. The human being (*der Mensch*) is "dem Ereignis er-eignet": appropriated by, given over to, and comes into his or her own through the coming-to-pass and coming-into-its-own of being.

122. Heidegger, *Beiträge zur Philosophie*, p. 92. I translate: an essential unfolding of its truth."

123. Heidegger, "The Thing," in *Poetry, Language, Thought*, pp. 174–81. For the German, see "Das Ding," VA, pp. 163–81. Read in German, this essay is an especially good example of how Heidegger thinks by listening to language—and in particular, by letting the play of the sensuous word-sounds, all their

echoes, reverberations, overtones, and undertones, give him something to think about. It also illustrates, therefore, how thinking must let itself be guided by the metaphorical "truth" of *aletheia,* the interplay of concealment and unconcealment always at work *beneath* the level of statements and assertions—the level of propositional truth. Statements and assertions take place in a dimension of language closed to the meta-phorical dynamics of concealment and unconcealment—there where words sound and resound. Heidegger's discourse comes from the *meta-phorical* dimension of language, speaks a "truth" deeply rooted in this subsoil. The "truth" it speaks, coming from the clearing, the openness of the field of meaning in the interplay of concealment and unconcealment, is thereby capable of breaching the *stasis* of settled meanings belonging to the discourse of statements and assertions.

124. See Heidegger, "The End of Philosophy," in *On Time and Being* (New York: Harper & Row, 1972), pp. 67–71; *Zur Sache des Denkens* (Tübingen: Max Niemeyer Verlag, 1969), pp. 74–79.

125. Friedrich Nietzsche, "On Truth and Lies in a Nonmoral Sense," in Daniel Breazeale (ed. and trans.), *Philosophy and Truth: Selections from Nietzsche's Notebooks of the Early 1870's* (New Jersey: Humanities Press International, 1979), p. 84.

126. Wallace Stevens, "On the Road Home," in *The Collected Poems of Wallace Stevens* (New York: Alfred E. Knopf, 1961), pp. 203–4.

127. See Merleau-Ponty, "The Child's Relations with Others," in *The Primacy of Perception* (Evanston, IL: Northwestern University Press, 1964), pp. 96–155.

128. See Rolf Wiggershaus, *The Frankfurt School: Its History, Theories, and Political Significance* (Cambridge, MA: MIT Press, 1994), p. 48.

129. Heidegger, *Beiträge zur Philosophie,* p. 306.

130. Ibid., p. 253. Adorno is quite mistaken when, in *Negative Dialectics,* he accuses Heidegger of suppressing difference and contradiction in his concept of being, treating it "as an identity, as pure Being itself, devoid of its otherness" (New York: Continuum, 1973), p. 104. The fact of the matter is rather that Heidegger challenged the traditional ways of thinking the concept of being on precisely these grounds. His careful examination of the experience of being as nothingness, as groundless, and his emphasis on the interplay of presence and absence in the moment of unconcealment certainly attest to the persistence of Heidegger's concern in this regard. Heidegger's concept of being cannot possibly be articulated in terms of a logic of identity.

131. Heidegger, *Beiträge zur Philosophie,* p. 264.

132. Ibid., p. 332.

133. Ibid., p. 335.

134. Ibid., p. 387.

135. Heidegger, "The Way Back into the Ground of Metaphysics," in Walter Kaufman (ed. and trans.), *Existentialism from Dostoevsky to Sartre* (New York: Meridian, New American Library, 1975), p. 265. For the German, see *Was Ist Metaphysik?* (Frankfurt am Main: Vittorio Klostermann, 1955), p. 7.

136. Heidegger, " . . . Poetically Man Dwells . . . ," in *Poetry, Language, Thought*, p. 223. For the original German, see " . . . Dichterisch Wohnet der Mensch . . . ," *Vorträge und Aufsätze*, p. 197.

137. Nietzsche, *Joyful Wisdom* (New York: Frederick Ungar, 1960), §78, p. 110.

138. G. W. F. Hegel, *The Encyclopaedia of the Philosophical Sciences*, in William Wallace (ed. and trans.), *The Logic of Hegel*, second edition revised and augmented (London: Oxford University Press, 1950), Part I, chapter 1, p. 20.

139. Heidegger, *Beiträge zur Philosophie*, p. 5.

140. Ibid., pp. 431–32.

141. Ibid., p. 112.

142. Walter Benjamin, "On Language as Such and On the Language of Man," in *Reflections: Essays, Aphorisms, Autobiographical Writings* (New York: Schocken, 1986), p. 326.

143. Herbert Marcuse, "On the Affirmative Character of Culture," in *Negations: Essays in Critical Theory* (Boston: Beacon Press, 1986), p. 98.

CHAPTER 5. THE FIELD OF VISION

1. Novalis (Friedrich von Hardenberg), "On Goethe," in *Philosophical Writings* (Albany: State University of New York Press, 1997), p. 118.

2. Maurice Merleau-Ponty, *The Visible and the Invisible* (Evanston, IL: Northwestern University Press, 1968), p. 247; *Le Visible et l'Invisible* (Paris: Gallimard, 1964), p. 300. The English translation will hereafter be cited as "VIE," and the French original will be cited as "VIF."

3. Theodor Adorno, "Sociology and Empirical Research," in *The Positivist Dispute in German Sociology* (London: Heineman, 1981), p. 69.

4. Max Horkheimer and Theodor Adorno, "Note," in *Dialectic of Enlightenment* (New York: Continuum Publishing, 19), p. 230.

5. For more on this, see my book, *The Opening of Vision: Nihilism and the Postmodern Situation* (London: Routledge, 1988) and "Decline and Fall: Ocularcentrism in Heidegger's Reading of the History of Metaphysics," in D. M. Levin (ed.), *Modernity and the Hegemony of Vision* (Los Angeles: University of California Press, 1994).

6. See Martin C. Dillon, "Gestalt Theory and Merleau-Ponty's Concept of Intentionality," in *Man and World*, vol. 4, no. 4 (November 1971), pp. 436–59.

7. Merleau-Ponty, *Phenomenology of Perception* (London and New York: Routledge & Kegan Paul, 1962), p. 406; *Phénoménologie de la perception* (Paris: Gallimard, 1945), p. 465. Hereafter, the English will be cited as "PPE" and the French as "PPF."

8. Merleau-Ponty, *The Visible and the Invisible*, p. 185; *Le Visible et l'Invisible*, p. 239.

9. Martin Heidegger, 1973 Seminar in Zähringen, in *Seminare, Gesamtausgabe* (Frankfurt am Main: Vittorio Klostermann, 1986), bd. 15, p. 385.

10. Horkheimer and Adorno, *Dialectic of Enlightenment*, p. 230.

11. Ludwig Wittgenstein, *Philosophical Investigations* (New York: Macmillan, 1953), p. 194.

12. Walter Benjamin, "On the Mimetic Faculty," in *Reflections: Essays, Aphorisms, Autobiographical Writings* (New York: Schocken Books, 1986), p. 333.

13. Ibid., p. 334.

14. Ibid.

15. Heidegger, *Parmenides* (Bloomington: Indiana University Press, 1992), p. 150. Italics added, and the translation has been altered: here, and throughout this present essay, the German word, *Sein,* will *not* be capitalized. For the German, see *Parmenides, Gesamtausgabe,* vol. 54 (Frankfurt am Main: Vittorio Klostermann, 1992), p. 223. Hereafter, the English will be cited as "PE" and the German as "PG."

16. Heidegger, "On the Essence of Truth," in *Basic Writings,* revised and expanded edition (New York: Harper & Row, 1993), p. 125. Italics added. For the original German, see *Vom Wesen der Wahrheit* (Frankfurt am Main: Vittorio Klostermann, 1949), p. 15.

17. Michel Foucault, Interview, *Le Monde,* July 22, 1961.

18. Heidegger, "The Anaximander Fragment," in *Early Greek Thinking* (New York: Harper & Row, 1975), p. 36: "Der Spruch des Anaximander," *Holzwege* (Frankfurt am Main: Vittorio Klostermann, 1950), p. 322. Hereafter, the English will be cited as "AXE," the German by "AXG."

19. Heidegger, "Plato's Doctrine of Truth," in H. Aiken and W. Barrett (eds.), *Philosophy in the Twentieth Century* (New York: 1962), vol. 3, p. 265. Also see pp. 261 and 267. For the German original, see *Platons Lehre von der Wahrheit* (Bern: Verlag A. Francke, 1947), p. 41.

20. Heidegger, *Discourse on Thinking* (New York: Harper & Row, 1966), pp. 58–59; *Gelassenheit* (Pfullingen: Günther Neske, 1959), pp. 31–32. Hereafter, the English will be cited as "DT" and the German as "G."

21. Benjamin, *The Origin of German Tragic Drama* (London: Verso, New Left Books, 1977), p. 36.

22. Heidegger, *Basic Concepts* (Bloomington: Indiana University Press, 1993), §1, Introduction, p. 17.

23. Heidegger, *What Is Called Thinking?* (New York: Harper & Row, 1968), p. 237; *Was Heißt Denken?* (Tübingen: Max Niemeyer Verlag, 1954), p. 144.

24. Heidegger, "What Are Poets For?," in *Poetry, Language, Thought* (New York: Harper & Row, 1971), p. 110; "Wozu Dichter?" *Holzwege,* p. 266.

25. Heidegger, "The Question Concerning Technology," in *The Question Concerning Technology and Other Essays* (New York: Harper & Row, 1977), p. 28. In German: *Die Technik und die Kehre* (Pfullingen: Güenther Neske, 1962), p. 27.

26. Heidegger, "The Word of Nietzsche: God Is Dead," in *Question Concerning Technology,* p. 107; "Nietzsches Wort 'Gott ist tot,' " *Holzwege,* p. 241.

27. Ibid.

28. Heidegger, *An Introduction to Metaphysics* (New York: Doubleday Publishing Co., 1961), p. 52; *Einführung in die Metaphysik* (Tübingen: Max Niemeyer Verlag, 1953), p. 48.

29. Heidegger, *Being and Time* (New York: Harper & Row, 1962), p. 88; *Sein und Zeit* (Halle: Max Niemeyer Verlag, fifth edition, 1941), p. 61.

30. Heidegger, "The Age of the World Picture," in *Question Concerning Technology*, p. 151; "Die Zeit des Weltbildes," *Holzwege*, p. 101.

31. Heidegger, *Basic Concepts* (Bloomington: Indiana University Press, 1993), pp. 98, 161; *Grundbegriffe, Gesamtausgabe*, vol. 51 (Frankfurt am Main: Vittorio Klostermann, 1981), pp. 113–15.

32. Heidegger, "The Origin of the Work of Art," in *Poetry, Language, Thought*, pp. 25, 82; "Ursprung des Kunstwerkes," *Holzwege*, pp. 15 and 66.

33. Heidegger, *Basic Concepts*, pp. 97–99; *Grundbegriffe*, pp. 113–15.

34. For more on the pathologies that are distinctive of our contemporary world, see D. M. Levin (ed.), *Pathologies of the Modern Self: Postmodern Studies on Narcissism, Schizophrenia, and Depression* (New York: New York University Press, 1987).

35. Heidegger, "What Are Poets For?," in *Poetry, Language, Thought*, p. 120; "Wozu Dichter?," p. *Holzwege*, p. 275.

36. See F. W. J. Schelling, *Schriften von 1794–1798* (Darmstadt: Wissenschaftliche Buchgesellschaft, 1980), p. 217.

37. Quoted without any bibliographical information in Rainer Nägele, *Theater, Theory, Speculation: Walter Benjamin and the Scenes of Modernity* (Baltimore: Johns Hopkins University Press, 1991), p. 110.

38. There are striking and significant similarities between the Buddhist epistemology of the *Abhidharmapitaka* and Heidegger's phenomenology of perception and its *Gestalt*-formations. Heidegger's phenomenology is grounded in the hermeneutics of the ontological difference between being and beings, and recognizes this difference in, and as, the event (*Ereignis*) of opening-up (*Lichtung*) by grace of which there is (*Es gibt*) a field for the taking-place of perceptual experience. In Buddhist epistemology, there are two fundamental, and mutually implicative concepts: *shunyata* and *pratityasamutpada*. The second of these, conventionally translated as "dependent origination," refers to the interdependence and interconnectedness of all things—the fact that all entities are contextualized, situated in a field. The first of these, as Guenther and Trungpa assert, "can be explained in a very simple way. When we perceive, we usually attend to the delimited forms of objects. But these objects are perceived within a field. Attention can be directed either to the concrete limited forms or to the field in which these forms are situated. In the *shunyata* experience, the attention is on the field rather than on the contents. By 'contents', we mean here those forms which are the outstanding features of the field itself. . . . This open dimension is the basic dimension of *shunyata*." Herbert V. Guenther and Chögyam Trungpa, *The Dawn of Tantra* (Berkeley: Shambhala Publishing Co., 1975), p. 27. They point out, further, that "this openness is present in and is actually presupposed by every determinate form. Every determinate entity evolves out of something indeterminate and to a certain extent maintains its connection with this indeterminacy; it is never completely isolated from it. Because the indeterminate entity is not isolated from the indeterminacy and be-

cause nevertheless there is no bridge between the two, our attention can shift back and forth between one and the other" (ibid.).

39. Heidegger, *An Introduction to Metaphysics*, p. 116. Italics added. For the German, see *Einführung in die Metaphysik*, p. 105.

40. Heidegger, "The Origin of the Work of Art," in *Poetry, Language, Thought*, p. 64. In *Holzwege*, see p. 52.

41. Heidegger, "On the Essence of Truth," in *Basic Writings*, p. 130. For the German original, see *Vom Wesen der Wahrheit*, p. 20.

42. Heidegger, "The Turning," in *Question Concerning Technology*, p. 45; "Die Kehre," *Die Technik und die Kehre* (Pfullingen: Günther Neske, 1962), p. 44.

43. Heidegger, "The Turning," op. cit., p. 45. "Die Kehre," op. cit., p. 43.

44. Ibid.

45. Rainer Maria Rilke, *Sämtliche Werke* (Frankfurt am Main: Insel Verlag, 1975), vol. 2, p. 697.

46. Benjamin, *Gesammelte Schriften* (Frankfurt am Main: Suhrkamp Verlag, 1980-), vol. 2, part 1, p. 311.

47. Merleau-Ponty, *Signs* (Evanston, IL: Northwestern University Press, 1964), p. 20.

48. The following texts have been useful in defining the classical conception of the *Gestalt* in the domain of psychology: Kurt Koffka, *Principles of Gestalt Psychology* (New York: Humanities Press, 1935); Wolfgang Köhler, *Gestalt Psychology* (New York: New American Library, 1947) and *Dynamics in Psychology* (New York: Washington Square Press, 1965); Kurt Lewin, *A Dynamic Theory of Personality* (New York: McGraw-Hill, 1935); and Mary Henle, Julian Jaynes, and John Sullivan (eds.), *Historical Conceptions of Psychology* (New York: Springer Publishing Co., 1973), especially the chapter by Edna Heidbreder, "Lewin's Principles of Topological Psychology" and the chapter by Fritz Heider, "Gestalt Theory: Early History and Reminiscences." Also useful: Fritz Perls, *Gestalt Therapy: Excitement and Growth in the Human Personality* (New York: Delta, 1951); Aron Gurwitsch, *Studies in Phenomenology and Psychology* (Evanston, IL: Northwestern University Press, 1966) and *Phenomenology and the Theory of Science* (Evanston, IL: Northwestern University Press, 1974); Alphonso Lingis, "The Elemental Background," in James M. Edie (ed.), *New Essays in Phenomenology* (Chicago: Quadrangle Press, 1969), pp. 24–38; and Samuel J. Todes, "Sensuous Abstraction and the Abstract Sense of Reality," in Edie (ed.), op. cit., pp. 15–23.

49. I have italicized my words, "to be seen as," words that should remind us of Wittgenstein's discussion of "seeing as" in his *Philosophical Investigations*, in order to bring out a point on which I have been insisting for many years, viz., that the logic of phenomenological "description" is *not* the logic of descriptive propositions, description pure and simple, but is in fact the logic of "performatives." In other words, the method of phenomenology cannot be understood in the static, reifying terms of the correspondence theory of truth, but must be understood in the dynamic, more radical terms of an "aletheic" theory of

disclosure. Also see Eugene Gendlin, "Experiential Phenomenology," in Maurice Natanson (ed.), *Phenomenology and the Social Sciences* (Evanston, IL: Northwestern University Press, 1973), pp. 281–319.

50. For more material on his three major new concepts, the "intertwining," the "chiasm," and "reversibility," see "The Intertwining—The Chiasm" and "Working Notes," in *The Visible and the Invisible*. I would insist, though, that there are important, and quite unmistakable *adumbrations* of these concepts already at work in his much earlier work, the *Phenomenology of Perception*.

51. See my "Visions of Narcissism: Intersubjectivity and the Reversals of Reflection," in M. Dillon (ed.), *Merleau-Ponty Vivant* (Albany: State University of New York Press, 1990.

52. Ralph Waldo Emerson, "Circles," in Joel Porte (ed.), *Essays and Lectures* (New York: Library of America, Viking Press, 1983), p. 403.

53. Heidegger, "The Turning," op. cit., p. 39; "Die Kehre," op. cit., p. 39.

54. Heidegger, "Aletheia: Heraclitus Fragment B16," in *Early Greek Thinking*, p. 103; for the German, see *Vorträge und Aufsätze* (Pfullingen: Günther Neske, 1954), p. 258. Hereafter the English will be cited as "AE" and the German as "AG."

55. Heidegger, "The Turning," op. cit., p. 47; "Die Kehre," op. cit., p. 45.

56. Heidegger, "The Age of the World Picture," op. cit., p. 131; "Die Zeit des Weltbildes," op. cit., p. 83.

57. The passages that follow, with their titles and page numbers, may all be found in English translation, assembled under the title *Early Greek Thinking* (New York: Harper & Row, 1975). The "Aletheia" essay was written in 1943; "The Anaximander Fragment" was written in 1946; and the "Moira" essay dates back to 1954. The German text of "The Anaximander Fragment" may be found in *Holzwege*. As for the German texts of "Aletheia" and "Moira," they may be found in *Vorträge und Aufsätze*.

58. See Heidegger, "On the Essence of Truth," in *Basic Writings*, pp. 117–38; *Vom Wesen der Wahrheit*, pp. 11–15, on the question of "exposure" ("Aussetzung in die Entborgenheit des Seienden").

59. Heidegger, *On Time and Being* (New York: Harper & Row, 1972), pp. 14–15; *Zur Sache des Denkens* (Tübingen: Max Niemeyer Verlag, 1969), p. 15.

60. Heidegger, "The Turning," op. cit., p. 37; "Die Kehre," op. cit., p. 37.

61. Samuel Beckett, *Endgame* (New York: Grove-Atlantic, 1983).

CHAPTER 6. OUTSIDE THE SUBJECT

1. Maurice Merleau-Ponty, *Humanism and Terror* (Boston: Beacon Press, 1969), p. xiv.

2. Merleau-Ponty, *Phenomenology of Perception* (London: Routledge & Kegan Paul, 1962), p. 127; *Phénoménologie de la perception* (Paris: Librairie Gallimard, 2nd edition, 1945), p. 147. Hereafter, the English title will be cited as "PPE" and the original French as "PPF."

3. Merleau-Ponty, *The Visible and the Invisible* (Evanston, IL: Northwestern University Press, 1979), p. 151; *Le Visible et l'Invisible* (Paris: Gallimard, 1964), p. 198. The English will be cited hereafter as "VIE," the French as "VIF."

4. Michel Foucault, "The Subject and Power," in H. Dreyfus and P. Rabinow, *Michel Foucault: Beyond Structuralism and Hermeneutics* (Chicago: University of Chicago Press, 1982), p. 216.

5. Charles Baudelaire, "La fausse monnaie," *Oeuvres Complètes* (Paris: Bibliothèque de la Pléiade, 1975), vol. 1, p. 319; *Paris Spleen* (New York: New Directions, 1970), p. 53.

6. Merleau-Ponty, "The Child's Relations with Others," in *The Primacy of Perception* (Evanston, IL: Northwestern University Press, 1964), p. 106; "Les Relations avec Autrui Chez l'Enfant" (Paris: Centre du Documentation Universitaire, 1975), p. 15. Hereafter, the English will be cited as "CRO," while the original French will be cited as "CROF."

7. Merleau-Ponty, "Eye and Mind," in *The Primacy of Perception*, 1964), p. 188. Hereafter, references to this essay will be cited as "EM."

8. See my essay, "Tracework: Experience and Description in the Moral Phenomenology of Merleau-Ponty and Levinas," in a forthcoming collection edited by Wayne Froman and published by Northwestern University Press.

9. Merleau-Ponty, "The Concept of Nature" I, in *Themes from the Lectures at the Collège de France, 1952–1960* (Evanston, IL: Northwestern University Press, 1970), p. 82; "Le Concept de Nature," 1956–57, in *Résumés de Cours, Collège de France, 1952–1960* (Paris: Gallimard, 1968), p. 115.

10. See David Michael Levin, "Visions of Narcissism: Intersubjectivity and the Reversals of Reflection," in Martin C. Dillon (ed.), *Merleau-Ponty Vivant* (Albany: State University of New York, 1991), pp. 47–90.

11. See David Michael Levin, "Justice in the Flesh," in Galen A. Johnson and Michael B. Smith (eds.), *Ontology and Alterity in Merleau-Ponty* (Evanston, IL: Northwestern University Press, 1990), pp. 35–44.

12. See David Michael Levin, "Transpersonal Phenomenology and the Corporeal Schema," in *The Humanistic Psychologist*, vol. 16, no. 2 (autumn 1988), pp. 282–313. Also see Giorgio Agamben, *Infanzia e Storia: Distruzione dell 'Esperienza e Origine della Storia* (Torino: Giulio Einaudi, 1979), and *Il Linguaggio e la Morte: Seminario sul Luogo della Negatività;* (Torino: Giulio Einaudi, 1982).

13. Stéphane Mallarmé, "Prose," in *Oeuvres complètes*, ed. by Henri Mondor and G. Jean-Aubry (Paris: Éditions Gallimard, 1945), p. 57.

14. Merleau-Ponty, *Sense and Non-Sense* (Evanston: Northwestern University Press, 1964), p. 143; for the French original, see *Sens et Non-sens* (Paris: Editions Nagel, 1948), p. 252.

15. See David Abram, *The Spell of the Sensuous: Perception and Language in a More-Than-Human World* (New York: Pantheon, 1996). I have also benefited, in writing this chapter, from reading Martin C. Dillon, *Merleau-Ponty's Ontology* (Evanston, IL: Northwestern University Press, 2nd edition, 1997),

Gary Brent Madison, *The Phenomenology of Merleau-Ponty* (Athens, OH: Ohio University Press, 1981), and Samuel Mallin, *Merleau-Ponty's Philosophy* (New Haven, CT: Yale University Press, 1979).

CHAPTER 7. THE INVISIBLE FACE OF HUMANITY

1. Anton Chekhov, "A Day in the Country," in Bernardine Kielty (ed.), *A Treasury of Short Stories* (New York: Simon and Schuster, 1947), p. 57.

2. Ludwig Wittgenstein, *Culture and Value* (Chicago: University of Chicago Press, 1980), p. 1.

3. Jürgen Habermas, "Historical Consciousness and the Post-Traditional Identity: The Federal Republic's Orientation to the West," in *The New Conservativism: Cultural Criticism and the Historians' Debate* (Cambridge, MA: MIT Press, 1989), p. 251.

4. Theodor Adorno, *Minima Moralia: Reflections from a Damaged Life* (London: New Left Books, 1988), §68, p. 105; *Minima Moralia: Reflexionen aus dem beschädigten Leben, Gesammelte Schriften* (Frankfurt am Main: Suhrkamp Verlag, 1980), bd. 4, p. 116.

5. Emmanuel Levinas, "Apropos of Buber: Some Notes," in *Outside the Subject* (Stanford: Stanford University Press, 1994), p. 43.

6. Levinas, "The Meaning of Meaning," in *Outside the Subject*, p. 94.

7. Adorno, *Minima Moralia*, p. 105 in the English, p. 116 in the German.

8. Adorno, *Negative Dialectics* (New York: Continuum Publishing Company, 1973), p. 191; *Negative Dialektik* (Frankfurt am Main: Suhrkamp Verlag, 1973), *Gesammelte Schriften*, bd. 6, p. 192.

9. Henry David Thoreau, "Economy," in *Walden*, in Carl Bode (ed.), *The Portable Thoreau* (New York: Viking Press, 1947), p. 266.

10. Rainer Maria Rilke, "Arrival," in *Poems 1912–1926* (Redding Ridge, CT: Black Swan Books, 1981), p. 113.

11. Franz Rosenzweig, *The Star of Redemption* (Notre Dame: Notre Dame Press, 1985), p. 423.

12. Hermann Hesse, "Iris," in *The Fairy Tales of Hermann Hesse* (New York: Bantam Books, 1995), p. 245.

13. See the discussion by Martin Jay, "Hostage Philosophy: Levinas's Ethical Thought," in *Tikkun*, vol. 5, no. 6 (1994), pp. 85–87.

14. On the double tonality that figures in Heidegger's writing, and in the corresponding hermeneutical experience of "hearkening," see David M. Levin, *The Listening Self* (New York: Routledge, 1989).

15. On this process, see Eugene Gendlin, *Experience and the Creation of Meaning* (Evanston, IL: Northwestern University Press, 2nd revised, 1997); "Experiential Phenomenology," in Maurice Natanson (ed.), *Phenomenology and the Social Sciences* (Evanston, IL: Northwestern University Press, 1973); and "How Philosophy Cannot Appeal to Experience—and How It Can," in David M. Levin (ed.), *Language Beyond Postmodernism* (Evanston, IL: Northwestern University Press, 1997).

16. Martin Heidegger, "The Essence of Truth," in David F. Krell (ed.), *Basic Writings of Martin Heidegger* (New York: Harper & Row, 1994), pp. 126 and 129; *Das Wesen der Wahrheit* (Frankfurt: Vittorio Klostermann, 1949), pp. 15 and 18.

17. Levinas, "Paix et Proximité," *Les Cahiers de la nuit surveillée,* ed. by Jacques Rolland (Lagrasse: Verdier, 1984), p. 343; quoted in Adriaan Peperzak et al., *Emmanuel Levinas: Basic Philosophical Writings* (Bloomington: Indiana University Press, 1996), p. 166.

18. See Simon Critchley, "Diskussion zu Axel Honneth: 'Das Andere der Gerechtigkeit,' " *Deutsche Zeitschrift für Philosophie,* vol. 42, no. 6 (1994), pp. 1028–29.

19. Levinas, "Language and Proximity," in *Collected Philosophical Papers,* trans. by Alphonso Lingis (The Hague: Martinus Nijhoff, 1987), p. 124.

20. Levinas, *Otherwise Than Being, or Beyond Essence,* trans. by Alphonso Lingis (Boston: Kluwer Academic Publishers, 1991, p. 193; *Autrement qu'être, ou au-delà de l'Essence* (The Hague: Martinus Nijhoff, 1974), p. 120. Hereafter the English translation will be cited as OB and the French original as AE. Also see Paul Davies, "On Resorting to an Ethical Language," in Adriaan Peperzak (ed.), *Ethics as First Philosophy* (New York: Routledge, 1995), pp. 95–104.

21. See Critchley, "Diskussion zu Axel Honneth," pp. 1028–29. Critchley argues that, "insofar as his [Levinas's] theses are phenomenological, they are descriptive and not prescriptive, and they claim to bring out something of the deep structure of subjectivity that remains hidden at the level of the empirical or the natural attitude." He is quite right with regard to what he takes to be their claim; but I would argue that the phenomenological descriptivity of Levinas's discourse is not incompatible with its being also prescriptive—or, as I would prefer to say, performative. For Levinas is no longer working in terms of the static correspondence theory of truth.

22. See Axel Honneth, "The Other of Justice: Habermas and the Ethical Challenge of Postmodernism," in Stephen White (ed.), *The Cambridge Companion to Habermas* (Cambridge, England: Cambridge University Press, 1995), pp. 289–323. The original paper, "Das Andere der Gerechtigkeit," was published in the *Deutsche Zeitschrift für Philosophie,* vol. 2 (1994), p. 195ff. Also see Honneth's *Kommunitarianismus: Eine Debatte über die moralischen Grundlagen moderner Gesellschaften* (Frankfurt am Main: Fischer Verlag, 1993).

23. Critchley, "Diskussion zu Axel Honneth," pp. 1025–36.

24. See Max Pensky, "The Limits of Solidarity: Discourse Ethics, Levinas, and the Moral Point of View," unpublished manuscript. Pensky attempts to think, after Levinas, the embodiment of moral experience; but he unfortunately perpetuates the old metaphysical dualism by continuing to think of a "physical substrate." This makes it quite impossible to understand how we could ever form a bodily felt sense of moral responsibility for the other in response to the face-to-face presence of the other. But he is correct in pointing out that Levinas's work shows that "Moral theory . . . cannot follow those [everyday] moral intuitions to the level of bodily movement itself." The task that this

problem poses is, therefore, to work out a phenomenology of moral experience capable of thinking how the dispositions of our bodily nature figure in our moral development and moral judgment. I take Levinas to have made some important moves in this direction, but his phenomenology is ultimately disappointing because of its abstractness and thinness.

25. See Heidegger, "The Origin of the Artwork," in Krell (ed.), *Martin Heidegger: Basic Writings*, pp. 192 and 198, where he speaks for the importance of escaping "captivity in that which is" and argues that "language alone brings what is, as something that is, into the Open for the first time."

26. See the discussion of "indirect communication" in Sören Kierkegaard, *Concluding Unscientific Postscript to the Philosophical Fragments* (Princeton: Princeton University Press, 1960), book 2, part 2, chs. 2 and 3 (especially perhaps p. 247, but also pp. 216–17, 221, 232, 235, 318, and 321 in this first Princeton edition).

27. I would like to mention, as especially helpful for my thinking in this study, the following texts: Robert Bernasconi, "Deconstruction and the Possibility of Ethics," in John Sallis (ed.), *Deconstruction and Philosophy* (Chicago: University of Chicago Press, 1987), pp. 122–139; Bernasconi, "The Trace of Levinas in Derrida," in David Wood and Robert Bernasconi (eds.), *Derrida and Différance* (Evanston, IL: Northwestern University Press, 1988), pp. 13–29; Bernasconi, "Levinas and Derrida: The Question of the Closure of Metaphysics," in Richard Cohen (ed.), *Face to Face with Levinas* (Albany: State University of New York Press, 1986), pp. 181–202; Bernasconi, "Failure of Communication as a Surplus: Dialogue and Lack of Dialogue between Buber and Levinas," in Bernasconi and Wood (eds.), *The Provocation of Levinas* (London: Routledge, 1988), pp. 100–135; Simon Critchley, *The Ethics of Deconstruction: Derrida and Levinas* (Oxford: Basil Blackwell, 1992); Critchley, "Eine Vertieferuing der ethischen Sprache und Methode: Levinas' 'Jenseits des Seins oder anders als Sein geschieht,' " *Deutsche Zeitschrift für Philosophie*, vol. 42, no. 4 (1994), pp. 643–51; Fabio Ciaramelli, "Levinas's Ethical Discourse Between Individuation and Universality," in Bernasconi and Critchley (eds.), *Re-Reading Levinas* (Bloomington: Indiana University Press, 1991), pp. 85–105; Richard Cohen, "The Face of Truth in Rosenzweig, Levinas and Jewish Mysticism," in Daniel Guerriere (ed.), *Phenomenology of the Truth Proper to Religion* (Albany: State University of New York Press, 1990); Paul Davies, "The Face and the Caress: Levinas's Alterations of Sensibility," in David M. Levin (ed.), *Modernity and the Hegemony of Vision* (Los Angeles: University of California Press, 1994), pp. 252–72; Alphonso Lingis, "Face to Face: A Phenomenological Meditation," in *International Philosophical Quarterly*, vol. 19, no. 2 (June 1979), pp. 151–63; Adriaan Peperzak, "From Intentionality to Responsibility: On Levinas's Philosophy of Language," in Arleen Dallery and Charles Scott (eds.), *The Question of the Other in Contemporary Continental Philosophy* (Albany: State University of New York Press, 1989), pp. 3–22; Peperzak, "Some Remarks on Hegel, Kant, and Levinas," in Richard Cohen (ed.), *Face to Face*, pp. 205–17; Peperzak, *Beyond: The Philosophy of Emmanuel Levinas*

(Evanston, IL: Northwestern University Press, 1997); Laszlo Tengelyi, *Der Zwitterbegriff Lebensgeschichte* (Munich: Wilhelm Fink Verlag, 1998); and Edith Wyschogrod, "Doing Before Hearing: On the Primacy of Touch," in Francois Laruelle (ed.), *Textes pour Emmanuel Levinas* (Paris: Editions Jean-Michel Place, 1980), pp. 179–202.

28. Levinas, "Diachrony and Representation," in *Time and the Other* (Pittsburgh: Duquesne University Press, 1987), pp. 97–98; "Diachronie et Représentation," *Entre Nous: Essais sur le Penser-à-l'Autre* (Paris: Editions Grasset et Fasquelle, 1991), p. 165. Hereafter, the English will be designated by "TO."

29. Jacques Derrida, "Violence and Metaphysics: An Essay on the Thought of Emmanuel Levinas," in *Writing and Difference* (Chicago: University of Chicago, 1978), p. 91.

30. See Giorgio Agamben, *Infancy and History: The Destruction of Experience and the Origin of History* (London: New Left Books, Verso Edition, 1993), p. 94; *Infanzia e Storia: Distruzione dell'Esperienza e Origine della Storia* (Torino: Giulio Einaudi, 1978), also p. 94.

31. Ibid., p. 92.

32. Ibid.

33. Levinas, *Totality and Infinity: An Essay on Exteriority* (Pittsburgh: Duquesne University Press, 1969), p. 78; for the French, see *Totalité et Infini: Essai sur Extériorité* (The Hague: Martinus Nijhoff, 1961), p. 51. Hereafter, the English will be referred to by the symbols "TaI," the French by "TeI."

34. See Paul Davies, "The Face and the Caress: Levinas's Ethical Alterations of Sensibility," in Levin (ed.), *Modernity and the Hegemony of Vision*, pp. 252–72.

35. Adorno, "Trying to Understand *Endgame*," in *Notes to Literature* (New York: Columbia University Press, 1991), vol. 1, p. 247.

36. For more on Levinas's relation to light, see, for example, Levinas, *Totality and Infinity*, pp. 189f, and *Existence and Existents* (The Hague: Martinus Nijhoff, 1978), pp. 46–51.

37. Levinas, *Time and the Other*, p. 68. For the French text, see *Le Temps et l'Autre*, p. 53. Hereafter, the English will be designated by "TO," the French by "TA."

38. See Levinas, "Diachrony and Representation," in TO, pp. 99–100; "Diachronie et Représentation," *Entre Nous*, p. 166.

39. Walter Benjamin, "Einbahnstraße," *Schriften* (Frankfurt am Main: Suhrkamp Verlag, 1955), vol. 1, p. 558.

40. Benjamin, *Ursprung des Deutschen Trauerspiels*, *Schriften* (Frankfurt am Main: Suhrkamp Verlag, 1955), vol. 1, pp. 150–51. For the English translation, see *The Origin of German Tragic Drama* (London: Verso, New Left Books, 1977), pp. 35–36.

41. Levinas, "Language and Proximity," in *Collected Philosophical Papers*, p. 118.

42. See, for example, Levinas, "The Transcendence of Words: On Michel Leiris's *Biffures*," in *Outside the Subject*, p. 147. This text originally appeared, in French, in 1949. Also see "Diachrony and Representation," in *Time and the*

470 / Notes to Pages 252–62

Other, p. 98; "Diachronie et Représentation," *Entre Nous,* p. 166: in our culture, the other, says Levinas, is typically seized by perception, by an ego-logical gaze, and re-presented, by this gaze, to itself.

43. On this question, see Paul Davies, "The Face and the Caress," in Levin (ed.), *Modernity and the Hegemony of Vision.*

44. Max Horkheimer, *Gesammelte Schriften* (Frankfurt am Main: Suhrkamp Verlag, 1985), vol. 7, pp. 385–404.

45. Benjamin, *The Origin of German Tragic Drama,* p. 31. For the original German text, see Benjamin's *Schriften,* vol. 1, p. 146: " . . . daß Wahrheit nicht Enthüllung ist, die das Geheimnis vernichtet, sondern Offenbarung, die ihm gerecht wird."

46. Levinas, "In Memory of Alphonse de Waelhens," in *Outside the Subject,* p. 115.

47. Levinas, "L'Ontologie Est-elle Fondamentale?," *Entre Nous,* p. 19. My translation.

48. Levinas, *Ethics and Infinity,* p. 60.

49. On intentionality, also see Levinas, *Otherwise Than Being, or Beyond Essence,* pp. 65–72, 96–97, and 101; *Autrement Qu'Être, ou au-delà de l'Essence,* pp. 81–91, 122–24, and 128–29. Also see "Bad Conscience and the Inexorable," in Cohen (ed.), *Face to Face with Levinas,* pp. 35–40.

50. See Rosenzweig, op. cit., pp. 213–14, 239, and 268–69: Rosenzweig here undertakes a critique of the bourgeois conception of the subject and its freedom that is quite similar to the critique that Levinas makes.

51. Levinas, "The Paradox of Morality: an Interview with Emmanuel Levinas," in Robert Bernasconi and David Wood (eds.), *The Provocation of Levinas: Rethinking the Other* (London: Routledge, 1988), p. 178.

52. The problem that the prohibition on utopian images must address is that there is a temptation to idolatry not conducive, of course, to transformative experience—all the more tragic when the images are images of a utopian fulfillment of desire. Idolatry would accordingly be desire fixated on the utopian image, rather than on making use of the image for the transformation of desire.

53. Levinas, "Diachrony and Representation," in *Time and the Other,* pp. 99–100; "Diachronie et Représentation," *Entre Nous,* p. 167. My translation.

54. Levinas, "L'Autre, Utopie, et Justice," *Entre Nous,* p. 239. My translation. Also see OB 116, AE 147. These are just two of the many instances where Levinas works with this double meaning.

55. Levinas, "The Rights of Man and the Rights of the Other," in *Outside the Subject,* p. 124.

56. Levinas, *Otherwise Than Being,* p. 27; *Autrement Qu'Être,* p. 34. Also see pp. 29–30 in the English, pp. 37–38 in the French.

57. Levinas, *Difficult Freedom* (London: Athlone Press, 1990), p. 293.

58. Levinas, "On Jewish Philosophy," in *In the Time of Nations* (Bloomington: Indiana University Press, 1994), p. 182. Also see Bernhard Waldenfels, "Re-

sponse and Responsibility in Levinas," in Adriaan Peperzak (ed.), *Ethics as First Philosophy*, pp. 39–52.

59. Michel de Montaigne, "Apology for Raymond Sebond," in Donald Frame (ed.), *The Complete Essays* (Stanford: Stanford University Press, 1958), book 2, no. 12, p. 436.

60. Ibid., p. 437.

61. Levinas, "L'Autre, Utopie et Justice," *Entre Nous*, p. 244. My translation.

62. See Rosenzweig, op. cit., p. 228.

63. Levinas, "The Pact," in Séan Hand (ed.), *The Levinas Reader* (Oxford: Basil Blackwell, 1989), pp. 211–26. For the French original, see *L'Au-Delà du Verset* (Paris: Editions de Minuit, 1981), pp. 82–106.

64. See Rosenzweig, op. cit., pp. 213–14, 217–18, 234–35, 252, and 259.

65. Levinas, *Nine Talmudic Readings* (Bloomington: Indiana University Press, 1990), p. 168. The passage quoted comes from a 1972 lecture.

66. Levinas, "The Meaning of Meaning," in *Outside the Subject*, pp. 93–94.

67. Ibid.

68. See Derrida, *Speech and Phenomena* (Evanston, IL: Northwestern University Press, 1973), pp. 45 and 103.

69. Heidegger, "The Origin of the Work of Art," in Krell (ed.), *Martin Heidegger: Basic Writings*, p. 192. Italics added. Also see p. 198, where he remarks that "language alone brings what is, as something that is, into the Open for the first time."

70. Levinas, "The Paradox of Morality," op. cit., p. 176.

71. Ibid., p. 168.

72. Ibid., p. 171.

73. Ibid., pp. 176 and 169.

74. Levinas, "Meaning and Sense," in *Collected Philosophical Papers*, p. 102. Also see p. 104.

75. Ibid., p. 102.

76. Levinas, "On Intersubjectivity: Notes on Merleau-Ponty," in *Outside the Subject*, p. 115.

77. Levinas, "Philosophy and the Idea of Infinity," in *Collected Philosophical Papers*, pp. 55, 56, and 59.

78. Levinas, "L'Ontologie Est-elle Fondamentale?" *Entre Nous*, p. 22. My translation.

79. Ibid.

80. Levinas, *Nine Talmudic Readings*, p. 168.

81. Levinas, "Diachrony and Representation," op. cit., p. 109; "Diachronie et Représentation," *Entre Nous*, p. 175.

82. For an anticipation of Levinas's distinction between *le Dit* and *le Dire*, see Rosenzweig, op. cit., pp. 108–11, 131–33, 145–51, 227–35, 250–53, and 295–96. On pp. 199 and 231–32, Rosenzweig distinguishes between the contents said by the saying and the tonality of the saying. He himself at times makes use of an incantatory rhetorical mode of discourse.

83. Benjamin, "Theses," in *Illuminations* (New York: Schocken, 1969), pp. 253–64.

84. Levinas, "Meaning and Sense," in *Collected Philosophical Papers*, pp. 100–2. Italics added.

85. Maurice Merleau-Ponty, *Phenomenology of Perception* (London: Routledge & Kegan Paul, 1962), pp. 351–52. The abbreviated reference to this text will be "PhP."

86. Ibid., p. 242.

87. Ibid., p. 347.

88. Levinas, "Meaning and Sense," op. cit., p. 103

89. Ibid., p. 106.

90. Ibid., p. 104.

91. For further discussion of Levinas's struggles with the language of phenomenology, see my "Tracework: Experience and Description in the Moral Phenomenology of Merleau-Ponty and Levinas," forthcoming in a collection edited by Bernard Flynn and Wayne Froman which will be published by Northwestern University Press.

92. See my "Tracework: Myself and Others in the Moral Phenomenology of Merleau-Ponty and Levinas," in the *International Journal of Philosophical Studies*, vol.6, no. 3 (1998), pp. 345–92.

93. Levinas, "The Ego and Totality," in *Collected Philosophical Papers*, p. 34; "Le Moi et la Totalité," *Entre Nous*, p. 34.

94. Levinas, "The Ego and Totality," op. cit., p. 42; "Le Moi et la Totalité," op. cit., p. 43. Concerning the question of whether or not the animal may be said to have a face, see "The Paradox of Morality," op. cit., pp. 169–72.

95. Karl Marx, *Capital*, vol. 1 (Harmondsworth: Penguin, 1976), p. 72.

96. Heidegger, *What Is Called Thinking?* (New York: Harper & Row, 1968), p. 61. See also Levinas's essay, "Philosophy and the Idea of Infinity," in *Collected Philosophical Papers*, p. 55: Levinas here says the same thing as Heidegger in defining the difference between the animal's head and the human face: the animal "is not yet in touch with itself." Heidegger says that the animal does not perceive itself, does not enjoy apperception, and cannot talk. However, in opposition to Heidegger, Levinas extends the ethical to all sentient beings: "It is clear," he says, "that, without considering animals as human beings, the ethical extends to all living beings." (Levinas, "The Paradox of Morality," op. cit., p. 172.)

97. Heidegger, *What Is Called Thinking?*, p. 62.

98. Horkheimer, "The Authoritarian State," in Andrew Arato and Eike Gebhardt (eds.), *The Essential Frankfurt School Reader* (New York: Continuum, 1987), p. 116.

99. Levinas, "And God Created Woman," a 1972 lecture published in *Nine Talmudic Readings* (Bloomington: Indiana University Press, 1990), p. 168.

100. Rilke, *The Notebooks of Malte Laurids Brigge* (New York: W. W. Norton, 1949), pp. 15–16.

101. Levinas, "And God Created Woman," a 1972 lecture published in *Nine Talmudic Readings*, p. 168. On masks and faces in relation to racial identity and

racism, see Linda Alcoff, "Toward a Phenomenology of Racial Embodiment," forthcoming in Robert Bernasconi (ed.), *Race and Racism in Continental Philosophy* (Indiana University Press).

102. Benjamin, *Reflections: Essays, Aphorisms, Autobiographical Writings* (New York: Schocken Books, 1986), p. 196. For the German, see *Gesammelte Schriften*, vol. 3, part 2, p. 443.

103. Levinas, "Ethics as First Philosophy," in Sean Hand (ed.), *The Levinas Reader*, p. 83.

104. See J. Hillis Miller, *Hawthorne and History* (Oxford: Basil Blackwell, 1991), p. 57.

105. On the face of the other as angel of judgment, as bringing judgment and awakening one's sense of "bad conscience," see "Diachrony and Representation," in *Collected Philosophical Papers*, pp. 117–18; "Diachronie et Représentation," *Entre Nous*, p. 182.

106. Rosenzweig's discussion of Gyges's ring in *Star of Redemption* (p. 207) may have suggested the story to Levinas.

107. Friedrich Nietzsche, *Beyond Good and Evil: Prelude to a Philosophy of the Future*, trans. by Walter Kaufmann (New York: Vintage Books, 1966), part 2, §40, p. 51.

108. Johann Wolfgang von Goethe, *Elective Affinities* (New York: Oxford University Press, 1994), p. 216.

109. Levinas, *In the Time of Nations* (Bloomington: Indiana University Press, 1994), p. 182; *À l'Heure des Nations* (Paris: Editions de Minuit, 1988), p. 214.

110. Levinas, "Diachrony and Representation," in *Collected Philosophical Papers*, p. 107; "Diachronie et Représentation," *Entre Nous*, p. 173.

111. Levinas, *In the Time of Nations*, p. 182; *À l'Heure des Nations*, p. 214.

112. I am indebted to Miller's reading of Hawthorne for parts of the interpretation I am formulating here.

113. Benjamin, *Gesammelte Schriften*, vol. 1, part 1, p. 211. For the English, see *The Origin of German Tragic Drama*, p. 31.

114. Levinas, *Totality and Infinity*, pp. 65–66. For the French, see *Totalité et Infini*, p. 37.

115. Levinas, *En Découvrant l'Existence avec Husserl et Heidegger* (Paris: Vrin, 1988), p. 208.

116. Rebecca Comay, "Facies Hippocratica," in Adriaan Peperzak (ed.), *Ethics as First Philosophy: The Significance of Emmanuel Levinas for Philosophy, Literature and Religion* (New York: Routledge, 1995), p. 227. Levinas also writes of the need to "efface" (*dévisager*) the face in order to let the "universal" claimed for justice shine forth. See, e.g., "On Jewish Philosophy," in *In the Time of Nations*, pp. 174–75.

117. Benjamin, *Charles Baudelaire: A Lyric Poet in the Era of High Capitalism* (London: Verso, 1983), pp. 147f.

118. Ibid., pp. 150–51. For the German, see *Gesammelte Schriften* (Frankfurt am Main: Suhrkamp Verlag, 1980–89), vol. 1, part 2, p. 648: "Blicke dürften

um so bezwingender wirken, je tiefer die Abwesenheit des Schauenden, die ihnen bewältigt wurde. In spiegelnden Augen bleibt sie unvermindert. Eben darum wissen diese Augen von der Ferne nichts."

119. Benjamin, fascinated by the allegorical significance of the baroque image of the death's-head, discusses it in a number of different texts: [1] *The Origin of German Tragic Drama*, p. 166. [2] "Baudelaire," *Das Passagen-Werk*, in *Gesammelte Schriften* (Frankfurt am Main: Suhrkamp Verlag, 19), vol. 5, part 1, p. 463, J78, 4. [3] "Einbahnstraße," *Schriften*, vol. 1, p. 544: "Unvergleichliche Sprache des Totenkopfes: völlige Ausdruckslosigkeit—das Schwarz seiner Augenhöhlen—vereint er mit wildesten Ausdruck—den grinsenden Zahnreihen."

120. Benjamin, *Ursprung des deutschen Trauerspiels*, in *Schriften* (Frankfurt am Main: Suhrkamp Verlag, 1955), vol. 1, p. 289.

121. Benjamin, *Ursprung des deutschen Trauerspiels*, *Schriften*, vol. 1, pp. 289–90. For the English translation, see *The Origin of German Tragic Drama* (London: Verso, New Left Books, 1977), pp. 165–66. In the "Introduction" to *The Genuine Works of Hippocrates* (New York: William Wood, 1886), p. 195, Francis Adams explains the *facies hippocratica* as follows: This countenance, suffering from "the worst," is marked by "a sharp nose, hollow eyes, collapsed temples, the ears cold, contracted, and their lobes turned out: the skin about the forehead being rough, distended and parched; the color of the whole face being green, black, livid, or lead-colored."

122. Daniel Casper von Lohenstein, *Hyacinthen*, quoted by Benjamin in his *Ursprung des Deutschen Trauerspiels*, *Schriften*, vol. 1, p. 340; also see pp. 357–58. For English translation, see p. 215; also see pp. 232–33.

123. Benjamin, *Gesammelte Schriften*, vol. 1, part 2, p. 682. Also see vol. 5, p. 72. Benjamin probably derived this dialectical image from Marx's reference to the Medusa-head in *Das Kapital*. See Karl Marx and Friedrich Engels, *Werke* (Berlin: Dietz Verlag, 1962), vol. 23, pp. 15, 146f. In the "Preface" (*Vorwort*) to the first (1867) edition, Marx writes: "Im Vergleich zur englischen ist die soziale Statistik Deutschlands und des übrigen kontinentalen Westeuropas elend. Dennoch lüftet sie den Schleier grade genug, um hinter demselben ein Medusenhaupt ahnen zu lassen." ("In comparison with those of England, the social statistics of Germany and the rest of continental Western Europe are wretchedly compiled. Nevertheless, they [the social statistics of continental Europe] lift the veil just enough to let us glimpse the Medusa-head behind it.") On the same page in this preface, Marx also draws on the mythic story of Perseus to call attention to the monsters of capitalism, from the sight of which we obstruct our gaze: "Perseus brauchte eine Nebelkappe zur Verfolgung von Ungeheurn. Wir ziehen die Nebelkappe tief über Aug und Ohr, um die Existenz der Ungeheuer wegleugnen zu können." ("Perseus wore a magic cap in order to hunt down the monsters [without their seeing him]. We pull the magic cap down over our eyes and ears—in order to deny the existence of the monsters.")

124. Merleau-Ponty, *Phenomenology of Perception*, p. 361.

125. Ibid., p. 362.

126. Ibid., p. 352. Also see pp. 129, 216, 254, and 352–53.

127. The fullest presentation of this point is to be found in Merleau-Ponty's published lecture material on "The Child's Relations with Others," in *The Primacy of Perception* (Evanston, IL: Northwestern University Press, 1964). For a discussion of this material, see my chapter on Merleau-Ponty in this book.

128. Adorno and Horkheimer, *Dialectic of Enlightenment* (New York: Continuum, 1986), pp. 102–3.

129. Benjamin, *The Origin of German Tragic Drama*, p. 166; "Der Ursprung des Deutschen Trauerspiels," *Gesammelte Schriften*, vol. 1, part 1, p. 343.

130. Berthold Brecht, "Die Auslöschung," *Werke*, Berliner und Frankfurter Ausgabe, Stücke, 3 (Frankfurt am Main: Suhrkamp, 1988), vol. 3, p. 78.

131. Interviews with Subcomandante Marcos, in John Ross, "Introduction," and Frank Bardacke (ed. and trans.), *Shadows of Tender Fury* (New York: Monthly Review Press, 1995), pp. 88, 102–5, 195–201, 205, and 246.

132. Adorno, "Trying to Understand *Endgame*," in *Notes to Literature*, vol. 1, p. 249.

133. Levinas, *Difficult Freedom* (Baltimore: Johns Hopkins University Press, 1990), pp. 135, 140.

134. Horkheimer, *Critique of Instrumental Reason* (New York: Continuum, 1974), p. 22.

135. René Char, "Recherche de la base et du sommet," *Oeuvres Complètes* (Paris: Gallimard, 1983), p. 728.

136. Char, "Sur la poésie," *Oeuvres Complètes*, p. 1298. Also in *Feuillets d'Hypnos* (Paris: Gallimard, 1946), p. 83: "Le poète, conservateur des infinis visages du vivant."

137. Robert Coles, "Children as Moral Observers," in *The Tanner Lectures on Human Values*, vol. 2 (Salt Lake City: University of Utah Press, 1981), p. 138.

138. Levinas, *Ethics and Infinity*, p. 92.

139. See Patrizia Magli, "The Face and the Soul," in Michel Feher (ed.), with Ramona Nadoff and Nadia Tazi, *Fragments for a History of the Human Body*, part 2 (New York: Zone Press, 1989), pp. 87–127.

140. See Robert Bernasconi, "Sartre's Gaze Returned: The Transformation of the Phenomenology of Racism," in *Graduate Faculty Philosophy Journal*, vol. 18, no. 2 (1995), pp. 201–21, and "The Double Face of the Political and the Social: Hannah Arendt and America's Racial Divisions," in *Research in Phenomenology*, vol. 16 (1996), pp. 3–24.

141. Jean-Paul Sartre, *Nausea* (New York: New Directions, 1964), p. 120.

142. Levinas, "Martin Buber, Gabriel Marcel and Philosophy," in H. Gordon and J. Bloch (eds.), *Martin Buber: A Centenary Volume* (1984), p. 320. Also see Levinas, "The Meaning of Meaning," in *Outside the Subject*, p. 94.

143. Michel Foucault, "How much does it cost for reason to tell the truth?" in *Foucault Live: Interviews 1966–84* (New York: Columbia University Press, Semiotext(e) Foreign Agent Series, 1989), p. 252. This reference to the face is all the more remarkable, coming as it does some years after his comments on the face in *The Order of Things* (*Les Mots et les Choses*). In the later reference,

476 / *Notes to Pages 300–308*

the face belongs to a singular, concrete other, and expresses the incorporation of social interactions and practices. In the two earlier references, appearing near the end of *The Order of Things*, the face is the face of Man, an abstract other, and it is identified with a metaphysics committed to essence, totality, homogeneity and a logic of the same. In the earlier references, the face, as the face of Man, is condemned to death. Here are the two references: "What Nietzsche's thought announces is not so much the death of God . . . as the end of his murderer; it is the shattering of man's face in laughter, and the return of masks." See *Les Mots et les Choses* (Paris: Gallimard, 1966), pp. 396–97. In the second, he says: "Man will be effaced, like a face traced in the sand at the edge of the sea" (op. cit., p. 398). The face in question here belongs to the modern representations of Man. This theme of the death of God and finally the death of Man was already prefigured by Foucault's Introduction to Kant's 1798 *Anthropologie in pragmatischer Hinsicht*. Foucault wrote this as an Introduction to his doctoral thesis. See David Macey, *The Lives of Michel Foucault* (New York: Pantheon, 1993), p. 89.

144. Levinas, *Totality and Infinity*, p. 219; p. 194 in French.

145. There is a useful paper in this regard by Fabio Ciaramelli, "Levinas's Ethical Discourse between Individuation and Universality," in Robert Bernasconi and Simon Critchley (eds.), *Re-Reading Levinas* (Bloomington: Indiana University Press, 1991).

146. Levinas, "Philosophy and the Idea of Infinity," in *Collected Philosophical Papers*, p. 69.

147. See Rosenzweig, op. cit., pp. 176, 185–86, 200, and 228, where there are discussions of the "third person" position that prefigure Levinas's discussions of the "le tiers," "third party."

148. See Derrida, "The Politics of Friendship," in *Journal of Philosophy*, vol. 85 (1988), pp. 632–45.

149. Levinas, *In the Time of Nations*, p. 174; à; *l'Heure des Nations*, p. 205.

150. Honneth, "The Other of Justice," op. cit., p. 291.

151. Thomas McCarthy, review of Stephen White (ed.), *The Cambridge Companion to Habermas*, in *Ethics* (January 1997), p. 372.

152. Nietzsche, *The Will to Power* (New York: Vintage Books, 1968), note 18, p. 16: "The most universal sign of the modern age: man has lost dignity in his own eyes to an incredible extent."

153. Heidegger, "Letter on Humanism," in Krell (ed.), *Basic Writings*, pp. 213–65.

154. See Immanuel Kant, *The Metaphysics of Morals*, trans. by Mary J. Gregor (Philadelphia: University of Pennsylvania Press, 1964), p. 37; *Gesammelte Schriften*, ed. Königliche Preussische Akademie der Wissenschaften (Berlin: Walter de Gruyter, 1902), vol. 6, p. 379. Also see Heidegger, *The Fundamental Concepts of Metaphysics: World, Finitude, Solitude* (Bloomington: Indiana University Press, 1995), §§38–39, where, in reference to the "*Dasein* in man," the "essence" of man, he speaks of the need "to liberate the humanity in man." For the original German, see *Die Grundbegriffe der Metaphysik: Welt,*

Endlichkeit, Einsamkeit (Frankfurt am Main: Vittorio Klostermann, 1983, 1992), §§38–39. For the argument that mirroring double-crosses narcissism, see my "Visions of Narcissism: Intersubjectivity and the Reversals of Reflection," in Martin C. Dillon (ed.), *Merleau-Ponty Vivant* (Albany: State University of New York Press, 1991), pp. 47–90.

155. See Bernhard Waldenfels, *Ordnung und Zwielicht* (Frankfurt am Main: Suhrkamp Verlag, 1987) on the ethical asymmetry of *Responsivität* and the moral-political symmetry of *Verantwortung.*

156. Levinas, "The Temptation of Temptation," in *Nine Talmudic Readings*, p. 47.

157. In the preface to the 1987 German translation of *Totalité et Infini*, Levinas says that, in the original French edition, justice is thought as a synonym for the ethical, just as Derrida had charged in "Force of Law." In *Otherwise Than Being*, however, he distinguishes these two and emphasizes that the question of justice first arises when the third, who presses for a decision between competing moral claims and puts the face-to-face ethical relation to the other in a specific sociopolitical context, comes on the scene. See, for example, OB, ch. 5, §3: "From the Saying to the Said, or the Wisdom of Desire" ("Du Dire au Dit, ou la Sagesse du Désir"). Also see "The Paradox of Morality," an interview by Tamra Wright, Peter Hughes, and Alison Ainley, in Robert Bernasconi and David Wood (eds.), *The Provocation of Levinas: Rethinking the Other*, p. 171: "In *Totality and Infinity* I used the word 'justice' for ethics, for the relationship between two people. I spoke of 'justice', although now 'justice' is for me something which is a calculation, which is knowledge, and which supposes politics; it is inseparable from the political. It is something which I distinguish from ethics, which is primary. However, in *Totality and Infinity*, the word 'ethical' and the word 'just' are the same word, the same question, the same language. When I use the word 'justice' there, it is not in the technical sense as something opposed to or distinct from the moral."

158. Levinas, "Humanism and An-archy," in *Collected Philosophical Papers*, pp. 135–36; "L'Humanisme et An-archie," *Entre Nous*, pp. 77–78.

159. Levinas, "The Youth of Israel," in *Nine Talmudic Readings*, p. 135.

160. Levinas, "Le Moi et la Totalité," *Entre Nous*, p. 38.

161. Merleau-Ponty, *The Visible and the Invisible* (Evanston, IL: Northwestern University Press, 1968, p. 148; *Le Visible et l'Invisible* (Paris: Gallimard, 1964), p. 195. Hereafter, the English translation will be cited as "VIE," and the French original will be cited as "VIF."

162. Merleau-Ponty, VIE 152, VIF 199.

163. Merleau-Ponty, VIE 260, VIF 313.

164. Benjamin, "On the Mimetic Faculty," in *Reflections: Essays, Aphorisms, Autobiographical Writings* (New York: Schocken, 1986), p. 336. Also see Levinas, "The Trace of the Other," in Mark Taylor (ed.), *Deconstruction in Context* (Chicago: University of Chicago Press, 1986), pp. 345–59, and "Enigma and Phenomenon," in *Collected Philosophical Papers*, p. 68. I also recommend Edward Casey, "Levinas on Memory and the Trace," in J. Sallis, G. Moneta, and J.

Taminiaux (eds.), *The Collegium Phaenomenologicum* (Boston: Kluwer Academic Publishers, 1988).

165. Levinas, "Ethics as First Philosophy," in Sean Hand (ed.), *The Levinas Reader* (Oxford: Basil Blackwell, 1989), p. 84.

166. Alphonso Lingis, "The Sensuality and the Sensitivity," in Cohen (ed.), *Face to Face with Levinas,* p. 227.

167. Adriaan Peperzak, "Some Remarks on Kant, Hegel, and Levinas," in Cohen (ed.), *Face to Face with Levinas,* p. 212.

168. See Robert Bernasconi, " 'Only the Persecuted': Language of the Oppressor, Language of the Oppressed," in Adriaan Peperzak (ed.), *Ethics as First Philosophy: The Significance of Emmanuel Levinas for Philosophy, Literature and Religion* (New York: Routledge, 1995), pp. 77–86.

169. Levinas, *Difficile liberté: Essais sur le Judaisme* (Paris: Albin Michel, 2nd edition, 1976), p. 290.

170. Sigmund Freud, *Civilization and Its Discontents* (New York: Doubleday, 1965), ch. 7, p. 80. Translation modified.

171. Levinas, "Messianic Texts," *Difficult Freedom,* p. 78.

172. Levinas, *Nine Talmudic Readings,* pp. 114–15.

173. For further discussion on the problematic of language and the problem of retrieving the trace, see my "Tracework: Experience and Description in the Moral Phenomenology of Merleau-Ponty and Levinas," forthcoming in an anthology on Merleau-Ponty edited by Bernard Flynn and Wayne Froman.

174. Adorno, *Negative Dialectics,* pp. 365–68; *Negative Dialektik,* in *Gesammelte Schriften* (Frankfurt: Suhrkamp Verlag, 1973), vol. 6, pp. 358–61. English translation modified, italics added.

175. Benjamin, *The Origin of German Tragic Drama,* p. 175; *Ursprung des deutschen Trauerspiels,* p. 299.

176. Derrida, *Of Grammatology* (Baltimore: Johns Hopkins University Press, 1976), p. 140.

177. Levinas, *Difficult Freedom,* p. 135.

178. Ibid., p. 140.

179. Merleau-Ponty, "The Child's Relations with Others," in *The Primacy of Perception,* p. 146.

180. Merleau-Ponty, VIE 159; VIF 211.

181. See Judith Butler, *The Psychic Life of Power: Theories in Subjection* (Stanford: Stanford University Press, 1997). This is an important book. Reading it after I had thought this chapter finished, I realized that I needed to say something here that would remind us that intercorporeality is not necessarily liberating and that the "persecution" and "trauma" of which Levinas speaks can be the "subjection" of oppression, of a recognition withheld, as well as the origin of responsibility and obligation. Thus I was provoked to add a new final section, indebted to her argument on behalf of the many whose lives have been irrevocably damaged by the pressures for normalization inherent in all processes of socialization, all forms of subjection.

182. On this theme, see Giorgio Agamben, *Infancy and History,* cited earlier.

183. Horkheimer, "The Authoritarian State," in Arato and Gebhardt (eds.), *Frankfurt School Reader*, p. 102.

184. Levinas, "De l'Unicité," *Entre Nous*, p. 202.

CHAPTER 8. JUSTICE IN THE SEER'S EYES

The following abbreviations are used throughout the chapter.

AX   Martin Heidegger, "The Anaximander Fragment," in *Early Greek Thinking*

B   Walter Benjamin, "Re the Theory of Knowledge, Theory of Progress," in Gary Smith (ed.), *Benjamin Philosophy, Aesthetics, History*

BT   Heidegger, *Being and Time*

GA   Heidegger, *Gesamtausgabe*

GS   Benjamin, *Gesammelte Schriften*

H   Heidegger, *Holzwege*

IL   Benjamin, *Illuminations*

OGT   Benjamin, *Origin of German Tragic Drama*

Sch   Benjamin, *Schriften*

SZ   Heidegger, *Sein und Zeit*

UDT   Benjamin, *Ursprung des Deutschen Trauerspiels*, in *Schriften*, vol. 1

1. Walter Benjamin, quoted in Theodor Adorno, *Negative Dialectics* (New York: Continuum, 1973), p. 359. Translation slightly modified.

2. Theodor Adorno, *Minima Moralia: Reflections from Damaged Life* (London: New Left Books, 1974), §128, p. 200.

3. Martin Heidegger, "The Origin of the Work of Art," in David Krell (ed.), *Martin Heidegger: Basic Writings*, revised second edition (New York: Harper & Row, 1994), p. 192. For the German text, see "Der Ursprung des Kunstwerkes," *Holzwege* (Frankfurt: Vittorio Klostermann, 1950), p. 55. Here, and in all my other transcriptions of translations made by others, I have reduced the word "Being," beginning with a capital letter, to "being," beginning with a small letter. Capitalization unnecessarily encourages metaphysical hypostatization, and only gives critics an easy reason to accuse Heidegger of metaphysical mystification.

4. Herbert Marcuse, "The Affirmative Character of Culture," in *Negations: Essays in Critical Theory* (Boston: Beacon Press, 1968), p. 98.

5. Jacques Derrida, *Of Grammatology* (Baltimore: Johns Hopkins University Press, 1976), p. 167.

6. Heidegger, "The Anaximander Fragment," in *Early Greek Thinking* (New York; Harper & Row, 1975), p. 13. The German text is to be found in "Der

Spruch des Anaximander," *Holzwege* (Frankfurt am Main: Vittorio Klostermann, 1950), p. 296.

7. But for Benjamin, "Andenken" has a quite different meaning: "What are sold in the arcades are *Andenken* [mementos, souvenirs]. In the arcades, the *'Andenken'* perpetuate the form of commodities." *Gesammelte Schriften* (Frankfurt am Main: Suhrkamp Verlag, 1982), vol. 5, part 2, p. 1034.

8. See Stephen David Ross, *Injustice and Restitution: The Ordinance of Time* (Albany: State University of New York Press, 1993), and want to note my indebtedness.

9. See Benjamin's letter to Gershom Scholem, dated January 20, 1930, GS, vol. 5, part 2, p. 1094.

10. For Benjamin's distinction, see his "Prologue" for the *Trauerspiel* essay, where he distinguishes between a "revelation" of truth and its totalizing, reifying "exposure": "truth is not a process of exposure [*Enthüllung*] which destroys the secret, but a revelation [*Offenbarung*] which does justice to it," from *Origin of German Tragic Drama* (London: New Left Books, 1977), p. 31; *Ursprung des Deutschen Trauerspiels*, in *Schriften*, (Frankfurt am Main: Suhrkamp Verlag, 1955), vol. 1, p. 146. This is related to his thesis that the truth—at least the truth of revelation, is "an intentionless state of being" and that the "proper approach" to it is "not one of intention and knowledge, but rather total immersion and absorption [*Eingehen und Verschwinden*] in it." "Truth," he argued, "is the death of intention" OGT 35–36; UDT 150–51. For Heidegger's equivalent, formulated in terms of a distinction between "truth" and "unconcealment" (*aletheia*), see *Being and Time* (New York: Harper & Row, 1962), §§33–34 and §44, and also his essay on "The Essence of Truth," in Krell (ed.), *Basic Writings*, pp. 115–38.

11. For an important and insightful discussion of the question of justice in Heidegger, see Robert Bernasconi, "Justice and the Twilight Zone of Morality," in John Sallis (ed.), *Reading Heidegger* (Bloomington: Indiana University Press, 1993), pp. 80–94.

12. Theodor W. Adorno, *Notes to Literature*, vol. II (New York: Columbia University Press, 1992), p. 165.

13. Adorno, "On the Final Scene of Faust," in *Notes to Literature* (New York: Columbia University Press, 1991), vol. 1, p. 120.

14. Friedrich Schlegel, *Philosophical Fragments*, trans. by Peter Firchow (Minneapolis: University of Minnesota Press, 1991), §80, p. 27.

15. Jürgen Habermas, *The Philosophical Discourse of Modernity* (Cambridge, MA: MIT Press, 1987), pp. 13–14. Habermas clearly recognizes, here, the difference between "fate" and "destiny." This is a crucial distinction for Heidegger, who uses "Schicksal" to refer to fate, a predetermined chain of events, and "Geschick" to refer to destiny, a future that can come to pass only if our appropriation of the past prepares for its arrival.

16. Schlegel, op. cit., §330, p. 66.

17. Benjamin, "Rückblick auf Stefan George," *Schriften*, vol. 1, p. 323: "Prophetie ist ein Vorgang in der moralischen Welt. Was der Prophet vo-

raussieht, sind die Strafgerichte." My translation. It can be useful to keep in mind that Benjamin's conception of the interaction between imagination and remembrance can be traced back to Novalis's discussion of *Erinnerung* and *Ahnung* in what he calls "Poesie," the work of the "poëtische Philosoph." Novalis, in turn, derived many of his thoughts (e.g., *Spielraum* and *Zufälligkeit*) from Fichte's *Grundriß des Eigentümlichen der Wissenschaftslehre* (1795) as well as from Fichte's *Grundlage* of 1794–95.

18. Adorno, *Dialectic of Enlightenment* (New York: Continuum, 1986), p. 230.

19. In this regard, see Howard Caygill's excellent discussion of the affinities and differences between Heidegger and Benjamin, in his chapter, "Benjamin, Heidegger and the Destruction of Tradition," in Andrew Benjamin and Peter Osborne (eds.), *Walter Benjamin's Philosophy: Destruction and Experience* (New York: Routledge, 1994), pp. 1–31.

20. See, for example, Benjamin's elegiac lament over the loss of narrative memory in modern, late capitalist culture, beautifully articulated in "The Storyteller," in *Illuminations* (New York; Schocken Books, 1969), pp. 83–109.

21. Adorno, "Was bedeutet Aufarbeitung der Vergangenheit?" in G. Knädelbach (ed.), *Erziehung zur Mündigkeit* (Frankfurt: Suhrkamp Verlag, 1970), p. 13. Quoted by Marcuse in *One-Dimensional Man* (Boston: Beacon Press, 1964), p. 99.

22. Benjamin, "Zum Bilde Prousts," in *Schriften*, vol. 2 (Frankfurt: Suhrkamp Verlag, 1955), p. 133.

23. Benjamin, GS, vol. 1, part 3, p. 1064.

24. Benjamin, "Theses on the Philosophy of History," in *Illuminations*, p. 254; *Schriften* I, p. 495.

25. Concerning the dialectical antinomies in Benjamin's relationship to images of redemption, see Rebecca Comay, "Materialist Mutations of the *Bilderverbot*," in David M. Levin (ed.), *Sites of Vision: The Discursive Construction of Sight in the History of Philosophy* (Cambridge, MA: MIT Press, 1997), pp. 337–78, and "Redeeming Revenge: Nietzsche, Benjamin, Heidegger, and the Politics of Memory," in Clayton Koelb (ed.), *Nietzsche as Post-Modernist: Essays Pro and Con* (Albany: State University of New York Press, 1990). Also see Michael W. Jennings, *Dialectical Images: Walter Benjamin's Theory of Literary Criticism* (Ithaca: Cornell University Press, 1987); Charles Rosen, "The Ruins of Walter Benjamin," in Gary Smith (ed.), *On Walter Benjamin: Critical Essays and Recollections* (Cambridge, MA: MIT Press, 1988), pp. 129–75; Rolf Tiedemann, "Dialectics at a Standstill: Approaches to the *Passagen-Werk*," in Smith (ed.), *On Walter Benjamin*, pp. 260–91; Hans Robert Jauss, "Reflections on the Chapter 'Modernity' in Benjamin's Baudelaire Fragments," in Smith (ed.), *On Walter Benjamin*, pp. 176–84; Habermas, "Consciousness-Raising or Rescuing Critique," in Smith (ed.), *On Walter Benjamin*, pp. 90–128. I am also greatly indebted to Susan Buck-Morss, whose work, published in *The Dialectics of Seeing: Walter Benjamin and the Arcades Project* (Cambridge, MA: MIT Press, 1989), has not only made my own work much easier, but enabled me to take my thinking much further than otherwise would have been possible.

26. Benjamin, "Imagination," in *Walter Benjamin: Selected Writings,* 1913–1926, vol. 1 (Cambridge, MA: Harvard University Press, 1996), p. 280.

27. Ibid., p. 282.

28. Benjamin, "Theses on the Philosophy of History," in *Illuminations,* p. 260; *Schriften,* vol. 1, p. 502.

29. Ibid., p. 256 in the English; p. 497 in the German.

30. Irving Wohlfarth, "On the Messianic Structure of Walter Benjamin's Last Reflections," in *Glyph, Johns Hopkins Textual Studies,* vol. 3 (Baltimore: Johns Hopkins University Press, 1978), p. 152. This is an excellent study, one from which I have learned much.

31. Benjamin, "The Storyteller," in *Illuminations,* p. 98; *Schriften,* vol. 2, pp. 245–46.

32. Emmanuel Levinas, *Totality and Infinity* (Pittsburgh: Duquesne University Press, 1969), pp. 74 and 99; *Totalité et Infini: Essai sur l'Extériorité* (The Hague: Martinus Nijhoff, 1961), pp. 47 and 92.

33. Levinas, *Totality and Infinity,* p. 28; *Totalité et Infini,* p. xvi.

34. See, for example, Heidegger's *Being and Time,* §44–45, pp. 256–273; *Sein und Zeit* (Halle: Max Niemeyer Verlag, fifth edition, 1941), pp. 212–230.

35. Benjamin, "Theses," in *Illuminations,* p. 255; *Schriften,* vol. 1, p. 497.

36. Ibid, p. 257 in the English; p. 499 in the German.

37. Caygill, op. cit., p. 21.

38. Ibid., p. 18.

39. Benjamin, "Theory of Knowledge, Theory of Progress," in Gary Smith (ed.), *Benjamin: Philosophy, Aesthetics, History* (Chicago: University of Chicago Press, 1983), p. 70. The Smith anthology contains a good translation of this important text. For the German, see "Zur Erkenntnistheoretisches, Theorie des Fortschritts," GS, vol. 5, part 1, pp. 598–99.

40. Benjamin, GS, vol. 5, part 2, p. 1027.

41. Ibid.

42. Ibid.

43. Ibid. Also see p. 1021

44. Benjamin, "Der Sammler," GS, vol. 5, part 1, p. 279.

45. Ibid., p. 271.

46. Benjamin, GS, vol. 5, part 2, 1027.

47. Benjamin, GS, vol. 5, part 2, p. 1036. See also p. 1027.

48. Benjamin, GS, vol. 5, part 1, p. 279.

49. See Benjamin, GS, vol. 5, part 1, pp. 993–1038, especially 524–69.

50. See Benjamin, GS, vol. 5, part 2, pp. 1052–53.

51. See Benjamin, "On Some Motifs in Baudelaire," in *Illuminations,* pp. 166–74. *Schriften,* vol. 1, pp. 437–46.

52. Adorno, "Introduction to Benjamin's *Schriften,*" in B, p. 9. This description echoes Benjamin's own "description of the world that emerges under the gaze of the melancholic." See Benjamin, GS, vol. 1, p. 318.

53. Derrida, "Force of Law: The 'Mystical Foundation of Authority,' " in Drucilla Cornell, Michael Rosenfeld, and David Carlson (eds.), *Deconstruction and the Possibility of Justice* (New York: Routledge, 1989), p. 44.

54. See Max Pensky, *Melancholy Dialectics: Walter Benjamin's Play of Mourning* (Amherst: University of Massachusetts Press, 1993). Pensky articulates the dialectical intricacies of mourning with admirable lucidity.

55. For more on the phenomenology of the essential relation between vision and weeping, see my book, *The Opening of Vision* (New York: Routledge and Kegan Paul, 1988). I argue there that crying is the root of seeing, and that, in terms of human experience, it is not mere coincidence that the eyes both weep and see.

56. Max Horkheimer, "Die Sehnsucht nach dem ganz Anderen," an interview with Helmut Gumnior (Hamburg: Furche, 1970).

57. Benjamin, "Baudelaire," GS, vol. 5, part 1, p. 465.

58. Ibid., p. 466.

59. Ibid., p. 439.

60. Ibid., p. 466.

61. See Pensky, op. cit., p. 121 for a discussion of the phases of this allegorical dialectic. For Benjamin's remark about the "death of intention," see OGT 35–36, UDT 150–51.

62. Benjamin, "Paris: Capital of the Nineteenth Century," in *Reflections: Essays, Aphorisms, Autobiographical Writings* (New York: Schocken Books, 1986), p. 162; "Paris: Die Hauptstadt des XIX. Jahrhunderts," *Schriften*, vol. 1, p. 422.

63. Adorno, *Kierkegaard: Construction of the Aesthetic* (Minneapolis: University of Minnesota Press, 1989), p. 126.

64. Pensky, p. 124.

65. Ibid., p. 122.

66. Adorno, "A Portrait of Walter Benjamin," in *Prisms* (Cambridge, MA: MIT Press, 1981), p. 235.

67. Benjamin, "Re the Theory of Knowledge, Theory of Progress," in B, p. 51. For the German original, see GS, vol. 5, part 1, p. 578.

68. Benjamin, GS, vol. 2, p. 299.

69. Benjamin, "On the Topic of Individual Disciplines and Philosophy," in *Walter Benjamin: Selected Writings 1913–1926* (Cambridge, MA: Harvard University Press, 1996), vol. 1, p. 405.

70. Benjamin, *Angelus Novus* (Frankfurt: Suhrkamp Verlag, 1966), pp. 202 and 215. This description also appears many times elsewhere, e.g., in the essay on Surrealism.

71. Benjamin, "Theses on the Philosophy of History," in *Illuminations*, p. 254; *Schriften*, vol. 1, p. 496.

72. Benjamin, GS, vol. 1, part 3, p. 1233.

73. Benjamin, "Theses on the Philosophy of History," op. cit., p. 263 in the English; p. 506 in the German.

484 / *Notes to Pages 369–77*

74. Benjamin, GS, vol. 1, part 3, p. 1243.

75. See Howard Caygill, "Benjamin, Heidegger, and the Destruction of Tradition," in Andrew Benjamin and Peter Osborne (eds.), *Walter Benjamin's Philosophy*, pp. 12–21. Caygill argues that a significant difference between Heidegger and Benjamin consists in the fact that the former, at least in *Being and Time*, continues to think of the site where tradition is gathered into the present, received and handed down, in terms of a subject. Although this is only in a certain sense correct—it must be kept in mind, first, that in the *Dasein* of *Being and Time* Heidegger attempts a deconstruction of the traditional subject, and second, that after his *Kehre* he carried this deconstruction so far that his critics, misunderstanding his philosophical moves, disturbed by his visionary turn to *Ereignis*, accused him of mystification and fatalism—it must not be overlooked, as Pensky astutely points out (op. cit., pp. 215–19), that Benjamin's virtual eradication of the subject, his insistence that the dialectical gaze be without intention, that it attempt to be purely receptive, holding itself open to involuntary memories, make the political relevance of this gaze and its images extremely problematic. As Foucault seemed to realize near the end of his life, the dangers in preserving the subject are matched by equal dangers in totally eliminating it. What is needed, instead, is a radical reconfiguration of the site occupied much too long by the conceit of the philosopher's "subject."

76. Benjamin, "Surrealism: The Last Snapshot of the European Intelligentsia," in *Reflections*, p. 192.

77. Levinas, *Otherwise Than Being, or Beyond Essence* (Dordrecht: Kluwer Academic Publishers, 1991), note 3, p. 194; *Autrement Qu'Être, ou au-delà de l'Essence* (The Hague: Martinus Nijhoff, 1974), note 3, p. 128.

78. Ibid., note 4, p. 194 in English; note 4, p. 128 in the French original.

79. Benjamin, "The Critique of Violence," in *Reflections*, p. 300; "Kritik der Gewalt," *Schriften*, vol. 1, p. 28.

80. Benjamin, GS, vol. 1, part 3, p. 1245.

81. Adorno, "The Actuality of Philosophy," in *Telos* 31 (spring 1974), pp. 120, 126; *Gesammelte Schriften* I: *Philosophische Frühschriften* (Frankfurt am Main: Suhrkamp Verlag, 1973), p. 76.

82. Heidegger, *Die Grundprobleme der Phänomenologie*, GA, vol. 24 (Frankfurt am Main: Vittorio Klostermann, 1975), p. 244; *The Fundamental Problems of Phenomenology* (Bloomington: Indiana University Press, 1982), p. 171. Translation altered.

83. Heidegger, "Overcoming Metaphysics," in *The End of Philosophy* (New York: Harper & Row, 1973), p. 110; "Überwindung der Metaphysik," *Vorträge und Aufsätze* (Pfullingen: Günther Neske, 1954), p. 99. English translation of *Ereignis* significantly modified.

84. Charles Taylor, *Hegel* (Cambridge, England: Cambridge University Press, 1975), p. 241.

85. Ibid., pp. 236–37.

86. Heidegger, "Overcoming Metaphysics," op. cit., p. 86; "Überwindung der Metaphysik," op. cit., p. 72.

87. Ibid., p. 110 in the English; p. 99 in the German.

88. Heidegger, *What Is Called Thinking?* (New York: Harper & Row, 1968), p. 166; *Was Heißt Denken?* (Tübingen: Max Niemeyer Verlag, 1954), p. 104. In part 1, lecture 1, and part 2, lectures 3–5 (1951–52), Heidegger discusses memory as gathering and attempts to think it, by way of its etymology, as a process of thanking.

89. Ibid.

90. Heidegger, "Recollection in Metaphysics," in *The End of Philosophy* (New York: Harper & Row, 1973), p. 83; "Die Erinnerung in die Metaphysik," *Nietzsche*, vol. 2 (Pfullingen: Günther Neske Verlag, 1961), p. 490. Translation of *Ereignis* as "Appropriation" altered.

91. Heidegger, "Overcoming Metaphysics," op. cit., p. 96; p. 83 in the German text. Also see his *Beiträge zur Philosophie (Vom Ereignis), Gesamtausgabe*, vol. 65 (Frankfurt: Vittorio Klostermann, 1989), especially §§89–100.

92. Heidegger, "The End of Philosophy and the Task of Thinking," in *On Time and Being* (New York: Harper & Row, 1972), p. 57; "Das Ende der Philosophie und die Aufgabe des Denkens," *Zur Sache des Denkens* (Tübingen: Max Niemeyer Verlag, 1969), pp. 62–63.

93. Heidegger, *Basic Concepts* (Bloomington: Indiana University Press, 1993), p. 105; *Grundbegriffe, Gesamtausgabe* (Frankfurt: Vittorio Klostermann, 1981), vol. 51, p. 123.

94. See Immanuel Kant, *Von einem neuerdings erhobenen vornehmen Ton in der Philosophie, Gesammelte Schriften*, ed. Königliche Preussische Akademie der Wissenschaften (Berlin and Leipzig: Walter de Gruyter, 1902), vol. 8, p. 405.

95. *Basic Concepts*, p. 73 in the English, p. 86 in the German.

96. Ibid., p. 73 in the English, p. 87 in the German.

97. Ibid., p. 87 in the English, p. 101 in the German.

98. Ibid., p. 13 in the English, p. 15 in the German.

99. Ibid.

100. Ibid., p. 78 in the English, p. 92 in the German.

101. Ibid., p. 10 in the English, p. 13 in the German.

102. Heidegger, "Der Zeitbegriff in der Geisteswissenschaft," *Frühe Schriften* (Frankfurt: Vittorio Klostermann, 1972), p. 368; trans. by Harry Taylor and Hans Uffelmann as "The Concept of Time in the Science of History," in *Journal of the British Society for Phenomenology*, vol. 9, no. 1 (January 1978), p. 8.

103. Heidegger, *Being and Time*, p. 359; *Sein und Zeit*, p. 311.

104. Heidegger, "The Turning," in *The Question Concerning Technology and Other Essays* (New York: Harper & Row, 1977), p. 38; "Die Kehre," *Die Technik und die Kehre* (Pfullingen: Günther Neske Verlag, 1962), p. 38.

105. Ibid., p. 47 in the English, p. 45 in the German.

106. Ibid., p. 37 in both the English and the German.

107. Ibid., p. 49 in the English, p. 46 in the German.

108. Ibid., p. 44 in the English, p. 43 in the German.

109. Ibid., p. 47 in the English, p. 45 in the German.

110. Ibid.

111. Ibid., p. 45 in the English, p. 43 in the German.

112. Heidegger, *Parmenides* (Bloomington: Indiana University Press, 1992), pp. 144–51; *Parmenides, Gesamtausgabe*, vol. 54 (Frankfurt: Vittorio Klostermann, 1982), pp. 214–26.

113. Heidegger, *Die Grundbegriffe der Metaphysik: Welt, Endlichkeit, Einsamkeit, Gesamtausgabe* (Frankfurt: Vittorio Klostermann, 1983), vol. 29/30, p. 225.

114. Theodor Kisiel, *The Genesis of Heidegger's Being and Time* (Los Angeles: University of California Press, 1993), p.494.

115. Heidegger, BT, p. 185; SZ, p. 145.

116. Caygill, op. cit., p. 10.

117. Heidegger, "The Origin of the Work of Art," in *Poetry, Language, Thought* (New York: Harper & Row, 1971), p. 59; "Die Ursprung des Kunstwerkes," *Holzwege* (Frankfurt: Vittorio Klostermann, 1950), p. 47.

118. Benjamin, "Theologico-Political Fragment," in *Reflections: Essays, Aphorisms, Autobiographical Writings*, p. 313.

119. Heidegger, GA, vol. 65, pp. 83–84.

120. See P. Christopher Smith, "Agon kai katallagê, Kampf und Versöhnung in Heidegger's Readings of the *Antigone*," in *1997 Proceedings of the Thirty-first Heidegger Conference* (Penn State University). In this important paper, Smith undertakes a reading of Heidegger's *Introduction to Metaphysics* and his essay on Hölderlin's hymn, "Der Ister," in order to document the changes in Heidegger's thinking about "resoluteness," the violence of heroic self-assertion, struggling against the forces of nature and the injustices of fate. The seer in some ways resembles the tragic hero of the *Introduction to Metaphysics*, in that he also "bolts into the unsaid, . . . breaks into the unthought, . . . forces what has not happened into happening, and makes the never-seen appear. . . . " See *Einführung in die Metaphysik* (Tübingen: Max Niemeyer Verlag, 1953), p. 123. But unlike this tragic hero, whose defiant self-assertion can only end in defeat and catastrophe, the seer undertakes a recollection of the justice, the *Diké*, of being, choosing to learn both the possible and the inevitable from its secret ordinance.

121. Heidegger, AX, p. 25; for the German, see H, p. 309.

122. Heidegger, *Introduction to Metaphysics* (New York: Doubleday, 1961), p. 135; *Einführung in die Metaphysik* (Tübingen: Max Niemeyer Verlag, 1953), p. 123.

123. Ibid.

124. Heidegger, *Wegmarken* (Frankfurt: Vittorio Klostermann, 1967), p. 191.

125. Heidegger, *Nietzsche*, trans. by David F. Krell (New York: Harper & Row, 1979), vol. 1: *The Will to Power as Art*; *Nietzsche* (Pfullingen: Günther Neske, 1961), vol. 1, p. 194.

126. Ibid., p. 165–66 in the English; p. 193–94 in the German.

127. See Heidegger's discussion of justice in the context of critical reflections on Nietzsche, in "The Word of Nietzsche: 'God is dead,' " in *Question Con-*

cerning Technology, pp. 88–93; "Nietzsches Wort 'Gott ist tot,' " *Holzwege,* pp. 224–29. I would argue that, with regard to the question of justice, the reading of Heidegger that I have laid out here is supported by Heidegger's discussion of justice in relation to Nietzsche. Heidegger challenges Nietzsche's conception of justice on the grounds that it is a manifestation of the ego-logical subject's will to power, its drive towards a nihilism that is willfully forgetful of being. "The justice thought by Nietzsche," he says, "is the truth of what is—which now *is* in the mode of the will to power." Rejecting a justice that is anthropocentric and grounded in domination, in the will to power, Heidegger pushes towards a representation of justice that is oriented, instead, by the questioning thought of being.

128. Adorno, *Minima Moralia,* §153, p. 247.

129. Benjamin, GS, vol. 3, part 1: *Kritik und Rezensionen* (Frankfurt: Suhrkamp Verlag, 1972), p. 259. My translation.

130. Adorno, *Minima Moralia,* §153, p. 247.

131. Novalis, Friedrich von Hardenberg, *Heinrich von Ofterdingen,* in Paul Kluckhohn and Richard Samuel (eds.), *Schriften,* vol. 1: *Das Dichterische Werk* (Stuttgart: Kohlhammer Verlag, third enlarged and revised edition, 1977), p. 286, ll. 6–7.

CHAPTER 9. SHADOWS

1. Ludwig Wittgenstein, *Culture and Value* (Chicago: University of Chicago Press, 1980), p. 1e.

2. Theodor Adorno, *Kierkegaard: Construction of the Aesthetic* (Minneapolis: University of Minnesota Press, 1989), p. 126.

3. Wallace Stevens, *The Collected Poems of Wallace Stevens* (New York: Alfred A. Knopf, 1961), p. 305.

4. Friedrich Nietzsche, *Gay Science* (New York: Vintage Books, 1974), p. 203. For the original German, see *Die Fröhliche Wissenschaft* (Frankfurt: Insel Verlag, 1982), p. 158: "Gedanken sind die Schatten unserer Empfindungen— immer dunkler, leerer, einfacher als diese."

5. René Char, "Pour un Prométhée Saxifrage: En touchant la main éolienne de Hölderlin," *Oeuvres Complètes* (Paris: Gallimard, 1983), p. 399: "God had lived too powerfully among us. We no longer knew how to rise and depart. The stars are dead in our eyes, after being sovereign in his gaze." (My translation.)

6. Walter Benjamin, "Das Passagen-Werk," *Gesammelte Schriften* (Frankfurt: Suhrkamp Verlag, 1982), vol. 5, p. 702 (T 2, 5), cited by Susan Buck-Morss in *The Dialectics of Seeing: Walter Benjamin and the Arcades Project* (Cambridge, MA: MIT Press, 1989), p. 308.

7. Immanuel Kant, *Critique of Practical Reason* (New York: Library of Liberal Arts, 1956), p. 166.

8. Blaise Pascal, *Pensées* (New York: E. P. Dutton & Co., 1958), §206, p. 61. See also §72, p. 17.

9. Georg Lukács, *Theory of the Novel: A Historico-Philosophical Essay on the Forms of Great Epic Literature* (Cambridge, MA: MIT Press, 1971), p. 29.

10. Benjamin, "Das Passagen-Werk," *Gesammelte Schriften*, vol. 5, part 1, (K6, 4), p. 505. My translation.

11. G. W. F. Hegel, *Introduction to the Philosophy of History*, trans. by Leo Rauch (Indianapolis: Hackett, 1988), p. 14.

12. Char, *Oeuvres Complètes*, p. 424. My translation: "They take for clarity the jaundiced laughter of shadows."

13. Plato, "The Republic," in Benjamin Jowett (ed. and trans.), *The Dialogues of Plato* (New York: Random House, 1937), vol. 1, p. 739.

14. Ibid., p. 761.

15. See Martin Heidegger, *Platons Lehre von der Wahrheit* (Bern: A. Francke, 1947).

16. Char, "Éclore en hiver," *Oeuvres Complètes*, p. 503. My translation: "to see, nearing, a shadow giving birth to a shadow through the slant of a luminous shaft, and to scrutinize it."

17. Nietzsche, *The Will to Power* (New York: Vintage Books, 1965), book 1, §91, p. 55.

18. Benjamin, "Charles Baudelaire: Ein Lyriker im Zeitalter des Hochkapitalismus," *Zentralpark*, part 3, §28, *Gesammelte Schriften*, vol. 1, part 2, p. 676. My translation.

19. Benjamin, *Gesammelte Schriften*, vol. 1, part 3, p. 1165. My translation.

20. Char, "Dans la Marche," *Oeuvres Complètes*, p. 411. My translation: "We can live only in the openness of the intermediate, precisely on the hermetic dividing line between shadow and light."

21. Rudolf Borchardt, "Epilegomena zu Dante, I" *Schriften* (Berlin: E. Rowohlt,1923), pp. 56–57, quoted by Benjamin in N1, 8, "Re: The Theory of Knowledge, Knowledge of Theory," in Gary Smith (ed.), *Benjamin: Philosophy, History, Aesthetics* (Chicago: University of Chicago Press, 1989), p. 44. For the original quotation, see Benjamin, "Das Passagen-Werk," *Gesammelte Schriften*, vol. 5, part 1, p. 571: "Das bildschaffende Medium in uns zu dem stereoskopischen und dimensionalen Sehen in die Tiefe der geschichtlichen Schatten zu erziehen."

22. Benjamin, "Das Passagen-Werk," *Gesammelte Schriften*, vol. 4: *Kritik und Rezensionen* (Frankfurt am Main: Suhrkamp Verlag, 1972), p. 259.

CHAPTER 10. WHERE THE BEAUTY OF TRUTH LIES

1. Henry David Thoreau, *The Journal of Henry David Thoreau*, vol. 2, ed. by B. Torry and F. Allen (New York: Dover, 1906), p. 43. Journal entry for June 21, 1852.

2. I would like to mention, here, *Is There Truth in Art?* by Herman Rapaport. This book, published in 1997 by Cornell University Press, has been of great value, not only as a stimulus and provocation, but also as a measured force of restraint.

3. Wallace Stevens, *The Collected Poems of Wallace Stevens* (New York: Alfred A. Knopf, 1961), pp. 203–4. In "Eye and Mind," an essay on vision and painting, Maurice Merleau-Ponty observes that "no grape was ever what it is in the most figurative painting and that no painting, no matter how abstract, can get away from being, that even Caravaggio's grape is the grape itself." This remark carries the implication that truth in painting cannot be understood in terms of its correctness, its correspondence with a fixed reality. See Merleau-Ponty, *The Primacy of Perception* (Evanston, IL: Northwestern University Press, 1964), p. 188.

4. Plato, *The Republic,* in Benjamin Jowett (ed. and trans.), *The Dialogues of Plato* (New York: Random House, 1937), vol. 2, book 5, p. 739.

5. Ibid., book 6, p. 761.

6. Ibid., book 7, p. 797.

7. Ibid., book 6, p. 770.

8. Ibid., book 7, pp. 791, 797.

9. Plato, *Symposium,* in ibid., pp. 301–45.

10. Plato, *Phaedrus,* in ibid., pp. 253–55.

11. Walter Benjamin, *The Origin of German Tragic Drama* (London: New Left Books, 1977), p. 31; *Ursprung des deutschen Trauerspiels, Schriften* (Frankfurt am Main: Suhrkamp Verlag, 1955), vol. 1, p. 145.

12. See, for example, Martin Heidegger, "Der Spruch des Anaximander," *Holzwege* (Frankfurt am Main: Vittorio Klostermann, 1950), p. 321; "The Anaximander Fragment," in *Early Greek Thinking* (New York: Harper & Row, 1975), p. 36.

13. Benjamin, *German Tragic Drama,* p. 31 in the English, p. 146 in the German.

14. Benjamin, *German Tragic Drama,* p. 33 in English; p.148.

15. Stevens, *Collected Poems,* p. 373.

16. Martin Heidegger, *Nietzsche,* vol. 1: *The Will to Power as Art,* trans. by David F. Krell (New York: Harper & Row, 1979), p. 166; *Nietzsche* (Pfullingen: Günther Neske, 1961), vol. 1, p. 195. Hereafter, the English will be designated "NA," the German "NK," the "A" standing in for "Art," the "K" standing in for "Kunst." I will use Krell's exemplary translations and follow them in every detail, except for one: I will not, anywhere in this chapter, write "being" with a capital letter. In my opinion, the capital letter only subjects being to unnecessary temptations to reify it or capture it for another ontotheological discourse.

17. Heidegger, "What Are Poets For?," in *Poetry, Language, Thought* (New York: Harper & Row, 1971), p. 120; "Wozu Dichter?," *Holzwege* (Frankfurt am Main: Vittorio Klostermann, 1950), p. 275.

18. See Heidegger, *Being and Time,* trans. by Macquarrie and Robinson (New York: Harper & Row, 1962), pp. 177 and 197; *Sein und Zeit* (Halle: Max Niemeyer Verlag, 1941), pp. 138 and 155. Heidegger's word is "abgeblendet."

19. John Sallis, "Twisting Free: Being to an Extent Sensible," in *Research in Phenomenology,* vol. 18 (1987), pp. 16–17. This essay has been reprinted in *Double Truth* (Albany: State University of New York, 1995), pp. 75–96. My

page references (hereafter "TF," followed by the page number) will, however, use the journal publication. Also see Sallis's important earlier work, *Being and Logos: The Way of Platonic Dialogue* (Atlantic Highlands: Humanities Press, 1986), pp. 153–59, where he takes up the question of Plato's metaphysical dualism, separating the sensuous and the intelligible. Also relevant is his *Echoes: After Heidegger* (Bloomington: Indiana University Press, 1990).

20. See Heidegger, *Being and Time*, §§33–34 and 44, pp. 195–211 and 257–73; *Sein und Zeit*, pp. 153–67 and 212–30.

21. Heidegger, "The Origin of the Work of Art," in *Poetry, Language, Thought*, p. 56; "Ursprung des Kunstwerkes," *Holzwege*, p. 44. Henceforth, the English translation will be cited as "PLT" and the German as "H."

22. Heidegger, "The End of Philosophy and the Task of Thinking," in David F. Krell (ed. and trans.), *Basic Writings* (New York: Harper & Row, first edition, 1977), p.386; "Das Ende der Philosophie und die Aufgabe des Denkens," in *Zur Sache des Denkens* (Tübingen: Max Niemeyer Verlag, 1969), p. 74. Hereafter, the English translation will be cited as "BW," while the German will be cited as "SD."

23. See Heidegger, "On the Essence of Truth," in *Basic Writings*, p. 123; *Vom Wesen der Wahrheit* (Frankfurt: Vittorio Klostermann, 1949), p. 11.

24. Heidegger, "The Question Concerning Technology," in *The Question Concerning Technology and Other Essays* (New York: Harper & Row, 1977), p. 34; "Die Frage nach der Technik," in *Die Technik und die Kehre* (Pfullingen: Neske, 1962), p. 34.

25. Heidegger, "The Word of Nietzsche: 'God is dead,' " in *Question Concerning Technology*, p. 83; "Nietzsches Wort: 'Gott ist tot,' " *Holzwege*, p. 220.

26. Heidegger, "The Question Concerning Technology," in *Question Concerning Technology*, p. 28; "Die Frage nach der Technik," op. cit., p. 27.

27. Theodor Adorno, *Philosophie der neuen Musik* (Frankfurt am Main: Europäische Verlagsanstalt, 1958), p. 126.

28. Rainer Maria Rilke, *Poems 1912–1926*, trans. by Michael Hamburger (Redding Ridge, CT: Black Swan Books, 1981), pp. 48–49: "Werk des Gesichts ist getan, / tue nun Herz-werk / an den Bildern in dir, jenen gefangenen; denn du / überwältigst sie: aber nun kennst du sie nicht."

29. Rilke, *Duino Elegies*, trans. by J. B. Leishman and Stephen Spender (New York: W. W. Norton, 1967), pp. 20–21. I have significantly modified their translation, staying closer to the original German, which is also provided in this edition, next to the English translation: "Denn das Schöne ist nichts / als das Schrecklichen Anfang. . . . "

Index of Names

Text: 10/13/Aldus
Display: Aldus
Composition: BookMasters, Inc.
Printing and binding: Haddon Craftsmen, Inc.